MW01000417

"Everyday Latin phrases spring to mind to describe *The Pastor's Book*. It is a *magnum opus*—a major work for all ministers, incorporating one and a half lifetimes of gathered pastoral resources. It will be a *vade mecum*—the go-to book and faithful companion for younger ministers, to guide, inform, and sometimes correct and restrain. It should prove to be a *sine qua non* for all who are engaged in gospel ministry over the long haul—the very book needed to help recalibrate and refresh. These pages constitute a love gift to their fellow undershepherds from Kent Hughes and Douglas Sean O'Donnell. They have put all who love Christ's church in their lasting debt."

Sinclair B. Ferguson, Professor of Systematic Theology, Redeemer Seminary, Dallas, Texas

"This is an immensely helpful, Scripture-saturated resource for busy pastors, explaining the practical 'how to's' of leading weddings, funerals, baptisms, the Lord's Supper, personal counseling, and weekly worship services. It reflects the accumulated wisdom of decades of ministry, and it comes from the pen of a godly, wise senior pastor for whom I have the highest appreciation and respect."

Wayne Grudem, Research Professor of Theology and Biblical Studies, Phoenix Seminary

"*The Pastor's Book* should be on the shelf of every young preacher heading out into gospel ministry. It is a resource volume—meant to guide you into good practice and provide you with language for a variety of pastoral settings. Its success comes from the authors' mutual hallmark of disciplined and careful preparation. With this book, they have been kind enough to do some of the heavy lifting for us as well!"

David R. Helm, Pastor, Holy Trinity Church, Chicago; Chairman, The Charles Simeon Trust

"This is an invaluable resource for every pastor or church leader, at whatever stage of life and ministry. Full of biblical and theological insights, practical applications, and excellent examples, it will become an essential companion and guide for a multitude of ministry opportunities and challenges."

David Jackman, Former President, Proclamation Trust, London, United Kingdom

"Veteran pastors Kent Hughes and Douglas O'Donnell have given to us a wonderful, biblically anchored, gospel-centered resource. This is an invaluable, go-to treasure for busy pastors. From invocations to benedictions and from weddings to funerals, this volume is a very helpful guide in confidently exercising our duties as ministers of the gospel. What a gift!"

Crawford W. Loritts Jr., Senior Pastor, Fellowship Bible Church, Roswell, Georgia; author, *A Passionate Commitment*

"I wish I had had this book when I began my ministry as a pastor! It pulls back the curtain to show us what we need to know about our calling and the expectations of our people. It gives a breadth and context to pastoral responsibilities I've not seen in other similar books."

Erwin W. Lutzer, Senior Pastor, The Moody Church, Chicago, Illinois

"*The Pastor's Book* is a remarkable resource, forged over four decades of Hughes's pastoral experience. It is historically informed, biblically grounded, thoroughly Christ-centered, and eminently practical. This is a book that the new pastor and the veteran minister alike will return to again and again as they press through the crucible of pastoral ministry."

Aaron Messner, Senior Minister, Westminster Presbyterian Church, Atlanta, Georgia

"Pastors must be prepared for almost any imaginable situation. From weekly sermons and counseling to hospital visitations and funerals, the pastoral tasks vary from day to day, even from hour to hour. Kent Hughes provides the type of theologically rich handbook every minister needs on his shelf. Hughes is a sagacious guide to the many facets of pastoral ministry, and his program for ministry is deeply rooted in Scripture. I am confident that pastors will be greatly served by this book and better equipped for faithful ministry in every avenue of life."

R. Albert Mohler Jr., President, The Southern Baptist Theological Seminary

"I can only imagine the benefits I would have received if I had been given this book on my ordination day. I not only look forward to having my own copy, but also to securing copies for the young men I have the privilege of mentoring for the gospel ministry. *The Pastor's Book* is a well-written and comprehensive compendium on pastoral ministry. Get it and use it, and may our Lord's church again be blessed by ministers called of God who give themselves to 'the ministry of prayer and the Word.'"

Harry L. Reeder III, Senior Pastor, Briarwood Presbyterian Church, Birmingham, Alabama

"Whether you are a newly minted pastor or a veteran, you will find this all-in-one resource for pastoral ministry a very helpful book. This book will actually remind pastors there are many wonderful resources to draw upon, all of which equip us to biblically minister in the various roles and contexts we find ourselves pastoring within."

Jay Thomas, Lead Pastor, Chapel Hill Bible Church, Chapel Hill, North Carolina

"Veteran pastor and author Kent Hughes has written what will surely prove to be one of the most widely used and useful guides to pastoral ministry available to young pastors. As I read through this volume, I was struck over and over again by the practical wisdom, measured assessment, and confident admonition that could come only from one who has pastored—and pastored thoughtfully and well—for many years. The benefit this book will be for pastors and their churches is incalculable. What a gift this is."

Bruce A. Ware, Professor of Christian Theology, The Southern Baptist Theological Seminary

The

PASTOR'S

BOOK

A COMPREHENSIVE AND PRACTICAL

GUIDE TO PASTORAL MINISTRY

R. KENT HUGHES

DOUGLAS SEAN O'DONNELL

Contributing Editor

∷ CROSSWAY®

WHEATON, ILLINOIS

The Pastor's Book: A Comprehensive and Practical Guide to Pastoral Ministry
Copyright © 2015 by Crossway
Published by Crossway
   1300 Crescent Street
   Wheaton, Illinois 60187

Cover design: Studio Gearbox

First printing, 2015

Printed in China

ISBN: 978-1-4335-4587-0
ePub ISBN: 978-1-4335-4590-0
PDF ISBN: 978-1-4335-4588-7
Mobipocket ISBN: 978-1-4335-4589-4

Library of Congress Cataloging-in-Publication Data
Hughes, R. Kent, 1942–
 The pastor's book : a comprehensive and practical guide to pastoral ministry / R. Kent Hughes, Douglas Sean O'Donnell.
  pages cm
 Includes bibliographical references.
 ISBN 978-1-4335-4587-0 (hc)
 ISBN 1-4335-4587-X (hc)
 ISBN 978-1-4335-4588-7 (PDF)
 ISBN 978-1-4335-4589-4 (Mobipocket)
 ISBN 978-1-4335-4590-0 (ePub)
 1. Pastoral theology. I. O'Donnell, Douglas Sean, 1972–
II. Title.
BV4211.3.H84 2015
253—dc23   2014036804

Crossway is a publishing ministry of Good News Publishers.

RRDS   25 24 23 22 21 20 19 18 17 16
16 15 14 13 12 11 10 9 8 7 6 5 4 3 2

To
Barbara Hughes
and
Emily O'Donnell

Contents

Detailed Contents

PART 2

PARTS OF THE WORSHIP SERVICE

Preface

When Dr. Lane Dennis, president of Crossway Books, asked me to consider authoring what is now *The Pastor's Book*, I was intrigued, but unsure of what course to follow. So in the following weeks, I began to reflect over my forty-plus years of pastoral ministry and upon those responsibilities that filled my week, as well as my duties on the Lord's Day. When Doug O'Donnell agreed to serve as contributing editor, my thinking was enlarged.

Having been busy pastors during our tenures, we hope to encourage and enhance the gospel ministries of our fellow busy pastors with the rich theology and resources that have sustained our own ministries. Thus, we have worked together to create a go-to resource that stands on the shoulders of those who have gone before, is theologically informed, and is crammed full of examples and ideas from which a pastor can selectively cull with an eye to elevating not only the weekly ministry of the Word in both contemporary and traditional settings, but the day-to-day pastoral ministry of the gospel.

We have limited the material we cover for various reasons. We wanted to center on pastoral tasks we have thought a lot about and that we feel are often neglected or overlooked, especially by the younger generation of pastors. We also thought that addressing many important topics, such as calling to ministry, personal character, family life, preaching, leading a pastoral staff, working with elders, church discipline, and church planting, would make this large go-to book too bulky to go to. Moreover, we know that excellent books and articles already have been written on each of these topics. We offer recommendations for some of these books in the section titled "Books for Further Reading."

A brief look at the chapter on Communion will give an idea of how the book's chapters work, as it includes a history of the Lord's Table, a biblical theology of the Table, resources for the Table (numerous invitations, prayers, and confessions for Communion; prayers for the bread and the cup; and benedictions), the outlines of four key Reformation liturgies, the complete texts of three Communion liturgies for today, select hymns and songs for Communion, a liturgy for Christmas Communion, and advice on questions about the frequency of and participation in the Lord's Table. The information is arranged so that a pastor may select elements that will elevate the observance of the Lord's Supper in the unique context of the church he serves. Hopefully, this and the other chapters will often serve as an inspiring one-stop resource for many busy pastors.

The Pastor's Book is grounded on the conviction that all Christian ministry must be gospel-centered. We believe, therefore, that the pulpit must be devoted to the regular proclamation of the full canonical gospel—"that Christ died for our sins in accordance with the Scriptures, that he was buried, that he was raised on the third day in accordance with the Scriptures" (1 Cor. 15:3–4). We believe that such preaching is at the heart of authentic ministry.

But to imagine that Christian ministry is accomplished solely by the faithful exposition of the Word is to diminish the expansive scope of the gospel and the pastoral calling, because the day-in-and-day-out ministry of the pastor is meant to be wholly gospel-infused. Take, for example, the responsibility for weddings—a duty that is often regarded by pastors as a waste of time, an ecclesial diversion from "the main thing." Time-consuming, yes! But a wedding is not a waste if the gospel is made so integral to premarital counseling that the bride and groom go on to portray, over the decades, the union of Christ and the church to a lost world. Likewise, time has not been siphoned from "the main thing" when the gospel is winsomely preached from a Christ-saturated wedding text to a "captive" gathering of souls that may include more non-Christians than will darken the door of the church in a month of Sundays. Indeed, properly understood, the day-to-day responsibilities of the pastor covered in the chapters on weddings, funerals, pastoral counseling, and hospital visitation all have to do with gospel events. All these chapters feature numerous templates and options.

This book argues and assumes that Sunday services will be gospel-centered through regular preaching that lifts up Christ through the exposition of the Word, and thus provides diverse orders of service that serve to exalt Christ. The book includes extended chapters on Sunday prayers; historic creeds; hymns and songs; baptism; and Communion, plus an "Enrichment" section on classic Christian poems—all crafted to enhance the exaltation of Christ in the Lord's Day services. Again, each of these chapters contains multiple examples and options.

The chapter on annual services necessarily follows the outline of the gospel—Christmas, Messiah's birth; Good Friday, Messiah's death; Easter,

Messiah's resurrection—providing orders of service and appropriate Scripture quotations, songs, and poems for each season of the gospel. A perusal of the detailed table of contents will acquaint the reader with the array of resources included in each of the eleven chapters and the appendix.

It is our hope that *The Pastor's Book* will:

- encourage a thoroughly gospel-centered ministry;
- refresh the church from the wells of historic orthodoxy;
- provide many of the best practical examples; and
- become a go-to resource for busy pastors.

Acknowledgments

Douglas O'Donnell, now senior lecturer in biblical studies and practical theology at Queensland Theological College in Brisbane, who serves as this book's contributing editor, is a man of many talents. He is the founding pastor of two churches, an accomplished Bible expositor, and an expert in biblical Wisdom Literature, having authored *The Beginning and End of Wisdom: Preaching Christ from the First and Last Chapters of Proverbs, Ecclesiastes, and Job*; the Preaching the Word commentaries *The Song of Solomon: An Invitation to Intimacy* and *Matthew: All Authority in Heaven and on Earth*; and the Reformed Expository Commentary volumes *Ecclesiastes: Enjoyment East of Eden* and *1–3 John: A Gospel-Transformed Life*. In addition, he has written *God's Lyrics: Recovering Worship through Old Testament Songs*, in which he includes some of his own original songs. Doug contributed three chapters to this book, "Sunday Worship," "The Historic Christian Creeds," and "Hymns and Songs," as well as the last half of the chapter on baptism, and he made many other additions and improvements. I am grateful not only for his contributions, but also for his patience, humor, wit, and elevated style, all of which have made this a better book.

I must also express my appreciation to my longtime friend, Milton scholar, and prodigious author Dr. Leland Ryken, retired Wheaton College professor of English, who researched and selected some of the finest Christian poems in the English language for inclusion in the enrichment section titled "Poetry to Enhance Worship and Preaching," and also supplied select poems for Christmas, Good Friday, and Easter, and the love poems and epithalamia for weddings. Lee's work will enrich many a wedding, special service, and sermon, and will grace some grateful hearts.

Deepest thanks must go to another close friend, Dr. Bob Evans, pastor of Christ Church in Pleasanton, California, for the superb chapter on pastoral counseling. Also, I have deep appreciation for Chuck King, who collaborated with me as music pastor for many years at College Church and is architect of many of the beautiful orders of service in the "Annual Services" chapter. Special thanks go to Tom Buck, pastor of the First Baptist Church of Lindale, Texas, for his baptism protocols and liturgies; Dr. Niel Nielson, for his confirmation liturgy; Dr. Matt Newkirk, for a number of the congregational prayers; K. Edward Copeland, for providing New Zion Baptist Church's order of service; and Dr. Gary Rownd, for allowing us to print his wonderful song "Gift from the Lord." Lastly, I am so grateful to those who provided the many homilies, as noted in the following pages: Tom Buck, Bob Evans, Randall Gruendyke, W. Carey Hughes, Arthur Jackson, Jim Johnston, Jay Thomas, and Todd Wilson.

This book was written during the early months of 2014 in Jupiter, Florida, where my wife, Barbara, and I wintered as I taught at The Expositor's Seminary on the campus of Grace Immanuel Bible Church. I am most grateful to the seminary's dean, Bob Whitney, for doing everything possible to make our stay pleasant and productive, and to Pastor Dr. Jerry Wragg, for his superb expositions and corporate worship under the direction of Dr. Dan Kreider, who provided his personal canon for many of the hymns in this book. Indeed, these pastors modeled much of what *The Pastor's Book* is about. Barbara and I must also express our gratitude to Jim and Sandy Koepnick, for opening their remarkable home to us during those warm winter months.

Many thanks also go to Dr. Lane Dennis and the editorial staff of Crossway Books, including Ted Griffin and Greg Bailey, for their superb, painstaking editing of this volume.

PART 1

CHRISTIAN GATHERINGS

1

Sunday Worship

By Douglas Sean O'Donnell

In this opening chapter, we will consider various aspects of what is undoubtedly the highest calling of the church—worship of our great God.

I should warn you—Kent has Quaker roots, and I Roman Catholic. What a former Quaker and Roman Catholic might together say about worship in the free-church evangelical tradition warrants careful and cautionary reading. Kent's first memory of Christianity is the 1949 Los Angeles Billy Graham crusade. His Southern Baptist grandmother took him to the huge tent set up on the corner of Washington and Hill Streets. "The dressed-up crowd, the young evangelist's blue eyes radiating in the spotlights, and cowboy Stuart Hamblen singing 'Just a Closer Walk with Thee'" are a few of the memorizes etched in his mind.[1] After the crusade, Kent attended Vermont Avenue Presbyterian Church. Of that experience, he recalls, "It was there, hushed and seated with my mother along with other reverent worshippers in the dark, Scottish-kirk ambience of that old church, that I began to sense the transcendence of God and to be drawn to Christ."[2]

Christ drew Kent to himself in a saving way as a teenager through the Christians at Granada Heights Friends Church. While this was a Quaker congregation, the worship style was eclectic, blending aspects from free-church traditions such as the Methodists, Nazarenes, and Baptists. The church's "liturgy" looked like that of many evangelical services today: a season of congregational singing (including gospel songs and choruses, with

---

[1] R. Kent Hughes, "Free Church Worship: The Challenge of Freedom," in *Worship by the Book*, ed. D. A. Carson (Grand Rapids: Zondervan, 1992), 136.

[2] Ibid.

perhaps a hymn and a choir number) followed by a sermon. It did, however, include a short time of silence, a vestige from the Quakers' traditional silent meetings. One aspect of worship this congregation was not silent about was evangelism! And like his church, Kent regarded evangelism as the Christian's highest calling. However, this emphasis, as God-ordained and honoring as it was, deemphasized, as least in Kent's mind, the purpose of corporate worship. He reflects: "I certainly never gave any thought as to the purpose of our Lord's Day gatherings, other than as a venue for preaching."[3] Even his embrace of Calvinism before seminary never led him to theological reflection on worship.

It was only after seminary, as Kent served as a youth pastor and then church planter, that serious reflection began. Hughes described the atmosphere from which his many thoughtful questions, such as, "Is this authentic worship or entertainment?" arose:

> Irreverence became widespread. Congregational prayers were often a mindless stream-of-consciousness offered in a "kicked-back" cannabis tone. Mantra-like music was employed to mesmerize worshippers, and preachers were replaced by "communicators" who offered bromides strung together with a series of relational anecdotes.[4]

During his twenty-seven years as the senior pastor at College Church in Wheaton, Illinois, Kent's philosophy and practice of congregational worship was honed. He has thought long and hard about answers to questions such as:

- What do the Scriptures have to say about corporate worship?
- Is our worship Christ-centered and God-honoring?
- How should the Bible be read, sung, and preached?
- Should we use creeds?
- How do we celebrate the sacraments?

In what follows, I have summarized some of his thoughts and added my own.

To say something of my path to serious reflection on the topic of corporate worship, I will simply add that the nineteen years I spent at St. Philip the Apostle Catholic Parish, two years at Willow Creek Community Church,

---

[3] Ibid., 137. For more on Kent's upbringing, see Randy Gruendyke, "Disciplines of a Godly Minister: A Biographical Sketch," in *Preach the Word: Essays on Expository Preaching: In Honor of R. Kent Hughes*, ed. Leland Ryken and Todd Wilson (Wheaton, IL: Crossway, 2007), 258–262.
[4] Hughes, "Free Church Worship," 137–138.

and nearly twenty years as a pastor/church planter with College Church all influenced me, with the emphasis of influence falling on the latter. My times at College Church and its church plants—Holy Trinity in Chicago, Christ the King in Batavia, Illinois, and New Covenant in Naperville, Illinois, where I helped develop various orders of service, write a philosophy of music, and plan and execute special services—refined my own thoughts on the matter. To see if I'll advocate a blend of the sign of the cross, a splash of holy water, smooth jazz soloists, comfortable auditorium seating, expository preaching, and "A Mighty Fortress" on the organ, you'll have to read on.

WORSHIP—ALL OF LIFE AND EVERY SUNDAY

Kent and I have both been to Oz and back—the island of Australia, that is. In fact, I am there now, serving as a lecturer at Queensland Theological College in Brisbane. Our major Oz influence, however, comes from the Sydney Anglicans, especially those associated with Moore Theological College. Kent credits Graeme Goldsworthy, William Dumbrell, Peter Jensen, and Phillip Jensen, among others, for clarifying his view that worship is more than what happens on Sunday. In the New Testament, worship clearly embodies all of life!

The biblical evidence is conclusive. Jesus's coming fulfilled Scripture's promise of a new covenant (cf. Jer. 31:31–34). And it is most significant that the entire text of this substantial prophecy is recorded in Hebrews 8:7–13, in the midst of a section (Hebrews 7–11) that asserts there is no longer any earthly sacrifice, priesthood, or temple because all have been fulfilled in Christ. There are no longer any sacred times or sacred places. Under the new covenant, Christians are thus to worship all the time—in their individual lives, in their family lives, and when they come together for corporate worship. Corporate worship, then, is a particular expression of a life of perpetual worship. This is what worship is: "Day-in-day-out living for Christ, the knees and heart perpetually bent in devotion and service."[5]

Thus, with the New Testament perspective in mind, as Christians we must center our worship on Christ as the temple, priest, and sacrifice; and we must reject traditions that advocate for sacred spaces—"sanctuaries," "tabernacles," and such—as well as for an ordained "priesthood," along with any elements of the levitical cultus of Aaronic vestments, altars, and bloodless sacrifices.

That said, the designated place where Christians worship is, in some

---

[5] Ibid., 139–140.

sense, set apart. It is not a *sanctified* place, but it is a *special* place—whether it is St. Paul's London or the DuPage Children's Museum (where my church worshiped for a number of months before we moved into another rented space). Moreover, while we embrace the priesthood of all believers, we recognize that a church is not a church without appointed leaders (elders and deacons), as the Pastoral Epistles make clear. Lastly, individual devotion does not negate gathering on the Lord's Day to worship the risen Lord until his return. We should make it our habit to gather to encourage one another (see Heb. 10:25), each person prepared to build others up (1 Cor. 14:26), knowing that Sunday through Saturday, as brothers, we are called "to present *your* [plural] bodies as a living sacrifice, holy and acceptable to God, which is *your* [plural] spiritual worship" (Rom. 12:1).

But why do we gather on Sunday? The New Testament, perhaps surprisingly, speaks little on this issue. The emphasis of the New Testament is on mutual edification, as is clear in Hebrews 10:25 ("encouraging one another"), 1 Corinthians 14:26 ("When you come together. . . . Let all things be done for building up"), and the gatherings described in Acts. Evangelism is also mentioned in 1 Corinthians 14. The hope of a Spirit-filled assembly would be the "unbeliever or outsider . . . falling on his face," worshiping God, and declaring that "God is really among you" (vv. 24–25).[6] Beyond edification and evangelism is the obvious: exaltation! If the church's desire is that the unbeliever "worship God" (v. 25), then there is little doubt the believers should be on their faces before God as well. Views that advocate that corporate assemblies are merely to edify believers or evangelize unbelievers miss the plain fact that if Christ is not lifted up in praise, no believer is edified and no unbeliever is saved. When the New Testament speaks of God's people gathering to pray (to God), sing (to God), and preach (God's gospel), it assumes exaltation. Christian worship encompasses the threefold goal of edification, evangelism, and exaltation. And those three aspects of public worship intersect and support each other on many levels.[7] From our

---

[6] In a broader sense, Douglas Wilson describes the effect in this way: "As we gather in the presence of the living God on the Lord's Day, He is pleased to use our right worship of Him as a battering ram to bring down all the citadels of unbelief in our communities. Just as the walls of Jericho fell before the worship and service of God, so unbelievers tremble when Christians gather in their communities to worship the living God rightly." *A Primer on Worship and Reformation: Recovering the High Church Puritan* (Moscow, ID: Canon, 2008), 32.
[7] In his excellent study of the biblical theology of worship, *Engaging with God: A Biblical Theology of Worship* (Downers Grove, IL: IVP Academic, 1992), David Peterson argues that edification and evangelism emerge "as a priority for those concerned to offer to God 'acceptable worship'" (188). By those means, we engage with the true and living God on his terms "and in the way that he alone makes possible" (20). Peterson likewise acknowledges the importance of exaltation. In his chapter on the book of Revelation, he writes, "the Revelation to John stresses the importance of praise and acclamation as a means of honouring God and encouraging his people to trust him and obey him" (279). However, with that said, he does summarize "the purpose of Christian gatherings" to be edification (287).

acclamation of God, the church is built up, and unbelievers tremble and (Lord willing) trust! As Hughes puts it:

> I have come to see that while all of life is worship, gathered worship with the body of Christ is at the heart of a life of worship. Corporate worship is intended by God to inform and elevate a life of worship. In this respect, I personally view how we conduct gathered worship as a matter of life and death.[8]

CLARIFYING CORPORATE CHRISTIAN WORSHIP

"Life and death"? Those are strong words. What does it matter how we conduct our Sunday worship service? As long as "all things [are] done decently and in order" (1 Cor. 14:40), aren't all aspects of our edification/evangelism/exaltation liturgy acceptable? Before I answer that important question, a history lesson is necessary. (You can blame this excursus on me and my church history obsession and education, or on Kent, whose work I'm hanging the following thoughts upon.)[9]

The free-church tradition—of which the majority of our readers are a part (just an educated guess)—grew from a protest against Protestant traditions ungrounded in Scripture. In early seventeenth-century England, groups labeled "Puritans" and "Separatists" desired to worship according to the Word. Even though Thomas Cranmer's Book of Common Prayer bled Bible, there was reason for reform. "What does the Word of God say about worship?" was a legitimate question. The Puritans wanted to explore what God's *pure* revelation said; Separatists (some Anglican Puritans included) wanted to *separate* from England's official but not God-ordained religion. The Church of England was not *the* church. Their critique, summarized with seven points, involved divergent views of (1) preaching, (2) Scripture, (3) prayer, (4) singing, (5) sacraments, (6) simplicity, and (7) vestments. In brief, they advocated the following changes:

1. As opposed to simply reading the Prayer Book homilies on diverse topics and for various occasions within the church calendar, they argued that preaching should be a plain, passionate, and orderly exposition of a biblical text created by the preacher and applicable to every congregant.
2. Instead of the few small assigned readings for the day from the lectionary of the Book of Common Prayer, larger sections of Scripture should

---

[8] Hughes, "Free Church Worship," 142.
[9] The following is my summary of Hughes's section "The Irony of Freedom," in ibid., 142–146.

be read. On most occasions, these passages should relate directly to the preacher's sermon.

3. Instead of reading the collects (short prayers) from the Prayer Book, ministers were encouraged to offer their own (often lengthy) prayers, which were either written down or prayed extemporaneously.

4. As opposed to having a professional choir singing choral pieces *on behalf of* the congregation, the voice of the congregation was desired, and thus simpler, singable congregational hymns were introduced and sung.

5. Dismissing extrabiblical traditions such as kneeling for Communion and giving the baptized child the sign of the cross, an emphasis on Paul's words of institution (1 Cor. 11:23–25) for the Lord's Supper and a return to the connection of faith to baptism were advocated.

6. Against the pomp of the high-church liturgy and the extravagance of Anglican ecclesial architecture, there was a call for simplicity in liturgical and architectural styles.

7. While not completely or in totality (some Puritan pastors wore the simple Geneva gowns), clerical vestments were rejected in favor of more simple attire, if any special attire at all.

Those of us in the free-church tradition worship in the liturgical world created by these reformers. While we should be respectful and appreciative of other Christian traditions (Cranmer's Prayer Book is incredibly thoughtful and rich), we should also celebrate these changes. The freedom to dress like the people in our congregations, structure the service with biblical simplicity, pray our own heartfelt words, preach our own expositional sermons from Bible texts, and administer the sacraments according to the clear dictates of the Word are reasons to rejoice.

However, there is little doubt today that these freedoms have been abused, and the freedom to worship according to the Word has deteriorated into the freedom to do what works. Pragmatism, not Biblicism, rules the day! From Charles Finney's "new measures" revivals of the nineteenth century to Bill Hybels's seeker-sensitive services of recent years, many evangelical churches do what is right in their own eyes. The regulative principle (that we worship based on biblical prescriptions)[10] regulates few independent evangelical churches today. Between the new cultuses of authentic spontaneity and programmatic anthropocentrism, we must find a scriptural center.

---

[10] As summarized by John Calvin: "God disapproves of all modes of worship not expressly sanctioned by his word." *The Necessity of Reforming the Church*, trans. Henry Beveridge (Philadelphia: Presbyterian Board of Publication, 1844), 17.

TWO OLD TESTAMENT PICTURES:
PARADIGMS, POSTURES, AND PURPOSES

What does God's Word say about corporate worship? We also can ask the question this more focused way: What scriptural characteristics help control Christian worship? The answer can be a hundredfold! There are many scriptural principles, practices, and paradigms we should use to guide us, such as: our worship should be Trinitarian ("Father-focused, Christ-centered, and Spirit-enabled"),[11] reflective of God's transcendence and immanence in balance, and salvation-celebratory as we focus on the life, death, resurrection, and return of Christ. Moreover, our worship should be exclusive (we worship Yahweh alone, not alongside other gods), dependent on God's initiative (we love God because he first loved us), eye-opening, heart-expanding, and mind-renewing. Or we can simply follow Terry Johnson's excellent summary that worship that is reformed according to the Bible is simple, spiritual, and substantial:

> [It is] *simple* because the New Testament does not describe a complex ritual of service as is found in the Old Testament; *spiritual* because when Jesus removed the special status of Jerusalem as *the* place where God was to be worshiped (Jn 4:7–24), He signaled the abolition of all the material forms that constituted the typological Old Testament system including not only the city, but all that gave the city significance—the temple, the altars, the priests, the sacrificial animals, and the incense; *substantial* because the God of the Bible is a great God and cannot be worshiped appropriately with forms that are light, flippant, or superficial; He must always be worshiped with "reverence and awe" (Heb 12:28).[12]

With all that is said above duly noted, perhaps the two most glaring omissions in the contemporary free-church tradition are (1) the fear of God and (2) the Word of God read, sung, prayed, and preached. When you can bet your Cadillac that there will be greater reverence ("godly fear," Westminster Confession of Faith 21.5) and more Bible reading(s), songs, and prayers at the local Roman Catholic Church than at the Bible church, you know something is terribly amiss. A new reformation is in order! We must protest all Protestantism that will not tremble before God as we listen to his

---

[11] J. Ligon Duncan III, "Foundations for Biblically Directed Worship," in *Give Praise to God: A Vision for Reforming Worship*, ed. Philip Graham Ryken, Derek W. H. Thomas, and J. Ligon Duncan III (Phillipsburg, NJ: P&R, 2003), 62.

[12] Terry L. Johnson, ed., *Leading in Worship: A Sourcebook for Presbyterian Students and Ministers Drawing from the Biblical and Historical Forms of the Reformed Tradition* (Powder Springs, GA: Tolle Lege, 2013), 9.

voice proclaimed. We must return to bibliocentric, God-fearing worship that exalts, edifies, and evangelizes.

If by God's sovereign grace liturgical reformation is to sweep through the contemporary free churches, a return to their Protestant liturgical traditions (which is a return to the Word) is in order. In *Worship Reformed according to Scripture,* Hughes Oliphant Old lists fifteen of "the most valuable worship traditions at the heart of the heritage of Reformed Protestantism." The first involves preaching the Bible: "At the head of the list should certainly be expository preaching. This has always been the glory of Protestant worship." The final valued tradition, but certainly not the least, involves our attitude: "The greatest single contribution that the Reformed liturgical heritage can make to contemporary American Protestantism is its sense of the majesty and sovereignty of God, its sense of reverence and simple dignity, its conviction that worship must above all serve the praise of God."[13] For these two often neglected characteristics of worship under the new covenant—(1) bibliocentric, (2) God-fearing worship—I will, ironically enough, explore two Old Testament texts. We will then conclude by answering how these characteristics and others listed above play out in our Sunday gatherings. We begin with Ecclesiastes 5:1–7.[14]

God-Revering

Many years ago, I went to a wealthy suburban church that had sermon titles such as "What Would Jesus Say to Bart Simpson?" and that, for its youth day, had its teenagers stream down the aisles dressed like inner-city gang members as they rapped out the opening "hymn," with the appropriate ganglike hand gestures. More recently, I attended a church that showed hilarious homemade video clips to season the sermonette. I have also heard about a church that hands out free popcorn as you enter the "sanctuary," and another where everyone bounces around a beach ball during the "worship" band's performance. Although these examples are perhaps extreme, they show a growing trend. Today, as our churches overflow with folksy entertainment and raw "authenticity," we live in one of the most sacrilegious and blasphemous church cultures in the history of Christianity. No joke.

Yet each generation has troubles of its own. In New Testament times,

---

[13] Hughes Oliphant Old, *Worship Reformed according to Scripture* (Louisville: Westminster John Knox, 2002), 172, 176. "Reverence and fear are at the heart of Christian worship." D. G. Hart and John R. Muether, *With Reverence and Awe: Returning to the Basics of Reformed Worship* (Phillipsburg, NJ: P&R, 2002), 119–120.
[14] Some of this section is taken from Douglas Sean O'Donnell's sermon "Sandals Off, Mouths Shut," chapter 9 in *Ecclesiastes: Enjoyment East of Eden,* Reformed Expository Commentary (Phillipsburg, NJ: P&R, 2014), 107–119; used with permission.

James criticized those in the church who were showing favoritism toward the rich (James 2:2–4), and Paul decried those in the Corinthian church who were getting drunk on the Communion wine (1 Cor. 11:21). Jesus got out a whip for those making a profit on the pilgrims to Jerusalem, treating the temple like a den of thieves (John 2:13–17). In Old Testament times, the prophets called out the hypocrites who walked through the sacrificial motions (e.g., Isa. 29:13; Mal. 1:14). And in Ecclesiastes 5:1–7, Pastor Solomon (Qoheleth) prophetically shares some choice words of his own for the recreationally religious person who is oblivious that his "worship" is highly offensive to God. Put simply, he warns the "fool" (vv. 1, 3, 4) to fear God (v. 7). Put differently and more broadly, he instructs all of God's people at all times on how to worship wisely.

Establishing a Safe Distance

As we approach God in worship, Pastor Solomon wants to establish a safe distance between us and the transcendent God. He does this with two imperatives given at the top (v. 1) and tail (v. 7) of the text. At the top, we are charged to watch out when we go to worship ("Guard your steps when you go to the house of God"), and at the tail, we are given the central charge of wisdom literature: to fear God. This *inclusio* of admonitions counsels "caution, reverence, restraint, moderation, and sincerity" before the Lord.[15]

In Ecclesiastes 1–4, we learn a number of things about God, including that whatever God does endures forever (3:14), that God has given us work to be busy with (3:10), that God grants us enjoyment in our work (2:24–25; 3:13) and the reward of wisdom, knowledge, and joy (2:26), that God has made everything beautiful in its time (3:11), and that in his time he will judge the righteous and the wicked (3:17).

In Ecclesiastes 5:1–7, we learn three truths about God. First, God has a house. In verse 1, "the house of God" references Solomon's temple, built in the tenth century BC and destroyed in 587 BC. While it stood, the temple was a visible testimony to God's absolute holiness. There Isaiah saw "the Lord sitting upon a throne, high and lifted up" (Isa. 6:1) as the seraphim called to one another, "Holy, holy, holy is the LORD of hosts" (v. 3). The temple symbolized God's holiness—that is, he was inaccessible except by sacrifice through a priestly mediator, and even such a priestly mediator could be incinerated by God's consuming fire (Lev. 10:1–2; cf. 15:31; 1 Sam. 6:19–20). Of course, God was not limited to this human-made house. In Solomon's

---

[15] Choon-Leong Seow, *Ecclesiastes*, Anchor Bible 18C (New York: Doubleday, 1997), 197.

dedication of the temple, he says as much: "But will God indeed dwell on the earth? Behold, heaven and the highest heaven cannot contain you; how much less this house that I have built!" (1 Kings 8:27). Solomon echoes that prayer in Ecclesiastes 5:2, proclaiming that "God is in heaven." Is God in the temple *and* in heaven? Yes, he is: "the whole earth is full of his glory!" (Isa. 6:3; cf. Deut. 4:39). Wherever God is, there is a distance and difference between the Creator and his creation. He is not our peer: "I am God and not a man, the Holy One" (Hos. 11:9).

Second, God knows and judges the way we worship. He sees into our hearts—the attitudes behind the actions—and judges whether our worship is "acceptable worship" (Heb. 12:28) or not. If it is not, he renders his judgment against "the [mere] appearance of godliness" (2 Tim. 3:5). He gets "angry" at the blabbering fool and "destroys" (i.e., does not accept) his sacrificed animal and retracted vow (Eccl. 5:5–6).

Third, unlike the gods of the Gentiles, which are deaf and dumb, Israel's God hears and speaks. In the temple, God's people were told "to draw near to listen" (Eccl. 5:1), and in the temple, God heard and accepted sincere sacrificial vows.

So, then, in light of God's transcendence, omnipresence, omniscience, and holiness (God has a house); justice (God knows and judges our worship); and forgiveness and accessibility (God hears and speaks), "God is the one you must fear" (Eccl. 5:7). Our perpetual posture before the Lord should be that of humility, awe, reverence, and faith. We are to come with boldness and confidence before our good, approachable King (mixed, of course, with a bit of shaking in our boots). As Annie Dillard fittingly describes:

> On the whole, I do not find Christians, outside of the catacombs, sufficiently sensible of conditions. Does anyone have the foggiest idea what sort of power we so blithely invoke? Or, as I suspect, does no one believe a word of it? . . . It is madness to wear ladies' straw hats and velvet hats to church; we should all be wearing crash helmets. Ushers should issue life preservers and signal flares; they should lash us to our pews. For the sleeping god may wake someday and take offense, or the waking god may draw us out to where we can never return.[16]

Drawing Near Wisely

This God "in heaven" (Eccl. 5:2), who rules time (3:1–15) and judges all peoples (3:16–22), nevertheless can be approached. The Preacher emphasizes

---

[16] Annie Dillard, quoted in R. Kent Hughes, *Disciplines of a Godly Man* (Wheaton, IL: Crossway, 2001), 114.

this approachability by changing in chapter 5 from his "reflective 'journaling' style" to sermonizing.[17] That is, he moves from first-person observations (e.g., "*I* saw" and "*I* considered") to second-person imperatives (e.g., "[*You*] pay what you vow" and "*You* must fear"). This is the first time in the book that the reader is addressed and admonished.

Having looked at *God*, let us turn our attention to *you*. Between the two imperatives that frame our text, we find a number of negative admonitions: "Be *not* rash with your mouth" (5:2), "do *not* delay paying it" (v. 4), and "let *not* your mouth lead you into sin" (v. 6). All the admonitions are warnings about words in worship, about nouns and verbs related to verbal communication: "Be not rash with your mouth, nor let your heart be hasty to utter a word" (5:2); "a fool's voice . . . many words" (v. 3); "not vow . . . and not pay" (v. 5); "let not your mouth . . . do not say . . . your voice" (v. 6); and "words grow many" (v 7).

Listening First

Drawing near to God requires that we listen before we speak:

> Guard your steps when you go to the house of God. To draw near to listen is better than to offer the sacrifice of fools, for they do not know that they are doing evil. Be not rash with your mouth, nor let your heart be hasty to utter a word before God, for God is in heaven and you are on earth. Therefore let your words be few. For a dream comes with much business, and a fool's voice with many words. (Eccl. 5:1–3)

Temple sacrifices were offered in silence. In effect, the silence shouted out the steadfast love of a holy, holy, holy God for undeserving sinners. Then the silence was broken by a reading from the Law of Moses and an explanation for the people. The response to hearing from God was to speak to God—through prayers, songs, and sometimes personal vows. The service closed with a benediction.

The emphasis in Ecclesiastes 5:1–3 is on listening to the Word of God. This listening ear is contrasted with the mouths of fools. Here the foolish worshipers are not necessarily those who bring blind, lame, or sick animals to be sacrificed ("they do not know that they are doing evil," v. 1); rather, the foolish are those who sin with their mouths. Instead of being like Moses before the burning bush—with their sandals off, mouths shut, and ears open,

---

[17] Kathleen A. Farmer, *Who Knows What Is Good? A Commentary on the Books of Proverbs and Ecclesiastes*, International Theological Commentary (Grand Rapids: Eerdmans, 1991), 167.

respectfully revering the Lord, Ex. 3:5)—they chatter on before their Creator. They mumble mantras before the Almighty! With hollow hearts and blank minds, they offer up "empty phrases" (Matt. 6:7), thinking that the more they talk, the more God will listen.

In the temple, Israel was to listen first. As Christians, we know and appreciate that through Jesus's death, our Lord judged the temple (Matt. 21:13; 23:38) and replaced it (Matt. 12:6; 24:2; 26:61; 27:40, 51). We do not journey to Jerusalem to worship God in some building. Under the new covenant in Jesus's blood, we have a perfect and permanent sacrifice and an intercessor for our sins (Heb. 7:23–28), as well as the gift of the Holy Spirit, who dwells within everyone who worships God in spirit and in truth (John 4:23–24; Eph. 2:13–22). Jesus is the temple we go through to worship God rightly, and in him we become the temple of the living God (1 Cor. 3:16; Eph. 2:19–22; 1 Pet. 2:5). Nevertheless, like Israel of old, we are to hear ("Hear, O Israel," Deut. 6:4) before we speak to God. In all walks of life, but especially in public worship, we are to "be quick to hear, slow to speak" (James 1:19). The words of God, rather than the words of the worshiper, are to take priority. Wise worship starts with locked lips.

Speaking Second

Those lips should not stay locked, however. Worshiping wisely also involves right words at the right time. We are to listen to God first and speak to God second. The second half of this Old Testament text covers the boundaries for this second lesson:

> When you vow a vow to God, do not delay paying it, for he has no pleasure in fools. Pay what you vow. It is better that you should not vow than that you should vow and not pay. Let not your mouth lead you into sin, and do not say before the messenger that it was a mistake. Why should God be angry at your voice and destroy the work of your hands? For when dreams increase and words grow many, there is vanity; but God is the one you must fear. (Eccl. 5:4–7)

If it is not obvious from the repetition of the word *vow* (five times), this section centers on temple vows. Such a vow involved a conditional promise; a worshiper coming to the temple asked God for something in return for something—usually money or an animal sacrifice (Lev. 27:1–25), although it could be just about anything or anyone. For example, barren Hannah vowed to give God her son if she was able to conceive and give birth (1 Samuel 1–2).[18] So the problem being addressed in Ecclesiastes is not the vow itself (it was a condoned but not commanded biblical practice), but the temptation to "delay" (Eccl. 5:4) or "not pay" (v. 5) the vow once the request has been granted. To say to the temple "messenger" (the spiritual bill collector sent to retrieve the coins for the temple treasury) that "It was a mistake" or "It was unintentional" is intentionally sinful (Num. 15:30–31; Deut. 23:21). It is better not to vow than to vow and refrain from keeping your end of the deal. "All you need to say is simply 'Yes' or 'No'; anything beyond this comes from the evil one" (Matt. 5:37 NIV), as Jesus said. Why? Because God doesn't take kindly to vows like that of Ananias and Sapphira (Acts 5:1–11). Or, as Solomon exhorted, God "has no pleasure in fools" (Eccl. 5:4) and "Why should God be angry at your voice and destroy the work of your hands?" (v. 6). All toying with God will be exposed ("You blind fools!" Matt. 23:16–22) and judged ("a rod for his back," Prov. 14:3). All lame excuses will be leveled by the Lord.

We all make vows to God and to one another. I vowed to remain faithful to my wife "'til death do us part." As an ordained minister, I vowed "to be zealous and faithful in maintaining the truths of the Gospel and the purity, peace and unity of the church, whatever persecution or opposition may arise." If you are a witness in a court of law, you vow (perhaps even with your hand on a Bible) to "tell the whole truth and nothing but the truth," so help you before God. Making vows is not the issue. Making impulsive promises that you have no intention of keeping or without any real idea of what you are saying is foolish (cf. Prov. 20:25). It is a dream-induced fantasy.

Twice Solomon compares "many words" (Eccl. 5:3, 7) to dreams. The sense of verse 3 is that just as an extremely busy day produces sound sleep (and the dreams that come with such sleep), so a fool produces verbosity. And the sense of verse 7 is that pious phrases uttered by "the mouth . . . [that] pours out evil things" (Prov. 15:28)—reciting God's covenant statutes (Ps. 50:16)—will prove to be as futile as the fantasies created in slumberland. Poof! They are gone the moment you awake. We should watch out for making dreamlike oaths. If we are to vow, let us "make [our] vows to the LORD [our] God and perform them" (Ps. 76:11). Let us not say to the Lord, "I will do this" and then fail to do it (cf. the parable of the two sons, Matt. 21:28–30). There is no value in mindless muttering and great danger in rash

---

[18] Other examples of vows are Jacob's vowing that if God protected and provided for him, he would give God "a full tenth" (Gen. 28:20–22), and David's vowing that he wouldn't go to bed until the temple was built (see the poetic exaggeration in Ps. 132:2–5).

vows (e.g., the story of Jephthah's daughter, Judg. 11:29–40). Perhaps the only vow we should make—certainly the safest, but never the easiest—is the vow to fear God. Pledge to do that today! "Lord, I will listen to you when you speak; and, Lord, when I speak to you I will not come before you with aimless chatter or deluded daydreaming, but with humble and honest admiration and heartfelt and reasonable requests."[19]

Not Fearing God

Beyond our speak-first, listen-second (if ever) world, the more foundational issue is the absence of the fear of God in the culture as well as in the church. Paul's quotation of Psalm 36:1, "There is no fear of God before their eyes" (Rom. 3:18), could be the contemporary church's motto. If it is not found in our actual vision statements, it is found in many worship services every Sunday. We have made glorious Jesus into our own inglorious image and serve him up to accommodate everyone's personal tastes.

Ecclesiastes 5:1–7 is an antidote for such cultural and religious rubbish. It especially protests against this new Protestantism. It gives us a sorely needed vision of God and a picture of wise worship. It moves us beyond God as "the Big Guy upstairs" and Jesus as our "homeboy." Instead, it takes us to the feet of "the One who is high and lifted up, who inhabits eternity, whose name is Holy" (Isa. 57:15) and of his Son, Jesus Christ, "the firstborn of the dead, . . . the ruler of kings on earth" (Rev. 1:5), the One whose eyes are a flame of fire, whose voice is like the roar of many waters, and whose face is like the sun shining in full strength (vv. 14–16), the One who nevertheless "loves us and has freed us from our sins by his blood" (v. 5). Such a view of God compels us to take our sandals off, keep our mouths shut, and listen first.

Scripture-Saturated

Writing in the same century as Nehemiah lived, the Greek historian Thucydides penned a popular saying: "It is the people, not the walls, that make a city."[20] We might build upon that concept, summarizing the book of Nehemiah in this way: as God's people rebuild the wall, God is rebuilding his covenant community under the authority of his Word. This theme is especially seen in chapter 8, which highlights how *God's people love, learn, and live his law.*

Nehemiah 8 features three main characters: Ezra (scribe, priest, and

---

[19] The phrase "aimless chatter or deluded daydreaming" comes from Carl Schultz, "Ecclesiastes," in *Evangelical Commentary on the Bible*, ed. Walter A. Elwell (Grand Rapids: Baker, 1989), 441.

[20] See Raymond Brown, *Nehemiah*, The Bible Speaks Today (Downers Grove, IL: InterVarsity, 1998), 127.

Scripture reader), the Levites (Scripture teachers, or we could call them Bible translators and/or exegetes), and "all the people." It is the laity, however, more than the leaders, that dominate this text. Note that "the people" is repeated eighteen times and "all the people" eleven times.[21] The God-centered worship service at the Water Gate is also, if you will, people-centered. It is people-centered in the sense that we learn here that it was a gathering of men, women, and children ("all who could understand," v. 2) who wanted to hear and heed the Word.

They Loved the Law

Having looked at the phrase "the people," we will next divide our summary phrase—*God's people love, learn, and live his law*—into three sections. First, God's people love his law. Verse 1 and the beginning of verse 4 show this point.

> And all the people gathered as one man into the square before the Water Gate. And they told Ezra the scribe to bring the Book of the Law of Moses that the LORD had commanded Israel. (v. 1)

> And Ezra the scribe stood on a wooden platform that they [the people] had made for the purpose. (v. 4a)

This was a megachurch. There were thousands in attendance. But this was no modern-day megachurch service. No one was sitting in the balcony, settling into his comfortable seat with a freshly brewed cappuccino in hand as he waited for the soft jazz/soft sermon entertainment to begin. No! Rather, here we find God's people gathering, building, speaking, listening, standing, and bowing. "Give me the Word!" was their sentiment.

Besides the gathering, building, speaking, listening, standing, and bowing, another action that demonstrates their affection toward the Word was their double "Amen" at the end of the Scripture reading.

> And Ezra opened the book in the sight of all the people, for he was above all the people, and as he opened it all the people stood. And Ezra blessed the LORD, the great God, and all the people answered, "Amen, Amen," lifting up their hands. (vv. 5–6a)

To say "Amen" is to express agreement. It means: "We believe it," "We agree," "It is true," or "So let it be!" The church father Jerome "commented

---

[21] Note also "the assembly" and the pronouns *they* and *them*.

that in the early church, when visitors used to come, they were commonly frightened at the *amen*." They said, "It had the sound of thunder."[22] Does your church say "Amen" after the Bible is read? How about a double "Amen"? How about raising your hands (as they did) and giving the double "Amen" so loud it wakes the babies in the nursery!

Because of the abuses that go with it, we underestimate the value of certain words and certain postures as real expressions of love. The typical story of an engagement proposal ends with the man upon his knees, confessing his love. It would seem odd to us if the proposal ended otherwise. Just imagine if a bride-to-be said her proposal happened this way: "He knocked on the door, turned his back to me, stared into the sky, and muttered under his breath, 'Um, will you marry me?'" Such a proposal would be preposterous. There can be a deadness in many churches that are full of rote confessions and robotic postures, but that does not mean that such confessions and postures can't be faithful and appropriate representations of the congregation's earnest love for God and his Word. In fact, the best worship is when both heart and hands are raised in devotion—when, for example, we stand to hear the Word read, we stand also in our hearts, lifting up our love to the Lord for his divine revelation. "Oh how I love your law! It is my meditation all the day" (Ps. 119:97).

They Learned the Law

Beyond loving the law, God's people also learned it. Without a doubt—from top to tail—Nehemiah 8 depicts a worship service centered on the written Word of God:

> *Top*: "And all the people gathered as one man. . . . And they told Ezra the scribe to bring the Book of the Law." (v. 1)

> *Tail*: "And day by day, from the first day to the last day, he read from the Book of the Law of God." (v. 18)

The law is mentioned nine times in this chapter! This emphasis is interesting in light of the fact that the books of Ezra and Nehemiah concentrate on the *temple*. Of course, what we have in Nehemiah 8 is not a new dedication of the temple, such as was done in Solomon's time. Rather, it is a reverent and royal reception of divine revelation. As Derek Kidner writes: "At the dedication of Solomon's Temple there had been glory and beauty, natural and

---

[22] This story is retold in Douglas Wilson, *Mother Kirk: Essays and Forays in Practical Ecclesiology* (Moscow, ID: Canon, 2001), 152.

supernatural, to overwhelm the worshippers. Here the focus, apart from a wooden platform, was a scroll—or more exactly, what was written in it."[23]

The Protestant Reformation introduced an important architectural shift—giving the pulpit, not the altar, the place of prominence. For projecting sound and the idea of authority, the Protestants built tall and large pulpits, and often in front of the church platform they placed a large, opened Bible translated into the language of the people. There was also a Communion table, but it was set to the side or behind the pulpit. It is this kind of deliberate positioning that we see in our text. "The book of the Torah," as William Dumbrell explains, "is literally placed at the center of the united people."[24] It was the Torah, not the temple, that then, as it does now, served as "the foundation" for covenant community life.[25]

In graduate school, I took a class on the history of revivals. We began with the "revivals" recorded in Scripture and then walked through the important revivals in Christian history. Our professor argued that there were three characteristics to all true works of Spirit-empowered revival: (1) emotions were shown, (2) order was established, and (3) the emphasis on the Word of God as the center of worship was restored. Nehemiah 8 certainly fits under this rubric.

Notice the emotions expressed. In verses 9–12, people express a mixture of sorrow and joy. At first, when they heard the Word, they grieved over their sins. With each commandment read, it must have felt like blows from a hammer as the perfect Word pounded them with its purity. "Yet, despite the seriousness of their sin, the people were urged to dry their tears," because it was the Feast of Booths, and within ten days of the Feast of Booths would be the Day of Atonement, that day of mercy when all their sins "would be fully, immediately and irrevocably pardoned."[26] So, as is true of any true work of the Spirit, there was the right mixture of emotions—sorrow over sin and joy over salvation.

Furthermore, as is true in any true work of the Spirit, we see the establishment of order. This characteristic may surprise readers who presume that the Holy Spirit is synonymous with spontaneity. There can indeed be spontaneity in worship, but it should all end in order. Recall how Paul concluded his section on spiritual gifts (or the abuse of them) in 1 Corinthians 12–14: "But all

---

[23] Derek Kidner, *Ezra & Nehemiah*, Tyndale Old Testament Commentaries (Downers Grove, IL: InterVarsity, 1979), 105–106.
[24] William J. Dumbrell, *The Faith of Israel: A Theological Survey of the Old Testament* (Grand Rapids: Baker, 2002), 320.
[25] Ibid.
[26] Brown, *Nehemiah*, 134.

things should be done decently and in order" (14:40). The apostle tells the super-spiritual Christians in Corinth that the Spirit desires the church service to have both decency and order.

For some Christians, especially in the free-church tradition, the word *liturgy* has a negative connotation. To them, that word fits churches that don't preach the Bible. But the word *liturgy* comes from the Greek word *latreuo* (meaning "to work or serve"), which is found in several places in the New Testament. So *liturgy* is a Bible word, and a good (not bad) one, and "one's work in worship" is not condemnable but commendable: "There must be some holy sweat if you are to please and glorify God."[27] Some think we can divide churches into two categories—liturgical and non-liturgical. However, in reality, every church is liturgical because all churches have an order of service. Even the most charismatic churches, which claim they just let the Spirit have his way, usually follow the same order of service every Sunday. As Hughes says elsewhere:

> All churches have liturgies, even those which would call themselves "non-liturgical." In fact, having no liturgy is a liturgy! Relaxed charismatic services may be as liturgical in their format as a high-church service—and in some cases more rigid.[28]

So the question is not whether such and such a church has a liturgy (order of service). Of course it does. All churches are liturgical in that sense. Rather, the question is this: Is its liturgy biblical or unbiblical? Is its worship governed by the Word or by something or someone else—perhaps the whims of culture or personal preference? Nehemiah 8 gives us a biblical picture of a God-honoring liturgy: a call to worship, a formal reading of Scripture, an oral exposition or explanation of Scripture, and a celebration of a sacred meal. Does this seem familiar? Yes! For nearly 2,500 years, God's people have followed that basic liturgy. God is not a God of disorder. Just as he sent his Spirit at the beginning of time to bring order to creation, so he still sends his Spirit in these last days to bring order to his new creation—the church.

In Nehemiah 8, we see a true work of the Spirit. It has all the marks: emotions are shown, order is established, and the emphasis on the Word of God as the center of worship is restored.

Speaking of the Word, don't be afraid to be a bookish church, if your bookishness is Bible-bookishness. We are a people of the Book *because* God

---

[27] Hughes, *Disciplines of a Godly Man*, 115.
[28] Ibid.

wrote a book. He didn't produce a movie. He didn't record a music video. He wrote a book! And the people in Nehemiah's day loved that book! And because they loved the Word of God, they learned it. Is there any *learning* in your church's liturgy? Does your service begin with "all who could understand" assembling to hear the Word (vv. 1–2) and "study" it (v. 13), and end with people understanding "the words that were declared to them" (v. 12b)? Hosea 4:6 reads, "My people are destroyed for lack of knowledge." Some of that destruction, it is our strong contention, is in our churches today because we have tossed out the bookishness of Christianity. It used to be said that God's people were "a people of the Book." Sadly, I don't think that would be an accurate assessment today. Perhaps "People of the YouTube Clip" or "People of the Three-Minute Skit" would be a more accurate assessment. Don't be ashamed to be a bookish church. Hold high the Book! Seek to teach men, women, and children the content of the Bible. Engrave Nehemiah 8:8 above the church doors, upon the preacher's pulpit, and within the pew Bibles: "They read from the book, from the Law of God, clearly, and they gave the sense, so that the people understood the reading."

They Lived the Law

Nehemiah 8 shows us that because God's people loved the law, they learned it, and they also *lived* it. Authentic worship effects our ethics! Notice how nicely what is said in verses 13–15 (learning) transitions into verse 16 and what follows (living). I highlight below this transition from learning the law to living the law:

> And they found it written in the Law that the LORD had commanded by Moses that the people of Israel should dwell in booths during the feast of the seventh month, and that they should proclaim it and publish it in all their towns and in Jerusalem, "Go out to the hills and bring branches of olive, wild olive, myrtle, palm, and other leafy trees to make booths, as it is written." *So the people went out and brought them and made booths for themselves*, each on his roof, and in their courts and in the courts of the house of God, and in the square at the Water Gate and in the square at the Gate of Ephraim. (vv. 14–16)

Verse 18 also highlights the transition from learning ("And day by day, from the first day to the last day, he read from the Book of the Law of God") to living ("They kept the feast seven days, and on the eighth day there was a solemn assembly, according to the rule"). From early morning until mid-day, all of them listened to the Bible being read to them—"the ears of all the people were attentive" (v. 3). As we think on the wandering, grumbling, rebellious people of the Old Testament, this is indeed "rare responsiveness."[29] What (or who) has gotten into them?

The Holy Spirit is the answer! We say this because the Spirit, while not mentioned in chapter 8, is mentioned in chapter 9. The prayer recorded there mentions the secret work of the Spirit in the life of Israel: "You gave your good Spirit to instruct them" (v. 20). Moreover, verse 30 states, "Many years you bore with them and warned them by your Spirit through your prophets." Like Joel 2 (cf. Acts 2), Nehemiah 8 is a down payment of the new covenant. But even a down payment is a real payment. Put differently, this is not the full, final work of the Spirit in the church, but it is a real work.

What does all this mean for those who live in and under the new covenant? It means that we are to "be doers of the word, and not hearers only" (James 1:22). We who love and have learned the Word ought to live the Word. We ought to live out, by the power of the Spirit, *all* that is written in the Bible for us.

Nehemiah 8 shows us a high moment in Israel's history, when God's people loved the law, learned the law, and lived out the law. Moreover, it teaches the church today—we who have Christ's indwelling Spirit—that we ought to (by the power of the Spirit) love/desire the Word, study/know the Word, and walk/live according to the Word. When so many churches don't know why they do what they do or don't do what they know they should do, we write this book with the desire to ground you in God's revelation about worship and about keeping the Bible at the center of our services on Sunday and throughout the week.

ORDERING WORSHIP

In answering which scriptural characteristics help control Christian corporate worship, we have seen that our worship should be, among other things, God-fearing (Ecclesiastes 5) and bibliocentric (Nehemiah 8). In other words, our worship should be God-revering and Scripture-saturated. Next, let's build upon that foundation by answering the more practical question: How, then, should we order our weekly Sunday gathering?

Our worship should be regulated *tota et sola Scriptura* ("by the Scriptures alone, and by all of Scripture").[30] True. But what does the Bible pre-

---

[29] Kidner, *Nehemiah*, 104.

[30] "Was David right to eat the showbread? . . . Was Christ right to worship in the synagogue, a pattern of worship generally required by God (Lev. 23:3; Ps. 74:8), but nowhere regulated in the details? To ask such questions is to answer them. Put another way, the requirements *of* the Word of God are broader than the

scribe regarding Christian *liturgy*?[31] Nothing. There is no command in the New Testament to (1) gather on Sunday, (2) say the *Shema*, immediately followed by the *Gloria Patri*, (3) read Genesis, Jeremiah, Matthew, and then Paul, (4) share some matzah bread, and (5) go in peace to love and serve the Lord. Rather, what we find throughout the New Testament are descriptive elements of worship. Does this allow for freedom of forms? Yes. Does it mean we ignore what is described? God forbid! "When something is not specifically commanded, prescribed, or directed or when there is no scriptural example to guide us in how we are to perform some particular aspect of worship we should try nevertheless to be guided by scriptural principles."[32]

JESUS'S WORSHIP HABITS

With that truth in mind, let's start with Jesus's worship habits. In Luke 4:16–21, we read:

> And he came to Nazareth, where he had been brought up. And as was his custom, he went to the synagogue on the Sabbath day, and he stood up to read. And the scroll of the prophet Isaiah was given to him. He unrolled the scroll and found the place where it was written,
>
> "The Spirit of the Lord is upon me,
>   because he has anointed me
>   to proclaim good news to the poor.
> He has sent me to proclaim liberty to the captives
>   and recovering of sight to the blind,
>   to set at liberty those who are oppressed,
> to proclaim the year of the Lord's favor."
>
> And he rolled up the scroll and gave it back to the attendant and sat down. And the eyes of all in the synagogue were fixed on him. And he began to say to them, "Today this Scripture has been fulfilled in your hearing."

Notice six details.

First, it was Jesus's "custom" to attend synagogue on Saturdays. To give a conservative estimate, if Jesus had attended synagogue on the Sabbath since age thirteen, then at this point in his ministry he had worshiped

requirements *in* the Word of God. Our worship is to be authoritatively regulated *tota et sola Scriptura*, by the Scriptures alone, and by all of Scripture." Wilson, *Mother Kirk*, 125.

[31] Again, the word *liturgy* is a Greek (also Latin) word that simply means "the work or service of the people." It need not have a high-church connotation.

[32] Hughes Oliphant Old, *Worship That Is Reformed According to Scripture* (Atlanta: John Knox, 1984), 171.

there about nine hundred times. Whatever else we might say about that fact, we must acknowledge that Jesus didn't find the "formal" liturgy (see what follows below) and regular attendance in a building designated for learning about God to be stultifying to his spiritual development (Luke 2:40).

Second, there was a Bible reading, and Jesus was the one who read it. Did he ask to do the reading or was he asked to do it? We don't know. Was it in Hebrew or Greek? We don't know. Diaspora synagogues would have read the Bible in Greek; for the Jews of Palestine, the reading would have been in Hebrew and translated into Aramaic. Perhaps the synagogue in Jesus's hometown read the Hebrew. Through the synagogue school, and perhaps through Joseph's business, Jesus would have learned Hebrew, Greek, and Aramaic.

Third, there was an "attendant" who handed him the scroll of Isaiah. Was Jesus given Isaiah because (1) it was the only scroll they had, (2) there was a set reading from Isaiah for the day and he knew where to find it, or (3) he asked for it and, as the teacher, had the liberty to preach from any text he desired? We cannot be certain, but most likely he simply was given the next section in the prophet Isaiah, following the previous Sabbath's reading.

Fourth, on this occasion, he preached Christ (himself) from the Old Testament (and it didn't go over well in his hometown).

Fifth, when he read the text, he was standing, yet when he taught, he was sitting. Sitting was a sign of authority. He spoke *ex cathedra* ("from the chair").

Sixth, this passage, along with a few passing references elsewhere in the Gospels and Acts,[33] gives us all we are told about the synagogue service in the New Testament. Why? Is it because the synagogue service was insignificant to Jesus's view of public worship? No. Was it then because the majority of the first readers of the New Testament knew very well all the elements of service? Yes.

I have read many explanations of the synagogue service over the years. Perhaps the clearest and simplest, and thus certainly one of the best, comes from a children's book that covers the topic. The full picture is in order:

> The synagogue was a place of meeting for reading . . . the Bible, and for prayer. . . . Within the synagogue there was nearly always a closet

---

[33] For example, Matthew 4:23; Mark 1:21–28; 3:1–6; 6:2; Luke 6:6; 13:10; John 6:59; 18:20; Acts 13:5; 14:1; 18:4, 19.

or chest which stood against the wall that faced toward Jerusalem. This closet or chest was the ark where the scrolls of the sacred books were kept. These were the Law, the Prophets, and the Writings. . . . In the center of the synagogue stood a platform on which a reading desk was placed. At the foot of the platform and facing the rest of the room were benches called chief seats. Here important persons sat during the services. . . . The leader of the synagogue conducted the service.[34] The Shema was said.[35] Benedictions were recited.[36] A procession of men and of boys over thirteen years of age brought the scrolls from the ark and placed them on the reading desk. Psalms were chanted. Then the leader chose someone to read from the Law. He began where the reading of the last Sabbath had ended. Then a portion from the Prophets was read. A member of the congregation was chosen to explain the Law or to preach a verse from the Prophets.[37] There were prayers. The service closed with a final benediction.[38]

There is little doubt that when the early church gathered regularly on Sundays (Acts 20:7; 1 Cor. 16:2) or what came to be called "the Lord's Day" (Rev. 1:10)—because it was the day Jesus rose from the dead (see Mark 16:1–2; John 20:1)[39] and bestowed the Spirit upon his church (Acts 2:1–3)—the pattern of the synagogue played a major role in the structure of their gatherings. Perhaps they simplified the structure, or perhaps what is recorded in the New Testament is only part of their gatherings. The picture we get from the gatherings mentioned in Acts 2:42–47 and 20:7–11 centers on table fellowship ("the breaking of bread"), apostolic teaching (Christians

---

[34] To this detail, Ralph P. Martin adds: "The 'ruler' summons the 'minister' (see Luke vi, 20) to invite someone from the congregation to commence the service with this 'call to worship'. He begins with the cry: 'Bless ye the Lord, the One who is to be blessed'; and the people respond with the benediction: 'Blessed be the Lord . . . for ever,' in the spirit of Nehemiah ix, 5. At the outset, then, the worshippers are invited to think of God and to acknowledge His greatness and blessing." *Worship in the Early Church* (Grand Rapids: Eerdmans, 1975), 25.

[35] Compare Deuteronomy 6:4–9 with 11:13–21 and Numbers 15:37–41.

[36] While there was no standardized prayer book, the *Eighteen Benedictions* show something of what the Jews of Jesus's generation would have prayed. These prayers "cover a wide range of themes . . . partly an expression of praise, partly petitions for spiritual and material benefits and partly supplications for those in need (exiles, judges and counsellors and chosen people)." Martin, *Worship in the Early Church*, 26.

[37] Cf. Josephus, *Contra Apionem* 2:175; Philo, *De Somniis* 2:127.

[38] Ethel L. Smither, illus. Ruth King, *A Picture Book of Palestine* (New York/Nashville: Abingdon, 1947), 46, 50–51. For more scholarly summaries, see Martin, *Worship in the Early Church*, 23–27; Andrew E. Hill, *Enter His Courts with Praise! Old Testament Worship for the New Testament Church* (Grand Rapids: Baker, 1993), 228–233; and Larry W. Hurtado, *At the Origins of Christian Worship: The Context and Character of Earliest Christian Devotion* (Grand Rapids: Eerdmans, 2000), 31–34.

[39] On the Lord's Day, cf. *Didache* 14.1; Ignatius, *To the Magnesians* 9.1; Justin, *Apology* I.67.3 (Justin speaks of the focus on Scripture reading [the writings of the Prophets and apostles "are read as long as we have time"], exhortation, and prayer). "*Each* Lord's Day was an Easter Festival, since this was not yet confined to one single Sunday in the year. . . . It is correct to say that from the time of Christ's resurrection, the day of rest appointed by God was transferred to the day of Christ's resurrection and was regarded as 'fulfilled' in it." Oscar Cullmann, *Early Christian Worship* (repr., Bristol, IN: Wyndham Hall, n.d.), 11.

"devoted themselves to the apostles' teaching"),[40] and prayer (*"the* prayers," to be precise, likely a reference to set prayers said in Jewish homes, at synagogue, and perhaps when traveling to the temple, no doubt Christianized where needed).

Again, while this pattern is not prescriptive, it would be foolish for us to dismiss a scriptural pattern as unimportant. We can't be dogmatic (we must order our services like this or else!)[41] and we shouldn't be stale (for example, insisting that Christian worship must always contain teaching, Communion, and prayer in that order and never with variance), but we can be wise. And to be wise is to understand patterns and principles we find in Scripture *and*, in general, followed throughout church history. As Old writes: "While the Reformers understood the Scriptures to be their sole authority, they were very interested in how generations of Christians down through history had understood the Scriptures. In the history of Christian worship they found many good examples of how the church had truly understood Scripture."[42] Later he comments that the contemporary church should "maintain [the Reformed liturgical] tradition because it witnesses to the authority of Scripture."[43] Its public worship practices are "above all, according to Scripture."[44]

WORSHIP THROUGH THE AGES

In this same vein, in his excellent essay "Worship Through the Ages," Nick Needham writes, "Unless we wish to make a virtue of solipsism, any serious consideration of worship must take into account the history of worship, as a sort of running commentary on Scripture, a commentary embodied in practice and preserved in literary monuments, especially liturgies."[45] Table 1 (page 49) is my summary of Needham's historical survey.[46]

---

[40] In 1 Timothy 4:13, Paul focused on the Word elements of worship, writing, "Until I come, devote yourself to the public reading of Scripture, to exhortation, to teaching."

[41] "Jesus attended the synagogue regularly and taught there (Luke 4:15–16), so there can be no question as to God's approval of the institution. It is interesting, however, to note that the synagogue and the temple were very different in their scriptural warrant: God regulated the sacrificial worship of the tabernacle and the temple in detail, charging the people to do everything strictly according to the revealed pattern. He hardly said anything to Israel, however, about the synagogue (or, for that matter, about the ministries of teaching and prayer carried out on the temple grounds), leaving the arranging of its services largely to the discretion of the people. Of course, they knew in general what God wanted: he wanted his word to be taught and prayer to be offered. But God left the specifics open-ended." John M. Frame, *Worship in Spirit and Truth: A Refreshing Study of the Principle and Practice of Biblical Worship* (Phillipsburg, NJ: P&R, 1996), 23.

[42] Old, *Worship That Is Reformed According to Scripture*, 4.

[43] Ibid., 170.

[44] Ibid., 172.

[45] Nick R. Needham, "Worship Through the Ages," in *Give Praise to God*, 375.

[46] Cf. Bryan Chapell, *Christ-Centered Worship: Letting the Gospel Shape our Practice* (Grand Rapids: Baker Academic, 2009). See his helpful charts—from Rome to Rayburn!—on historic liturgical structures (see Charts 1.1 to 6.2).

Table 1. The Basic Liturgies of the Western Church

APOSTOLIC FATHERS	THE PATRISTIC AGE	THE MIDDLE AGES	MARTIN LUTHER	ULRICH ZWINGLI*	JOHN CALVIN	ENGLISH PURITANS
Scripture readings: OT and NT	Greeting/response	Greeting/response	Hymn or psalm	Set prayer	Scripture reading; Psalm 124:8	Call to worship
The sermon	Scripture reading: OT	*Kyrie elesion:* "Lord, have mercy"	*Kyrie elesion:* "Lord, have mercy"	Scripture reading: NT Epistles	Opening set prayer: Confession of sin	Prayer of adoration and supplication
The collection	Psalm or hymn	Hymn: *Benedictus dominus* (Luke 1:68–79) or *Gloria in excelsis*	Set prayer	*Gloria in excelsis* (said, not sung)	Scriptural words of pardon/absolution	Psalm
The Lord's Supper	Scripture reading: NT (Acts—Rev.)	Collect (set prayer for the day)	Scripture reading: NT (Acts—Revelation)	The Apostles' Creed	Ten Commandments with *Kyrie elesion*: sung	Scripture reading: OT
	Psalm or hymn	Scripture reading: OT	Hymn: Sung by choir	Prayer: The Lord's Prayer	Prayer for illumination	Psalm
	Scripture reading: Gospels	Scripture reading: NT Epistles	Scripture reading: Gospels (chanted)	Set prayer	Scripture reading	Scripture reading: NT
	Sermon	Hymn	The Apostles' Creed	The Lord's Supper	Sermon	Prayer of confession and intercession
	Prayers	Scripture reading: Gospels	Sermon	Psalm (said, not sung)	Collection (offering)	Sermon
	Lord's Supper	Chants: Trisagion	Prayer: The Lord's Prayer	Set prayer	Set prayer of intercession, then Lord's Prayer	Prayer of thanks and intercession
	Benediction	Sermon	The Lord's Supper	Benediction	The Apostles' Creed or a psalm sung	The Lord's Prayer
		Litany (responsive liturgical prayers)	Set prayer		The Lord's Supper (once a month)	The Lord's Supper
		Offertory/psalm sung	Benediction: (Num. 6:24–26)		Benediction: (Num. 6:24–26)	Psalm
		Kiss of peace				Benediction
		Lord's Supper				
		Prayer: The Lord's Prayer				
		Dismissal				

*This is the order for Zwingli's communion service. "The normal Sunday morning worship in Zwinglian Zurich was essentially a preaching service, consisting of Bible readings, prayers, and a sermon. Zwingli was unique among the Reformers in not regarding the Lord's Supper as integral to Sunday worship; he was happy that it should be celebrated four times a year: Christmas, Easter, Pentecost and a local Zurich festival on September 11." Nick R. Needham, "Worship Through the Ages," in *Give Praise to God: A Vision for Reforming Worship,* ed. Philip Graham Ryken, Derek W. H. Thomas, and J. Ligon Duncan III (Phillipsburg, NJ: P&R, 2003), 399.

Four elements shared by all the liturgies on page 49 include (1) the reading and singing of Scripture, (2) the sermon on Scripture, (3) prayer according to Scripture, and (4) the Lord's Supper modeled after what is recorded in Scripture.[47] The purpose behind the survey and summary, however, is not to pick a liturgy from above or to pick and choose some elements from each of them. Rather, it is to encourage and exhort the contemporary church to be as thoughtful and biblically conscious in ordering our worship as our forefathers were.[48] We must let the Word inform *and comprise* our worship. Furthermore, we must understand that there are right and wrong, as well as better and worse, ways to worship God; and our best efforts now will pale in comparison to our future new-heaven-and-new-earth orthodoxy and doxology. Finally, we must be aware that many of today's trends in worship are powered by subjectivism rather than thoughtful scriptural reflection. As Needham bravely and rightly critiques the contemporary church:

> The congregation has become an audience, the minister has become an orator, and everything else in the service can be safely ignored or even treated with casual contempt. Liturgy, creed, Scripture lections, confession, intercessory prayers, psalms and hymns, Eucharist—all have either been dropped or emptied of existential engagement. The only thing that matters is to be uplifted through the sermon. Subjectivity has won its first victory.[49]

If we are to resist the lure of subjectivity, we must reset our sights on Scripture, as was done in the past, and, for God's sake and our good, stop squandering the rich inheritance that has been handed down to us! Because Scripture allows for some flexibility of form, and perhaps of elements,[50] we should acknowledge this God-given flexibility and adjust our liturgies to our con-

---

[47] Note Westminster Confession of Faith 21.5, which speaks of "the ordinary religious worship of God" consisting of "the reading of Scriptures . . . the sound preaching . . . singing of psalms . . . [and] the sacraments."
[48] Throughout the centuries—in many cases, even millennia—God's people have sought to chain their worship to Scripture itself. In fact, the Book of Common Prayer (1552)—the gem of the English Reformation—consists largely of biblical quotations. Also in the Reformed tradition is the Dutch Liturgy, adopted at the beginning of the seventeenth century, the Book of Common Order (commonly called "John Knox's Liturgy"), which is only slightly freer in style, and the Directory for the Public Worship of God, produced by the Westminster Assembly in the mid-seventeenth century. Martin Luther's service was an evangelical revision of the Mass, and John Calvin produced a simplified yet structured liturgy, as well as the Form of Prayers, for public worship. "What the Reformers and their heirs opposed was the imposition of a particular liturgy on the church as a necessary form for the true worship of God." Michael Horton, *A Better Way: Rediscovering the Drama of God-Centered Worship* (Grand Rapids: Baker, 2002), 147.
[49] Needham, "Worship Through the Ages," 409.
[50] While we might debate some of Frame's critiques of the regulative principle, he is nevertheless correct to point out that "Scripture nowhere divides worship up into a series of independent 'elements,' each requiring independent scriptural justification." *Worship in Spirit and Truth*, 53. Also, he is right to note (and critique) those who use that principle to "enforce traditionalism in worship" (45). For more on "formality and informality," see Peterson's helpful critique of the idea that formality over informality is "acceptable worship." *Engaging with God*, 160.

text. However, while much is permissible, not everything is profitable! For example, if a service does not contain a Bible reading and an explanation of the Bible (which, sadly, the services in many of the world's largest evangelical churches do not), something is devilishly wrong. As Oscar Cullman wrote: "Our sources of investigation of the early Christian service of worship do not yield a perfectly clear picture of the outward development of the gatherings for worship; they do disclose, however, a fairly clear tendency in worship."[51] That clear tendency is far removed from today's liturgical innovators, who have eliminated godly reverence because it is "irrelevant" and public Bible readings because they are "dull." Let us flee that subjectivity of our age and return to the timeless truths of Scripture.

SAMPLE WORSHIP SERVICES FROM CONTEMPORARY CHURCHES

In the spirit of subjectivity, I thought I'd start with myself. More seriously, I wanted to show some of the thought process that went into two liturgies I designed for two church plants. These plants were birthed from College Church, and thus were consciously dependent on our mother church's liturgy.

In his chapter "Discipline of Worship" in *Disciplines of a Godly Man* and in Appendix A of his chapter "Free Church Worship" in *Worship by the Book*, Kent provides an order of service and its rationale. Below is a summary of his thoughts, often in his own words, as well as my own additional comments based on my experience at College Church as a student and intern:

The Details of Corporate Worship at College Church (1999)

Every Christian "must understand that worship
is the ultimate priority of his life."[52]

—Kent Hughes

Prelude.

Welcome. Sometimes brief announcements (goal: less than two minutes long) would be done during the Welcome, as they were less intrusive to the flow of worship. However, since people often come late to service,

---

[51] Cullmann, *Early Christian Worship*, 7.
[52] Hughes, *Disciplines of a Godly Man*, 111. On that same page, Hughes further comments: "A look at the massive emphasis on worship in the Old Testament reveals God's mind on worship's priority. Exodus devotes twenty-five chapters to the construction of the Tabernacle, the locus of divine worship. Leviticus amounts to a twenty-seven chapter liturgical manual. And the Psalms are a spectacular 150-chapter worship hymnal. Divine worship has always been the occupation and sustenance, the priority, of the believing soul."

moving them to the middle might make better sense—especially for important announcements that affect the whole body.

Silence. Americans seem to be obsessed with the need for unending sound. Some consider silence in worship a breach of etiquette. They want no "dead spots." But silence slows the frantic pace and gives time for reflection and individual dialogue with God. It bows to Habakkuk's call: "The LORD is in his holy temple; let all the earth keep silence before him" (Hab. 2:20). The time is brief, perhaps even ten seconds, but it helps us "center down" (as the Quakers say).

Call to Worship and Invocation. Properly done, the call is from God, who is inviting us corporately into his presence. We listen to God's words (often a Psalm) with reverent, prayerful anticipation. As the call ends, we offer an invocation (a pastor prays or the choir sings) that invites God to meet us and calls us to submit ourselves in worship, for his glory.

Doxology. The Doxology is meant to draw us upward in music for the purpose for which we have come—to give God glory. It should be sung with our whole hearts.

Apostles' Creed. We employ the creed for three reasons: (1) to affirm the essentials; (2) to emphasize that we are in the stream of historic orthodoxy; and (3) to provide a familiar reference to visitors and new Christians from mainline and Roman Catholic backgrounds. The Nicene Creed is often used during Advent, for the same reasons given above.

Hymn. While we sing to each other (and we hear and see each other sing), God is our ultimate audience. We sing to him with heart and *head*, thus fulfilling Paul's determination: "I will sing praise with my spirit, but I will sing with my mind also" (1 Cor. 14:15). What a glory it is to God when a hundred, two hundred, or a thousand all truly sing to God with their minds and spirits in the sublime labor of praise!

Congregational Prayer. When the congregational prayer begins, all minds must engage in unison with silent or verbal agreements—"Yes, Lord" or "Amen." Ending with a congregational "Amen" (said loudly or sung in unison) is very fitting, as this is *our* prayer to God. The person praying (most often the senior pastor) should be prepared. As Kent writes: "Next to preaching, I spend most of my preparation time on prayer. My hope is not to pray a beautiful prayer . . . rather it is to be so filled with the Word and the needs of my people that we are all borne up to God." The thoughtful pastor knows that this prayer on behalf of his people has a dynamic potential for exaltation (it lifts us up to God), edification (it builds us up in Christ), equipping (it teaches us how to pray), and even evangelism (it might be used by the Spirit to draw unbelievers into a saving relationship through the prayed truths of the gospel and the communion of the saints).

Often included at the end of the congregational prayer is the Lord's Prayer. When used, it must never be merely recited but rather prayed with the head and heart. Worshipers are never to babble out (see Matt. 6:7) that perfect model prayer.

Anthem. Church choirs have their precedent in the choirs of voices and instruments in the Old Testament. Thirty-five of the psalms have the superscription "To the choirmaster." Others were sung according to recommended tunes such as "The Hind of the Dawn," tunes no doubt well known to many in Israel. Choirs offer music in a way that is beyond the average person's capacity. It is the congregation's way of offering its best to God and is an especially beautiful gift for him.

Tithes and Offerings. Giving ought to be an act of conscious worship rather than a reflexive religious act. The givers, as they give of their substance, ought to first give *themselves* to God (cf. Rom. 12:1; 2 Cor. 8:5).

God at Work. This heading provides the place for the many variations that are part of our corporate worship pattern. *God at work in families*: infant baptisms and dedications take place. *God at work in missions*: a missionary focus. *God at work in our lives*: testimonies.

Scripture Reading. The reading of Scripture is purely the sharing of God's Word, while it remains to be seen whether the sermon that follows is. When Ezra read the law, all Israel stood (Neh. 8:5), and we should stand in solidarity with such respect for God's Word, symbolizing our submission to it. By standing, responding with our corporate "Amen," and then singing the *Gloria Patri*, we acknowledge and celebrate the centrality of God's written revelation.

Sermon. Admittedly the hardest work during the liturgy may be listening to the sermon. Here the minister should have done his work (in preparing to expound and deliver the Word), but the congregation has its work to do as well. It is helpful to keep one's Bible open to better follow the textual argument and look up possible references. It is also helpful to take notes: identify the theme; list points, subpoints, observations, and applications. Pray for God's grace to hear and understand what he wants you to hear and to apply his voice preached into your life and the life of the body.

Lord's Supper. Celebrated once a month. (See chapter 6 for more information.)

Hymn. See "Hymn" above. (Also note that sometimes three hymns were sung during the worship hour.)

Benediction. A scriptural blessing is given.

Postlude.

When you look at an actual liturgy from College Church, you can see how these principles are applied:

Sample Worship Service at College Church
Prelude
 "Morning," Edvard Grieg
 "O Sons and Daughters, Let Us Sing," arr. F. Gramann
 Jubilation Ringers, Bryan Park, conductor

  And we with holy church unite
  As evermore is just and right
  In glory to the King of Light.
Choral Call to Worship
 Make a joyful noise to the LORD, all the earth!
 Serve the LORD with gladness!
 Come into his presence with singing!
 (Psalm 100:1–2)
Welcome
 Pastor Marc Maillefer
Silence
Invocation
Doxology
 Lasst Uns Erfreuen (congregation standing)
Apostles' Creed (congregation standing)
Hymn
 "The Day of Resurrection"
Congregational Prayer and Lord's Prayer
 Pastor Kent Hughes

Hymn

"Good Christian Men, Rejoice and Sing"

Anthem

"Christ Is Now Arisen," Chancel Choir, Greg Wheatley, conductor

Tithes and Offerings

Offertory

"Alleluia! The Strife Is O'er," arr. F. Gramann, Jubilation Ringers

Scripture Reading

2 Timothy 2:8–13, Mrs. Diane Jordan (congregation standing)

Gloria Patri

Sermon

"The Essential Memory," Pastor Kent Hughes

Hymn

"Jesus Lives, and So Shall I" (congregation standing)

Benediction

Pastor Kent Hughes (congregation standing)

The congregation will be seated for a moment of reflection.

Postlude

"Good Christians All, Rejoice and Sing," piano: Ed Childs, organ: H. Willnan

With my experience of worship at College Church and a basic knowledge of the thoughtful rationale for the elements of worship, before I helped plant Christ the King Church and New Covenant Church, I walked the core groups of those plants through some ideas I had for our corporate gatherings. (On an ironic side note, when I showed something similar at a church-planting assessment center, many of the progressively minded twentysomething pastors thought my ideas were fresh, novel, and even hip. Oh, if they only knew I was simply standing on the shoulders of giants.)

The list below shows excerpts from the draft I gave to the core group for the first church. I have kept some of the rough-draft feel to it to give you the sense that this was a work in progress. The pastors (myself and Ken Carr), with the congregation's feedback, wanted to decide how to worship on Sundays at our new church. As you read through this list, notice how we consciously built upon College Church's firm foundation at Christ the King. Also notice, in the list further below, how various aspects of the service for New Covenant stayed the same and various ones changed from Christ the King. The changes might have involved theological developments in my own understanding of liturgy, or, more likely, they reflected doing worship in a different context.

The Details of Corporate Worship at Christ the King (2000)

"The heart of the Christian life is to be found
in the act of public worship"

—Hans Lietzmann.[53]

Prelude. What is the purpose of the prelude? The prelude is not a musical filler or a piano recital; it functions to set a "suitable atmosphere for the preparation of heart and mind for the exalted activity of worship."[54]

Welcome. This is not necessary, but is obviously beneficial—for setting the tone, informing people that worship is soon to start, acknowledging visitors, and giving the congregation any necessary announcements about body life.

Greeting. What is the purpose of the greeting? We should not seek communion with God if we are not reconciled with our brother (Matt. 5:23–24). Why do we have it at the beginning of the service? Traditionally it is placed before Communion (peace between each other/peace with God). However, if we are to be reconciled with our brother, why wait until the time before Communion? (Some pragmatic honesty: I found it to be disruptive in the middle.) What sign do we give of greeting/peace? A handshake or a hug (that's just our culture). What did people in the ancient church do? "A holy kiss" (Rom. 16:16; 1 Cor. 16:20; 2 Cor. 13:12; 1 Thess. 5:26).

Call to Worship. What is its purpose? To call us to worship God! The notion is seen throughout the Psalms (95:1; 145–150) and also dates back to Nehemiah 8:1, where the people wanted to worship.

Music/Singing. What are all the musical components of our service? The Doxology, five congregational songs, the offertory, the *Gloria Patri*, prelude, and postlude. We try to emulate what we see in Scripture. We sing songs from all periods of Christian history to show our solidarity with the whole body of Christ throughout the ages (no chronological snobbery!). The Doxology is a song of praise to God as Trinity. The tune comes from *Pseaumes Octante Trois de David* (1551); the words, however, come from Isaac Watts's paraphrasing of Psalm 117, with the third verse written by Thomas Ken in 1709. It functions as a musical call to worship.

---

[53] Hans Lietzmann, *The Founding of the Church Universal* (London: Lutterworth Press, 1950), 124, quoted in Martin, *Worship in the Early Church*, 133.
[54] Robert G. Rayburn, *O Come, Let Us Worship: Corporate Worship in the Evangelical Church* (Grand Rapids: Baker Book House, 1987), 171–172.

The *Gloria Patri* is also called the "lesser or minor doxology." It praises the Holy Trinity. It probably originated as an adaptation of the Jewish "blessings" addressed to God (cf. Rom. 16:27; Phil. 4:20; Rev. 5:13). Its form was influenced by the Trinitarian baptismal formula (e.g., Matt. 28:19). Variations of it were used in the Arian controversy. It was written in the second century. The form we now sing comes from the seventh century. It reflects both Jewish and Gregorian chant. Psalm-singing is modeled in the New Testament (see Eph. 5:19; Col. 3:16; James 5:13) and was also used throughout church history.

Creed. Why the Apostles' Creed? It is not necessary, but it is helpful for three reasons: (1) it reflects the language of Scripture (cf. Philippians 2; Colossians 1; 1 Corinthians 15) and is a good summary of the content (not the effects) of the gospel; (2) it is a defense against heresy; and (3) it reflects the "common faith" of the church universal. The creed:

- comes from the Old Roman Creed (first century);
- was recited at baptism;
- deals with many second-century issues (e.g., Gnosticism) and with Jesus's true humanity and death;
- was reintroduced by the Protestant Reformers (even Zwingli); and
- is very agreeable to a wide range of Christians.

There are some confusing words in the Creed:

- Why V rather than v for "Virgin"? This is due to Isaiah 7:14, the idea being that Mary is *the* Virgin.
- The word *catholic* means "universal" (note that Martin Luther used "Christian").
- "Descended into hell" is not in the original. This can be taken spiritually (Matt. 27:46) or physically (1 Pet. 3:19).

Note: we will use scriptural "creeds" (Phil. 2:1–11; Col. 1:15–20) as well as other historic creeds (e.g., the Nicene Creed).

Congregational Prayer. Who should give the congregational prayer? The leaders, typically the pastors. This is due to three factors: (1) we have the time to do it, (2) we are your overseers, and (3) we know what is going on in the church better than others. We might also have couples from the congregation (an elder and his wife?) do this.

What should be its content and form? We usually follow ACTS (borrowing from Origen)—adoration, confession, thanksgiving, supplication. The prayer should be brief (Matt. 6:9–13); usually written out (as modeled in Scripture, e.g., "the prayers," Acts 2:42, and certainly in history); not preachy; not sentimental or extremely personal; and not overly detailed (e.g., "We pray that you would stop the pus from coming out of Aunt Martha's right big toe").

Offering/Offertory. Why is this part of the "worship" service? Why not simply place a box at the exit? There are several reasons:

- Tithing was practiced in the Old Testament.
- Collections were taken in the New Testament (see 1 Cor. 16:1–4; cf. Acts 11:27–30).
- Jesus and the apostles saw giving as a token of the heart response to the gospel.
- Part of the gospel ministry is remembering the poor (Gal. 2:10).

Offertory music is to be meditative.

King's Court/Children in Worship. Why do we have children in the service?

- There is value in family worship.
- Through immersion and example, the children are learning the language of worship.

How do we help the children grasp what is happening?

- The Kingdom Kids sermon handout
- Repetition: e.g., memorization of creed and songs
- Kid's Court

Scripture Reading. Why do we have a Scripture reading? The Bible tells us to (1 Tim. 4:13). Why do we read the Scripture the way we do? What's with the ceremony? See Nehemiah 8 (standing, saying "Amen").

Sermon. Where do we get the idea of giving a sermon?

- The sermons in Acts
- The book of Hebrews
- "Prophets" in Acts (13:1; 15:32)

Exegetical homilies/sermons were the "standard homiletical form, as it was almost the only sermonic genre in the church before the High Middle Ages."[55] Why do we do expository preaching?

- We see examples in the Bible.
- We see examples in church history (Chrysostom and Augustine).
- God's questions, not ours, are answered.
- Texts are not ignored if one goes systematically through a book.

---

[55] O. C. Edwards Jr., *A History of Preaching* (Nashville: Abingdon, 2010), 67.

The Lord's Supper. Why do we celebrate Communion? Christ commanded us to partake of Communion (Matt. 26:26–28). Why do we celebrate it once a month? Jesus did not explicitly state how often we are to partake. There are two major practices: (1) quarterly or seasonally: this draws the connection between the Old Testament feasts (especially Passover) and the vagueness of the phrase "as often as you" (1 Cor. 11:25–26); and (2) weekly: this seems to be what happened in the early church; it seems to be the pattern of worship in the Bible to end with a covenant meal; and it was what many of the Protestant Reformers did or wanted to do. What elements do we use? Bread and wine (should we use wine or grape juice?).

Benediction. The idea for a benediction derives from benedictions in the Bible: Numbers 6:22–27; Romans 15:13; 16:24; 1 Thessalonians 5:23; Hebrews 13:20–21; 2 John 3; Jude 24–25. Note that biblical benedictions are often not about what people do for God, but about what God does for people. What is the purpose? *Bene* means "good" (as in *benefit*); *diction* means "pronouncement." It is a short invocation (to God) for divine help, blessing, and guidance, usually given after or at the end of the service.

The following is the bulletin from our first service at Christ the King:

Sample Worship Service at Christ the King

Welcome/Announcements
  Pastor Ken Carr
A Reading from the Psalms
  Psalm 1
Opening Hymn
  "O Worship the King" (insert)
The Apostles' Creed
  Pastor Douglas O'Donnell
Congregational Prayer
  John and Debbie Seward
Greeting
  Pastor Ken Carr
Congregational Singing
  "Praise to the Lord"
  "You Are My King"
  "Lord, We Are Few" (all inserts)
Offering/Prayer
  Pastor Douglas O'Donnell
Elders Commissioning
  Elders

Gloria Patri
Reading from God's Word
   Philippians 2:1–11, Pastor Douglas O'Donnell
Sermon
   "United by the King," Pastor Ken Carr
Closing Hymn
   "How Great Thou Art" (insert)
Benediction
   Pastor Ken Carr

Seven years later, as I was planning to plant New Covenant Church, I refined some of my earlier liturgical thoughts and added new ideas. In the list below, I have included only components or part of the explanation that changed. I prefaced this handout with a document titled "Foundations for our Fellowship," which listed three priorities for our worship:

- Faithful to the non-negotiable, timeless, and principled components of the New Testament assemblies—Word, prayer, and the Lord's Supper.
- Reflective of certain necessary, neutral, or good values of the culture in which we gather—English language, song selection and instrumentation, etc., thoughtful throughout, efficient, orderly, simplicity of style and flow.
- Promoting the purposes of Christian assemblies:
  - Exaltation. There is reverent, joyful, thankful, God-centered exaltation (so that people say, "That gathering was about God!").
  - Edification. This gathering helps Christians grow in their reliance upon God, his Scriptures, his gospel, and his church; also, it helps people build one another up.
  - Equipping. This gathering serves to equip Christians to live the Christian life, witness to the world, and serve one another, the lost, and the good of the city.
  - Evangelism. Unbelievers encounter God through his Word and his people.

The Sunday Morning "Heavenly Gathering"[56] at New Covenant Church (2008)

Public worship is "the finest of the fine arts."[57]

—Andrew Blackwood

---

[56] Original explanation: Because God has gathered his people to himself in Christ (through his election and our faith, we have been raised up with Christ in "the heavenly places"), we gather together here and now, with Christ in our midst, for the purpose of fellowshipping with him and with one another, with the practical effect of stirring one another up to love and good works.
[57] Andrew Blackwood, *The Fine Art of Public Worship* (Nashville: Cokesbury, 1939), 8.

Prelude. What is the purpose of the prelude? What atmosphere? Festive resurrection music (fast but subtle)—a joyous sound! We are coming to celebrate God's work through Christ!

Welcome. Welcome all, especially visitors (tell them how to get connected). State our vision, then go into no more than three announcements.

Call to Worship. What is its purpose? To call us to recognize the presence of God and come before him with reverence, praise, and thanksgiving. Usually a short Scripture passage is read, and then a prayer is offered.

Congregational Singing. A group of two to four songs (the best songs of the old and new that flow well together)—very well liked, singable, etc. If needed, instruction is given (singing, history, Bible verses), but rarely.

The Prayers. The key here is diversity of form (as determined by the pastor). The typical pastoral prayer is interactive ("Let us pray")—on the spot or received during that week. We together recite/pray a thoughtful, beautifully written prayer.

The Offering. Why is this part of the gathering? Why not simply place a box at the exit? There are several reasons:

- Tithing was practiced in the Old Testament.
- Collections were taken in the New Testament (see 1 Cor. 16:1–4; cf. Acts 11:27–30).
- Jesus and the apostles saw giving as a token of the heart response to the gospel.
- Part of the gospel ministry is remembering the poor (Gal. 2:10).

Offertory music sets the stage for the Scripture reading (thus, it is to be meditative). Children K–5th grade are dismissed.

Scripture Reading. Same as Christ the King.

Sermon. Same as Christ the King.

Doxology. Led by the pastor. Follows his prayer (perhaps sung *a capella*).

The Lord's Supper. Why do we celebrate Communion? What is the goal? Christ commanded us to partake of Communion (Matt. 26:26–28). It is a "love feast"—a communal meal (how can we accomplish this in our context?). What elements should we use? Bread (unleavened) and wine (non-alcoholic wine). The bread is broken. How will the elements be distributed and by whom? People will come forward. The elements will be distributed by the pastor/s and elders. One hymn (cross-centered) will be sung as people are coming forward.

Closing Hymn. Joyful, well-known resurrection song (such as the Hillel Psalms).

Benediction. Same as Christ the King.

Postlude. See notes on prelude, similar purpose.

Below is the bulletin from our first service at New Covenant Church on June 1, 2001.

Sample Worship Service at New Covenant Church
Our Gathering In Christ's Presence, June 1, 2008
Prelude
Welcome
   Pastor Douglas O'Donnell
Musical Invocation (Introit)
   "Let All Mortal Flesh Keep Silence"
Invocation
   Pastor Andrew Fulton
   Psalm 95
Hymn of Adoration
   "Holy, Holy, Holy"
Creed
   Pastor Douglas O'Donnell
The Prayers
   Pastor Andrew Fulton
Hymns to Christ
   "My Heart Is Filled with Thankfulness"
   "O the Deep, Deep Love of Jesus"
The Collection
   Pastor Andrew Fulton
Scripture Reading
   Paul Adams
   Luke 19:1–10
Scripture Teaching
   Pastor Douglas O'Donnell
   "A Camel Gets Through"

Song of Response
  "Be Thou My Vision"
The Breaking of the Bread
  "O Sacred Head, Now Wounded"
Benediction
  Pastor Douglas O'Donnell
Postlude

In that first bulletin, and for months afterward (as well as at least once a year), we included the insert below. This insert shows a more finalized form of our thoughts in the list above. Any recent additions are in *italics*:

New Covenant Order of Service

Welcome: Our welcome serves three purposes: (1) to warmly greet those who have gathered in Christ's name, (2) to remind us of the vision of this church, and (3) to inform us of and invite us to its ministries.

Introit and Invocation: Sometimes it is difficult to focus on the things of God. The Introit (a musical entrance) and the Invocation (a call to worship, *which often includes a Psalm,*[58] *the confession of sin, and acknowledgment of God's acceptance in Christ*) serve to turn our thoughts to God, his Word, and his people.

Hymn of Adoration: Some Christian liturgies walk through the life of Christ, the storyline of the Bible, a re-enactment of the events of personal salvation, or the formula of a covenant renewal. Our liturgy seeks to blend all of these as best we can. While we acknowledge we are sinners as we come into the presence of Christ, we also recognize we are saved sinners, all by the grace of God. Thus, we begin with a hymn in which the melody and lyrics are God-centered, joyous, and reverent—befitting our great God and his great work of salvation in history and in our very lives.

Creed: Through a historic creed of the church (e.g., the Apostles' Creed) or a creedal statement of Scripture (e.g., Phil. 2:1–11; Col. 1:15–20), we join the communion of saints—past and present—as we together affirm some of the essential Christian beliefs (*credo* is Latin for "I believe"). Also, as we weekly recite various orthodox statements of faith—which have been believed by all Christians everywhere at all times—we renew

[58] On the first Sunday night of every month, New Covenant Church hosts "Psalms and Sermon." This is a half-hour worship gathering where we (1) sing Psalms and (2) listen to a short expositional sermon. The Psalms are very valuable in teaching us that worship: (1) is Godward, (2) is done with joy and reverence, (3) can be musical, (4) can be done both by individuals and as an assembly, and (5) is historically focused (recalls and celebrates the acts of God in history).

our minds in the basic truths of God's revelation to us in Christ, thus combating heretical views about God, man, and salvation.

The Prayers (Acts 2:42): Each week an elder of the church leads us in the congregational prayer. He does so using the "prayers" of Scripture and often following a traditional pattern of prayer.[59]

Hymn to Christ: Here we sing a Christ-centered scriptural song that reminds us of God, his plan of redemption, and our saving relationship with him through Christ.

The Collection (1 Cor. 16:1): We worship God when we give generously to the work of the gospel in the world (*here we always pray before the collection for one of our missionaries*) and to the needs both within and without the body of Christ (*here we also pray for those who are sick or for those grieving loss*). As we listen to meditative music and also read silently the Scripture passage that is about to be read aloud (printed in our bulletin or in the pew Bibles), we prepare ourselves to listen to the Word of God read and proclaimed.

Scripture Reading: Following the pattern set forth in Nehemiah 8 (and subsequently followed in the liturgy of the synagogue and almost all liturgies within the Christian church), we stand to listen to God speak to us through the reading of his Word. *After the reading, we sing the* Gloria Patri—*praising God for his revelation to us. In the tradition of Nehemiah 8:6, we encourage people to lift their hands in praise, in a sense affirming the reading with our hands and hearts, "Amen, Amen."*

Scripture Teaching: As we seek to exalt Jesus Christ and to show forth his excellencies, as well as to encourage and equip the saints, each Sunday we gather as God's people around God's Word to hear it explained and applied. *We also hope and pray that those who do not know Christ might, through our worship, bow before him in saving faith and adoration.*

The Breaking of the Bread: Perhaps the most forgotten words of our Lord Jesus's institution of the Lord's Supper are the words "as often." Throughout history, the church has widely differed on how often we are to gather to partake of this meal. We at New Covenant Church gather once a month as a full corporate body to remember, through this visible and tangible drama, the death of our Lord, and also to commune with God as we commune with each other. *On Good Friday—at our*

---

[59] Examples of such prayers can be found in chapter 5.

special annual service—the elders stand at the front, and the people walk forward as we sing to one another of our shared salvation and then receive the elements as the elders say each person's name and the words of remembrance (e.g., "Joe/Jane, Christ died for your sins. Eat this in remembrance of him").

Song of Response: Reflective of the text of Scripture just preached, we seek to offer our response to the Word of God and the work of God in our lives. Knowing our sinful tendency to love self or the things of this world more than God, we recommit ourselves to loving him with all our heart, soul, strength, and mind.

Benediction: This word comes from the Latin *benedicere* ("to speak well of" or "bless"). Following an ancient form, the pastor raises his hand, and in a fatherly fashion—as if laying his hand upon the heads of his sons and daughters—asks for God's continued blessing upon the family of God. *This blessing reminds us that it is God who has called us out of the world to worship him and loves to extend more grace each time we gather in his name.*

THOUGHTFUL VARIETY: OTHER NEW LITURGIES

While there is much liturgical reformation still to be done in evangelical churches, we must acknowledge that we are living in a time when many young Christians have returned to biblical thoughtfulness in worship. This can be seen, for example, at Bruce Benedict's website, Cardiphonia (www.cardiphonia.org), which hosts a wide variety of worship resources, including sample liturgies. Two liturgies we especially liked are from Covenant Presbyterian Church in Chicago and Redeemer Presbyterian Church in Indianapolis. Their bulletins can be found at http://www.covenantchicago.org/pdf/Covenant_Chicago_order_of_worship.pdf and www.redeemindy.org/worship/worship-bulletins. Benedict also gives an excellent liturgy example from St. Barnabas Anglican Church in London (see his post on September 13, 2013; http://cardiphonia.org/2013/09/13/worshipping-with-st-barnabas-anglican-church-in-london/). Other examples on his website and other websites abound.[60] Some excellent ones include:

[60] In an e-mail dated March 24, 2014, Bruce Benedict also suggested to me orders of service from the following churches: All Souls Church, http://allsoulschristianchurch.com/blog/post/liturgy-recap-03-29-14; City Church, http://www.citychurchphilly.com/bulletins; First Presbyterian Augusta, http://repository.firstpresaugusta.org/bulletins/currentbulletin.pdf; Resurrection Park Slope, http://www.resurrectionparkslope.org/Sunday-Worship-Bulletins

GRACE IMMANUEL BIBLE CHURCH

Grace Immanuel Bible Church in Jupiter, Florida, has no printed order of service that the congregation sees. Instead, the church uses a projection system during its time of corporate singing, and the only printed material those in the congregation see is their own copies of the Scriptures.

Although the service order is not displayed, the elements themselves are carefully and consistently prepared based on a pattern of the gospel narrative. Broadly speaking, the services are structured around two parts: (1) worship through singing and giving and (2) worship in the Word. Through singing, Scripture, and prayer, four elements are presented: (1) adoration, (2) confession, (3) assurance of grace, and (4) response. Sometimes the music leader will explain the role of a particular song or Scripture passage ("Now we'll confess our sin by singing . . ."), but over time the congregation has begun to pick up on the flow of the elements without needing them to be expressly stated. These elements are the essence of the gospel: God is holy, we are sinful, there is forgiveness offered to us in Christ, and we respond to God in faith and obedience. The advantage of this structure is that it gives purpose and intentionality to the flow of the service; but because it is not visible, it frees up the congregation to participate and respond without feeling restricted by a printed page.

The presence of a liturgical structure does not of itself guarantee gospel-centered, doctrinally rich content. Corporate worship is edifying and Christ-exalting only when the leadership commits and plans to make it so.

Grace Immanuel Bible Church (March 16, 2014)
Welcome/Body-Life
Worship through Singing and Giving
   Adoration: "O Worship the King"
   Confession: Scripture: Psalm 51:1–3, 10–12
   "Merciful God"
Scripture Reading
   Psalm 96
Offering
   Assurance of Grace: "Great Is Thy Faithfulness"
   "Resurrection Hymn"
Worship in the Word
   Response: "O Great God"

Grace Immanuel Bible Church (March 23, 2014)
Call to Worship
   "Come, People of the Risen King"

Welcome/Body-Life
Worship through Singing and Giving
   Adoration: "Fairest Lord Jesus"
   Confession: Scripture: 2 Corinthians 5:21, Isaiah 53:3–6
   Assurance of Grace: "His Robes for Mine"
Scripture Reading
   Exodus 19 (sermon text)
Offering
   Assurance of Grace: "Now Why This Fear"
   Response: "I Will Glory in My Redeemer"

Friendly Temple Missionary Baptist Church

In his book *Christ-Centered Worship*, Bryan Chapell provides a few example services, including an "African American Baptist" service from Friendly Temple Missionary Baptist Church in St. Louis:[61]

Gathering Music
   "We Bring the Sacrifice of Praise"
Choral Call to Worship
   "The Lord Is Worthy of Praise"
Responsive Reading
   Psalm 1
Song of Assurance
   "Welcome to This Place"
Pastoral Prayer for Church Needs
Preparation for Thanksgiving
   Reading: Malachi 3:8–12
Offering
   Collection with choral and congregational songs of thanksgiving
Announcements and Greeting of Guests
Choral Anthem
   "Praise to the Lord"
Choral and Congregational Preparation for the Word
   "Holy Spirit, Come Down"
Proclamation of the Gospel
Prayer
   Text Reading: Matthew 27:27–32
Preaching
   Matthew 27:27–32

---

[61] Chapell, *Christ-Centered Worship*, 270–271.

Prayer of Consecration
Invitation to Discipleship
Benediction
Postlude

NEW ZION BAPTIST CHURCH

I asked my friend K. Edward Copeland, senior pastor of New Zion Baptist Church, Rockford, Illinois, to send me his typical Sunday morning worship service (along with some brief explanation). Note the feel, but also see the structure that allows for various freedoms of expression:

Opening Praise
Corporate singing
Baptism
(We don't do baptism every Sunday morning, but when we do, we include it here.)
Scriptural Prayer
(We gather in small groups and individually read a verse from the psalm for the day to the group and pray it back in our own words.)
Ministry Highlights
(Ministry opportunities we are emphasizing for the week.)
Welcome
(Corporate singing while we give hugs and handshakes to guests and one another.)
Worship in Giving
(Choir sings during this element.)
Worship through Music
(Choir sings or praise dancers dance, or both.)
Sermon
Call to Commitment
(We always call for a commitment, but often include an "altar call.")
Communion
(We don't observe Communion every Sunday morning, but when we do, we include it here.)
Final Blessing/Benediction

CHRIST THE REDEEMER

Christ the Redeemer in Spokane, Washington, is a Baptist church with Episcopalian roots. Its pulpit is expository, its theology is Reformed, and its worship is a mixture of hymns and Keith Getty/Stuart Townend and Sovereign Grace fare interspersed with a few elements of the church's liturgical past:

Christ the Redeemer, June 22, 2014
"A Mighty Fortress," Martin Luther
"I Sing the Mighty Power of God," Isaac Watts
Welcome and Announcements
  Pastor Brian Hoch
High School Senior Acknowledgments
Old Testament Scripture Reading
  Isaiah 6:1–13

  Minister: "This is the Word of the Lord."
  Congregation: "Thanks be to God."
Confession
  Heavenly Father, in spite of the everlasting love You have shown us, we still go our own way . . .
Offering
  "The Risen Christ," Phil Madeira and Keith Getty
  "O Great God," Bob Kauflin
New Testament Scripture Reading
  Luke 8:1–21

  Minister: "This is the Word of the Lord."
  Congregation: "Thanks be to God."
Congregational Prayer
Sermon
  "Gospel Farming," Pastor Carey Hughes
  "Oh How Good It Is," Keith Getty, Ross Holmes, Stuart Townend
  "Come People of the Risen King," Keith and Kristyn Getty and Stuart Townend
Benediction
  Pastor Loren Baker

In his book *A Better Way: Rediscovering the Drama of God-Centered Worship*, Michael Horton writes, "Regardless where we find ourselves on the ecclesiastical map, it can hardly be disputed that all churches have some sort of liturgy."[62] True. And as he rightly notes: "the structure and content of the service are never neutral, nor should they be regarded as matters of preference":

---

[62] Horton, *A Better Way*, 141.

Unlike the "gods of the nations," the God of Abraham and Jesus does not leave the matter of how we approach him in our hands. While there may not always be a clear black-and-white answer to all our questions about which style to use in a given context, it should be fairly obvious that liturgical style is more than the window dressing of worship. In fact, it is that which brings into an embodied form all our beliefs about God, ourselves, redemption, and the chief end of human existence.[63]

Therefore, while we cannot claim that our church's liturgy is the only way to worship God rightly, we should be able to say that there is great intention as to how we order our public worship. We know what we do and why we do it.[64] We can defend our motives and motions as biblical, as being "draw[n] from the depths of 'the whole counsel of God'" rather than from the whims of the world.[65] We recognize that "church services will vary in entirely appropriate ways; some things are necessary [e.g., the Bible is taught] while other things depend on circumstances of time and place"[66] (e.g., the Bible is taught from a raised pulpit or behind a music stand). The key, at least as we have argued, is God-revering, Scripture-saturated, corporate worship that exalts God, edifies believers, and evangelizes unbelievers.

PUTTING IT INTO PRACTICE

In this chapter, as we have attempted to journey away from solipsism (from the Latin *solus* and *ipse*, which, in the context of public worship, we might define as "self alone") to standing on the shoulders of others (modern and ancient), we conclude with a call to repentance. Or, less pointedly, we end with a request for recalibration. After reading about the biblical foundations, historical practices, and a few contemporary applications of public worship, how might you change your church's Sunday morning gatherings? Below are some questions to walk through with the church leadership:

1. What is your "liturgical" background? How might it influence the way you think about corporate worship—in both positive and perhaps negative ways?
2. During Sunday morning gatherings, how do you emphasize that worship is *all of life* (living for God Sunday through Saturday)?

---

[63] Ibid., 143.
[64] Ibid., 142. For Horton's own "rough outline of [the elements of] a typical worship service" (143), a "biblical liturgy . . . in new covenant worship" (148), see 148–160.
[65] Ibid., 143.
[66] Ibid., 148.

3. If Christian worship has a threefold goal of edification, evangelism, and exaltation, how does your service reflect that?

4. We must let the Word inform and *comprise* our worship! What scriptural characteristics for corporate worship were listed in this chapter? What Old Testament and New Testament principles, practices, and paradigms does your church use to help control Christian worship? For example, would you classify your corporate gatherings as being God-fearing and Scripture-saturated? If not, what changes should be made?

5. What did you learn from the history lesson (about the roots of the free-church tradition) and the historical liturgies (including the synagogue service of Jesus's time)? What might you add or subtract from your liturgy based on this historical reflection?

6. Review the order of services for College Church and two of its church plants (Christ the King and New Covenant Church). Also review and check out some of the other new liturgies listed. How might these resources help your church think through how and why you do what you do? For example, how would you answer such questions as:

   • How many Scripture readings should be included in our services? None? One from the Old Testament? Two—one from the Old Testament and one from the New Testament? Where in the service should that reading or those readings come?

   • Will we use a creed or creeds? If so, which ones, and where in the service, on what occasions, and with what frequency?

   • Should we include a separate prayer of confession, or should it be included in the congregational prayer?

   • Should we use traditional songs, such as the Doxology and the *Gloria Patri*? If so, where, when, and how often?

   Once you have answered these questions and many more like them, then structure a couple of "ideal" orders of worship. Use the extensive resources in this book to help.

THE IMAGINARY BUT IDEAL CHURCH

We conclude this chapter with David Peterson's "brief portrait of an imaginary church."[67] Read it! It is beautiful. Then ask yourself: What does your biblical ideal of corporate worship look like? Write or list your own thoughts.

Anyone could tell from the way the members of this congregation related to one another that their Sunday gathering was an expression of genuine Christian community. It was clearly a high point in their week, but not

---

[67] This excerpt is from Peterson, *Engaging with God*, 289–292.

the only time when most of them met together or engaged in ministry together. Their conversation, their prayers and their contributions during the service reflected an obvious concern for one another in a whole range of situations. This was no spiritual ghetto, since it was clear that members desired to welcome strangers and to minister to the needs of those outside their fellowship. Many seemed to be actively involved in evangelism, pastoral care, or social action groups in the wider community.

The service began with a time of informal singing, as the congregation remained seated and latecomers continued to arrive. Songleaders and instrumentalists had carefully planned this segment so that people were reminded of the significance of their gathering together, distractions were removed, and minds were focused on God's character and promises. Every contribution to the service seemed to be motivated by a desire to encourage the congregation in their relationship with God and with one another. This was no entertainment extravaganza, but it was certainly an involving experience that was far from dull. The time of informal singing led quite naturally to the reading of a few verses from Scripture and a challenge to draw near to God with repentance and faith.

Perhaps the most surprising aspect of this service was the fact that it happily combined a set "liturgical form" with informal and spontaneous elements. The prayer of confession, which all said together, and the assurance of God's forgiveness which followed, were the beginnings of the formal liturgy. Song leaders and instrumentalists then led another segment of praise and thanksgiving, responding to the reminder of gospel promises which had just been given. When two members of the congregation read the set lessons from the Bible, one from the Old Testament and one from the New, it was obvious that they had prepared well and anticipated that God would encounter his people through this ministry.

The sermon which followed was based on one of the readings for the day, though it incorporated insights from the other readings as well. Sometimes sermons were topical or thematic and sometimes they involved the explanation and application of key verses from Scripture. Mostly they were systematic expositions of biblical passages, working through a series of chapters for six to eight weeks, and then moving to another part of Scripture for variety of content and style. When a sermon series proceeded systematically through a segment of the Bible, home groups were encouraged to discuss several set questions each week, based on the exposition given that Sunday. Such questions were prepared in advance by the preachers, to enable members of the congregation to work hard at discovering the implications of the text. With such an integrated programme of adult education in the parish, people were more motivated to listen to the Sunday sermon and were actively involved with one another in implementing its teaching. Many prepared for the next Sunday by studying the relevant Bible passage in advance.

On this occasion the sermon was a careful explanation of a brief passage, well applied to the situation of the listeners and delivered in a compelling fashion. Since the subject was coping with suffering, at an appropriate point in the sermon the preacher asked a lady to share briefly how God had helped her in her recent distress. This unusual contribution really helped to bring the message home. It was one of several creative techniques used from time to time to involve people in the public teaching ministry, giving a voice to their hopes and fears, their victories and defeats. You could tell from the way the preacher handled the Scriptures, exalting the Lord Jesus Christ and challenging the congregation to relate every aspect of their lives to God and his promises, that this was viewed as an opportunity for the congregation to engage with God, in the Holy Spirit, through his words. The prayer before and after the sermon certainly conveyed something of that expectation.

The hymn after the sermon was carefully chosen to draw out some of the consequences of the sermon and enable the congregation to make a further response to what they had just heard. Then followed a time of announcements and informal ministry. A married couple asked for prayer about important family matters. A girl shared how God had answered a recent prayer and challenged the congregation to be bold themselves in intercession. Another person gave news of some missionaries who had gone out from the church and offered prayer for them. A man and a woman made specific responses to the sermon, giving ideas about the practical application of the biblical text. When this activity was first introduced into the Sunday services, people were slow to contribute, but the right sort of leadership encouraged even some of the most timid to share after a while. It was really an extension of the sort of ministry that members of the congregation were already exercising in home groups throughout the week.

The service leader then began a time of corporate prayer, in which he nominated areas of concern and called upon people to pray spontaneously about these concerns, closing each segment with a set prayer. On other Sundays a few people would be asked to prepare the prayer segment in advance and to lead it from the front. Sometimes the whole congregation broke into small groups, sharing in prayer with those seated near them. The matters that were contributed during the announcements and time of informal ministry were incorporated into the intercessions. The focus was not merely on the needs of the local church, however, but on the world and its problems.

On this particular Sunday, a hymn formed a bridge to the celebration of the Lord's Supper. A time of preparation was followed by a prayer of thanksgiving for Christ's saving work and a recollection of his words at the Last Supper. To express their commitment to one another as the body of Christ, members of this fairly large congregation passed the bread and the wine to each other, using appropriate words. On other occasions, they were encouraged to come forward in groups, stand in a circle and share the bread and wine with one another. When segments of the church were away together for weekends of teaching and fellowship, they celebrated the Lord's Supper quite informally, in the context of an ordinary meal.

The meeting finished on a note of thanksgiving and rededication to God. This was expressed in prayer and singing. In fact, much of the service seemed to be concerned with what would come after—in the time of informal conversation after church, in home groups during the week, and in the opportunities for ministry that many shared in the neighbourhood, in the workplace and beyond. Although the focus of the gathering was on heavenly or spiritual realities, the relevance of these truths to the world in which they lived was the preoccupation of those who participated.

Such an outward-looking emphasis, in the teaching, the prayers and other contributions, served to enhance and not to diminish the importance of the Sunday gathering. The congregation enjoyed meeting together to renew their relationship with God and with one another. But it was not the sum total of their involvement with each other or the ultimate expression of their commitment to Christ! It was a time to draw collectively on all the resources available to them in Christ, through the local congregation. It was a time to serve the Lord by participating in the building up of his body, and to be encouraged together to honour him in everyday life.

2

Annual Services

When the Passover was instituted, the Lord specified to Moses, "This day shall be for you a memorial day, and you shall keep it as a feast to the LORD" (Ex. 12:14). That same day, when Moses concluded his instructions for observing the first Passover, he said: "And when you come to the land that the LORD will give you, as he has promised, you shall keep this service. And when your children say to you, 'What do you mean by this service?' you shall say, 'It is the sacrifice of the LORD's Passover, for he passed over the houses of the people of Israel in Egypt, when he struck the Egyptians but spared our houses'" (Ex. 12:25–27). Thus, we understand that the celebration of the Passover was not an option. It was not man's idea but God's. Remembering God's saving work was essential to the faith of the generations to come and ultimately to their embracing "Christ, our Passover" (1 Cor. 5:7).

In the same way, the annual celebrations of the saving work of the Lamb of God through his incarnation, death, and resurrection (the gospel) are essential to the spiritual well-being of God's children and their children's children. These are, without reservation, the greatest events of world history. As such, they are events that the faithful pastor uses to instill the essentials of the gospel in the lives of his people by the prayerful preparation of sermons and services that evoke the question, "What do these things mean?" to which he then heralds the eternal answers.

In this chapter, we will provide some wisdom for the three singular gospel events of the year. You will note that we have not followed the full liturgical calendar of the traditional Western church year (e.g., we do not treat Lent or Holy Week), though we do include a simple liturgy for the four Sundays of Advent and for Good Friday. Our selection is based on our belief that celebrating the birth, death, and resurrection of Christ is central to the apostolic vision of the gospel.

CHRISTMAS

On Christmas Eve, the eternal Son of God stood poised, so to speak, at the rim of the universe, radiating light. Then he dove headlong through the galaxies and over the Milky Way toward our planet and into the watery warmth of the Virgin's womb, where he first became a zygote, then an embryo, then a fetus, and then a baby, who would be born of Mary in a barnyard on what we call Christmas Day. Isn't that the most beautiful story ever told? But today it is lost amid the glittering and plastic sentiment of our culture, which, without the Christ, is a yellow brick road to darkness.

Our task as pastors is to put together services in which the great story is preached in its rich biblical context amid hymns and songs that lift up the glories of the incarnation, so that our children and children's children will wonder at and understand its meaning. The following resources will aid the busy pastor.

SELECT CHRISTMAS SCRIPTURES

The following Bible passages make excellent preaching texts. They can also be read, directly or responsively, at the various services of the Christmas season.

Old Testament

Numbers 24:15–17	Isaiah 11:1–10
Psalm 2	Isaiah 40:1–11
Psalm 8	Ezekiel 34:22–24
Isaiah 9:1–7 (esp. v. 6)	Micah 5:2

New Testament

Matthew 1:18–25	John 1:1–4
Matthew 2:1–11	John 1:1–14
Matthew 2:13–23	2 Corinthians 8:9
Luke 1:5–25	2 Corinthians 9:15
Luke 1:26–38	Galatians 4:4–6
Luke 1:39–45	Philippians 2:1–8
Luke 1:46–56	Colossians 1:15–20
Luke 1:57–66	1 Timothy 1:15
Luke 1:67–80	1 Timothy 3:16
Luke 2:1–7	Hebrews 2:14–18
Luke 2:1–20	Hebrews 4:14–16
Luke 2:21	Hebrews 10:5–7
Luke 2:22–38	

Select Advent and Christmas Hymns and Songs

There is so much high-quality Advent and Christmas music that we can't possibly list it all here, but we have chosen many of what we consider to be the best hymns and songs.

Classic Advent and Christmas Hymns

"All My Heart This Night Rejoices" (Gerhardt)
"Angels from the Realms of Glory" (Montgomery)
"Come, Thou Long-Expected Jesus" (Wesley)
"Comfort, Comfort Ye My People" (Olearius)
"Gabriel's Message" (Basque carol)
"Good Christian Men, Rejoice" (Suso)
"Hark, the Glad Sound" (Doddridge)
"Hark! The Herald Angels Sing" (Wesley)
"How Great Our Joy" (Baker)
"Joy to the World" (Watts)
"Let All Mortal Flesh Keep Silence" (Liturgy of St. James)
"Lo, How a Rose E'er Blooming" (15th c. German)
"O Come, All Ye Faithful (*Adeste Fideles*)" (Wade)
"O Come, O Come Emmanuel" (Latin hymn)
"O Holy Night" (Cappeau)
"Of the Father's Love Begotten" (Prudentius)
"On Jordan's Bank the Baptist's Cry" (Coffin)
"On This Day Earth Shall Ring" (*Piae Cantiones*)
"Once in Royal David's City" (Alexander)
"Rejoice, Rejoice Believers" (Laurenti)
"Savior of the Nations, Come" (Ambrose)
"Silent Night! Holy Night" (Mohr)
"The First Noel" (trad. English carol)
"Thou Didst Leave Thy Throne" (Elliott)
"Wake, Awake, for Night is Flying" (Nicolai)
"What Child Is This?" (Dix)

Recent Advent and Christmas Hymns and Songs

"Anthem for Christmas" (Gaither/Smith)
"Awake! Awake, and Greet the New Morn" (Haugen)
"Christ the Lord Is Born Today" (Altrogge)
"Exult in the Savior's Birth" (Carson/Boswell)
"From the Squalor of a Borrowed Stable" (Townend)
"Glory Be to God" (Wesley; alt. Kauflin)

"Jesus, Joy of the Highest Heaven" (Getty/Getty)
"Joy Has Dawned" (Getty/Townend)
"O Come, Our World's Redeemer, Come" (Perry)
"O Savior of Our Fallen Race" (Getty/Getty)
"People, Look East" (Farjeon)
"Thou Who Wast Rich Beyond All Splendour" (Houghton)
"Wonderful Counselor" (Altrogge)

SELECT CHRISTMAS POEMS

The following represent the finest poems in the English language and are meant for reading at appropriate places in Christmas services and for quotation in total or in part where they serve the text of the sermon. We also recommend that you read this section annually, so that its content will be in your mind as you prepare for the Christmas season.

The four oldest Christmas poems are found in the Gospel of Luke: Mary's *Magnificat* (1:46–55), Zechariah's *Benedictus* (1:68–79), the angels' hymn to the shepherds (2:14), and Simeon's *Nunc Dimittis* (2:29–32).

"As with Gladness Men of Old" (William C. Dix)

As with gladness men of old
Did the guiding star behold;
As with joy they hailed its light,
Leading onward, beaming bright;
So, most gracious Lord, may we
Evermore be led to Thee.

As with joyful steps they sped
Savior, to Thy lowly bed,
There to bend the knee before
Thee, whom heaven and earth adore;
So may we with willing feet
Ever seek Thy mercy seat.

As they offered gifts most rare
At Thy manger, rude and bare,
So may we with holy joy,
Pure and free from sin's alloy,
All our costliest treasures bring,
Christ, to Thee, our heav'nly King.

Holy Jesus, every day
Keep us in the narrow way;
And when earthly things are past,
Bring our ransomed souls at last
Where they need no star to guide,
Where no clouds Thy glory hide.

In the heavenly country bright,
Need they no created light;
Thou its light, its joy, its crown,
Thou its sun which goes not down;
There forever may we sing
Alleluias to our King!

"Brightest and Best of the Sons of the Morning" (Reginald Heber)

Brightest and best of the sons of the morning,
Dawn on our darkness and lend us Thine aid;
Star of the East, the horizon adorning,
Guide where our infant Redeemer is laid.

Cold on His cradle the dewdrops are shining;
Low lies His head with the beasts of the stall;
Angels adore Him in slumber reclining,
Maker and Monarch and Savior of all!

Say, shall we yield Him, in costly devotion,
Odors of Edom and offerings divine,
Gems of the mountain and pearls of the ocean,
Myrrh from the forest, or gold from the mine?

Vainly we offer each ample oblation,
Vainly with gifts would His favor secure.
Richer by far is the heart's adoration;
Dearer to God are the prayers of the poor.

"A Christmas Folk-Song" (Lizette Woodworth Reese)

The little Jesus came to town;
The wind blew up, the wind blew down;
Out in the street the wind was bold;
Now who would house Him from the cold?

Then opened wide a stable door,
Fair were the rushes on the floor;

The Ox put forth a horned head:
"Come, Little Lord, here make Thy bed."

Up rose the Sheep were folded near:
"Thou Lamb of God, come, enter here."
He entered there to rush and reed,
Who was the Lamb of God, indeed.

The little Jesus came to town;
With Ox and Sheep He laid Him down;
Peace to the byre, peace to the fold,
For that they housed Him from the cold!

"A Christmas Hymn" (Richard Wilbur)
A stable-lamp is lighted
Whose glow shall wake the sky;
The stars shall bend their voices,
And every stone shall cry.
And every stone shall cry,
And straw like gold shall shine;
A barn shall harbor heaven,
A stall become a shrine.

This child through David's city
Shall ride in triumph by;
The palm shall strew its branches,
And every stone shall cry.
And every stone shall cry,
Though heavy, dull, and dumb,
And lie within the roadway
To pave His kingdom come.

Yet he shall be forsaken,
And yielded up to die;
The sky shall groan and darken,
And every stone shall cry.
And every stone shall cry
For stony hearts of men:
God's blood upon the spearhead,
God's love refused again.

But now, as at the ending,
The low is lifted high;
The stars shall bend their voices,
And every stone shall cry.
And every stone shall cry
In praises of the child
By whose descent among us
The worlds are reconciled.

"Descent" (Luci Shaw)

Down he came from *up*,
and *in* from *out*,
and *here* from *there*.
A long leap,
an incandescent fall
from magnificent
to naked, frail, small,
through space,
between stars,
into our chill night air,
shrunk, in infant grace,
to our damp, cramped
earthy place
among all
the shivering sheep.

And now, after all,
There he lies
fast asleep.[1]

"The Girlhood of Mary Virgin" (Dante Gabriel Rossetti)

This is that blessed Mary, pre-elect
God's Virgin. Gone is a great while, and she
Was young in Nazareth of Galilee.
Her kin she cherished with devout respect:
Her gifts were simpleness of intellect
And supreme patience. From her mother's knee
Faithful and hopeful; wise in charity;

[1] Luci Shaw, *Accompanied by Angels: Poems of the Incarnation* (Grand Rapids: Eerdmans, 2006). Reprinted by permission of the publisher. All rights reserved.

Strong in grave peace; in duty circumspect.
So held she through her girlhood; as it were
An angel-watered lily, that near God
Grows, and is quiet. Till one dawn, at home,
She woke in her white bed, and had no fear
At all,—yet wept till sunshine, and felt awed;
Because the fullness of the time was come.

"Holy Sonnet 15" (John Donne)

Wilt thou love God, as he thee? then digest,
My soul, this wholesome meditation,
How God the Spirit, by angels waited on
In heaven, doth make his temple in thy breast.
The Father having begot a Son most blest,
And still begetting (for he ne'r begene)
Hath deigned to choose thee by adoption,
Coheir to his glory, and Sabbath's endless rest;
And as a robbed man, which by search doth find
His stolen stuff sold, must lose or buy it again;
The Son of glory came down, and was slain,
Us whom he had made, and Satan stolen, to unbind.
'Twas much, that man was made like God before,
But, that God should be made like man, much more.

"A Hymn on the Nativity of My Savior" (Ben Jonson)

I sing the birth was born tonight,
The Author both of life and light;
The angels so did sound it,
And like the ravished shepherds said,
Who saw the light, and were afraid,
Yet searched, and true they found it.

The Son of God, the eternal King,
That did us all salvation bring,
And freed the soul from danger;
He whom the whole world could not take,
The Word, which heaven and earth did make,
Was now laid in a manger.

The Father's wisdom willed it so,
The Son's obedience knew no "No,"

Both wills were in one stature;
And as that wisdom had decreed,
The Word was now made Flesh indeed,
And took on Him our nature.

What comfort by Him do we win?
Who made Himself the price of sin,
To make us heirs of glory!
To see this babe, all innocence,
A martyr born in our defense,
Can man forget this story?

"In the Bleak Midwinter" (Christina Rossetti)

In the bleak midwinter, frosty wind made moan,
Earth stood hard as iron, water like a stone;
Snow had fallen, snow on snow, snow on snow,
In the bleak midwinter, long ago.

Our God, Heaven cannot hold Him, nor earth sustain;
Heaven and earth shall flee away when He comes to reign.
In the bleak midwinter a stable place sufficed
The Lord God Almighty, Jesus Christ.

Enough for Him, whom cherubim, worship night and day,
Breast full of milk, and a manger full of hay;
Enough for Him, whom angels fall before,
The ox and ass and camel which adore.

Angels and archangels may have gathered there,
Cherubim and seraphim thronged the air;
But His mother only, in her maiden bliss,
Worshipped the beloved with a kiss.

What can I give Him, poor as I am?
If I were a shepherd, I would bring a lamb;
If I were a Wise Man, I would do my part;
Yet what I can I give Him: give my heart.

"Mary's Song" (Luci Shaw)

Blue homespun and the bend of my breast
keep warm this small hot naked star
fallen to my arms. (Rest . . .

you who have had so far
to come.) Now nearness satisfies
the body of God sweetly. Quiet he lies
whose vigor hurled
a universe. He sleeps
whose eyelids have not closed before.
His breath (so light it seems
no breath at all) once ruffled the dark deeps
to sprout a world.
Charmed by dove's voices, the whisper of straw,
he dreams,
hearing no music from his other spheres.
Breath, mouth, ears, eyes
he is curtailed
who overflowed all skies,
all years.
Older than eternity, now he
is new. Now native to the earth as I am, nailed
to my poor planet, caught that I might be free,
blind in my womb to know my darkness ended,
brought to this birth
for me to be new-born,
and for him to see me mended
I must see him torn.[2]

"On the Morning of Christ's Nativity" (John Milton)
This is the month, and this the happy morn,
Wherein the Son of Heaven's eternal King,
Of wedded maid and virgin mother born,
Our great redemption from above did bring;
For so the holy sages once did sing,
That he our deadly forfeit should release,
And with his Father work us a perpetual peace.

That glorious form, that light unsufferable,
And that far-beaming blaze of majesty,
Wherewith he wont at Heaven's high council-table
To sit the midst of Trinal Unity,
He laid aside, and, here with us to be,

---

[2] Used by permission of the author, Luci Shaw.

Forsook the courts of everlasting day,
And chose with us a darksome house of mortal clay.

"Rejoice and Be Merry" (anonymous medieval hymn)

Rejoice and be merry in song and in mirth!
O praise our Redeemer, all mortals of earth!
For this is the birthday of Jesus our King,
Who brought us salvation—His praises we'll sing!

"Yet If His Majesty" (Thomas Ford)

Yet if his majesty our sovereign lord [i.e., the king]
Should of his own accord
Friendly himself invite,
And say "I'll be your guest to-morrow night,"
How should we stir ourselves, call and command
All hands to work! "Let no man idle stand.
Set me fine Spanish tables in the hall,
See they be fitted all;
Let there be room to eat,
And order taken that there want no meat.
See every sconce and candlestick made bright,
That without tapers they may give a light.
Look to the presence: are the carpets spread,
The dazie o'er the head,
The cushions in the chairs,
And all the candles lighted on the stairs?
Perfume the chambers, and in any case
Let each man give attendance in his place."
Thus if the king were coming would we do,
And 'twere good reason too;
For 'tis a duteous thing
To show all honor to an earthly king,
And after all our travail and our cost,
So he be pleased, to think no labor lost.
But at the coming of the King of Heaven
All's set at six and seven:
We wallow in our sin,
Christ cannot find a chamber in the inn.
We entertain him always like a stranger,
And as at first still lodge him in the manger.

Other Beautiful Christmas Poems
"BC–AD" (U. A. Fanthorpe)
"Journey of the Magi" (T. S. Eliot)
"O Simplicitas" (Madeleine L'Engle)
"The Risk of Birth" (Madeleine L'Engle)
"What the Donkey Saw" (U. A. Fanthorpe)

Additional note: Among the greatest Christmas poems are hymns, some of which hold up with the best as printed poems quite apart from the music that accompanies the singing of them. In fact, the oral reading of these texts that are usually sung can bring out new meanings and emotional responses. The list of great poetic Christmas hymns includes the following:

"Angels from the Realms of Glory"
"Come, Thou Long-Expected Jesus"
"Hark! The Herald Angels Sing"
"Joy to the World"
"O Come, All Ye Faithful"
"O Little Town of Bethlehem"
"Silent Night, Holy Night"

ADVENT LITURGY
For ideas for Advent remembrance and celebration, we recommend Bruce Benedict's amazing website: http://cardiphonia.org/church-year/.

Here is a simple template for involving families, singles, and other groups of the church in leading the church's focus on Christ through the successive Sundays of Advent. Advent is eschatological in its focus and lifts our eyes beyond the incarnation to Christ's triumphant, glorious return.

First Sunday of Advent
Directions to the family or group lighting the first candle of Advent: plan to arrive before the prelude and sit near the front. When the pastor announces your names, gather your family/group around the Advent wreath. A microphone will be available, and all speaking participants must use it. A butane lighter for lighting the candle will be there. Check out both the mike and the lighter before the service.

The pastor introduces the lighting of the Advent candle.

Minister: "*Advent* means 'coming.' It is the season of the year, taken up by the four Sundays before Christmas, in which the church prepares to celebrate the two comings of Christ: first, his coming through his incarnation in Bethlehem, and second, his future coming in glory to judge the living and the dead.

"Advent is a time for serious reflection on both comings of Christ.

"Christ has come, and is coming again!

"This morning, [the names of the family or group] will lead us in lighting the first candle of Advent."

Reader: "As we come to light the first candle of Advent, let us again hear the prophecy of Micah: 'But you, O Bethlehem Ephrathah, who are too little to be among the clans of Judah, from you shall come forth for me one who is to be ruler in Israel, whose coming forth is from of old, from ancient days' (5:2)."

The candle at the twelve o'clock position is lit.

First speaker: "We light the first candle of Advent to remind us to look up and center our thoughts upon a loving God who sent us his Son, who is coming again."

The pastor then prays, and when he finishes the family/group returns to their seats.

(Note: all participants are expected to have practiced their parts ahead of time.)

Second Sunday of Advent

Directions to the family or group lighting the second candle of Advent: see First Sunday of Advent.

The pastor introduces the lighting of the Advent candle.

Minister: "*Advent* ("coming") means that Christ has come in the flesh and is coming again in his glorious body to take us to be with him. This morning, [the names of the family or group] will lead us in lighting the second candle of Advent."

Reader: "Let us together hear the prophecy of Isaiah: 'A voice cries: "In the wilderness prepare the way of the LORD; make straight in the desert a highway for our God. . . . And the glory of the LORD shall be revealed, and all flesh shall see it together, for the mouth of the LORD has spoken"' (40:3–5)."

The candle at the twelve o'clock position is lit.

First speaker: "We light the first candle of Advent to remind us to look up and center our thoughts on a loving God who sent us his Son, who is coming again."

The candle at the three o'clock position is lit.

Second speaker: "As we light the second candle of Advent, let it remind us that this is a time to look back two thousand years to the moment when God's great gift came to us in Bethlehem and to look forward to his coming again."

The pastor then prays, and when he finishes the family/group returns to their seats.

(Note: all participants are expected to have practiced their parts ahead of time.)

Third Sunday of Advent

Directions to the family or group lighting the third candle of Advent: see First Sunday of Advent.

The pastor introduces the lighting of the Advent candle.

Minister: "As the Christmas tract *Christmas Is a Promise* says: 'Every Christmas is still a "turning of the page" until Jesus returns. Every December 25th marks another year that draws us closer to the fulfillment of the ages, that draws us closer to our heavenly home. Every Christmas carol is a beautiful echo of the heavenly choir that will one day fill the universe with joy and singing. Each Christmas gift is a foreshadowing of the gifts of golden crowns to be cast at the feet of the King of kings.'

"This morning, [the names of the family or group] will lead us in lighting the third candle of Advent."

Reader: "Let us together hear the prophecy of Isaiah: 'The people who walked in darkness have seen a great light; those who dwelt in a land of deep darkness, on them has light shone' (9:2)."

The candle at the twelve o'clock position is lit.

First speaker: "We light the first candle of Advent to remind us to look up and center our thoughts on a loving God who sent us his Son, who is coming again."

The candle at the three o'clock position is lit.

Second speaker: "As we light the second candle of Advent, let it remind us that this is a time to look back two thousand years to the moment when God's great gift came to us in Bethlehem and to look forward to his coming again."

The candle at the six o'clock position is lit.

Third speaker: "As we light the third candle, let it remind us that Christmas is a time to look within ourselves and prepare our hearts for the coming of Christ."

The pastor then prays, and when he finishes, the family/group returns to their seats.

(Note: all participants are expected to have practiced their parts ahead of time.)

Fourth Sunday of Advent

Directions to the family or group lighting the fourth candle of Advent: see First Sunday of Advent.

The pastor introduces the lighting of the Advent candle.

Minister: "Christ has come in the flesh, and so now we are 'waiting for our blessed hope, the appearing of the glory of our great God and Savior Jesus Christ' (Titus 2:13). This morning, [the names of the family or group] will lead us in lighting the fourth candle of Advent."

Reader: "Let us together hear the words of praise from Zechariah, the father of John the Baptist, for the coming Messiah: 'Blessed be the Lord God of Israel, for he has visited and redeemed his people and has raised up a horn of salvation for us in the house of his servant David' (Luke 1:68–69)."

The candle at the twelve o'clock position is lit.

First speaker: "We light the first candle of Advent to remind us to look up and center our thoughts on a loving God who sent us his Son, who is coming again."

The candle at the three o'clock position is lit.

Second speaker: "As we light the second candle of Advent, let it remind us that this is a time to look back two thousand years to the moment when God's great gift came to us in Bethlehem and to look forward to his coming again."

The candle at the six o'clock position is lit.

Third speaker: "As we light the third candle, let it remind us that Christmas is a time to look within ourselves and prepare our hearts for the coming of Christ."

The candle at the nine o'clock position is lit.

Fourth speaker: "As we light the fourth candle, let it remind us that the message of Christmas calls us to open our hearts to Christ and give him glory, honor, and love until his great return."

The pastor then prays, and when he finishes, the family/group returns to their seats.

(Note: all participants are expected to have practiced their parts ahead of time.)

The Christ Candle (Lit on Christmas Eve or Christmas Sunday)

Directions to the family or group lighting the third candle of Advent: see First Sunday of Advent.

The pastor introduces the lighting of the Christ candle.

Minister: "Tonight/Today, [the names of the family or group] will lead us in lighting the Christ candle."

Reader: "On this Christmas Eve/Christmas Day, let us together hear the prophecy of Christ from the Law of Moses: 'I see him, but not now; I behold him, but not near: a star shall come out of Jacob, and a scepter shall rise out of Israel' (Num. 24:17)."

The candle at the twelve o'clock position is lit.

First speaker: "We light the first Advent candle to remind us to look up and center our thoughts on a loving God who sent us his Son, who is coming again."

The candle at the three o'clock position is lit.

Second speaker: "As we light the second Advent candle, let it remind us that this is a time to look back two thousand years to the moment when God's great gift came to us in Bethlehem and to look forward to his coming again."

The candle at the six o'clock position is lit.

Third speaker: "As we light the third candle, let it remind us that Christmas is a time to look within ourselves and prepare our hearts for the coming of Christ."

The candle at the nine o'clock position is lit.

Fourth speaker: "As we light the fourth candle, let it remind us that the message of Christmas calls us to open our hearts to Christ and give him glory, honor, and love until his great return."

The Christ candle, the candle at the center of the wreath, is lit.

Fifth speaker: "As we light the Christ candle, let it remind us of the night of Christ's birth, when he veiled his glories, taking the form of a servant. May it also cause us to look forward to the day of his coming again, when he will return in all his glory."

Congregational response: "God our Father, on this night/day, we are reminded afresh of the coming of our Lord Jesus Christ. Sustain our faith and fix our eyes on him until the Day dawns and Christ the Morning Star rises in our hearts. To him be the glory both now and forevermore. Amen."

The pastor then prays, and when he finishes, the family/group returns to their seats.

(Note: all participants are expected to have practiced their parts ahead of time.)

Evening Christmas Services

The four Sunday evenings of Advent provide prime opportunities to focus on the incarnation. Some larger churches use two consecutive evenings for a grand Christmas pageant that serves the surrounding communities. Others use several evenings for distinctly different Christmas services, such as a children's Christmas program/musical, a sing-along *Messiah*, a traditional service of lessons and carols, or Christmas Communion. Most churches, however, choose to do only one or two of these. Then, on Christmas Eve, some churches offer an early-evening family Christmas service, followed at midnight by a candlelight service to welcome in Christmas Day.

How are we to respond to this array of options? Certainly not like the man who got on his horse and "rode off in all directions." Pastors and their leadership are responsible to choose only those Christmas services that best serve their local churches. Three factors determine the best choice(s): context, resources, and the gospel. A new urban church full of twentysomethings is not the right context for a children's Christmas program, but such a service would be very appropriate in a suburban church. A large-scale Christmas pageant might work in certain older middle-class contexts, but would be a turnoff in another place. And, of course, resources are always a consideration. For example, a trained choir is necessary to do a classic service of lessons and carols.

But the overriding consideration is: how does this service focus on the gospel of the incarnation of Messiah Jesus? Happily, this question is not answered primarily by resources or context, though contextualizing (knowing where you are and to whom you are ministering) is always a consideration. This said, the pastor must make sure that the gospel is central in all services. For example, if hosting a sing-along *Messiah*, it would be a disservice to the gospel to imagine that visiting non-Christian music lovers will understand the gospel simply from hearing Handel's magnificent, Scripture-infused text. Rather, the responsible thing to do would be to take ten minutes to give a winsome, articulate introduction to *The Messiah*, providing Handel's history and purpose, and walking the audience through the prophetic texts of the great oratorio, giving their gospel sense. Then the choir and soloists can sing it to the hearers' hearts!

Likewise, the traditional service of lessons and carols is simply nine Scripture readings/lessons (four from the Old Testament and five from the New Testament) interspersed with traditional Christmas choral music and hymns. Again, a pointed gospel explanation and a prayer inviting the Holy Spirit to do his work may well be a prelude to a work of Christmas grace. Here it must be said that if the music is too heavy for the context in which you serve, the nine lessons could prove to be a fine template for a more contemporary version, say, the Scriptures and songs of the incarnation.

This kind of gospel care must be given to everything—right down to the cute first-graders wearing shepherd costumes, halos, and sheep's ears as they sing about the Christmas star. All is good and well if it is part of a service where the "good news of great joy that will be for all the people" is preached. If not, a pastoral miniword to all may be in order.

The possible orders for the various Sunday evening Christmas services are too many to list. Moreover, you want to choose and design your own services to fit your context and the needs of your people. We have provided the extended sections of "Select Christmas Scriptures," "Select Advent and Christmas Hymns and Songs," and "Select Christmas Poems" in this section, along with an "enrichment" section on "Poetry to Enhance Preaching and Worship" and a chapter on "The Historic Christian Creeds," so that you will have a fine Christmas treasury from which to create meaningful services.

We have, however, included several sample orders of service for Christmas Eve candlelight services, including the College Church Christmas Eve service for 2006 (see the first sample in the next section), my (Kent's) last service as pastor there. Though the service is traditional and may not be an appropriate template for more contemporary candlelight services, it is well-constructed and utilizes the resources that we provide in this chapter. The reader will note that the Advent wreath's Christ candle was lighted by my pastoral colleagues and that the congregation's affirmation of the Nicene Creed was interspersed with the singing of "Of the Father's Love Begotten," making a very powerful affirmation of the incarnation.

SAMPLE CHRISTMAS EVE CANDLELIGHT SERVICES
Sample Christmas Eve Candlelight Service #1
Prelude
Norm Ruiz, guitar
Introit
"O Little Town of Bethlehem," Robin Wiper, soprano
Processional Hymn
"O Come, All Ye Faithful" (congregation standing)
Invocation
Pastor Todd Wilson
Christmas Carol Sing
"Angels We Have Heard on High"
"Joy to the World"
"Away in a Manger"
Christmas Anthem
"Lo, How a Rose E'er Blooming"
Chancel Choir, Michael Praetorius
The Christmas Narrative
Luke 2:1–20, pastoral staff
The Lighting of the Christ Candle
Pastoral staff
A Christmas Prayer
Pastor Bruce Wilson

Interlude

"Mary, Did You Know?" Robin Wiper, soprano, Norm Ruiz, guitar

Affirmation of the Incarnation

(Note: this was printed on an insert, but is included here for easy reference.)

Choir: "Of the Father's love begotten, ere the worlds began to be,
He is Alpha and Omega, He the Source, the Ending He,
Of the things that are, that have been,
And that future years shall see, evermore and evermore!"

Congregation: "We believe in one God, the Father, the Almighty, maker of heaven and earth, all that is, seen and unseen."

Choir: "O that birth, forever blessed, when the virgin full of grace,
By the Holy Spirit conceiving, bare the Savior of our race;
And the Babe, the world's Redeemer,
First revealed His sacred face, evermore and evermore!"

Congregation: "We believe in one Lord, Jesus Christ, the only Son of God, Light from Light, true God from true God, begotten, not made, of one being with the Father. Through him all things were made. For us and for our salvation he came down from heaven: by the power of the Holy Spirit he became incarnate from the virgin Mary, and was made man. For our sake he was crucified under Pontius Pilate; he suffered death and was buried. On the third day he rose again according to the Scriptures; he ascended into heaven and is seated at the right hand of the Father. He will come again in glory to judge the living and the dead, and his kingdom will have no end."

Choir: "O ye heights of heaven adore Him; angel hosts, His praises sing,
Pow'rs, dominions, bow before Him, and extol our God and King!
Let no tongue on earth be silent,
Every voice in concert ring, evermore and evermore!"

Congregation: "We believe in the Holy Spirit, the Lord, the giver of life, who proceeds from the Father and the Son. With the Father and the Son he is worshiped and glorified. He has spoken through the Prophets. We believe in one holy catholic Church. We acknowledge one baptism for the forgiveness of sins. We look for the resurrection of the dead, and the life of the world to come."

All: "Christ, to Thee with God the Father, and, O Holy Ghost, to Thee,

Hymn and chant with high thanksgiving, and unwearied praises be:
Honor, glory, and dominion,
And eternal victory, evermore and evermore!"
Christmas Message
"Incarnation's Night," Pastor Kent Hughes, Hebrews 10:1–7
Christmas Eve Candlelight Service
Chancel choir, Norm Ruiz, "Peace, Peace"
The pastors will bring the light from the Advent Christ candle
to each row. As the flame is passed, please tip the candle that is
being lighted. Please do not tip the lighted candle.
When all the candles have been lighted, the congregation
will sing "Silent Night." When we come to the final lines, which
begin, "Son of God, love's pure light . . ." we will lift our candles
high and extinguish them together at the song's conclusion.
Hymn
"Silent Night"
Benediction
Pastor Hughes
Choral Response
"How Great Our Joy" (Arranged by John Rutter)
Postlude
"Carillon on a Ukrainian Bell Carol," H. E. Singley, piano
Gerald Near, organ

Sample Christmas Eve Candlelight Service #2
Gathering in Christ's presence.
Prelude
The prelude music is listed on the back of the bulletin.
Entrance Hymn
"O Come, All Ye Faithful," bulletin insert (congregation standing)
Welcome
Dr. Nick Perrin
Lighting of the Advent Candle
The James family lights the Christ candle
Choral Song
"Sussex Carol" (English carol, arr. Lau), choir
Christmas Carols
Bulletin insert:
"Once in David's Royal City" (v. 1 solo, vv. 2–5 all)
"Angels We Have Heard on High"
"Joy to the World"

Scripture Reading
Luke 1:26–38, Lily O'Donnell
Vocal Solo
"O Holy Night," Grace Canfield
The Birth Story
Brad Alstadt
Luke 2:1–20 (children third grade and under are invited to the steps)
Christmas Hymn
"Infant Holy, Infant Lowly," bulletin insert
Christmas Reflection
"A Glorious Humility," Pastor Douglas O'Donnell
Carol and Candle Lighting
"Silent Night," bulletin insert (congregation standing)
For candle lighting: (a) Hold lighted candles upright, and tip
the unlit candle to the lighted one; (b) on the final verse, when
we sing, "love's pure light," please raise your candle up until the
end of the song; and (c) wait for the pastor to blow out his candle
before you blow out yours.
Postlude
"Joy to the World"

Sample Christmas Eve Candlelight Service #3
Instrumental Prelude
"O Holy Night" (solo)
Opening Prayer
Worship through Singing and Scripture
All congregational:
"Joy Has Dawned"
"What Child Is This?"
Scripture: Luke 1:28–56
"Hark the Herald Angels Sing"
Scripture: Matthew 1:18–25
"O Little Town of Bethlehem"
"O Come, O Come Emmanuel"
Scripture: Luke 2:1–7, Galatians 4:1–7
"Hallelujah! What a Savior"
Prayer of Thanksgiving
"Infant Holy, Infant Lowly"
Worship in the Word
Sermon

Candle Lighting
"The First Noel"
"Silent Night, Holy Night"
Closing Prayer

Sample Christmas Sunday Services

As these services fall on the Sunday prior to Christmas (or on Christmas Day), they demand celebrative care as to the choice of the Scripture reading(s) and the hymns and carols. A good rule of thumb is to include the reading of the nativity in Luke 2 in addition to the text that is being preached that morning. In a similar vein, the grand, well-known Christmas hymns and carols should be chosen, and the most singable of them. This particular morning is one of those that non-churchgoers frequent, and the unfamiliar may add to their discomfort. Preachers, our task of making the Christmas gospel clear is a privilege and our burden!

Sample Christmas Sunday Service #1
Prelude
Daniel and Barbara Fackler
Is Est Ne, arr. Fackler
Welcome
Pastor Bruce Wilson
Carol Sing
"Angels from the Realms of Glory"
"What Child Is This?"
"The First Noel" (congregation standing) (verses 1 and 2 all; verse 3 women; verse 4 all; verse 5 men; verse 6 all)
Christmas Creed
Pastor Jay Thomas
John 1:1–5, 14:

> *Minister*: "In the beginning was the Word,"
> *Congregation*: "And the Word was with God,
> And the Word was God."
> *Minister*: "He was in the beginning with God.
> All things were made through Him,"
> *Congregation*: "And without him was not any thing made that was made."
> *Minister*: "In him was life,"
> *Congregation*: "And the light was the light of men."
> *Minister*: "The light shines in darkness,"

Congregation: "And the darkness has not overcome it. . . ."
Minister: "And the Word became flesh and dwelt among us,"
Congregation: "And we have seen his glory,
Glory as of the only Son from the Father,
Full of grace and truth."

Hymn
"Hark! The Herald Angels Sing"
Christmas Interviews
Mrs. Diane Jordan
Christmas Prayer
Wendell Hawley
Tithes and Offerings
Pastor Kent Hughes
Offertory
Mrs. Robin Wiper
"Some Children See Him," words: Hutson, music: Burt
Scripture Reading
Pastor Todd Augustine with daughter Eleah (congregation standing)
Luke 2:1–20

Reader: "This is God's Word."
Congregation: "Amen."

Sermon
"The Nativity"
Pastor Kent Hughes
"Angels We Have Heard on High" (congregation standing)
Benediction
Pastor Chuck King (congregation standing)
Postlude
Debbie Hollinger, piano; Carol Medley, arr. Mark Hayes

Sample Christmas Sunday Service #2
Prelude
"Angels We Have Heard on High" (arr. D. Wischmeier),
D. Wischmeier, organ
"O Little Town of Bethlehem" (arr. Smith),
B. Thompson, piano; D. Wischmeier, organ
"Silent Night" (arr. Smith),
B. Thompson, piano; D. Wischmeier, organ
Welcome
Pastor Andrew Fulton

Introit and Invocation
Pastor Douglas O'Donnell
"God Rest Ye Merry, Gentlemen" (traditional),
Andy Peterson, French horn
Hymn of Adoration
"How Great Our Joy" (congregation standing)
Lighting of the Advent Candles
Ed and Edith Blumhofer
Revelation 1:12–16; 21:23–25
Prayers with the Lord's Prayer
Pastor Donald Limmer
Christmas Carols
"The First Noel"
"What Child Is This?"
The Collection
Pastor Donald Limmer
"My Soul Doth Magnify the Lord" (R. Thompson),
Gretchen Canfield, vocals; Beth Jones, piano
Scripture Reading
Angela Walters
Luke 1:46–55 (congregation standing)
Gloria Patri
"Glory be to the Father, and to the Son, and to the Holy Ghost;
As it was in the beginning, is now, and ever shall be:
world without end. Amen. Amen."
Scripture Teaching
"Magnify God," Pastor Douglas O'Donnell
Song of Response
"The Song of Mary," bulletin insert
Benediction
Pastor Douglas O'Donnell
Postlude
"Joy to the World" (arr. D. Wischmeier), D. Wischmeier, organ

Sample Christmas Sunday Service #3
Welcome
Pastor Garrett Nates
Prelude
"Christmas Morn Is Dawning," arr. Morten J. Luvas
"Angels from the Realms of Glory"

The Divinity of Christ
Pastor James Seward
John 1:1–4 (congregation standing)
Advent Reading and Candle
Reading by the Charlie Warner family:

The people who walked in darkness have seen a great light; those who dwelt in a land of deep darkness, on them has light shone. (Isa. 9:2)

It shall come to pass in the latter days that the mountain of the house of the LORD shall be established as the highest of the mountains, and shall be lifted up above the hills; and all the nations shall flow to it, and many peoples shall come, and say: "Come, let us go up to the mountain of the LORD, to the house of the God of Jacob, that he may teach us his ways and that we may walk in his paths." . . . O house of Jacob, come, let us walk in the light of the LORD. (Isa. 2:2–3a, 5)

Blessed be the Lord God of Israel, for he has visited and redeemed his people and has raised up a horn of salvation for us in the house of his servant David . . . that we, being delivered from the hand of our enemies, might serve him without fear, in holiness and righteousness before him all our days. . . . [T]he sunrise shall visit us from on high to give light to those who sit in darkness and in the shadow of death, to guide our feet into the way of peace. (Luke 1:69–69, 74–75, 78b–79)

At one time you were darkness, but now you are light in the Lord. Walk as children of light (for the fruit of light is found in all that is good and right and true), and try to discern what is pleasing to the Lord. (Eph. 5:8–10)

And I saw no temple in the city, for its temple is the Lord God the Almighty and the Lamb. And the city has no need of sun or moon to shine on it, for the glory of God gives it light, and its lamp is the Lamb. By its light will the nations walk, and the kings of the earth will bring their glory into it, and its gates will never be shut by day—and there will be no night there. (Rev. 21:22–25)

No longer will there be anything accursed, but the throne of God and of the Lamb will be in it, and his servants will worship him. They will see his face, and his name will be on their foreheads. And night will be no more. They will need no light of lamp or sun, for the Lord God will be their light, and they will reign forever and ever. (Rev. 22:3–5)

Advent Prayer
Pastor Kent Hughes
"Once in Royal David's City"

Anthem
"Carol of the Holy Child," Jerry and Jane Sundberg, arr. Mary E. Caldwell

Tithes and Offerings

Offertory
Christmas music, A. Schoenberg; Jonathan Blumhofer, Diane Johnson, violins; Pippa Downs, cello; Elaine MacWatt, piano; H. E. Singley, organ

Scripture Reading
Pastor Todd Wilson
Luke 1:46–55 (congregation standing)

Sermon
"Song of the Incarnation, 2"
Pastor Kent Hughes
"Hark! The Herald Angels Sing"

Benediction
Pastor Kent Hughes

Postlude
"Hark! The Herald Angels Sing," Henry Kihlken

Sample Christmas Sunday Service #4

"Good Christian Men Rejoice," Heinrich Suso, 1328; trans. John M. McNeale, 1855

Welcome
Pastor Carey Hughes
Nicene Creed
"Joy to the World"

Announcements
Pastor Carey Hughes

Congregational Prayer
Scripture reading
Luke 1:67–79

> *Minister*: "This is the Word of the Lord."
> *Congregation*: "Thanks be to God."

Offering
"O Come All Ye Faithful"
Sermon
Dave Hammond
"Angels We Have Heard on High"
Benediction
Pastor Carey Hughes

GOOD FRIDAY

When Jesus said to the paralytic, "Take up your bed and walk" (Mark 2:9), it required a mere exercise of Jesus's creational power. He healed the man with the ease of omnipotence. Power went out from Jesus without affecting the infinity of his power. It was easy! But the hardest thing of all was to say, "Son, your sins are forgiven" (Mark 2:5), because that meant his death on the cross.

In the garden of Gethsemane, the prospect of the cross was so horrific that Jesus "began to be greatly distressed and troubled. And he said to them, 'My soul is very sorrowful, even to death. Remain here and watch.' And going a little farther, he fell on the ground and prayed that, if it were possible, the hour might pass from him. And he said, 'Abba, Father, all things are possible for you. Remove this cup from me. Yet not what I will, but what you will'" (Mark 14:33–36). And when the hour came, he did it by dying the lowest death of all, "even death on a cross" (Phil. 2:8).

In retrospect, the apostle Paul described what took place in just fifteen Greek words: "For our sake he made him to be sin who knew no sin, so that in him we might become the righteousness of God" (2 Cor. 5:21). Jesus was sinless through all his thirty-three years; he "knew no sin." And he remained sinless when he became sin for us. So Christ became sin while remaining inwardly and outwardly impeccable.

During those three dark hours of Good Friday, his heart, so to speak, became a sea surrounded by the festering mountains of our sin, into which flowed all our evils. There the loathsome mass of our corruption poured over him. There our sins were focused on Christ as he bore the fiery wrath of God, having become a curse for us (see Gal. 3:13). Jesus, in full, lucid consciousness, writhing like a serpent in the gloom of Good Friday, took your sins and mine with a unity of understanding and pain that none can fathom. And he did it willingly, so he could say, "Son [or daughter], your sins are forgiven" (Mark 2:5).

On Good Friday, Jesus did the hardest thing ever done in time or eternity for you and me! His death means that he is committed to forgiving you if you turn to him.

These words bear the essence of a brief sermon prepared for the observance of the Lord's Table at a Good Friday Communion service. Our experience has been that such services have been extraordinary occasions for a powerful, saving focus on Christ's substitutionary death and atonement on the cross. And for this reason, it is regrettable that many evangelical churches ignore Good Friday. Likely this is due to an aversion to any association with the liturgical churches' traditional Holy Week nexus of Ash Wednesday-Maundy Thursday-Good Friday, or with the liturgical calendar in general. These aversions must be overcome because the death of Christ is central to Paul's definition of the gospel: "Christ died for our sins in accordance with the Scriptures, . . . he was buried, . . . he was raised on the third day in accordance with the Scriptures" (1 Cor. 15:3–4).

In terms of the Savior's gospel chronology of birth, death, and resurrection, Jesus Christ was incarnated in Bethlehem; thirty-three years later, he was crucified and buried in Jerusalem; and three days later, he was resurrected in Jerusalem. Good Friday, if you will, is the bleak launching pad for the explosive victory of Easter Sunday. Therefore, to give Good Friday (the hardest thing ever done in time or eternity) a mere passing nod on the way to celebrating the glorious resurrection is pastorally irresponsible.

Several things can be done to elevate the observance of Good Friday, and none of them contains elements that appeal to the flesh. They are: 1) announce the service as a solemn preparation for the joys of Resurrection Sunday; 2) maintain a fitting reverence throughout the service; 3) choose a text to preach that focuses on Christ's atoning death and labor hard over it, asking God to first plow your own heart and then the hearts of your people; 4) choose well from the treasury of Christian hymns and songs that speak of Christ's death; 5) include several readings from both Testaments; 6) do not approach the Lord's Table perfunctorily, but rather slow it down so the people can reflect on what Christ has done and on the state of their own hearts (here it is effective to "set the Table" by using a bell or chime to slowly toll the thirty-three years of Christ's life); and 7) at the benediction, ask the congregation to refrain from greeting one another or have unnecessary conversation as they depart.

At College Church in Wheaton (which I, Kent, pastored for nearly three decades), the ministry of this service was remarkable, as families went home to have significant spiritual discussions involving all their school-age children. Many came to regard the Good Friday service as a significant spiritual event in their year. The 6 p.m. service grew to fill the building, and an 8 p.m. service was added, which again filled the church. We also discovered that people from other churches that did not have Good Friday services attended because the solemn worship and time for serious reflection met their unrequited spiritual needs. The service was also effective in evangelizing unbelieving Roman Catholics.

As with the Christmas services, we here include some resources to aid in your planning of Good Friday services.

SELECT GOOD FRIDAY SCRIPTURES

Old Testament

The texts listed here are full chapters, but they contain sections that will make excellent Good Friday texts.

Genesis 22
Exodus 12
Psalm 22
Isaiah 53
(Compare Luke 22:14–15 and 1 Cor. 5:7)

In the upper room, Christ directed his disciples to Isaiah 53 by quoting its final verse, indicating that he himself "was numbered with the transgressors," thus alerting them to the fact that every line of Isaiah 53 referred to him (Luke 22:37; cf. Isa. 53:12b).

New Testament

The four Gospels contain the primary texts in their individual accounts of Jesus's crucifixion and burial. These accounts should be searched in full for texts. Indeed, whole sections can be skillfully summarized into brief, pointed sermons. The outtakes from these chapters are suggestive, not determinative.

Matthew 26:26–29	Mark 15:33–34
Matthew 26:36–46	Mark 15:42–47
Matthew 27:15–23	Luke 22:7–23
Matthew 27:32–44	Luke 22:39–46
Matthew 27:45–54	Luke 23:26–43
Matthew 27:57–61	Luke 23:44–49
Mark 14:3–9	Luke 23:50–56
Mark 14:32–42	John 19:1–16
Mark 15:1–15	John 19:17–30
Mark 15:16–32	John 19:31–42

Other New Testament texts include:

Mark 10:45	Galatians 3:10–14
John 3:14–18	Colossians 1:15–20
John 10:11–18	Colossians 1:19–23
John 12:24, 32–33	Colossians 2:13–15
Romans 3:22b–26	Hebrews 2:9–17
Romans 4:25a	Hebrews 10:1–10
Romans 5:6–11	Hebrews 13:10–13
Romans 8:32	1 Peter 1:18–19
1 Corinthians 1:22–24	Revelation 1:1–18
2 Corinthians 5:21	

Texts that speak of our sins being laid on Christ or his bearing our sins include:

Isaiah 53:6, 12	Galatians 3:13
John 1:29	Hebrews 9:28
2 Corinthians 5:21	1 Peter 2:24

SELECT GOOD FRIDAY HYMNS AND SONGS

Classic Good Friday Hymns

"Ah, Holy Jesus, How Hast Thou Offended" (Heermann)
"Alas! and Did My Savior Bleed?" (Watts)
"King of My Life, I Crown Thee Now" (Hussey)
"My Song Is Love Unknown" (Crossman)
"O Sacred Head, Now Wounded" (Bernard of Clairvaux)

Recent Good Friday Hymns and Songs

"Amazing Love, O What Sacrifice" (Kendrick)
"Beneath the Cross of Jesus" (Getty/Getty)
"Gethsemane" (Getty/Townend)
"His Robes for Mine" (Anderson)
"Lamb of God" (Paris)
"Let Us Draw Near" (Clarkson)
"Man of Grief and Man of Sorrows" (Kendrick/Getty)
"My Jesus Fair" (Anderson)
"On the Cross" (Baker)
"The Look" (Newton; alt. Kauflin)
"Through the Precious Blood" (Altrogge)

SELECT GOOD FRIDAY POEMS

Again, the following represent the finest poems and are meant for reading in appropriate places in Good Friday services and for quotation, all or in part, where they serve the text of the sermon.

The first "Good Friday poems" are found in the Bible: they are Psalm 22 and the song of the suffering servant in Isaiah 53. Good Friday poems include:

"The Agony" (George Herbert)

>Philosophers have measured mountains,
>Fathomed the depths of the seas, of states, and kings,
>Walked with a staff to heaven, and traced fountains:
>But there are two vast, spacious things,
>The which to measure it doth more behove:
>Yet few there are that sound them: Sin and Love.
>
>Who would know Sin, let him repair
>Unto mount Olivet; there shall he see
>A man so wrung with pains, that all his hair,
>His skin, his garments bloody be.
>Sin is that press and vice, which forceth pain
>To hunt his cruel food through ev'ry vein.
>
>Who knows not Love, let him assay,
>And taste that juice, which on the cross a pike
>Did set again abroach, then let him say
>If ever he did taste the like.
>Love is that liquor sweet and most divine,
>Which my God feels as blood, but I, as wine.

"Good Friday" (Christina Rossetti)

>Am I stone and not a sheep
>That I can stand, O Christ, beneath Thy Cross,
>To number drop by drop Thy blood's slow loss,
>And yet not weep?
>
>Not so those women loved
>Who with exceeding grief lamented Thee;
>Not so fallen Peter weeping bitterly;
>Not so the thief was moved;
>
>Not so the Sun and Moon
>Which hid their faces in a starless sky,

A horror of great darkness at broad noon—
I, only I.

Yet give not o'er,
But seek Thy sheep, true shepherd of the flock;
Greater than Moses, turn and look once more
And smite a rock.

"He Bore Our Griefs" (Jacob Revius)

No, it was not the Jews who crucified,
Nor who betrayed you in the judgment place,
Nor who, Lord Jesus, spat into your face,
Nor who with buffets struck you as you died.
No, it was not the soldiers fisted bold
Who lifted up the hammer and the nail,
Or raised the cursed cross on Calvary's hill,
Or, gambling, tossed the dice to win your robe.
I am the one, O Lord, who brought you there,
I am the heavy cross you had to bear,
I am the rope that bound you to the tree,
The whip, the nail, the hammer, and the spear,
The blood-stained crown of thorns you had to wear:
It was my sin, alas, it was for me.
(Translated by Henrietta ten Harmsel)

"Holy Sonnet 11" (John Donne)

Spit in my face, you Jews, and pierce my side,
Buffet, and scoff, scourge, and crucify me,
For I have sinned, and sinned, and only He,
Who could do no iniquity, hath died.
But by my death can not be satisfied
My sins, which pass the Jews' impiety.
They killed once an inglorious man, but I
Crucify him daily, being now glorified.
O let me then His strange love still admire;
Kings pardon, but He bore our punishment;
And Jacob came clothed in vile harsh attire,
But to supplant, and with gainful intent;
God clothed Himself in vile man's flesh, that so
He might be weak enough to suffer woe.

"In Evil Long I Took Delight" (John Newton)
  In evil long I took delight
  Unawed by shame or fear,
  Till a new object met my sight,
  And stopped my wild career.

  I saw One hanging on a tree,
  In agony and blood,
  Who fixed His languid eyes on me,
  As near His cross I stood.

  Sure, never to my latest breath,
  Can I forget that look;
  It seemed to charge me with His death,
  Though not a word He spoke.

  My conscience owned and felt the guilt,
  And plunged me in despair,
  I saw my sins His blood had shed,
  And helped to nail Him there.

  A second look He gave, which said,
  "I freely all forgive;
  This blood is for thy ransom paid;
  I die that thou mayest live."

  Thus, while His death my sin displays
  In all its blackest hue,
  Such is the mystery of grace,
  It seals my pardon, too.

  With pleasing grief and mournful joy,
  My spirit now is filled,
  That I should such a life destroy,
  Yet live by Him I killed.

"Now Goeth Sun under Wood" (medieval, anonymous)
  Now goeth sun under wood,
  Me reweth, Mary, thy fair rode.
  Now goeth sun under tree,
  Me reweth, Mary, thy son and thee.

  Glosses: pun on *sun* and *son*; *me reweth* means "I pity";
      rode means "face"

From *Paradise Lost*, Book 3 (John Milton)

> And now without redemption all mankind
> Must have been lost, adjudged to death and hell
> By doom severe, had not the Son of God,
> In whom the fullness dwells of love divine,
> His dearest mediation thus renewed:
> "Father, thy word is passed, man shall find grace;
> And shall grace not find means, that finds her way . . . ?
> Behold me then, me for him, life for life,
> I offer; on me let thine anger fall;
> Account me Man; I for his sake will leave
> Thy bosom, and this glory next to thee
> Freely put off, and for him lastly die
> Well pleased; on me let Death wreak all his rage."

"Redemption" (George Herbert)

> Having been tenant long to a rich lord,
> Not thriving, I resolved to be bold,
> And make a suit unto him, to afford
> A new small-rented lease, and cancel the old.
>
> In heaven at his manor I him sought;
> They told me there that he was lately gone
> About some land, which he had dearly bought
> Long since on earth, to take possession.
>
> I straight returned, and knowing his great birth,
> Sought him accordingly in great resorts;
> In cities, theatres, gardens, parks, and courts;
> At length I heard a ragged noise and mirth
> Of thieves and murderers; there I him espied,
> Who straight, *Your suit is granted*, said, and died.

"The Windhover" (Gerard Manley Hopkins)

The Good Friday aspect of the following poem is implied rather than ex-plicit. The ostensible subject of the poem is the speaker's catching sight of the motion of a kestrel (a small hawk) on an early morning walk. The bird first masters the morning wind in a spiral ascent; then the bird submits to the wind, plummeting downward (probably in pursuit of prey). The principle that this motion embodies (what Hopkins called the inscape or individuating principle of something) is strength that stoops to conquer (the bird is even more impressive when submitting to the wind than when mastering it). The supreme example of this principle is the atoning death of Christ. There are two hints in the poem that Hopkins intends us to see this analogy or application—the inscription ("To Christ our Lord") and the last line, with its christological imagery of gall and gashing gold vermilion.

> *To Christ our Lord*
> I caught this morning morning's minion, king-
> dom of daylight's dauphin, dapple-dawn-drawn Falcon, in his riding
> Of the rolling level underneath him steady air, and striding
> High there, how he rung upon the rein of a wimpling wing
> In his ecstasy! then off, off forth on swing,
> As a skate's heel sweeps smooth on a bow-bend: the hurl and gliding
> Rebuffed the big wind. My heart in hiding
> Stirred for a bird,—the achieve of; the mastery of the thing!
>
> Brute beauty and valor and act, oh, air, pride, plume, here
> Buckle! AND the fire that breaks from thee then, a billion
> Times told lovelier, more dangerous, O my chevalier!
>
> No wonder of it: sheer plod makes plough down sillion
> Shine, and blue-bleak embers, ah my dear,
> Fall, gall themselves, and gash gold-vermilion.

SAMPLE GOOD FRIDAY SERVICES

Sample Good Friday Service #1

Prelude

> "Lamb of God, Pure and Sinless," piano, H. E. Singley; organ, Edwin T. Childs
> "Jesus, Priceless Treasure"
> "My Faith Looks Up to Thee," arr. Mark C. Jones

Responsive Call to Worship

> *Minister*: "The stone that the builders rejected has become the Cornerstone . . ."
> *Congregation*: "This was the Lord's doing, and it is marvelous in our eyes."
> *Minister*: "Lift up your hearts."
> *Congregation*: "We lift them up to the Lord."

Hymn

> "King of My Life, I Crown Thee Now" (congregation standing)

Anthem
"When I Survey the Wondrous Cross," arr. Gilbert Martin
CHRIST'S REJECTION
Reading
Pastor Jim Johnston
Matthew 26:36–46
Anthem
"Alone You Go Out, O Lord"
Reading
Pastor Randy Gruendyke
Matthew 26:57–64
Anthem
"Gladsome Radiance," Sergei Rachmaninoff
CHRIST'S CRUCIFIXION
Responsive Reading
Matthew 27:11–26 (congregation standing)
Pastors Niel Nielson and Dave White and congregation

Now Jesus stood before the governor, and the governor asked him, "Are you the King of the Jews?"

Jesus said, "You have said so."

But when he was accused by the chief priests and elders, he gave no answer. Then Pilate said to him, "Do you not hear how many things they testify against you?"

But he gave him no answer, not even to a single charge, so that the governor was greatly amazed.

Now at the feast the governor was accustomed to release for the crowd any one prisoner whom they wanted. And they had then a notorious prisoner called Barabbas. So when they had gathered, Pilate said to them, "Whom do you want me to release for you: Barabbas, or Jesus who is called Christ?" For he knew that it was out of envy that they had delivered him up. . . .

Now the chief priests and the elders persuaded the crowd to ask for Barabbas and destroy Jesus.

The governor again said to them, "Which of the two do you want me to release for you?"

And they said, "Barabbas."

Pilate said to them, "Then what shall I do with Jesus who is called Christ?"

They all said, "Let him be crucified!"

And he said, "Why, what evil has he done?"

> *But they shouted all the more, "Let him be crucified!"*
> So when Pilate saw that he was gaining nothing, but rather that a riot was beginning, he took water and washed his hands before the crowd, saying, "I am innocent of this man's blood; see to it yourselves."
> *And all the people answered, "His blood be on us and on our children!"*
> Then he released for them Barabbas, and having scourged Jesus, delivered him to be crucified.

Hymn
"Ah, Holy Jesus, How Hast Thou Offended"
Reading
Pastor Dave White
Matthew 27:27–38
Philippians 2:8: Jesus "humbled himself by becoming obedient to the point of death, even death on a cross."
Hymn
"O Sacred Head, Now Wounded"
Reading
Pastor Clem Escudero
Matthew 27:39–45
Anthem
Tenebrae Factae Sunt, G. Palestrina
Reading
Pastor Garrett Nates
Matthew 27:46–54
Anthem
"Christ, We Do All Adore Thee"
Remembrance: The Lord's Table
Communion meditation: Pastor Kent Hughes
Chimes toll thirty-three times, representing the thirty-three years of our Savior's sinless life on earth.
Nicene Creed
Pastor Niel Nielson (congregation standing)
Words of Institution
THE BREAD
"Jesus, Thou Joy of Loving Hearts"
THE CUP
"Alas! and Did My Savior Bleed?"
Reading
Pastor Dave White

Matthew 27:57–60

Hymn

"My Song is Love Unknown" (congregation standing)

Benediction

Pastor Kent Hughes

The service ends in quiet and darkness.

The congregation departs in silence.

Resurrection is coming!

Sample Good Friday Service #2

Prelude

"Come, Ye Disconsolate," Emily Gerdts, vocals; Randy Benware, piano

Invocation

Pastor Douglas O'Donnell

Opening hymn

Bulletin insert

"My Song Is Love Unknown" (congregation standing)

Scripture Readings

Pastor Andrew Fulton

Matthew 26:57–68; 27:27–31, 45–54

Meditation on the Cross

George Ridgeway

Song on Meditation

"Stricken, Smitten, and Afflicted," bulletin insert

The Lord's Supper

Pastor Douglas O'Donnell

"Let Thy Blood in Mercy Poured," bulletin insert

"Alas! and Did My Savior Bleed," I. Watts and H. Wilson; arr. R. Smith

"Alas! and Did My Savior Bleed," I. Watts and G. Wilbur

Chimes ring thirty-three times, remembering Jesus's thirty-three years of sinless life on earth.

As a sign of respect, the congregation is asked to leave in silence.

Sample Good Friday Service #3

Prelude

"O the Deep, Deep Love of Jesus," Russell Callender, organ

"O Sacred Head, Now Wounded," arr. J. J. Bach; Russell Callender, organ

Welcome and Invocation
Pastor Douglas O'Donnell
Scripture Reading
Pastor Andrew Fulton
Matthew 27:45–46 (congregation standing): "Now from the sixth hour there was darkness over all the land until the ninth hour. And about the ninth hour Jesus cried out with a loud voice, saying, 'Eli, Eli, lema sabachthani?' that is, 'My God, my God, why have you forsaken me?'"

> *Minister*: "Blessed be the Lord, the great God."
> *Congregation*: "Amen. Amen."

First Reflection
Pastor Douglas O'Donnell
Hymn to Christ
"O Sacred Head, Now Wounded"
Scripture Reading
Pastor Andrew Fulton
Matthew 27:47–49 (congregation standing): "And some of the bystanders, hearing it, said, 'This man is calling Elijah.' And one of them at once ran and took a sponge, filled it with sour wine, and put it on a reed and gave it to him to drink. But the others said, 'Wait, let us see whether Elijah will come to save him.'"

> *Minister*: "This is the Word of the Lord."
> *Congregation*: "Thanks be to God!"

Second Reflection
Pastor Douglas O'Donnell
Hymn to Christ
"What Wondrous Love Is This?"
The Breaking of the Bread
Pastor Andrew Fulton
Hymn to Christ
"Stricken, Smitten, and Afflicted"
Scripture Reading
Pastor Andrew Fulton
Matthew 27:50–53 (congregation standing): "And Jesus cried out again with a loud voice and yielded up his spirit. And behold, the curtain of the temple was torn in two, from top to bottom. And the earth shook, and the rocks were split. The tombs also were opened. And many bodies of the saints who had fallen asleep were raised, and coming out of the tombs after his resurrection they went into the holy city and appeared to many."

Minister: "Glory be to the Father and to the Son and to the Holy Ghost."

Congregation: "As it was in the beginning, is now, and ever will be, world without end. Amen."

Third Reflection

Pastor Douglas O'Donnell

Hymn to Christ

"Fairest Lord Jesus"

Minister: "When the centurion and those who were with him, keeping watch over Jesus, saw the earthquake and what took place, they were filled with awe and said . . ."

Congregation: "Truly this was the Son of God!"

Bells

Chimes toll thirty-three times, each stroke symbolizing one year of Jesus's life on earth.

Silence

In reverence for the death of our Lord, the congregation is asked to exit in silence.

Sample Good Friday Service #4

Opening Prayer

Worship through Singing and Scripture

"Gethsemane" (choir)

Scripture reading: Isaiah 53

"Lamb of Glory" (choir)

"How Deep the Father's Love For Us" (congregation)

Scripture reading: Psalm 22:1–8, 19–24

Christ lag in Todesbanden (BWV 4), verses 2 and 7 (4, English translation, soloists and choir)

Scripture Reading

Luke 23:33–45

"*Kyrie eleison* (It Is Finished!)" (chamber choir)

"The Perfect Wisdom of Our God" (congregation)

Prayer of Thanksgiving

Worship in the Word

Communion

"Here is Love (Grace Takes My Sin)" (congregation)

"My Jesus, I Love Thee" (congregation)

Closing Prayer

Sample Good Friday Service #5

Welcome and Call to Worship

Pastor Carey Hughes

"The Power of the Cross," Keith Getty and Stuart Townend

"When I Survey," Watts/Mason

"O Sacred Head Now Wounded," text P. Gerhardt;
music J. S. Bach

Old Testament Scripture Reading

Isaiah 53

> *Minister*: "This is the Word of the Lord."
> *Congregation*: "Thanks be to God."

Prayer

"Behold the Lamb," Keith and Kristyn Getty and Stuart Townend

New Testament Scripture Reading

Mark 15:21–32

> *Minister*: "This is the Word of the Lord."
> *Congregation*: "Thanks be to God."

Sermon

Pastor Brian Hoch

Communion

Pastor Carey Hughes

Please leave in silence, reflecting on the powerful significance of Christ's death on the cross and the anticipation of His glorious resurrection.

EASTER

According to Philippians 2, Christ's downward self-humiliation was due to his own eternal resolve. First, there was *his humility in heaven*—"who, though he was in the form of God, did not count equality with God a thing to be grasped" (v. 6). Christ viewed his equality with God as qualifying him for his humble descent to save his people. Second, there was *his humility in his incarnation*—"but emptied himself, by taking the form of a servant, being born in the likeness of men" (v. 7). Jesus fully identified with the human race and donned a towel as he took on the appearance and being of a slave. Third, there was *his humility in death*—"And being found in human form, he humbled himself by becoming obedient to the point of death, even death on a cross" (v. 8). Nothing could be lower.

Of course, as we know from the flow of the text, Christ's self-humiliation was followed by his grand resurrection and exaltation by God the Father. So the down, down, down of Christ's humiliation was followed by his soaring resurrection.

To get a feel for this, picture the gears of a catapult being ratcheted down ever tighter with the three movements of his self-humiliation, so that the final groaning click of the gears creates explosive tension (infinite spiritual compression). Thus, we have the explosive moment on Easter morning when Jesus came right through his graveclothes in the sacred body of his humiliation, glorious and radiant. And in the following moments, as Matthew records, "there was a great earthquake, for an angel of the Lord descended from heaven and came and rolled back the stone and sat on it" (Matt. 28:2). *Look, world—Jesus has risen from the dead!*

Following the pattern of this chapter, below are some resources to help you and your church celebrate that crowning day.

SELECT EASTER SCRIPTURES

Old Testament

Genesis 22:1–19. Cf. Hebrews 11:17–19.

Exodus 3:6. Cf. Matthew 22:23–33; Mark 12:18–27; Luke 20:37–38; Acts 3:13–16.

Psalm 16:1–11. Cf. Acts 2:22–33.

Hosea 6:2. Cf. Luke 24:46 and 1 Corinthians 15:4, which both say that the Old Testament Scriptures prophesied that Christ would rise on the third day. And Hosea 6:2 is the prophecy: "After two days he will revive us; on the third day he will raise us up, that we may live before him." This prophecy was given to sinful Israel, but there is nothing in their long history to correspond to it, except that when Christ rose from the dead on the third day, he raised with himself believing Israel (cf. Gal. 3:29; 6:16).

New Testament

Each of the four Gospels devotes a chapter to the resurrection narrative: Matthew 28, Mark 16, Luke 24, and John 20. Before acceding to other preachers' suggestions as to textual divisions, read them through, making the natural homiletical divisions yourself. Of course, each chapter can be preached in its entirety if the preacher has a good eye to economy of time. The following list also includes other key New Testament Easter texts:

Matthew 22:23–33; Mark 12:18–27; Luke 20:37–38. Cf. Exodus 3:6.
Matthew 27:51–54

Matthew 28:1–20
Mark 16:1–20
Luke 24:1–53
John 5:25–29
John 11:1–44, esp. vv. 21–27
Acts 2:22–33. Cf. Psalm 16:1–11.
Acts 3:12–26
Acts 13:26–41
Romans 1:1–4
1 Corinthians 15:1–58
Philippians 3:10–11
Colossians 3:1
1 Peter 1:3–5
Revelation 1:9–18
Revelation 5:1–14

SELECT EASTER HYMNS AND SONGS

Classic Easter Hymns

"Christ Jesus Lay in Death's Strong Bands" (Luther)
"Christ the Lord Is Risen Today" (Wesley)
"Crown Him with Many Crowns" (Bridges/Thring)
"The Day of Resurrection" (John of Damascus)
"The Head That Once Was Crowned with Thorns" (Thomas Kelly)
"Thine Be the Glory" (Budry)

Recent Easter Hymns and Songs

"All Praise to Thee" (Tucker)
"Alleluia! Jesus Is Risen" (Brokering)
"Behold Our God" (Baird/Baird/Altrogge/Baird)
"Christ Is Risen" (Maher)
"Christ Is Risen, He Is Risen Indeed" (Getty/Getty/Cash)
"Hail the Day" (Wesley; adapted Cook/Cook)
"In Christ Alone" (Getty/Townend)
"Jesus Lives" (Romanacce/Kauflin)
"See What a Morning" (Getty/Townend)

SELECT EASTER POEMS

"Angels, Roll the Rock Away" (Thomas Scott)
    Angels, roll the rock away,
    Death, yield up the mighty prey:

See! he rises from the tomb,
Glowing with immortal bloom.
Hallelujah.
'Tis the Savior, angels, raise
Fame's eternal trump of praise;
Let the earth's remotest bound
Hear the joy-inspiring sound.
Hallelujah.
Now, ye saints, lift up your eyes,
Now to glory see him rise,
In long triumph up the sky,
Up to waiting worlds on high.
Hallelujah.
Heaven displays her portals wide,
Glorious Savior, through them ride;
King of glory, mount thy throne,
Thy great Father's and thy own.
Hallelujah!
Praise him, all ye heavenly choirs,
Praise and sweep your golden lyres;
Shout, O earth, in rapturous song,
Let the strains be sweet and strong.
Hallelujah.
Every note with wonder swell,
Sin o'erthrown, and captived hell;
Where is hell's once dreaded king?
Where, O death, thy mortal sting?
Hallelujah.

"Easter" (Gerard Manley Hopkins)
Break the box and shed the nard;
Stop not now to count the cost;
Hither bring pearl, opal, sard;
Reck not what the poor have lost;
Upon Christ throw all away:
Know ye, this is Easter Day.
Build His Church and deck His shrine;
Empty though it be on earth;
Ye have kept your choicest wine—
Let it flow for heavenly mirth;

Pluck the harp and breathe the horn:
Know ye not 'tis Easter morn?
Gather gladness from the skies;
Take a lesson from the ground;
Flowers do ope their heavenward eyes
And a Spring-time joy have found;
Earth throws Winter's robes away,
Decks herself for Easter Day.
Beauty now for ashes wear,
Perfumes for the garb of woe,
Chaplets for disheveled hair,
Dances for sad footsteps slow;
Open wide your hearts that they
Let in joy this Easter Day.
Seek God's house in happy throng;
Crowded let His table be;
Mingle praises, prayer, and song,
Singing to the Trinity.
Henceforth let your souls alway
Make each morn an Easter Day.

"Easter Hymn" (Henry Vaughan)

Death and darkness, get you packing:
Nothing now to man is lacking.
All your triumphs now are ended,
And what Adam marred is mended.
Graves are beds now for the weary;
Death a nap, to wake more merry;
Youth now, full of pious duty,
Seeks in thee for perfect beauty;
The weak and aged, tired with length
Of days, from thee look for new strength;
And infants with thy pangs contest,
As pleasant, as if with the breast.
Then unto him who thus hath thrown
Even to contempt thy kingdom down,
And by his blood did us advance
Unto his own inheritance—
To Him be glory, power, praise,
From this unto the last of days!

"An Easter Hymn" (Richard Le Gallienne)
   Celestial spirit that doth roll
   The heart's sepulchral stone away,
   Be this our resurrection day,
   The singing Easter of the soul:
   O Gentle Master of the Wise
   Teach us to say, "I will arise."

"Easter Song" (George Herbert)
   I got me flowers to strew thy way,
   I got me boughs off many a tree;
   But thou wast up by break of day,
   And brought'st thy sweets along with thee.

   The Sun arising in the East,
   Though he give light, and the East perfume,
   If they should offer to contest
   With thy arising, they presume.

   Can there be any day but this,
   Though many suns to shine endeavour?
   We count three hundred [365], but we miss:
   There is but one, and that one ever.

"Sonnet 68" (Edmund Spenser)
   Most glorious Lord of life, that on this day
   Didst make thy triumph over death and sin,
   And having harrowed hell, didst bring away
   Captivity thence captive us to win;
   This joyous day, dear Lord, with joy begin,
   And grant that we for whom thou didst die,
   Being with thy dear blood clean washed from sin,
   May live for ever in felicity.

   And that thy love we weighing worthily,
   May likewise love thee for the same again,
   And for thy sake that all like dear didst buy,
   With love may one another entertain.

   So let us love, dear love, like as we ought:
   Love is the lesson which the Lord us taught.

Other Beautiful Easter Poems
"Seven Stanzas at Easter" (John Updike)
"The Stone Has Rolled Away" (Chad Walsh)

SAMPLE EASTER SERVICES

Sample Easter Service #1
Prelude
"Thine Is the Glory, Risen, Conquering, Son"
"The Strife Is Over," arr. C. Kohlmann
"Christ the Lord Is Risen Today," arr. C. Kohlmann
"Easter Song"
Welcome
Pastor Andrew Fulton

Minister: "Why do you look for the living among the dead? He is not here; the Lord has risen!"
Congregation: "He has risen indeed!"
Minister: "The Lord has risen!"
Congregation: "He has risen indeed!"
Minister: "The Lord has risen!"
Congregation: "He has risen indeed!"
Minister: "Where, O death, is your victory? Where, O death, is your sting? Death has been swallowed up in victory!"
Congregation: "Christ has risen indeed!"
Minister: "Jesus said, 'I am the resurrection and the life. Whoever believes in me, though he die, yet shall he live, and everyone who lives and believes in me shall never die.'"
Congregation: "Thanks be to God! He gives us the victory through our Lord Jesus Christ."
Minister: "The Lord has risen!"
Congregation: "He has risen indeed! Alleluia!"
Introit and Invocation
Andy Nussbaum
"Christ Is Risen! Alleluia!" choir and organ
Hymn of Adoration
"Christ the Lord Is Risen Today"
The Apostles' Creed
Pastor Douglas O'Donnell

I believe in God the Father Almighty,
creator of heaven and earth.
I believe in Jesus Christ,

his only Son, our Lord,
who was conceived by the Holy Spirit,
born of the virgin Mary,
suffered under Pontius Pilate,
was crucified, died, and was buried;
he descended into hell.
On the third day he rose again from the dead;
he ascended into heaven,
and is seated at the right hand of the Father;
from there he will come to judge
the living and the dead.
I believe in the Holy Spirit,
the holy catholic church,
the communion of the saints,
the forgiveness of sins,
the resurrection of the body,
and the life everlasting. Amen.

Prayers
Dr. Nick Perrin

Hymn to Christ
Bulletin insert
"See What a Morning"

The Collection
Pastor Andrew Fulton
"An Easter Fanfare," choir, instruments, and piano

Scripture Reading
Rhett Austin
Matthew 27:62–28:15 (congregation standing)
Gloria Patri
"Glory be the Father, and to the Son, and to the Holy Ghost;
As it was in the beginning, is now, and ever shall be:
World without end. Amen. Amen."

Scripture Teaching
Pastor Douglas O'Donnell
"Behold Him That Was Crucified"

Hymn of Response
Bulletin insert
"Jesus Is Lord" (congregation standing)

Benediction
Pastor Douglas O'Donnell (congregation standing)

Postlude
"Thine Is the Glory, Risen, Conquering Son," organ

Sample Easter Service #2

Prelude

"In Christ Alone" (J. S. Bach), orchestra

> Christ lay in bonds of death, sacrificed for our sins.
> He is now arisen and has brought life to us;
> therefore we shall be joyful, praise God and be thankful to Him
> and sing hallelujah. Hallelujah!
> (Martin Luther)

Fanfare

Brass ensemble

Hymn

"Christ the Lord Is Risen Today" (congregation standing)

Acclamation

Pastor Jay Thomas

> *Minister*: "The Lord is risen!"
> *Congregation*: "The Lord is risen!"
> *Minister*: "The Lord is risen! Alleluia!"
> *Congregation*: "He is risen indeed! Alleluia!"

Doxology

Lasst Uns Erfreuen (congregation standing)

The Apostles' Creed

Pastor Bruce Wilson

> *Minister*: "I believe in God, the Father Almighty, maker of
>   heaven and earth.
> I believe in Jesus Christ, his only Son, our Lord;
> He was conceived by the Holy Spirit, born of the virgin Mary,
> suffered under Pontius Pilate, was crucified, dead, and buried;
> He descended into hell."
> *Congregation*: "I believe on the third day he arose again from
>   the dead.
> He rose again! Alleluia!"
> *Minister*: "He ascended into heaven
> and is seated at the right hand of God,
> the Father Almighty.
> He is coming again to judge the living and the dead.
> I believe in the Holy Spirit, the holy catholic [universal] church,
> the communion of saints, and the forgiveness of sins."
> *Congregation*: "I believe in the resurrection of the body;
> the resurrection of the body and the life everlasting.
> Because he lives, we too shall live.

He is risen indeed! Alleluia!"
  All: "Amen!"
Eye-Opener
  Testimony of new life by Keith Conley
Hymn
  "Thine Is the Glory, Risen, Conquering Son"
Congregational Prayer
  Pastor Kent Hughes
Tithes and Offerings
  Offertory anthem:
  "Achieved Is the Glorious Work," chancel choir; orchestra

  Achieved is his glorious work.
  Our song must be to the praise of God!
  Glory to His name forever!
  He sole on high exalted reigns.
  Alleluia!
Scripture Reading
  Pastor Todd Augustine
  John 11:21–27
Sermon
  "I Am the Resurrection"
  Pastor Kent Hughes
Hymn
  "I Know That My Redeemer Lives" (congregation standing)
Response of Praise
  "Hallelujah Chorus" (from *Messiah* by George Frideric Handel)
  The congregation is invited to sing or listen with joy!

  Minister: "The Lord is risen!"
  Congregation: "He is risen indeed! Alleluia!"
Postlude
  Tocatta (from Suite op. 5)

Sample Easter Service #3

Sunrise Service

Quem Quaertis
  The congregation gathers at the entrance to the church.
  Minister: "Whom do you seek?"
  Women: "Jesus of Nazareth, who was crucified, died, and
    was buried."

Minister: "He is no longer in the grave. He is risen, just as he said. Go tell the others!"

Women: "Alleluia! The Lord is risen!"

All: "The Lord is risen! Alleluia!"

The doors are opened, and all process with joy into the church.

Choral Fanfare and Processional

"Joy to the Heart"

Processional Hymn

"Christ the Lord Is Risen Today" (congregation standing)

Acclamation

Pastor Todd Wilson, congregation (standing)

> *Minister*: "The Lord is risen!"
>
> *Congregation*: "He is risen indeed!"
>
> *Minister*: "The stone that the builders rejected has become the cornerstone."
>
> *Congregation*: "This is the Lord's doing; it is marvelous in our eyes!"
>
> *Minister*: "Christ died for our sins, in accordance with the Scriptures . . ."
>
> *Congregation*: ". . . he was buried, and he was raised on the third day, in accordance with the Scriptures."
>
> *Minister*: "Christ has been raised from the dead, the firstfruits of those who have fallen asleep."
>
> *Congregation*: "For as by man came death, by a man has come also the resurrection of the dead."
>
> *Minister*: "For as in Adam all die, so also in Christ shall all be made alive. This is the day that the Lord has made."
>
> *Congregation*: "Let us rejoice and be glad in it!"
>
> *Minister*: "The sting of death is sin, and the power of sin is the law."
>
> *Congregation*: "But thanks be to God, who gives us the victory through our Lord Jesus Christ!"
>
> *Minister*: "The Lord is risen!"
>
> *Congregation*: "He is risen indeed! Hallelujah!"

Doxology

Last Uns Erfreunen (congregation standing)

Hymn

"In Christ Alone," words by Stuart Townend, music by Keith Getty

Easter Prayer

Pastor Kent Hughes

Tithes and Offerings
Offertory anthem:
"See What a Morning (Resurrection Hymn)," Keith Getty and
Stuart Townend
Congregation joins on final stanza
Scripture Reading
Pastor James Seward
John 11:21–27
Message
"I Am the Resurrection"
Pastor Kent Hughes
Hymn
"I Know That My Redeemer Lives," arr. Edwin T. Childs
(congregation standing)
Acclamation and Benediction
Minister: "The Lord is risen!"
Congregation: "The Lord is risen indeed! Hallelujah!"
Postlude
Toccata (from Suite op. 5)

Sample Easter Service #4
Prelude
"Were You There?" (orchestra)
Call to Worship
"Christ Is Risen, He Is Risen Indeed!" (congregation)
Welcome/Body Life
Worship through Singing and Giving
Adoration: "Christ Is Risen," choir and orchestra; "Behold Our
God," congregation
Confession: "Come, Ye Sinners, Poor and Needy," congregation
Scripture Reading
Revelation 1
Prayer and Offering
Assurance of Grace: "E'en So, Lord Jesus, Quickly Come," choir;
"Before the Throne of God Above," congregation
Response: "Be Thou My Vision," congregation
Worship in the Word

Sample Easter Service #5
"Christ the Lord Is Risen Today," Charles Wesley
"Thine Be the Glory," text Edmund L. Budrey; music G. F. Handel

Welcome and Announcements
Pastor Carey Hughes
Scripture Reading
Luke 24:1–12

> *Minister*: "This is the Word of the Lord."
> *Congregation*: "Thanks be to God."

Confession
Offering
"How Great Thou Art," stringed ensemble
"Come People of the Risen King," Keith and Kristyn Getty and Stuart Townend
"Christ Is Risen, He is Risen Indeed," Keith and Kristyn Getty and Ed Cash
Scripture Reading
1 Peter 1:3–9

> *Minister*: "This is the Word of the Lord."
> *Congregation*: "Thanks be to God."

Congregational Prayer
Sermon
Pastor Carey Hughes
"Resurrection Hymn," Stuart Townend and Keith Getty
Baptism
"In Christ Alone," Stuart Townend and Keith Getty
Benediction
Pastor Brian Hoch

3

Weddings

Weddings are wonderful opportunities for pastors to minister to others and to provide a beautiful picture of the gospel.

It may be tempting for the busy pastor to regard weddings as a time-consuming waste of pastoral energy. Admittedly, they do take precious time. Just the rehearsal and the dinner following can occupy a whole evening, and the wedding plus the reception requires half a day or more. The proverbial uptight bride and her mother and the sometimes awkward moments that accompany any wedding ("Where's my bowtie?" and "The flower girl is locked in the bathroom!") often drench the perspiring bridal party with tension that the presiding pastor somehow has to manage with a benign, calm, and ecclesiastical smile. Nevertheless, we pastors must understand that a Christian wedding is of immense pastoral importance for reasons that are at once theological, domestic, and evangelistic.

The *theological* significance of Christian marriage is enthroned at the summit of the apostle Paul's instruction on marriage in Ephesians 5, where he quotes Genesis 2:24, "Therefore a man shall leave his father and mother and hold fast to his wife, and the two shall become one flesh." To this the apostle solemnly adds, "This mystery is profound, and I am saying that it [Genesis 2:24] refers to Christ and the church" (Eph. 5:31–32). So we see that in primeval history, with Eve fresh from Adam's side, the couple's one-flesh marital intimacy was prophetic of the union of Christ and the church! And more, Christian marriages today are to be a window through which the church and the world glimpse the mystery of Christ and the church. So, pastors, we are to do our best to tie knots that are redolent with Christ and his union with and love for the church. This means that pastoral counseling, marriage preparations, and the way we conduct the service are all of eternal importance.

As to the *domestic* importance of performing a truly Christian wedding, no more needs to be said than is told by the sad statistics of divorce and broken homes among professing Christians. Intrusive secular culture can be blamed, but the underlying reason is that the church has not done its job in conveying the exalting, life-elevating teaching of Scripture on marriage and the family, and in many places does not provide for or insist on adequate biblical premarital counseling. There is a sense in which a marriage in the Christian community is a matter of life and death, because that is what it will mean to the coming generations. Advice is provided later in this chapter.

Christian weddings are not commonly thought of as *evangelistic*, but they are, and here's why: First, the presiding pastor (you) is a Christian minister charged to ". . . do the work of an evangelist, fulfill your ministry" (2 Tim. 4:5). This means, at the very least, that your preaching is to be gospel redolent, full of the good news. The marriage texts supply just that, with a deep emphasis on Christ's atoning work. This does not suggest that the hearers of the brief sermon/homily will be challenged to receive Christ. But it does mean that you lift up the cross. Second, the celebrants, at least the bride and groom, are Christians whom you can directly address with an affectionate intimacy that allows you to say "hard" gospel realities, which the non-Christian in the congregation must then overhear, to his soul's education and benefit. Third, you normally have more non-Christians, proportionally, in a wedding service than on any Sunday service! Fourth, the whole service is built around the Scriptures that are variously read and are the ground upon which the exchange of vows and rings is based. Finally, the hymns and songs (rightly chosen) are also full of scriptural truth. So it all works together to paint a beautiful picture of what the gospel has done for the bride and groom and what it demands of them in marriage. Such a service can be used by Christ to make attendees thirsty for the water of life.

Truly Christian weddings can have a vast influence over the years on the contours of the church and the surrounding culture.

THE IMPORTANCE OF PREMARITAL COUNSELING

Premarital counseling must necessarily be preceded by an initial meeting with the pastor. When the couple schedules an appointment, have the office send them a questionnaire to be filled out and returned to the office prior to the meeting with the pastor. This will enhance the meeting as well as save time.

Sample Wedding Questionnaire[1]

BRIDE/GROOM

(B) Name_____

(G) Name_____

(B) Address_____

(G) Address _____

(B) Phones _____

(G) Phones _____

(B) Birthplace _____

(G) Birthplace _____

(B) Date of birth _____

(G) Date of birth _____

(B) Schooling _____

(G) Schooling _____

(B) Occupation _____

(G) Occupation _____

(B) Employer _____

(G) Employer _____

(B) Church membership _____

(G) Church membership _____

(B) Previously married? _____

(G) Previously married? _____

(B) Father _____

(G) Father _____

(B) Mother _____

(G) Mother _____

Proposed wedding and rehearsal dates _____

Crucial Questions

The scheduled meeting with the bride and groom is almost always with a much-in-love, very excited couple, and it is generally most enjoyable, notwithstanding some necessary, penetrating questions (listed below).

---

[1] For a downloadable version of this questionaire, please visit Crossway.org/WeddingWorksheet1

1. *Christians?* The faith of the bride and groom is not always a simple matter to discern, because there are times when either the man or the woman is not a believer, and both attempt to make you think otherwise, even using bits and pieces of pious, evangelical jargon. Discernment is especially difficult for the pastor when the couple is nice, especially non-Christians who are, indeed, morally upright people. But some key questions can cut to the quick. One that is always revealing is, "Can you explain to me what the gospel is?" or perhaps the well-traveled Evangelism Explosion question: "If you were to die tonight and stand before God, and if he were to say to you, 'Why should I let you into my heaven?' what would you say?" Also, questions that inquire about their commitment can help the pastor discern the couple's spiritual condition: "What are some of the ways you serve Christ?" or "When do you pray?" In any case, if the prospective bride or groom is not a believer, it is an appointed opportunity to share the gospel and, as has sometimes been our experience, begin a pastoral relationship in which you have the joy of introducing a person or couple to Christ and then, as God would have it, to perform a joyous wedding!

In cases where the nonbeliever remains in his or her unbelief, so that you cannot perform the wedding, you have done the couple and the body of Christ a gracious favor.

2. *Chaste?* If a Christian couple is sexually active (*fornicating* is the biblical word), they are by definition living in sin (a quaint expression to the modern mind, but altogether accurate). Their flagrant lack of restraint, should they marry, may sow the seeds of distrust in what would have otherwise been a healthy marriage. As it stands, that lack is a cautionary reason to think hard and seek prayer and counsel about future wedlock. Nevertheless, if the couple repents and submits to pastoral guidance and, in consultation with the pastoral leadership, commits to living chastely apart from each other for an agreed space of time, and does so in fellowship with the body of Christ, then holy matrimony may be pursued. The pastoral imperative here is to ask the appropriate questions and then minister appropriately under the graced wisdom of God's Word. We have had the particular joy of performing weddings for couples who have submitted to such care and have seen their lives and growing families prosper over the years.

3. *Family support?* This is not a deal breaker. There is a generation of disordered parents out there. But the question needs to be asked because marriage is not easy amid the pressures of modern culture, and a couple needs all the support they can get. Parental distaste for or disapproval of one's spouse can add substantial stress to a marriage. So if the parents of the

bride or groom object to the marriage, the pastor should explore the reasons before consenting to perform the wedding.

4. *Life direction?* A woman who has a passion for missions must think twice about marrying a man whose passion, for example, is golf. He will be on the fairway and she in the air as the shadow of her jet crosses over the links on the way to Zimbabwe. Seriously, the pastor needs to ask a few probing questions about their values and goals in life. Mutuality foreshadows harmony. Dissonance augurs trouble.

5. *Children?* The Scriptures teach that "children are a heritage from the LORD, the fruit of the womb a reward" (Ps. 127:3) and that God seeks "godly offspring" through faithfulness to the covenant of marriage (Mal. 2:15). In accord with this, the wedding service of the 1662 Book of Common Prayer gives as the first reason for marriage "the procreation of children." So couples that marry and covenant with each other to forgo children are at odds with the Scriptures and with the historic church. Certainly there can be valid reasons not to have children, which may be health-related or genetic. But if the rationale is to "save the planet" from overpopulation (contra Gen. 1:28), "to be free to be all that you can be," or even "to be free to minister the gospel" (all of which are specious arguments), or the fear that they will be "bad parents" (a credible argument), then marriage ought to be set aside. Indeed, singleness must be the logical option. And more, if a couple is in sharp disagreement about having a family, they should consider whether to pursue marriage at all. It is pastorally imperative to explore the couple's thinking on this crucial subject.

6. *"'Til death do us part"?* Some final questions for the prospective bride and groom are:

• Are your vows for life?
• Do you conceive of any way that your marriage could be dissolved other than by the death of your spouse or his or her unrepentant, serial adultery or willful desertion?
• What if your wife loses her mind and is institutionalized? Would you divorce her? Will you file for divorce if your husband loses his physical, mental, or even his spiritual health?
• Is there any escape clause hidden in the recesses of your minds?

If the answer to any of these questions is yes, we suggest that a responsible pastor must say no to performing the wedding. Otherwise, "for better or for worse, for richer or for poorer, in sickness and in health, to love and to cherish, 'til death do us part" is a conscious fraud.

When the pastor has completed the initial meeting with the couple and approved the wedding (which is happily almost always the case), the rehearsal and wedding dates can be entered on the church calendar and arrangements made for premarital counseling.

IMPLEMENTING EFFECTIVE PREMARITAL COUNSELING: EXAMPLES AND CURRICULA

Dr. Robert W. Evans notes in his chapter on "Pastoral Counseling" in this book:

> Countless wide-eyed young people are gleefully bounding down the aisle every year and standing before us to vow before God their lifelong devotion to a person whom they don't really know, covenant to live in a "mystery" that they don't really understand, and assume roles and responsibilities based upon expectations that they don't really share. It seems that most couples spend more time preparing for a two-week cruise than for a fifty-year marriage.

To counter this, Dr. Evans articulates his own rigorous pastoral template for premarital counseling. The class requires attendance at eight ninety-minute sessions that focus on the crucial aspects of marriage. He also requires one to three hours of weekly homework utilizing *Preparing for Marriage: The Complete Guide to Help Discover God's Plan for a Lifetime of Love*, edited by Dennis Rainey. See pages 513–515 for Pastor Evans's approach and the subjects covered.

Premarital counseling is necessarily wide-ranging due to the varied topics that need to be addressed, and some pastors do not feel equipped to deal adequately with the diverse topics. So they opt to arrange for a premarital course that utilizes godly members of their church and surrounding churches, and to work in concert with them to effect a strong premarital curriculum. The following is an effective model for a *five-session class* that meets weekly for two-hour sessions, providing a total of ten hours of instruction. Each session requires homework, and class attendance is not optional. Couples are required to read three short books and to submit written evaluations of the books.

1. *The biblical basis for Christian marriage.* This session can be taught by the pastor.
2. *Needs assessment and goal formation.* Couples come into marriage with needs that they expect their spouses to fulfill, and often those needs are

unexpressed. This class will help the couple identify and express them, which is both necessary and salutary, especially at the beginning of marriage. Along with this, the couple is asked to articulate four long-range goals and four short-term goals, and to choose one of the goals and map out a strategy to meet it. This session can be taught by a wise, mature couple in the church, ideally an elder and his wife.

3. *Communication and conflict management.* This session stresses the necessity of good communication and lays out tried-and-true methods of communication. Along with this, the instructor shares wisdom on how the couple can manage the conflicts that normally arise in marriage. This session can be taught by a trained Christian counselor.

4. *Finances and family relationships.* Prior to the class, the couple is asked to fill out a personal finance form and to bring it for their own reference as they interact with a financial expert. The first part of this session should be taught by a respected financial counselor or banker. A private session may then be arranged if a couple sees that it is necessary. The second half on family relationships can again be taught by a mature Christian couple.

5. *Sexuality and in-laws.* The first part of this session should be taught by a biblically informed Christian gynecologist, who, in addition to his/her expertise on sex and human reproduction, is articulate on the subject of contraception and the now widespread use of abortifacients. The second part of the session can be taught by a wise, mature couple.

If a longer premarital course is desired, here is an extended curriculum used by College Church in Wheaton, Illinois: (1) biblical foundations of marriage, (2) the gospel and marriage, (3) family—context for relationships, (4) family—communication, (5) roles of husbands and wives, (6) intimacy and romance, (7) conflict, (8) finances, and (9) panel discussion and wrap-up/evaluation.

The genius of this class/session approach, apart from the basic curriculum (and its allowance for expertise, creativity, and expansion), is that the attending couples naturally involve themselves in lively discussion and exchange that may not occur in private one-on-one counseling. Sometimes lifelong friendships are formed between the couples.

Some of the books widely used for premarital counseling are:

• David Boehl, Brent Nelson, Jeff Schulte, and Lloyd Shadrach, *Preparing for Marriage*, ed. Dennis Rainey (Ventura, CA: Gospel Light, 1998, 2010).

- Bryan and Kathy Chapell, *Each for the Other: Marriage as It Is Meant to Be* (Grand Rapids: Baker, 2006).
- Dave Harvey, *When Sinners Say "I Do"* (Wapwallopen, PA: Shepherd Press, 2007).
- Timothy Keller and Kathy Keller, *The Meaning of Marriage* (New York: Dutton, 2011).
- Gary and Betsy Ricucci, *Love That Lasts* (Wheaton, IL: Crossway, 2006).
- Winston T. Smith, *Marriage Matters* (Greensboro, NC: New Growth Press, 2010).
- Paul David Tripp, *What Did You Expect? Redeeming the Realities of Marriage* (Wheaton, IL: Crossway, 2010).

PLANNING THE WEDDING SERVICE
THE NECESSITY OF A CHURCH WEDDING COORDINATOR

Planning the wedding ceremony is a big deal for most brides, and some come to the busy pastor with details best left to someone else—such as the request to include a selection from a popular song before the wedding vows, which forces the pastor to tell the tearful bride that, notwithstanding that the song has become "their song," it is inappropriate, especially because of a few double entendres. Or, on another awkward occasion, having to inform a disappointed couple that their homemade wedding vows won't be used in the wedding ceremony because (ever so gently, pastor) such connubial intimacies are better suited to the bedroom. Of course, apart from such memorable requests, there are a myriad of worthy details that must be dealt with kindly—but by someone *other* than the pastor, namely, a wedding coordinator with the church wedding policy in hand.

The importance of having a church wedding coordinator remains constant regardless of the size of the church because the complexity of the whole event, from the rehearsal to the end of the reception, remains constant regardless of the church's size (a wedding coordinator's checklist typically runs five pages, and church wedding policies can be extensive). Some churches are fortunate enough to have a woman who finds fulfillment in volunteering her services. Others retain a coordinator by including her fee in the cost of using the church facility. No matter how the arrangement is structured, the coordinator must be the kind of woman who loves helping the bride and groom and sees herself as serving Christ and the church. The following sample job description is a helpful template for designing a description that fits your church's needs.

Sample Job Description

Title: Church Wedding Coordinator

Reporting: Reports to and is under the supervision of the presiding pastor (or designated pastor or staff member).

Objective: To oversee wedding logistics, planning, rehearsals, and wedding day activities.

Duties:

1. Meet with the bride two months before the wedding and again two weeks before the event to discuss and advise on all aspects of the wedding checklist as they pertain to the rehearsal, the wedding, and the reception (if it is held on church premises).

2. Inform the bride of the church's wedding policies and be responsible to see that they are observed.

3. Fill out audio sound sheet forms for the technicians and setup sheets for the custodians detailing the setup of the rooms that the wedding will utilize, including the dressing rooms, and submit them to the presiding pastor two weeks before the wedding.

4. Assist the pastor in directing the wedding rehearsal.

5. Assist the wedding party and the family on the wedding day. Serve as a troubleshooter. Oversee the photo schedule, the sound check, the ushers, the processional, and the departure.

6. Remain on the premises until all people involved in the wedding have left. Leave the church premises as they were before the wedding party arrived.

7. Perform additional duties as directed by the presiding pastor.

RESOURCES FOR DESIGNING A CHRIST-EXALTING WEDDING SERVICE

To assist pastors in designing a Christ-exalting wedding, the following section includes:

- A chart detailing the general structure and components of Protestant wedding services.
- Guidance on the optional unity candle.
- Select hymns and songs for weddings.
- A sample wedding service, composed of the choice elements of the wedding services included in Appendix A.
- A sample wedding ceremony planning worksheet.

In addition, the Appendix (p. 541) includes (1) the full texts of standard wedding services for comparison and culling in preparation for planning a wedding service and (2) select outtakes from the standard wedding services, arranged under standard headings.

The Scriptures are very clear about what Christian marriage is, but if you look to the Bible for specific instructions on how to conduct a Christian wedding ceremony, you will find little help. Yet today there is a shared tradition in Western culture that effects a similarity among Christian wedding services. This is because standard denominational wedding services draw their structure and language from the deep theological and literary well of The Form and Solemnization of Matrimony in Thomas Cranmer's 1662 Book of Common Prayer. Many of the elements and phrases from Cranmer's service live on in contemporary renderings. Baptist and independent churches are more eclectic, as they have borrowed freely from each other's traditions, but Cranmer's fingerprints are still there.

STRUCTURE OF STANDARD WEDDING SERVICES

The following headings indicate the general structure and flow of the standard Protestant wedding service, though the terms for the headings differ among the traditions.

- Prelude
- Processional
- Presentation of the bride
- Call to worship
- Preface ("We have come together . . .")
- Charge
- Consent ("Will you take . . .")
- Prayer/invocation
- Scripture readings
- Homily/brief sermon
- Vows
- Rings
- Pronouncement ("Forasmuch as . . .")
- Prayer(s) and benediction
- Kiss
- Introduction of the bride and groom
- Recessional
- Postlude

A quick scan of the wedding services listed in the Appendix (in which we have inserted the headings/divisions in bold type) will acquaint the reader with the structure, components, and flow of the standard services.

Though most weddings today feature a brief sermon (homily), only the Lutheran and Anglican services designate a place for one. The Lutheran order places the sermon toward the beginning of the service, and the Anglican at the end, after the pronouncement of marriage. The Presbyterian, Methodist, and Baptist services omit the homily from the ceremony outline simply because it is not essential to solemnizing a marriage. So if your denominational order of service does not include a homily, you will have to decide where to insert it. Usually it fits best after the exchange of vows and rings.

Since many of today's wedding services (including those that are denominationally structured) allow for some variation, we have included some outtakes from them for your appreciation and possible incorporation into your order of service. They can be used in full or in part, and where the language is stilted, they can be easily adapted for use in your setting. See the Appendix for an extended list.

The Optional Unity Candle

The unity candle is of recent and inexact origin, having risen in America in the expressionistic late 1960s or early 1970s. And while it rose out of apparent Christian sentiment, it is used today in Jewish and interfaith ceremonies (the latter for symbolizing the uniting of two distinct traditions). The Roman Catholic Church hesitatingly permits the unity candle because its nuptial rites are already full of symbolism, but it forbids placement of the candle on the altar. This said, an Internet search reveals a thriving unity candle industry, complete with expensive candles and special unity candle poems.

The lighting of the unity candle usually involves the arrangement of three candles side by side near where the bride and groom will exchange their vows. The two outside candles are lighted during the prelude by the couple's mothers. Then (customarily after the exchange of vows or after the pronouncement), the bride and groom each take their respective candles and jointly light the center candle, after which they extinguish the two candles, thus completing the symbolism: their lives now burn as one.

Certainly this new tradition is not bad or unacceptable. The genesis of it is Christian. But the ceremony can be blandly secular (witness soap operas' fond use of it) unless the presiding pastor infuses the symbolism with explicit Christian significance, such as the following:

As Jesus Christ has declared that he is the light of the world, and inasmuch as he lives in your hearts by faith, and because he therefore calls you to be lights in a dark world, will you now live out his command to "Let your light shine before others, so that they may see your good works and give glory to your Father who is in heaven" (Matt. 5:16)?

The bride and groom then proceed to light the candles.

Select Hymns and Songs for Weddings

Though a wedding is ostensibly horizontal, celebrating romantic love and commitment, a Christian wedding ceremony must also be vertical, rejoicing in the God who is love and who gives his people the gift of love. As we eye the beautiful couple, our hearts should be lifted heavenward. The Essence and Author of love is to be exalted! One way to do this is through songs that focus on the person and works of God, notably his glorious gospel. The opening hymn sets the tone for the wedding. The other songs complement that vertical tone while introducing the horizontal.

The placement of music in the order of service is a matter of individual preference, but a good rule of thumb is not to feature more than two hymns or songs in a service and to place them at natural junctures—say, for example, after the call to worship or after the initial prayer/invocation before the Scripture readings or after the pronouncement of marriage.

As to the choice of congregational hymns and songs, you should choose only those that are well known and *eminently* singable. This is because weddings are attended by many who otherwise never darken the door of a church, not to mention the fact that weak singing detracts from the ceremony.

Below is a short collection of some fitting songs:

"Although I Speak with Angel's Tongue" (Donaldson)
"Beloved, God's Chosen" (Cherwien)
"Give Praise to God" (Boice/Jones)
"God Himself Is with Us" (Tersteegen)
"How Great Thou Art" (Hine)
"Jesus Is Lord" (Townend)
"O God, Beyond All Praising" (Perry)
"O Great God" (Kauflin)
"Praise to the Lord, the Almighty" (Neander)
"Rejoice, the Lord Is King" (Wesley)
"This Is a Day, Lord, Gladly Awaited" (Rowthorn)
"Where Love Is Found" (Schutte)

WEDDING SERVICE

The following ceremony, composed from choice elements of the standard services, is laid out in some detail, so that it includes suggestions about where to insert hymns and special music, when the congregation should stand and be seated, and where to insert additional elements (such as a unity candle).

Please note that the contents of the nondenominational ceremony have been freely edited.

Prelude

Processional (congregation stands at the entrance of the bride)

Presentation of the Bride

> *Minister*: "Who gives this woman in marriage?"
>
> *Father*: "Her mother and I do."

Father kisses his daughter and gives her to the groom.

Call to Worship

> Our Lord Jesus said: "From the beginning of creation, 'God made them male and female.' 'Therefore a man shall leave his father and mother and hold fast to his wife, and the two shall become one flesh.' So they are no longer two but one flesh" (Mark 10:6–8).
>
> Let us worship God as we now witness the marriage of _____ and _____ (full names).

Hymn (optional)

> Congregation stands for hymn and is seated at conclusion.

Preface

> We have come together here in the sight of God and in the presence of this congregation to join together this man and this woman in holy matrimony, which is an honorable state of life, instituted in the beginning by God himself, signifying to us the spiritual union that is between Christ and the church.
>
> Christ adorned and beautified matrimony with his presence and with the first sign by which he revealed his glory at a marriage in Cana of Galilee; and Holy Scripture demands that all should hold it in honor.
>
> It is therefore not to be entered upon unadvisedly, lightly, or merely to satisfy physical desires, but prayerfully, with careful thought and with reverence for God, duly considering the purposes for which it was ordained.
>
> It was ordained for the procreation of children and that they might be brought up in the nurture and instruction of the Lord, to the praise of his holy name.

It was ordained so that those to whom God has granted the gift of marriage might live a chaste and holy life, as befits members of Christ's body.

And it was ordained for the mutual companionship, help, and comfort that the one ought to have to the other, both in prosperity and adversity.

Charge (written by Dr. Merrill Tenney)

_____ and _____ (full names), today you are presenting yourselves before this congregation to declare your intention of uniting your lives voluntarily and honorably for the service of God and man. You are making a double dedication: to each other, in a lasting and indivisible union that shall endure for the remaining years of your lives, and to God, that he may make you his dual instrument for the accomplishment of his purpose both in and by your personalities. The achievement of this purpose will require appreciation of each other's abilities and virtues, forgiveness of each other's faults, and unfailing devotion to each other's welfare and development. There must be on your part a united consent to the purpose of God as he progressively reveals it to you by his Word and by his Spirit, and an unhesitant acceptance by faith of the challenges that he sets before you.

I charge you, therefore, first of all to consider that your promises to each other are made in the presence of a God who remembers your pledges and who holds you responsible for performing them. They must be kept inviolable before him.

I admonish you to keep in mind that each of you is the object of Christ's redemption and should be valued accordingly. Neither should be neglected or belittled by the other. Esteem each other as God's gift for mutual aid, comfort, and joy, and as a repository of complete confidence and trust.

I encourage you to share willingly and sympathetically your joys and worries, your successes and your struggles, and to be neither conceited by the former nor depressed by the latter. Whichever may prevail, cling closely to each other, that defeats may be met by united strength, and victories by united joy.

I charge you to make your home a place where you can have a refuge from the storms of life, not only for yourselves, but also for others who may be your guests. Let it be a haven for the weary, a source of uplift for the discouraged, and a convincing testimony to a cynical world.

In short, recognize the Lord Jesus Christ as head of the house, the ruler of your destinies, and the object of your deepest affection. If you do, he will confirm your marriage by his guidance and will overshadow it by his peace.

I charge you to love each other, to support each other, and to serve him with sincere hearts and determined wills until your mutual service for him shall be completed.

Consent

Minister: "(G)_____, will you have (B)_____ as your wife, to live together as God has ordained, in the holy state of matrimony? Will you love her, cherish her, in sickness and in health, and, forsaking all others, be faithful to her as long as you both shall live?"

Groom: "I will."

Minister: "(B)_____, will you have (G)_____ as your husband, to live together as God has ordained, in the holy state of matrimony? Will you love him, obey him, honor and protect him, in sickness and in health, and, forsaking all others, be faithful to him as long as you both shall live?"

Bride: "I will."

Prayer/Invocation

Hymn (optional)

Congregation stands for hymn and is seated at conclusion.

Reading of Scriptures

Old Testament reading

New Testament reading

Homily

Vows

Repeated after the minister:

Groom: "I, (G) _____, take you, (B)_____, to be my wedded wife, to have and to hold from this day forward, for better or for worse, for richer or for poorer, in sickness and in health, to love and to cherish, until we are parted by death. This is my solemn vow."

Bride: "I, (B)_____, take you, (G)_____, to be my wedded husband, to have and to hold from this day forward, for better or for worse, for richer or for poorer, in sickness and in health, to love and to cherish, until we are parted by death. This is my solemn vow."

Rings

Minister: "Lord, bless these rings, that as (G)_____ and (B)_____ wear them, they may abide in you and continue in your favor until their lives shall end, through Jesus Christ our Lord. Amen."

Groom (repeating after the minister): "(B)_____, this ring I give you, in token and pledge of my constant faith and abiding love."

Bride (repeating after the minister): "(G)_____, this ring I give you, in token and pledge of my constant faith and abiding love."

Pronouncement

Minister: "Forasmuch as (G) _____and (B) _____ have consented together in holy wedlock and have witnessed the same before God and this people and have pledged their faith to each other and have declared the same by the giving and receiving of rings, I pronounce them husband and wife together, in the name of the Father and of the Son and of the Holy Spirit. Amen.

"Those whom God has joined together let no one put asunder."

Unity Candle (optional)

Hymn (optional)

Congregation stands for hymn and is seated at conclusion.

Prayer/Benediction

Specially prepared prayer for the couple (kneeling or standing).

Minister: "The Lord bless you and keep you; the Lord make his face shine upon you; the Lord lift up his countenance upon you and give you peace. Amen."

Kiss

Minister: "You may kiss your bride."

Introduction

Minister: "May I present Mr. and Mrs. (full name of the groom)."

Recessional

Postlude

SAMPLE WEDDING CEREMONY PLANNING WORKSHEET[2]

The sample worksheet below is meant to be suggestive as to how you may construct your own worksheet. You may prefer a different or abbreviated order of service. You also may be using a denominational template. Regardless, the best approach is to read through the traditional wedding services in the Appendix, observing the inserted headings while comparing what they say as to vows, preface, or consent. Then choose what you consider to be best for use in your context. And, of course, if the language is too archaic or stilted, you should do some editing.

---

[2] For a downloadable version of the worksheet, please visit crossway.org/WeddingWorksheet2

Among the benefits of composing a service that you have thought through and like is that it leaves only a few things for the bride and groom to determine, namely, the prelude and postlude, the hymns, the special music, the Scripture reader(s), and the question of the unity candle.

Prelude
Processional
Presentation _____
Call to worship _____
Hymn (optional) _____
Preface _____
Charge _____
Consent _____
Prayer/invocation _____
Hymn (optional) _____
Reading of Scriptures
    Old Testament _____
    New Testament _____
Homily
Vows _____
Rings _____
Pronouncement _____
Unity candle (optional)
Hymn (optional) _____
Prayer/benediction _____
Kiss
Introduction
Recessional
Postlude

THE WEDDING HOMILY: RESOURCES AND EXAMPLES

As we said earlier, the wedding homily, when it is based on the biblical texts that inform marriage, is naturally gospel-centered. And the fragrance of Christ, coupled with the first-person intimacy used by the pastor in directly addressing the bride and groom, gives the message a flesh-and-blood reality and piquancy that the Holy Spirit may be pleased to use in making some wedding guests thirsty for the water of life. This means that the brief wedding sermon is of great importance.

The following resources are included to encourage careful, prayerful work on the homily.

SELECT SCRIPTURES FOR WEDDINGS
Old Testament

For easy recall, key lines from each passage are included. The opening lines and some outtakes of some psalms (in entirety or in part) will serve to focus a wedding upward as well as upon the occasion.

Genesis 1:26–31: "So God created man in his own image, in the image of God he created him; male and female he created them" (v. 27).

Genesis 2:18–25: "Therefore a man shall leave his father and his mother and hold fast to his wife, and they shall become one flesh" (v. 24).

Psalm 45: "My heart overflows with a pleasing theme; I address verses to the king; my tongue is like the pen of a ready scribe. You are the most handsome of the sons of men" (vv. 1–2a).

Psalm 67: "May God be gracious to us and bless us and make his face to shine upon us, that your name may be known on earth, your saving power among all nations" (vv. 1–2).

Psalm 103: "Bless the LORD, O my soul, and all that is within me, bless his holy name!" (v. 1; note the multiple statements of "Bless the LORD" in this psalm).

Psalm 121: "I lift up my eyes to the hills. From where does my help come? My help comes from the LORD, who made heaven and earth" (vv. 1–2).

Psalm 127: "Unless the LORD builds the house, those who build it labor in vain. . . . Behold, children are a heritage from the LORD" (vv. 1, 3a).

Psalm 128: "Blessed is everyone who fears the LORD, who walks in his ways! . . . Your wife will be like a fruitful vine" (vv. 1, 3a).

Psalm 148: "Praise the LORD! Praise the LORD from the heavens; praise him in the heights! Praise him all his angels; praise him, all his hosts!" (vv. 1–2).

Psalm 150: "Praise the LORD! Praise God in his sanctuary; praise him in his mighty heavens!" (v. 1).

Song of Solomon 2:1–4: "his banner over me was love" (v. 4b).

Song of Solomon 2:7–17: "My beloved speaks and says to me: 'Arise, my love, my beautiful one, and come away'" (v. 10).

Song of Solomon 4:12–15: "A garden locked is my sister, my bride, a spring locked, a fountain sealed" (v. 12).

Song of Solomon 6:3a: "I am my beloved's and my beloved is mine."

Song of Solomon 8:6–7: "Set me as a seal upon your heart, as a seal upon your arm, for love is as strong as death. . . . Many waters cannot quench love" (vv. 6–7a).

New Testament
The following texts directly address marriage:

Matthew 19:3–12
Mark 10:6–9
Ephesians 5:21–33
Colossians 3:18–19
1 Peter 3:1–7
Revelation 19:5–9

The following texts encourage love for God and one another:

Matthew 22:35–40
Romans 12:9–10
1 Corinthians 13:1–3
Ephesians 3:14–21
Colossians 3:12–17
1 John 4:7–12

The following texts encourage godliness:

Matthew 5:3–12
Romans 12:9–21
Galatians 5:22–23
Philippians 2:1–4
Philippians 4:8–9

Select Poems for Weddings
The following poems (some from Scripture itself) have been selected by Dr. Leland Ryken. They represent the very best love poems and epithalamia (wedding poems) in the English language. As such, they provide extraordinary resources for the wedding message, perhaps in full, or just a choice stanza or indelible line. Some could be read aloud at an appropriate place

in the ceremony or by a member of the wedding party at the reception (for example, Sidney Lanier's "Wedding Hymn"). Any of them could be used effectively in a printed wedding program. We suggest that pastors read through this brief section before they prepare their wedding homilies.

Ecclesiastes 4:9–12 (NIV)

Two are better than one,
    because they have a good return for their labor:
If either of them falls down
    one can help the other up.
But pity anyone who falls
    and has no one to help them up.
Also, if two lie down together, they will keep warm.
    But how can one keep warm alone?
Though one may be overpowered,
    two can defend themselves.
A cord of three strands is not quickly broken.

Song of Solomon 2:10–13, 16

Arise, my love, my beautiful one,
    and come away,
for behold, the winter is past;
    the rain is over and gone.
The flowers appear on the earth;
    the time of singing has come,
and the voice of the turtledove
    is heard in our land.
The fig tree ripens its figs,
    and the vines are in blossom;
    they give forth fragrance.
Arise, my love, my beautiful one,
    and come away. . . .
My beloved is mine, and I am his.

Song of Solomon 8:6–7 (AT)

Set me as a seal upon your heart,
    as a seal upon your arm,
for love is strong as death,
    passion as fierce as the grave.
Its flashes are flashes of fire,

the very flame of the LORD.
Many waters cannot quench love,
    neither can floods drown it.
If a man offered for love
    all the wealth of his house
    it would be utterly despised.

"A Birthday" (Christina Rossetti)
    My heart is like a singing bird
    Whose nest is in a watered shoot;
    My heart is like an apple-tree
    Whose boughs are bent with thick-set fruit;
    My heart is like a rainbow shell
    That paddles in a halcyon sea;
    My heart is gladder than all these,
    Because my love is come to me.

    Raise me a dais of silk and down;
    Hang it with vair and purple dyes;
    Carve it in doves and pomegranates,
    And peacocks with a hundred eyes;
    Work it in gold and silver grapes,
    In leaves and silver fleurs-de-lys;
    Because the birthday of my life
    Is come, my love is come to me.

From "Love" (Roy Croft)
    I love you,
    Not only for what you are,
    But for what I am
    When I am with you.

    I love you,
    Not only for what
    You have made of yourself,
    But for what
    You are making of me. . . .

    I love you
    For putting your hand
    Into my heaped-up heart

And passing over
All the foolish, weak things
That you can't help
Dimly seeing there,
And for drawing out
Into the light
All the beautiful belongings
That no one else had looked
Quite far enough to find.

I love you because you
Are helping me to make
Of the lumber of my life
Not a tavern
But a temple;
Out of the works
Of my every day
Not a reproach
But a song. . . .

"My True Love Hath My Heart" (Sir Philip Sidney)

My true-love hath my heart and I have his,
By just exchange one for the other given:
I hold his dear, and mine he cannot miss;
There was never a better bargain driven.
His heart in me keeps me and him in one;
My heart in him his thoughts and senses guides:
He loves my heart, for once it was his own;
I cherish his because in me it bides. . . .
My true love hath my heart and I have his.

"Sonnet 68" (Edmund Spenser)

Sixteenth-century English poet Edmund Spenser penned this poem and addressed it to his fiancée on Easter Day. A Christian literary scholar once expressed the wish that this poem be read at every Christian wedding.

Most glorious Lord of life, that on this day
Didst make thy triumph over death and sin,
And having harrowed hell, didst bring away
Captivity thence captive, us to win:
This joyous day, dear Lord, with joy begin,

And grant that we, for whom thou didst die,
Being with thy dear blood clean washed from sin,
May live for ever in felicity.
And that thy love we weighing worthily,
May likewise love thee for the same again,
And for thy sake, that all like dear didst buy,
With love may one another entertain.
So let us love, dear love, like as we ought,
Love is the lesson which the Lord us taught.

"Sonnet 116" (William Shakespeare)

This poem is a celebration of the permanence of true love that lasts over the course of an entire lifetime.

Let me not to the marriage of true minds
Admit impediments. Love is not love
Which alters when it alteration finds,
Or bends with the remover to remove:
O no; it is an ever-fixéd mark,
That looks on tempests, and is never shaken;
It is the star to every wandering bark,
Whose worth's unknown, although his height be taken.
Love's not Time's fool, though rosy lips and cheeks
Within his bending sickle's compass come;
Love alters not with his brief hours and weeks,
But bears it out even to the edge of doom [the final judgment].
If this be error and upon me proved,
I never writ, nor no man ever loved.

"To My Dear and Loving Husband" (Anne Bradstreet)

If ever two were one, then surely we.
If ever man were loved by wife, then thee.
If ever wife was happy in a man,
Compare with me, ye women, if you can.
I prize thy love more than whole mines of gold,
Or all the riches that the East doth hold.
My love is such that rivers cannot quench,
Nor ought but love from thee give recompense.
Thy love is such I can no way repay.
The heavens reward thee manifold, I pray.

Then while we live, in love let's so persever [persevere]
That when we live no more we may live ever.

"Wedding Hymn" (Sidney Lanier)
Thou God, whose high, eternal Love
Is the only blue sky of our life,
Clear all the Heaven that bends above
The life-road of this man and wife.
May these two lives be but one note
In the world's strange-sounding harmony,
Whose sacred music e'er shall float
Through every discord up to Thee.
As when from separate stars two beams
Unite to form one tender ray:
As when two sweet but shadowy dreams
Explain each other in the day:
So may these two dear hearts one light
Emit, and each interpret each.
Let an angel come and dwell tonight
In this dear double-heart, and teach.

THE COMPLETE TEXTS OF TEN WEDDING HOMILIES
Sample Wedding Homily #1 (Kent Hughes)
On Ephesians 5:22–33; cf. Genesis 2:23

_____and _____, there will never be another day like today.

There will never be a day so anticipated, dreamed of, discussed, prepared for, choreographed, or *expensive*!

The uniqueness of this day lies in this: God has called you to become one. Your parents have recognized this and stand with you in joyous support. Your family and friends realize the same and are here to celebrate. Your church, along with everyone else, recognizes that these are holy moments and supports you with her prayers. What a great day this is! May God fix in your minds the sweet memory of this—your wedding day.

The Well

This is a Christian marriage. Both of you know and love Christ, and you desire that he be at the very center of your lives and first in your marriage. As a consciously Christian marriage, the intimacy and commitment that you desire is drawn from the well of the sixth day of creation, when Eve was taken out of Adam's side so that he might embrace with great love a part of himself. Adam's shout of ecstasy upon seeing Eve was:

> "This is at last bone of my bones
> and flesh of my flesh;
> she shall be called Woman,
> because she was taken out of Man." (Gen. 2:23)

This rapturous cry records the first human words quoted in the Bible, as well as the first poetic couplet in God's Holy Word. Such astonished ecstasy! Adam had found his longed-for love. And because God had just honed Adam's naming powers, he spontaneously declared:

> "She shall be called Woman,
> because she was taken out of Man."

The sound play of their names celebrated their relationship.

Adam had restated his own name embedded in hers, trumpeting the greatest intimacy.

Adam's shout echoes down to this day (your wedding day), proclaiming loudly the joy and intimacy of marriage. There in Genesis, Adam's voice subsides, and the voice of Moses concludes, "Therefore a man shall leave his father and his mother and hold fast to his wife, and they shall become one flesh" (Gen. 2:24).

Moses's words became the deep well for the Bible's teaching on marriage. Jesus himself would quote them as the very Word of God: "Therefore a man shall leave his father and his mother and hold fast to his wife, and the two shall become one flesh" (Matt. 19:5).

The apostle Paul drew from the deep well of Genesis when he concluded his teaching on marriage by again quoting Moses, saying: "'Therefore a man shall leave his father and mother and hold fast to his wife, and the two shall become one flesh.' This mystery is profound, and I am saying that it refers to Christ and the church" (Eph. 5:31–32).

Christian Marriage and the Cross

_____ and _____, in the light of Paul's teaching that marriage evokes the mystery of Christ and the church, you must understand that without the cross, your marriage is not a Christian marriage. Marriage is about dying, because that is what Christ did for his bride: "Husbands, love your wives, as Christ loved the church and gave himself up for her" (Eph. 5:25).

Today, as you are joined in marriage, a single man and a single woman will die, and the two of you shall become one flesh. These sacred moments (witnessed by God, the angels, and the church here in festal assembly) mark the end of your former life. Your joyous wedding is the beginning of a sacred death. Christian wedding vows mark the sweet inception of a lifelong death to self, giving over not only all that you have but all that you are. This is a daunting reality, and it is so beautiful—an enduring glory to Christ and his church.

So on this your long-awaited wedding day, I challenge you to raise the cross over your lives, so that it towers over all, because that is what makes your marriage Christian. And, of course, the cross is the road to a particular joy: "For whoever would save his life will lose it, but whoever loses his life for my sake will find it" (Matt. 16:25). May you find your life together ever more full and joyous.

_____ and _____, lift high the cross!

The Covenant

Along with the cross, you must embrace the fact that marriage is not a contractual relationship but a lifelong covenant. It is not a Christian marriage if it is conditional or contractual. Christian marriage calls for a solemn oath before God—swearing together before him that you will never, ever break your promise. In preparation for this day, I have asked you hard questions about your covenant, and you have affirmed that it is for life, whatever may come.

God is smiling on you on this day of your public covenant before the church and the state. This is so liberating, because your solemn word— ". . . in sickness and in health . . . to love and to cherish as long as we both shall live, until death do us part"—frees you to work things out through the ups and downs of life.

_____and _____, you have a lifetime to explore and celebrate your oneness! You have the space to grow because you can always be sure of each other's commitment.

The Christ

There is the *cross*, there is the *covenant*, and there is the *Christ*—the grand key to marriage. As believers, you are married to him for eternity. And because Christ is the center of your lives, he will grace your intimacy as you draw near to him. Temple Gardner caught it perfectly with this prayer:

> That I may come near to her,
> draw me nearer to Thee than to her,
> make me know Thee more than her,
> That I may love her with a perfect love. . . .
> Cause me to love Thee more than her.

_____and _____, determine to draw nearer to Christ than to each other, to know him more than one another, so that you will love each other with a perfect love!

_____and _____, go to the well of the sixth day.

May you always be dazzled with each other.

May you be amazed that God has given you such a love.

May you plumb the depths and heights of each other's being.

May every season of life be graced with a deeper love.

May your love grace your families.

May your love grace the church.

May your love grace a needy world.

Lift high the *cross*.

Keep the *covenant*.

Run to Jesus, the *Christ*.

Sample Wedding Homily #2 (Kent Hughes)
On Ephesians 5:25–33

_____and _____, becoming one in Christ is a profound mystery. So deep is it that the ancient Christians referred to it as a mystical union, because they knew the truth that is often forgotten today—the depth of the marital union is illustrative of the relationship of Christ and the church.

Furthermore, Christ's love for the church informs all Christians as to how marriage is to be lived.

To the Groom
An incarnational life: The Holy Scriptures, at the end of the fifth chapter of Ephesians (the most explicit teaching on marriage in the Bible), command you to love your wife, "as Christ loved the church and gave himself up for her" (Eph. 5:25), calling you to lead an incarnational life in relation to _____.

_____, such a life means that you are to be a *sensitive man*, realizing that your masculinity is elevated by your sensitivity to your wife's femininity. You must set yourself to understanding her heart and the subtleties of her mind and her emotions—the Fahrenheit of her soul. You never will perfectly! But the pursuit will make you Christlike and a better husband. Your actions are to say to _____, "My life for yours."

An incarnational life also demands that you be a *caring man*.

The depth of caring is described by the apostle: "Husbands should love their wives as their own bodies. . . . For no one ever hated his own flesh, but nourishes and cherishes it" (Eph. 5:28–29b). In effect, the Scriptures call you to a sublime other-directed narcissism. "[So] shall she be placed in my constant soul" (*Merchant of Venice*, Act II, Scene VI). Her body is to be your body, her comfort your comfort, her adornment yours, her care your care. _____, cherish your constant soul.

An incarnational life also demands *dying*, because that is what the incarnation ultimately meant for Christ. Marital love is like death, because it demands all of you. Mike Mason dramatized this when he likened marital love to a great cosmic shark: "And who has not been frightened almost to death by love's dark shadow gliding swift and huge like an interstellar shark, like a swimming mountain, through the deepest waters of our being, through depths we never knew we had?"[3]

_____, "love's dark shadow" is the recurrent experience of every loving husband, as there will come a frightening love that fills our horizons, sounding the depths of our beings. A foreboding call? Not at all. In truth, husbands who love like this are those who enjoy the greatest marital joy and deepest love.

The shark smiles as he glides by,
And from his wake
Flow ripples of grace. (Hughes)

A redemptive life: _____, loving your wife "as Christ loved the church" not only requires an incarnational life, but also a redemptive life, as the apostle further says of Christ: "[He] gave himself up for her, that he might sanctify her, having cleansed her by the washing of water with the word, so that he might present the church to himself in splendor, without spot or wrinkle or any such thing, that she might be holy and without blemish" (Eph. 5:25–27).

Your bride, so radiant and beautiful in her wedding dress, is a bright shadow of this. This is what Christ will do to both of you through your divine marriage to him, because at his return the washed and regenerated church will be presented to him in absolute perfection. This is the sealing of the romance of the ages!

Meanwhile, Christ's care for the bride is an illustration of what ought to be the loving husband's sanctifying effect on his wife. _____, you are to promote your wife's godliness and sanctification. You are to prepare her for the future marriage of Christ and the church.

In this grand venture, you are to be her *prophet*, filling yourself with God's Word so that you will be a wise leader. You are to be her *priest* as you pray for her in loving detail. You are to be her *king*, not by strength

---

[3] Mike Mason, *The Mystery of Marriage* (Colorado Springs: Multnomah, 2005), 62.

but because you lead a princely life. You are to be her *servant* because "the Son of Man came not to be served but to serve" (Mark 10:45).

To the Bride

A Spirit-filled life: _____, as I have likened _____'s love for you to that of the Son of God, I will liken yours to that of the Spirit of God. The Holy Spirit is called the Paraclete, the one who comes alongside God's children and *comforts, encourages,* and *exhorts*. When you hitch your life to another in marriage, you are in for a wild ride that at times will take you to the stars and sometimes will drive you to the depths. When _____ gets down, comfort him with the comfort of God.

Encourage him to be a man of God who loves God more than he loves you. Challenge him to be a man—a man of his word, a man who always speaks the truth, a man who never compromises his ethics, a generous man, a man who loves the poor, a man who loves the church, a man who loves the gospel and the lost world.

_____, pray for your husband following the analogy of the Holy Spirit, who "helps us in our weaknesses. For we do not know what to pray for as we ought, but the Spirit himself intercedes for us with groanings too deep for words" (Rom. 8:26). As his wife, his "one flesh," his constant soul, you will know his inarticulate center and the things that he cannot express. May you then intercede for him in the things too deep for words.

_____, in a day when the culture is telling you to seek the place of power, to put yourself first, God's Word still speaks: "Wives, submit to your own husbands, as to the Lord. For the husband is the head of the wife even as Christ is the head of the church, his body. . . . And let the wife see that she respects her husband" (Eph. 5:22, 23, 33). There is a divinely ordained order for the home, even as there is in the Holy Trinity.

_____, live and love in it to the fullest.

To the Couple

_____and _____, in just a few moments you are going to exchange solemn vows to each other that are very similar to those that your parents and their parents and their ancestors said to one another. In doing so, you will be announcing your solidarity with the past and your fidelity to the high call of God.

Your vows are for life. They must never be broken! God and this congregation are your witnesses. Beautiful and handsome as you are today, there will come a time when the blossom will fade. But when the petals fall, may your love radiate the beauty of Christ.

Sample Wedding Homily #3 (Doug O'Donnell)
On the Song of Solomon (suggested reading Song 8:5–7)

"Love Stronger Than Death"

A kiss. A white dress. People standing when the bride appears. A father placing his daughter upon the groom's arm. One candle lit by the couple. A gold ring.

A wedding ceremony is full of symbols: symbols of passion, purity, respect, leaving and cleaving, unity, and longevity. In the Bible, there is a wedding poem drenched in symbolism. Solomon's greatest song! The Song of Songs is a poem about covenant love *and* erotic love, a combination so rare today that our world does not know what to do with it. It is, of course, this erotic or physically romantic part of this Song that must be read with care and caution. In fact, the rabbis of the first century thought this book so dangerous to the immature and impure imagination that they forbade men under the age of thirty to read it. (You both are of age, aren't you?)

Listen to its language. It begins, "Let him kiss me with the kisses of his mouth! For your love is better than wine!" (Song 1:2), and it climaxes at the end of chapter 4 and the beginning of chapter 5, where the bride says:

> Awake, O north wind,
>   and come, O south wind!
> Blow upon my garden,
>   let its spices flow.
> Let my beloved come to his garden,
>   and eat its choicest fruits. (4:16)

The bridegroom gladly indulges and then replies:

> I came to my garden, my sister, my bride,
> I gathered my myrrh with my spice,
> I ate my honeycomb with my honey,
> I drank my wine with my milk. (5:1a)

He then turns to his audience (i.e., the wedding attendants *and* the reader) and invites them to feast as well: "Eat, friends, drink, and be drunk with love!" (v. 1b).

This is the book you wanted me to talk on, right? Is everyone still comfortable? If not, we will be done in just a moment. Well, the Song of Songs ends, thankfully so, with some sobriety. In the passage that was read, we learn that all this emotional and physical affection occurs within the context of the covenant bond of marriage.

In chapter 8, as the curtain closes on this greatest love song, the characters emerge to take their final bow and to declare their last and lasting vow. In verse 5, we see that the bride has left her family to join her husband, similar to what we all witnessed just a moment ago. And as she leans upon him at the very place their love began and acknowledges her union with him publicly, she urges him to assure her that their love is all-encompassing. She says, "Set me as a seal upon your heart, as a seal upon your arm" (v. 6a). In other words, she is saying, "Promise me your comprehensive devotion—your internal commitment ("your heart") and your external commitment ("your arm")." She asks for such commitment because she understands the nature of genuine love. She continues:

For love is strong as death,
 jealousy is fierce as the grave.
Its flashes are flashes of fire,
 the very flame of the Lord. (v. 6b)

This is no ordinary fire! It is, as Roland Murphy said, "the flame of divine love," or, as Robert Browning labeled it, "his fire of fires."

Many waters cannot quench love,
 neither can floods drown it.
If a man offered for love
 all the wealth of his house,
 he would be utterly despised. (v. 7)

This covenant love that characterizes marriage is as active, irresistible, and irreversible as death. It is passionately but purely jealous (single-minded in its devotion and protection). It is like an eternal flame, one fueled by divine love and power. And it is not something that can be purchased, for there is nothing you could exchange for it that is of equal or greater value.

Like a wedding ceremony itself, as the Song of Songs speaks of the beauty, power, goodness, and purity of human love, it symbolizes something greater, namely the love of God in Christ. Most people know John 3:16: "For God so loved the world, that he gave his only Son, that whoever believes in him should not perish but have eternal life." But listen also to how 1 John 3:16 begins, "By this we know love, that he [Jesus] laid down his life for us." How do we know the essence of love, both human and divine? "Jesus Christ and him crucified" (1 Cor. 2:2) is how Christians define love.

"Now, wait a minute," some might say. "This is a wedding. And we can take some subtle talk about sex, but not about death, and certainly not about crucifixion." Ah, but _____and _____wouldn't have it otherwise. For they know that we do not know love except in this: Jesus selflessly and sacrificially laid down his life. You see, it is in the death of Christ that the unchangeable, unquenchable, and invaluable love described in the Song of Songs gains definition.

So, _____ and _____, on this day I promise you that I will not bombard you with marital advice other than to say, in your marriage, look to the love of God in the cross of Christ! In times of joy, look to the cross. In times of sorrow, look to the cross. In times of confusion, look to the cross. In times of sin, look to the cross. For in the cross of Christ you will find all the comfort, wisdom, strength, hope, and forgiveness you need to love each other as husband and wife.

My brother and sister in Christ, may the love that you have expressed and will express this day, in word and action, be the kind of love described here in God's Word, a love that is ultimately embodied in the drama of our redemption, in our Lord Jesus Christ and him crucified. So as you soon exchange vows, rings, and (if I allow you by the power vested in me by the state of _____) a kiss, may your love for each other *symbolize* to this lost world what you have found in Jesus!

Sample Wedding Homily #4 (Doug O'Donnell)

On 1 John 3:16 (suggested readings include: 1 John 3:16–18; cf. 1 John 4:16, 19; 1 Corinthians 13)

"By This We Know Love"

In Ecclesiastes 3:11, Solomon writes: "He [God] has made everything beautiful in its time." The context of that summary saying is the famous poem on time, which begins: "For everything there is a season, and a time for every matter under heaven" (v. 1). Then it lists fourteen human activities under heaven, such as "a time to weep, and a time to laugh; a time to mourn, and a time to dance," and it includes those two great wedding sermon lines "a time to love . . . a time to embrace" (see vv. 2–8). Today we celebrate God's beautiful timing—that is, how he has made everything beautiful in its time in your lives.

The Song of Solomon, the great marriage poem in the Bible, also celebrates God's timing as it relates to love. There is the refrain to the young maidens to wait—"[do] not stir up or awaken love until it pleases" (Song 2:7; cf. 3:5; 8:4). But there are also passages like 2:10–13, which reads:

My beloved speaks and says to me:
"Arise, my love, my beautiful one,
    and come away,

for behold, the winter is past;
    the rain is over and gone.
The flowers appear on the earth,
    the time of singing has come,
and the voice of the turtledove
    is heard in our land.
The fig tree ripens its figs,
    and the vines are in blossom;
    they give forth fragrance.
Arise, my love, my beautiful one,
    and come away."

I won't read the rest of that text lest I blush. But I don't blush in saying to you now that God has perfectly timed your love, and that is what we celebrate today. It is a time—finally!—to love.

But what is love? How shall we define it?

In the 1960s, a young woman named Kim was engaged to a young man named Roberto Casali. Before they were married, Kim would write little love notes and slip them into Roberto's fishing box, his back pocket, or whatever secret place she could find. Her notes were simple. Each one featured a drawing of a childlike couple, a man with dark black hair and a woman with blonde hair, and both modestly undressed. And beneath each drawing was a short inscription, which always began *Love is* . . . Perhaps you have seen one of these comic strips, for Roberto took them to Tribune Media Services, and the rest is history. They became a worldwide success, featured in nearly every major newspaper for decades. Their appeal was the mixture of simple art with universal themes.

Here is how Kim defined love. (I'll give you just a few examples.)

Love is . . . giving each other silly pet names.

Love is . . . someone who makes you weak in the knees.

Love is . . . showing her the house where you spent your
        childhood.

Love is . . . making her queen.

Love is . . . keeping a light burning for him.

Love is . . . patching up a quarrel.

Love is . . . telling her she looks wonderful on a down day.

Love is . . . when the passion slows down and the friendship
        speeds up.

Love is . . . massaging her toes.

Love is . . . like wine, better as it matures.

Those are healthy definitions, certainly better than some of what passes as definitions and expressions of love today, such as:

Love is . . . tolerance without truth.
Love is . . . never insisting on changing or challenging some-
    one's views.
Love is . . . refusing to label anything "wrong."

Today, *love* is defined by the cult of "tolerance," which is the moralistic invention of the modern secular world. This cult borrows Christian language—like the word *love*—to mean something very different than Jesus did, and then accuses Christians of being arrogant, unloving, and ironically *unchristian*. (I digress.)

Kim Casali's definitions of love are commendable. However, there is something even more commendable than those cartoon captions—the living Word of God, the Bible. The Bible gives its own definitions of love. There is, for example, the famous 1 Corinthians 13 text: "Love is patient and kind," and so on. There is also the first epistle of John, part of which you chose to have read at your wedding.

John has been called "the theologian of love," for in his little epistle of 1 John, love (as in the words *love, beloved, loves,* and *loved*) is mentioned more than fifty times! He doesn't define love, as some do today, as tolerance of moral choices and theological perspectives (or even by a cute Casali saying, "Love is . . . counting every freckle"). Rather, his definition of love centers on God in Christ.

Here is a sampling of what he has to say. In 1 John 3:16, we read, "By this we know love, that he [Jesus] laid down his life for us, and we ought to lay down our lives for the brothers." In 4:8–11 he adds: "Anyone who does not love does not know God, because God is love. In this the love of God was made manifest among us, [how?] that God sent his only Son into the world, so that we might live through him. In this is love, not that we have loved God but that he loved us and sent his Son to be the propitiation for our sins. Beloved, if God so loved us, we also ought to love one another." Then, in 4:16, 19, he writes: "So we have *come to know* and to believe the love that God has for us. God is love, and whoever abides in love abides in God, and God abides in him. . . . We love because he first loved us."

You see, to John, love is orthodox, active, and assuring. And it is modeled in Jesus Christ's compassion, concern, consideration, and care for others, but ultimately in his self-sacrifice on the cross. To John, love is not mysticism, emotionalism, or anything-goes-ism. Rather, it is "Jesus Christ and him crucified" (1 Cor. 2:2). *That* is the love that we celebrate today, and that is the love that you are called to in marriage.

As Christians, your marriage should look like a *crucifixion*. It should look like Christ's crucifixion—where selfless love and selfless submission collide (see Eph. 5:22–33), and where both husband (_____) and wife (_____) can say, "God has given me a lover who preaches to me every day the glorious gospel of Jesus Christ, a spouse who sings to me the story of our salvation—of God having reconciled selfish sinners through his selfless Son." You reveal the "mystery" of marriage to the world (cf. Eph. 5:32)!

_____ and _____, today we celebrate. We celebrate God's beautiful timing—that is, how he has made everything beautiful in its time in your lives. And today we celebrate God's incredible love, which you now get to display daily to one another. May God help you!

Sample Wedding Homily #5 (Doug O'Donnell)
On Matthew 19:3–6; cf. Genesis 2:24

"What God Has Joined Together"
_____ and _____, today you enter into the covenant of marriage. This is indeed a joyous occasion—for you, for me, for us!

Yet, as you know (as we all know), there are many different perspectives on marriage, oftentimes very negative ones. For example, Ambrose Bierce, in his humorous, sarcastic *Devil's Dictionary*, defines love in this way: "a temporary insanity curable by marriage." In a similar vein, Woody Allen puts it this way: "There are three rings involved with marriage: the engagement ring, the wedding ring, and the suffering."

We laugh because there is some truth in these overly negative assessments of marriage. There is some truth because we all naturally tend to love ourselves and live for ourselves rather than for God and others. The Bible calls this "sin." We are all sinners! And sinners (at least I've found this to be the case) are sometimes quite difficult to work with, to live with, and to love day after day, year after year, decade after decade . . . 'til death do us part.

It is for this reason that Paul prays in Ephesians 3 the way he does—praying for inward strength, that you two (and we all, whether married or not)—would be "rooted and grounded in love" and that "Christ may dwell in our hearts through faith" (Eph. 3:17). We all need Jesus, who saves us from our sin. And we all need the power of the Holy Spirit to live within us so that we might live for God and for others more than we live for ourselves. This is the great challenge in any relationship, and especially in the covenant of marriage. Will I (a sinner) serve you (a sinner), sacrifice for you, and be committed to you? Will I love you? That is what you are asking and answering each other this day. And so, because we are sinners, we need God and his power.

And it is because we are sinners that we resonate with Jesus's disciples after they heard him talk about marriage. In Matthew 19, the Pharisees came to Jesus and, trying to trip him up, asked, "Is it lawful to divorce one's wife for any cause?" (v. 3). That's a tough question, isn't it?

I'll get to Jesus's response in a minute. But after his first response and then his second to their follow-up question, the disciples stood there at the end of this theological debate, dumbfounded by Jesus's seemingly strict view of marriage. They said to him, "If such is the case of a man with his wife, it is better not to marry" (v. 10). They were not far removed from Woody Allen and Ambrose Bierce. The sentiment is, "If I'm stuck with her forever, if I can't just easily divorce her whenever and for whatever, then why marry in the first place?"

"Well," you say, "what did Jesus say that was so controversial and unacceptable to them?" He answered the Pharisees by turning their attention to Genesis 2: "Have you not read [in your Bible!] that he who created them from the beginning made them male and female, and said, 'Therefore a man shall leave his father and his mother and hold fast to his wife, and the two shall become one flesh'?" (Matt. 19:4–5). Commentary on this (and Jesus's answer to their divorce question) is: "So they are no longer two but one flesh. What therefore God has joined together, let not man separate" (v. 6).

There are many interesting implications from Jesus's answer. We could talk about in-laws and what Jesus says here about leaving and cleaving. But I won't talk about that (especially in front of them). We could talk about sex and the metaphorical language Jesus uses for it. I could flesh out that stuff about "one flesh." But I certainly won't do that. We are all too modest for such a discussion. I could even talk about the last phrase he uses—"let not man separate"—and talk about your role in this relationship and the priority of your purity, faithfulness, and commitment. But I won't even talk about that today, as important as it is. The only thing—or, better, the one *person*—I want to talk about on your wedding day is *God*! In this great marriage text, Jesus said, "What therefore *God* has joined together . . ."

Have you ever thought about that statement? It is an incredible statement! What is the claim here? The claim is that when you two said, "I will," when you two will say, "With this ring, I thee wed," and when you two will join those longing lips together and then turn around and run down this aisle with smiles on your faces, it is not a mistake. It is part of God's plan. He joined you together. In the power of his providence, he is wedding you this day. And the purpose for such union is not yet known to you. Will you be rich together or poor? Will you both enjoy great health and live long lives, or will one or both of you get sick, perhaps much sooner than expected? The vow is this: "I will wed you, have you as my wife/husband from this day forward, no matter what—for better or for worse." Does *better* mean "better"? Indeed, it means "better." Does *worse* mean "worse?" Yes, it means "worse."

God has brought you together, but God hasn't told you why. Is it for joy and gladness or for struggles and sorrows? But whatever befalls you (and I hope and pray as you do and as we do for happiness and lots of [surname _____] children and grandchildren), I want you to know that marriage is not primarily about happiness, reproduction, or whatever else we might think most important in this life. Rather, it is primarily about sanctification, about learning to love as God does, to love the unlovely, to love the sinner, to love when love is the last thing we want to do.

_____ and _____, when times are good (and for you two I know there will be many good times!) and when times are bad or difficult, remember this one phrase of Jesus, read and talked about on this day—"What . . . God has joined together." Remember that, and learn to rejoice in that reality no matter what sorrows or joys come your way.

Sample Wedding Homily #6 *(James A. Johnston)*
Genesis 1:27; cf. Ephesians 5:22—28; Genesis 2:24

_____ and _____, we all want to thank you for the honor of being part of this special day. We are so thrilled to see what God has done in your lives. It's a wonderful day!

When you decided to get married, you could have gone to the courthouse to be married by a judge in a civil wedding. A mayor, governor, county clerk, or notary could have done the job for you. Instead, you decided to have a Christian wedding in a church.

What are you saying? You are embracing God's purposes for marriage as revealed in the Bible. You are committing yourself to his leadership for your family. You are recognizing his place in this intimate, personal, core part of your life.

This is why you chose Psalm 127:1 to mark this special day: "Unless the LORD builds the house, those who build it labor in vain." You are asking God to build your house.

So what is God's purpose for marriage? We honor him and find our greatest joy when we follow his directions in his Word. I'd like to share with you some principles rooted in the opening chapters of Genesis.

God Created You Each in His Image

First, remember that God created you both in his image. "So God created man in his own image, in the image of God he created him; male and female he created them" (Gen. 1:27).

As husband and wife, you each bear God's image—you are pictures of God himself. At the rehearsal dinner last night, we could all see the family resemblance with your brothers, sisters, and parents. If the Lord gives you children, you will gaze at their faces to see whose eyes they have, whose chin they inherited, what family they favor. Children look like their parents, and as human beings, we look like God.

Both husbands and wives have equal value because they both bear God's image. As you enter into marriage, remember that you are living with, talking to, sleeping with, caring for a picture of God himself. Be gentle and speak kindly to each other. Protect each other. See God's reflection in each other. Honor each other.

God Created You Male and Female

The second principle is that God designed and invented gender. We live in a world that is increasingly confused about sexuality. In several states, boys are allowed to play on girls' sports teams and vice versa. Germany recently changed its birth certificates to allow parents to designate their children as male, female, or neither. But the two sexes are not an accidental, evolutionary adaptation. Gender is not something we can change or decide for ourselves. God created us male and female.

And he made us distinct and different as men and women. The balance of male and female hormones in the womb affects our organs, so that male and female fetuses have different heart rates, respiration rates, red blood cell counts, and even brain structures! And differences continue into adulthood, of course.

Your marriage will honor God and give you the most joy when you recognize that you are the same, yet different. You shouldn't expect each other to have the same strengths, the same perspectives, the same roles. God created you to complement each other, to fit together like pieces of a puzzle.

_____, God calls you to be a man. He calls you to be a woman, _____. To do this, you will need to listen to God's Word. The world is full of advice on what it means to be a woman or a man. Watch the ads during *Monday Night Football* and you will see the world's definition of a man. Spend an hour watching *The View* and you'll get our culture's idea of what a woman should be.

_____, God says that a real man takes the responsibility to lead, protect, and provide for his wife. You are to lay down your life for her good:

> Husbands, love your wives, as Christ loved the church and gave himself up for her, that he might sanctify her, having cleansed her by the washing of water with the word, so that he might present the church to himself in splendor, without spot or wrinkle or any such thing, that she might be holy and without blemish. In the same way husbands should love their wives as their own bodies. He who loves his wife loves himself. (Eph. 5:25–28)

Christ is your model for manhood. Study the way Christ gave himself for us and follow in his steps.

And, _____, the Bible teaches us that a real woman—a mature woman—freely embraces an attitude that affirms, receives, and supports her husband's strength and leadership:

> Wives, submit to your own husbands, as to the Lord. For the husband is the head of the wife even as Christ is the head of the church, his body, and is himself its Savior. Now as the church submits to Christ, so also wives should submit in everything to their husbands. (vv. 22–24)

This is the role God created for you uniquely as a woman. Study the way the church loves Christ and follows him as her head.

God created harmonious roles for husband and wife—equal, yet different. Matthew Henry noticed that Eve was "not made out of his head to rule over him, nor out of his feet to be trampled upon by him, but out of his side to be equal with him, under his arm to be protected, and near his heart to be loved."[4]

God Creates a New Family

When God created marriage, he also created a new family. Genesis 2:24 tells us, "Therefore a man shall leave his father and his mother and hold fast to his wife."

This means that your marriage takes priority over every other relationship in your life, even with your own parents. The covenant you are making today is a picture of the faithful relationship between Christ and his church. Nothing comes before it.

---

[4] Matthew Henry, *Matthew Henry's Commentary on the Whole Bible*, 6 vols. (McLean, VA: McDonald Publishing, n.d.), I.20.

Some marriages end up in trouble because the husband and wife never leave their parents. They clean out the rooms they grew up in, set up their own home, buy their own furniture, even have their own children—but their first loyalty stays stuck to Mom and Dad. They fail to leave and cleave.

Today, your relationship with each other is your first loyalty. _____, you can't go home anymore—home is where your husband is. _____, home is where your wife is. Your parents will love you, support you, and cheer you on, but your relationship with each other comes first.

God Created Physical Intimacy

Finally, when God created marriage, he created intimacy. The man and woman were "naked [together] and were not ashamed" (Gen. 2:25). Before they sinned, it never occurred to them to put clothes on; they experienced complete openness and vulnerability with each other—physically, emotionally, spiritually.

The intimacy of a husband and wife is a gift God gives in this fallen world. In a sense, it is a taste of life before the fall, untainted by sin. Sex is to be enjoyed in the covenant of marriage. It burns like fire. Keep it in the fireplace and it will warm the whole house; but if you light this fire outside the bounds of your marriage, you will set your life on fire.

When you chose a Christian wedding, you chose to embrace God's purposes for marriage as you begin your life together. And so you chose a blessing for yourself, because God says, "Those who honor me I will honor" (1 Sam. 2:30). May you find your deepest joy as you follow God's direction.

Sample Wedding Homily #7 (James A. Johnston)
On Genesis 1:27–28

_____ and_____, we all feel a special sense of joy as God has brought you here today. Who could have known that when you first met, one day you would be standing here? But a spark grew to a flame, a flame into a fire, and now we all feel the warmth of your love. God brought you together and blessed you and your two families. And that is a joy for all of us.

And with this in mind, it is good to remember that today is not the end of the road, but the start of a lifelong journey. Just as Lewis and Clark set off across the continent, you are setting off across great unknown lands before you. You have before you the new experience of marriage, of living together as husband and wife. No matter how close you have become during your engagement, this will be different! And you have before you a new experience in ministry, of serving God together as husband and wife.

No one here today can tell you with certainty what these new lands will look like—what rivers you will have to cross, what canyons you will have to bridge, the beauty of the sunsets you will see, or the quiet fields where you will find rest. These are all ahead, and no one finds the journey quite the same.

What we can do is look at the map God has given us in his Word and consider the cartography of marriage as he planned it. We do not have to go beyond the first chapter of Scripture to see the *pattern and purpose* God has for marriage and ministry. We read in Genesis 1:27–28:

> God created man in his own image, in the image of God he created him; male and female he created them. And God blessed them. And God said to them, "Be fruitful and multiply and fill the earth and subdue it, and have dominion over the fish of the sea and over the birds of the heavens and over every living thing that moves on the earth."

Created by God

Notice first that these verses clarify your relationship to God. He created you, and so you owe your very life to him. This is why Paul would later say we need to "walk in a manner worthy of the Lord, fully pleasing to him" (Col. 1:10). Whether single or married, our ambition is to please the God who made us in his image.

And since you are created by God, you are incredibly valuable. I was watching *Antiques Roadshow* and saw an expert comparing two silver soup ladles. It turned out that one of them was made by Paul Revere, and the other was made at the same time by another Boston silversmith. What amazed me was that the ladle made by Revere with his mark on it was worth $20,000, but an absolutely identical ladle by the other silversmith was worth only $2,000. Revere's work was ten times more valuable. The value came from the maker and his mark! We are created by God, and so each of us has dignity and value as the work of his hands.

But not only did he create you, he created both of you—as a man and a woman—in his image. He put his mark on both of you. And what's even more, Jesus gave his life to redeem you and to re-create you in his image. You are both priceless.

As you explore the new lands of married life, remember that you are walking next to, talking to, and sleeping with a priceless picture of God himself. Treat each other with care. Look past the other's sin to see the image of Christ himself being renewed in the other. Protect each other and handle each other gently, for God created both of you in his image, and you are precious.

Created to Extend the Blessings of God's Kingdom

Genesis 1:28 tells us why he brought male and female together. As God's agents in his image, we are to "fill the earth and subdue it."

What does this mean? God placed the man and woman on earth to care for it and rule over it in his place. God's plan was for men and women to multiply on the earth, and God would spread his loving rule—his kingdom—around the world through them. As men and women in God's image moved across the globe, they would carry God's presence and his loving authority with them. This is still the purpose for your life and your marriage—you are to spread God's kingdom in this world.

So how do we spread God's kingdom? Since you and I sinned and turned away from God, God raised his Son, Jesus Christ, from the dead to rule over all creation. We become citizens of God's kingdom when we turn to Jesus and follow him as our Ruler. This is the gospel: Christ died on the cross for sinners and rose again to be our King.

The gospel is the center of everything in your life, including your relationship as husband and wife. Your marriage is a relationship God has ordained to bring spiritual blessing to this world as the gospel grows in your own life and as the gospel grows through you in the world.

This begins with each of you personally. So make your own spiritual growth a priority, and encourage each other to grow in your love and obedience to God. As husband and wife, you will be in a unique place to bless through the roles God has given you.

_____, you are to love your wife "as Christ loved the church" (Eph. 5:25). This means that you need to place her welfare before your own and give your life for her spiritual growth to make her holy through God's Word. Many a man has said that he would take a bullet for his bride in a moment of crisis. Jesus calls you to do something harder—to die to yourself daily for her good.

_____, you are to respect your husband and submit to his leadership in the same way Jesus Christ submitted to God the Father's will. Christ Jesus is fully God and fully equal in his divinity with the Father. Yet he became a servant, submitting to the Father's will so we could be saved. In the same way, God will use your gentle and quiet spirit to bring blessing to your family and all those around you.

As two believers, live out the "one anothers" of Scripture with each other: encourage each other; be patient with each other; "be kind to one another, tenderhearted, forgiving one another, as God in Christ forgave you" (Eph. 4:32); stir up one another to love and good works; pray for each other daily. Model what it means to live together in the kingdom of God.

And as you do, you will bless each other for eternity. Your marriage may last fifty years, maybe even sixty years if God gives you long lives. But these decades together can lead to rewards you will enjoy thirty thousand years from now!

An anonymous author reminds us what eternity with God means:

The stars shine over the earth,
The stars shine over the sea,
The stars look up to the mighty God,
The stars look down on me.
The stars will live for a million years,
For a million years and a day!
But God and I shall live and love
When the stars have passed away.

_____ and _____, I'm sure you will be investing as a couple for the twenty or thirty years you will be retired. Retirement is so short, just a few decades. Don't forget to invest for eternity. By encouraging each other to grow in Christ now, you can bless each other for countless ages, after even the stars are a distant, faded memory.

For the same reason, if God should bless you with children, either naturally or through adoption, their growth in Jesus Christ must be a top priority for you. You will have more influence on your children than on anyone on earth. You can bless your children for eternity as they learn to love Jesus from their earliest days.

And make it a goal for your marriage to reach out together in ministry. God has not brought you together just to serve each other; he is making you one so that together you can do more for his kingdom than you could alone.

The body of Christ needs you as a couple. This fallen world needs you. Christians are salt and light. The light of Christ should shine out from your home as you serve in the church and engage our culture with the gospel. God brought you together to extend the blessings of his kingdom around the world as you live for Christ.

No one can tell you what the land ahead of you is like, what the coming years have for you. Like Lewis and Clark, you stand on the edge of an unknown land; marriage and ministry, love and service are ahead of you. The years ahead will be ones of discovery as you serve God together as husband and wife.

The beginning of this journey is a time of special joy. So may God give you the grace to grow as followers of Jesus Christ, both for now and into eternity.

Sample Wedding Homily #8 (Jay Thomas)
On Genesis 2:18–24

It is that time in this ceremony where we pull back and take a few moments to think about and reflect upon just what we are doing here in this place with you two. _____ and _____, I address this primarily to you as your wedding charge, yet ultimately this is for us all.

You did not have to get married in a church like this or have a ceremony at all. Nothing in Scripture commands it. You are not more married or fulfilling a legal requirement of any kind. Rather, you are making a point—that this marriage is one based in Christ and one carried out in the midst of his people.

We are not here merely to watch, but to participate. You are not the only ones making a covenant today, for we are all called to covenant with you—to support you, pray for you, and watch you through as a new mini-community in the midst of a greater community. _____ and _____, you are parts of a whole.

Two as One

That is where I want to begin, with this idea of the part in the midst of the whole—in other words, defining this commitment you are making today by the big picture. One of the worst things you could do, which so many end up doing, is to begin this journey together defined by your expectations—the image you have for marriage. This is a recipe for disaster, and not only that, it goes against everything God's Word says about marriage.

The beginning chapters of Genesis are a foundation for marriage, and they lay the groundwork for what the rest of Scripture says or assumes about marriage, not least Ephesians 5. They tell us why marriage was created—its purpose: "It is not good that the man should be alone; I will make him a helper fit for him" (Gen. 2:18). God did not take another piece of earth, nor did he form his helper from another outside source. Rather, he took something from *within* Adam, a rib, and fashioned it into his wife, Eve. It is crucial to note that God did not take the two and form them into one. He took one and formed them into two—the parts from the whole, the whole in the parts. Why? Because God created man in *his image*, to reflect himself to the world. God designed into marriage the great reality of his own being: he is one and yet three. His threeness does not contradict his oneness, nor does his oneness contradict his threeness. They work together perfectly.

Now, before you worry that I am heading off into the esoteric reality of the Trinity, I am not. I say all this simply to show the power of the Genesis 2 text for our understanding of what is going on here before us—namely, that marriage is defined by the one who fashioned it, and it is to be lived out in light of the way in which the Creator fashioned it.

_____ and _____, the first key to a powerful marriage is that you do not attempt to live as two people struggling to become one, but that you realize you are inextricably one, living life as two. Realize your unity, then live out your diversity in light of that.

This is not just physical unity, but holistic, mysterious unity. As you drive in the car, as you brush your teeth together, and in the most precious of moments, you are one.

> Then the man said, "This at last is bone of my bones and flesh of my flesh; she shall be called Woman, because she was taken out of Man." Therefore a man shall leave his father and his mother and hold fast to his wife, and they shall become one flesh. (Gen. 2:23–24)

Oneness Demonstrated in Love

You must live like one because you are in fact one. So what does that look like? How does this play out practically? Your oneness, as God has designed you, is demonstrated in *love*.

Though the Genesis text does not say this explicitly, it is implicit and is stated more and more clearly as the Scriptures unfold. God loved his people. The covenant he made with them was one of promise indeed, but promise united with love. This again is part and parcel of who God is and how he considers his creation.

If love is a central feature of our relationship to God, and if this relationship is the blueprint for marriage, then love is the greatest expression of the covenant you are making today. If oneness is the fabric of your relationship, then love is the color and drape. It is the evidence to the world of who you are as a married couple, and it is the evidence of its Creator.

I began by examining how the two of you add up to one rather than two, a reflection of God's unity (and the way God does math), but the Lord has given us another rich image of what exactly marriage is designed for, and that is the reflection of Christ's relationship to the church. Ephesians 5 is a great example of this. It says that marriage is a bold demonstration in living color of how Christ loves the church. Marriage is a sermon. It is a sermon of the gospel to those who have eyes to see and ears to hear.

Some are put off by Paul's statement that "the husband is the *head* of the wife" (Eph. 5:23). But what does headship look like? Love. Christlike love. It is portrayed by the priestly stewardship of a husband to lead his wife by love and her willing and joyful response to follow, out of love. Again, marriage is not defined by how we conceive of love and promise, but by how God illustrated it above and beyond us in his Son, the Lord Jesus Christ, and his love for us, his church. Marriage becomes so much more meaningful when we see it in the *big picture*—not what we make of it, but what God has made *for* it.

Marriage Must Be Grace-Laden, Christ-Centered

Christ's love is the model for marriage. As beautiful as that is, it also strikes terror into my heart, especially as a husband whom Paul is primarily addressing as the one who models Jesus in the marriage.

In 1 Corinthians 13, Paul says love never fails, never! No qualifications. No sometimes. No exceptions. Love never fails.

I have been married to my wife many years now, and I have failed her innumerable times. I even failed to love her during the honeymoon, perhaps within the first hours of our marriage.

_____ and _____, who am I to charge you with these ideals? Who are any of us to strive after such a pattern of love?

As much as I hope and pray for the best for the both of you, you will fail each other. Your love will never actually attain the perfection of Christ's love in this life.

So what are we to do? Many decide they cannot answer this and end up letting the gravity of sin and fallenness pull them down. What, then, is our hope? Actually, the better question is, *who is our hope?*

Our hope becomes gloriously clear when we realize that Christ is not only the pattern but the constant reminder that *his* perfection is requisite, not ours. He is the model because he is the enabler of marriage. Why can you strive and exert yourselves for this love? It is because you are the recipients of the greatest promise and the greatest love—you are the recipients of God's grace in Christ. Therefore, strive under the banner of the Lord Jesus Christ. Define your marriage by his work, his Word, and his presence in the center of your lives. He defines love. He defines your promises. He is your ability to love without your inevitable failures meaning disaster.

He knows that you will fall short, and he therefore calls you to trust in grace and to depend on him.

Powerful, God-glorifying marriage knows its source, *our Lord.*

It knows its design—*oneness.*

It knows its function—*love.*

It knows its power—*grace.*

Sample Wedding Homily #9 *(Randall Gruendyke)*
On Genesis 2:18–25; cf. Ephesians 5:28–30

What is marriage? That is the question of our day. How it is answered will have a profound effect upon the future of our world. The first two chapters of the Bible reveal that marriage was not born out of the mind of man. Rather, it is *God's* idea—an idea first expressed when the Lord said, "It is not good that the man should be alone" (Gen. 2:18a).

So Adam by himself in God's creation was not a good thing. That's interesting, because up to that point God had declared everything in his new creation to be good, and man in particular to be *very* good! But Adam alone—that was not good. What was not good about it? The answer is seen in God's response to the problem: "I will make a helper fit for him" (v. 18b).

God identified and answered man's first problem by making him a helper, one who was fit, suitable, or corresponding to him—a helpmate or "an help meet," as the old King James puts it. But first, Scripture goes on to tell us:

> Now out of the ground the LORD God had formed every beast of the field and every bird of the heavens and brought them to the man to see what he would call them. And whatever the man called every living creature, that was its name. The man gave names to all livestock and to the birds of the heavens and to every beast of the field. But for Adam there was not found a helper fit for him. (Gen. 2:19–20)

Adam *did* find helpers. In fact, he found *many* helpers: oxen to plow his field, horses to pull his wagon, dogs to bring him his paper! But Adam did not find a helper who *corresponded* to him. So, having dramatically heightened Adam's appetite for such a helper, God continued to solve this problem by doing five things:

- He made Adam sleep.
- He took one of his ribs.
- He closed up the place where he'd taken the rib.

- He made the rib into a woman (notice that she was from Adam, not from the earth like the animals).
- He brought her to the man.

Upon waking up, Adam's response to God's solution was literally a poem. The first recorded human words are a poetic couplet:

Then the man said,

"This at last is bone of my bones
     and flesh of my flesh;
she shall be called Woman,
     because she was taken out of Man." (Gen. 2:23)

In a deliberate and methodical way, God showed Adam that he was alone, he needed a partner, and he wouldn't find it among the animals made from the earth. So he created a wonderfully mind-blowing, deeply satisfying, and wholly complementary helper from Adam's own body. The outworking of that partnership is expressed in marriage. We see it at the end of this account, where God said, "Therefore a man shall leave his father and his mother and hold fast to his wife, and they shall become one flesh" (Gen. 2:24).

So, _____ and _____, what is marriage? Basically it is this:

- A *man* leaves his father (man) and mother (woman) and thereby shifts his ultimate human commitments so that he may
- hold fast to his wife (woman)—entirely and exclusively—and in so doing
- become with her one flesh.

Jesus later accentuated this teaching by saying: "So they are no longer two but one flesh. What therefore God has joined together, let not man separate" (Matt. 19:6).

God put it this way in Ephesians 5:28–30:

Husbands should love their wives as their own bodies. [Why?] He who loves his wife loves himself. For no one ever hated his own flesh, but nourishes and cherishes it [now get this], just as Christ does the church, because we are members of his body.

Marriage, established at the beginning of time, is a lifelong role play of God's loving relationship with his people in Christ and a standing invitation for men and women everywhere to the great wedding at the end of time, when the heavenly host will cry, "The kingdom of the world has become the kingdom of our Lord and of his Christ, and he shall reign forever and ever" (Rev. 11:15).

_____ and _____, these are God's foundational words on marriage. Now, by his grace, build on them with the Lord's remaining words as found throughout the Bible—words that not only express his intentions for a legal and well-ordered marriage, but words that give life to the new person you are becoming today.

Sample Wedding Homily #10 (Todd Wilson)
On Ephesians 5:22–33

Introduction

_____ and _____, the first thing I would like to say to you is: *Congratulations!* You've made it. You're almost married. You've done very well to get this far, and we all want to congratulate you.

Of course, you have not gotten to this point alone. You've had lots of help. No one gets to the marriage altar without loads of support and encouragement from others. Your parents have obviously been a huge part in preparing you for this day. And I know I speak for both of you in saying, "Thank you, Mom and Dad." Your siblings have also had a major hand in your lives, as have many other friends and family members, many of whom are here today, some of whom are on this platform with you.

I also want to congratulate you on your decision to take on a new part in the play. Did you know that today you're getting a new part in a play? Yes, you are. By choosing to get married, you have chosen to take up new roles in an amazing drama. This is a drama, a play, like none other, and it lasts your whole life.

The Mystery of Marriage—a Drama

The play is called *The Mystery of Marriage*. At least, that's what the Bible calls it. Your dear friends and marriage mentors just read from Ephesians 5, where we learn about the mystery of marriage. There, you'll remember, Paul quotes from Genesis 2:24, where it says, "Therefore a man shall leave his father and his mother and hold fast to his wife, and they shall become one flesh." Now, this is an amazing concept, an amazing truth: two very different people become "one flesh."

Remarkably, however, this passage of Scripture says that the marriage of a man and woman is even more amazing than that. Paul says that the union of husband and wife points to something beyond itself. He calls it a mystery and says that it points not ultimately to the relationship between the husband and wife, but to the relationship between Christ and the church. Paul says, "This mystery is profound, and I am saying that it refers to Christ and the church" (Eph. 5:32).

So marriage, the Bible says, is a mystery. Not that it's something mysterious that is to be kept secret. Rather, marriage is something symbolic, something that exists to draw attention to something else. Thus, your marriage is to be a drama, a play, that depicts the relationship between Christ and the church.

But what are your parts in this play?

The Wife's Part

_____, as a wife, you're to play the part of the church. That's your role in the drama of marriage.

Your responsibility, then, is to submit willingly to the loving leadership of your husband, as the church would willingly submit to the loving leadership of Christ: "Wives, submit to your own husbands, as to the Lord" (v. 22). That final phrase is the key phrase: "as to the Lord."

Now, you are called to submit to _____'s loving leadership because of who God has called him to be in the relationship and because of the part he plays in the drama of marriage. It is your responsibility to submit to him, as this passage says: "For the husband is the head of the wife even as Christ is the head of the church" (v. 23). And so, as Paul says, "as the church submits to Christ, so also wives should submit in everything to their husbands" (v. 24).

The Husband's Part

Now, _____, if _____'s role is to play the part of the church, then yours is to play the part of Christ. And if her responsibility is to submit to you as the head, as the church submits to Christ, then your responsibility is to love your wife as Christ loved the church (v. 25).

But how did Christ love the church? As our passage says, and as we know from the story of the Gospels, Christ gave himself up for the church. That's how he loved the church—he died for the church.

This, then, is your responsibility as the husband: to love her as Christ loved the church. That is, to lay down your life for your wife, to die for her. Did you know that's what you were signing up for today?

Now this is not a swift and easy death, but one that lasts your whole life. As the husband, _____, you are called to lay down your life for your wife on a daily basis. This means, in essence, looking out not for your own interests but hers. This means prioritizing her best interests over your own. This means denying what you might want in order to serve her. In a word, this means sacrifice.

This is, after all, precisely what Christ did for us. Christ Jesus was in the very form of God, yet he did not count equality with God a thing to be grasped. Instead, he made himself nothing, taking the form of a servant. Being born in the likeness of men, he humbled himself even to the point of enduring death. But not just any kind of death, the most ignominious and humiliating kind of death—death on a cross! And he died this death—he endured the scorn and the shame of the cross—as an expression of his love and in order to deal with the sin that separates us from the Father.

In your role as Christ in this divine drama, this mystery called marriage, you are to love your wife as Christ loved the church and gave himself up for her.

Conclusion

Marriage is, in itself, as you'll no doubt come to realize, a wonderful mystery and a wonderful joy. It is wonderfully thrilling and fulfilling. But marriage is ultimately intended to point not to itself, but to the relationship between Christ and the church. When a wife willingly yields her prerogatives for the sake of her husband, and when a husband lovingly lays down his life for his wife, then they are truly playing the part of Christ and the church. Then they are truly living out the gospel in the context of their own relationship. Then they are truly enacting something worth seeing.

_____ and _____, as you seek to live out in your marriage the relationship that exists between Christ and the church, may I leave you with several encouragements to help you along the way? My wife and I received three pieces of advice at our wedding. I'd like to pass those along to you. As you seek to play your parts as Christ and the church, think of these three sayings as lines you should say to one another.

The first thing to say is very simple: "I love you." Perhaps because it's so simple, it's so easily neglected. But say "I love you" to one another often, every day, multiple times a day. Yes, you know—we all know—that you love one another, but it's good to say it to each other regularly.

The second is to say, "I'm sorry." It's very easy to verbalize, but we often find it very difficult to say, don't we? These words are massively powerful in any relationship, not least in a marriage, because, as you will soon realize, _____, if you don't already, _____'s not perfect; so, too, _____, _____ is not perfect. You're both going to fall short in this marriage. But be quick to say, "I'm sorry," and seek forgiveness.

The third and final thing to say is this: "How can I help?" You will need each other's help every day. That's what a marriage is all about:

mutual encouragement, support, love, and sacrifice. So make it your ambition to be regularly asking the other person: "How can I help you? How can I serve you? Is there anything you need? Is there an errand I can run for you? Can I do anything around the house?"

_____ and _____, marriage is a profound mystery, for it is ultimately about Christ's love for the church and the church's adoration of Christ. May you live out this most profound mystery in your marriage, for your own joy, for the good of others, and for the glory of God.

4

Funerals

Funerals provide unique opportunities for pastoral ministry. The finality of death, the pain of permanent loss, is so sobering that it naturally occasions reflection on eternal things, because, as the Preacher said, "[God] has put eternity into man's heart" (Eccl. 3:11). This tender state often is a time when souls become reflective as to their eternal destiny and the condition of their hearts—especially those who knew the deceased well, such as family members, friends, and coworkers. Thus, pastoral care is part and parcel of comforting loved ones, helping them prepare for the services, and then presiding over the funeral itself, all of which provides immense opportunities for sharing the gospel.

However, before we talk about the pastoral care involved in this occasion, it is important that we take to heart the divinely ordained value of a funeral. For a biblical perceptive on funerals, we turn to Ecclesiastes 7:1–4,[1] where we read twice that attending a "house of mourning" is better than going to a "house of feasting" or "mirth":

A good name is better than precious ointment,
    and the day of death than the day of birth.
It is better to go to the house of mourning
    than to go to the house of feasting,
for this is the end of all mankind,
    and the living will lay it to heart.
Sorrow is better than laughter,
    for by sadness of face the heart is made glad.
The heart of the wise is in the house of mourning,
    but the heart of fools is in the house of mirth.

---

[1] This opening section on Ecclesiastes 7:1–4 was taken, with permission from the publisher, from Douglas Sean O'Donnell, *Ecclesiastes: Enjoyment East of Eden*, Reformed Expository Commentary (Phillipsburg, NJ: P&R, 2014).

The Preacher's counterintuitive teaching is reminiscent of Jesus's Beatitudes. Jesus didn't label the courageous, the agreeable, the funny, the intelligent, the attractive, and the fit "blessed." Rather, he attached that description to those who mourn, are persecuted, and are poor in spirit. Similarly, Solomon speaks of sorrow as better than laughter, the day of death as better than the day of birth, and going to a funeral as better than going to a festival.

These three conditions or occasions are better because they help us focus on our character and reputation. Verse 1 claims, "A good name is better than precious ointment," or, as Proverbs puts it, "than great riches . . . than silver or gold" (Prov. 22:1). The title of Alister Chapman's biography of John Stott, *Godly Ambition*, fittingly summarizes the point. We should be ambitious to make a good name for ourselves by glorifying God's name on earth.

How does a funeral help with this task? At a birthday bash, frat party, wedding reception, or whatever kind of party one might attend, people do not evaluate how well and wisely they are living their lives. Even the most celebratory New Year's Eve parties are superficial. We would do better to stay home that night, shake our heads in dismay, and read Ecclesiastes until falling asleep. So do not underestimate the divinely appointed opportunity that every funeral allows. Outside each funeral home, God holds up his picket signs: "Life is brief," "Death is inevitable," and "Walk wisely!" And within each funeral home, every casket cautions us ("Redeem the time!") and questions us ("How are you spending your time?"). What will be said of you when people gather at the house of mourning to mourn over you? Will you be remembered as someone wise or foolish?

In her brilliant song "Laughing With," Regina Spektor juxtaposes how God can be the butt of a "God-themed joke" at "a cocktail party," but how no one laughs at God "in a hospital . . . in a war . . . when they're starving or freezing or so very poor," how no one laughs at God "when the doctor calls after some routine test . . . when their airplane starts to uncontrollably shake."[2] We may add to Spektor's thought-provoking lyrics that no one laughs at God when asked to sign the death certificate at the hospital or when standing at a graveside, watching a loved one being lowered into the ground.

As much as Western culture is a culture of death (we play violent video games, watch documentaries on serial killers, and murder our unborn), we nevertheless deny death when it gets uncomfortably close. This aversion is shown in our language (we say compassionately, "She has passed away" or "She has gone to a better place," or crudely, "He has kicked the bucket"),

---

[2] Available at www.reginaspektor.com/songs/laughing.

as well as in our entertainment. British scholar Carl Trueman bemoans the American obsession with happy endings. In his book *Fools Rush in Where Monkeys Fear to Tread*, he writes:

> I remember my jaw hitting the floor some years ago when I watched a Disney version of *Notre Dame de Paris* where the Hunchback does not die but lives happily ever after. . . . The point of the story of Quasimodo is that the guy with the hump dies at the end and it's all terribly sad. My wife is meant to cry, and I am meant to feel angry at the raw deal Quasimodo has been dealt in the poker game of life.[3]

In a similar but even more serious vein, in his novel *The Second Coming*, Walker Percy writes:

> The present-day unbeliever is crazy because he finds himself born into a world of endless wonders, having no notion how he got here, a world in which he eats, sleeps . . . works, grows old, gets sick, and dies . . . takes his comfort and ease, plays along with the game, watches TV, drinks his drink, [and] laughs . . . as if his prostate were not growing cancerous, his arteries turning to chalk, his brain cells dying by the millions, as if the worms were not going to have him in no time at all.[4]

Death is an enemy (1 Cor. 15:26), but also an evangelist. Death "is the great mentor for diligence, sobriety, love, generosity, reverence and humility. Death forces the most profound questions to be asked, but mercilessly mocks those who sleep through its lessons."[5] Death is like a detox clinic—it sobers us up. It is not the emotionally abusive father ("You'll never amount to anything."), but rather the effective drill sergeant ("Attention! Move out. Time is short. Get to a funeral. Sit there. Think.").

Jimmy Carr, father of our friend Pastor Ken Carr, played in the National Football League. Typical of professional athletes, he thought he was invincible. It wasn't until he was nearing sixty and went to the funeral of a close friend that he saw his invincibility as an illusion. God used the corpse of his close friend as a mirror. For the first time, the great Jimmy Carr reexamined his own less-than-great life. Shortly after the funeral, he gave his life to Christ.

[3] Carl R. Trueman, *Fools Rush in Where Monkeys Fear to Tread: Taking Aim at Everyone* (Phillipsburg, NJ: P&R, 2012), 169–170.
[4] Quoted in Philip Graham Ryken, *Ecclesiastes: Why Everything Matters*, Preaching the Word (Wheaton, IL: Crossway, 2010), 153–154.
[5] Daniel C. Fredericks, "Ecclesiastes," in Daniel C. Fredericks and Daniel Estes, *Ecclesiastes and the Song of Songs*, Apollos Old Testament Commentary (Downers Grove, IL: InterVarsity, 2010), 177.

When we go to funerals, we should think about our reputations. Who are we? What have we done with our lives? How will we stand before God? Moreover, as Christians, we should think beyond our earthly reputations to our heavenly resurrections. While the Preacher believed in an afterlife (Eccl. 12:7, 14), he certainly did not express an exalted view of it. As Christians, however, if we do not hold out hope for the resurrection of our bodies, we are to be most pitied. After the glorious resurrection of Jesus, we are not left groping in the dark. We know for certain that our Redeemer lives and that we will abide with him forever. As Jesus said, "Whoever believes in me, though he die, yet shall he live" (John 11:25). In light of Christ's trampling down of death by his death, we see death differently. It is not the exit to extinction, but the entrance to eternity. True, our bodies are wasting away. But it is also true that our inner nature is being renewed day by day as we pass through slight, momentary afflictions into an eternal glory that is beyond our comprehension (2 Cor. 4:16–18). Thus, we affirm with Paul that "to die is gain" (Phil. 1:21). We also affirm with Solomon (in a way he could not have comprehended) that "the day of death" *is* better than "the day of birth" (Eccl. 7:1).

INITIAL PASTORAL CARE
IMMEDIATE VISIT WITH THE GRIEVING

Regardless of whether the death was expected or unexpected, the event requires a lot of hands-on ministry—"weep[ing] with those who weep" (Rom. 12:15), just as Jesus did amid the mourning of Lazarus's sisters (John 11:33–36). The wise shepherd has well-chosen Scriptures at hand to read at tender moments and can offer fresh prayers during his stay, especially as others arrive to offer comfort.

The pastor must be sensitive in regard to the length of his stay. His initial comfort can morph into awkwardness if, for example, the grieving family feels that they have to be attentive to the pastor as they are making and receiving calls from loved ones. In most cases, the pastor will know when to leave. A business card, left in plain sight, is always appreciated.

Sometimes the necessary details regarding the times for the visitation, funeral, and burial can be discussed at the initial visit with the family. Some request this to get it off their minds. But in most cases, the pastor should offer his services in making arrangements, which may occasion a further brief meeting with the bereaved in consultation with the mortuary. Several questions may arise at this time that require thought-through answers.

ANTICIPATED CONSIDERATIONS

Should the Casket Be Open at the Visitation?

The answer is a qualified yes. If the deceased has been so disfigured by disease or trauma as to render him or her grotesque, the casket should be closed. However, under "normal" circumstances, it should be open for viewing. The reason is that in this death-denying culture, where death is the "ultimate obscenity," it is good for people to face the grim reality. In past generations, viewing the dead was common. Typically, the deceased's homemade casket lay in the living room, surrounded by flowers to distill any unpleasant odors, with pennies on his or her closed eyelids, while family members, friends, and children gathered around for one last look and to pay their respects as they sipped refreshments. Viewing helps mourners understand and accept the reality of death. In modern terms, it is therapeutic, regardless of what some may say.

Should the Funeral Be in the Church or Funeral Home?

The answer is the church. While some funeral homes are visually Christian, most are not, because the industry wants to be religion-neutral and devoid of symbols that would offend potential clients such as Jews, Buddhists, Muslims, Mormons, Jehovah's Witnesses, and today's secularized pagans. If the church has been a home for your soul, a nourishing "mother" (as Cyprian called it), that is where your funeral should take place, where the cross is lifted high, even if it is in a warehouse.

Can military honors be incorporated into the service? The answer is no and yes. The no is in respect to military participation in the funeral service itself, because civil rites and Christian rites should not be interwoven in a service, though a flag-draped coffin is acceptable. Traditionally, military ceremonies, such as the solemn and moving presentation of the flag and "Taps," take place at the cemetery after the pastor has concluded the committal service.

Is Cremation Acceptable in Place of Burial?

The answer is a qualified yes. Cremation as a way of disposing of the body has come into vogue in general culture and among Christians only recently. The first recorded cremation in the United States took place in 1876. Cremation was not practiced among God's people in the Old Testament. Burning was reserved largely for idolators, criminals, or enemies. Christ himself was buried in a tomb, from which he was resurrected on the third day (1 Cor. 15:3–4). Christian reverence for the body and the burial of the body is with an eye to the resurrection of the physical bodies of Christians at the coming of Christ, "who will transform our lowly body to be like his glorious body" (Phil. 3:21). Christian burial is a sacred nod to this eschatological reality. But most certainly Christian burial does *not* pave the way for the resurrection. We believe that cremated and unburied believers will undergo resurrection because "the sea will give up her [unburied] dead," as say the classic words of the committal service.

Cremation is not a gospel issue. And today many Christians, especially those on limited incomes, have little choice other than cremation because of the increasing costs of traditional burial. Pastors must be careful not to make traditional burial a putative symbol of fidelity to the faith or a measure of Christian commitment. This said, the spate of cremations fits very well with the disposal mentality of our death-denying culture, whereas Christian burial underlines a belief in the resurrection and a reverent witness to that belief. However, regardless of whether cremation or burial is employed, Christians should show reverence for the body, believing that Christ shall raise the believer's body up on the last day.

One option for those who choose cremation is to have a "graveside" committal service and bury the deceased's ashes, commending the soul of the departed and committing the body to the ground, "earth to earth, ashes to ashes, dust to dust, in the sure and certain hope of the resurrection to eternal life; through Jesus Christ our Lord."

Whatever your church's position on burial and cremation, it will prove helpful to the pastor and the congregation to have it made clear in the church's polity.

PREPARATION FOR THE FUNERAL

The first step in preparing for a funeral is an initial meeting with the larger family a day or two after the death, when the siblings and children of the deceased have arrived. Sometimes the "family" includes a best friend or two. The purpose of this meeting is twofold: (1) to gather information about the deceased in preparation for a fitting personal remembrance, and (2) to plan a Christ-honoring funeral service. Both of these tasks are almost always a pastoral pleasure. The meeting may take place in the family home or in the pastor's office.

GATHERING INFORMATION ABOUT THE DECEASED

Gathering information for the remembrance is good for the grieving family, especially when the family members are guided through their memories by their caring pastor with questions that proceed from the facts to the personal and the spiritual. These sessions are usually times of tears and unexpected laughter, and the family predictably leaves feeling better and more relaxed as they anticipate the next few days. The following questions represent a helpful order. The answers should be culled by the pastor to present a ten- to fifteen-minute portrait/remembrance composed with the goal of glorifying Christ for his grace in the life of the deceased.

- When and where was the deceased born? What were the parents' names and occupation(s)? What are the siblings' names and what was the order of their births?
- Early schooling? Childhood memories that the deceased or the siblings have recounted? Church experiences and early spiritual memories?
- What was the deceased like as a child?
- Names of middle schools and high schools attended? Interests as a teenager? Achievements and honors? Spiritual experiences and commitments? Date of high school graduation?
- Further education?
- Spiritual biography? Story of conversion?
- If the deceased was married, some information about the deceased's and his or her spouse's courtship and the wedding, including the location and date of the wedding.
- Children? Their names and dates of birth?
- Professional or domestic history?
- Last, very personal questions. What was the deceased like as a husband, as a father, as a person, as a Christian?

Following the meeting with the family, the busy pastor can best conserve his time by immediately typing or dictating a brief remembrance while the conversation is still fresh. It can be shortened or edited later.

Having gathered the information for the remembrance, the other item of business is the funeral itself—which need not take too much time if the pastor has two worksheets in hand: a Funeral Information Worksheet and a Funeral Service Planning Worksheet (see pp. 190–192). The first deals with the necessary times and logistics, as is evident in the following sample. Note: much of this form should be completed by an administrative assistant or deaconess in a call with a family member, so that the pastor will not have to deal with too many details. Of course, the sample work sheet should be modified to each church's unique needs.

Sample Funeral Information Worksheet[6]
Deceased's full name_____
Dates of birth/death _____

Contact person
Name _____ Phone # _____

Pastor in charge _____

VISITATION
Date _____
Time _____
Place_____
Light refreshments? _____
     # in family _____
     Serving time _____

FUNERAL SERVICE
Date _____
Time _____
Place _____
Organist? _____ Confirmed? _____
Pianist? _____ Confirmed? _____
Musicians? _____ Confirmed? _____
Bulletin cover selected? _____
     How many bulletins needed? _____
Order of funeral service completed? _____
Memorials/funds designation? _____
Sound technician contacted? _____
     Phone # _____
     Music, etc. given to technician? _____

BURIAL
Date _____
Time _____
Place _____
Refreshments or meal requested? _____
Date _____
Serving time _____
Location _____

in family attending? _____
(Be realistic with travel plans for those out or town)
close friends attending? _____
Is family/deceased a member of a Sunday school class or small group?
_____

Have close friends volunteered to help with food? _____
Names? _____
    Phone #s _____
Will there be a general invitation for all who attend the service to stay for
the meal? _____
Does the family need a meal at home? _____
Are there dietary restrictions? _____
Set-up directions for the custodian(s) completed? _____

Additional instructions
    Copy to:
    Pastor in charge
    Receptionist
    Deaconesses

Planning the Funeral

When the pastor meets with the family to plan the funeral service, he can
save a lot of time by having a Funeral Service Planning Worksheet, even if he
has an order of service in his head. This is because a sheet that lays out the
shape of the service helps the family quickly understand what needs to be
done, with a minimum of explanation. The following is a sample template.

Sample Funeral Service Planning Worksheet[7]
Funeral Service for _____
Date and time _____
Location _____

Prelude
Welcome and invocation (Pastor)
Hymn
    Title and #_____
Old Testament readings
    Reader _____
    Selections _____

[7] For a downloadable version of this worksheet, please visit crossway.org/FuneralWorksheet2

_____

_____

Remembrance _____

Music _____

New Testament readings
    Reader _____
    Selections _____

_____

_____

Message/homily (Pastor)
Prayer (Pastor)
Hymn
    Title and # _____
Benediction (Pastor)
Postlude

A Selection of Songs for Funerals
  Old Hymns
    "Abide with Me" (Lyte)
    "All Things New" (Bonar; new music by Wells)
    "Be Still, My Soul" (von Schlegel)
    "For All the Saints" (How)
    "God Moves in a Mysterious Way" (Cowper)
    "It Is Well with My Soul" (Spafford)

  New Hymns
    "All Must Be Well" (Bowley-Peters; alt. Smith)
    "It Is Not Death to Die" (Malan; alt. Kauflin)
    "O Father, You Are Sovereign" (Clarkson)
    "Out of the Depths" (Kauflin)
    "Still, My Soul, Be Still" (Getty/Getty/Townend)
    "The Perfect Wisdom of Our God" (Getty/Townend)
    "There Is a Hope" (Townend)

THE FUNERAL SERVICES
THE VISITATION SERVICE

The visitation normally takes place at the funeral home, but sometimes at the church, especially if the church has an inviting reception area or if the funeral is unusually large. The focus is, of course, upon the open casket, set against a backdrop of flowers, where mourners may have a last look at the deceased and then express their condolences and prayers to the family seated before the casket. A guest book is always provided so that the family will have a record of those attending.

As to the time of the visitation, it usually is set in the late afternoon or evening of the day prior to the funeral service. This is because it is easier for the elderly to attend while it is still light, and likewise families with children can more easily attend after work and school. The generations of young and old gathered around the body of a loved one is a beautiful part of the Christian tradition. Visitation may extend for two to three hours so as to accommodate the mourners' schedules. But a lengthy visitation can prove stressful to the family.

Again, the salutary effects of facing the reality of death by viewing the lifeless body of a friend or loved one can help the process of grieving and the consideration of eternal things.

THE FUNERAL SERVICE

The apparent reason for a funeral service is to confront loss, mourn the deceased, and offer comfort to the family. All Christian funerals have this as a purpose. But this is where the cultural drift toward disposing of the body, thereby eliminating a visitation service, a coffin at the funeral service, and a burial service, misses the mark. The effect is to anesthetize those attending to the reality of death. It is as if "good old John" just stepped into a jet plane, and the funeral service is his aloha. Instead of hymns, there are John's favorite songs. Everyone stands for the seventh inning stretch, sings "Take Me Out to the Ballgame," and toasts John. Balloons are released. "Best of luck, John. You gave it your best. If anyone will make it to the extra innings, you will." A parody? Well, almost. But this is what is, in effect, common in segments of contemporary culture—and has begun to enter the church.

This is not to say that a Christian funeral service is devoid of happiness, but rather that a Christian funeral looks death directly in the face in all its earthly finality. There is real grief. But then the gaze of the mourning is joyfully directed up to heaven, where the departed has become like Christ, because he has seen "him as he is" (1 John 3:2).

The conscious purpose of a Christian funeral must be to glorify Christ by declaring the good news of his death, burial, and resurrection—"that Christ died for our sins in accordance with the Scriptures, that he was buried, that he was raised on the third day in accordance with the Scriptures" (1 Cor. 15:3–4). And, more, this gospel of Christ's *death*, *burial*, and *resurrection* is the template for the Christian's hope. Indeed, in this life we were baptized into the death and resurrection of Christ. Therefore, the sweet logic is: "For if we have been united with him in a death like his, we shall certainly be united with him in a resurrection like his" (Rom. 6:5; cf. 1 Cor. 15:50–55). This, of course, means cosmic comfort and transcending joy for those who mourn.

The responsibility of the pastor who conducts a Christian funeral is to lift high the cross and the empty tomb—in other words, to preach the gospel!

Important Considerations

The pastor has the responsibility to maintain a congenial control over what takes place in the funeral service. Inappropriate music, rambling remembrances by family members, embarrassing revelations, and emotional sermonettes are not uncommon if there is no one keeping a steady hand at the helm. Therefore, here is some helpful counsel:

1. *Scripture.* The reading of God's Word from both Testaments should be given prominence in a Christian funeral service. And the readings ought to address the issues of death: the brevity of life, the work of Christ on the cross, the hope of the resurrection and the realities of heaven (see the list of Scriptures that follows). Often, the pastor is asked to read favorite texts of the deceased, which is fine if the essential texts are not deleted to make room for the favorites. Happily, more is truly more!

2. *Music.* The pastor or his music director must have final say as to the music used in the service. Generally, a couple of well-known and loved congregational hymns or songs will be enough. Not only must the choices be theologically sound and God-centered, they also must be *singable*. Remember, too, that a funeral is not the place for a performance. So any special music must be limited and, when allowed, carefully vetted as to content and competency. A reflective violin rendition of a hymn is one thing; a rising piece from Mozart that evokes an ovation and a bow is another. The same reasoning applies to any genre. So much rests on the heart of the musician and who is being glorified. Remember, too, that additional music adds to the length of the service. Maintain godly control, pastor!

3. *Remembrance.* Some traditions, such as those of the Anglicans and the Lutherans, do not allow for remembrances or eulogies in the funeral service. They reason that the funeral is not a celebration and that a remembrance (which is necessarily person-focused) prevents the service being Christ-centered or may detract from Scripture's teaching that salvation is by grace alone. This is a substantive argument. And, indeed, a remembrance can

become a tasteless man/woman-exalting monologue brimming with Pelagian sentimentality that contradicts the gospel or, on regrettable occasions, an opportunity for inappropriate candor and humor that is an embarrassment to all. But this need not be if the pastor (or a reliable, gospel-focused family member or friend) does the remembrance himself and briefly celebrates the grace of God in the deceased's life, including certain of the joys and woes over the years that shaped his/her life, as well as the experience of saving grace. If the deceased was uniquely used by God, a humble public account of the grace of God in and through him/her will bring glory to God and his saving grace. As the self-effacing apostle Paul said, "But by the grace of God I am what I am, and his grace toward me was not in vain" (1 Cor. 15:10).

4. *Family recollections and memories.* These should be reserved for the meal or reception that normally follows the funeral service. This is the place to display photographs, show home movies, and invite the sharing of memories, provided they are presided over by a family member or friend who understands the boundaries and can cheerfully control the mike.

Funeral Protocol

The funeral director is expert in matters of protocol and should be consulted in advance, unless he and the pastor already have a working relationship. In most cases, the pastor and the funeral director should arrange to meet at the church with the family and pallbearers thirty minutes before the service to go over the order of service and to answer questions. This meeting is important not only for the smoothness of the service but to calm nerves, because nearly everyone will feel stress, even the pallbearers. The director should explain that after the guests have arrived, he will arrange the family in proper order and lead them as a group to their seats, at which time the service will begin.

He should also give directions about how the family will recess at the end of the service, with the pastor leading them. Typically, the pastor pronounces the benediction, motions the congregation to be seated, descends the platform, approaches the nearest to the deceased (the spouse or sibling), offers quiet condolences and extends them to others sitting nearby, and then motions the family to stand and leads them out, with the principal mourner at the front. When the family has exited, the funeral director announces that the service has concluded and invites the people to stand and exit.

Sometimes the casket is borne to the waiting hearse by the pallbearers at the conclusion of the service or at the conclusion of the reception. Traditionally, the pastor leads the pallbearers to the hearse.

The Burial Service

Sometimes the burial service is held before the funeral service because of scheduling problems with the mortuary or family travel schedules. This is to be avoided if at all possible because it contradicts the flow of the visitation (open casket) to the funeral (closed casket) to the burial (burying the casket). It also means that the casket cannot be present before the people at the funeral as a poignant testimony to the reality of death. Lastly, the finality of death and the hope of the resurrection are sealed visually when the body is committed to the earth from which it came. The progression from visitation to funeral to burial is important for all in the process of grieving, as well as for instilling in the younger members of the family a sense of their own mortality and that Jesus is "the way, and the truth, and the life" (John 14:6)—the only hope of heaven.

Graveside Protocol

A limousine bearing the immediate members of the family usually follows the hearse in procession to the cemetery, followed by the cars of close friends. The pastor leads the pallbearers to the graveside, where they place the casket over the grave. The family members take seats on chairs under a canopy, friends gather around, and the service begins.

Graveside Order of Service

Numerous brief denominational liturgies are available. Most of the various Protestant services are variations of the classic 1662 Book of Common Prayer service. The following suggested service is such a variation.

Welcome and opening prayer
Scripture readings
   The readings are brief and center on the hope of the resurrection
   (see selections from the list below).
Words of committal
   Three versions are presented here for comparison:

   Book of Common Prayer, 1662
   "Forasmuch as it hath pleased Almighty God of his great mercy to take unto himself the soul of our dear brother here departed: we therefore commit his body to the ground; earth to earth, ashes to ashes, dust to dust; in sure and certain hope of the resurrection to eternal life, through our Lord Jesus Christ; who shall change our vile body, that it may be like his glorious body, according to the mighty working, whereby he is able to subdue all things to himself."

The Book of Common Worship, 1956
"Unto the mercy of Almighty God, we commend the soul of our brother departed and we commit his body to the ground, earth to earth, ashes to ashes, dust to dust, in the sure and certain hope of the resurrection to eternal life; through Jesus Christ our Lord. Amen."[8]

The Christian Minister's Manual, 1945
"Forasmuch as it hath pleased Almighty God, in His wise providence, to take out of this world the soul of our deceased brother, we therefore commit his body to the ground, earth to earth, ashes to ashes, dust to dust, looking for the resurrection on the last day, and the life of the world to come through our Lord Jesus Christ; at whose coming in glorious majesty to judge the world, the earth and the sea shall give up their dead; and the corruptible bodies of those who sleep in Him shall be changed, and made like unto His glorious body; according to the mighty working whereby He is able to subdue all things unto Himself."[9]

Benediction
"'Blessed are the dead who die in the Lord from now on.' 'Blessed indeed,' says the Spirit, 'that they may rest from their labors, for their deeds follow them!'" (Rev. 14:13).

Lord's Prayer
Copies of the Lord's Prayer (so there will be no awkwardness in respect to the version prayed) and the Doxology (for those who have never sung it) are handed out.

Doxology
Military honors (if any)
With the service concluded, the pastor(s) should approach the seated family and offer some personal words to each member and then begin to interact with the attenders.

FOLLOW-UP AFTER THE FUNERAL

Pastoral care can be easily enhanced with a simple plan for follow-up, monitored through the church office or administrative assistant. The following is a sequence that honors the anniversaries of the day of death.

---

[8] The Book of Common Worship (Philadelphia: The Board of Education of the Presbyterian Church in the United States of America, 1956).
[9] James DeForest Murch, *The Christian Minister's Manual* (Cincinnati: Standard, 1945), 137.

One-month anniversary—call or visit
Three-month anniversary—send a card
Six-month anniversary—call
One-year anniversary—visit
Two-year anniversary—visit

THE FUNERAL HOMILY: RESOURCES AND EXAMPLES

Because "the house of mourning" (Eccl. 7:2, 4) is a place where people become reflective as to eternity and the condition of their souls, the funeral message is a God-given opportunity to preach the gospel. Indeed, the gospel can be preached with an intimacy and directness that is unique as the preacher brings comfort to the family. The pastor should direct many of his remarks to the family, including the younger children, with pastoral tenderness as he speaks of the resurrection and the realities of heaven—realizing that the unregenerate will be drawn to listen in and absorb the gospel.

The privilege and responsibility of the pastor is immense, and the faithful pastor rejoices in it and prays long and works hard to craft a message that will comfort the believing and present Christ to the lost. Following a list of appropriate Scripture passages for funeral homilies, several brief messages are included below as examples of some ways to do this.

SELECT SCRIPTURES FOR FUNERALS

Here are some texts regarding the brevity of life, death, heaven, protection, resurrection, and suffering:

Brevity of Life

Job 8:9	Psalm 103:15–18
Psalm 39:4–5	James 4:13–15
Psalm 90:1–17	

Death

Job 9:23–26	Ecclesiastes 12:1–8
Ecclesiastes 3:1–2	Hebrews 9:27
Ecclesiastes 5:15	Revelation 1:18

Heaven

John 14:1–3	1 John 3:2–3
1 Corinthians 2:9	Revelation 14:13
2 Corinthians 4:13–18	Revelation 21:1–4, 9–27
2 Corinthians 5:1–5	Revelation 22:1–5

Protection

Psalm 23:1–6	Psalm 121:1–8
Psalm 27:1–5	Romans 8:26–39
Psalm 46:1–11	Romans 14:8–9
Psalm 91:1–16	

Resurrection

Daniel 12:2–3	John 20:1–23
Matthew 28:1–15	1 Corinthians 15:12–20
Mark 16:1–13	Philippians 3:20–21
Luke 24:1–49	1 Thessalonians 4:13–18
John 5:25–29	1 Peter 1:3–5
John 11:21–27	

Suffering

Romans 8:18	Philippians 1:29
2 Corinthians 4:16–18	Philippians 3:10

The Complete Texts of Ten Funeral Homilies

Sample Funeral Homily #1 (R. Kent Hughes)

There is a grand passage from Paul's letter to the Romans that is known in church history as the Golden Chain: "For those [God] foreknew he also predestined to be conformed to the image of his Son. . . . And those whom he predestined he also called, and those whom he called he also justified, and those whom he justified he also glorified" (8:29–30).

_____ has held each of these golden links—and now grasps the ultimate gleaming link, as she is glorified with Christ. She is the possessor of riches that challenge the imagination, a joint heir with Christ, inheritor of the promised riches of Christ Jesus.

It is the glory of this ultimate golden prize that we will consider in these next moments. The reason for this is that at times of grief, we are most impressionable regarding eternity. The death of a loved one opens the lives of family members, friends, and even casual acquaintances to the vision of heaven. So these are moments of grace. That is why the teacher in Ecclesiastes tells us that "It is better to go to the house of mourning than to go to the house of feasting, for this is the end of all mankind, and the living will lay it to heart" (Eccl. 7:2). So as we consider the place where _____ now resides on this _____ day of _____, we have some grace moments for some sweet work to be done on our souls. You, _____'s family—her children and her grandchildren—and you, her circle of friends, are meant to benefit from today as we consider that final golden link.

Where _____ *is today is a definite locality, not just a spiritual state.* She's not floating around on some cloud, as Jesus made so clear: "In my Father's house are many rooms. If it were not so, would I have told you that I go to prepare a place for you? And if I go and prepare a place for you, I will come and will take you to myself, that where I am you may be also" (John 14:2–3). The language that Jesus uses indicates that he has prepared *permanent* rooms, dwelling places for his children— real, habitable, personal abodes. What a thought! It is difficult for us to grasp, and it was not easy for the original writers to communicate. Joe Bayly, a man who thought long and hard on heaven (as he lost three of his six children in their youth), put it this way: "How would the Eskimo describe a pineapple to others in his village, even if he were transported to Hawaii and then returned? 'Sweet and juicy blubber' is still about as close as he could come."[10] In the same way, how would you describe ice to a desert tribe? How could you tell people of heaven? Yet the thought is clear enough.

_____ is in an abode designed for her by the architect of the universe and the Savior of her soul. Her room is perfect for her, because he has always known her every thought and desire. It is more than she ever conceived of or wished for. This is not sentiment. This is *reality*—eternal reality. This said, it is a wonder that believers try to delay their entrance into heaven as long as possible.

The apostle Paul had it right: "I am hard pressed. . . . My desire is to depart and be with Christ, for that is far better" (Phil. 1:23). It is always "far better" to be with Christ. It is "far better" whether you are nine months or nine years or nineteen or thirty-nine or eighty-nine.

We know where _____ is, and it is so much better than anything she experienced here on earth. So when Jesus says, "Let not your hearts be troubled" (John 14:1), he means it. In fact, it is a command!

_____ *is also in a glorious state because of what is not there.* There is no longer any death. Jesus says of departed believers, "They cannot die anymore, because they are equal to angels and are sons of God, being sons of the resurrection" (Luke 20:36). Relentless, unremitting, eternal life courses through their souls.

As a pastor, I have seen death far more than I wish. It is not natural. Adam and Eve were not created to die. Death was "naturalized" by sin.

---

[10] Joseph Bayly, *A Voice in the Wilderness* (Colorado Springs: David C. Cook, 2000), 261.

It is always wrenching, regardless of the godliness of the departed. A beloved family member or friend is torn from this earth—from us! It hurts. But now, for _____, there is no death.

What a great thought! Those in heaven will never again experience death and separation. The dark specter will never come. Here we sorrow. And it is right that we do so. Love invites sorrow. Deep love; deep sorrow. Our Lord himself wept tears over young Lazarus and his sisters, though he would raise Lazarus from the dead. And at this moment, Christ sympathizes with our human pain and mourning, because as God incarnate, he experienced human sorrow. Tears are a language he understands. As the psalmist wrote: "Put my tears in your bottle. Are they not in your book?" (Ps. 56:8).

But now for _____, there is no sorrow.

Revelation says that in heaven, "He will wipe away every tear from their eyes, and death shall be no more, neither shall there be mourning, nor crying, nor pain anymore, for the former things have passed away" (Rev. 21:4). We have had tears, and rightly so. But not so with _____.

Though the stars fade and the sun turns to ice, she will never suffer hurt, bereavement, grief, or even a lump in her throat.

For _____, there is no longer any pain. It's tough to suffer the process of aging, as did _____. It's tough to suffer the ravages of death, as did _____. But in heaven, there is no pain, ever. In fact, there is no weariness—no need to end a conversation because of an ache. Neither is there ever the pain of misunderstanding and hurt feelings.

No relational sorrow of any kind. Free, open, unimpeded, unending exchange.

Along with this, there is nothing that defiles. Revelation again says of heaven, "But nothing unclean will ever enter it, nor anyone who does what is detestable or false, but only those who are written in the Lamb's book of life" (Rev. 21:27).

Over the years, God's grace had woven godliness into _____'s soul. And she felt a dissonance with the course of this world—with its blasphemies, perversions, cruelties, deceptions, and unfairness.

But now there is nothing to vex her sweet soul. She lives in a constant stream of truth and goodness. So heaven is glorious indeed, and not simply for what *is not* there.

Heaven is glorious because of what is there. Jesus Christ is the centerpiece of heaven. As the hymn puts it: "The Lamb is all the glory of Immanuel's Land." And _____ has seen him and has become like him, as the Scriptures promised: "Beloved, we are God's children now, and what we will be has not yet appeared; but we know that when he appears we shall be like him, because we shall see him as he is" (1 John 3:2). So _____ is right now like him!

John Donne, the preacher/poet, reveled: "I shall so be like God that the devil himself shall not know me from God. He will not be able to tempt me anymore than he can tempt God. Nor will there be any more chance of falling out of the kingdom than of God being driven out of it."[11] Such stupendous thoughts. We pray "Our Father in heaven" because heaven is the place of his throne and the perfect place of his worship.

As believers, we are filled with a worshipful sense of divine paternity, and the Holy Spirit within us causes us to cry out "Abba, Father"— "Dearest Father!" "Abba, Father" is the lyric of _____'s existence. Her experience is one of total well-being—*shalom*—wrought by the Father, the Son, and the Holy Spirit. While here on earth, _____ shared a unity with those who preceded her to heaven.

The same spiritual blood, the same spiritual DNA that infuses their perfected souls (from Abraham, the apostles, and believers from all the ages), courses through her soul. Now she's with "the spirits of the righteous made perfect" (Heb. 12:23). And she is talking with the saints of the centuries and joining them in singing recurrent choruses of "Worthy is the Lamb" (Rev. 5:12). Ecstasy is too small a word to describe what she is experiencing.

Everything that we have described—from what is not there to what is there—is _____*'s experience in all its fullness.*

She had a glimpse of these things while here on earth and understood the words of the apostle: "For this light momentary affliction is preparing for us an eternal weight of glory beyond all comparison, as we look not to the things that are seen but to the things that are unseen. For the things that are seen are transient, but the things that are unseen are eternal" (2 Cor. 4:17–18). Now she's traveled through the unseen to the eternal— *the real.* And the reality that is now hers makes earth a distant, fading shadow.

So this day, as you have entered the house of mourning, these are some of the things that will benefit your souls. And in these tender moments, may this knowledge grace the souls of the children and grandchildren of _____ in the succeeding generation.

What would _____ say to us if she were to stand before us today here at her funeral service? We can have a good idea because of her commitment to Christ. She would tell us:

[11] Quoted by A. J. Gossip in *The Interpreter's Bible*, vol. 8 (New York: Abingdon, 1952), 703.

- Everyone we meet is of great importance. They all are made in the image of God; they are immortal souls. And their destiny rests on whether they believe the gospel or not.
- Jesus Christ is the sole hope of every soul.
- Christ's death was sufficient for her sins and, indeed, for the sins of anyone who comes to him.
- The gift of forgiveness comes from grace alone, not by works: "If it is by grace, it is no longer on the basis of works; otherwise grace would no longer be grace" (Rom. 11:6).
- Salvation comes by faith in Christ: "For by grace you have been saved through faith. And this is not your own doing; it is the gift of God, not a result of works, so that no one may boast" (Eph. 2:8–9).

She would urge us to give first priority to these matters, "for what does it profit a man to gain the whole world and forfeit his soul?" (Mark 8:36). As for _____ herself, she would tell us not to mourn for her because, though she has experienced death, now she is perfect, complete, and whole. She is "with Christ," which is "far better" (Phil. 1:23).

Sample Funeral Homily #2 (R. Kent Hughes)

To introduce this homily, it is helpful to include a reference to the brevity of life and how time flies, or perhaps a reference to Isaiah 40:6–7: "All flesh is grass . . ."

If today, on the day of his funeral, as we are mourning his loss, _____ could materialize and stand before us in radiant health, what would he say?

Christ

He would tell us that he has seen the face of Christ and that he cannot get over it.

He would explain that he has experienced what has been promised to all of God's children in 1 John 3:2: "Beloved, we are God's children now, and what we will be has not yet appeared; but we know that when he appears we shall be like him, because we shall see him as he is."

In a dazzling, sacred moment—when _____ breathed his last and his heart lay still—he saw the radiant, welcoming face of the Creator of the universe and the Savior of his soul! He saw Jesus face to face, eye to eye, soul to soul. He looked into Christ's gaze. And because he saw the face of Christ, he became like him!

In this world, _____'s sins had been forgiven through the blood of Christ, but in that instant, he became sinless like his Savior. In fact, sin became an impossibility for him. In this world, _____, by grace, had been given the imputed righteousness of Christ. But in that blazing moment, righteousness became the air he breathed.

And then he was freed from the limitations of his miserable body, so ravaged by illness, that had bound him for years, but at the consummation Christ "will transform [his] lowly body to be like his glorious body, by the power that enables him even to subject all things to himself" (Phil. 3:21).

A body transformed *by* Christ to be like that of Christ himself? Astonishing!

Astonishingly true.

How was it for _____ in that first minute in heaven?

The first five minutes?

The first hour?

The first day?

Do they have days in heaven?

Heaven

_____ would also assure us earthbound souls (who are conditioned to think that only what we can touch is real) that heaven is the solid reality. Perhaps he would quote the apostle Paul: "The things that are seen are transient, but the things that are unseen are eternal" (2 Cor. 4:18). He believed this by faith. And now his faith has become sight. _____ is living in the *real*—the eternal.

Joseph Bayly, a man who did a lot of thinking about heaven because three of his young children went there while Joe was a young father, put it this way in his book *The View from a Hearse*:

> I cannot prove the existence of heaven. I accept it by faith, on the authority of Jesus Christ: "In my Father's house are many mansions: if it were not so, I would have told you. I go to prepare a place for you."
>
> For that matter, if I were a twin in a womb, I doubt that I could prove the existence of earth to my mate. He would probably object that the idea of an earth beyond the womb was ridiculous, that the womb was the only earth we'd ever know.
>
> If I tried to explain that earthlings live in a greatly expanded environment and breathe air, he would only be more skeptical. After all, a fetus lives in water; who could imagine its being able to live in a universe of air? To him such a transition would seem impossible.

It would take birth to prove the existence of earth to a fetus. A little pain, a dark tunnel, a gasp of air—and then the wide world! Green grass, laps, lakes, the ocean, horses (could a fetus imagine a horse?). With enough room that you don't have to shove, and a universe beyond.[12]

On _____, when _____ passed through the dark tunnel into the light, he found far more than a mere "universe beyond," and what he now is experiencing makes the dark watery womb a fit picture of our earthly existence. He has gone from black and white to color to polychrome to the textured, pungent, sensual existence of an unfolding heaven, where each chapter is as wonderful as the first.

Christ is real! Heaven is real! And in this sense, _____ is *more real* than he has ever been—because "we look not to the things that are seen but to the things that are unseen. For the things that are seen are transient, but the things that are unseen are eternal" (2 Cor. 4:18).

_____ would not come back if he could—except to tell us what is real and to urge us to make knowing Christ the focus of our lives.

Coheirs

It is customary to refer to the church on earth as "the church militant" and the church in heaven as "the church triumphant." Sometimes the church on earth fails in its task, but in heaven it is always victorious.

_____ is part of the church triumphant, part and parcel of "the spirits of the righteous made perfect," as the writer of Hebrews calls those who have gone to heaven (Heb. 12:23). And what is that perfection? Certainly it is perfection that comes from being delivered from our sins. But it includes more. It is the absolute perfection of our humanity, not only our moral defects but our mental defects and physical defects. So a Down syndrome child will be his or her perfect self—what God intended the child to be from eternity. _____ is perfect morally, mentally, and physically. And he is glorious, too, sharing in the "eternal weight of glory beyond all comparison," as the apostle Paul calls it (2 Cor. 4:17).

In *The Weight of Glory*, C. S. Lewis said that if we could see _____ now, our impulse would be to worship him. And there is more. As a member of the church triumphant, he is a firstborn son, which means that along with every true believer, he is a number one heir of everything in the universe. Indeed, he is a "fellow heir" with Christ (Rom. 8:17). This is mind-boggling. But this is what the Scriptures tell us.

[12] Joseph Bayly, *The View from a Hearse: A Christian View of Death* (Bloomington, IN: Clearnote Press, 2014), 86.

The Gospel

What else would _____ tell us? He would passionately affirm that the gospel is our only hope. The reason that the gospel is our only hope is that we are so utterly sinful that we could never in a billion lifetimes atone for our sins. And this is why Christ did the hardest thing ever done in time and eternity for us.

The creation of the universe was merely an exercise of his creational power. He did it with a word—with the ease of omnipotence. But the hardest thing ever was/is to say, "My son, my daughter, your sins are forgiven," because it meant his death on the cross.

In the garden of Gethsemane, the prospect of it was so horrific that the Gospel writer tells us he "began to be greatly distressed and troubled. And he said to [his disciples], 'My soul is very sorrowful, even to death. Remain here and watch.' And going a little farther, he fell on the ground and prayed that, if it were possible, the hour might pass from him. And he said, 'Abba, Father, all things are possible for you. Remove this cup from me. Yet not what I will, but what you will'" (Mark 14:33–36).

And when the hour came, he did the Father's will by dying the lowest death of all, even death on a cross. During those three dark hours on Good Friday, Jesus's heart, so to speak, became a sea into which poured the mountains of our festering sin. There the mass of our corruption poured over him. There our sins were focused on Christ as he bore the fiery wrath of God, having become a curse for us (Gal. 3:13). Jesus, in fully lucid consciousness, writhing like a serpent in the gloom, took your sin and mine with a unity of understanding and pain that none can fathom. And he did it willingly, so that he could say, "My son, my daughter, your sins are forgiven."

If _____ were standing here today, he would tell us all that Jesus did the hardest thing ever done in time or eternity for you and me! And that means that Jesus is committed to forgiving you as you turn to him. Nothing is so beautiful as the gospel at a time like this.

Time

Perhaps last _____ would tell us that life on this earth is short, as the Psalms remind us:

> My days are like an evening shadow; I wither away like grass. (Ps. 102:11)

> The years of our life are seventy, or even by reason of strength eighty; yet their span is but toil and trouble; they are soon gone, and we fly away. (Ps. 90:10)

_____ was once a young groom holding his newlywed bride's hand.

He blinked, and he was holding his firstborn son in his arms.

He blinked, and he was holding his firstborn's daughter.

He blinked again, and he was holding Jesus's hand.

Now is the time to get it right.

There is no other time.

Sample Funeral Homily #3 (Doug O'Donnell)

"Memorial Homily for the Death of a Child"

In 2 Corinthians 1:3–4, the apostle Paul, who suffered much in his life, wrote these words: "Blessed be the God and Father of our Lord Jesus Christ, the Father of mercies and God of all comfort, who comforts us in all our affliction, so that we may be able to comfort those who are in any affliction, with the comfort with which we ourselves are comforted by God." _____ and _____, we gather today to comfort you and to comfort one another by together dwelling on the God of all comfort and the truths of his Word.

First of all, let us *be comforted that* _____ *(child's name) is in the hands of our loving and merciful God.* Our Lord Jesus, who suffered for us and for the sins of the world, cried aloud while dying upon the cross, "Father, into your hands I commit my spirit!" (Luke 23:46). In the ancient world, the pagan peoples who surrounded Israel offered child sacrifices to their gods. Their gods were made of stone in the shapes of people. Upon an idol's stony cold hands, they would place a child for sacrifice. Such a wicked practice! The God to whose hands our Lord Jesus committed his spirit was no cold and lifeless god, but the living and loving God of the universe. _____ and _____, you have placed _____ into the hands of our gracious and good God, a God who loves that little boy/girl more than you ever could. So be comforted this day that the God who weeps over sin and death—as Jesus did when he came to Lazarus's tomb—is the same God who comforts us with the fact that his hands are better hands in which to place the body and soul of your dear child.

Moreover, *be comforted by the fact that suffering is for our good.* The apostle Peter writes words of healing and comfort, explaining why bad things happen to good people:

> Blessed be the God and Father of our Lord Jesus Christ! According to his great mercy, he has caused us to be born again to a living hope through the resurrection of Jesus Christ from the dead,

to an inheritance that is imperishable, undefiled, and unfading, kept in heaven for you, who by God's power are being guarded through faith for a salvation ready to be revealed in the last time. In this you rejoice, though now for a little while, if necessary, you have been grieved by various trials, so that the tested genuineness of your faith—more precious than gold that perishes though it is tested by fire—may be found to result in praise and glory and honor at the revelation of Jesus Christ. Though you have not seen him, you love him. Though you do not now see him, you believe in him and rejoice with joy that is inexpressible and filled with glory, obtaining the outcome of your faith, the salvation of your souls. (1 Pet. 1:3–9)

Later, Peter adds, "Beloved, do not be surprised at the fiery trial when it comes upon you to test you, as though something strange were happening to you" (4:12). Suffering—whether in the form of persecution or loss—is to be expected. It is to be expected because such suffering is for our good. Suffering wakes us up to reality. Suffering helps us long for eternal life and final justice. Suffering helps us to love not the world nor the things of the world.

Be comforted that _____ is in the hands of our loving God. Be comforted that suffering is for our good. Finally, *be comforted by the knowledge that the death of death is coming soon!* Through the sin of Adam and Eve, sin was introduced into the world. In the genealogical record in Genesis 5, there is a repeated phrase: "and he died." So and so lived this many years, "and he died." That is at the beginning of the Bible and the beginning of the effect of sin in the world. But listen now to how the Bible ends. It ends with a vision of the death of death:

Then I saw a new heaven and a new earth, for the first heaven and the first earth had passed away, and the sea was no more. And I saw the holy city, new Jerusalem, coming down out of heaven from God, prepared as a bride adorned for her husband. And I heard a loud voice from the throne saying, "Behold, the dwelling place of God is with man. He will dwell with them, and they will be his people, and God himself will be with them as their God. He will wipe away every tear from their eyes, and death shall be no more, neither shall there be mourning, nor crying, nor pain anymore, for the former things have passed away." (Rev. 21:1–4)

In John Donne's famous sonnet "Death Be Not Proud," throughout the poem the preacher/poet mocks death and its apparent power, ending with these words:

One short sleep past, wee wake eternally,
And death shall be no more; death, thou shalt die.

_____ and _____, family and friends, be comforted that Jesus has risen from the grave and that his death is the death of death, eternal life. _____ (name and/or middle name of the child), as you know, means "_____." We rejoice today in the God of comfort, who comforts, saves, and heals. Amen.

Sample Funeral Homily #4 (James A. Johnston)

Begin with personal words of sympathy to the family, such as, "(Names), we want you to know that our hearts are with you."

Whenever we face death, even the death of a strong believer like _____, whose faith was strong to the end, we are left with questions. So this morning we're going to think about two questions to help us understand what has happened and what is yet to come, to help give us strength and hope in hard days and to help us know what to do.

What happened to _____ on Monday? We can analyze and describe what went on in his body. But we're not talking about vital signs, heartbeats, or disease. What happened to the part of _____ you can't monitor or hear with a stethoscope? What happened to _____, the eternal soul created in God's image?

To know this, the only place we can turn is the Bible. On Monday, _____ went to be with God. The Bible says that if we are absent from the body, we are at home with the Lord (2 Cor. 5:8).

There is no safer place to be. God's Word tells us, "For I am sure that neither death nor life, nor angels nor rulers, nor things present nor things to come, nor powers, nor height nor depth, nor anything else in all creation, will be able to separate us from the love of God in Christ Jesus our Lord" (Rom. 8:38–39). Not even death itself can separate us from God's love.

When we come face to face with the end of life, we need to remember that death is not all-powerful. We all die, so it might seem that nothing can stand against death. But there is someone greater than death!

Where did death come from? When Adam and Eve sinned in the garden of Eden, God set the curse of death on humanity. So we realize that death ravages this world not because it is more powerful than God, but because almighty God has made death the penalty for our sins.

The good news we discover in the Bible, though, is that Jesus "bore our sins in his body on the tree, that we might die to sin and live to righteousness. By his wounds you have been healed" (1 Pet. 2:24).

The Bible tells us that this same Jesus is greater than death! He says, "I died, and behold I am alive forevermore, and I have the keys of Death and Hades" (Rev. 1:18). So death is not the end, because our Jesus holds the keys! Jesus is stronger than death. And this is the hope that _____ so clearly had.

Jesus said: "Truly, truly, I say to you, whoever hears my word and believes him who sent me has eternal life. He does not come into judgment, but has passed from death to life" (John 5:24). _____ heard Jesus's words when (mention the circumstances of his/her salvation), and he believed them—he trusted in Jesus to take away his sins and became a follower of Jesus. And according to Jesus's words, he passed from death to life _____ years ago.

This is the hope of all God's people. Dietrich Bonhoeffer's last known words before being executed for treason in Nazi Germany, written in complete confidence to a friend, were, "This is the end, for me the beginning of life."[13]

If _____ is with God, death is not the end. _____ will live again!

The Bible says: "Behold! I tell you a mystery. We shall not all sleep, but we shall all be changed, in a moment, in the twinkling of an eye, at the last trumpet. For the trumpet will sound, and the dead will be raised imperishable, and we shall be changed" (1 Cor. 15:51–52).

These weak bodies will be made new:

- No more eyeglasses, or even Lasik
- No more prescriptions
- No more cancer, no more coughing
- No more fear of the latest virus
- No more aging, frailties, limping, or pain, for God will make all things new!

A stethoscope can tell what happened to _____'s old body. God tells us what is going to happen to him when Christ comes again!

What will happen to your soul after you die? We have all disobeyed God; we have all sinned in our thoughts, words, and deeds. "The soul who sins shall die" (Ezek. 18:4).

_____ put his trust in Jesus as his Savior. "God so loved the world, that he gave his only son, that whoever believes in him should not perish but have eternal life" (John 3:16). What are you trusting? Death comes to us all, but are we ready to meet God after we die?

[13] Quoted in Randy Alcorn, *Eternal Perspectives: A Collection of Quotations on Heaven, the New Earth, and Life after Death* (Wheaton, IL: Tyndale, 2012), 133.

What do we have to look forward to? God isn't just transforming people. His plan is much bigger. He's transforming the world! He is making a new heaven and a new earth. Isaiah 65:17 says, "For behold, I create new heavens and a new earth, and the former things shall not be remembered or come into mind."

The joy of what God is creating will be so overwhelming. We will forget the pain and sorrows of this life. Light will dawn and chase away the shadows. God knows we have tears and tragedies, and he will heal our hearts and lift the sorrows from our minds. The whole world will be made new!

The first detail we need to know about heaven is that a service like this won't happen there. No funerals! There will be no evil, no sin, no one who hurts another, no disease, no random violence, no terrorism, no threat warnings, no AIDS, no smallpox, no congenital defects. "'They shall not hurt or destroy in all my holy mountain,' says the Lord" (Isa. 65:25).

God is making all things new. If you love God, if you belong to Christ, this is what you have to look forward to! In that new creation, those of us who know Jesus will meet _____ again.

Someone asked W. A. Criswell, pastor of First Baptist Church in Dallas, whether we'd know each other in heaven, and he answered, "We won't really know each other until we get to heaven!"[14] When we see _____ again someday, we will see him as God has seen him all along, perfect and complete, shining with glory in God's presence.

So just wait! If you loved _____, you ain't seen nothing yet.

Donald Grey Barnhouse's wife died when their three children were still young. They were driving to her funeral, and Barnhouse was thinking about how he could comfort his children. It was a bright, sunny day, and as they came up to a stoplight, a big truck pulled up beside them and put them in its shadow.

Just then Barnhouse had an idea. He asked his daughter, "Which would you rather be hit by, that truck or the shadow of the truck?" "The shadow, of course," she answered. "That's right," Barnhouse said, "and that's the way it is with death for a Christian. Jesus was hit by death so we would only be hit by the shadow of death."[15]

This is our confidence and our strong hope.

---

[14] Quoted in Jeff Lasseigne, *Unlocking the Last Days: A Guide to the Book of Revelation and the End Times* (Grand Rapids: Baker, 2011), 314.

[15] Mark Hitchcock, *55 Answers to Questions about Life After Death* (Portland, OR: Multnomah, 2005), 77.

Sample Funeral Homily #5 (W. Carey Hughes)

The remarkable thing about Psalm 23 is that it is so simple and beautiful, and I think that because of this, we naturally assume that its great beauty and simplicity is where the psalm's comfort comes from.

But actually the comfort of Psalm 23 comes from its *strength*! In its simple beauty, there is incredible strength, like an arched bridge. If you've ever taken the time to look at an old arched bridge, you probably noticed that it is made up of a few large main arches that are connected and supported by many smaller arches and cross members, and that the overall effect is an intricate, lattice-like structure that is pleasing to the eye—it is beautiful! But in that beauty, of course, there is incredible support and strength. In fact, the structure is so strong that we entrust our lives to that bridge as we cross over it!

You see, when we actually think about the beautiful words of this psalm, we see that there are two strong promises imbedded in its beauty— promises that we can trust.

The Lord Is My Shepherd

King David is going through some tough times in his life. He is being despised and abused by his enemies, and feels completely overwhelmed by the circumstances of his life, as he describes it so memorably in verse 14 of the preceding psalm, where his personal miseries are prophetic of Christ's sufferings.

He thinks he is going to die! So David cries out with what he understands to be true of his God, saying, "The LORD is my shepherd" (Ps. 23:1).

Shepherd is the most intimate metaphor yet used in the Psalms. Other powerful metaphors, such as *king, deliverer, rock*, and *shield*, have been used to describe God, but those are comparatively distant and somewhat impersonal terms. But here we have *shepherd*!

The shepherd lives with his flock. He is everything to it: provider, protector, and physician. The flock is his life. The sheep live because of his care.

This is the thought that gives comfort to David in his time of need. God Almighty, the Maker of heaven and earth, Sustainer of all things, is David's Shepherd! This is a good shepherd to have. This is a shepherd who goes beyond dealing with daily provision and protection. He cares for David's very heart and soul: "He makes me lie down in green pastures. He leads me beside still waters. He restores my soul. He leads me in paths of righteousness for his name's sake" (vv. 2–3).

You see, this isn't just about refreshment, like the guy in the Irish Spring soap commercial, who is whistling a cheery tune as he enjoys a refreshing outdoor mountain shower and is revived as he takes a long whiff of the tingly scent of the soap. No! This is spiritual. We see this in verse 3: "He restores my soul. He leads me in paths of righteousness for his name's sake."

God guides David in honoring him. He shepherds David's soul! Therefore, the psalmist can say, "Even though I walk through the valley of the shadow of death, I will fear no evil, for you are with me; your rod and your staff, they comfort me" (v. 4). This shepherd has a rod and a staff that can deal with death!

All other guides turn back at this point—doctors, therapists, counselors, life coaches, teachers, family members, friends. The traveler must go it alone at this point. But not so for the psalmist, because the Lord, the Great Shepherd, takes him through that dark valley.

And there is even more, as there is a second deed that the shepherd does: "You prepare a table before me in the presence of my enemies; you anoint my head with oil; my cup overflows. Surely goodness and mercy shall follow me all the days of my life, and I shall dwell in the house of the LORD forever" (vv. 5–6). The metaphor changes. The Shepherd becomes the Host!

The Host

You see, what is being promised here is not merely surviving death, but triumph! A victory party! A homecoming party.

King David knows that the Lord is *his* Host—a good host who has prepared for him a home and a place at his table so that he may be part of God's family for eternity.

The Shepherd *Who Is* Host—*a Promise to Hold*

What I love about this psalm is how *timeless* it is. It is not just some ancient text that we read and say: "Good for David. I'm glad that it comforted him." No, we can truly find comfort here, in times like this today, because as we read in our Bibles, the Lord God has come down into history and has come as our Shepherd to lead us through "the valley of the shadow of death" (v. 4).

Jesus says in the Gospel of John: "I am the good shepherd. The good shepherd lays down his life for the sheep" (John 10:11). And we know that he did; the Shepherd became the slaughtered Lamb. He gave his life on the cross in our place, paying for our sins and taking our punishment in order to open the way to the Father's home.

Jesus says: "In my Father's house are many rooms. . . . I go to prepare a place for you" (John 14:2). The *Shepherd* is now the *Host*, waiting for his flock.

You see, the comfort and strength of Psalm 23 is not in its beauty but in its truth—its reality. Here is reality to hold on to this day and for eternity.

Sample Funeral Homily #6 (Arthur Jackson)

"Memorial Homily for the Death of a Child"

If McKinley could speak . . .

Dear Mommy and Daddy, Sierra and Whitney, Grandma and Grandpa Whitlock, Grandma and Grandpa Smith, Uncle Paul and Aunt Robyn, Aunt Samantha and Uncle Chuck, and all my mommy's and daddy's friends who are here today.

Thank you for being here. I am honored that you feel that I am so special. Thanks also for being my mommy's and daddy's friends. They are overwhelmed by your love and kind expressions.

I have some messages on my heart and from the heart of God that I want to share with you. Please remember them. I didn't know just how to say them to you, so I got together with Pastor Jackson. Forgive him if he doesn't say it just right; after all, he's one of those . . . I believe you call them grownups. They are always making mistakes.

The first thing I want to say is: Mommy and Daddy, I am glad you are my parents. I wouldn't have it any other way. I love the name that you gave me. It fits so well; I wear it with honor. From the time I came into being—the child of Randy and Linda Smith—I knew I was loved, the fruit of your love for each other. I felt so safe inside of you, Mommy.

My imperfect condition was the result of living in an imperfect world, and no direct fault of your own. Thank you for providing the best of care when I was in the hospital—the doctors and nurses were so great. I anticipated your visits when I was in the hospital. I learned to recognize your voices. Thank you for holding me and touching me—I felt so loved by you. And thanks for bringing my big sisters to see me.

I appreciate the way that you planned for me and anticipated my coming home to our house in Berwyn, and I know it hurts you that I will never sleep in my bed or romp with my sisters or help you make cookies or all the things that little girls do. But our heavenly Father had another plan for me.

His plan for some people includes many years, and his plan for others includes just a few days. His plan for your organist, Mr. Dunlop, has included many years (I've heard him play; he's good!). My time with you was but a few days. But both plans are good.

His ways have been called mysterious. A man by the name of William Cowper wrote about this in his hymn "God Moves in a Mysterious Way":

> God moves in a mysterious way
> His wonders to perform;
> He plants His footsteps in the sea
> And rides upon the storm.
>
> Ye fearful saints, fresh courage take;
> The clouds you so much dread
> Are big with mercy, and shall break
> In blessings on your head.[16]

Great words, Mommy and Daddy, and I want you to remember them.

A Bitter Cup

As much as we want sweet water, sometimes our cups, our portions in life, include things that are bitter. From cups that are bitter *and* cups that are sweet, we all are often called to drink.

Remember the Lord Jesus in the garden of Gethsemane. He would rather not have tasted the bitter cup of death. Just like our Lord, you have been called to drink a very bitter cup. This cup is not one you would have chosen. But drink. Cowper's song continues:

> His purposes will ripen fast,
> Unfolding every hour;
> The bud may have a bitter taste,
> But sweet will be the flower.

Everyone, please pray for my mommy and daddy as they drink. Support them as they drink. The cup has the Smiths' name on it today; it may have yours on it tomorrow.

Daddy and Mommy, I could say more, but I have some things to say to others who have come to honor me and say hello and good-bye.

I was born into such a wonderful extended family. Thanks for all the ways you supported my daddy and mommy. It's been hard, but the Lord has used you to hold them up. Uncle Paul, you are awesome. I was flattered by your McKinley reports. Thanks for that kind of support.

---

[16] From the hymn "God Moves in a Mysterious Way" by William Cowper, 1774.

An Imperfect Heart

I entered into this life with an imperfect heart physically. That condition demanded repair. The doctors worked to fix my condition as best they could.

But all come into this world with damaged hearts, not the physical organ at the center of their bodies, but the spiritual core of their lives.

Our hearts are sinful, and they need the work of the divine cardiologist. He gives new hearts at the time of new birth. If you don't yet have yours, if you ask him, he will give you one.

Perhaps some of you are wondering about how the Lord handles little people like me, people who have not made a choice for him, people who can't believe for themselves.

Some of you would be inclined to appeal to my innocence and to refer to me as a sweet little baby. Though I have not sinned, still I was born with a sin nature, and it would have just been a matter of time before I acted on it. Like others, I needed new birth.

God in his grace and mercy provides that rebirth for little people like me. For remember, "unless one is born again, he cannot see the kingdom of God" (John 3:3). He has chosen to redeem us, to include us in the work of his Son, the Lord Jesus. He even says that the kingdom of God is made up of people like me. I would remind you of that.

A Perfect God

I know this is a difficult time for many of you. The figures don't add up, the puzzle pieces don't fit for you; some of you here are trying to make sense of all of this. Others are angry. You're saying: "It's not fair! The Smiths' home is a great home. They are such great parents."

In matters like this, there are several ways you can respond—curse, question, or worship God.

As Job's wife in the Bible suggested, you can curse God. You can indiscriminately spew out words of judgment against God. You can judge him as unjust, unfair, uncaring, and unwise. None of those words fit. Such spouting says more about the speaker than the one spoken about.

Another option is that you can question God. Certainly questioning God is better than cursing God. That may be where some of you are. Again Cowper helps us. Listen:

Judge not the Lord by feeble sense,
But trust Him for His grace;
Behind a frowning providence
He hides a smiling face.

Blind unbelief is sure to err
And scan His work in vain;
God is His own interpreter,
And He will make it plain.

Question if you must; just don't rely on human wisdom to supply the answers.

In the Bible, David faced a similar situation for different reasons. His infant son was sick. He fasted and prayed for his son, just like people fasted and prayed for me. His son died. Scripture says: "Then David arose from the earth and washed and anointed himself and changed his clothes. And he went into the house of the LORD and worshiped" (2 Sam. 12:20).

Similarly Job, when stripped of children and possessions, worshiped God: "Then Job arose and tore his robe and shaved his head and fell to the ground and worshiped. And he said, 'Naked I came from my mother's womb, and naked shall I return. The LORD gave, and the LORD has taken away; blessed be the name of the LORD'" (Job 1:20–21).

John Piper, in his book *Seeing and Savoring Jesus Christ*, asks:

> Will we worship or will we curse the One who rules the world? Shall sinners dictate who should live and who should die? Or shall we say with Hannah, "The LORD brings death and makes alive; he brings down to the grave and raises up" (I Sam. 2:6, NIV)? And shall we, with ashes on our heads, worship with Job, "Blessed be the name of the LORD" (Job 1:21)? Will we learn from James that there is good purpose in it all: "You have heard of the steadfastness of Job, and you have seen the purpose of the Lord, how the Lord is compassionate and merciful" (James 5:11, RSV).

I know I'm a child, but I would ask that you apply the "yes, no, maybe so" saying in this situation. Say yes to worship, no to cursing, and maybe to the questions, as long as they are honest inquiries.

Worship God as God all-wise. Worship him as God with a purpose. Things are not just disjointed happenings. God has an appointed purpose. The bottom line is his glory.

You can worship him as the God of comfort. Some of you have experienced that today. Worship him as the God of grace who knows our limitations. Worship him as the God who provides friends like you. Worship him as the God of life.

Worship him as the God and Father of the Lord Jesus Christ, who will one day transform this earth to its renewed state, in which there will be no more diabetes, heart problems, cancer, crime, and death. There will be no more crying and tears.

From McKinley Ruth Smith, with love.

Sample Funeral Homily #7 (Randall Gruendyke)[17]

One of the things for which I am especially grateful is the perspective that God's Word provides for a time like this. Here are three things I find helpful as I wrestle my way through these difficult days.

First, our brother and sisters are alive! Their existence did not end thirteen days ago. Nor will they be any less alive as their memories fade in the months and the years to come. They are alive because Jesus said:

> As for the resurrection of the dead, have you not read what was said to you by God: "I am the God of Abraham, and the God of Isaac, and the God of Jacob"? He is not God of the dead, but of the living. (Matt. 22:31–32)

In other words, if Abraham, Isaac, and Jacob were no longer alive, God would no longer be their God. But they *are* alive. And so are our friends with them.

Second, not only are our brother and sisters alive, but they are also *with* the Lord. Paul told the Corinthians that to "be away from the body [is to be] at home with the Lord" (2 Cor. 5:8)—that is, in his physical presence. So the Christ whom our friends once knew by faith they now know by sight. The moment that they could only imagine is now a Technicolor reality.

Finally, our brother and sisters are worshiping Christ in community with those of us here tonight. The book of Hebrews says that in Christ, you and I have come:

- "to the city of the living God, the heavenly Jerusalem,"
- "to innumerable angels in festal gathering,"
- "to the assembly of the firstborn who are enrolled in heaven,"
- "to God, the judge of all," and
- "to the spirits of the righteous made perfect" (Heb. 12:22–23).

So as we worship the Lord together, we do so in solidarity with those who have gone before us and in anticipation of the day when, once again, we will do so in each other's physical presence.

Until that day, there remains a task to be completed. As the old gospel hymn "We've a Story to Tell to the Nations" says:

---

[17] This homily was delivered soon after four students and one staff member of Taylor University died when the van in which they were traveling was struck by a tractor-trailer on Interstate 69 in Indiana on April 26, 2006.

We've a story to tell to the nations
That shall turn their hearts to the right,
a story of truth and mercy,
a story of peace and light.[18]

This past week has been filled with testimonies about how our friends told that story in word and deed.

So who will go and continue carrying the gospel to the worlds in which they were involved and the ones toward which they were headed?

Who will complete what they began?

May many be raised up, even tonight, to fulfill that mission.

Sample Funeral Homily #8 (Randall Gruendyke)

Five months and seventeen days ago, _____ was promoted to glory. The reality of glory and _____'s presence there is a great consolation. But the prospect of finishing this life without him is, to say the least, an enduring burden. In Philippians, Paul expresses three ways that he worked at bearing up under the burdens of this world.

First, no matter where he happened to be in the race of life, Paul's eyes were fixed on the last day. In chapter 3, he writes that false Christians place their confidence in the here and now, while real Christians place their confidence in what's to come—their "heavenly citizenship," as he put it (v. 20). They keep their eyes on the finish line.

As a junior higher, I anchored the 440 relay team. When I was handed the baton, my eyes went to neither my competitors nor the crowd. Instead, they locked onto the finish line. You may remember, in the movie *Chariots of Fire*, coach Sam Mussabini showing Harold Abrahams why the great American sprinter Jackson Scholz could be beaten—he always looked back! Paul didn't look back. He ripped off the rearview mirror aimed at his past and continued "straining forward" for the prize in Christ (Phil. 3:13). That's the first way to bear up under the weight of _____'s absence.

Second, Paul was sustained—and thirteen times he exhorts the Philippians to be sustained—by joy. He did not exhort his readers toward happiness, which is fleeting, rising and falling on the vicissitudes of our happenings. Rather, Paul exhorted the Philippians to rejoice. Joy is rooted in Christ, transcends death, and, as one scholar puts it, is "the emotion of heaven." In Philippians 4, joy is part of the equation that enables Paul to do all things—even the hard things—through Christ.

Third, Paul understood that "to live is Christ, and to die is gain" (Phil. 1:21). Now, I'll tell you what you might have heard: "To live is

---

[18] From the hymn "We've a Story to Tell to the Nations" by H. Ernest Nichol, 1896.

gain, and to die is *Christ.*" And here's why you might have heard it that way. In our extremity, we all pray to live—that would be gain. But to die, well, at least we get Christ. But that's not what the verse says! It says, "To live is *Christ*, and to die is *gain.*" What does that mean?

How did Christ live? Certainly he lived against the headwinds of this world, but not without joy (John 15:11; 16:33)! How did Christ die? He died as the resurrection and the life! John 11:25 says, "Whoever believes in me [like _____], though he die [like _____], yet shall he live [like _____]." That is gain—enduring gain that ultimately overrides the weight of living in this world, even a world without _____.

So, with the help of God's Spirit, let's imitate Paul by keeping our eyes fixed on the last day, cultivating a spirit of joy and understanding that to live is Christ and to die is truly gain—gain that is enjoyed even now by _____.

Sample Funeral Homily #9 *(Tom Buck)*

Introduction

What do we say in moments like this, as family members and friends gather and we are confronted with the awfulness of death? When we experience the sting of death, surely we realize there must be more than the perpetual cycle of living, dying, and grieving. What do we make of the fact that _____ was a faithful and committed Christian in his/her life? And where is God in the midst of all of this?

Well, I can assure you that death is not a sign that God has forgotten us or that God has forgotten _____. If we are to believe the glorious truth of the gospel, he/she is more alive today than he/she has ever been—free from the grip of sin and the sufferings of this life, and free from the grip of death.

But what is the basis for such a hope? Knowing that we all will face our own deaths someday, what does God say to us today in our pain?

Our hope is in the good news of the gospel of Jesus Christ. If we want to make sense of life and death, we need to look no further than Jesus himself in John 11:17–36 and the circumstances surrounding the death of Lazarus. In this story, we see a God who has entered the pain of our world, fully understands the awful results of death, and offers us an everlasting hope in the person of Jesus Christ.

A Caring God Broken by a Sin-Sick World

There is nothing more difficult than facing the death of a friend or loved one. Even when it is a believer who has died, there is still great sadness.

Death causes a painful separation that can be fully understood only if you have personally walked through it.

But one encouraging truth is that God is not uncaring about the sadness we feel when our lives are touched by death. The mourning at the funeral of Lazarus sounds all too familiar to us—people weeping at the grave of their beloved friend. But in a surprising turn, Jesus himself joins in and weeps. Jesus is fully aware that he will raise Lazarus from the dead. Yet he still weeps.

It appears that he weeps for at least two reasons. First, he is moved with compassion for those who are grieving over their loss. Jesus is not insensitive to the hurts of those around him. He is personally moved by their pain. These are his friends, and he shares in their suffering.

Second, Jesus weeps from the personal grief he experiences as he sees the effects of death. When God created the world, there was no death. But ever since Adam and Eve rebelled in their sin, mankind has been shrouded in death's darkness. Death is the result of sin. If there were no sin in this world, there would be no death.

Gathering here today at a funeral and parting with a loved one does not indicate something that is right in this world, but rather is evidence that there is something terribly wrong with it. Jesus looked at the pain, suffering, and destruction that sin had brought into this world, and he wept—not out of sentimentalism, but over the hopelessness of a world ravaged by death.

A Glorious Savior

How comforting it is to have a God who is willing to enter our world, experience our pain, and be moved with compassion in response to the dreadful course of a sin-sick world. But it is a far greater thing to have a God who is willing to *do* something and change the entire trajectory. The wonderful news of the gospel is that Jesus came to do something about sin. He was not just moved by its effects, but he entered our sin-sick world to offer hope to those living in it. The hope of the gospel is found in Jesus Christ, and this is the central revelation of the story.

The hope of the gospel comes in Jesus's words to Martha: "I am the resurrection and the life. Whoever believes in me, though he die, yet shall he live, and everyone who lives and believes in me shall never die" (John 11:25).

This is said in response to Martha's troubled spirit as she tries to understand why everything has happened the way it has. She rightly concludes that Jesus would have been the answer if he could have arrived sooner. She declares, "Lord, if you had been here, my brother would not have died" (John 11:21). She had hope in the past, before Lazarus died, that Jesus would have made a difference, had he been there. In addition, Martha has a certain hope in the future. When Jesus declares that Lazarus will rise again, she expresses her confident belief in the resurrection "on the last day" (v. 24). However, although Martha had great confidence in what could have been and has confidence in what ultimately will be, she appears to be confounded in the fog of her present circumstances.

Jesus wants Martha to see him as more than one who could have prevented Lazarus from dying and to understand who is the source of the future resurrection in which she is confident. Therefore, he does not declare to her what he is capable of doing, but makes a more profound declaration of who he truly is: "Do you understand who I am, Martha? I am the resurrection and the life. The way of escape from the powerful grip of sin and the destructive nature of death is to believe in me."

Jesus is the source of the future resurrection in which Martha hopes and the source of life in the face of death's seeming victory. Martha's hope needs to go beyond what Jesus could have done before and beyond the promise of future resurrection. She needs to place her hope in the very person who stands before her right then—the Lord Jesus Christ.

The same Jesus stands before you today as you face the fog of your own circumstances. All our hope—past, present, and future—is wrapped up in the person of Christ. If you want to escape the horrific consequences of death, you need to be delivered from the tyranny of sin. Jesus is the answer! First Corinthians 15:54–57 says it is Christ who has swallowed up death in victory and has taken away its sting. When he died on the cross, Jesus experienced death in our place so that we might be freed from death. When a believer faces death, we certainly grieve over the loss. But Paul wrote in 1 Thessalonians 4:13 that we don't grieve like those in this world, who have no hope. We know that for the one who truly believes in Christ, death is not final. Death's sting has been replaced with a promised resurrection and life because of who Jesus is and what he has done.

If Martha wants hope in the midst of her pain and grief, it is to be found in her belief that Jesus is who he declares himself to be. Therefore, Jesus calls upon her to respond by asking, "Do you believe this?" (John 11:26).

Do You Believe This?

In times like this, we have an opportunity to face our own mortality. What do we make of life and our inevitable death? The grief must be unbearable for those who do not have the hope offered in Christ Jesus. Life loses all meaning.

The good news today is that hope is offered to each of us in the gospel of the Lord Jesus Christ. He entered our sin-sick world, died to pay for our sins, and arose from the grave victorious over sin and death. That saving hope is given to all who turn to Christ in faith and believe he is the resurrection and the life.

Do you believe what Jesus declares about himself? The question is as pertinent for you and me today as it was for Martha in the hour of her grief. Do *you* believe this? Do you believe Jesus is the resurrection and the life?

There is no better time to evaluate this question than when we see the inescapable reality of death. We know what _____'s answer to that question was. He/she faced death with great certainty because he/she had entrusted his/her life to the one who is the resurrection and the life. If you share this hope in Christ Jesus, then even in your sorrow you can rejoice that this is not the end. Jesus Christ is your hope!

Sample Funeral Homily #10 *(Robert W. Evans)*
1 Peter 3:15–16a

"On Real Hope"
First Peter 3:15 says, "In your hearts honor Christ the Lord as holy, always being prepared to make a defense to anyone who asks you for a reason for the hope that is in you; yet do it with gentleness and respect." Such is my aim this afternoon—to give you a reason for the hope that is in me. The Bible says that the Christian is to be *always* ready to do so. No, not merely when it is convenient, comfortable, easy, or well-received, but always. Yes, in *this* moment as much as in any other—perhaps *especially* in this moment, when all seems so dark and lost. And surely the circumstances that bring us here today beg for such a defense, for it is exceedingly difficult to stare into the face of a lifeless fifteen-year-old girl and not struggle in the effort to make sense of such a tragic loss.[19]

Hope. Is there *any* reason to hold on to such a thing at a time like this? For some, the confusion and pain associated with such a loss washes

---

[19] Dr. Evans writes: "I preached this sermon at the funeral of a well-known and much-loved youth in our community who was tragically killed. This sermon has been 'sanitized' of all identifying information and slightly edited to remove my personal remarks made during the funeral service. I express my deep love and appreciation to the parents of this child, who join me in praying that God might see fit to use the testimony of their child's life, and the future life of this sermon, to bring others to embrace the real hope found only in the gospel of Jesus Christ."

over them like a flood, and any hope for hope itself is lost. Others continue to hope that something good might still come out of this tragedy, even though they have no solid ground for hope at all. Quite frankly, theirs is a false hope, which is a kind of hope that is really worse than having no hope at all.

But is there ground for *real* hope? What reasons can be given to anchor real hope at a time such as this? Well, I know of no better way of finding out whether we have solid grounding for the hope that is in us than to look at the Bible. The Scriptures form the worldview—the vantage point, if you will—from which the Christian examines *all* of life—in its good times and in its bad. And when we come to the Bible, what do we find? Does it say anything about hope? And if so, does it provide us with any reason for real hope in the midst of this seemingly senseless tragedy?

The Counterfeits of Real Hope

The Bible has much to say about the ground for true hope, but to get at it, we must first be careful to avoid some very common pitfalls. To begin, we must distinguish between wishing, faith, and hope. Many confuse those three and regard them as the same. But that is wrong. Wishing is one thing, faith another, and hope yet a third.

Wishing is a thing of chance—in other words, something wholly fortuitous—which is a concept that is completely foreign to the Bible. Rather, at all points, the Bible presents a God who is in full control, so that even events that appear random and meaningless remain under his sovereign direction. For example, in Proverbs 16:33 we read: "The lot is cast into the lap, but its *every* decision is from the LORD." So let us set wishing aside. I'm not talking about wishing this afternoon; I'm talking about hope—a concept about which, by contrast, the Bible has *much* to say.

Neither should we confuse faith with hope. While closely related, they are distinct. Someone has said that faith *works* and trusts, while hope *waits* and trusts. In other words, faith acts in the present based upon what we know to be true, while hope expects for the future based upon what we know to be true. Faith labors in the light; hope sings in the darkness, even when all seems most bleak and desperate. Though the circumstances of life draw around one as a cloak of midnight black, still hope sings and heralds a new and glorious morning.

Now, a trusting faith produces a confident hope, and therefore it should be obvious that you can't have real hope if you don't have true faith. And this is the condition of some. Lacking faith in anything, they lack hope in everything. And when all hope in this life has been lost, discouragement and despair follow close behind. When there is no hope—in this life or the next—some see no reason to press on. To their minds, life is meaningless and futile, signifying nothing.

I rather doubt there is anyone listening to me today who has no hope at all. Given that you are here, I rather suspect that you are trying to make sense of things, and such a disposition exists only in those who are holding out hope. If you are attentively listening to me today, you have hope; so the only question that remains is whether you are holding on to a false hope or a true hope.

If you are holding on to false hope in this life, I would suggest that you are actually worse off than the one who has no hope at all, for at least the one who has no hope may one day come to the realization that he needs what he lacks and be motivated to seek a hope worth having. But if you embrace false hope, you are more likely to remain as you are. And that is sad, for false hope is always grounded in something other than truth.

For some, their hope in both this life and the life to come is based on their church membership. "I joined the church twenty years ago," one will say. "I attend faithfully, give generously, and even invite my friends to come along with me so that they may find a comfort and peace that will lead them to hope too." But, my friend, church membership assures you of nothing in light of eternity. Nowhere does the Bible say that you must join a local church to be made acceptable before God. And, to be sure, there are many who belong to churches but know nothing of the grace of God in the gospel of Jesus Christ. If you are resting in a hope that is built upon your church membership, you may be quite sure that yours is a false hope.

Others base their hope on their own goodness and believe that when this life is through, their good intentions and works will earn them favor with God. "Just look at me," some insist. "Am I not better than many? Am I not more honest, more compassionate, more loving, more giving, more tender, more concerned, more generous than most? Surely I am living a moral life that will commend me to God when my time before him comes." But again, my friend, good intentions and works, as wonderful as they may be, assure you of nothing in light of eternity. The Bible states that God's only acceptable standard is perfection, not goodness, and further states that no one is perfect—no one is righteous—save Jesus Christ alone. My friend, if you are pointing to your good character or reputation, your praiseworthy deeds or intentions, you may be quite sure that yours is a false hope.

Others base their hope on their assumption of who God is and what he is like. They are often heard saying something like this: "God is loving and merciful, is he not? And given that he is loving and merciful, I believe that things will come out all right in the end for me." But, my friend, the same God who is loving and merciful is also just and honest, and he has said throughout Scripture that he will not pardon the guilty. If you believe him to be loving and merciful, would you also take him at his word that he will not do what he said he cannot do? If you presume that God will pardon you because he is loving and merciful, you may be quite sure that yours is a false hope.

Still others base their hope on their feelings. With a cool shrug, they say, "I just feel that all will work out well, both now and in the future." But of what assurance is that? What confidence can you have in either this life or the next if your convictions are pinned to that which can change? If you are of the impression that when everything is said and done all will turn out just fine, you are merely whistling in the dark and may be quite sure that yours is a false hope.

These are all examples of false hope—counterfeit hope—which is really worse than having no hope at all. And if your hope is false, it is best to find out today, for you do not know whether this day may be your last. _____ did not know that last Saturday would be her last on this earth. And you have no assurance that you will see the setting of the sun tonight. So be very sure that you don't have a false hope. Make very sure that your hope is grounded in the truth.

The Character of Real Hope

You may be wondering, "How can I know whether mine is a false hope?" Well, here is a test that I think that we can each apply to ourselves: Does your sense of hope change with your circumstances? Are you here today with doubts and discouragement that you did not have a week ago? Has this tragedy shaken your confidence? Then you may have a false hope.

My friend, you can have real hope—a hope that is built on a solid foundation—a foundation that cannot be swept away. The storm clouds of life's circumstances can gather, the rains of disappointment can pound, the hail of discouragement can punish, and the winds of despair can howl, and your hope can remain sure because it is built upon the right foundation.

Nothing but Jesus Christ will do. A hope built on any other foundation is built on shifting sand and will not stand the test of time or trial in either this life or the next. Only Jesus Christ will do. Anything else is a false hope propped up by self-delusions. Anything else will wither and be swept away by either the disappointments of this life or the judgment of the next. Only Jesus Christ will do. Without Christ, the foundation for your life is good for nothing. Without Christ, all is lost. Without Christ, all hope is lost.

Listen to what God himself says, as recorded in Isaiah 28:16: "Therefore, thus says the Lord God, 'Behold, I am the one who has laid as a foundation in Zion, a stone, a tested stone, a precious cornerstone, of a sure foundation.'" And what is this tested, precious cornerstone that lays the sure foundation for real hope? Listen to what the apostle Peter said in Acts 4:11: "This Jesus is the stone that was rejected by you, the builders, which has become the cornerstone." The apostle Paul said something similar in Ephesians 2:20: ". . . Christ Jesus himself being the cornerstone." And then listen to what Peter said just after stating that Jesus Christ is the cornerstone: "And there is salvation in no one else, for there is no other name under heaven given among men by which we must be saved" (Acts 4:12).

You may belong to a wonderful church, but that's an inadequate foundation. You may have built up a very good character, but that foundation will not stand. You may have good feelings about God or yourself, and you may cross your fingers and hope that everything will just turn out all right, but that will not do.

There is only one foundation upon which true hope stands. Only one foundation will withstand the storms and tragedies of life. Only one foundation will not be swept away when all is said and done. Only one foundation is acceptable to God—having been given by him, tested by him, proven by him, and found precious and sure: it is Jesus Christ. *Nothing* but Jesus Christ will do!

The Confidence of Real Hope

Let me ask you, suppose death should come and place his icy hand upon your shoulder this afternoon, as it did _____ a week ago, and say to you, "It is time to go," and usher you into the presence of God—would you be ready to meet your Maker? That's the real issue before us today, isn't it? How would you answer?

"Well, I'll deal with that another day," some may be thinking. But, you see, you do not know that you have another day—_____ didn't. And we must be ready every day for what may happen any day. So again I ask, "Are you ready to meet God this very moment?"

If you say, "I hope so," please know that is not a good answer, for your hope reveals itself to be actually nothing more than a wish, and, remember, a wish has no surety. We're not talking about wishing, we're talking about hope—a settled confidence, a quiet assurance—that something is so. When the Bible speaks of real hope, it leaves no room for doubt.

If you were to ask me if I am a man, I would not reply, "I hope so." If you were to ask me if I am married, you would think me highly odd if I said, "I hope so." If you were to ask me if I am a father, the answer, "I hope so," would not do. Similarly, if I were to ask you if you are a Christian and ready to meet almighty God, you cannot say, "I hope so." That's a statement of wishing, not fact, and it reveals that the foundation for your hope is not sure. By contrast, the Bible speaks of hope as the disposition that confidently rests on and waits in the moment for a future reality as though it had already come to pass.

I recall watching a recording of a football game after I had been told the final score. While the team for which I was rooting was down by a significant margin at the half and all would have normally seemed bleak, I sensed no anxiety at all, for I already knew the outcome of the game. I watched with absolute confidence, completely assured that what seemed improbable in the moment would eventually occur. Such is the character of real hope. Such is the hope that the Bible holds out for you this day. Such is the hope that belongs to all who have placed their full trust in the accomplished work of Jesus Christ at Calvary.

Hope is the word that the Bible uses most often in connection with either the Christian's hope of the resurrection or the return of our Lord Jesus Christ. There is no doubt that those who have died in Christ will be made alive again in him. There is no doubt that those bodies that have died in weakness will be raised with power. There is no doubt that the graves of every cemetery will burst open and that the dead in Christ shall rise first. There is no doubt that those who have built their hope on the solid foundation of Jesus Christ shall see _____ again! There is no doubt!

Real hope holds fast at all times and in all circumstances. It holds fast in the midst of confusion. It holds fast in times of trial. It holds fast when disappointments buffet and discouragements assail. And it holds fast in this very hour when we will lay _____'s body in the grave, for we have hope that her body will come back again. We lay _____ down with a sure hope, a sound hope, a precious hope, a blessed hope, a glorious hope. We lay her down with real hope!

So is there a reason for the hope that is in me? Oh, yes! And it is *real* hope.

The Call of Real Hope

In John 5:24, Jesus is recorded as saying: "Truly, truly, I say to you, whoever hears my word and believes him who sent me has eternal life.

He does not come into judgment, but has passed from death to life." And what is the "word" that Jesus would have us hear? It is that he is the very Son of God come in human flesh. And that he lived a sinless life and died on a cross to pay the penalty for your sin and mine. And that he was raised again from the grave, thereby triumphing over both sin and its consequence, death. And that if you acknowledge your sin and your need for him, ask God to forgive you, turn from your sinful ways, and place your faith in Christ as your Savior, Lord, and King, then, like _____, the sting of death will be removed, and you will have hope—true hope; real hope; the sure hope of life everlasting in God's glorious presence.

John 1:11–12 says: "He came to his own, and his own people did not receive him. But to all who did receive him, who believed in his name, he gave the right to become children of God." My friend, the full confidence and absolute surety of hope is yours, if you accept the foundation that God has provided in the person and accomplished work of his Son, Jesus Christ.

Don't hope in your church affiliation, in having a good reputation or sterling character, in an appeal to the love or goodness of God, or in the subjectivity of your feelings. Real hope is found only in a personal relationship with Jesus Christ—the tested, precious, and sure foundation.

If you turn from sin and believe this good news, you will become a child of God and will have a confident hope. This good news lay at the foundation of _____'s hope. And this is why I can declare to you this day, with full confidence, that *she* is not dead, only her body is dead. _____ has never been more alive than she is at this very moment. Hers is a realized hope.

God gave all that he had when he gave his Son, and he wants us to accept his gracious gift of salvation. _____ did. _____ had laid hold of that marvelous gift, and it established the foundation of her sure hope of forgiveness of sin and everlasting life in the very presence of God.

What about you? Will you trust God and receive, through faith and repentance, that which he has so graciously provided for you? Let not anyone here leave this place with fingers crossed. Rather, seize the assurance of forgiveness and salvation, and allow God to give you a sure foundation for your hope—a *real* hope that will never fail and that will never end.

SAMPLE FUNERAL REMEMBRANCES

Leslie Harris, 1924–1986 (R. Kent Hughes)

Leslie Harris was born May 21, 1924, in Glen Ridge, New Jersey, to Edward and Madeline Woodruff. Her father sold real estate and her mother was a contented homemaker.

The Woodruff home was a happy place, as her parents were kind and attentive to Leslie—their only child. She was something of a tomboy because all her friends were boys, and she referred to herself as "spoiled" because her grandparents lived next door. Whether that was true or not, it didn't have a lasting effect, as we all know. One of her cousins regarded Leslie as "perfect, but nice."

Early on, Leslie took to the piano. As a teenager, she had many healthy interests, but above all, she loved to skate. In spring and summer, she would strap skates to her shoes, skate to a nearby bridge that had a smooth macadam surface, and "cut figures." She also enjoyed tennis, spending hours hitting the ball against the garage. And, of course, she loved to sing and developed a lovely solo voice. One of the great disappointments of her young life came from having been elected to sing at her high school graduation, and then catching the measles. Leslie Woodruff was a charming, spirited girl who brimmed with enthusiasm—the operative word for her life.

During these years, her brushes with church didn't interest her very much. However, her grade school principal, Miss Reeves, who was a Christian and read from a large Bible to the entire assembly of students, left such an impression on Leslie that she persuaded her father to buy her an inexpensive edition.

When Leslie was fifteen years old, her context changed radically. Her father died of a brain tumor in 1939, and a year later, her mother died of cancer. Her loving grandfather, Joe, became her guardian. But the year of her parents' deaths also brought some great things into Leslie's life. On August 19, 1940, she went roller skating accompanied by her ailing mother, and Franklin Harris asked the tiny brunette if she would skate the "couples-only waltz" with him. Franklin was impressed with Leslie. Not only was she a great skater, but her energy and love for life magnetized him. Franklin also skated with her mother, because she too wanted to skate. Two weeks later, Leslie's indomitable mother passed away. Franklin remarks that four months ago, when Leslie was told by her doctors that she had about three months to live, they went ice skating, And as they skated, they remembered her mother's dedication to Leslie when she skated with her daughter just before her death.

Franklin and Leslie did a good deal of courting on skates, with obligatory stops at Stubb's Ice Cream Parlor for a double dish of chocolate ice cream and orange ice. Franklin was busy studying engineering, so they would often study together and then go skating to relax. Oh, could they skate!

Leslie was not yet a Christian. Their long walks together, such as the one to Eagle Rock, from which they could view New York City, afforded time to discuss important things. Leslie attended church with Franklin and was fascinated as Pastor McNiele preached from the Old Testament. Franklin prayed for her and, on one occasion, sang for her all the verses of "I Have a Savior, He's Pleading in Glory." Leslie came to Christ when the pastor preached on the Passover. As Franklin remembers her at that time, she was energetic, enthusiastic, fragile, prudent, and in love with Jesus!

They were married on May 29, 1943, in her home on Woodlawn Avenue. Franklin was in the Navy and stationed in Washington, DC, so he was in uniform. Leslie found a statuette of a Navy enlisted man to top the cake.

Soon they bought a large old farmhouse on twelve acres about ten miles south of Washington. Franklin continued his career with the Navy Research Lab as a civilian (1942–1974), and they began a family. They wanted a dozen children, but four proved enough: Kathy in 1944, Bob in 1945, Jean in 1947, and John in 1948. Later came their adopted daughter Debby. Leslie was busy with the four children, hauling water to the house from the hand pump in the front yard, supplying coal to the furnace, and heating water. Ultimately, Franklin designed and built a water heater.

As their children tell it, the spiritual atmosphere of the house was wonderful. Every morning, Leslie played the piano with enthusiasm. She and Franklin would wake the children for prayers, a Bible reading, and singing. As they grew older, it took place after dinner, when Leslie would relax at the piano. Of course, there was church, especially Sunday evening, with two pianos (Leslie at one). They were led by John Wittinger, solo trombone for the Navy Band, and accompanied by various other musicians from the Naval School of Music.

Leslie was nicknamed "The Bible Club Lady" because she taught Child Evangelism Fellowship "Good News" Clubs for twenty-five years—on Thursday, grades one through three, and on Friday, grades four through six. She served as school secretary for a time and president of the PTA.

Leslie Harris loved her family and was a lover of Christ—that is the consistent testimony of her children. When Leslie learned that she had only three months to live, her faith did not waver. She accepted her situation from the beginning, believing that God could heal her if he pleased, but if not, "so be it." She repeatedly sang the words, "It is well with my soul."

Her last weeks were remarkable. On Christmas Sunday, she sang in the choir for the last time, and it concluded with the "Hallelujah Chorus." On her last Sunday, she held court after the service, saying her good-byes. This last week, she was reasonably comfortable, and on Wednesday morning, January 29, at 7:05 a.m., Leslie Harris saw Christ and became like him, for she saw him as he is!

Lois Griffin, 1938–2014 (Todd Wilson)

Lois Grace (Watts) Griffin was born in Pasadena, California, in 1938, the middle child of five. She graduated from Pasadena High School and then Pasadena City College. During those years, she marched in the Rose Parade seven times as a member of the Tournament of Roses Band, playing clarinet. She also began many years of receiving piano instruction at that time. In the late years of her life, she also learned to play the saxophone (using her brother's sax that he had used in the Marine Band during the Korean War) and also the recorder.

As a child, she came to know Jesus Christ as her personal Savior at Forest Home Bible Camp, where she later served as a counselor numerous times; she also counseled at Verdugo Pines Bible Camp. Both camps are in Southern California. In later years, she also counseled at Lake Geneva Youth Camp (in southern Wisconsin), as well as at Lake Helen Bible Camp (in far northern Wisconsin), where she also taught archery.

Lois began her studies at Moody Bible Institute (MBI) in January 1964, graduating with a B.A. in Bible theology in 1967, the first graduating class to receive a degree from MBI. It was during that time that she met Ted Griffin, who a few years later became her husband.

Lois and Ted were married on April 26, 1969, after a growing relationship developed mainly through long-distance letter writing while Ted served on a missions team in the Philippines for two years and then served in the U.S. Army. As they sought God's will for them during that time, breaking up several times along the way, they encouraged each other many times with Proverbs 3:5–6: "Trust in the LORD with all thine heart; and lean not unto thine own understanding. In all thy ways acknowledge him, and he shall direct thy paths" (KJV).

A few months after their wedding, Ted and Lois returned to Chicago so Ted could earn his B.A. In 1970, they lost a child due to a miscarriage, but they believed God would give them children to raise for his glory. In 1978, they adopted Charles, and then Joy in 1980. Today, Ted and Lois have six grandchildren and one great grandchild.

When their children were in school, Lois often drove many of Chuck and Joy's friends to or from school, their friendly taxi driver. She also often drove church friends to doctor's appointments, shopping, etc. She loved helping others any way she could.

Lois was very involved in various local churches for many years (Avenue 54 Gospel Chapel in Los Angeles, Woodside Bible Chapel in Maywood, Illinois, and Calvary Memorial Church in Oak Park, Illinois), especially in children's ministries (Sunday school, VBS, Awana, Pioneer Girls, Caraway Street, etc.). For several years, she directed a children's choir at Woodside Bible Chapel. She sang in choirs at Woodside Bible Chapel and at Calvary Memorial Church. She also started an orchestra at Woodside.

She played in several orchestras and bands over the years (Christian Fellowship Band, Triton Concert Band, Concordia Symphony Orchestra, Calvary Memorial Church Orchestra, Senior Suburban Orchestra), and even more so after she retired from the Metropolitan Water Reclamation District in 2004.

Lois was a talented musician (vocally and instrumentally), cook, gardener, and seamstress. She loved making special pillowcases for friends and family, designed especially for them. She loved creating and enjoying works of beauty. But most of all, she loved serving her Savior, Jesus Christ, by serving her family and the church. She made friends easily wherever she went and impacted many, many more lives than she realized.

Today we grieve because she is not with us here any longer, but we rejoice because she is now home. Her suffering and pain are over, and we can say with absolute confidence that she has never been better!

Enrichment

Poetry to Enhance
Preaching and Worship

Listed below are the full texts of some of the finest Christian poems in the English language, selected by Dr. Leland Ryken, retired professor of English at Wheaton College, author of numerous books on literature and theology, and a member of the Translation Oversight Committee for the English Standard Version. (Dr. Ryken also graciously supplied the select poems for Christmas, Good Friday, and Easter listed in chapter 2, "Annual Services," as well as the select poems for weddings in chapter 3.)

Why this selection of Christian poems in *The Pastor's Book*? Well, certainly not to promote the impression that we are well-read preachers given to poetic diction and fancy language. Rather, it is to increase our powers of expression by acquainting us with what the greatest Christian poetic minds have thought and said over the centuries on the key issues of life, thereby enhancing our powers of devotional expression. Reading these enduring masterpieces will enrich our stores of metaphor, as, for example, does George Herbert's image of "reversed thunder" as a description of the power of petitionary prayer. Likewise, aphoristic expressions, such as William Shakespeare's depiction of his soul as "the center of my sinful earth," say it perfectly for every honest soul. Poetic expressions are compact and pithy, and have a way of penetrating and detonating in the soul. Stored in the preacher's consciousness, they elevate the preaching of the Word.

This said, poetry must be carefully employed in pulpit discourse. Great poetry is often initially opaque, which means that preachers must be selective in choosing outtakes because the preaching of God's Word must be clear. Generally, the quotations must be short and readily comprehensible—

perhaps a shimmering phrase or a stanza or two, such as this stanza from Alfred, Lord Tennyson's "Strong Son of God":

> Our little systems have their day;
> They have their day and cease to be:
> They are but broken lights of thee,
> And Thou, O Lord, art more than they.

We know that God intends for you and your parishioners to understand and love poetry because at least a third of the Bible comes to us in poetic form. We suggest that you take the time to read these magnificent poems through so that you are acquainted with the best of the best, noting the lines and thoughts that particularly strike you and elevate your devotion to Christ—and that will likely prove useful in your preaching of God's holy Word.

"Aaron" (George Herbert)

> Holiness on the head,
> Light and perfections on the breast,
> Harmonious bells below, raising the dead
> To lead them unto life and rest:
> Thus are true Aarons dressed.
>
> Profaneness in my head,
> Defects and darkness in my breast,
> A noise of passions ringing me for dead
> Unto a place where is no rest:
> Poor priest, thus am I dressed.
>
> Only another head
> I have, another heart and breast,
> Another music, making live, not dead,
> Without whom I could have no rest:
> In him I am well dressed.
>
> Christ is my only head,
> My alone-only heart and breast,
> My only music, striking me even dead,
> That to the old man I may rest,
> And be in him new-dressed.
>
> So, holy in my head,
> Perfect and light in my dear breast,

My doctrine tuned by Christ (who is not dead,
But lives in me while I do rest),
Come people; Aaron's dressed.

"As Kingfishers Catch Fire" (Gerard Manley Hopkins)

As kingfishers catch fire, dragonflies draw flame;
As tumbled over rim in roundy wells
Stones ring; like each tucked string tells, each hung bell's
Bow swung finds tongue to fling out broad its name;
Each mortal thing does one thing and the same:
Deals out that being indoors each one dwells;
Selves—goes itself; *myself* it speaks and spells,
Crying *Whát I dó is me: for that I came.*

I say móre: the just man justices;
Keeps grace: thát keeps all his goings graces;
Acts in God's eye what in God's eye he is—
Chríst—for Christ plays in ten thousand places,
Lovely in limbs, and lovely in eyes not his
To the Father through the features of men's faces.

"At the Round Earth's Imagined Corners" (John Donne)

The speaker in the following poem contemplates the last judgment in light of his personal sinfulness. First he invokes the last day to happen immediately, and then he reconsiders and asks that it be delayed so he can repent.

At the round earth's imagined corners, blow
Your trumpets, angels, and arise, arise
From death, you numberless infinities
Of souls, and to your scattered bodies go;
All whom the flood did, and fire shall o'erthrow,
All whom war, dearth, age, agues, tyrannies,
Despair, law, chance hath slain, and you whose eyes
Shall behold God and never taste death's woe.
But let them sleep, Lord, and me mourn a space,
For if above all these my sins abound,
'Tis late to ask abundance of thy grace
When we are there; here on this lowly ground
Teach me how to repent; for that's as good
As if thou hadst sealed my pardon with thy blood.

"Batter My Heart" (John Donne)

Batter my heart, three-personed God, for you
As yet but knock, breathe, shine, and seek to mend;
That I may rise and stand, o'erthrow me, and bend
Your force to break, blow, burn, and make me new.
I, like an usurped town to another due,
Labor to admit you, but oh, to no end;
Reason, your viceroy in me, me should defend,
But is captived, and proves weak or untrue.
Yet dearly I love you, and would be loved fain,
But am betrothed unto your enemy;
Divorce me, untie or break that knot again,
Take me to you, imprison me, for I,
Except you enthrall me, never shall be free,
Nor ever chaste, except you ravish me.

"The Collar" (George Herbert)

I struck the board, and cried, "No more;
I will abroad!
What? shall I ever sigh and pine?
My lines and life are free, free as the road,
Loose as the wind, as large as store.
Shall I be still in suit?
Have I no harvest but a thorn
To let me blood, and not restore
What I have lost with cordial fruit?
Sure there was wine
Before my sighs did dry it; there was corn
Before my tears did drown it.
Is the year only lost to me?
Have I no bays to crown it,
No flowers, no garlands gay? All blasted?
All wasted?
Not so, my heart; but there is fruit,
And thou hast hands.
Recover all thy sigh-blown age
On double pleasures: leave thy cold dispute
Of what is fit and not. Forsake thy cage,
Thy rope of sands,
Which petty thoughts have made, and made to thee

Good cable, to enforce and draw,
And be thy law,
While thou didst wink and wouldst not see.
Away! take heed;
I will abroad.
Call in thy death's-head there; tie up thy fears;
He that forbears
To suit and serve his need
Deserves his load."
But as I raved and grew more fierce and wild
At every word,
Methought I heard one calling, *Child!*
And I replied *My Lord.*

"Crossing the Bar" (Alfred, Lord Tennyson)

Sunset and evening star,
And one clear call for me!
And may there be no moaning of the bar,
When I put out to sea,

But such a tide as moving seems asleep,
Too full for sound and foam,
When that which drew from out the boundless deep
Turns again home.

Twilight and evening bell,
And after that the dark!
And may there be no sadness of farewell,
When I embark;

For though from out our bourne of Time and Place
The flood may bear me far,
I hope to see my Pilot face to face
When I have crossed the bar.

"Death, Be Not Proud" (John Donne)

Death, be not proud, though some have called thee
Mighty and dreadful, for thou art not so;
For those whom thou thinkest thou dost overthrow
Die not, poor Death, nor yet canst thou kill me.
From rest and sleep, which but thy pictures be,

Much pleasure; then from thee much more must flow,
And soonest our best men with thee do go,
Rest of their bones, and soul's delivery.
Thou art slave to fate, chance, kings, and desperate men,
And dost with poison, war, and sickness dwell,
And poppy or charms can make us sleep as well
And better than thy stroke; why swellest thou then?
One short sleep past, we wake eternally
And death shall be no more; Death, thou shalt die.

"The Elixir" (George Herbert)

Teach me, my God and King,
In all things Thee to see,
And what I do in anything
To do it as for Thee.

Not rudely, as a beast,
To run into an action;
But still to make Thee prepossest,
And give it his perfection.

A man that looks on glass,
On it may stay his eye;
Or it he pleaseth, through it pass,
And then the heaven espy.

All may of Thee partake:
Nothing can be so mean,
Which with his tincture—"for Thy sake"—
Will not grow bright and clean.

A servant with this clause
Makes drudgery divine:
Who sweeps a room as for Thy laws,
Makes that and the action fine.

This is the famous stone
That turneth all to gold;
For that which God doth touch and own
Cannot for less be told.

"Epitaph on Himself" (Samuel Taylor Coleridge)
Stop, Christian passer-by! Stop, child of God,
And read with gentle breast. Beneath this sod
A poet lies, or that which once seemed he.
O, lift one thought in prayer for S. T. C.;
That he who many a year with toil of breath
Found death in life, may here find life in death!
Mercy for praise—to be forgiven for fame
He asked, and hoped, through Christ. Do thou the same!

"For His Wife, on Her Birthday" (Charles Wesley)
Come away to the skies.
My beloved, arise,
And rejoice in the day thou wast born;
On this festival day,
Come exulting away,
And with singing to Zion return.

We have laid up our love
And our treasure above,
Though our bodies continue below,
The redeemed of the Lord
Will remember his word,
And with singing to paradise go.

Now with singing and praise,
Let us spend all the days,
By our heavenly Father bestowed,
While his grace we receive
From his bounty, and live
To the honor and glory of God.

For the glory we were
First created to share,
Both the nature and kingdom divine!
Now created again
That our souls may remain,
Throughout time and eternity thine.

We with thanks to approve,
The design of that love
Which hath joined us to Jesus's name;

So united in heart,
Let us never more part,
Till we meet at the feast of the Lamb.

There, O! there at his feet,
We shall all likewise meet,
And be parted in body no more;
We shall sing to our lyres,
With the heavenly choirs,
And our Savior in glory adore.

Hallelujah we sing,
To our Father and King,
And his rapturous praises repeat:
To the Lamb that was slain,
Hallelujah again,
Sing, all heaven and fall at his feet.

"God's Grandeur" (Gerard Manley Hopkins)

The world is charged with the grandeur of God.
It will flame out, like shining from shook foil;
It gathers to a greatness, like the ooze of oil
Crushed. Why do men then now not reck his rod?
Generations have trod, have trod, have trod;
And all is seared with trade; bleared, smeared with toil;
And wears man's smudge and shares man's smell: the soil
Is bare now, nor can foot feel, being shod.

And for all this, nature is never spent;
There lives the dearest freshness deep down things;
And though the last lights off the black West went
Oh, morning, at the brown brink eastward, springs—
Because the Holy Ghost over the bent
World broods with warm breast and with ah! bright wings.

"The Good Shepherd" (Lope de Vega)

Shepherd! who with thine amorous, sylvan song
Hast broken the slumber that encompassed me,
Who mad'st Thy crook from the accursed tree,
On which Thy powerful arms were stretched so long!
Lead me to mercy's ever-flowing fountains;

For Thou my shepherd, guard, and guide shalt be;
I will obey Thy voice, and wait to see
Thy feet all beautiful upon the mountains.

Hear, Shepherd!—Thou who for thy flock art dying.
O, wash away these scarlet sins, for Thou
Rejoicest at the contrite sinner's vow.
Oh, wait! to Thee my weary soul is crying,
Wait for me: Yet why ask it, when I see,
With feet nailed to the cross, Thou'rt waiting still for me!
(trans. Henry W. Longfellow)

"Hark, My Soul" (John Austen)
Hark, my soul, how everything
Strives to serve our bounteous King;
Each a double tribute pays;
Sings its part, and then obeys.

Nature's chief and sweetest choir
Him with cheerful notes admire;
Chanting every day their lauds,
While the grove their song applauds.

Though their voices lower be,
Streams have too their melody;
Night and day they warbling run,
Never pause, but still sing on.

Only we can scarce afford
This short office to our Lord;
We, on whom His bounty flows,
All things gives, and nothing owes.

Wake! for shame, my sluggish heart,
Wake! and gladly sing thy part;
Learn of birds, and springs, and flowers,
How to use thy nobler powers.

Live for ever, glorious Lord,
Live, by all Thy works adored;
One in Three, and Three in One,
Thrice we bow to Thee alone.

"How Soon Hath Time" (John Milton)

How soon hath Time, the subtle thief of youth,
Stolen on his wing my three-and-twentieth year!
My hasting days fly on with full career,
But my late spring no bud or blossom showeth.
Perhaps my semblance might deceive the truth
That I to manhood am arrived so near;
And inward ripeness doth much less appear,
That some more timely-happy spirits endueth.
Yet be it less or more, or soon or slow,
It shall be still in strictest measure even
To that same lot, however mean or high,
Toward which Time leads me, and the will of Heav'n:
All is, if I have grace to use it so,
As ever in my great Task-Master's eye.

"Hymn" (Caedmon)

Written in Old English, "Caedmon's Hymn" (as it is familiarly known) is the oldest extant English poem. The version that appears below is the editor's translation.

Now we must praise the Keeper of Heaven's Kingdom,
The power of the Lord and his wisdom,
The work of the Glory-Father, when he of every wonder,
The eternal Lord, the beginning established.
He first created for the sons of earth
Heaven as a roof, Holy Creator.
Then middle-earth the Protector of mankind,
Eternal Lord, afterwards made
For men, the earth, the Lord almighty.

"I Never Saw a Moor" (Emily Dickinson)

I never saw a moor,
I never saw the sea;
Yet know I how the heather looks,
And what a wave must be.
I never spoke with God,
Nor visited in heaven;
Yet certain am I of the spot
As if the chart were given.

"The Kingdom of God" (Francis Thompson)
> O world invisible, we view thee,
> O world intangible, we touch thee,
> O world unknowable, we know thee,
> Inapprehensible, we clutch thee!
>
> Does the fish soar to find the ocean,
> The eagle plunge to find the air—
> That we ask of the stars in motion
> If they have rumor of thee there?
>
> Not where the wheeling systems darken,
> And our benumbed conceiving soars!—
> The drift of pinions, would we hearken,
> Beats at our own clay-shuttered doors.
>
> The angels keep their ancient places—
> Turn but a stone and start a wing!
> 'Tis ye, 'tis your estrangèd faces,
> That miss the many-splendored thing.
>
> But (when so sad thou canst not sadder)
> Cry—and upon thy so sore loss
> Shall shine the traffic of Jacob's ladder
> Pitched betwixt Heaven and Charing Cross.
>
> Yea, in the night, my Soul, my daughter,
> Cry—clinging to Heaven by the hems;
> And lo, Christ walking on the water,
> Not of Genesareth, but Thames!

"Lady That in the Prime of Earliest Youth" (John Milton)
> Lady that in the prime of earliest youth
> Wisely has shunned the broad way and the green,
> And with those few art eminently seen
> That labor up the hill of heavenly Truth,
> The better part with Mary and with Ruth
> Chosen thou hast, and they that overween
> And at thy growing virtues fret their spleen,
> No anger find in thee, but pity and ruth.
> Thy care is fixed and zealously attends
> To fill thy odorous lamp with deeds of light,

And hope that reaps not shame. Therefore be sure
Thou, when the Bridegroom with his feastful friends
Passes to bliss at the mid-hour of night,
Hast gained thy entrance, virgin wise and pure.

"The Lamb" (William Blake)

Little Lamb, who made thee?
Dost thou know who made thee,
Gave thee life and bid thee feed
By the stream and o'er the mead,
Gave thee clothing of delight,
Softest clothing wooly bright;
Gave thee such a tender voice,
Making all the vales rejoice?
Little Lamb, who made thee?
Dost thou know who made thee?

Little Lamb, I'll tell thee,
Little Lamb, I'll tell thee!
He is called by thy name,
For he calls himself a Lamb:
He is meek and he is mild,
He became a little child:
I a child and thou a lamb,
We are called by his name.
Little Lamb, God bless thee.
Little Lamb, God bless thee.

"Leave Me, O Love" (Sir Philip Sidney)

This poem belongs to the genre known as palinode—a poem in renunciation of romantic love. The devotional aspect of the poem emerges if we read
it as (1) a mosaic of biblical allusions and (2) a meditation on Colossians
3:2—"Set your minds on things that are above, not on things that are on
earth."

Leave me, O Love, which reachest but to dust;
And thou, my mind, aspire to higher things;
Grow rich in that which never taketh rust;
Whatever fades but fading pleasure brings.
Draw in thy beams and humble all thy might
To that sweet yoke where lasting freedoms be;

Which breaks the clouds and opens forth the light,
That both doth shine and give us sight to see.
O take fast hold; let that light be thy guide
In this small course which birth draws out to death,
And think how evil becometh him to slide,
Who seeketh heaven, and comes of heavenly breath.
Then farewell, world; thy uttermost I see:
Eternal Love, maintain thy life in me.

"Love (III)" (George Herbert)

Love bade me welcome. Yet my soul drew back
Guilty of dust and sin.
But quick-eyed Love, observing me grow slack
From my first entrance in,
Drew nearer to me, sweetly questioning,
If I lacked any thing.

A guest, I answered, worthy to be here:
Love said, You shall be he.
I the unkind, ungrateful? Ah my dear,
I cannot look on thee.
Love took my hand, and smiling did reply,
Who made the eyes but I?

Truth Lord, but I have marred them: let my shame
Go where it doth deserve.
And know you not, says Love, who bore the blame?
My dear, then I will serve.
You must sit down, says Love, and taste my meat:
So I did sit and eat.

From "The Marshes of Glynn" (Sidney Lanier)

As the marsh-hen secretly builds on the watery sod,
Behold, I will build me a nest on the greatness of God:
I will fly in the greatness of God as the marsh-hen flies
In the freedom that fills all the space 'twixt the marsh and the skies:
By so many roots as the marsh-grass sends in the sod
I will heartily lay me ahold on the greatness of God:
Oh, like to the greatness of God is the greatness within
The range of the marshes, the liberal marshes of Glynn.

"Methought I Saw My Late Espousèd Saint" (John Milton)
>Methought I saw my late espousèd saint
>Brought to me like Alcestus from the grave,
>Whom Jove's great Son to her glad husband gave,
>Rescued from Death by force though pale and faint.
>Mine as whom washed from spot of child-bed taint
>Purification in the Old Law did save,
>And such as yet once more I trust to have
>Full sight of her in heaven without restraint,
>Came vested all in white, pure as her mind:
>Her face was veiled, yet to my fancied sight
>Love, sweetness, goodness in her person shined
>So clear as in no face with more delight.
>But O, as to embrace me she inclined,
>I waked, she fled, and day brought back my night.

"My Song Is Love Unknown" (Samuel Crossman)
>My song is love unknown,
>My Savior's love to me;
>Love to the loveless shown,
>That they might lovely be.
>O who am I,
>That for my sake
>My Lord should take
>Frail flesh and die?

>He came from His blest throne
>Salvation to bestow;
>But men made strange, and none
>The longed-for Christ would know:
>But O! my Friend,
>My Friend indeed,
>Who at my need
>His life did spend.

>Sometimes they strew His way,
>And His sweet praises sing,
>Resounding all the day
>Hosannas to their King.
>Then "Crucify!"
>Is all their breath,

And for His death
They thirst and cry.

Why, what hath my Lord done?
What makes this rage and spite?
He made the lame to run,
He gave the blind their sight,
Sweet injuries!
Yet they at these
Themselves displease,
And 'gainst Him rise.

They rise and needs will have
My dear Lord made away;
A murderer they save,
The Prince of life they slay.
Yet cheerful
He to suffering goes,
That He His foes
From thence might free.

Here might I stay and sing,
No story so divine;
Never was love, dear King!
Never was grief like Thine.
This is my Friend,
In Whose sweet praise
I all my days
Could gladly spend.

"None Other Lamb" (Christina Rossetti)
None other Lamb, none other Name,
None other hope in heaven or earth or sea,
None other hiding place from guilt and shame,
None beside thee!
My faith burns low, my hope burns low;
Only my heart's desire cries out in me
By the deep thunder of its want and woe,
Cries out to thee.
Lord, thou art Life, though I be dead;
Love's fire thou art, however cold I be:

Nor heaven have I, nor place to lay my head,
Nor home, but thee.

"O Deus, ego amo te" (Gerard Manley Hopkins)
O God, I love thee, I love thee—
Not out of hope of heaven for me
Nor fearing not to love and be
In the everlasting burning.
Thou, thou, my Jesus, after me
Didst reach thine arms out dying,
For my sake sufferedst nails, and lance,
Mocked and marred countenance,
Sorrows passing number,
Sweat and care and cumber,
Yea and death, and this for me,
And thou couldst see me sinning:
Then I, why should I not love thee,
Jesu, so much in love with me?
Not for heaven's sake;
Not to be out of hell by loving thee;
Not for any gains I see;
But just the way that thou didst me
I do love and I will love thee:
What must I love thee, Lord, for then?
For being my king and God. Amen.
(trans. Francis Xavier)

"O What Their Joy" (Peter Abelard)
O what their joy and their glory must be,
Those endless Sabbaths the blessèd ones see;
Crown for the valiant, to weary ones rest:
God shall be All, and in all ever blest.
What are the Monarch, his court and his throne?
What are the peace and the joy that they own?
O that the blest ones, who in it have share,
All that they feel could as fully declare!
Truly, "Jerusalem" name we that shore,
City of peace that brings joy evermore;
Wish and fulfillment are not severed there,
Nor do things prayed for come short of the prayer.

There, where no troubles distraction can bring,
We the sweet anthems of Zion shall sing;
While for thy grace, Lord, their voices of praise
Thy blessed people eternally raise.
Now, in the meantime, with hearts raised on high,
We for that country must yearn and must sigh,
Seeking Jerusalem, dear native land,
Through our long exile on Babylon's strand.
Low before him with our praises we fall,
Of whom and in whom and through whom are all;
Of whom, the Father; and in whom, the Son;
And through whom, the Spirit, with them ever One.
(trans. John Mason Neale)

From "Ode on the Death of Mrs. Anne Killegrew" (John Dryden)

John Dryden's ten-stanza poem is a panegyric and eulogy for musician Anne Killegrew. In the last stanza, Dryden's imagination soars above the occasion of the poem as he takes us to the last day and final judgment.

When in mid-air, the golden trump shall sound,
To raise the nations under ground;
When in the valley of Jehosophat,
The Judging God shall close the book of fate,
And there the last Assizes keep,
For those who wake, and those who sleep;
When rattling bones together fly,
From the four corners of the sky,
When sinews o'er the skeletons are spread,
Those clothed with flesh, and life inspires the dead;
The sacred poets first shall hear the sound,
And foremost from the tomb shall bound:
For they are covered with the lightest ground,
And straight, with in-born vigor, on the wing,
Like mounting larks, to the new morning sing.
There thou, sweet saint, before the choir shall go,
As harbinger of Heaven, the way to show,
The way which thou so well hast learned below.

From "On Another's Sorrow" (William Blake)

He doth give His joy to all:
He becomes an infant small,

He becomes a man of woe,
He doth feel the sorrow too.
Think not thou can sigh a sigh,
And thy Maker is not by:
Think not thou canst weep a tear,
And thy Maker is not near.
O He gives to us his joy,
That our grief He may destroy:
Till our grief is fled and gone
He doth sit by us and moan.

"On Time" (John Milton)

Fly envious Time, till thou run out thy race,
Call on the lazy leaden-stepping hours,
Whose speed is but the heavy Plummet's pace;
And glut thy self with what thy womb devours,
Which is no more then what is false and vain,
And merely mortal dross;
So little is our loss,
So little is thy gain.
For when as each thing bad thou hast entombed,
And last of all, thy greedy self consumed
Then long Eternity shall greet our bliss
With an individual kiss;
And Joy shall overtake us as a flood,
When every thing that is sincerely good
And perfectly divine,
With Truth, and Peace, and Love shall ever shine
About the supreme Throne
Of him, to whose happy-making sight alone,
When once our heavenly-guided soul shall clime,
Then all this Earthy grossness quit,
Attired with Stars, we shall for ever sit,
Triumphing over Death, and Chance, and thee O Time.

From *Paradise Lost*, Book 12 (John Milton)

The following passage appears just before the conclusion of Milton's grand epic. The context is that Adam has received a vision of fallen history, ending with the atoning death of Jesus. Adam's response is the moment of epiphany toward which the whole poem moves.

Henceforth I learn, that to obey is best,
And love with fear the only God; to walk
As in his presence, ever to observe
His providence, and on him sole depend,
Merciful over all his works, with good
Still overcoming evil, and by small
Accomplishing great things, by things deemed weak
Subverting worldly strong, and worldly wise
By simply meek; that suffering for truth's sake
Is fortitude to highest victory,
And, to the faithful, death the gate of life;
Taught this by his example, whom I now
Acknowledge my Redeemer ever blest.

"Peace" (Henry Vaughan)

My Soul, there is a country
Far beyond the stars,
Where stands a wingéd sentry
All skillful in the wars;
There, above noise and danger
Sweet Peace sits, crowned with smiles,
And One born in a manger
Commands the beauteous files.
He is thy gracious friend
And (O my Soul awake!)
Did in pure love descend,
To die here for thy sake.
If thou canst get but thither,
There grows the flower of peace,
The rose that cannot wither,
Thy fortress, and thy ease.
Leave then thy foolish ranges,
For none can thee secure,
But One, who never changes,
Thy God, thy life, thy cure.

"Pied Beauty" (Gerard Manley Hopkins)

Glory be to God for dappled things—
For skies of couple-color as a brinded cow;
For rose-moles all in stipple upon trout that swim;

Fresh-firecoal chestnut-falls; finches' wings;
Landscape plotted and pieced—fold, fallow, and plough;
And áll trádes, their gear and tackle and trim.
All things counter, original, spare, strange;
Whatever is fickle, freckled (who knows how?)
With swift, slow; sweet, sour; adazzle, dim;
He fathers-forth whose beauty is past change:
Praise him.

"Prayer" (George Herbert)

Prayer, the church's banquet, angel's age,
God's breath in man returning to his birth,
The soul in paraphrase, heart in pilgrimage,
The Christian plummet sounding heaven and earth;
Engine against the Almighty, sinner's tower,
Reversed thunder, Christ-side-piercing spear,
The six-days world transposing in an hour,
A kind of tune, which all things hear and fear;
Softness, and peace, and joy, and love, and bliss,
Exalted manna, gladness of the best;
Heaven in ordinary, man well dressed;
The milky way, the bird of Paradise;
Church-bells beyond the stars heard, the soul's blood,
The land of spices; something understood.

"The Pulley" (George Herbert)

When God at first made man,
Having a glass of blessings standing by,
"Let us," said he, "pour on him all we can.
Let the world's riches, which dispersèd lie,
Contract into a span."
So strength first made a way;
Then beauty flowed, then wisdom, honor, pleasure.
When almost all was out, God made a stay,
Perceiving that, alone of all his treasure,
Rest in the bottom lay.
"For if I should," said he,
"Bestow this jewel also on my creature,
He would adore my gifts instead of me,
And rest in Nature, not the God of Nature;

So both should losers be.
"Yet let him keep the rest,
But keep them with repining restlessness;
Let him be rich and weary, that at least,
If goodness lead him not, yet weariness
May toss him to my breast."

"The Quality of Mercy" (from *The Merchant of Venice*)
(William Shakespeare)

> The quality of mercy is not strained,
> It droppeth as the gentle rain from heaven
> Upon the place beneath; it is twice blest:
> It blesseth him that gives and him that takes;
> 'Tis mightiest in the mightiest; it becomes
> The thronéd monarch better than his crown;
> His scepter shows the force of temporal power,
> The attribute to awe and majesty,
> Wherein doth sit the dread and fear of kings;
> But mercy is above this sceptered sway;
> It is enthroned in the hearts of kings,
> It is an attribute to God himself;
> And earthly power doth then show likest God's
> When mercy seasons justice.

"Sonnet 14, On the Religious Memory of Mrs. Catherine Thomson,
My Christian Friend, Deceased Dec. 16, 1646" (John Milton)

> When Faith and Love, which parted from thee never,
> Had ripened thy just soul to dwell with God,
> Meekly thou didst resign this earthy load
> Of death, called life, which us from life doth sever.
> Thy works and alms and all thy good endeavor
> Stayed not behind, nor in the grave were trod,
> But as Faith pointed with her golden rod,
> Followed up to joy and bliss for ever.
> Love led them on, and Faith who knew them best,
> Thy hand maids, clad them o'er with purple beams
> And azure wings, that up they flew so dressed,
> And spake the truth of thee in glorious themes
> Before the Judge, who thenceforth bid thee rest
> And drink thy fill of pure immortal streams.

"Sonnet 146" (William Shakespeare)

The Middle Ages produced a religious and literary tradition known by the Latin phrase *contemptus mundi*—"contempt of the world." Poems in this tradition elevate the heavenly and spiritual over the earthly and physical. The following sonnet by Shakespeare belongs to this tradition (as does "Leave Me, O Love" by Philip Sidney, cited above).

> Poor soul, the center of my sinful earth,
> [Foiled by] these rebel powers that thee array,
> Why dost thou pine within, and suffer dearth,
> Painting thy outward walls so costly gay?
> Why so large cost, having so short a lease,
> Dost thou upon thy fading mansion spend?
> Shall worms, inheritors of this excess,
> Eat up thy charge? is this thy body's end?
> Then soul, live thou upon thy servant's loss,
> And let that pine to aggravate thy store;
> Buy terms divine in selling hours of dross;
> Within be fed, without be rich no more:
> So shalt thou feed on Death, that feeds on men,
> And, Death once dead, there's no more dying then.

"Spring" (Gerard Manley Hopkins)

> Nothing is so beautiful as Spring—
> When weeds, in wheels, shoot long and lovely and lush;
> Thrush's eggs look little low heavens, and thrush
> Through the echoing timber does so rinse and wring
> The ear, it strikes like lightnings to hear him sing;
> The glassy pear tree leaves and blooms, they brush
> The descending blue; that blue is all in a rush
> With richness; the racing lambs too have fair their fling.
> What is all this juice and all this joy?
> A strain of the earth's sweet being in the beginning
> In Eden garden.—Have, get, before it cloy,
> Before it cloud, Christ, lord, and sour with sinning,
> Innocent mind and Mayday in girl and boy,
> Most, O maid's child, thy choice and worthy the winning.

"The Starlight Night" (Gerard Manley Hopkins)

> Look at the stars! look, look up at the skies!
> O look at all the fire-folk sitting in the air!

The bright boroughs, the circle-citadels there!
Down in dim woods the diamond delves! the elves'-eyes!
The grey lawns cold where gold, where quickgold lies!
Wind-beat whitebeam! airy abeles set on a flare!
Flake-doves sent floating forth at a farmyard scare!
Ah well! it is all a purchase, all is a prize.
Buy then! bid then!—What?—Prayer, patience, alms, vows.
Look, look: a May-mess, like on orchard boughs!
Look! March-bloom, like on mealed-with-yellow sallows!
These are indeed the barn; withindoors house
The shocks. This piece-bright paling shuts the spouse
Christ home, Christ and his mother and all his hallows.

"Strong Son of God" (Alfred, Lord Tennyson)

Strong Son of God, immortal Love,
Whom we, that have not seen thy face,
By faith, and faith alone, embrace,
Believing where we cannot prove;

Thine are these orbs of light and shade;
Thou madest Life in man and brute;
Thou madest Death; and lo, thy foot
Is on the skull which thou hast made.

Thou wilt not leave us in the dust:
Thou madest man, he knows not why,
He thinks he was not made to die;
And thou hast made him: thou art just.

Thou seemest human and divine,
The highest, holiest manhood, thou.
Our wills are ours, we know not how,
Our wills are ours, to make them thine.

Our little systems have their day;
They have their day and cease to be:
They are but broken lights of thee,
And thou, O Lord, art more than they.

We have but faith: we cannot know;
For knowledge is of things we see;

And yet we trust it comes from thee,
A beam in darkness: let it grow.

Let knowledge grow from more to more,
But more of reverence in us dwell;
That mind and soul, according well,
May make one music as before,

But vaster. We are fools and slight;
We mock thee when we do not fear:
But help thy foolish ones to bear;
Help thy vain worlds to bear thy light.

Forgive what seemed my sin in me,
What seemed my worth since I began;
For merit lives from man to man,
And not from man, O Lord, to thee.

Forgive my grief for one removed,
Thy creature, whom I found so fair.
I trust he lives in thee, and there
I find him worthier to be loved.

Forgive these wild and wandering cries,
Confusions of a wasted youth;
Forgive them where they fail in truth,
And in thy wisdom make me wise.

"Up-Hill" (Christina Rossetti)

The following poem has been interpreted in a variety of ways. It becomes
a devotional poem on the hope of heaven if we read the questions in each
stanza as expressing the weariness that we feel on the journey of life and the
answers to the questions (perhaps even spoken by Christ) as affirming the
reality of heaven.

Does the road wind up-hill all the way?
Yes, to the very end.
Will the day's journey take the whole long day?
From morn to night, my friend.

But is there for the night a resting-place?
A roof for when the slow dark hours begin.

May not the darkness hide it from my face?
You cannot miss that inn.

Shall I meet other wayfarers at night?
Those who have gone before.
Then must I knock, or call when just in sight?
They will not keep you standing at that door.

Shall I find comfort, travel-sore and weak?
Of labor you shall find the sum.
Will there be beds for me and all who seek?
Yea, beds for all who come.

"Virtue" (George Herbert)

Sweet day, so cool, so calm, so bright,
The bridal of the earth and sky;
The dew shall weep thy fall to-night,
For thou must die.

Sweet rose, whose hue angry and brave
Bids the rash gazer wipe his eye;
Thy root is ever in its grave,
And thou must die.

Sweet spring, full of sweet days and roses,
A box where sweets compacted lie;
My music shows ye have your closes,
And all must die.

Only a sweet and virtuous soul,
Like seasoned timber, never gives;
But though the whole world turn to coal,
Then chiefly lives.

"When I Consider How My Light Is Spent" (John Milton)

When I consider how my light is spent,
Ere half my days, in this dark world and wide,
And that one Talent which is death to hide
Lodged with me useless, though my Soul more bent
To serve therewith my Maker, and present
My true account, lest he returning chide;
"Doth God exact day-labor, light denied?"

I fondly ask. But patience, to prevent
That murmur, soon replies, "God doth not need
Either man's work or his own gifts; who best
Bear his mild yoke, they serve him best. His state
Is Kingly. Thousands at his bidding speed
And post o'er Land and Ocean without rest:
They also serve who only stand and wait."

Also see selections from the following works by T. S. Eliot:
"Little Gidding"
"The Rock"
Murder in the Cathedral

PART 2

PARTS OF THE
WORSHIP SERVICE

5

Public Prayers

Public prayers are an important part of church services and the ministry of the gospel.

However, in his book *A Better Way: Rediscovering the Drama of God-Centered Worship*, Michael Horton makes a telling observation:

> One of the most disappointing features of contemporary worship is the absence of prayer, and one suspects that few of the youth in evangelical or mainline churches today even know the Lord's Prayer, which covenant children have prayed—and used as a model for their prayers—for two thousand years. If corporate prayer does not play an important part in our worship, it should not be surprising that it is marginalized in the individual lives of Christians.[1]

Certainly Horton is right, and in the broader contexts of evangelicalism, doubly so. Today it is not uncommon for there to be no pastoral/congregational prayer amidst the flow of contemporary worship, with no worship leader opening in prayer, no prayer at the offering, and no pastor praying that God will bless his message. It seems that prayer is regarded as something that interferes with the movement of worship. Other times, the congregational prayer, such as it is, is an existential stream of consciousness inspired by the singing that preceded it amidst equally existential riffs on the acoustic guitar. A caricature? Yes, but one that is based on an actual Sunday morning service that happened in time and space. This said, most Sunday services are not so overtly prayerless.

Likewise, most or certainly many extemporaneous prayers are beautiful and edifying. But often they are not. There are the "just" prayers, in which the

---

[1] Michael Horton, *A Better Way: Rediscovering the Drama of God-Centered Worship* (Grand Rapids: Baker, 2003), 156.

one praying repeats the word *just* before every clause as he considers what to say next: "Lord, we just . . . want to say that we love you and that we are just . . . sinners, but we just . . . want to be right with you, so just . . . forgive our sins . . ." The thinking behind this kind of prayer apparently is that inarticulate fumbling for what to say is a sign of a humble dependence on the Spirit rather than "just" having nothing to say. There are also the "heavenly Father" prayers, in which the title is used twenty times in two minutes, with no thought that the Father has many other appellations, such as almighty Father, loving Father, holy Father, gracious Father, merciful Father, and eternal Father—not to mention the title *God* and the dozens of other titles used for him in the Scriptures. Such praying suggests a limited knowledge of God and his Word.

Again, these are caricatures, and somewhat cranky ones. But it is God's name that is being blithely abused by mindless repetitions and pious empty fumblings. This kind of public prayer also abuses the body of Christ.

THE IMMENSE IMPORTANCE OF PUBLIC PRAYERS IN THE WORSHIP SERVICE

The conviction that informs this chapter is this: our public prayers in our corporate worship services have a massive impact on the prayer lives of God's people, in that such prayers teach the church how to approach our transcendent but immanent God. They also bring power to our churches.

OUR PUBLIC PRAYERS TEACH OUR PEOPLE HOW TO PRAY

The early Reformation worship liturgies were rich in prayer, with specific designations for the kinds of prayers included. There were prayers of:

- invocation (invoking God's care for his people and the adoration of his character);
- confession of sin;
- thanksgiving for his provision;
- petition for needs;
- intercession for others;
- illumination for the reading and preaching of the Word; and
- benediction, a good word upon all.

All of these prayers (and others for the sacraments) were included variously in the Reformers' two- to three-hour-long services on the Lord's Day. This, of course, raises the question of whether we must be denied the rich variety of prayer because our worship services are shorter. Actually, no, because the various prayers can be subsumed under as few as two headings: Invocation and Pastoral/Congregational Prayer. For example, the invocation can invoke God's presence and naturally include adoration and confession, and the pastoral prayer can include confession, thanksgiving, petition, intercession, and a prayer for illumination. Therefore, our services can instruct our people on how to pray in multidimensional richness.

Because of this, we must work on our prayers, as D. A. Carson has strongly admonished:

> **If you are in any form of spiritual leadership, work at your public prayers.** It does not matter whether the form of spiritual leadership you exercise is the teaching of a Sunday school class, pastoral ministry, small-group evangelism, or anything else: if at any point you pray in public as a leader, then work at your public prayers. . . .
>
> In brief, public praying is a pedagogical opportunity. It provides the one who is praying with an opportunity to instruct or encourage or edify all who hear the prayer. In liturgical churches, many of the prayers are well-crafted, but to some ears they lack spontaneity. In nonliturgical churches, many of the prayers are so predictable that they are scarcely any more spontaneous than written prayers, and most of them are not nearly as well-crafted. The answer to both situations is to provide more prayers that are carefully and freshly prepared.[2]

So much depends on how well pastoral leaders prepare to lead the people in prayer. If they prepare well and create a prayer-rich context, children through adults will learn how to adore God, confess sin, give thanks, petition, intercede, ask for the illumination of the Word, offer a good word of benediction, and, we may add, pray the Lord's Prayer. Prayer is more easily caught than taught.

The resources provided throughout this chapter have been carefully selected to inform and elevate the prayers under the headings of Invocations, Confessions, Pastoral/Congregational Prayers, and Benedictions.

OUR PUBLIC PRAYERS BRING POWER TO THE CHURCH

The immense importance of the corporate prayers of the body of Christ rests on Scripture's direct accounts of the power wrought by such prayers and the apostolic dependence on the prayers of the church.

---

[2] D. A. Carson, *A Call to Spiritual Reformation: Priorities from Paul and His Prayers* (Grand Rapids: Baker Academic, 1992), 34–35 (emphasis original).

The book of Acts tells us that it was after a mighty corporate prayer for boldness (Acts 4:24–30) that "the place in which they were gathered together was shaken, and they were all filled with the Holy Spirit and continued to speak the word of God with boldness" (v. 31). Acts also recounts how the church's corporate prayers brought deliverance for the imprisoned apostle Peter. The manacled apostle felt an angel tap him on the side, heard his chains rattle to the ground, and saw the iron prison gate automatically open for him (12:7–10). After Peter collected himself and went to the house of Mary, he found the church praying for him (v. 12).

The same thing happened to Pastor Zebedayo Idu, who, having been imprisoned by a Marxist dictator (who had given orders for his immediate execution), suddenly found himself free and on the street due to a "mechanical" malfunction. As he ran back to his village, he glanced into the church, where he saw his congregation united in fervent intercession for him.[3]

The apostle Paul's intimate knowledge of the power of corporate prayer prompted him to conclude his teaching on spiritual warfare with the ringing challenge for his readers to take "the sword of the Spirit, which is the word of God, praying at all times in the spirit, with all prayer and supplication . . . for all the saints" (Eph. 6:17b–18). And then, very significantly, Paul asked for the church's prayer for *himself*, adding, "And [pray] also for me, that words may be given to me in opening my mouth boldly to proclaim the mystery of the gospel" (v. 19).

There is mighty power when the church comes together for focused, corporate prayer, because when the prayers are not perfunctory but thought through, and when the people are truly engaged and praying in concert, great grace is poured out on world mission, local evangelism, national leaders, the preaching of the Word, the sanctification of God's people, and the ill and grieving.

PREPARING FOR PUBLIC PRAYER

Preparation for public prayer requires preparation of the heart and of the head. Preparation of prayers apart from the heart may result in accuracy and eloquence, but of a frigid sort. Preparation of the heart is indispensable, but apart from some thought, prayers may be pious and vacuous. Pulpit prayer requires a melding of both types of preparation.

---

[3] Kent and Barbara Hughes, *Liberating Ministry from the Success Syndrome* (Wheaton, IL: Crossway, 2008), 73–74.

SPIRITUAL PREPARATION

The public prayers of the pastor must be a reflection of his private prayer; public prayer must flow from our communion and intercession with God in secret. Congregational prayers can be theologically precise and beautiful but hollow if they are not rooted in the heart and practice of the pastor. Samuel Miller, of the old Princeton Seminary, argued in his *Thoughts on Public Prayer* that our prayers must be deeply felt and must engage the whole heart:

> When the heart is engaged, and in proportion that it is deeply and warmly engaged; when the value of spiritual things is cordially felt, and the attainment of them earnestly desired; when the soul has a heartfelt sense of its own unworthiness, and an humble, tender confidence in the Saviour's love and grace—in a word, when the whole soul is prepared to flow out in accordance with the language uttered, in faith, love, gratitude and heavenly desire;—then, and only then, will every petition, and word, and tone be, in some good degree, in happy keeping with the nature and scope of the exercise.[4]

The takeaways for those of us who are charged with leading in corporate prayer are significant:

- We must be pastors who have deep, regular, private communion with God.
- The emotion that we express in public prayer must be consonant with the feeling that we express in private prayer. We must be real.
- Apart from personal, family, and confidential matters, the things that we pray for in public must be consistent with the things we have been praying for in private. Our private prayer burdens should inform our public prayer burdens.
- We must be utterly engaged in our prayers, so that God fills our horizons, not our "audience."
- We must ask God to work in our hearts first those things that we would like worked in the hearts of our people.
- We must go "prayed up" and prepared when we stand before God's people to lead them in prayer.

PREPARING PRAYERS

When we speak of "preparing prayers," we are not referring to set prayers that are sometimes used for invocation or confession, but prayers that the pastor may compose for any part of corporate worship, including invoca-

---

[4] Samuel Miller, *Thoughts on Public Prayer* (Harrisonburg, VA: Sprinkle Publications, 1985), 262.

tions and confessions. Some advice about the use of set prayers appears at the end of this section.

First, we must understand how *not* to pray, a negative that must certainly inform the subject of preparation. Significantly, just before Jesus told his disciples how they ought to pray, giving them the example of the Lord's Prayer, he told them how they ought not to pray: "And when you pray, do not heap up empty phrases as the Gentiles do, for they think that they will be heard for their many words" (Matt. 6:7). Jesus warned against two kinds of prayers: those full of empty phrases (today's pious, vacuous jargon) and lengthy prayers (inflated by such empty jargon). This is not an argument against extemporaneous prayer, but a warning to take care as to the words and content of our prayers. This can best be done by writing out our prayers, as this personal anecdote from Douglas Wilson illustrates:

> I grew up in evangelical circles and knew the public prayer ropes. I could pray readily in public settings, particularly in church, and did so in accordance with the accepted canons for many years. When I finally began to write my prayers out before the service, I noticed something funny. I had *stopped* repeating myself. I found myself praying in new territory. In short, the previous situation had allowed me to pray predictable prayers that I had not really thought about. Composing prayers beforehand, sitting down and actually thinking through what I was going to say, brought in a whole new world of possibilities in prayer. Too many people, when they pray extemporaneously, pray in the same way they comb their hair. It is a habitual action that requires no thought.[5]

At this point, readers may think that we are down on extemporaneous prayers in public worship. We are not. If we are Spirit-filled Christians, our waking hours are filled with extemporaneous prayer, and not just before meals and meetings. As pastors, we may be called on to offer extemporaneous prayer several times a day. In this sense, extemporaneous prayer is a barometer of spiritual health. It can even be said that at times an extemporaneous prayer is the height of spiritual expression and heartfelt devotion.

We are saying that thought-through public prayers will enrich and elevate public worship and the prayer life of the congregation. In fact, preparation often provides the ground for remarkable extemporaneous prayers. And because of this, we pastors should embrace the discipline of writing out our prayers.

---

[5] Douglas Wilson, *Mother Kirk: Essays and Forays in Practical Ecclesiology* (Moscow, ID: Canon Press, 2001), 147.

Years ago, in the Princeton days of Miller, it was noted that Rev. John Gillies, a visiting Scottish preacher, prayed with remarkable pastoral grace and depth. When asked why that was, after demurring, he explained that if there was anything in his public prayer different from the prayers of others, it was due, "under God," to the fact that in the first ten years of his ministry he never wrote a sermon "without writing a prayer, in part or in whole, corresponding with it in its general strain."[6] This kind of discipline pours grace on the gathered worship of the church.

Having made the case for the discipline of writing out our prayers for public worship, we are not suggesting that those prayers be read verbatim. They can be used as "security blankets" in making sure that we pastors stay on target. They can even be reduced to suggestive outlines or their contours committed to memory. In any case, they must be internalized so that they come from the depths of our hearts with much affection. Likewise, the set prayers and prayers of confession, some of which are listed below, must never be "said," but *prayed* with the full engagement of our minds and hearts. Our people can sense the difference. And by the way, never invite your people to "say" the Lord's Prayer (the ultimate of all set prayers), but rather invite them to "pray" it: "Let us now pray the prayer that the Lord taught his disciples to pray, praying, 'Our Father . . .'"

The prayers that follow under their categorized headings are meant to be used in full or in part—for outtakes or for inspiration for writing your own prayers. Some of the prayers are ancient and others quite contemporary (written as recently as last year).

INVOCATIONS

We begin with Puritan Richard Baxter's Savoy Liturgy of 1661. It is full of deep theology and unique expressions, and is therefore a mine for excellent thoughts for composing invocations. From there, we will look at the brief, classic invocation from The Book of Common Worship, followed by invocations made from various biblical texts.

BAXTER'S SAVOY LITURGY

O eternal, almighty, and most gracious God: heaven is thy throne, and earth is thy footstool; holy and reverend is thy name. Thou art praised by the heavenly hosts, and in the congregation of thy saints on earth, and wilt be sanctified in all that come nigh unto thee. We are sinful and

---

[6] Miller, *Thoughts on Public Prayer*, 295–296.

unworthy dust; but being invited by thee, we are bold, through our blessed Mediator, to present ourselves and our supplications before thee. Receive us graciously; help us by thy Spirit: let thy fear be upon us; let thy word come to us in power, and be received in love, with attentive, reverent, and obedient minds. Make it to us a savour of life unto life. Cause us to be fervent in prayer, and joyful in thy praises, and to serve thee this day without distraction; that we may find that a day in thy courts is better than a thousand, and that it is good for us to draw near to God; through Jesus Christ our Lord and Saviour. *Amen.*[7]

THE BOOK OF COMMON WORSHIP, 1946

ALMIGHTY God, unto whom all hearts are open, all desires known, and from whom no secrets are hid: Cleanse the thoughts of our hearts by the inspiration of the Holy Spirit, that we might perfectly love Thee, and worthily magnify Thy holy name; through Jesus Christ our Lord. *Amen.*[8]

AN INVOCATION BUILT FROM A TAPESTRY OF TEXTS

Our Father in heaven, we have come to worship and bow down, and kneel before You the Lord our Maker, for You are our God, and we are the people of Your pasture, the sheep of Your hand (Ps 96:6–7).

We come to You in the name of the Lord Jesus Christ, the Lamb of God that takes away the sin of the world; He is our advocate with the Father; He is the only Mediator between God and man; He always lives to make intercession for us. Through Him we come boldly to Your throne of Grace. In His name we earnestly seek You. O Lord, our soul thirsts for You, our flesh yearns for You, in a dry and weary land where there is no water (1 Jn 2:1; 1 Tim 2:5; Heb 2:18; 7:25; Ps 63:1).

Bow Your heavens and come down. Inhabit the praises of Your people; remember Your promise, O Spirit of Christ, to be present in the midst of Your worshipping people when two or more are gathered in Your name. Condescend to us; grant us the joy of Your fellowship; speak to us through Your word; and be blessed by our prayer and adoration (Ps 22:3; 144:5; Mt 18:20); even as we pray as our Lord taught us to pray . . .[9]

---

[7] Quoted in Bard Thompson, *Liturgies of the Western Church* (Philadelphia: Fortress, 1980), 386.
[8] The Book of Common Worship (Philadelphia: The Board of Christian Education of the Presbyterian Church in the United States of America, 1946), 46.
[9] Terry L. Johnson, ed., *Leading in Worship: A Sourcebook for Presbyterian Students and Ministers Drawing from the Biblical and Historical Forms of the Reformed Tradition* (Powder Springs, GA: Tolle Lege Press, 2013), 26.

An Invocation from Several Psalms

Almighty Father, the Psalms provide us with the heart language for a proper passion for you, and so as we begin our worship we invoke the Psalms for ourselves as we pray in the first-person intimacy of these longings of the soul:

- "One thing have I asked of the LORD, that will I seek after: that I may dwell in the house of the LORD all the days of my life, to gaze upon the beauty of the LORD and to inquire in his temple" (27:4).
- "As a deer pants for flowing streams, so my soul pants for you, O God. My soul thirsts for God, for the living God" (42:1–2).
- "O God, you are my God; earnestly I seek you; my soul thirsts for you . . . as in a dry and weary land where there is no water" (63:1).
- "Whom have I in heaven but you? And there is nothing on earth that I desire besides you" (73:25).
- "How lovely is your dwelling place, O LORD of hosts! My soul longs, yes, faints for the courts of the LORD; my heart and flesh sing for joy to the living God" (84:1–2).
- "My soul waits for the Lord more than watchmen for the morning, more than watchmen for the morning" (130:6).
- "I stretch out my hands to you; my soul thirsts for you like a parched land" (143:6).

Indeed, Father, we do *pant* and *thirst* and *seek* and *desire* and *long* and *faint* for you because it is going to be so wondrous when we see your Son and become like him, for we shall see him as he is and will gaze on the beauty of the Lord and join "every creature in heaven and on earth and under the earth and in the sea, and all that is in them, saying, 'To him who sits on the throne and to the Lamb be blessing and honor and glory and might forever and ever!'" (Rev. 5:13).

So now, Father, receive our worship as we long for you and your Son and for the Holy Spirit. Amen.

An Invocation Based Partly on Genesis 2

The following invocation is based on Genesis 2:2–3 ("And on the seventh day God finished his work that he had done. . . . So God blessed the seventh day and made it holy, because on it God rested from all his work that he had done in creation") and, in part, on the Lutheran Book of Prayer:

Heavenly Father, who on this day began your work of creation, we ask that you would renew us—your new creation—in your creating and saving love. Lord Jesus, who on this day conquered death and rose from the grave, help us to die to sin and to rise to new life with you.

O Holy Spirit, who on this day came upon our Lord's disciples with power, come upon us now afresh, giving us victorious faith and humble obedience.

O blessed Trinity—Father, Son, and Spirit—our God, who cannot be contained in houses of worship made with our hands, we ask that you make your presence known among us now as we worship you. Gracious God, as we gather together this Sunday as your people, on this day of worship and rest, we pause now to lift our hearts in adoration and thanksgiving to your throne. And so with grateful hearts, we praise you for your Son, our Lord Jesus, for his life and death and resurrection, for all the work he has done on our behalf to make us sons and daughters of God. For while we have stumbled, through him you have lifted us up. And while we have sinned, through faith in him we have received full pardon and a complete and final Sabbath rest.

An Invocation Based on the *Shema*

Our mighty Savior, the words of the *Shema* echo down to us today: "Hear, O Israel: The LORD our God, the LORD is one. You shall love the LORD your God with all your heart and with all your soul and with all your might" (Deut. 6:4–5). And this, our Lord, you identified as the "great and first" commandment (Matt. 22:38). And more, you drove it home when you asked Peter three times if he loved you. Love for you, our risen Christ, is meant to fill all our horizons.

You know everything—you know the temperature of our souls. You know that as we are gathered here in worship today, we vary in our love for you, and you discern every degree. We cannot fool you. What do we need to do? We need to see your death and resurrection more clearly.

So we pray that as we, your body, greet one another, we will see your life in our brothers and sisters, and that as we praise you in hymn and song, our hearts and minds will focus upward to the cross, and that as we confess our sins, it will be with the transparency demanded by your all-knowing gaze, and that as the Word is preached, you will be exalted and love for you will rise in our souls.

Christ Jesus, we love you for dying on the cross for our sins and rising to new life for our salvation. Refresh us by that love.

In your name we pray. Amen.

An Invocation Based on Philippians 2:9–11

Our Lord Jesus, after your resurrection from the grave and ascension into heaven, God the Father highly exalted you and gave you a name that is above every name so that at your return and the judgment, every knee will bow in heaven (the knee of every angel and archangel and the saints above), and every knee will bow on earth (the knee of every believer and nonbeliever alike), and every knee will bow under the earth (the knee of every demon and Satan himself) and confess that "Jesus Christ is Lord, to the glory of God the Father."

On this Lord's Day, your day, we confess as we begin our worship that you are Jesus (the incarnate Son of God), we confess that you are the Christ (the Messiah, the yes to every promise of God), and we confess that you are the Lord, the God of both covenants.

Jesus—Christ—Lord, may we worship you this day in the fullness of your name! Amen.

CONFESSIONS

Corporate confession of sin was a primary feature in all the liturgies of the early Protestant churches. The Strassburg Liturgy of Martin Bucer, John Calvin's The Form of Church Prayers, John Knox's The Forme of Prayers, The Middleburg Liturgy of the English Puritans, The Westminster Directory for the Publique Worship of God, and The Savoy Liturgy of Baxter, the consummate pastor, were all heavily loaded with substantial corporate confession of sin.[10] The Savoy Liturgy contains a 1,500-word confession. Certainly the decline of prayer that has spread to so many churches, bringing with it the infrequency or even absence of confession, ought to concern us. More, if church is the place where Christians learn to pray, what will happen to the souls of those who neglect to confess their sins? Corporate confession of sin is of vast importance to the health of the evangelical church and the future of her children.

Before we move to examples, we must say loudly and clearly that we are not advocates of a *pro forma* weekly confession in which brain-numbed worshipers repeat a confession of sin in muffled Latinate cadences. Rather, we are advocating transparent, engaged, passionate confession by the assembled body of Christ. We believe it should never be routine. Corporate confession of sin must be varied. Sometimes there needs to be no more than a reading of a Scripture passage along with the pastoral invitation, "Let us confess our sins" (or, "Let us confess our sins, as is fitting to each of our souls"), followed by sixty seconds of silence (real silence, without musical accompaniment) in which the

---

[10] Thompson, *Liturgies of the Western Church*, 168–169, 197–198, 295–297, 322–323, 368–369, 387–391.

congregation may do so! Another time it may be done by the use of an ancient confession with a brief pastoral rubric about praying it from the heart and then praying it slowly enough for people to do it. Then, perhaps the majority of the time, there can be a prayer of confession by the pastor written by the pastor for himself and his people. This can take the form of a set confession said in unison or one prepared specifically for the service. The pastor can also decide to include this crucial component of confession as part of his pastoral prayer.

Below are several examples of early Protestant Confessions, followed by examples of three types of corporate Protestant confessions: (1) pastoral prayers of confession, (2) unison prayers of confession, and (3) responsive prayers of confession. We have also provided suggested Scripture passages to facilitate silent confession of sin.

Early Protestant Confessions

We have chosen three early Protestant confessions that are representative of the penetrating vitality of corporate confession. Note that the prayer from The Strassburg Liturgy is followed in the original by a lengthy alternative confession that works through all the Ten Commandments, confessing that the pastor and his people have broken them all. These older prayers are theologically rich and lend themselves to easy translation to modern English for theological grist for our own written confessions.

The Strassburg Liturgy, Second Alternative Confession

Almighty, eternal God and Father, we confess and acknowledge that we, alas, were conceived and born in sin, and are therefore inclined to all evil and slow to do all good; that we transgress thy holy commandments without ceasing, and evermore corrupt ourselves. But we are very sorry for the same, and beseech thy grace for help. Wherefore have mercy upon us, most gracious and merciful God and Father, through thy Son our Lord Jesus Christ. Grant to us and increase in us thy Holy Spirit, that we may recognize our sin and unrighteousness from the bottom of our hearts, attain true repentance and sorrow for them, die to them wholly, and please thee entirely by a new and godly life. Amen.[11]

John Calvin, The Form of Church Prayers

My brethren, let each of you present himself before the face of the Lord, and confess his faults and sins, following my words in his heart.

---

[11] Ibid., 168.

O Lord God, eternal and almighty Father, we confess and acknowledge unfeignedly before thy holy majesty that we are poor sinners, conceived and born in iniquity and corruption, prone to do evil, incapable of any good, and that in our depravity we transgress thy holy commandments without end or ceasing: Wherefore we purchase ourselves, through thy righteous judgment, our ruin and perdition. Nevertheless, O Lord, we are grieved that we have offended thee; and we condemn ourselves and our sins with true repentance, beseeching thy grace to relieve our distress. O God and Father most gracious and full of compassion, have mercy on us in the name of thy Son, our Lord Jesus Christ. And as thou dost blot out our sins and stains, magnify and increase in us day by day the grace of thy Holy Spirit: that as we acknowledge our unrighteousness with all our heart, we may be moved by that sorrow which shall bring forth true repentance in us, mortifying all our sins, and producing in us the fruits of righteousness and innocence which are pleasing unto thee; through the same Jesus Christ &c. [our Lord. Amen].[12]

The Book of Common Prayer (1662)
A General Confession to Be Said of the Whole Congregation after the Minister, All Kneeling

ALMIGHTY and most merciful Father, We have erred and strayed from thy ways like lost sheep, We have followed too much of the devices and desires of our hearts, We have offended against thy holy laws, We have left undone those things which we ought to have done, And we have done those things which we ought not to have done, And there is no health in us: But thou, O Lord, have mercy upon us miserable offenders; Spare thou them, O God, which confess their faults, Restore thou them that are penitent, According to thy promises declared unto mankind in Christ Jesu our Lord: And grant, O most merciful Father, for his sake, That we may hereafter live a godly, righteous, and sober life, To the glory of thy holy Name. Amen.[13]

PASTORAL PRAYERS OF CONFESSION
A Prayer of Confession Based on Psalm 32
Our merciful Father, we thank you that you never allow us comfort when we are not walking with you. When we refuse to confess our sins you give us an inward ache, as though our bones are wasting away, and we

---
[12] Ibid., 197–198.
[13] The Book of Common Prayer (Cambridge: Cambridge University Press, n.d.), 18.

groan with an inaudible roar of guilt. You keep your hand heavy upon us, always pressing and depressing us. And our energy evaporates as dried up by the heat of a summer night. O Lord, the misery of unconfessed sin is a grace; it is a sign of being your child, and that we are loved. Thank you for the gift of guilt.

Merciful Father, thank you for forgiveness—because when we confess our sins there is *real* forgiveness for our *real* guilt, and the ache and the heaviness and the apathy disappear. And our hearts sing: "Blessed is the one whose transgression is forgiven, whose sin is covered" (v. 1). "You are a hiding place for me . . . you surround me with shouts of deliverance" (v. 7).

Loving Father, thank you for the blessed discomfort that you bring to us when we are away from you.

Hear us as we now confess our sins in these moments of silence.

A Prayer of Confession Based on Psalm 139

Almighty God, unto whom all things are open, we set ourselves before you.
Where can we go from your Spirit?
Where can we flee from your presence?
If we ascend to heaven, you are there!
If we make our bed with the dead, you are there!
If we dwell in the deepest part of the sea, you are there!
Darkness and light are alike to you.

You observed us before we were born, and in your book all our days were written.

There is nothing hidden from you. And we take great comfort in this. We are your relentless focus, "the apple of your eye" (Ps. 17:8). You have numbered the hairs on our heads.

Your loving knowledge of us also disquiets our souls. We can fool others (and we do), we can fool ourselves (and we do), but we cannot fool you! Your intimate knowledge of us demands honesty. You have seen our outward sins, which we now confess: our deceptions; our lies; our gossip; our hurtful words; our loveless actions; our "me first" self-focus; our irritability; our anger. Hear our confession of these sins, as it fits our own souls.

We confess our inner sins, the attitudes that are contrary to the fruits of the Spirit: our jealousies; our hatreds; our malice. Hear our confession of these sins, Lord, as it fits our own souls.

Thank you, merciful Father, that the blood of your Son cleanses us from all sin and that "If we confess our sins, he is faithful and just to forgive us our sins and to cleanse us from all unrighteousness" (1 John 1:9).

A Prayer of Confession Based on Luke 19:10

Our eternal, loving God, we celebrate your missionary heart—that, although you are completely self-sufficient, having no need of us, you sought us. The greatest missionary enterprise ever undertaken began when "the Word became flesh and dwelt among us" (John 1:14). And Jesus, the living Word himself, would announce, "For the Son of Man came to seek and save the lost" (Luke 19:10). And truly we would not be yours if you were not, indeed, the awesome Son of Man to whom the Ancient of Days gave "dominion and glory and a kingdom, that all peoples, nations, and languages should serve him" (Dan. 7:14). You sought us with ineluctable power. Sovereign Lord Jesus, you are the Hound of Heaven, and we bear testimony to your glorious footfall. We celebrate that in all our wandering and seeking, we were sovereignly sought.

Merciful Lord, your pursuing love causes us to see ourselves for what we are, ever-wandering sheep. We confess that we have strayed from your ways like lost sheep. We have followed the sinful desires of our own hearts. We have broken your laws. We have left undone those things we ought to have done, and we do things that are wrong. There is no forgiveness or comfort in ourselves. Some of us have done things that we feel are beyond forgiveness. We wish that we could take back what we have done. We have wrongly kept back our confession of sin and suffer from guilt.

Hear our confession. Hound of Heaven, we repent of our sinful wandering. Forgive us our sins and cause us to follow you faithfully. Amen.

A Prayer of Confession to God the Father by Virtue of Jesus's Name

Our mighty God, we come to you only by virtue of Jesus's name. Were it not for his blood, we would find no place before you. There is an infinite distance between your holiness and us, your sinful creatures. Your purity and perfection forbid our access—except through your Son. So we come to you by his perfection, which has been given to us through his death and resurrection.

Lord God, your beauty overwhelms us. We long to dwell in your temple and behold that splendor. Our hearts are drawn to you. We desire your presence. Our souls thirst for you.

Our joyous confession is that you are light and life and joy. We believe that you are good, we believe that you are merciful, we believe that you are gracious, we affirm your steadfast love, and we believe that you are unchangeable in all these things.

And, Father, in confessing you as the holy God of all perfection, we see ourselves for what we are, and we humbly confess our sins in the silence of the following moments, trusting in Christ's blood alone for forgiveness.

UNISON PRAYERS OF CONFESSION

The most widely used and influential unison confession comes from Thomas Cranmer's Book of Common Prayer, included above in the early Protestant confessions. It appears verbatim in the Presbyterian Book of Common Worship, and its expressions turn up variously in modern confessions, especially "We have left undone those things that we ought to have done, and done those things that we ought not to have done." The first unison confession below is a nice modern rendering of this prayer from *Common Prayer: Resources for gospel-shaped gatherings*, while the remainder are our own compositions. Note that we begin these confessions with the phrase, "Let us join together in confessing our sins." In practice, it would be good to vary the invitation to confession.

A Modern English Unison Confession from the Book of Common Prayer

Let us join together in confessing our sins.
Merciful Father,
we have strayed from your ways like lost sheep.
We have followed too much the schemes and desires
of our own hearts,
and have broken your holy laws.
We have left undone what we ought to have done,
and we have done what we ought not to have done.
Yet, good Lord, have mercy on us;
restore those who repent,
according to the promises declared to us
through your Son, Jesus Christ.
Grant, merciful Father, for his sake,
that from now on,
we may live godly and obedient lives,
to the glory of your holy name. Amen.[14]

Additional Unison Prayers of Confession

Let us join together in confessing our sins:
Heavenly Father,
you have loved us with an everlasting love,
but we have gone our own way,
and rejected your will for our lives.
We are sorry for our sins

---

[14] *Common Prayer: Resources for gospel-shaped gatherings* (Sydney: Anglican Press Australia, 2012), 10.

and turn away from them.
For the sake of your son who died for us,
forgive us, cleanse us, and change us.
By your Holy Spirit, enable us to live for you,
and to please you in every way,
for the glory of our Lord Jesus Christ. Amen.[15]

Let us join together in confessing our sins.
Almighty God, Father of our Lord Jesus Christ,
you made all things, and you call everyone to account.
With shame we admit that we have sinned against you
in what we have thought, said, and done,
and we deserve your judgment.
We turn from our sins and are truly sorry for them.
Have mercy on us, most merciful Father.
Because of the cross of your Son,
our Lord Jesus Christ, forgive us.
Enable us to serve and please you in new life,
to your honor and glory,
through Jesus Christ our Lord. Amen.

Let us join together in confessing our sins.
Father, we gather together with the expectant knowledge that,
through your Son, you freely pardon
all who repent and turn to him.
We have sinned against you this week
in our thoughts, our words, and our actions.
We have not loved you, or others, as you told us.
Grant us the mercy,
the forgiveness, and the cleansing
that Jesus gives to those who confess their sin.
Grant that we may worship you in Spirit and in truth,
to the glory of your name. Amen.

Let us join together in confessing our sins.
Almighty God, Father of our Lord Jesus Christ,
maker of all things, judge of all people,
we acknowledge and confess the grievous sins and wickedness
that we have so often committed by thought, word, and deed
against your divine majesty, provoking most justly your anger

---

[15] Ibid., 22.

and indignation against us.
We earnestly repent and are deeply sorry for these our wrongdoings;
the memory of them weighs us down,
the burden of them is too great for us to bear.
Have mercy upon us, have mercy upon us, most merciful Father;
for your Son our Lord Jesus Christ's sake, forgive us all that is past;
and grant that from this time onward we may always serve
and please you in newness of life, to the honor and glory of
     your name,
through Jesus Christ our Lord. Amen.

RESPONSIVE PRAYERS OF CONFESSION

In the following prayers, paragraphs in bold are to be spoken by the congregation.

Eternal God, You do not change. You have revealed Yourself to us in Your Word. You call us to worship You in spirit and in truth.
But we confess that we often worship a god made in our image and who we wish You to be.
We frequently ask You to bless what we do, rather than seeking to do what You bless.
Forgive us for seeking concessions when we should be seeking guidance.
You command us to be generous with our love and resources, for the sake of the church and the lost.
But we have been selfish and insensitive to the needs and opportunities around us.
Display Your glory before us.
That we might bow before Your unspeakable majesty and so live for You now and forever in Christ. Amen.
Individual confession of sin.[16]

Our lips are ready to confess,
But our hearts are slow to feel, and our wills are reluctant to repent.
We bring our entire selves to You, this morning—
Bend us, wound us, and, if necessary, break us.
We have seen the purity of Your perfect word, the happiness of those in whose heart it reigns, the calm dignity of the walk to which it calls—
Yet we daily violate its precepts.

---

[16] See *The Worship Sourcebook*, 2nd ed. (Grand Rapids: Calvin Institute of Christian Worship/Faith Alive Christian Resources/Baker Books, 2013).

Your loving Spirit strives within us, brings us Scripture warnings, speaks in startling providences, allures by secret whispers—
Yet we make shameful choices that grieve Him and quench His influence.
We mourn and lament these sins, crying to You for pardon.
Grant that through the tears of repentance we may see more clearly the goodness and glory of our Savior and His cross.
Individual confession of sin.[17]

Father, we gather together with the expectant knowledge that, through your Son, you freely pardon all who repent and turn to him.
We have sinned against you this week in our thoughts, our words, and our actions. We have not loved you, or others, as you told us.
Grant us the mercy, the forgiveness, and the cleansing that Jesus gives to those who confess their sin. On that basis, grant that we may continue to worship you in Spirit and in truth, to the glory of your name. Amen.

Scripture Passages for Silent Confession

A meaningful time of solemn confession can be created by the reading of a text that evokes reflection and confession, followed by the simple pastoral injunction, "Let us confess our sins." The following texts are suggested in Robert Rayburn's *O Come, Let Us Worship.*[18]

The LORD is in his holy temple;
the LORD's throne is in heaven;
his eyes see, his eyelids test the children of man.
The LORD tests the righteous,
but his soul hates the wicked and the one who does violence. . . .
For the LORD is righteous;
he loves righteous deeds;
the upright shall behold his face. (Ps. 11:4, 5, 7)
Let us confess our sins.

O LORD, who shall sojourn in your tent?
Who shall dwell on your holy hill?
He who walks blamelessly and does what is right
and speaks truth in his heart;
who does not slander with his tongue
and does no evil to his neighbor,

[17] Ibid.
[18] Robert G. Rayburn, *O Come, Let Us Worship* (Eugene, OR: Wipf & Stock, 2010).

nor takes up a reproach against his friend. (Ps. 15:1–3)
Let us confess our sins.

Who can discern his errors?
   Declare me innocent from hidden faults.
Keep back your servant also from presumptuous sins;
   let them not have dominion over me!
Then I shall be blameless,
   and innocent of great transgression. (Ps. 19:12–13)
Let us confess our transgressions.

Who shall ascend the hill of the LORD?
   And who shall stand in his holy place?
He who has clean hands and a pure heart,
   who does not lift up his soul to what is false
   and does not swear deceitfully.
He will receive blessing from the LORD
   and righteousness from the God of his salvation. (Ps. 24:3–5)
Let us confess our sins.

O Lord, open my lips,
   and my mouth will declare your praise.
For you will not delight in sacrifice, or I would give it;
   you will not be pleased with a burnt offering.
The sacrifices of God are a broken spirit;
   A broken and contrite heart, O God, you will not despise.
      (Ps. 51:15–17)
Let us confess our sins.

O LORD, you have searched me and known me!
You know when I sit down and when I rise up;
   you discern my thoughts from afar.
You search out my path and my lying down
   and are acquainted with all my ways.
Even before a word is on my tongue,
   behold, O LORD, you know it altogether. (Ps. 139:1–4)
Let us confess our sins.

Seek the LORD while he may be found;
   call upon him while he is near;
let the wicked forsake his way,
   and the unrighteous man his thoughts;

let him return to the LORD, that he may have compassion on him,
   and to our God, for he will abundantly pardon. (Isa. 55:6–7)
Let us confess our sins.

"Yet even now, "declares the LORD,
   "return to me with all your heart,
with fasting, with weeping, and with mourning;
   and rend your hearts and not your garments."
Return to the LORD your God,
   for he is gracious and merciful,
slow to anger, and abounding in steadfast love. (Joel 2:12–13)
Let us confess our sins.

PASTORAL/CONGREGATIONAL PRAYERS

Carson emphasizes the importance of the congregational prayer, citing Charles Spurgeon's regard for the responsibility:

> In the last century the great English preacher Charles Spurgeon did not mind sharing his pulpit: others sometimes preached in his home church even when he was present. But when it came to the "pastoral prayer," if he was present, he reserved that part of the service for himself. This decision did not arise out of any priestly conviction that his prayers were more efficacious than others. Rather, it arose from his love for his people, his high view of prayer, his conviction that public prayer should not only intercede with God but also instruct and edify and encourage the saints.[19]

Leading God's people in praise, intercession, and petition is an immense privilege and responsibility because of the power that corporate prayer brings to the church and also because of how it informs and strengthens the prayer life of the body of Christ. The following prayers are provided as examples of how we as pastors have gone about it. Readers should note that the prayers do not include the typical weekly petitions for the ill or for God's blessing on the coming ministry events in the life of the church. These important things were prayed for in the context of the congregational prayers.

Sample Congregational Prayers

Sample Congregational Prayer #1

Lord God Almighty, we come before you today and ask that you would enable us to pass all the time of our pilgrimage here on earth in such a

---

[19] Carson, *A Call to Spiritual Reformation*, 35.

way that when we pass from this world we may be prepared to meet you in your heavenly kingdom.

When we think of this life and its various temptations, when we look around and see the wickedness of the world, and then contemplate also the weakness and corruption of our own nature, we recognize how easy it would be to fall under the power of such temptation. But we praise you, O Lord, for that abundant grace that is treasured up for us in Christ Jesus. We thank you for all the promises and encouragements given to us in your gospel, which is "the power of God for salvation to everyone who believes" (Rom. 1:16). So we exalt you because your Son has died as a sacrifice for sin and the Spirit of Christ has been given to sanctify us. And so we pray now for the filling of that same Spirit; we ask that you would fill us with the Holy Spirit so that in all we think and say and do this world might also be filled with the righteousness of God, your will, O heavenly Father.

Prepare us, we ask you, for every task of this day and coming week; arm us for every trial that may come upon us. Sanctify us, O Lord, in body, soul, and spirit. Help us this week to devote ourselves more fully to you; and may we, by your grace, be found walking in the fear of the Lord, fulfilling, each of us, our proper vocation with Christian humility and simplicity.

Deliver us from a careless and unbelieving life, from a life of idleness and foolishness, as well as of wickedness and vice. Save us from the sins that in times past may have most easily beset us and from those temptations to which we may now, through our age and our circumstances, be most exposed.

May our hearts be filled with love to you; and may all our abilities be so used in doing good that no place may be given for those temptations that continually overcome those who do not know the gospel of salvation. And may your grace increase in us and our corruptions be weakened day by day. At the same time, forgetting the things that are behind and looking forward to those things before us, may we continue to press toward the mark of the prize of our high calling in Christ Jesus.

O Lord, help us this day to remember how short and uncertain is the time of our pilgrimage here on earth, so that, whatever work we might do, we may do it with all our might, and to the glory of your name. Amen.[20]

Sample Congregational Prayer #2

Lord Jesus Christ, when you took on flesh, you humbled yourself "by becoming obedient to the point of death, even death on a cross" (Phil. 2:8).

---

[20] This prayer is a slight revision of a "morning prayer" from Henry Thornton's personal prayer book, published as *Devotional Prayers* (Chicago: Moody, 1993), 49–51. This is an incredible resource for public and private prayers.

Your obedience did not begin in heaven. Unlike your love, which is eternal, your obedience is not eternal. Today, exalted Christ, you obey nothing in the heavens above or on the earth or under the earth. Your obedience began when you became a man, the one obedient man of all history. You lived in full obedience to your Father all your years as a man, and though you were God, when you prayed for deliverance, it was not God praying to God, but man praying to God, who "In the days of his flesh . . . offered up prayers and supplications, with loud cries and tears, to him who was able to save him from death, and he was heard because of his reverence" (Heb. 5:7). Lord Jesus, when you asked to have the cup taken from you, your loving Father heard you and answered no. And you, as a man, the Man, obeyed. Your Word tells us that you "learned obedience through what [you] suffered. And being made perfect, [you] became the source of eternal salvation to all who obey . . . being designated by God a high priest after the order of Melchizedek" (Heb. 5:8–10).

Suffering Servant, your incarnate obedience made you "obedient to the point of death, even death on a cross" (Phil. 2:8). Apart from your obedience as a man who became the sacrificial lamb who took away the sin of the world, we would be lost and without hope. And more, your obedience in suffering in human flesh has made you to be our merciful and faithful high priest, because having suffered when you were tempted, you are able to help those who are tempted (cf. Heb. 2:10, 18). So when we are tempted by life's difficulties to engage in doubt and disobedience, you will help us. Therefore:

> Since . . . we have a great high priest who has passed through the heavens, Jesus, the Son of God, let us hold fast our confession. For we do not have a high priest who is unable to sympathize with our weaknesses, but one who in every respect has been tempted as we are, yet without sin. Let us then with confidence draw near to the throne of grace, that we may receive mercy and find grace in time of need. (Heb. 4:14–16)

So, Lord, when we are tempted by suffering to doubt and disobey you, we know that you understand our humanity and weaknesses, and there is not a note that can strike in our humanity that does not sound a sympathetic chord in your exalted humanity. So we now, with confidence, draw near to the throne of grace, that we may receive mercy and find grace in our time of need.

Merciful Savior, we pray for those in our midst who are being tempted to engage in disbelief and disobedience by the difficult circumstances of life—perhaps a difficult marriage, perhaps the loss of a job, perhaps the loss of a spouse or a child, perhaps a series of failures, perhaps the unremitting pressure of debt or problems at every turn—and as a result want to bail and resort to their own devices. Lord, assure all believers that you do understand and sympathize, and draw them to the throne of grace for unremitting mercy and endless grace. Amen.

Sample Congregational Prayer #3

Almighty and everlasting God, our creator, sustainer, redeemer, and friend, we now enter into your sacred presence under a deep sense of our weakness and unworthiness and your unspeakable greatness, holiness, and majesty. We approach you, at the same time, as a God of goodness, grace, and mercy; for you have made yourself known to us in Jesus Christ your Son and have proclaimed pardon to every repenting sinner through faith in the sacrifice that Christ has offered on the cross for us. We desire to honor you for this strong and sure foundation of hope, and we would now address you in the full assurance of faith, renouncing all confidence in ourselves, rejoicing in him who has become the hope of all the ends of the world. We praise the Lamb who died for us, has risen again, and is now exalted at your right hand, where he ever lives to make intercession for us.

So we ask you, our God, to accept for Christ's sake our imperfect worship that we offer up to you both now and throughout this week. Having been taught through your Word to know your will, may we be diligent to fulfill it. Grant us a faith that loves, obeys, and works! Within our homes, workplaces, and this church, give us a spirit of humility and kindness and patience. Our great God, you have been bountiful and gracious to us. You have multiplied our temporal comforts, and you pardon our many transgressions. Grant that we may follow the example of your generosity and that we may also be like you, ready to forgive. May we, by your assistance, be watchful over ourselves but tender toward the infirmities and weaknesses of others.

Strengthen us, our Lord, in our seasons of trials and temptation; guide us through all the difficulties into which we may fall; and bless us in all the scenes of life through which we may pass. Prepare us by all the events and circumstances of this life for the last day and the life of the world to come. When the shadows of the evening shall come upon us, when age and sickness shall arrive and human help fail, O Lord, be the strength of our hearts and our portions forever.

We pray all this in Christ's name and for his glory. Amen.[21]

---

[21] Much of this prayer is taken from ibid., 160–162.

Sample Congregational Prayer #4

Lord Jesus Christ, incarnate Son of God, the firstborn of all creation, you are the Creator of everything in the universe, for the Scriptures speak of you when they say, "For by him all things were created, in heaven and on earth, visible and invisible, whether thrones or dominions or rulers or authorities—all things were created through him and for him. And he is before all things, and in him all things hold together" (Col. 1:16–17). You created every texture, every aroma, the unseen beauties under the sea, the gliding rainbow of a cell, the stripes on a bumblebee, the trackless, fleeing galaxies, every speck of stellar dust. You were existing before these things were, and you hold all things together by the word of your power (Heb. 1:3). And, as the firstborn of all creation, you are the heir of everything in the universe and, indeed, its very goal—as you, Christ, affirmed at the end of the Revelation: "I am the Alpha and the Omega, the first and the last, the beginning and the end" (Rev. 22:13).

Sovereign Lord, you are the Creator, the Sustainer, the Goal who became our Redeemer when you took on human flesh, lived among us, and then died on the cross for our sins. Lord Jesus, help us grasp the immensity of who you are and what you have done for us, and then believe it with all of our hearts—because the most important thing about us is what we believe about you. You are the Creator, Sustainer, Goal, Redeemer, and Lover of our souls. We believe; help our unbelief!

May those who are doubting their significance in this uncaring world grasp the immensity of your person and the vast love with which they are loved, and likewise those reeling from rejection, overcome with loneliness, struggling to provide, dealing with errant children, or aging and facing the loss of a loved one. May the astonishing wonder of your death on the cross for us, eternal Son and Creator and Sustainer, and the unending tide of your love cause us to rest in you.

We pray this in the name that is above every name. Amen.

Sample Congregational Prayer #5

"The LORD reigns, let the earth rejoice; let the many coastlands be glad! Clouds and thick darkness are all around him; righteousness and justice are the foundation of his throne" (Ps. 97:1–2). Our great and sovereign God, we bow before you this morning and recognize your righteousness and justice, your holiness and love. And we recognize that you alone are worthy to be praised. So we lift our voices and hearts in praise of you!

Our gracious and merciful God, as we dwell upon the perfect requirements of your holy law, we quickly recognize that we are great sinners—

our flesh still battles with our spirit; our new hearts still long for the new day of the resurrection of our bodies. But until then, O Lord, please hear again our confession of sin. Please forgive us our sin. And please help us by the power of the Holy Spirit to overcome sin.

We thank you for our Savior, the Lord Jesus Christ, the only mediator between God and man. We thank you for his perpetual cleansing blood, for your constant forgiveness through him. We thank you for the gospel—the good news of salvation through Christ. And we thank you for the work of the Holy Spirit in our hearts, minds, and wills to embrace this glorious message of salvation.

Lord, you have commanded us, through your Word, to give thanks in all circumstances, for such is your will for us in Christ. But while we admit how easy it is to rejoice in your gospel and the good news of our salvation, and to rejoice when we see all things working together for our good, we also admit how hard it is to give thanks when we cannot see through the storm. Help us, O Lord, to see through our trials, to have a divine perspective on them, to see them as you see them, and thus to trust in you so that we indeed can rejoice and give thanks even now. Lord, come to the rescue of those who cry out to you. Heal the bodies and souls of those who cry out to you, or of those on whose behalf others cry out. Be the God of all grace and comfort.

On this Lord's Day, our Lord, we acknowledge you as Lord. And so we bow before you, Lord of the universe and Lord of the church and Lord of this church, trusting that you alone hear our prayers and you alone have the power to answer them. So do answer them, our gracious Lord and Father, according to your perfect will and for the sake of your perfect glory. We pray this in Christ's name. Amen.

Sample Congregational Prayer #6

Father, we have gathered this morning because of the resurrection of your Son and our Savior, Jesus Christ. So this is a day of great rejoicing, and a time in which our hearts are raised up to you in adoration and praise. Hear us, O God. Hear now our heartfelt praise and thanksgiving for all you have given us in Christ.

But hear also, our gracious and merciful God, our confession of sin. Lord, we know that you are faithful and just to forgive all our sins if we come to you, like the prodigal son, saying: "I am no longer worthy to be called your son. . . . I have sinned against heaven and before you" (Luke 15:19, 21). We know that you, as a kind and loving Father, will forgive us all our trespasses. So, Lord, listen now to our confession of all that we have sinned against you in body and in mind.

(Pause.)

Lord, have mercy upon us. Forgive us our sins against you and against one another.

Our God in heaven, you have taught us in your Word that "the prayer of a righteous person has great power as it is working" (James 5:16). So, Father, knowing that you have heard our confession of sin and have absolved us through the righteous blood of Christ, our Advocate before you, we ask now that you would hear our prayers. Lord, we pray for our government officials—the president, the members of the Senate and the House of Representatives, as well as our governor, mayor, and all other local officials. We ask that you would give them knowledge, wisdom, and virtue. We pray that they will know and accomplish their duties, namely, that they would punish the wicked and administer justice according to your law.

Lord, we also lift up the leaders of this church and ask that you would help the elders and deacons to make wise and prudent decisions. Help us to have clarity of mind and vision. Give us patience and wisdom, and bestow upon us a spirit of humility and unity in Christ as we seek to be servants of the servants of God.

Lord, we "rejoice with those who rejoice" and we "weep with those who weep" (Rom. 12:15). We rejoice especially with _____. And, Father, we weep for those who weep—whether it is due to some sickness or distress. And we ask that you would be the God of comfort to them. Be especially with _____.

Lord, we gathered today to worship you. So we look forward now to honoring you through the songs we sing, the words we hear, and the response we give. To you, Father, Son, and Spirit, be all the glory in the church, both now and forevermore. Amen.

Sample Congregational Prayer #7

Our loving Savior, your Word tells us that the light of the gospel has been entrusted to us in the frail "jars of clay" of our humanity "to show that the surpassing power belongs to God and not to us" (2 Cor. 4:7). And, Lord Jesus, you told the apostle Paul directly, "My grace is sufficient for you, for my power is made perfect in weakness" (2 Cor. 12:9a). The reality is that all through history, you, our God, have chosen and used nobodies because their unusual dependence on you made possible the unique display of your power; you chose and used somebodies only when they renounced dependence on their natural abilities and relied on you. So you don't need our strengths, if they are what we depend upon. You need our weaknesses, and, Lord, we have a lot to give!

Lord, you are telling us that the ministry of the gospel goes out when we live in profound dependence upon you. Regardless of our wealth, education, or standing in the world, you are pleased to use only clay pots. This is humbling, but so beautiful. Paul, a man of immense abilities, understood it and lived it out, saying, "Therefore I will boast all the more gladly of my weaknesses, so that the power of Christ may rest upon me" (2 Cor. 12:9b)—because Paul knew that you pitch your tent with us in our weaknesses. Jesus, you camp with those who depend upon you. Lord, apart from you, we can do nothing. So now as we pray for the spread of the gospel, we pray for full dependence upon you.

We pray for the children of this church. While we instruct them, we are helpless to open their eyes. Open their eyes, Lord.

We pray for our community as we endeavor to share the gospel through our ministries, realizing that a ministry never won anyone to Christ.

We pray for our missionaries, _____ in _____, that you would encourage their efforts with new believers.

We pray for our government leaders—for _____, _____, and _____. You hold the hearts of kings in your hand. Turn their hearts to you.

Our Lord, we are "not ashamed of the gospel, for it is the power of God for salvation to everyone who believes" (Rom. 1:16). It is your power. You can save anyone, anywhere, anytime. And you can use clay pots to do it—"to show that the surpassing power belongs to God and not to us" (2 Cor. 4:7). Amen.

Sample Congregational Prayer #8

For the congregational prayer this morning, I want to involve you—the congregation—in the prayer itself. I will do this by using a traditional formula for congregational prayer—namely, I will give a series of brief petitions, ending each one with the words, "We pray to the Lord." Then you will reply by saying, "Lord, hear our prayer." After six brief petitions, I will give a short concluding prayer. After that, we can all reply with a hearty "Amen." Let us pray.

Heavenly Father, you have called us as Christians to remember to pray for the church, the world, and the ongoing ministry of the gospel, that it might increase and make disciples of all nations. And so we pray to the Lord.

Lord, hear our prayer.

For those in need—the poor and the hungry, the homeless and the unemployed, the sick and the lonely—that they may receive help in their distress, we pray to the Lord.

Lord, hear our prayer.

For those who do not yet believe, and for all those in spiritual need—that they may find faith, hope, and comfort, we pray to the Lord.

Lord, hear our prayer.

For our nation and for all who govern—that justice and freedom may be preserved for all citizens, and that we may dwell in peace, as so to give a greater opportunity for the spread of the gospel, we pray to the Lord.

Lord, hear our prayer.

For the church throughout the world, and especially for our missionaries in _____—that these brothers and sisters of ours may remain faithful to their calling (help them to proclaim the gospel boldly even in the midst of much conflict) and so prove to be the light of Christ among the nations, we pray to the Lord.

Lord, hear our prayer.

And for our own congregation—for parents and children in the home, and for each of us in our vocations, that we may prove to be Christ's disciples in both word and deed, that we might walk in a manner worthy of God, we pray to the Lord.

Lord, hear our prayer.

Heavenly Father, source of all good and Savior of mankind, grant grace to your people to live as faithful followers of Christ our Lord and worthy witnesses of your gospel. Have mercy on the peoples of the earth, and draw the lost into your gracious kingdom. Help us meet the needs of the poor and suffering through the love of Jesus Christ, in whose name we pray.

Amen.

SAMPLE CONGREGATIONAL PRAYERS BASED ON TEXTS OF SCRIPTURE

A Prayer Based on Exodus 20:2

Father, you are the Lord our God, who brought Israel out of Egypt, out of the house of slavery, and who has brought us out of darkness and into your marvelous light, out of slavery in our sins and into the freedom of the gospel.

You have commanded that we are to have no other gods before you. Lord, help us resist the gods of this world—the constant temptations of our society that war against our hearts and minds. By your Spirit, renew us day by day, that we may not only resist false gods, but actively seek after you, the true God, with all our heart, soul, mind, and strength.

You have commanded that we not make any idols in the form of anything in heaven or on earth. Lord, help us not to recast you in our image. Help us not to try and change you according to how we see fit, if even inadvertently, but rather re-form us by your Word and Spirit to be conformed to the likeness of your Son.

You have commanded that we not misuse your name. While most of us probably don't misuse your name by speaking it hastily, we are much more likely to misuse it by not representing it well. As those born again and given a new name—Christian—may we not be found to misuse the name of Christ by our words or deeds. Help us not only to avoid misusing your name, but also to excel in using it—to represent our Savior Jesus in the ways that we speak and live.

You have commanded us to remember the Sabbath. Lord, help us to be faithful to work diligently for six days, and to treat this Lord's Day as holy. May we not merely rest from our work, but may we remember and worship you, the Creator God, who rested on the seventh day.

You have commanded that we honor our father and mother. Lord, help us to do this not only by refraining from disrespecting our parents, but also by actively seeking ways to honor and bless them.

You have commanded that we not murder. Lord, forgive us for how we murder in our hearts through hatred and bitterness. Free those who are even now in bondage to animosity toward others. Renew us by your Spirit, that we would learn to love those who do us wrong, just as you have loved us.

You have commanded that we not commit adultery. Lord, forgive us when this command is transgressed, whether physically, emotionally, or mentally. Renew and strengthen our marriages, that we might reflect well Christ's forgiving and reconciling relationship with the church, and foster purity among those who are single, that they might be holy servants of you, our pure and holy God.

You have commanded that we not steal. Lord, help us not only to refrain from taking what is not ours, but also to give generously to those in need.

You have commanded that we not give false testimony. May we not only refrain from lies in our words, but may we also live truthfully. May how we live behind closed doors coincide with how we live in view of all.

You have commanded that we not covet. Lord, may we not scorn your goodness by coveting your providence upon others, but develop in us hearts that are grateful for your providence in our lives.

As we consider your commands, Lord, we must confess that they are good and right. We also confess that we fall short of them, and so we rely on your mercy through Jesus. Thank you for forgiving our shortcomings. Thank you for your grace in imputing to us Christ's perfect obedience of your law. Enable us to grow in holiness by loving you the ways you have commanded us, that you might be glorified in our lives. In Jesus's name. Amen.

A Prayer Based on Deuteronomy 4:5–8

> See, I [Moses] have taught you decrees and laws as the Lord my God commanded me. . . . Observe them carefully, for this will show your wisdom and understanding to the nations, who will hear about all these decrees and say, "Surely this great nation is a wise and understanding people." What other nation is so great as to have their gods near them the way the Lord our God is near us whenever we pray to him? And what other nation is so great as to have such righteous decrees and laws as this body of laws I am setting before you today? (NIV)

Father, you are the mighty God Most High, El Shaddai, the one who called Abram and graciously promised that his descendants would be more numerous than the stars. You made a covenant with Abraham, Isaac, and Jacob, to be their God, and by your mighty hand you rescued their descendants Israel out of bondage in Egypt and gathered them as a kingdom of priests. In your mercy, Lord, you dwelled with them in the tabernacle and the temple, and in your goodness you gave Israel laws and decrees for how to live holy lives in your presence in the Land of Promise. But they rebelled, Lord, and did not seek after your wisdom and did not abide by your statutes.

Our Father, how much are we your people today like Israel. You have graciously made promises to us. You have sent your Son Jesus to rescue us from our bondage in sin, and you have given your churches a covenant in his blood, that through his sacrifice we are made to be your people—a royal priesthood and a holy nation. And like Israel, Lord, you have given us laws and decrees by which to live—commands from the very lips of our Lord Jesus himself, that we might live holy lives in your presence as we move toward the new heaven and new earth that you have promised. In your mercy, you dwell with us by your Holy Spirit, transforming us into the very temple of God.

And like Israel, Lord, we acknowledge that we are prone to rebellion. Although you are holy, true, righteous, and good, our flesh is weak. So we pray, Lord, that you would quicken our hearts, grow us in holiness, change us from the inside out, and enable us to grow in our obedience and adherence to your word, so that your great wisdom and understanding would be manifest to our neighbors and to the nations, who will hear about your grace and mercy to us and say, "What other religion, what other people, is so great as to have their God near them the way Jesus has drawn near to his church?"

Lord, we pray for those here who are struggling with persistent sins. Whether it be anger, lust, vanity, sloth, envy, or pride—whatever it may be, you know our hearts—we pray that you would, by your Word and Spirit, bring sharp conviction where it is needed here today. We pray you would give us eyes that see and ears that hear, that we may not be blind and deaf to our sin, and that we would turn from it. And, Lord, in the midst of this struggle, we pray for your comfort. We pray that those here who are struggling in obedience to Jesus's words would remember that you are slow to anger and rich in love, and that you will finish the good work that you have started in them.

We thank you that our obedience to your Word is a reflection of our salvation and not a means to it. We thank you that Jesus's words are righteous, that they are words of life that are for our good. We praise you that you are a God who is worthy of obedience. All glory, honor, majesty, and dominion be yours, our God, now and forever. In Jesus's name. Amen.

A Prayer Based on Psalm 19:1–14

The heavens declare the glory of God,
    and the sky above proclaims his handiwork.
Day to day pours out speech,
    and night to night reveals knowledge. (vv. 1–2)

Our God, we are not hidden from your power and your grace. And we praise you this day for the wonders of your creation, which reveal to us but a fragment of your holiness, sovereignty, mercy, and love. Yet we realize, our Creator God, without your gracious revelation of your Son, our Lord Jesus Christ (the Word incarnate), as well as your gracious revelation of the written Word (the Bible), we, with our sinful hearts, would likely worship the creation rather than the Creator, who is forever to be praised. We thank you, our Lord, for your Word, and praise you for the way it emits your glory and warms our souls. For,

The law of the Lord is perfect,
    reviving the soul;
the testimony of the Lord is sure,
    making wise the simple;

the precepts of the LORD are right,
    rejoicing the heart;
the commandment of the LORD is pure,
    enlightening the eyes;
the fear of the LORD is clean,
    enduring forever;
the rules of the LORD are true,
    and righteous altogether.
More to be desired are they than gold,
    even much fine gold;
sweeter also than honey
    and drippings of the honeycomb.
Moreover, by them is your servant warned;
    in keeping them there is great reward. (vv. 7–11)

Teach us this day, O God, to know, understand, and obey your Word; for your testimony is the only truth that can enlighten our minds and revive our hearts. Your truth is pure, as sweet as honey, and reveals your righteousness and our impurity. For as the psalmist said,

Who can discern his errors?
    Declare me innocent from hidden faults.
Keep back your servant also from presumptuous sins;
    let them not have dominion over me!
Then I shall be blameless,
    and innocent of great transgression. (vv. 12–13)

Our gracious Lord, who can declare us innocent from hidden faults? Who can save us from the lust of the flesh, the lust of the eyes, and the pride of life? Your Son and his atonement is our only refuge! So take all our sins of this week and even this moment, and nail them to his saving cross. Lord Jesus, our advocate, speak kindly on our behalf and resurrect in us obedience to your Father's will.

Our righteous Savior, we ask you to watch our church, to keep its people from temptations and from the bite of the Evil One. Heal our sick. Provide for those in need (financially, emotionally, and spiritually). Save the lost in our midst and in our neighborhoods. May this church, by the strength of your Spirit, radiate the light of your gospel throughout this lost city and dark world.

Father, Son, and Spirit,

Let the words of [our] mouth and the meditation of [our] heart
    be acceptable in your sight,
    O LORD, [our] rock and [our] redeemer. (v. 14)

A Prayer Based on Psalm 73:25–28

> Whom have I in heaven but You? And besides You, I desire nothing on earth. My flesh and my heart may fail, but God is the strength of my heart and my portion forever. For behold, those who are far from You will perish; You have destroyed all those who are unfaithful to You. But as for me, the nearness of God is my good; I have made the Lord GOD my refuge, that I may tell of all Your works. (NASB)

Father, along with the psalmist, we turn to you for perspective. When all in this world seems to go against us, when life is apparently unfair, and when trials fall upon us like a rock, we turn to you, our Rock of redemption. We come into your sanctuary and see things as they truly are—with you upon the throne, and with the loving purpose of your perfect plan in place.

Lord, we pray this day, the Lord's Day—as we take but a momentary break from our weekly labors, to rest in you, to fellowship with one another, and to speak of that which matters most—that you would help us to see well the wonders of your works, the glory of your name, and the holiness of your person, so that we might bow in reverence, adoration, and praise.

For, Father, we recognize how little we understand your holiness, your perfect holiness. And this is why we so often fail to see ourselves as we should, as less than holy, as so unholy in your perfect light. But teach us even now how far we fall from your glory, and how much we need daily, hourly to come to you, to cling to Christ and his perfect holiness—his birth for us, his life for us, his death for us, his resurrection for us, his ascension for us, his sending of the Holy Spirit for us, his exaltation for us, his moment-by-moment mediation for us and for all our sins. To him be all the glory in the church and in this church—for Christ alone, and his deep, deep love, is worthy of our deepest love and commitment.

Help us to know his commandments, to walk in them, to teach them to others, and to share with others the way that leads to life. Give us the grace to serve you, to tell of all your works.

And, Lord, as we now come to sing unto Christ, and as we stand to hear your Word read and then sit to listen to it explained and applied, and then as we celebrate the Lord's Supper, we ask that you will help us to acknowledge our need, and to run to Christ with outstretched arms—for love, safety, and salvation. We pray this in his name, and for the glory of the Father, Son, and Holy Spirit. Amen.

A Prayer Based on Psalm 89:6–8

> For who in the heaven can be compared unto the Lord? who among the sons of the mighty can be likened unto the Lord? God is greatly to be feared in the assembly of the saints, and to be had in reverence of all them that are about him. O Lord God of hosts, who is a strong Lord like unto thee? or to thy faithfulness round about thee? (KJV)

Our strong and faithful God, we come before you this day, acknowledging that you are to be worshiped with reverence and awe. In a world that mocks you, so often debases your name, and forgets you as its Creator and Savior, we have gathered in this assembly on this Lord's Day to acknowledge and praise you as our God, Creator, Savior, and Lord.

But who are we, O God, to speak to you? Who are we to so come into your presence? Who are we to call upon the name of the Lord God Most High—we who are so small, sinful, and full of pride and presumption? We who think this world revolves around us—centers on our desires, on our needs, and on our wills being done.

Lord, if the perfect angels bow in fear and reverence in your very presence, we who are imperfect, earthbound, and of the flesh ought to cover our mouths, ought to hold our tongues, and ought to guard our hearts until we come to know you, to accept you, and to acknowledge you as holy, holy, holy, the Lord God Almighty, the Maker of heaven and earth. If you answer not one of our petitions, answer this one: Humble us, O Lord. Humble us! Make us this day to tremble under this privilege of prayer, under this privilege of coming into your presence through Christ.

We take you too lightly, O Lord. We call you "Father," and yet we so often think and act not like sons and daughters. We wander from your commands. We trample on your decrees. We say, "Yes" with our lips and "No" with our lives. We need forgiveness more than favors. We need grace more than goods. So give us this grace. Give us this forgiveness. Hide us now, hide us again, in the shadow of Christ's wings. Wash us clean in the blood of your Son. Touch our lips with your burning coals and we, like Isaiah, shall be healed, healed so that we might serve and speak.

Fill these empty vessels, O Lord, with your Holy Spirit, so that we might be holy as you are holy, so that we might strive to live a life that is pleasing to you—a life that considers others better than ourselves, a life that works to advance the kingdom of God on earth, a life that seeks the welfare of the poor: the orphans and the widows of our world. We, your prodigal sons and daughters, ask you now to take us and to make us pleasing children of God.

And, Lord, as we consider what we should be and ask that you would make us that, we also ask that you would come to us today and have your hand upon those who are in need. Touch those who need healing in their bodies. Touch those who need healing in their marriages. Touch those who need healing in their homes, healing with their children, or healing with their parents or with siblings. Touch those who need healing at work, with employers or employees. Touch those who need healing here within this church, with our brothers and sisters in Christ, those we are called to love and be at peace with. Lord, for these needs and many more, we ask of your provision through the only name that gains acceptance before your throne of grace, the name of Jesus, our only mediator. Amen.

A Prayer Based on Psalm 118:1–4, 19–21

> Oh give thanks to the Lord, for he is good;
>> for his steadfast love endures forever.
> Let Israel say,
>> "His steadfast love endures forever."
> Let the house of Aaron say,
>> "His steadfast love endures forever."
> Let those who fear the Lord say,
>> "His steadfast love endures forever."

Our gracious God, we praise you this morning for your goodness and enduring love. We praise you as the Maker, Creator, and Sustainer of all things. We praise you for your mighty acts in history. We praise you for our great redemption in Christ.

Our gracious God, we are a sinful people. Our minds and hearts have wandered this week from the way of life, from steadfast obedience to your righteous Word. And so we come to you now, confessing our sins and asking you, through the holy blood of Jesus Christ, to forgive us our sins and cleanse us from all iniquities.

Our Lord, we ask that you would purify our souls of the acts of our sinful nature, and fill us with your Spirit. Conquer our sin, and generously bestow upon us the gifts of love, joy, peace, patience, kindness, goodness, faithfulness, gentleness, and self-control.

> Open to me the gates of righteousness;
>> That I may enter through them
>> and give thanks to the Lord.
> This is the gate of the Lord;

the righteous shall enter through it.
I thank you that you have answered me
and have become my salvation.

Our Lord, we thank you for our salvation. And we thank you for the gift of the church, and the gift of this church. And we pray this day for our marriages, our homes, our jobs, and our ministries. We pray that you would bring an extraordinary spirit of humility, unity, and love within this body of believers.

Lord, we also pray for our nation and our world. We lift up our president and all who are in authority. Give them great wisdom in these days of internal and external conflict. And we lift up missionaries around the world. Use them to grow your gospel.

Father, we have gathered this day, the Lord's Day, in the name of our Lord Jesus Christ; our Jesus, who has taught us how to live, how to love, how to die to self, and also how to pray. And so we pray now the prayer he taught his disciples to pray:

Our Father, who art in heaven, hallowed be thy name.
Thy kingdom come, thy will be done, on earth as it is in heaven.
Give us this day our daily bread; and forgive us our debts, as we
forgive our debtors.
And lead us not into temptation, but deliver us from evil.
For thine is the kingdom, the power, and the glory forever. Amen.

A Prayer Based on Isaiah 40:27–31

Why do you complain, Jacob?
Why do you say, Israel,
"My way is hidden from the LORD;
my cause is disregarded by my God"?
Do you not know?
Have you not heard?
The LORD is the everlasting God,
the Creator of the ends of the earth.
He will not grow tired or weary,
and his understanding no one can fathom.
He gives strength to the weary
and increases the power of the weak.
Even youths grow tired and weary,
and young men stumble and fall;
but those who hope in the LORD
will renew their strength.

They will soar on wings like eagles;
>   they will run and not grow weary,
they will walk and not be faint.

Our Most High and supreme God, who exists from everlasting to everlasting, you spoke, and by your very word the earth and all that is in it came into being. Just as you have created the ends of the earth, so shall one day your glory be recognized unto the ends of the earth.

As your people, Lord, we come to you as those who can relate to the words of Isaiah. Because of the fall, and because of our ongoing sin, we undergo much pain and heartache in our lives, and sometimes we feel that our way is hidden and disregarded by you. Some of us go through personal struggles in our hearts and in our minds. We have an ache inside that has gone untreated for so long. We think that our way is hidden from your sight—that there is no hope. Some of us have struggles in our homes, families, marriages, or with our children, and when days and weeks and months go by with little or no change, we feel as if we're at the end of our rope and we find ourselves saying, "My cause is disregarded by my God." All of us here, Lord, feel the effects of the sin that has been brought on by humanity's rebellion against you, and all of us, at one time or another, and maybe even right now, feel weak and weary.

And so we call upon you, O Lord, and we ask you to revive us. Your Word here declares that you give strength to the weary, and so we pray that you would send your Spirit to comfort and strengthen those who struggle. We pray for those whose struggles are unseen to the world, who struggle within themselves with anger, sadness, dissatisfaction, or even despair. We pray that you would come to them, comfort them, and instill in them the hope of trusting in you, the One who does not grow tired or weary. We pray for those whose struggles are with others, whether within the family, within the church, or elsewhere. We pray, Lord, that you would increase the power of the weak and that you would mend broken relationships. We are prone to become hard—Lord, make us soft. We are prone to despair—Lord, give us hope.

And our hope is in your Word, that those who trust in you will have their strength renewed, not in our time, Lord, but in yours. Our hope is in your Word, that those who trust and hope in you will soar on wings like eagles, not by our own strength, but by yours. Our hope, O Lord, is in your promises, that you are making all things new, that you have started this process through the work of your Son, Jesus, that one day there will be no more tears, and that you are able to bring it to completion because, unlike us, you do not tire or grow weary.

We praise you, our sovereign Lord, and we cling to your Son Jesus as our hope and our Savior. In his powerful name we pray. Amen.

A Prayer Based on Isaiah 66:22–24

"As the new heavens and the new earth that I make will endure before me," declares the LORD, "so will your name and descendants endure. From one New Moon to another and from one Sabbath to another, all mankind will come and bow down before me," says the LORD. "And they will go out and look on the dead bodies of those who rebelled against me; the worms that eat them will not die, the fire that burns them will not be quenched, and they will be loathsome to all mankind." (NIV)

Our God, in the beginning you created the heavens and the earth. Your power is shown forth in creation. And in the end you will create the new heaven and the new earth. Your power is again shown forth as you conquer the death brought about by Satan and establish your creation as a place of righteousness and peace. Your majesty will then be fully revealed, as all mankind will come and bow down before you, the King of kings and Lord of lords.

Lord, we confess here this morning that left to ourselves we are rebels and deserve nothing but death. But because of your patient mercy, you have taken us, who were dead in our sins, and made us alive in Christ. You have turned us from rebels to servants, from enemies to your children. Although we have never deserved it, you have given us a place in your new creation as sons and daughters of the High King. Praise be to you for your great mercy!

Our Father, we pray for this city in which we live. We pray because there are many, many people here who remain dead in their sins, imprisoned by Satan's deception that you are not real, convinced that they face no judgment from you upon their death, and persistent in rebelling against you. Although they have been created in your royal image, Lord, they do not reflect you by their words and actions. Our God, even as you will create a new heaven and a new earth for those who profess faith in you through Jesus Christ, so does your Word say that those who rebel against you unto death will be punished with unquenchable fire.

Our God, this grieves us, not merely for the sake of the lost and the dreadful fate that awaits them, but especially because of your great name. Lord, would you show your power, grace, and mercy to this city by redeeming the lost by your Word and Spirit? For your great name's sake, Lord, would you take many in this city who are dead and make them alive? Would you conquer those who do not give their allegiance to you as King, renew their hearts and minds, and give them a new name—Christian—bringing them into your kingdom to enjoy the new heaven and new earth, all for the glory of your name?

Lord, we pray for us as a church. We pray that you would embolden and enable us, as the body of Christ, to be faithful witnesses to these truths. We pray that you would give us the ability to live and serve now in this present creation with our eyes fixed on the new creation. We pray for humility of character, that we would not hinder your gospel by our pride. We pray for wisdom and understanding, that we would know your Word well in order to communicate it to others. We pray for perseverance under opposition, that we would not fear mocking or scorning. And we pray for peace and unity within our church and among all the churches that believe your gospel—that division would not taint your message of peace. We worship and adore you, our God Most High. May your kingdom come on earth as it is in heaven. In Jesus's name. Amen.

A Prayer Based on Jeremiah 10:6–10

No one is like you, LORD;
    you are great,
    and your name is mighty in power.
Who should not fear you,
    King of the nations?
    This is your due.
Among all the wise leaders of the nations
    and in all their kingdoms,
    there is no one like you.
They are all senseless and foolish;
    they are taught by worthless wooden idols.
Hammered silver is brought from Tarshish
    and gold from Uphaz.
What the craftsman and goldsmith have made
    is then dressed in blue and purple—
    all made by skilled workers.
But the LORD is the true God;
    he is the living God, the eternal King.
When he is angry, the earth trembles;
    the nations cannot endure his wrath. (NIV)

O Lord, our God, as Jeremiah says, so do we say here this morning: Great is your name. You are mighty in power and worthy of all honor, adoration, and reverence, and so we gather together as your people this morning to give you your due. We praise you as the true God, the Creator of heaven and earth, the King of kings and the Lord of lords.

Lord, your Word here describes the foolishness of idolatry—the giving of allegiance to created things that cannot provide life and do not provide satisfaction. Father, although we here are not guilty of fashioning wooden idols, we are certainly guilty of being taught by and often following the worthless idols of our society. Although we are not tempted to bow down to hammered silver, the temptation is hammered into our heads that happiness is found in the attainment of the ideal. We are guilty of idolizing the ideal life, the ideal job, the ideal spouse, the ideal home—the ideal situation—and in idolizing such things, we distract ourselves from the true source of joy and satisfaction, *you.*

Lord, we confess this to you today, and we confess along with Jeremiah that you are a righteous God who would be just in bringing your wrath upon us. Because of this, it is only upon your great mercy that we cast ourselves. Our only hope is that you will be pleased to forgive, and it is with great joy, therefore, that we look upon the work of your Son, Jesus. As a faithful Son, Jesus never bowed to idols or sought to better his situation by manipulating his circumstances, and because you are indeed a God of great mercy, you have credited us with his faithfulness, and have placed the punishment for our idolatry upon him. Praise be to you, our God. Thank you for your grace and mercy upon us, and may this truth be the garment of joy and hope in which we dress ourselves.

We read in this text also that you are not only the King of Jeremiah, the King of Israel, but that you are the King of the nations as well. And, Lord, we know that there are many nations even now that are steeped in great idolatry. Some still have literal idols of wood, silver, and gold, and some have idols similar to those of our own society. And we know that in many of these places, this good news of your Son Jesus is not known—many nations do not know the God who made them, and the only God who can save them. We pray for these nations, Father, and as Jesus instructed us to pray, we pray that your kingdom would come, that your will would be done, on earth—over the whole earth—as it is in heaven. We pray that you would show your mercy to the nations because they cannot endure your wrath. Although you are just to judge, we pray that you would use your church to extend your mercy across creation. In Jesus's name. Amen.

A Prayer Based on Daniel 7:13–14

In my vision at night I looked, and there before me was one like a son of man, coming with the clouds of heaven. He approached the Ancient of Days and was led into his presence. He was given authority, glory and sovereign power; all nations and peoples of every language worshiped him. His dominion is an everlasting dominion that will not pass away, and his kingdom is one that will never be destroyed. (NIV)

Our Father, you are the Ancient of Days, the one who has existed from eternity past, who created this world out of nothing, and who decreed that your glory should fill this earth as far as the waters cover the seas.

Lord, you have made us, humanity, as your image bearers, those you created to reflect you and to represent you obediently throughout this earth. But like Adam and Eve before us, all of us have gone astray. We have all eaten the forbidden fruit of misplaced priorities and disbelief. None of us, Lord, have sought first your kingdom and your righteousness. Instead of being preoccupied with your glory throughout this earth—of seeing your gospel preached to all nations—we often prioritize our own agendas of our comfort, happiness, and security. Instead of investing our energies in your kingdom that will never be destroyed, we try to erect our own little futile kingdoms, where we are the rulers, where we are served, but which are ultimately like mist that vanishes in an instant.

Father, because of our sin, we are in need of one to take our place. We are in need of a human like us—one like a Son of Man—to obey where we have failed. Lord, we see this Son of Man in your Son Jesus, whom you sent to this earth to redeem us. We confess that we are cracked images of you in need of forgiveness, and that our hope is built on nothing less than Jesus's blood and righteousness. We thank you that in your mercy, you laid our punishment upon him, and we praise you that the grave could not hold our Savior in, but that you raised him up, that he has ascended on the clouds to your presence, and that all authority in heaven and on earth has been given to him. We praise you, Lord, that Jesus's authority is over all nations, all peoples, and that as Daniel's vision shows us, one day people from every tribe, language, and nation will worship him. May this make us bold as we serve you, our God.

We pray for our missionaries—for those who serve in _____, as well as the many others in our sphere who labor amidst the nations with your gospel—that the power of your everlasting dominion would empower their efforts. We pray that the fact that they serve you, the Ancient of Days, whose plan for your own glory throughout this earth will not be thwarted, would encourage them when they are discouraged, would strengthen them when they are weak, and would enable them to spread the glories of Jesus Christ, the Son of Man, who suffered on our behalf, yet who has been vindicated in glory.

Lord, we pray also for ourselves, the congregation of _____. We pray that you would shape our hearts and minds so we would view this world the way that you do—as the display case of your majesty, which you have called us to participate in filling with the redeemed from every nation. May we view our resources, money, and time as instruments to be used by you. May we become preoccupied with your plan for the nations, and may you use us despite our shortcomings for your glory, by your Sprit. We praise you for your mercy, and we long for the day when you will consummate your plan for the world, when all peoples will worship Jesus as King, and when sin will be no more on this earth. Amen, come Lord Jesus. Amen.

A Prayer Based on Habakkuk 2:2–4

Then the LORD replied:

"Write down the revelation
  and make it plain on tablets
  so that a herald may run with it.
For the revelation awaits an appointed time;
  it speaks of the end
  and will not prove false.
Though it linger, wait for it;
  it will certainly come
  and will not delay.
See, the enemy is puffed up;
  his desires are not upright—
but the righteous person will live by his faithfulness." (NIV)

Lord, you are great and most worthy of praise, and we your people ascribe to you glory, honor, and majesty, for you are the one true God, the Maker of heaven and earth, and you and you alone are due our allegiance and our worship. We praise you that throughout the ages you have required the same thing from your people—faith—trust in you and in your words. From Adam in the garden, you required faith. From Israel during the time of Habakkuk, you required faith. And from us now, you also require faith.

However, Lord, we confess that even as your requirement of faith has been consistent, our failure to meet that requirement has also been consistent. Adam did not trust your word in the garden, and so sin entered this world. Israel did not trust your word, and so you exiled them out of their land. And we, too, Lord, like them, are often guilty of a lack of faith.

Father, our lack of faith is reflected by our worries, stresses, and fears that often consume us. We worry about the future—how our jobs will hold up, how our kids will grow up, whether or not we'll achieve what we want to achieve. We stress about the present—how our relationships are going or not going, how we are perceived by others, and how we will manage the workload of our busy lives. And we fear the unknown—what will happen tomorrow, whether or not we can handle what is coming next. Father, our tendency is to dwell on things like these, to focus on them, instead of focusing on you, the one who sustains all things by your power and might, and putting our faith and trust in your ability to provide for us in every way.

Lord, forgive us this tendency not to trust you. Forgive us, and restore in us hearts that are prone, not to wander from you, but to wait faithfully upon you and to trust your good providence. Free us from our tendency to want to walk by sight—to see the path ahead and to know the particulars of it. Instead, give us eyes and hearts that are content to walk by faith, even when it means we cannot see.

Lord, we pray for those here today who are struggling with various issues. We pray for those with concerns about jobs. Lord, give them faith to trust and rest in your sustaining providence. We pray for those with concerns about relationships. Give them faith to forgive where necessary or to ask for forgiveness where necessary. We pray for those whose hearts hurt for one reason or another. May you put lenses of faith over their eyes through which to view their pain—not lenses that ignore their pain, but lenses that put it in the proper perspective.

Most of all, we pray for those in this room, in this city, and in the world who have not put their ultimate faith in you for this life and the next life. We pray for those who have not turned from their rebellion against you and have not yet trusted Jesus for their salvation. Lord, would you give them eyes of faith to turn to you and find forgiveness and life everlasting?

May we not be a puffed-up people who trust in ourselves, but may we be a people characterized by radical faith in you. In Jesus's name we pray. Amen.

A Prayer Based on the Sermon on the Mount (Matthew 5–7)

Our Father in heaven, as we pray now the words of your Son, we ask—for the sake of your glory and our blessedness—that you would help us to be poor in spirit, to mourn over our own sins and the sins of the world, to be meek, to hunger and thirst for righteousness, to be merciful, to be pure in heart, and to endure persecution for righteousness' sake.

And, Father, we ask that you would encourage us, through your Holy Spirit, to be active in good works, making us the salt of the earth and the light of the world, so that many might give glory not to us but to you.

Lord, make us quick to forgive our enemies and those who have trespassed against us, quick to serve those in need, and slow to murder through thought, word, or deed. Purify our minds of all wicked and adulterous thoughts, allowing us to be faithful both to you and our loved ones. And, Lord, in these days when lies are the norm, make us abnormal—enable us to speak the truth always.

Father, as we reflect on our righteousness in and through Christ (what a gift to us!), we ask that you would give us even more "righteousness"— that is, an unseen life of righteous prayer, righteous fasting, and righteous service; and yet make us ever aware of trumpeting our faith in order to be seen and esteemed by others.

Lord, may you and you alone be our only Master; and thus keep our hearts from the love of money and any other earthly treasure, and help us instead to lay up eternal treasures in heaven.

Gracious God, help us with our worries. Make us anxious only about your rule on earth. Grant that we may seek first the kingdom of God and your righteousness; so calm our cares over life, and even over the necessities of food, drink, clothing, and shelter.

Our holy and loving God, help us not to be judgmental, but to judge rightly; so allow us first to see our own sin, and then, if necessary, the sins of others. Lord, help us to be prayerful—to knock upon the door of heaven in the trust and hope that you will give us only good things, even your Holy Spirit. Lord, remind us always of the narrow gate, that the way that leads to life is hard and that few find it. And, Father, for the sake of our very souls, keep us aware of and away from false teachers and their works of lawlessness; Lord, kept by your grace, may we never in thought or deed follow their wide path, incurring your judgment.

Father, Son, and Spirit, make us always attentive to Christ's words, these words we have now prayed, so that we might build the house of our lives upon the rock of your truth. And give us a renewed vision for your kingdom priorities as we now pray the prayer Jesus taught his disciples to pray:

Our Father, who art in heaven, hallowed be thy name.
Thy kingdom come, thy will be done, on earth as it is in heaven.
Give us this day our daily bread; and forgive us our debts, as we
    forgive our debtors.

And lead us not into temptation, but deliver us from evil.
For thine is the kingdom, the power, and the glory forever. Amen.

A Prayer Based on Mary's Magnificat *(Luke 1:46–55)*

Lord, we rejoice as Mary did years ago, that you have sent to us a Savior—your Son and our Lord, Jesus Christ. And we come to you this day, as humble servants, in order that we might magnify your holy name; that we might give praise to you as our exalted King, as the God who has fulfilled his promise to Abraham and to his offspring in the person of Jesus.

Father in heaven, you are a God who scatters the proud and lifts up the humble, who brings down the mighty from their thrones and exalts those of low estate. So, Lord, we come now in humility, in low estate, in poverty of spirit, recognizing our need for the riches that Christ alone provides. And so give to us again and again the wealth of his mercy. Forgive us our sins against you. Forgive us our sins against others. Cleanse our hands and hearts from all iniquities, and wash us clean in the blood of our Lord.

Father, you are the Lord who fills the hungry with good things and sends the rich away empty. You are a God of provision, protection, and promise for your people, and a Judge to those who oppose your ways. And so, Lord, we ask that you would judge the wicked; that you would soon send your Son again, to judge the living and the dead, to bring upon the earth an eternal kingdom of righteousness and peace. Yet, Lord, in the meantime, for those of us who are your people and who live now between the first and second advents of Christ, we ask that you would continue to meet all our spiritual and physical needs. And we ask in the way your Son taught us to ask for provision and protection, praying together the Lord's Prayer:

Our Father, who art in heaven, hallowed be thy name.
Thy kingdom come, thy will be done, on earth as it is in heaven.
Give us this day our daily bread; and forgive us our debts, as we
     forgive our debtors.
And lead us not into temptation, but deliver us from evil.
For thine is the kingdom, the power, and the glory forever. Amen.

A Prayer Based on 2 Corinthians 1:3–5

Praise be to the God and Father of our Lord Jesus Christ, the Father of compassion and the God of all comfort, who comforts us in all our troubles, so that we can comfort those in any trouble with the comfort we ourselves receive from God. For just as we share abundantly in the sufferings of Christ, so also our comfort abounds through Christ. (NIV)

Father, we do praise you as a God who comforts the afflicted, as a God who mercifully draws near to your children with fatherly compassion. You are the true expression of a loving Father, and we exalt you and glorify you this morning.

But, Lord, although you have shown yourself compassionate, we often find ourselves living with a lack of compassion toward others and a lack of passion toward you—like children who have been given a bounty of good gifts, yet thanklessly and thoughtlessly have cast them aside.

We view our troubles and sufferings, not as a unifying participation with the suffering that Jesus went through on our behalf, but rather as obstacles to be avoided. We view our troubles and sufferings, not as opportunities to trust you and be filled with your supreme comfort and so show your glory, but rather as barriers to the shortsighted happiness and pleasure for which we foolishly thirst. We want comfort from you, but we are unwilling to suffer for you. And when suffering does come, we proclaim with our lips that you are our Great Comforter, but we often look to find our comfort from every other futile source we know of before turning to you. Lord, we confess these things to you and ask you, as our great Father of compassion, to forgive us.

We pray, Lord, not that you would spare us from suffering for your sake, but rather that you would comfort us and sustain us in the midst of that suffering—to the glory of your great name—and that through that comforting, we would receive unspeakable joy and would attest to your great compassion.

We pray that you would indeed comfort those of us who are troubled and suffering here. But do not allow us to be unchanged by your compassion. Rather, Lord, let it overflow in and through us to others, both within and without the church, that your glory as the Father of compassion may spread throughout this church, this city, and this world.

We pray for the brokenhearted, that you would mend them.

We pray for the sick, that you would heal them.

We pray for the proud, that you would humble them.

We pray for the weak, that you would strengthen them.

We pray for the apathetic, that you would enliven them.

We thank you for purchasing us from death and giving us life in Christ, our Savior.

We pray, Lord, most of all, that we would be a people who find our rest and comfort in you and, in turn, who offer your rest and comfort to others—to the glory of your name. In Christ's name we pray. Amen.

A Prayer Based on Ephesians 4:2–6

> Be completely humble and gentle; be patient, bearing with one another in love. Make every effort to keep the unity of the Spirit through the bond of peace. There is one body and one Spirit, just as you were called to one hope when you were called; one Lord, one faith, one baptism; one God and Father of all, who is over all and through all and in all. (NIV)

Our Father, we praise you as the mighty Creator, the Most High King of kings, the exalted Lord of lords, the one who is over all and in all; yet you have condescended to dwell with humanity—in relationship with us—and you even call us your children. In the garden with Adam, in the temple with Israel, in the flesh through your Son, and even now in our hearts by your Spirit, you are a God who has drawn near to us, our Immanuel.

Your Son Jesus, in his incarnation and throughout his life, provided the ultimate demonstration of humility, gentleness, patience, and love. He did not consider equality with God something to be grasped, but he made himself nothing, becoming a servant and humbling himself even unto death for sinners such as us. In light of his obedience, Lord, and in light of your commands for us to imitate him, we are acutely struck by how we struggle to keep them.

Lord, give us humility. Relieve us of the inborn pride that fights in our flesh and replace it with a recognition that we are sinners saved by grace, brought into your kingdom to reflect the humble One who has purchased us with the high price of his life. Lord, give us gentleness. O how we are prone to anger, yet your Word says that man's anger does not bring about the righteous life that you desire. Lord, cultivate in our hearts a softness toward those around us. When our flesh moves us toward intemperance in our relationships, help us to display gentleness. Help us to remember that we are recipients of your gentle forgiveness of our deep transgressions, that we might show such gentleness toward others. Lord, give us patience. We feel our impatient tendencies—our quickness to point out the faults of others and our forgetfulness of our past faults. Rebuke our haughtiness, Lord. When a spouse disappoints us or a friend hurts us, give us the patience of heart and mind to extend grace to them, and in so doing to reflect well the grace and patience you have shown to us.

Lord, in learning to grow in these ways, may we bear with one another in love. May the love that we display to one another be a reflection of the sacrificial love that your Son Jesus has shown to us. May we be willing to sacrifice for one another—our time, our money, our emotions—in order to build one another up, and so that the world may look upon us, see that we are one, and know that you have called us and changed us. By our unity in the Spirit, may they see your love reflected and come to you, the great King who is worthy of their praise and allegiance.

We thank you, Lord, that you have given us redemption by your Son and new birth by your Spirit, and that you have promised that you will bring to completion this work that you have started in us. In Jesus's name. Amen.

BENEDICTIONS

A benediction is simply a "good word" prayed by the pastor at the conclusion of a worship service, though there may be occasions for one during the service. Generally it is done by use of a brief sentence or two of Scripture, but not always. For example, the following benediction, based on a line from Philippians 4:7, comes from the Book of Common Prayer and is used verbatim in the Presbyterian Book of Common Worship:

> The peace of God which passeth all understanding, keep your hearts and minds in the knowledge and love of God, and of his Son Jesus Christ our Lord: And the blessing of God Almighty, the Father, the Son and the Holy Ghost, be amongst you and remain with you always. *Amen.*

Another venerable example that contains no explicit scriptural citation reads as follows:

> Grant, we beseech thee, Almighty God, that the words, which we have heard this day with our outward ears, may through thy grace be so grafted inwardly in our hearts, that they may bring forth in us the fruit of good living, to the honour and praise of thy name; through Jesus Christ our Lord. *Amen.*

Both these prayers (in modern English) make wonderful benedictions to the preaching of God's Word.

This said, most benedictions do well to quote or stay close to the rich treasury of benedictions in Scripture. Some are explicit benedictions in their contexts, while others are implicit benedictions that, with a couple of introductory words, work well. Also, nice benedictions can be created by conflating texts—for example, Romans 16:25, "Now to him who is able to strengthen you," and verse 27, "to the only wise God be glory forevermore through Jesus Christ! Amen."

We have listed numerous examples of scriptural benedictions in the following pages. The list makes it easy for the pastor to locate a benediction that fits a particular situation. We have not included Old Testament possibilities for benedictions because the Old Testament Scriptures do not abound with explicit benedictions as do the epistolary writings of the New Testament. However, when preaching from the Old Testament, the preacher will find that most texts contain memorable lines that can be easily crafted into perfect benedictions. It must be mentioned that the two most used benedictions in Protestant worship are the Aaronic benediction, "The LORD bless you . . ." (Num. 6:24–26), and the Pauline blessing, "The grace of the Lord Jesus Christ . . ." (2 Cor. 13:14).

Benedictions are not to be pronounced or "said," but prayed with the pastor's heart and mind fully engaged. Offering a benediction at the conclusion of worship on behalf of God's people is a high privilege, and an opportunity to remind them of the preached Word and to send them out with a sense of blessing and mission as they depart for their week.[22]

NEW TESTAMENT BENEDICTIONS

Grace to you and peace from God our Father and the Lord Jesus Christ. (Rom. 1:7b)

[Let us remember that] from him and through him and to him are all things. To him be glory forever. Amen. (Rom. 11:36)

May the God of endurance and encouragement grant you to live in such harmony with one another, in accord with Christ Jesus, that together you may with one voice glorify the God and Father of our Lord Jesus Christ. (Rom. 15:5–6)

May the God of hope fill you with all joy and peace in believing, so that by the power of the Holy Spirit you may abound in hope. (Rom. 15:13)

May the God of peace be with you all. Amen. (Rom. 15:33)

The God of peace will soon crush Satan under your feet. The grace of our Lord Jesus Christ be with you. (Rom. 16:20)

Grace to you and peace from God our Father and the Lord Jesus Christ. (1 Cor. 1:3)

[22] Bryan Chapell, *Christ-Centered Worship: Letting the Gospel Shape Our Practice* (Grand Rapids: Baker Academic, 2009), 252–254, details the rich pastoral theology underlying the benediction.

Therefore, my beloved brothers, be steadfast, immovable, always abounding in the work of the Lord, knowing that in the Lord your labor is not in vain. (1 Cor. 15:58)

The grace of the Lord Jesus be with you. (1 Cor. 16:23)

Grace to you and peace from God our Father and the Lord Jesus Christ. (2 Cor. 1:2)

Blessed be the God and Father of our Lord Jesus Christ, the Father of mercies and God of all comfort, who comforts us in all our affliction, so that we may be able to comfort those who are in any affliction. (2 Cor. 1:3–4a)

And God is able to make all grace abound to you, so that having all sufficiency in all things at all times, you may abound in every good work. (2 Cor. 9:8)

The grace of the Lord Jesus Christ and the love of God and the fellowship of the Holy Spirit be with you all. (2 Cor. 13:14)

Grace to you and peace from God our Father and the Lord Jesus Christ. (Gal. 1:3)

Grace to you and peace from God our Father and the Lord Jesus Christ. (Eph. 1:2)

Blessed be the God and Father of our Lord Jesus Christ, who has blessed us in Christ with every spiritual blessing in the heavenly places. (Eph. 1:3)

[May] Christ . . . dwell in your hearts through faith—that you, being rooted and grounded in love, may have strength to comprehend with all the saints what is the breadth and length and height and depth, and to know the love of Christ that surpasses knowledge, that you may be filled with all the fullness of God. (Eph. 3:17–19)

Now to him who is able to do far more abundantly than all that we ask or think, according to the power at work within us, to him be glory in the church and in Christ Jesus throughout all generations, forever and ever. Amen. (Eph. 3:20–21)

Peace be to the brothers, and love with faith, from God the Father and the Lord Jesus Christ. Grace be with all who love our Lord Jesus Christ with love incorruptible. (Eph. 6:23–24)

Grace to you and peace from God our Father and the Lord Jesus Christ. (Phil. 1:2)

[May] the peace of God, which surpasses all understanding, . . . guard your hearts and your minds in Christ Jesus. (Phil. 4:7)

The grace of the Lord Jesus Christ be with your spirit. (Phil. 4:23)

Grace to you and peace from God our Father. (Col. 1:2b)

Now may the God of peace himself sanctify you completely, and may your whole spirit and soul and body be kept blameless at the coming of our Lord Jesus Christ. He who calls you is faithful; he will surely do it. (1 Thess. 5:23–24)

The grace of our Lord Jesus Christ be with you. (1 Thess. 5:28)

Grace to you and peace from God our Father and the Lord Jesus Christ. (2 Thess. 1:2)

Now may our Lord Jesus Christ himself, and God our Father, who loved us and gave us eternal comfort and good hope through grace, comfort your hearts and establish them in every good work and word. (2 Thess. 2:16–17)

Now may the Lord of peace himself give you peace at all times in every way. The Lord be with you all. (2 Thess. 3:16)

The grace of our Lord Jesus Christ be with you all. (2 Thess. 3:18)

Grace, mercy, and peace from God the Father and Christ Jesus our Lord. (1 Tim. 1:2b)

To the King of the ages, immortal, invisible, the only God, be honor and glory forever and ever. Amen. (1 Tim. 1:17)

He who is the blessed and only Sovereign, the King of kings and Lord of lords, who alone has immortality, who dwells in unapproachable light, whom no one has ever seen or can see. To him be honor and eternal dominion. Amen. (1 Tim. 6:15–16)

Grace be with you. (1 Tim. 6:21b)

Grace, mercy, and peace from God the Father and Christ Jesus our Lord. (2 Tim. 1:2b)

The Lord be with your spirit. Grace be with you. (2 Tim. 4:22)

Grace to you and peace from God our Father and the Lord Jesus Christ. (Philem. 3)

The grace of the Lord Jesus Christ be with your spirit. (Philem. 25)

Now may the God of peace who brought again from the dead our Lord Jesus, the great shepherd of the sheep, by the blood of the eternal covenant, equip you with everything good that you may do his will, working in us that which is pleasing in his sight, through Jesus Christ, to whom be glory forever and ever. Amen. (Heb. 13:20–21)

Grace be with all of you. (Heb. 13:25)

According to the foreknowledge of God the Father, in the sanctification of the Spirit, for obedience to Jesus Christ and for sprinkling with his blood: May grace and peace be multiplied to you. (1 Pet. 1:2)

After you have suffered a little while, the God of all grace, who has called you to his eternal glory in Christ, will himself restore, confirm, strengthen, and establish you. To him be the dominion forever and ever. Amen. (1 Pet. 5:10–11)

Peace to all of you who are in Christ. (1 Pet. 5:14b)

Grace, mercy, and peace will be with us, from God the Father and from Jesus Christ the Father's Son, in truth and love. (2 John 3)

May mercy, peace, and love be multiplied to you. (Jude 2)

Now to him who is able to keep you from stumbling and to present you blameless before the presence of his glory with great joy, to the only God, our Savior, through Jesus Christ our Lord, be glory, majesty, dominion, and authority, before all time and now and forever. Amen. (Jude 24–25)

To him who loves us and has freed us from our sins by his blood and made us a kingdom, priests to his God and Father, to him be glory and dominion forever and ever. Amen. (Rev. 1:5b–6)

Worthy are you, our Lord and God, to receive glory and honor and power, for you created all things, and by your will they existed and were created. (Rev. 4:11)

To him who sits on the throne and to the Lamb be blessing and honor and glory and might forever and ever! (Rev. 5:13b)

Amen! Blessing and glory and wisdom and thanksgiving and honor and power and might be to our God forever and ever! Amen. (Rev. 7:12)

The grace of the Lord Jesus be with all. Amen. (Rev. 22:21)

6

The Historic
Christian Creeds

By Douglas Sean O'Donnell

John H. Leith has written in *Creeds of the Churches*:

> Christianity has always been a "creedal" religion in that it has always
> been theological. It was rooted in the theological tradition of ancient
> Israel, which was unified by its historical credos and declaratory affir-
> mations of the faith. No pretheological era has been discovered in the
> New Testament or in the history of the Christian community. From the
> beginning Christianity has been theological, involving men in theologi-
> cal reflection and calling them to declarations of faith. A nontheological
> Christianity has simply never endured.[1]

In *The Abolition of Man*, C. S. Lewis writes: "An open mind, in questions
that are not ultimate, is useful. But an open mind about ultimate foundations . . . is idiocy. If a man's mind is open on these things, let his mouth at
least be shut."[2]

In this chapter, we will discuss the ultimate foundations of our faith as
expressed in the historic Christian creeds, notably the Apostles' Creed and the
Nicene Creed (or, more technically accurate, the "Niceno-Constantinopolitan
Creed"). We will begin with the *importance* of creeds (What is the value in
saying creeds?), move to their *origins* (What is the content and history behind
these creeds?), and end with *expressions* (How might we use them today?).

---

[1] John H. Leith, *Creeds of the Churches*, 3rd ed. (Louisville: John Knox, 1982), 1.
[2] C. S. Lewis, *The Abolition of Man* (New York: HarperOne, 1974), 48.

IMPORTANCE

Everyone believes in God. Demons do (James 2:19). Atheists do (Rom. 1:18–21). And, of course, Christians do. The historic Christian creeds are simply condensed statements about what the church universal has believed and continues to believe about God. They are not Spirit-inspired or exhaustive summaries, but they do reflect scriptural language and theology,[3] represent historical consensus, and encapsulate the basics of the Christian faith. They are the church's effort to articulate concisely and coherently what God has revealed to us in Christ through the Bible. As Carl Trueman notes:

> No Christian, if asked by a friend what the Bible teaches, is simply going to start reading aloud at Genesis 1:1 and not stop until Revelation 22:21. Instead, when asked by friends what the Bible teaches, we all try to offer a synthesis, a summary of what the Bible says. And as we move from biblical text to theological statement, we offer what is, in terms of content, something akin to a creed or confession.[4]

Thus, creeds are "theological mirrors of the Bible's fundamental doctrine."[5] Likewise, "They are the product of many centuries of Bible study by a great company of believers. They are a kind of spiritual 'road map' of the teaching of the Bible, already worked out and proved by others before us."[6] They provide a "concise rendering of the Christian story and . . . vision of reality," being instruments "that can at once define the community of faith and challenge alternative stories and visions of reality."[7] Therefore, for these reasons and many more, creeds are useful, reliable, and even authoritative truths that every Christian should know and be able to say from the heart. In our ever-more-anti-confessional age (with its many creedless churches), these ancient but timeless documents are essential to Christianity's stability

---

[3] The ancient ecumenical creeds and Protestant confessions, as Carl E. Trueman notes, "are often referred to as *normed norms* or, to use the Latin, *norma normata*, in contrast with Scripture which is the *norming norm*, or *norma normans*." *The Creedal Imperative* (Wheaton, IL: Crossway, 2012), 17. He explains how the Reformation did not pit Scripture versus tradition, but rather "scriptural tradition versus unscriptural tradition." He continues: "Thoughtful Protestants then, and ever since, have understood the Reformers as arguing for what we might call a tradition that is *normed* by Scripture. In other words, Protestants know that they use language and conceptual terminology not found explicitly in the Bible; but they understand such are useful in understanding what Scripture says and, at the point where they are found to be inadequate for this task, or even to contradict Scripture, there they must be modified or abandoned" (16). Thus, as argued throughout his book, "creeds and confessions are thoroughly consistent with the belief that Scripture alone is the unique source of revelation and authority" (19).
[4] Ibid., 160.
[5] Burk Parsons, *Why Do We Have Creeds?* Basics of the Faith (Phillipsburg, NJ: P&R, 2012), 19.
[6] G. I. Williamson, quoted in ibid., 21.
[7] Luke Timothy Johnson, *The Creed: What Christians Believe and Why It Matters* (New York: Doubleday, 2003), viii. In this quote, Johnson is speaking specifically about the Nicene Creed, but in our view, it is applicable to all the early Christian creeds.

and spiritual growth. While the postmodern world balks at religious truth as implausible and distasteful, we boast in Christ as "God of God . . . who . . . for our salvation came down from heaven."

In the earlier chapter "Sunday Worship," we stated some of our pastoral motives for including creeds in the Sunday service. For College Church, Kent has written:

> We employ the Creed for three reasons: (1) to affirm the essentials; (2) to emphasize that we are in the stream of historic orthodoxy; and (3) to provide a familiar reference to visitors and new Christians from mainline and Roman Catholic backgrounds. The Nicene Creed is often used during Advent, for the same reasons given above.[8]

And for New Covenant Church, Doug stated:

> Through a historic creed of the church (e.g., the Apostles' Creed) or a creedal statement of Scripture (e.g., Phil. 2:1–11; Col. 1:15–20), we join the communion of saints—past and present—as we together affirm some of the essential Christian beliefs (*credo* is Latin for "I believe"). Also, as we weekly recite various orthodox statements of faith—which have been believed by all Christians everywhere at all times—we renew our minds in the basic truths of God's revelation to us in Christ, thus combating heretical views about God, man, and salvation.

Others have given fuller rationales for the inclusion of creeds. For example, in his book *Why Do We Have Creeds?* Burk Parsons answers that question with his "practical ten-point summary of the purpose of creeds in the church."[9] This list is worth quoting in full. The purpose of creeds is:

1. To *glorify* God according to his truth and to enjoy him forever by believing, confessing, and proclaiming our doctrine in accordance with what he has revealed and not according to the superstitions of men, the deceitful schemes of Satan, or the arrogant and presumptuous notions of our own hearts.
2. To *affirm* the one true God almighty who has revealed himself to us and whose glorious attributes, gracious laws, and grand story of redemption point us to himself as our only Lord to the end that we might love him rightly and as fully as possible with all our heart, with all our soul, with all our mind, and with all our strength.

---

[8] R. Kent Hughes, "Free Church Worship: The Challenge of Freedom," in *Worship by the Book*, ed. D. A. Carson (Grand Rapids: Zondervan, 1992), 175.
[9] Parsons, *Why Do We Have Creeds?* 30.

3. To *guard* the unchanging, sound doctrine of Scripture against false teachers and heretics outside the church, and to guard against the vain and false notions of Scripture from within the church as a shining witness of God's truth to the watching world out of which God calls his elect through the preaching of the gospel and inward call of the Holy Spirit.

4. To *discern* truth from doctrinal error and to discern truth from half-truth as we contend earnestly for the faith once delivered to the saints that we might grow up in every way into Christ, who is the living head of the church, who is the way, the truth, the life, and the only way to the Father.

5. To *remain* steadfast through the ages until Christ's return as one, holy, catholic, and apostolic church of Christ who believe, confess, and proclaim the pure and unadulterated Word of God and who rightly administer the sacraments of baptism and the Lord's Supper, including our consistent exercise of church admonition, correction, and discipline.

6. To *uphold* the life-encompassing doctrine of the inspired and inerrant Word of God as our sole, infallible authority that is profitable for doctrine, for reproof, for correction, for instruction in righteousness to the end that every man of God might be complete, thoroughly equipped for every good work.

7. To *maintain* freedom for individual Christians as well as the entire church from extra-biblical laws, traditions, and superstitions of men that bind men's consciences, perplex men's souls, lead our children astray according to their sin, and bring about man-exalting pride instead of God-exalting humility.

8. To *confirm* men according to the church's doctrinal standard who have been elected to serve as officers of the church as well as to equip, examine, and prove those men who have been called as pastors and elders over the flock of God, and to ascertain their suitability to teach as they feed, care for, and pray with and for the sheep of Christ for whom he gave his life.

9. To *preserve* the purity and, thereby, the peace and unity of the church visible as the outward witness of Christ and his elect bride, the church invisible, to the end that we might stand together as one family with one Father, one Lord, one faith, one baptism, unwaveringly according to and because of the truth, never in spite of, disregard for, or ignorance of it.

10. To *fulfill* the Great Commission in our united affirmation and proclamation of the one true gospel of Jesus Christ, which is the only power of God unto salvation to all who believe, by making disciples in our homes, churches, communities, and in all nations, baptizing them in the name of

the Father, Son, and Holy Spirit and teaching them to observe all things that our Lord Jesus Christ commanded us.[10]

Each Sunday, as we gather with God's people in God's presence, we renew our vision and communal identity. And when we recite one of the historic Christian creeds, we take a few minutes to remind ourselves of our story, one drawn from the great storyline of Scripture itself. We begin by announcing God's creation and end with his awesome eschatology. And between the start and stop, we announce the gospel: our salvation in the birth, sufferings, death, resurrection, ascension, and return of the God-man, Jesus Christ. What could be more important than that!? "[C]reeds are central to Christian doxology."[11] What a wise way to spend but two minutes out of our 10,080-minute week.

ORIGINS

While there is no command in the Bible to recite creeds, the earliest church— that of the New Testament—speaks often of commonly held theological truths by a variety of different names: "the gospel" (Rom. 1:1; 1:16; Gal. 1:6), "the/our confession" (Heb. 3:1; 4:14; 10:23), "the tradition" (2 Thess. 3:6), "the faith" (Acts 6:7; Col. 2:7; Jude 3), "the testimony of Jesus" (Rev. 1:2; 12:17; 19:10), and "the teaching" or "doctrine" (1 Tim. 4:16; Heb. 6:1). And texts such as Matthew 28:18–20 and Ephesians 4:11–16 (printed below) imply the imperative of Christian leaders disciplining through a recognizable set and summary of doctrine:

> And Jesus came and said to them, "All authority in heaven and on earth has been given to me. Go therefore and make disciples of all nations, baptizing them in the name of the Father and of the Son and of the Holy Spirit, teaching them to observe all that I have commanded you. And behold, I am with you always, to the end of the age." (Matt. 28:18–20)

> And he gave the apostles, the prophets, the evangelists, the shepherds and teachers, to equip the saints for the work of ministry, for building up the body of Christ, until we all attain to the unity of the faith and of the knowledge of the Son of God, to mature manhood, to the measure of the stature of the fullness of Christ, so that we may no longer

---

[10] Ibid., 30–32.
[11] Trueman, *The Creedal Imperative*, 19. "Historically, one could make the argument that Christian theology as a whole is one long, extended reflection upon the meaning and significance of that most basic doxological declaration, 'Jesus is Lord!' and thus an attempt to provide a framework for understanding Christian praise" (135).

be children, tossed to and fro by the waves and carried about by every wind of doctrine, by human cunning, by craftiness in deceitful schemes. Rather, speaking the truth in love, we are to grow up in every way into him who is the head, into Christ, from whom the whole body, joined and held together by every joint with which it is equipped, when each part is working properly, makes the body grow so that it builds itself up in love. (Eph. 4:11–16)

Moreover, the New Testament *does* offer imperatives to confess (*homologein*). We are to confess Jesus before others (Matt. 10:32)—to confess that he is "Lord" (Rom. 10:9–10) and God's Son who has "come in the flesh" (1 John 2:23; 4:2–3; 4:15; 2 John 7). This is our corporate "confession" (see 2 Cor. 9:13; Heb. 3:1; 4:14), one that bears witness to our basic beliefs (John 18:37; 19:35; Acts 2:40; 8:25; 1 Cor. 15:15; Rev. 22:18).[12]

Beyond these imperatives, there are certainly biblical *examples* of compressed creedal expressions in the Word's doctrine. Two creedal formations from the Old Testament are the Ten Commandments (Exodus 20) and the *Shema* (Deut. 6:4–5; cf. Matt. 22:34–40). For example, the two short verses of the *Shema* ("Hear, O Israel: The Lord our God, the Lord is one. You shall love the Lord your God with all your heart and with all your soul and with all your might") make at least three significant theological points.

First, the *Shema* is a call for communal and not simply individual commitment. Second, in the context of surrounding polytheistic cultures, it is exclusive. "The Lord" (the proper name of Israel's God, Yahweh) is both the "one" God and the only God to whom Israel owes allegiance. Finally, it is a personal commitment: Israelites are to "love" the Lord God with their whole heart, whole soul, and whole might. In other words, the *Shema* both defines the One to whom loyalty is given and defines Israel among the nations by its unique loyalty to this deity.[13]

Based on Old Testament creedal formulas like the *Shema*, the apostle Paul likewise formulated a number of mini-creeds (some based on the *Shema* itself—e.g., Rom. 3:29–30; 1 Cor. 8:4–6) to preserve and protect orthodoxy and to promote the "one faith" (Eph. 4:5) in Jesus as "Lord of all" (Acts 10:36). Below are his apostolic "creeds":

- ". . . the gospel of God, which he promised beforehand through his prophets in the holy Scriptures, concerning his Son, who was descended from David according to the flesh and was declared to be the Son of God

---

[12] For these references, see Johnson, *The Creed*, 42.
[13] Ibid., 11.

in power according to the Spirit of holiness by his resurrection from the dead, Jesus Christ our Lord, through whom we have received grace and apostleship to bring about the obedience of faith for the sake of his name among all the nations" (Rom. 1:1–5).

- "If you confess with your mouth that Jesus is Lord and believe in your heart that God raised him from the dead, you will be saved" (Rom. 10:9).
- "For I delivered to you as of first importance what I also received: that Christ died for our sins in accordance with the Scriptures, that he was buried, that he was raised on the third day in accordance with the Scriptures, and that he appeared to Cephas, then to the twelve. Then he appeared to more than five hundred brothers at one time, most of whom are still alive, though some have fallen asleep. Then he appeared to James, then to all the apostles" (1 Cor. 15:3–7).
- "[Jesus], though he was in the form of God, did not count equality with God a thing to be grasped, but emptied himself, by taking the form of a servant, being born in the likeness of men. And being found in human form, he humbled himself by becoming obedient to the point of death, even death on a cross. Therefore God has highly exalted him and bestowed on him the name that is above every name, so that at the name of Jesus every knee should bow, in heaven and on earth and under the earth, and every tongue confess that Jesus Christ is Lord, to the glory of God the Father" (Phil. 2:6–11).
- "He is the image of the invisible God, the firstborn of all creation. For by him all things were created, in heaven and on earth, visible and invisible, whether thrones or dominions or rulers or authorities—all things were created through him and for him. And he is before all things, and in him all things hold together. And he is the head of the body, the church. He is the beginning, the firstborn from the dead, that in everything he might be preeminent. For in him all the fullness of God was pleased to dwell, and through him to reconcile to himself all things, whether on earth or in heaven, making peace by the blood of his cross" (Col. 1:15–20).

Finally, "one of the most extensive and 'creedlike'" statements comes from Paul's first epistle to Timothy, where, in 1:5 and 3:16, Paul "incorporates the *Shema* and then expands it into a Christian rule of faith."[14] As Jaroslav Pelikan divides (and translates) the texts:

> There is one God;
>   there is also one mediator

---

[14] Jaroslav Pelikan, *Credo: Historical and Theological Guide to Creeds and Confessions of Faith in the Christian Tradition* (New Haven, CT: Yale, 2003), 133.

between God and
humankind;
Christ Jesus, himself human,
who gave himself a ransom for all. (1 Tim. 2:5–6)
He was revealed in flesh,
vindicated in spirit,
seen by angels,
proclaimed among Gentiles,
believed in throughout the world,
taken up in glory.[15]

When we consider what follows in 2 Timothy—namely, Paul's command to "follow the pattern of the sound words that you have heard from me, in the faith and love that are in Christ Jesus" (2 Tim. 1:13)—we can reasonably assume what Paul has in mind.

These miniature apostolic creeds are "like biblically sown seeds in the rich soil of the early church—seeds that grew into the more-advanced creedal formulations of the church in subsequent centuries,"[16] formulations such as the earliest Christian creeds (i.e., the Apostles' Creed and the Nicene Creed) and the later Protestant confessional standards (the Anglican Articles and Homilies; the Lutheran Book of Concord; the Three Forms of Unity; the Westminster Standards; and the 1689 Baptist Confession of Faith).[17]

SECOND- AND THIRD-CENTURY PROFESSIONS OF FAITH

Before we look more closely at some of those creeds and confessions, it is important to see how the scriptural seeds of the New Testament grew in the second and third centuries. While there was no uniform creedal statement that was recited in every church, it is amazing how local extant expressions show an orthodox catholicity of Christian belief. As you read the creedal formulas tucked within various occasional writings below,[18] note the differences. But also note the similarities. Christians throughout the Roman Empire confessed God as Trinity and focused on the person and work of Christ and the coming judgment.

---

[15] Ibid.
[16] Parsons, *Why Do We Have Creeds?* 28.
[17] In section 5.2, "Scripture in the Creeds and Confession," Pelikan says that the Protestant confessions "bristle with biblical quotations and references." *Credo*, 137. For example, the Westminster Confession of Faith (1647) listed more than 1,500 biblical texts in its "Quotations and Texts of Scripture Annexed."
[18] For the majority of these statements, see Leith, *Creeds of the Churches*, 16–23.

Ignatius of Antioch, Letter to the Trallians, *9:1–2 (ca. 107)*

Be deaf, therefore, whenever anyone speaks to you apart from Jesus Christ, who is of the stock of David, who is of Mary, who was truly born, ate and drank, was truly persecuted under Pontius Pilate, was truly crucified and died in the sight of beings of heaven, of earth and the underworld, who was also truly raised from the dead . . .

Epistula Apostolorum *(ca. 150)*

In the Father, the Ruler of the Universe,
And in Jesus Christ, our Redeemer,
In the Holy Spirit, the Paraclete,
In the Holy Church,
And in the Forgiveness of Sins.

Justin Martyr, Dialogue with Trypho, *85.2 (second century)*

In the name of this very Son of God and first-begotten of all creation, who was born through the Virgin, and became a passible man, and was crucified under Pontius Pilate by your people [Trypho was a Jew], and died, and rose again from the dead, and ascended to heaven, every demon is exorcised, conquered, and subdued.

Attributed to Justin Martyr (ca. 165)

We worship the God of the Christians, whom we consider One from the beginning, the creator and maker of all creation, visible and invisible. And the Lord Jesus Christ, the Servant of God, who had also been proclaimed beforehand by the prophets as about to be present with the race of men, the herald of salvation and teacher of good instructions.

Profession of the Presbyters of Smyrna (ca. 180)

We also know in truth one God, we know Christ, we know the Son, suffering as he suffered, dying as he died, and risen on the third day, and abiding at the right hand of the Father, and coming to judge the living and the dead. And in saying this we say what has been handed down to us.

Irenaeus (ca. 190)

The Church, though dispersed throughout the whole world, even to the ends of the earth, has received from the apostles and their disciples this faith: [She believes] in one God, the Father Almighty, Maker of heaven, and earth, and the sea, and all things that are in them; and in one Christ

Jesus, the Son of God, who became incarnate for our salvation; and in the Holy Spirit, who proclaimed through the prophets the dispensations of God, and the advents, and the birth from a virgin, and the passion, and the resurrection from the dead, and the ascension into heaven in the flesh of the beloved Christ Jesus, our Lord, and His [future] manifestation from heaven in the glory of the Father "to gather all things in one," and to raise up anew all flesh of the whole human race, in order that to Christ Jesus, our Lord, and God, and Savior, and King, according to the will of the invisible Father, "every knee should bow, of things in heaven, and things in earth, and things under the earth, and that every tongue should confess" to Him, and that He should execute just judgment towards all; that He may send "spiritual wickednesses," and the angels who transgressed and became apostates, together with the ungodly, and unrighteous, and wicked, and profane among men, into everlasting fire; but may, in the exercise of His grace, confer immortality on the righteous, and holy, and those who have kept His commandments, and have persevered in His love, some from the beginning [of their Christian course], and others from [the date of] their repentance, and may surround them with everlasting glory.

Tertullian, Against Praxeas *(ca. 200)*

We however as always, the more so now as better equipped through the Paraclete, that leader into all truth, believe (as these do) in one only God, yet subject to this dispensation (which is our word for "economy") that the one only God has also a Son, his Word who has proceeded from himself, by whom all things were made and without whom nothing has been made: that this [Son] was sent by the Father into the virgin and was born of her both man and God, Son of man and Son of God, and was named Jesus Christ: that he suffered, died, and was buried, according to the scriptures, and, having been raised up by the Father and taken back into heaven, sits at the right hand of the Father and will come to judge the quick and the dead: and that thereafter he, according to his promise, sent from the Father the Holy Spirit the Paraclete, the sanctifier of the faith of those who believe in the Father and the Son and the Holy Spirit. That his Rule has come down from the beginning of the Gospel, even before all former heretics, not to speak of Praxeas of yesterday, will be proved as well by the comparative lateness of all heretics as by the very novelty of Praxeas of yesterday.

Der Balyzeh Papyrus (ca. 200 or later)

Confesses the faith . . .

I believe in God the Father Almighty

And in his only begotten Son,
Our Lord, Jesus Christ,
And in the Holy Spirit,
And in the resurrection of the flesh
In the holy catholic Church.

THE APOSTLES' CREED

Finally, in our historic overview of the development of creedal formulas, we turn to the creeds we know best and use most in the Western church. We begin with the Apostles' Creed, the creed used liturgically in many Protestant churches, and devotionally and catechistically in Protestant and Roman Catholic churches alike.

Legend holds that each of the twelve apostles wrote a line of the creed. But while it was named after them and reflects apostolic teaching, it was certainly not penned by them. The earliest version we have found dates to the *Apostolic Tradition* of Hippolytus (ca. 215).[19]

In the following adaptation of the creed, the new believer would respond in the affirmative ("yes" or "I believe") to the questions:

- Do you believe in God, the Father Almighty?
- Do you believe in Christ Jesus, Son of God, who was born by the Holy Spirit out of Mary the Virgin, and was crucified under Pontius Pilate, and died and was buried, and rose on the third day alive from among the dead, and ascended into heaven, and sits at the right hand of the Father, to come to judge the living and the dead?
- Do you believe in the Holy Spirit, and the Holy Church, and the resurrection of the flesh?

Minor variations of this creedal formula can be found in a number of fourth- and fifth-century manuscripts, including Pope Julius I's letter to Marcellus, the bishop of Ancyra (ca. 340), and Sermons 213 and 215 by Augustine, the bishop of Hippo (354–430). In the early fifth century, Rufinus of Aquileia coined the name "the Apostles' Creed," gave the legend of its apostolic authorship, and added the phrase "descended into hell." Even though that controversial clause was a later addition, due to its biblical foundations (1 Pet. 3:18–20; cf. Acts 2:27)[20] it gained approval from Rome in the seventh century, was formalized under Charlemagne (ca. 800), and has remained a

---

[19] Cf. *Didache* 7:2, 9:5. For a later version of a creedlike formula used in baptism, see Ambrose of Milan, *De sacramentis* 2.7.70.

[20] For further study, see Daniel R. Hyde, *In Defense of the Descent: A Response to Contemporary Critics* (Grand Rapids: Reformation Heritage Books, 2010).

part of the confession of the Western church ever since. That final version, which has been a test of orthodoxy for at least 1,400 years, reads as follows:

> I believe in God, the Father Almighty,
> maker of heaven and earth:
> and in Jesus Christ, his only Son, our Lord;
> who was conceived by the Holy Ghost,
> born of the Virgin Mary,
> suffered under Pontius Pilate,
> was crucified, dead, and buried;
> he descended into hell;
> the third day he arose again from the dead;
> he ascended into heaven,
> and sitteth on the right hand of God the Father Almighty;
> from thence he shall come to judge the quick and the dead.
> I believe in the Holy Ghost;
> the holy catholic church;
> the communion of saints;
> the forgiveness of sins;
> the resurrection of the body;
> and the life everlasting. Amen.[21]

THE NICENE CREED

In 325, the emperor Constantine called the Council of Nicea. Its primary purpose was to deal with the christological errors of Arius (256–336). Arius taught that "God's essence (*ousia*) could not be shared," and therefore Jesus "cannot be fully God, but must be a creature that the Father formed."[22] The orthodox bishops responded with the Nicene Creed, a statement that affirmed Jesus's divinity by describing him as being "one in essence" (*homoousios*) with the Father. That creed was expanded at the First Council of Constantinople (381) and adopted by the Council of Chalcedon (451), and it serves as the form used by Roman Catholics, Anglicans, Lutherans, Calvinists, and a number of other Christian fellowships. We might more accurately call it the Constantinopolitan Formula or Niceno-Constantinopolitan Creed.

> We believe in one God, the Father Almighty,
> maker of heaven and earth,

---

[21] The wording for this creed and the three that follow comes from Terry L. Johnson, ed., *Leading in Worship: A Sourcebook for Presbyterian Students and Ministers Drawing from the Biblical and Historical Forms of the Reformed Tradition* (Powder Springs, GA: Tolle Lege, 2013), 269–275.

[22] As summarized by Johnson, *The Creed*, 33.

of all things visible and invisible.
And in one Lord Jesus Christ,
the only-begotten Son of God,
begotten of his Father before all worlds,
God of God, Light of Light,
very God of very God,
begotten, not made,
being of one substance [*homoousios*] with the Father;
by whom all things were made;
who for us men and for our salvation
came down from heaven,
and was incarnate by the Holy Spirit of the virgin Mary,
and was made man;
and was crucified also for us under Pontius Pilate;
he suffered and was buried;
and the third day he rose again
according to the Scriptures,
and ascended into heaven,
and is seated at the right hand of the Father;
and he shall come again, with glory,
to judge both the living and the dead;
whose kingdom shall have no end.
And we believe in the Holy Spirit,
the Lord and giver of life,
who proceeds from the Father and the Son;
who with the Father and the Son
together is worshipped and glorified;
who spoke by the prophets;
and we believe in one holy catholic and apostolic church;
we acknowledge one baptism for the remission of sins;
and we look for the resurrection of the dead,
and the life of the world to come. Amen.

THE ATHANASIAN CREED

The final ancient creed we will consider is the Athanasian Creed, which is named after Athanasius (d. 373), but was certainly not written by him (scholars estimate that it was penned between 380 and 430).[23] However, following Athanasius's theology, it "incisively and clearly articulates the

---

[23] The dating might be later, as the earliest extant copy of the creed comes from the prefix of sermons by Caesarius of Arles (d. 542).

doctrines of the Trinity, the incarnation, and the dual nature of Christ."[24] Echoes of Nicene orthodoxy are everywhere in this creed! Part of the reason it is still used liturgically in the West is due to its inclusion in the liturgy of the Anglican Book of Common Prayer and the Lutheran Book of Concord.

Whoever desires to be saved must above all things hold to the catholic faith. Unless a man keeps it in its entirety inviolate, he will assuredly perish eternally. Now this is the Catholic faith, that we worship one God in Trinity and Trinity in unity, without either confusing the persons or dividing the substance. For the Father's person is one, the Son's another, the Holy Spirit's another; but the Godhead of the Father, the Son, and the Holy Spirit is one, their glory is equal, their majesty is coeternal.

Such as the Father is, such is the Son, such is also the Holy Spirit. The Father is uncreated, the Son uncreated, the Holy Spirit uncreated. The Father is infinite, the Son infinite, the Holy Spirit infinite. The Father is eternal, the Son eternal, the Holy Spirit eternal. Yet there are not three eternals, but one eternal; just as there are not three uncreateds or three infinites, but one uncreated and one infinite. In the same way the Father is almighty, the Son almighty, the Holy Spirit almighty; yet there are not three almighties, but one almighty.

Thus the Father is God, the Son God, the Holy Spirit God; and yet there are not three Gods, but there is one God. Thus the Father is Lord, the Son Lord, the Holy Spirit Lord; and yet there are not three Lords, but there is one Lord. Because just as we are compelled by Christian truth to acknowledge each person separately to be both God and Lord, so we are forbidden by the Catholic religion to speak of three Gods or Lords.

The Father is from none, not made nor created nor begotten. The Son is from the Father alone, not made nor created but begotten. The Holy Spirit is from the Father and the Son, not made nor created nor begotten but proceeding. So there is one Father, not three Fathers; one Son, not three Sons; one Holy Spirit, not three Holy Spirits. And in this trinity there is nothing before or after, nothing greater or less, but all three persons are coeternal with each other and coequal. Thus in all things, as has been stated above, both Trinity and unity and unity in Trinity must be worshipped. So he who desires to be saved should think thus of the Trinity.

It is necessary, however, to eternal salvation that he should also believe in the incarnation of our Lord Jesus Christ. Now the right faith is that we should believe and confess that our Lord Jesus Christ, the Son of God, is equally both God and man.

---

[24] Johnson, *Leading in Worship*, 335.

He is God from the Father's substance, begotten before time; and he is man from his mother's substance, born in time. Perfect God, perfect man composed of a human soul and human flesh, equal to the Father in respect of his divinity, less than the Father in respect of his humanity.

Who, although he is God and man, is nevertheless not two, but one Christ. He is one, however, not by the transformation of his divinity into flesh, but by the taking up of his humanity into God; one certainly not by confusion of substance, but by oneness of person. For just as soul and flesh are one man, so God and man are one Christ.

Who suffered for our salvation, descended to hell, rose from the dead, ascended to heaven, sat down at the Father's right hand, from where he will come to judge the living and the dead; at whose coming all men will rise again with their bodies, and will render an account of their deeds; and those who have done good will go to eternal life, those who have done evil to eternal fire.

This is the Catholic faith. Unless a man believes it faithfully and steadfastly, he cannot be saved. Amen.

THE WESTMINSTER CREED

Since the classic orthodox Protestant confessions self-consciously followed "the basic Trinitarian and christological framework laid out in the early church creedal formulations" and are often based explicitly on these early creeds,[25] it is fitting to add a recently created creed based mostly on the Westminster Shorter Catechism. This creed, which is especially helpful, clarifies (as the great consensus of the Protestant confessions do) the nature of salvation.

I believe man's chief end is to glorify God, and to enjoy him forever.

I believe that the word of God, contained in the Scriptures of the Old and New Testaments, is the only rule given to direct us how to glorify and enjoy God.

I believe God is a Spirit, infinite, eternal, and unchangeable in his being, wisdom, power, holiness, justice, goodness, and truth; I believe there is but one true and living God; that there are three persons in the Godhead: the Father, the Son, and the Holy Ghost; and that these three are one God, the same in substance, equal in power and glory; I believe God has foreordained whatever comes to pass; that God made all things of nothing, by the word of His power, in the space of six days, and all very good; and that God preserves and governs all His creatures and all their actions.

---

[25] Trueman, *The Creedal Imperative*, 130.

I believe our first parents, though created in knowledge, righteousness, and holiness, sinned against God, by eating the forbidden fruit; and that their fall brought mankind into an estate of sin and misery; I believe God determined, out of His mere good pleasure, to deliver His elect out of the estate of sin and misery, and to bring them into an estate of salvation by a Redeemer; I believe the only Redeemer of God's elect is the Lord Jesus Christ, who, being the eternal Son of God, became man, and so was, and continues to be, God and man in two distinct natures, and one person, forever; I believe Christ, as our Redeemer, executes the office of a prophet, of a priest, and of a king; I believe Christ as our Redeemer underwent the miseries of this life, the wrath of God, the cursed death of the cross, and burial; He rose again from the dead on the third day, ascended up into heaven, sits at the right hand of God, the Father, and is coming to judge the world at the last day.

I believe we are made partakers of the redemption purchased by Christ, by the effectual application of it to us by his Holy Spirit; I believe God requires of us faith in Jesus Christ, and repentance unto life to escape the wrath and curse of God due to us for sin; I believe by His free grace we are effectually called, justified, and sanctified, and gathered into the visible church, out of which there is no ordinary possibility of salvation; I believe that we also are given *in this life* such accompanying benefits as assurance of God's love, peace of conscience, joy in the Holy Ghost, increase of grace, and perseverance therein to the end; that *at death*, we are made perfect in holiness, and immediately pass into glory; and our bodies, being still united in Christ, rest in their graves, till the resurrection; and *at the resurrection*, we shall be raised up in glory, we shall openly be acknowledged and acquitted in the day of judgment, and made perfectly blessed in the full enjoying of God to all eternity. (Emphasis in original.)

EXPRESSIONS IN THE SUNDAY GATHERING

Critics of creedal Christianity—inside and outside the church—remind us of potential dangers of adhering to historic creeds. We should never accept creeds uncritically. While creeds can be a helpful framework to understand Scripture, they are not Scripture and thus do not have Scripture's authority. Our theological frameworks must be shaped by Scripture first.

Moreover, when we recite the creeds, we should not "sleepwalk through the words."[26] Even if we memorize these creeds from the cradle, we should still say them *from the heart* and with our heads on straight. We should be

[26] Johnson, *The Creed*, 6.

well aware of the controversial and countercultural ideas to which we are publicly declaring our allegiance. Do we really believe that God made heaven and earth? Do we really believe that Jesus came down from heaven and was incarnate by the Holy Spirit through the virgin?

The recitation of the creed in worship can be introduced by the question, "Christian, what do you believe?" followed by a thunderous rendition of our common faith. It can also be introduced by means of a short, thought-provoking paragraph, such as one of the following:

> My brothers and sisters, there are many ways we identify ourselves as God's people. We sing the great hymns of the faith. We pray in the Spirit. We celebrate the sacraments. We listen to God's Word proclaimed. Now we come to profess God's story of our salvation through words of the _____ Creed. And in doing so, we seek to acknowledge the past and present communion of saints and long for the time when all God's people from every tongue, tribe, and nation will acknowledge together the truths of God's Word before his throne. Let us now confess wholeheartedly the faith of the universal church.

> We come now to say the _____ Creed. We do so for a number of reasons. It is a fitting response to [or "a fitting preparation for"] the Word of God proclaimed, an expression of the unity in the church across time and space, a witness to our individual participation in something greater than ourselves, a summary of the whole gospel, a recollection of our baptism and of the faith into which we have been baptized, and an expression of the common faith of the church, whose unity we affirm at the Lord's Supper.[27] We therefore join our voices together, saying . . .

> What we are about to do, in reciting the _____ Creed, is "one of the most countercultural things that Christians can do."[28] Together, as we announce "We believe in one God," we rebel against the claims of man-made religion, we demolish the throne of self, and we put the pretenders (our cultural idols) of sex, money, and power in their place. Join me now in insulting the world as we exalt the one, true God.

Furthermore, we should sing the creeds! In 1848, Cecil Frances Alexander published *Hymns for Little Children*. In this collection are her songs on the Apostles' Creed. For example, the hymn "All Things Bright and Beauti-

---

[27] These six "goals" come from *The Worship Sourcebook*, 2nd ed. (Grand Rapids: Calvin Institute of Christian Worship/Faith Alive Christian Resources/Baker Books, 2013), 151.
[28] Trueman, *The Creedal Imperative*, 154.

ful" expounds the phrase "maker of heaven and earth"; "Once in Royal David's City" covers "who was conceived by the Holy Ghost, born of the Virgin Mary"; and "There Is a Green Hill Far Away" explains "suffered under Pontius Pilate, was crucified, dead, and buried." These were originally children's songs! Thankfully, these three and other hymns of hers are in most hymnals. Now even adults can enjoy them as they learn the ABCs of historic Christianity.

Others have followed in Alexander's tradition (actually a tradition for Protestants that dates back to John Calvin's liturgy—see the *Genevan Psalter of 1542*—and for the whole church that dates all the way back to songs such as the *Te Deum*). Most hymnals have songs on the Apostles' and Nicene Creeds. For example, see Thomas Tallis's "Credo" in the hymnal *Cantus Christi*, the section "Creeds and Confessions" in *Lift Up Your Hearts*, as well as Timothy Dudley-Smith's "Though One with God in Form Divine," based on Philippians 2:6–11, and Christopher Idle's "All Things in Jesus Were First Created," based on Colossians 1:16–20.[29] There are many more songs available online. Enjoy the search and use the new tunes you find.[30]

BEYOND THE SUNDAY GATHERING

The historic creeds and confessions have much value beyond Sunday gatherings. Traditionally, churches have used them for discipling new believers and/or members, as well as for personal and family devotions. A final way to use them is as part of a church's articles of faith.

We end this chapter with the Articles of Faith of Christ the King Church in Batavia, the second church plant from College Church in Wheaton, Illinois. The first plant (Holy Trinity Church) adopted the Westminster Confession of Faith, the third plant (New Covenant Church) ascribes to The Gospel Coalition Statement of Faith, and the fourth plant (New Hope Fellowship) adheres to its own doctrinal statement, which is "built upon the historic creeds of the Protestant Reformation" and is "similar to statements in use today in many evangelical, reformed, Christian churches . . . [such as] the confessional statement of the Gospel Coalition."[31] The Christ the King articles are an example, albeit an imperfect one (Doug was young when he wrote them!), of what an independent evangelical church can do in the hope

---

[29] The Dudley-Smith song can be found in *A Door for the Word: 36 New Hymns Written between 2002 & 2005* (Carol Stream, IL: Hope, 2006), 33; the Idle song in *Walking by the River: 100 New Hymn and Song Texts with Other Verses* (Carol Stream, IL: Hope, 1998), 95.
[30] Start your search at http://cardiphonia.org/2010/10/28/hymns-of-faith-songs-for-the-apostles-creed/
[31] See http://www.myhopefellowship.org/about/what-we-believe

of aligning itself with both the creeds of early Christians and the confessions of the Protestant Reformation.

ARTICLES OF FAITH

The Nicene Creed, as written in AD 325 at the Council of Nicea and revised at the Council of Constantinople in AD 381, has been affirmed by the church throughout the ages, and thus serves as a good summary of the biblical and historical Christian faith. This creed, as explained in these Articles of Faith, shall be affirmed for membership into our particular Christian fellowship.

Section One: Of the One Triune God

> We believe in one God the Father almighty. . . . And in one Lord Jesus Christ, the only-begotten Son of God. . . . And in the Holy Spirit.

There is but one living and true God,[32] the God revealed to us in the Scriptures. Our communion with God and our comfortable dependence on Him relies on the knowledge that He consists of three distinct Persons,[33] of one substance, eternity, and unity: the Father, the Son, and the Holy Spirit, and is thus rightly worshiped in Trinity.[34] Although coequal in creation, sovereignty, holiness, wisdom, knowledge, justice, love, grace, mercy, and every other divine attribute and perfection,[35] God, as Father, Son, and Spirit, has and continues to execute distinct and harmonious offices in the glorious work of redemption.[36] And thus, as creator and redeemer, He is due from all humanity highest love, honor, and obedience.[37]

Section Two: Of Creation and the Fall

> We believe in one God the Father almighty; maker of heaven and earth, and of all things visible and invisible. And in one Lord Jesus Christ, . . . by whom all things were made. . . . And in the Holy Spirit, the Lord and giver of life.

---

[32] Deut. 4:35, 39; 6:4; Neh. 9:6; Mark 12:29. Cf. Thirty-Nine Articles, I; Anathema I of the Second Council of Constantinople.
[33] Gen. 1:2–3; Matt. 28:18–19; 2 Cor. 13:14. Cf. College Church in Wheaton, Statement of Faith, II; Heidelberg Catechism, Question 25; Baptist Confession of Faith: God and the Holy Trinity.
[34] Rom. 15:16; Eph. 3:4; Gal. 4:4. Cf. Athanasian Creed; Scottish Confession of Faith, I; College Church in Wheaton, Statement of Faith, II; Westminster Shorter Catechism, Question 6.
[35] Ex. 34:6; Ps. 33:5; Rev. 4:8. Cf. Westminster Confession of Faith, II; Second Helvetic Confession, III.
[36] 2 Thess. 2:13; Titus 3:4; 1 John 4:2. Cf. New Hampshire Baptist Confession, II.
[37] Ps. 148:13; Col. 2:6; Rev. 15:4. Cf. Westminster Shorter Catechism, Question 1; Baptist Faith and Message: God.

It pleased God the Father, Son, and Holy Spirit, for the manifestation of the glory of His eternal power, wisdom, and goodness, to create out of nothing the heavens and the earth.[38] As God did in the beginning, so even now unto all ages He continues to sustain and govern all of creation, according to His wise, holy, eternal, almighty, and ever present providence, in such a way that nothing happens in all the universe without His knowledge and will.[39]

Human beings, the crowning work of God's creation, were created in the image and likeness of God, in knowledge, righteousness, and holiness, with dominion over the creatures.[40] However, by the sin of Adam, humanity fell from original righteousness and communion with God, thereby bringing physical and spiritual death to all people, and making Adam and his posterity by nature children of wrath, servants of sin, subjects of death and all other miseries, spiritual, temporal, and eternal.[41] This inherited depravity, often called "original sin," continues to be the root of every kind of sin in us, and is so offensive in the sight of God, our holy creator, as to justly deserve His wrath and condemnation.[42]

Section Three: Of Jesus Christ, the Incarnate Son

And in one Lord Jesus Christ, the only-begotten Son of God, begotten of the Father before all the worlds, God of God, Light of Light, very God of very God, begotten, not made, being of one substance with the Father; by whom all things were made; who, for us men and for our salvation, came down from heaven, and was incarnate, by the Holy Spirit, of the virgin Mary, and was made man.

In the fullness of time, the Son of God, the second person of the Trinity, being fully and eternally God, of one substance and equal with the Father,[43] conceived of the Holy Spirit and born of the virgin Mary,[44]

[38] Gen. 1:1—2:3; Isa. 40:12–28; Acts 4:24. Cf. Westminster Confession of Faith, IV; Westminster Shorter Catechism, Question 9; Belgic Confession, XII; Apostles' Creed.
[39] Job 12:10; Col. 1:17; Heb. 1:2. Cf. Belgic Confession, XII, XIII; Westminster Confession of Faith, V; Westminster Shorter Catechism, Question 9; Heidelberg Catechism, Questions 26, 27; Second Helvetic Confession, VI; Scottish Confession of Faith, I; Baptist Confession of Faith: Divine Providence.
[40] Gen. 1:26–27, 31; Ps. 8:3–8; James 3:9–10. Cf. Westminster Shorter Catechism, Question 10; Belgic Confession, XIV; Heidelberg Catechism, Question 6; Baptist Faith and Message, III.
[41] Gen. 3:1–21; Ps. 51:5–7; Rom. 3:9–18; 5:12–19. Cf. Westminster Confession of Faith, V; Scottish Confession of Faith, II, III; College Church in Wheaton, Statement of Faith, III; Belgic Confession, XV; Baptist Confession of Faith: The Fall of Man, Sin, and Punishment; Canons of Dort—Human Corruption, Conversion to God, and the Way it Occurs, Article I.
[42] Ps. 5:4; Eph. 2:1–12, 18; 2 Thess. 1:8–9. Cf. Belgic Confession, XV; Thirty-Nine Articles, IX; Second Helvetic Confession, VIII; Council of Orange, Canons 1 and 2; London Baptist Confession of Faith, V; Heidelberg Catechism, Question 7; Canons of Dort—Divine Election and Reprobation, Article I, cf. Human Corruption, Conversion to God, and the Way it Occurs, Articles II, III.
[43] John 1:1–5, 14, 18; 10:30, 36–38; 17:19, 21–23; 1 John 2:23; Rev. 22:3.
[44] Matt. 1:1, 18–25; Luke 2:4–7; Gal. 4:4.

became fully man, yet without sin.[45] These two distinct natures, however, were joined together in one person, without change, separation, or confusion.[46] Thus the person and nature of Jesus is very God, and very man, yet one Christ, the only mediator between God and man.[47]

Section Four: Of the Gospel and the Kingdom

And in one Lord Jesus Christ . . . who, for us men and for our salvation, came down from heaven, and was incarnate, by the Holy Spirit, of the virgin Mary, and was made man; and was crucified also for us under Pontius Pilate; He suffered and was buried; and on the third day He rose again, according to the Scriptures . . . whose kingdom will have no end.

For God's glory and by His eternal plan, Jesus Christ, as the second Adam, the seed of Abraham, and the son of David, fulfilled the law and promises of God spoken through the prophets.[48] This gospel is the good news that Jesus Christ, our Prophet, Priest, and King, died for our sins according to the Scriptures, that He was buried, and that He was raised on the third day according to the Scriptures.[49] And by His perfect obedience and sacrifice of Himself which He, through the eternal Spirit, once offered up to God, our Lord Jesus Christ has fully satisfied the justice of God, has procured reconciliation, and has purchased an everlasting inheritance in the kingdom of heaven for all those whom the Father has given to Him,[50] a people born anew from every tongue, tribe, and nation, who live in humble and holy submission to the lordship of Christ,[51] and await the consummation of the kingdom at the return of Christ and the end of the ages.[52]

Section Five: Of Salvation in Christ

And in one Lord Jesus Christ . . . who, for us men and for our salvation . . .

---

[45] Matt. 2:1; John 8:48; 19:30–42; Heb. 4:14–15. Cf. Westminster Confession of Faith, VIII; Belgic Confession, XVIII; Second Helvetic Confession, XI; Apostles' Creed; Baptist Faith and Message: God the Son.
[46] Matt. 1:18, 23; Acts 2:22–36; Rom. 1:3–4; Cf. Definition of the Council of Chalcedon (AD 451); Anathemas III, VIII, X of the Second Council of Constantinople, and the Statement of Faith of the Third Council of Constantinople; the Scottish Confession of Faith, VI.
[47] Acts 9:20–22; Gal. 4:3–7; 1 Tim. 2:5. Cf. College Church in Wheaton, Statement of Faith, IV; Belgic Confession, XIX; Athanasian Creed; Heidelberg Catechism, Question 18; Canons of Dort—Christ's Death and Human Redemption Through It, Article IV.
[48] Matt. 5:17–18; Acts 3:12–26; Gal. 3:16. Cf. Belgic Confession, XXV; Second Helvetic Confession, XIII; New Hampshire Baptist Confession, IV.
[49] Acts 10:34–43; Rom. 1:1–5; 1 Cor. 15:1–5. Cf. Westminster Shorter Catechism, Question 23; Thirty-Nine Articles, II; College Church in Wheaton, Statement of Faith, IV; Heidelberg Catechism, Question 1; Apostles' Creed.
[50] John 3:16–17; 2 Cor. 5:20–21; Col. 1:19–22. Cf. Baptist Confession of Faith: Christ the Mediator.
[51] Mark 8:34; John 4:7; Rev. 5:9. Cf. Canons of Dort—Christ's Death and Human Redemption Through It, Articles V, VIII.
[52] 2 Thess. 4:13–18; 5:8–11; 2 Pet. 3:10–15; Rev. 22:11–17. Cf. Baptist Faith and Message: The Kingdom.

God made known His justice toward His Son, who was charged with our sin, and He poured out His goodness and mercy on us, giving to us His Son to die, by a most perfect love, and raising Him to life for our justification, in order that by Him we might receive righteousness, forgiveness, and eternal life.[53] By His free and absolute grace, God gives us true knowledge of His gospel wherein He kindles in our hearts an obedience of faith that embraces Jesus Christ alone for salvation, sanctification, perseverance, and glorification.[54] To us for whom Christ has obtained eternal redemption, God certainly and effectually applies and communicates this redemption, uniting us to Himself by His Spirit, and revealing to us in the Word and by the Word the mystery of salvation.[55]

Section Six: Of the Holy Spirit

And in the Holy Spirit, the Lord and giver of life; who proceeds from the Father and the Son; who with the Father and the Son together is worshipped and glorified; who spoke through the prophets.

The Holy Spirit, proceeding from the Father and the Son, is of one substance, majesty, and glory with the Father and the Son, very and eternal God.[56] As testified in Scripture, the Holy Spirit manifests the active presence of God in the world and in the church through the creation of the heavens and earth, the inspiration and illumination of Scripture, the exaltation of Christ, the conviction of sin, righteousness, and judgment, the effectual calling and regeneration of the saints, the cultivation of holiness, assurance, and comfort, the bestowment of spiritual gifts, and the sealing of the promise of the final redemption.[57]

Since it is wholly a gift of God to love God, it is right to praise the Spirit, who pours into our hearts the love of the Father and the Son,[58] giving us the faith, the will, and the strength to obey the law that is now written on our hearts and to proclaim the excellencies of Him who has called us out of darkness into His marvelous light.[59]

---

[53] John 3:16–18; Rom. 4:25; 5:6–11; Col. 1:13; 2:13. Cf. Belgic Confession, XX, XXI; Heidelberg Catechism, Questions 37, 45; Canons of Dort—Christ's Death and Human Redemption Through It, Article II; Second Helvetic Confession, XV.

[54] Rom. 6:1–11; 8:28–30; 1 Pet. 1:1–5; 2 Pet. 1:1–11. Cf. Belgic Confession, XXII, XXIII, XXIV; New Hampshire Baptist Confession, VI, VII, VIII; Baptist Faith and Message: Salvation; Second Helvetic Confession, XIV, XV; Canons of Dort—Human Corruption, Conversion to God, and the Way it Occurs, Article XI and The Perseverance of the Saints, Article III; The Council of Orange, Canons 9, 19.

[55] Rom. 10:17; Eph. 1:1–14; 3:6–9; 2 Thess. 2:13–14. Cf. Baptist Confession of Faith: Christ the Mediator.

[56] Luke 1:35; 24:9; John 14:26; 15:26; 16:13–15; Eph. 4:4–6. Cf. Thirty-Nine Articles, V; Belgic Confession, XI; Apostles' Creed; Athanasian Creed.

[57] John 16:8, 14; 1 Cor. 6:11; Gal. 5:22. Cf. Baptist Faith and Message: The Holy Spirit; Scottish Confession of Faith, XIII.

[58] Eph. 2:8–10; Phil. 3:3; Titus 3:5. Cf. Council of Orange, Canon 25.

[59] Jer. 31:33; Heb. 9:14; 1 Pet. 2:9–10. Cf. Council of Orange, Canon 6; Belgic Confession, XXV; Canons of Dort—Human Corruption, Conversion to God, and the Way it Occurs, Article XI.

Section Seven: Of the Holy Scriptures

... according to the Scriptures.... And in the Holy Spirit ... who spoke through the prophets.

Although the works of creation and providence manifest the goodness, wisdom, and power of God, so as to leave men without excuse, yet they are not sufficient to give that knowledge of God, and of His will, which is necessary for salvation.[60] Therefore it pleased the Lord, at various times, and in different ways, to reveal Himself, and to declare His word to His people in order that true knowledge of Him might be preserved and propagated throughout the world, unto the end of the ages.[61]

The Scriptures, both the Old and New Testaments, are given by inspiration of God and are the only infallible rule of faith and practice, thus serving the church as the supreme and sufficient standard by which Christian union and all human conduct, creeds, and opinions should be tried.[62]

The whole counsel of God, concerning all things necessary for God's own glory, man's salvation, faith, and life, is clearly recorded in Scripture. Consequently, all the words in Scripture are God's words in such a way that to disbelieve or disobey any word of Scripture (as rightly understood) is to disbelieve or disobey God.[63]

Under the name of Holy Scripture, or the Word of God written, are now contained all the books of the Old and New Testaments. We receive all these books and these only as holy and canonical, for the regulating, founding, and establishing of our faith.

Genesis, Exodus, Leviticus, Numbers, Deuteronomy, Joshua, Judges, Ruth, 1 Samuel, 2 Samuel, 1 Kings, 2 Kings, 1 Chronicles, 2 Chronicles, Ezra, Nehemiah, Esther, Job, Psalms, Proverbs, Ecclesiastes, Song of Songs, Isaiah, Jeremiah, Lamentations, Ezekiel, Daniel, Hosea, Joel, Amos, Obadiah, Jonah, Micah, Nahum, Habakkuk, Zephaniah, Haggai, Zechariah, Malachi.

Matthew, Mark, Luke, John, Acts of the Apostles, Romans, 1 Corinthians, 2 Corinthians, Galatians, Ephesians, Philippians, Colossians, 1 Thessalonians, 2 Thessalonians, 1 Timothy, 2 Timothy, Titus, Philemon, Hebrews, James, 1 Peter, 2 Peter, 1 John, 2 John, 3 John, Jude, Revelation.

---

[60] Ps. 19:1–6; Acts 14:15–17; 17:24–28; Rom. 1:18–21. Cf. Westminster Confession of Faith, I; Belgic Confession, II; Second Helvetic Confession, I.
[61] Prov. 22:19–21; Jer. 36:28; Heb. 1:1–2.
[62] 1 Thess. 2:13; 2 Tim. 3:14–16; 2 Pet. 1:19–21. Cf. College Church in Wheaton, Statement of Faith, I; Scottish Confession of Faith, XIX; New Hampshire Baptist Confession, I; Westminster Shorter Catechism, Question 2.
[63] Isa. 66:2; John 15:20; 2 Pet. 3:2.

Section Eight: Of the One Church

And one holy, catholic and apostolic Church. We acknowledge
one baptism . . .

Out of the whole creation, from the beginning of the world until its end,
God has called a people to Himself, whom He adopts for Himself, by
the Spirit and the Word, a Church chosen unto eternal life.[64] This one,
holy, catholic, and apostolic Church, as it is perceptible to us, is an assembly of visible saints, called and separated from the world, ordered,
empowered, and commissioned to worship and glorify God by extending
His kingdom to all nations by declaring and demonstrating the reign of
Christ, its King and Head.[65]

The Church, under Christ's rule, consists of those united on the basis
of the gospel and the doctrines of the Scripture, not outward liturgical
forms, traditional ecclesiastical structures, or any other basis however
supposedly beneficial to the unity and perseverance of God's people.
Thus, it is neither catholic nor apostolic to decree any teaching as an
essential doctrine that is contrary or additional to that which is taught
in the Scriptures. The true Church, under the authority of the Word, has
endured and will endure until the end of time, even through many perse-
cutions and evils within and without.[66]

The local church assembles, especially on the Lord's Day, for the
praise of God and the mutual sanctification, edification, and perseverance
of the elect.[67] Thus, the communal worship of any particular church is
pleasing and obedient to God when marked by the proper teaching of
the Scripture, administration of the ordinances of Baptism and the Lord's
Supper, and the sanctity of its members.[68]

Our good God, mindful of our weakness, has given the church the
sacraments or ordinances of Baptism and the Lord's Supper as visible
signs of his internal work in us, and eternal promise of sustaining grace
to us.[69]

Baptism, as ordained by the example and command of our Lord Jesus
Christ, is a perpetual and personal signification of the death, burial, and

---

[64] Rom. 4:16; Eph. 1:3–6; 2:19. Cf. Heidelberg Catechism, Question 54; Second Helvetic Confession, XVII;
Baptist Faith and Message: The Church.
[65] Eph. 4:15; 2 Pet. 2:9–12; Rev. 1:6; 5:10. Cf. London Baptist Confession of Faith, XXXIII.
[66] Matt. 16:18; 1 Tim. 3:15; Rev. 19:11–16; 21:2–3. Cf. Scottish Confession of Faith, V.
[67] Col. 1:28; 1 Thess. 1:4; 3:2; 4:18; 5:11; Heb. 10:25. Cf. Canons of Dort—Perseverance of the Saints,
Article XIV.
[68] Acts 2:42; Eph. 5:3; 1 Tim. 4:13. Cf. College Church in Wheaton, Statement of Faith, VIII; Scottish Confession of Faith, XVIII, XXV; Apostles' Creed.
[69] Matt. 26:17–30; Acts 2:38; 1 Cor. 11:23–26. Cf. Westminster Shorter Catechism, Questions 92, 93; Belgic
Confession, XXXIII; Heidelberg Catechism, Question 66; Second Helvetic Confession, IXX.

resurrection of Christ.[70] The outward element of water is to be used, wherein the person is baptized in the name of the Father, and of the Son, and of the Holy Spirit.[71] Although it be a sin to condemn or neglect this ordinance, yet grace and salvation are not so inseparably annexed unto it as that no person can be regenerated or saved without it, or that all that are baptized are undoubtedly regenerated.[72]

The Lord's Supper was ordained by Jesus Christ as the perpetual remembrance of the sacrifice of Himself in His death. It also results in our spiritual nourishment and growth in Him, and is a bond and pledge of our communion with Him, and with each other, as members of the mystical body.[73] It is a symbolic act of obedience whereby members of the church, through partaking of the bread and cup, remember the death of Christ until He comes again.[74]

Section Nine: Of the Return, Judgment and World to Come

And in one Lord Jesus Christ . . . [who] ascended into heaven, and sitteth on the right hand of the Father; and He shall come again, with glory, to judge both the living and the dead; whose kingdom will have no end. . . . We look for the resurrection of the dead, and the life of the world to come.

As our Lord Jesus Christ ascended into heaven,[75] and now sits on the right hand of the Father, He will soon bodily and visibly return to the world in power and glory as the King of kings and Lord of lords,[76] and finally triumph over evil by establishing a new heaven and earth, wherein dwells righteousness.[77]

Upon Christ's return, God has appointed a day where Christ will judge the world, in all righteousness.[78] Upon that day, all people that have ever lived shall appear before the tribunal of Christ to give an account of their thoughts, words, and deeds, and to receive reward or punishment according to what they have done, whether good or evil.[79]

---

[70] Matt. 3:13–17; 21:25–26; Rom. 6:3–8; Gal. 3:26; Col. 2:9–15.
[71] Matt. 28:19; Acts 8:36–38; Heb. 10:22. Cf. Westminster Confession of Faith, XXXVIII:II.
[72] Matt. 28:19; Acts 2:38; 8:13; 9:18; 10:2, 4, 22, 31, 45, 47; Rom. 4:9–12. Cf. Westminster Confession of Faith, XXXVIII:V.
[73] Mark 14:22–25; Acts 2:42, 46; 1 Cor. 10:16–17. Cf. Scottish Confession of Faith, XXI; Heidelberg Catechism, Question 75; Second Helvetic Confession, XXI; Westminster Confession of Faith, XXXIX:I.
[74] Acts 2:42; Luke 22:14–20; 1 Cor. 11:23–26. Cf. Baptist Faith and Message: Baptism and the Lord's Supper.
[75] Luke 24:51; Acts 1:9; 1 Tim. 3:16. Cf. Scottish Confession of Faith, IX; Heidelberg Catechism, Questions 21, 43.
[76] Acts 2:32–33; 5:31; 7:55–56; 2 Pet. 3:10; Rev. 19:11–16. Cf. Belgic Confession, XXXVII.
[77] Isa. 51:6; 2 Pet. 3:7–13; Rev. 21:1–2. Cf. College Church in Wheaton, Statement of Faith, X.
[78] John 12:48; Rom. 2:5; Heb. 9:27. Cf. The Apostles' Creed.
[79] Matt. 25:31–46; Rev. 20:11–15. Cf. Westminster Confession of Faith, XXXIII; The Athanasian Creed.

On this day, the righteous, who know God and trust in Christ, will go into everlasting life; while the wicked, who do not know God and have disobeyed the gospel, shall be cast into eternal torments, and be punished with everlasting destruction away from the presence of the Lord, and from the glory of His power.[80]

---

[80] Dan. 12:2–3; John 5:28–29; 2 Thess. 1:9. Cf. Westminster Confession of Faith, XXXIII; Belgic Confession, XXXVII; Heidelberg Catechism, Question 11; New Hampshire Baptist Confession, XVIII; College Church in Wheaton, Statement of Faith, IX; Canons of Dort—Christ's Death and Human Redemption Through It, Article I; The Apostles' Creed; The Athanasian Creed; Baptist Confession of Faith: The Last Judgment.

7

Hymns and Songs

By Douglas Sean O'Donnell

In the sixteenth chapter of C. S. Lewis's book *The Screwtape Letters*, Wormwood, the minor demon, is counseled by his mentor, Screwtape, on how to deal with the fact that his "patient"—a new convert to Christianity—is now regularly attending church. Normally this would present a problem. However, Screwtape recommends a number of "healthy" churches in the area that would assist in tainting this new Christian's view of Christianity:

> At the first of these [churches] the Vicar is a man who has been so long engaged in watering down the faith to make it easier for a supposedly incredulous and hard-hearted congregation that it is now he who shocks his parishioners with his unbelief, not *vice versa*. He has undermined many a soul's Christianity. His conduct of the services is also admirable. In order to spare the laity all "difficulties" he has deserted both the lectionary and the appointed psalms and now, without noticing it, revolves endlessly round the little treadmill of his fifteen favourite psalms and twenty favourite lessons. We are thus safe from the danger that any truth not already familiar to him and to his flock should ever reach them through Scripture. But perhaps your patient is not quite silly enough for this church—or not yet?[1]

Sadly, many Christians have moved beyond the "not yet." Today there are a lot of "silly" Christians. The reason (or part of it)? A lot of silly churches have a lot of silly pastors who allow a lot of silly worship leaders to select a

---

[1] C. S. Lewis, *The Screwtape Letters* (New York: Macmillan, 1948), 82–83. Sections from this chapter, including part of this introduction, can be found in Douglas Sean O'Donnell, *God's Lyrics: Rediscovering Worship through Old Testament Songs* (Phillipsburg, NJ: P&R, 2010). Used with the publisher's permission.

lot of silly songs from a lot of silly songwriters. The result? We sing songs that "water down the faith" and spare us "all 'difficulties,'" undermining "many a soul's Christianity." Whether that statement is too strong or not strong enough, we all must admit that there is silliness in our churches. This chapter, through scriptural solutions, offers an escape from the traps of triviality.

THE PURPOSE OF CHURCH MUSIC

Although music has been consistently part of Christian worship, it is not itself a distinctly Christian reality.[2] Martin Luther famously referred to music as "the excellent gift of God."[3] And indeed it is! Music is a divine gift for all people—Christians and non-Christians alike. "Music is one of those aspects of creation which God gives generously to all humanity. Like money and sex, it is something which sinners pervert by not acknowledging their creator and believers accept with thanksgiving."[4]

What, then, is the place of music in the church? Thankfully, Scripture sheds some light on this question. In view of its references to music or illustrations of music,[5] we discover that the three main purposes of ecclesiastical music well reflect the three main reasons why Christians are to gather for corporate worship. According to Scripture, and in line with the goals for Christian worship, Christians gather together in loving fellowship for at least three reasons: (1) to praise God (that is, to recall and proclaim his person and works), (2) to learn from God about God through his Word, and (3) to mutually encourage one another in the faith.

The music used in our Sunday morning worship services should be chosen and prepared with these reasons in mind. Therefore, we seek to draw

---

[2] We disagree with the notion of "sacred" music. There are only "sacred" lyrics, most notably the very songs of Scripture. Opening to the Psalms—the songbook of Israel and the church—demonstrates this point. The Psalms are composed of divinely inspired words, not text-plus-tunes. While certainly tunes are mentioned in some of the superscriptions (e.g., "the Doe of the Dawn" for Psalm 22), we have no record of what those songs sounded like.

[3] Martin Luther, *Luther's Works*, 55 vols., ed. Jaroslav Pelikan and Helmut T. Lehmann (St. Louis: Concordia; Philadelphia: Fortress, 1955–), 53:321, quoted in Miikka E. Anttila, *Luther's Theology of Music: Spiritual Beauty and Pleasure* (Berlin: De Gruyter, 2013), 70.

[4] John Woodhouse, "The Key to Church Music," in *Church Musicians' Handbook*, ed. Sally McCall and Rosalie Milne (Kingsford, NSW, Australia: Matthias Media, 1999), 11.

[5] For the following references, see Greg Clarke, "Music in the Bible," in ibid., 47–49:

- For "music," see Gen. 31:27; Judg. 5:3; 1 Sam. 18:6–7; 1 Chron. 6:31–32; 15:16; 23:5; 26:6–7; 2 Chron. 5:13; 7:6; Neh. 12:27; Ps. 27:6; 33:2; 57:7; 81:1–2; 87:7; 92:1–3; 95:1–2; 98:4–9; 144:9; Isa. 30:32; Amos 5:23; Eph. 5:19.
- For "sing," see Ex. 15:1; Judg. 5:3; 2 Sam. 22:48–50; 1 Chron. 16:8–9, 23, 33; Ps. 7:17; 9:11; 13:6; 27:6; 33:1–3; 47:6; 51:7; 61:8; 68:4; 71:22–23; 89:1; 95:1–2; 96:1–2; 98:1; 101:1; 105:2; 135:3; 145:7; 147:1; 149:1, 5; Isa. 12:5; 52:8–9; Jer. 20:13; 1 Cor. 14:15; Eph. 5:19–20; Col. 3:16; James 5:13; Rev. 5:13; 15:2–3.
- For "song," see Deut. 31:19–22; Ps. 18 (title); 28:7; 40:3; 42:8; 45 (title); 69:30; 92 (title); 144:9; Isa. 42:10; Rev. 5:9.

the head and heart together by selecting and singing "psalms and hymns and spiritual songs" (Col. 3:16) that teach God's Word, express our response to that revelation, and encourage and exhort one another to persevere in the faith. Our focus is both *vertical* (addressing God, declaring his worthiness, extolling his name, and rejoicing in his glories revealed in Jesus Christ) and *horizontal* (addressing one another, declaring the promises we have in Christ, comforting each other through trials and temptations, and reminding and encouraging one another to respond to God with faith, repentance, love, hope, joy, reverence, obedience, and gratitude).

GUIDELINES FOR CONGREGATIONAL SONGS

The glory of the gospel is to unite people of every language and culture under the lordship of Christ (Eph. 2:11–22; 4:3–6, 13; Rev. 7:9–17). So we should not be content with divisions created by different musical tastes and traditions. As we grow to maturity in Christ we should be looking for ways to express the unity that is God's goal for us: in gospel action, in the exchange of ministries and gifts, in combined services and in the sharing of musical resources and experiences.[6]

What is often missing in the debate on church music is a discussion on the virtue of love. As Christians, we must be committed to pleasing God by serving one another in love. We should value unity of the Spirit over and above uniformity of musical opinion. And so, taking into account the variety of musical tastes, experiences, and skills of a particular congregation, each local church should develop a musical tradition that is lovingly appropriate for that group of believers. Austin Lovelace and William Rice are right in saying: "All church music should have the ability to speak to the entire congregation. If the music is divisive, if most of the people do not understand what is happening, if it does not have meaning to most, then it is probably improper and wrong."[7]

Perhaps at your church such love expresses itself in a balance of classic hymns and contemporary choruses, or the addition of an Isaac Watts psalm paraphrase to your exclusive psalm-singing repertoire. But no matter how it looks, love should be expressed by careful and intentional song selection for the Sunday morning service. A hymn or song may be textually sound and its tune may be consistent with the text, but it may be either too formal or too informal for a certain congregation in its particular setting. The loving

---

[6] David G. Peterson, *Encountering God Together: Leading Worship Services That Honor God, Minister to His People, and Build His Church* (Phillipsburg, NJ: P&R, 2013), 143.
[7] Austin C. Lovelace and William C. Rice, *Music and Worship in the Church* (New York: Abingdon, 1960), 203.

worship leader will be "attuned both to the Word and to the people who are served."[8]

PRINCIPLES FOR LYRICS

Realizing the central importance of biblically accurate lyrics as well as the reality that certain musical styles "simply cannot carry various texts,"[9] we should acknowledge that the musical praise of the body of Christ should reflect and honor Christ. Aware that "the selection and use of music for public worship should always have as its primary motive the glory and honor of God (Rev. 4:8, 11; 1 Cor. 1:31),"[10] each church, under the oversight of its leaders, should use the following criteria for the selection of lyrics.

OUR LYRICS SHOULD REFLECT GOD'S LYRICS

First and most important, song lyrics must be biblical, echoing the words and reflecting the themes expressed in song from Genesis to Revelation. In the book *God's Lyrics*, the themes found in the songs of Scripture are summarized as follows:

1. The Lord is placed at the center; that is, God is addressed, adored, and "enlarged."
2. His mighty acts in salvation history are recounted.
3. His acts of judgment are rejoiced in.
4. His ways of living (practical wisdom: "instruction in wise behavior," Prov. 1:3 NASB) are encouraged.[11]

There are three ways to assure our songs are biblical. First, we can sing the inspired words of Scripture directly (or as directly as possible, as all songs set to patterns of English poetry are in a sense *paraphrases* of the original Greek or Hebrew). This would include the Psalms (see Paul's admonitions in Eph. 5:19; Col. 3:16), which have been sung throughout history:

A historical study of sung psalms in worship of the church reveals multiple traditions: from Gregorian psalmody to the metrical psalms of Calvin's psalters, to the early American *Bay Psalm Book* (1640), to Anglican chant; and from the psalm-hymns of Martin Luther, Isaac Watts, and

---

[8] R. Kent Hughes, "Free Church Worship: The Challenge of Freedom," in *Worship by the Book*, ed. D. A. Carson (Grand Rapids: Zondervan, 1992), 171.
[9] Leonard Payton, "How Shall We Sing to God?" in *The Coming Evangelical Crisis*, ed. John H. Armstrong and R. Kent Hughes (Chicago: Moody, 1996), 194.
[10] Douglas Wilson, *Mother Kirk: Essays and Forays in Practical Ecclesiology* (Moscow, ID: Canon, 2001), 142.
[11] O'Donnell, *God's Lyrics*, 113.

James Montgomery to small- and large-scale psalm settings by a great many composers. In other words, the psalms must be sung.[12]

It would also include the Bible's doxologies (e.g., Rom. 11:33–36; Rev. 1:4–7), canticles (e.g., Mary's *Magnificat* and Simeon's *Nunc Dimittis*), and Christ hymns (see next paragraph). As Christ's disciples, it is imperative that we sing songs that worship our Lord Jesus Christ (Rev. 5:12), reflecting the great truths and promises of God's gospel. He is the center of the canon!

Poetic texts in the New Testament are often thought to be "Christ hymns" or "hymn fragments" of early Christian songs (Phil. 2:5–11; Col. 1:15–20; 1 Tim. 3:16; perhaps John 1:1–5, 9–11; Rom. 10:9ff.; 1 Cor. 12:3; Eph. 5:14; 1 Tim. 2:5–6; Heb. 1:3; 1 Pet. 3:18c–19, 22).[13] They focus on the person and works of Jesus, at times highlighting his divinity. The most obvious example of the worship of "the Word [made] flesh" (see John 1:14) is the Song of the Lamb (Rev. 5:9–10).[14] We are to sing to this "Man," to slightly revise Pliny's observation of early Christian worship, "as to God."[15] Therefore, like the lyrics of the early church, the lyrics we write, select, and sing must proclaim the gospel and uplift the only name under heaven whereby we can be saved. We must join in the chorus of 1 Timothy 3:16:

Great indeed, we confess, is the mystery of godliness:
He was manifested in the flesh [incarnation],
    vindicated by the Spirit [death],
        seen by angels [resurrection],
proclaimed among the nations,
    believed on in the world [Pentecost and its aftermath],
        taken up in glory [ascension].

---

[12] Paul S. Jones, *What Is Worship Music?* Basics of the Faith (Phillipsburg, NJ: P&R, 2012), 13. Also, as John M. Frame notes: "We can also learn from the Psalms about the variety of songs that may be used in worship. Some psalms are long, while others are short. Some are didactic, while others are more lyrical. Some are very simple, while others are highly complex. Some utilize elaborate literary forms such as acrostics and multilevel chiasms, other do not. Some are addressed to God, while others are addressed to human beings." *Worship in Spirit and Truth: A Refreshing Study of the Principles and Practice of Biblical Worship* (Phillipsburg, NJ: P&R, 1996), 136.
[13] See Paul S. Jones, *Singing and Making Music* (Phillipsburg, NJ: P&R, 2006), 104. For a list of New Testament hymns, see Daniel Liderbach, *Christ in the Early Christian Hymns* (New York: Paulist Press, 1998), 42–50.
[14] Ralph P. Martin states correctly, "Christology was born in the atmosphere of worship." *Worship in the Early Church* (Grand Rapids: Eerdmans, 1974), 33. Cf. Larry W. Hurtado, *At the Origins of Christian Worship: The Context and Character of Earliest Christian Devotion* (Grand Rapids: Eerdmans, 1999), 86–92. On the possible connection between the worship service (including singing) of the early church and the book of Revelation, see Oscar Cullmann's chapter "The Gospel According to St. John and Early Christian Worship" in his *Early Christian Worship* (London: SCM, 1953).
[15] In *Ep.* x, xcvi, 7 Pliny writes of Christians: *"Camenque Christo quasi deo dicere"* ("They sing a song to Christ as if to a god").

Second, beyond the songs of Scripture, we can sing other biblical texts. We applaud the growing trend of taking non-poetic texts and setting them to music. For example, see the new songs written on the Gospel of Luke (http://thegospelcoalition.org/lukealbum/). If you are preaching through Jonah or John, Ecclesiastes or Ephesians, why not flip through the Scripture index in a few hymnals, search the Web to see what songs have been written, or commission your church musicians to write new contributions to the local and universal church?

Third, we can sing the great doctrines and themes of Scripture. Following Scripture's lead—notably the Psalms[16]—we can rehearse together God's attributes and acts displayed in creation and redemption. We can select and sing lyrics that echo and teach the great history of redemption—God's saving work from Genesis to Revelation. The new hymnal *Lift Up Your Hearts* has done this:

> God's people have learned many times throughout history how important it is that we tell the whole story of God—from creation to re-creation. . . . It is this story that forms the outline for the first half of *Lift Up Your Hearts*. Beginning with creation and our fall into sin, through the Old Testament narratives and the hope of Advent, to the birth, life, death, and resurrection of Christ, and onward to the gift of the Holy Spirit at Pentecost and the promise of the new creation, we find our story woven into the fabric, creating a beautiful testimony to the grace of God in our own lives.[17]

And we must write new songs that recount and celebrate the works of Christ, such as the Keith Getty and Stuart Townend song "In Christ Alone." The lyrics of the song address major themes:

Incarnation—"In Christ alone, who took on flesh"
Death—"Till on that cross as Jesus died"
Resurrection—"Up from the grave He rose again!"
Return—"Till He returns or calls me home"

Songwriter Caroline Cobb is another good model. Starting with creation and ending with Christ's return, she has created congregational songs that

---

[16] In the preface of his German translation of the Bible, Martin Luther referred to the Psalms as a "small Bible reduced to the loveliest and most concise form so that the content of the whole Bible exists in them as a handbook." Quoted in Payton, "How Shall We Sing to God?" 193. Payton adds, "In the 150 psalms, we find all the great biblical doctrinal themes presented poetically—themes such as our depravity, the Atonement, our redemption, God's creation and providence, and so on" (194).

[17] *Lift Up Your Hearts: Psalms, Hymns, and Spiritual Songs* (Grand Rapids: Faith Alive, 2013), vii.

tell the greatest story ever told (see her album *The Blood and the Breath: Songs That Tell the Story of Redemption*). Cobb has also written three insightful, encouraging, and practical posts on writing scriptural songs: "When the Power of Scripture Meets the Power of Music," "How to Write a Song from Scripture," and "Six Ideas for Writing Songs from Scripture." These can all be found on the Gospel Coalition Worship blog.

Join the movement! Return to singing God's Word in worship.[18]

Our Lyrics Should Edify Others and Exalt God

Have you ever noticed that many of the great hymns have us singing to one another? Think of "Come, Christians, Join to Sing," or that famous Christmas carol, "Good Christian Men, Rejoice," or of one of my favorites, "If Thou But Suffer God to Guide Thee":

> If thou but suffer God to guide thee
> And hope in Him through all thy ways,
> He'll give thee strength, whate'er betide thee,
> And bear thee through the evil days.

At first, we might think that such a focus is out of place in a worship service. But in Scripture, singing to one another is not merely condoned but in fact commanded. Little is said about music and singing in the New Testament. And what is said often turns our attention toward one another. For example, in Ephesians 5:15–21, Paul is exhorting Christians to be careful how they walk. So he writes, "And do not get drunk with wine, for that is debauchery, but be filled with the Spirit, addressing *one another* in psalms and hymns and spiritual songs" (vv. 18–19a). With the Spirit in us, we are commanded to sing to "one another." In Colossians 3:16, we find a similar command: "Let the word of Christ dwell in you richly, teaching and admonishing *one another* in all wisdom, singing psalms and hymns and spiritual songs." Our musical worship should engender opportunity, as Douglas Wilson has it, "to confess personal and corporate sins (Ps. 32:1), to receive comfort (Ps. 46), to find assurance of our faith and hope (Ps. 74; 77), to gain encouragement in times of trial and temptation (Acts 16:25; Ps. 102), to demonstrate the communion of the saints (Ps. 133:1–2), to remember God's great love and mercy to all generations (2 Chron. 20:21; Ps. 101), to express heartfelt joy and gratitude with reverence and respect (Ezra 3:10–11; Ps. 100), and to

---

[18] For an album to which Doug contributed a song, see http://cardiphonia.bandcamp.com/album/canticles. See also his new songs to old tunes in *God's Lyrics*, 179–187.

declare our personal and corporate faith in Jesus Christ as Lord and Savior (Phil. 2:10–11)."[19]

So we are to sing God's songs to one another. There is to be a horizontal dimension to our singing. But, of course, there is to be a vertical dimension as well. We are to raise our hearts and voices heavenward. Augustine defined a hymn as "a song containing praise of God." He went on to say:

> If you praise God, but without song, you do not have a hymn. If you praise anything, which does not pertain to the glory of God, even if you sing it, you do not have a hymn.[20]

While Augustine's definition is narrower than the horizontal dimension just discussed, it nevertheless makes the basic point of all the songs of Scripture: no focus on God, no hymn.[21] In the Bible's songs, God's people sing *to* the Lord and also *about* the Lord. In his book *Select Hymns* (1761), John Wesley gives seven standards for "inspired singing," the seventh being: "Above all sing spiritually." He goes on to define that trait in this way: "Have an eye to God in every word you sing. Aim at pleasing Him more than yourself, or any other creature."[22] Amen! Our lyrics should exalt him *and* edify others.

Our Lyrics Should Raise Religious Affections, Not Ridiculous Emotionalism

In his *Homily on Psalm 42*, John Chrysostom begins his treatment of the familiar first verse—"As a deer pants for flowing streams, so pants my soul for you, O God"—with these words:

> Nothing, in fact, nothing so uplifts the soul, gives it wings, liberates it from the earth, looses the shackles of the body, promotes its values and its scorn for everything in this world as harmonious music and a divine song rhythmically composed.[23]

In this sermon, the church father explains why this "piece of inspired composition in particular is recited to music."[24] His answer is twofold.

---

[19] Wilson, *Mother Kirk*, 143.

[20] Quoted in Andrew Wilson-Dickson, *The Story of Christian Music* (Minneapolis: Fortress, 1992), 25.

[21] Following Paul, Augustine used the term "hymn" to refer to a poem, usually sung in praise of a deity. See Calvin M. Johansson, *Discipling Music Ministry: Twenty-first Century Directions* (Peabody, MA: Hendrickson, 1992), 125.

[22] John Wesley, *Select Hymns with Tunes Annext: Designed chiefly for the Use of the People Called Methodists* (Bristol: William Pine, 1761, 1770).

[23] John Chrysostom, *Old Testament Homilies*, trans. Robert Charles Hill (Brookline, MA: Holy Cross Orthodox Press, 2003), 3:69.

[24] Ibid.

First, God uses music to make "the knowledge of spiritual things" (in the lyrics of the Psalms) more desirable.[25] Just as a fussing baby is soothed by a nurse's lullaby or beasts of burden are pacified by a wayfarer's tune, so God's Word, when set to music, "lightens the load" of carrying spiritual truths into our hearts.[26]

Second, God gave us his own songs as an edifying option. As opposed to "profane" and "lascivious songs," which upset "everything" and allow demons to "congregate," spiritual melodies allow the Spirit to attend and to sanctify.[27] Chrysostom explains:

> From profane songs, you see, harm and damage and many dire consequences would be introduced; the more intemperate and lawless of these songs lodge in the parts of the soul, and render it weaker and more remiss. From the psalms, by contrast, being spiritual, there comes great benefit, great advantage and much sanctification, and the basis for every value would be provided, since the words purify the soul and the Holy Spirit quickly alights on the soul singing such things.[28]

While we can debate the legitimacy of Chrysostom's critique of secular songs and the verity of his philosophical worldview, his admonition to the church to sing "divine" songs, as he calls them—songs taken from God's Word—is, narrowly speaking, what this entire first section is a call to do. And his conviction that the Word of God set to music is indeed a means by which, as he puts it, "the Holy Spirit quickly alights on the soul," is, broadly speaking, what we have sought to explore and teach in this third principle on lyrics.

Music has the innate ability to impact our emotions. The Bible acknowledges this reality and even "encourages the expression of emotion in song, especially joy."[29] As James writes: "Is anyone among you suffering? Let him pray. Is anyone cheerful? Let him sing praise" (James 5:13). Yet, without overreacting to the current culture of contemporary Christian music, we must nevertheless recognize the dangers of affected and inappropriate emotion. As John Woodhouse acutely observes, Christian "music needs to be demystified."[30] It should be "appreciated for what it is: a good, enjoyable,

---

[25] Ibid.
[26] Ibid., 69–70.
[27] Ibid., 70. Similarly, in his preface to the *Geneva Psalter*, John Calvin uses strong language for the "secular" songs of his times. He calls them "dishonest and shameless." Quoted in Calvin R. Stapert, *A New Song for an Old World: Musical Thought in the Early Church* (Grand Rapids: Eerdmans, 2007), 195.
[28] Chrysostom, *Old Testament Homilies*, 70.
[29] Tony Payne, "Riding the Tiger: Dealing with Music and Emotions," in *Church Musicians' Handbook*, 67.
[30] John Woodhouse, "The Key to Church Music," 19.

and useful gift of God. Music can be an appropriate way of expressing emotions, just like shouting or laughing."[31] But our emotions should be elevated by the truths of the gospel rather than just by the sweetness of the tune.

During a worship service, the emotions music causes are an unreliable "barometer of spiritual authenticity."[32] It is not necessarily true that "the more you are affected by the 'praise,' the more you are in tune with God."[33] Neither is it always right to "identify the emotions generated by singing with the work of God's Spirit."[34] At our churches, we should seek to impact the emotions of God's people through the glorious truths of the gospel expressed in Word and song. Thus, we should not promote the goal of having a "heaven now" experience. Rather, we should encourage one another to "sing in hope" of the world to come, and to "sing in order to build up each other to live more faithfully *in this world*—not to escape from it."[35]

Our Lyrics Should Be Theologically Comprehensive and Balanced

The lyrics we sing need to reflect the whole counsel of God. They need to be both comprehensive and balanced:

> The range of our singing of psalms, hymns, and spiritual songs should reflect faithfully the whole counsel of God and avoid the temptation of limiting our music to only *some* truths, or to *some* favorite text (Ps. 103:22). . . . Lyrics in public worship must not be limited only to some portions of the Word of God, but must reflect the fullness of God's infallible revelation (Ps. 145:10). Just as there is one Lord, one faith, one hope, and one baptism, so our music must reflect and encourage the true unity of all believers throughout the world and through all ages (Ps. 31:23; 89:7).[36]

Part of this comprehensiveness is that our lyrics should reflect the essential doctrines of the Christian faith—convictions expressed in historic Christian creeds, confessions, and catechisms. Comprehensiveness also includes catholicity: the acceptance and promotion of old hymns and spiritual songs that have been part of the church throughout the ages. On any given Sunday, people should expect to hear and sing songs that reflect the whole of God's

---

[31] Ibid., 20.
[32] Ibid., 19.
[33] Ibid.
[34] Rob Smith, "Pleasing All the People All the Time and Other Myths," in *Church Musicians' Handbook*, 24.
[35] Ibid., 23–24.
[36] Wilson, *Mother Kirk*, 142.

work in history and in the believer's life, promote sanctification, raise godly emotions, and embody all of the texts and themes of God's sacred revelation, whether found in classic hymns or new songs.

PRINCIPLES FOR MUSIC

In the context of the church, "words must take priority over music."[37] This is why we have dealt with lyrics first. Yet the music that accompanies the lyrics is not neutral. We affirm the notion that the lyrics (message) and the music (medium) should be compatible, and that musical credibility, while not as important as lyrical content, does matter! Below are four basic principles to help bring some compatibility to this marriage between the message and the medium.

MUSIC SHOULD ENHANCE THE LYRICS

Good words can be robbed of their richness if the tune doesn't fit the text. "The best congregational songs are those in which biblical truth is beautifully expressed and enhanced by appropriate music, in which tunes are not so awkward to sing that they distract from the words, and in which the structure is balanced and easy to follow."[38] Certain styles and melodies simply cannot carry the great truths of God's lyrics. For example, the theme to the old television show *Gilligan's Island* doesn't fit with the lyrics to "Amazing Grace," even though it works musically (i.e., those lyrics can be sung with that tune). A bouncy, happy, sunshiny chorus about Christ's passion and crucifixion is borderline blasphemous. This is not a matter of aesthetic snobbery, but of Christian seriousness. When we sing of God's righteous judgment, it is imperative that the tune's theme complement the text's theology. And when we sing of the joy of our salvation, a minor key might be inappropriate:

> The tune must support the meaning of the text. It is inevitable that a sentimental melody attached to a hortatory text will deflate the force of the text. Thus, the essentials for evaluating a tune are answered by the questions: Does its character fit the text? Does it have a melody capable of standing alone? These are not esoteric questions that can only be answered by the "experts." Anyone with some musical understanding, some common sense, and a willingness to think about it can make good decisions.[39]

---

[37] David Peterson, "The Old and the New," in *Church Musicians' Handbook*, 31.
[38] Peterson, *Encountering God Together*, 141.
[39] Hughes, "Free Church Worship," 170.

MUSIC SHOULD COMPLEMENT THE PREACHING

Music must be "the servant of preaching."[40] This means that the lyrics of the songs used during the service should reflect the text of Scripture preached that day and that the music attached to those lyrics needs to maintain the integrity of the words in an enhancing and confirming manner. We believe that the Word of God read and preached is the central component of our public worship, but the music helps raise our affections—provided they are raised primarily by the truth of God's revelation. As Luther declared, "Music and notes, which are wonderful gifts and creations of God, do help gain a better understanding of the text, especially when sung by a congregation and when sung earnestly."[41]

MUSIC SHOULD BE CONDUCIVE TO CONGREGATIONAL SINGING

The congregation must be able to sing the songs that are chosen for worship. The selection of tunes, along with the instrumentation,[42] should facilitate, not stifle or overwhelm, the congregation's voice. Music should be relevant to the congregation because "the congregation is the chief instrument of praise, the one indispensable choir!"[43] Under the new covenant of Christ's saving blood, music is every Christian's responsibility. As a kingdom of priests, like the Levitical choirs of the Old Testament, we are all enjoined to lift our voices. Therefore, sensitive to our specific congregations' vocal abilities and knowledge of music, as well as issues of pitch, tempo, and rhythm, we must select songs that are singable.

This does not mean, however, that we avoid difficult, global/ethnic, or new (or ancient!) songs that do not fit our current style or ability. Nor does it mean that we dismiss the notion of aesthetic objectivity—that some music is better or more beautiful than other music. Instead, we desire to learn songs—new or old, hard or easy—and to include in our congregational singing a wide array of musical styles, along with varying instrumental accompaniments and tunes from various times and cultures. So, for example, when teaching new or more difficult songs, we encourage the song leader (or choir, if you have one) to sing the song through before inviting the congregation

---

[40] Ibid., 167.
[41] Luther, quoted in Jones, *What Is Worship Music?* 27.
[42] Strings, winds, and percussion (2 Sam. 6:5; 1 Chron. 15:16; 25:6; 2 Chron. 5:12–14; 7:6; 29:25–28; Neh. 12:27) are all mentioned in Scripture. Both College Church and New Covenant Church seek to reflect this biblical balance. For example, at New Covenant, it is accomplished through the use of organ, piano, guitar, flute, violin, cello, oboe, trumpet, French horn, and other instruments.
[43] Hughes, "Free Church Worship," 171.

to sing. We want the church to become a school of music because we want worship to be a symphony of praise! Great congregational singing "builds up God's people in his Word and also draws unbelievers to consider both the reality and the substance of the faith."[44] In other words, public worship through song exalts, edifies, and even evangelizes!

Music Should Be Selected and Played by Godly and Competent Musicians

This final point should be obvious, but sadly, it is often neglected. We all understand that when the wrong notes are played, the lead singer is flat and loud, or the song is slightly off beat, it is difficult to be edified and easy to be annoyed and distracted. Wilson speaks of this point in this way: "Those in the church who select the music should be equipped and trained to do so. This means those who are equipped to evaluate and make such determinations are mature (1 Chr. 23:3–5), musically talented and trained (1 Chr. 25:6–8), theologically astute (Heb. 5:14), and personally holy (Amos 5:23–24)."[45] To that we add:

> Musicians must see themselves as fellow laborers in the Word and must lead with understanding and an engaged heart. Those who minister in worship services must be healthy Christians who have confessed their sins and by God's grace are living their lives consistently with the music they lead. The sobering fact is that over time the congregation tends to become like those who lead.
>
> Musicians are also called to render their very best to God. Qualitative standards can be expressed classically (unity, clarity, proportion), and biblically (creativity, beauty, craft). In Christian worship, where music is a servant of the Word of God, musical standards are a requisite to clear communication. Church music must be judged by universal standards of musicianship: it must be good music, well performed, with due attention paid to intonation, rhythmic accuracy, articulation, and tone. Happy is the congregation led by godly, competent musicians.[46]

As former church planters, we recognize that in small churches, musicians may not have much training compared to those in larger churches. Nevertheless, pastors should encourage those who lead in music to pursue

---

[44] Ibid., 172.
[45] Wilson, *Mother Kirk*, 145.
[46] Hughes, "Free Church Worship," 171. Jones summarizes the same point this way: "Pastoral musicians, irrespective of title, should be qualified, trained, spiritual, mature, humble, accountable, and aware of their responsibilities." *What Is Worship Music?* 37.

such training, and those currently leading should defer to better-trained musicians that are in the church or later join. Excellence in music, coupled with humility, both honors God and raises the hearers to proclaim God's glories without distraction by error, pride, or performance.

PASTORS TO LEAD IN WORSHIP

In some places, biblical worship principles are entirely ignored; in many others, they have not been thoroughly explored. And there is little wonder how this came to be. Protestant seminaries exclude virtually any musical training for pastors, even though churches depend on ministers to set good practices for them.[47]

Luther thought that "before a youth is ordained into the ministry, he should practice music in school."[48] Elsewhere, he scorned those who aspired to be theologians even though they couldn't sing![49] While the times have surely (and sadly) changed, every pastor should understand enough about music and singing to draw up a philosophy of church music that would help his particular local congregation. As Keith Getty admonishes in his first point on "Five Ways to Improve Congregational Singing":

> Begin with the pastor. Look at any congregation not engaged in worship through singing and the most consistent correlation is a senior pastor equally as disengaged. Ultimately the buck stops with him in congregational worship. . . . Pastors not only have a duty to be involved in preparing for the time of congregational singing, they also have a responsibility to personally model and demonstrate the importance of it.[50]

For New Covenant Church in Naperville, Illinois, we developed the "Five S Principles":

THE FIVE S PRINCIPLES

Scriptural: We will sing songs of Scripture and other lyrics which reflect biblical language, themes, and theology. Also, like Scripture itself, our songs will center on Christ. While the Bible teaches that we gather on the Lord's Day for the purpose of mutual edification, encouragement, and exhortation, we also gather in the presence of Christ (Rev. 2–3). Thus,

---

[47] Jones, *What Is Worship Music?* 6.
[48] Quoted in Carl F. Schalk, *Luther on Music: Paradigms of Praise* (St. Louis: Concordia, 1988), 30.
[49] See Martin Luther, "Lecture on Titus" (1527), in *Luther's Works*, 55 vols., ed. Jaroslav Pelikan and Helmut T. Lehmann (St. Louis: Concordia; Philadelphia: Fortress, 1955–), 41:176.
[50] Keith Getty, "Five Ways to Improve Congregational Singing," http://thegospelcoalition.org/blogs/tgc worship/2014/02/18/five-ways-to-improve-congregational-singing/

following the pattern of some of the "Christ hymns" of the New Testament, notably the Song of the Lamb (Rev. 5), we focus our singing on the person and work of Christ, together giving him the worship due his holy name. This does not mean, from time to time, we won't sing a song about our fellowship, the Bible, the church, or a doctrine of Scripture, but this will not be the main focus.

Supportive: The music will support the service and the preaching of the Word, not have its own agenda or serve its own end. Thus (1) the tune will fit the text, (2) the instruments will not override the human voice, but rather support and complement it, and (3) we avoid certain musical styles and art forms that would be otherwise appropriate in a different context (e.g., drum solo, folk-style singalong, beat box, ostentatious operatic duets, show tunes, etc.)—since such have the "power" to draw people to itself, rather than to heighten the Word and prepare us for it.

Skilled: The musicians will be skilled, trained, and prepared. A goal will be to train the church in music and congregational singing. Thus, we will use a hymnal and/or inserts which have musical notation.

Sacred: While there is technically no "sacred" music, we recognize and appreciate Christian tradition, and thus we will use the rich and established tradition often called "sacred music" (i.e., Christian hymnody and choral music). We will also sing the best contemporary worship songs—those which reflect well the above principles.

Sundry: We will use a variety ("sundry") of instruments and songs from different times (e.g., "ancient"—songs from the early church, Reformation, etc.) and places ("global"—a song now popular in South Korea translated into English, or even learned in the original). We will also attempt to balance simple songs (e.g., children's songs or certain contemporary choruses) with more complex (e.g., learning to sing a Psalm from the Genevan Psalter).

When I (Doug) gathered the core group to plant the church, I walked through these principles with them. When the church hired a new music director a few years ago, I walked her through them. These are just guidelines, but I do expect that all our church musicians are aware of them and agree with them (or at least agree not to be disagreeable about their disagreement over minor differences). Expectations are important. The musicians and the congregation need to understand and, for the most part, support the church's philosophy of music and singing.

The pastor, along with the elders, should also set guidelines for a variety of other issues related to music. For example, how would you answer the following questions?

- How should musicians dress?
- Should there be a lead singer (traditionally called a cantor)?
- Should there be more than one singer?
- Should the singer/s wear microphones?
- Should there be a choir?
- If so, should the choir (not a lead singer) lead in singing?
- How skilled must the musicians be (able to read music, improvise, etc.)?
- Should anyone talk before a song or songs?
- If so, what are some guidelines for what can or should be said?
- If our goal is to hear the human voice (this is *congregational* singing!), how loud should the instruments and/or miked voices be?
- What type of instruments are acceptable for our church?
- Should we pay musicians?
- Can non-Christian musicians play for special numbers (e.g., a certain choral piece on Easter)?
- If so, why?
- Should we use a hymnal?
- If so, which one?
- If not, is there any "canon" of what songs we can or cannot sing?

As you can see, there are many philosophical and practical questions to be answered before and after the first note of the first service is hit. This is just part of a longer list. Be intentional. Be thoughtful. Explain to the musicians and congregation what you are doing and why you are doing it. Get feedback. Be willing to change with the congregation. But whatever you do, lead!

THE HYMNBOOK: A GREAT TREASURE-STORE

One of the major contributing factors to the superficiality of the lives of evangelical Christians in our country today [the 1980s] is the failure of the churches to teach and use the great hymns of the church universal in their services of worship. We have reared a generation or two [or three now!] of Christians who prefer sentimental songs with highly questionable theology to the greatest Christian poetry which has even been penned. . . . Aside from the Bible itself there is no book which offers the devotional material found in the hymnbook, but it is not primarily for individual devotions. Its rich resources should be mastered, not by the ministers alone, but by every earnest Christian who desires to offer to God the very highest and best in the praise of His name. We are faithful to the very finest motivations for corporate worship when we are careful to sing those great expressions of praise and devotion which have stood the test of time in the worship of multitudes of believers.[51]

The last question from the list in the last section—about a song "canon"—leads to a final practical point. *What specific songs shall we sing?* When I (Doug) planted New Covenant Church, I decided that "less would be more" regarding song selection. That is, I wanted the congregation to learn a small number of songs well. "Better to have a small repertoire of great songs (that you will sing well) than a catalog full of songs recycled for sentimental reasons or chased after because they are the 'latest' thing.'"[52] Thus, I created a "canon" (a group of approved songs that also functions as a criterion to judge other songs).

Also and obviously, this canon made it much easier to select songs week by week. What a help for a busy pastor! I would, of course, plan a few months out, but admittedly some weeks forced last-minute song selection. I certainly had the freedom (and exercised that freedom often enough) to select songs not on the list. But the list helped tremendously to make the workload manageable and to insure that God's people under my care were growing in some of the ways explained earlier in this chapter. When we hired a part-time music director, I explained my purpose for creating this canon, walked through the list, and then (because I trust her) invited her to add to or subtract from it as she desired. Admittedly we have disagreed from time to time about song selection, but those conversations have been fruitful and helped me grow musically *and* spiritually.

If you recall from the first chapter, the *congregational*[53] musical components at New Covenant include the introit, hymn of adoration, hymns to Christ, and song of response. I have also included songs we often sing for the Lord's Supper (for other suggestions, see chapter 9).

---

[51] Robert G. Rayburn, *O Come, Let Us Worship: Corporate Worship in the Evangelical Church* (Grand Rapids: Baker, 1987), 233, 240–241.
[52] Getty, "Five Ways to Improve Congregational Singing."
[53] Our choir sings choral anthems once a month. The music director always selects those. I usually comment on pieces I especially like (my way of saying, "Let's sing that one again!"). Also the choir often sings the introit.

New Covenant Church Song "Canon"

Introits[54]

"All Glory, Laud and Honor"
"All Praise to Thee, My God, This Night"
"Be Thou My Vision"
"Christ the Lord Is Risen Today"
"Doxology"
"Earth Has Many a Noble City"
"Holy God, We Praise Thy Name"
"Holy Is the Lord"
"I Love Thy Kingdom, Lord"
"In the Bleak Midwinter"
"Jesus, Priceless Treasure"
"Jesus, the Very Thought of Thee"
"Jesus, Thou Joy of Loving Hearts"
"Joyful, Joyful We Adore Thee"
"Lead Me, Lord"
"Let All Mortal Flesh Keep Silence"
"Let All Things Now Living"
"Let Thy Blood in Mercy Poured"
"Little Children, Rise and Sing"
"Love Divine, All Loves Excelling"
"O Come Let Us Adore Him"
"O God of Earth and Altar"
"O Lord, We Praise Thee"
"O Love, How Deep"
"Of the Father's Love Begotten"
"Speak, O Lord"
"Spirit of God, Descend Upon My Heart"
"The Servant Song"
"We Gather Together"
"What Wondrous Love Is This?"

Hymns of Adoration

"A Mighty Fortress Is Our God"
"All Glory, Laud, and Honor"
"All Hail the Power of Jesus's Name"
"Christ the Lord Is Risen Today"

---

[54] The introit is typically only the first verse or chorus of a hymn—sung by the choir or a soloist, or played by the musicians without voice/s.

"Come and See"
"Crown Him with Many Crowns"
"For All the Saints"
"Give Praise to God"
"God Himself Is with Us"
"God of Triumph" (O'Donnell)
"Holy God, We Praise Thy Name"
"Holy, Holy, Holy"
"How Great Thou Art"
"Immortal, Invisible, God Only Wise"
"Jesus Is Lord"
"Let All Things Now Living"
"Lift High the Cross"
"Lord Most High"
"Marvelous Grace of Our Loving Lord"
"My Strength, My Song, My Salvation" (O'Donnell)
"Now Thank We All Our God"
"O Church Arise"
"O Great God"
"O Love, How Deep"
"O Worship the King"
"Praise, My Soul, the King of Heaven"
"Praise the Lord! O Heavens, Adore Him"
"Praise to the Lord, the Almighty"
"Rejoice, the Lord Is King"
"Round the Throne in Radiant Glory"
"See What a Morning"
"Tell Out My Soul"
"The God of Abraham Praise"
"The King Shall Come"
"The Risen Christ"
"There Is a Higher Throne"
"To God Be the Glory"
"Why Should We Now Not Adore Thee?" (O'Donnell)

Songs to Christ

"Before the Throne of God Above"
"Beneath the Cross"
"Christ Beside Me"
"Come to the Waters"
"Come Thou Fount"

"Fairest Lord Jesus"
"Give Thanks"
"How Deep the Father's Love for Us"
"In Christ Alone"
"Jesus, Lover of My Soul"
"King of the Ages"
"Lamb of God"
"Mercy Speaks by Jesus's Blood"
"My Heart Is Filled with Thankfulness"
"My Song Is Love Unknown" (Ed Childs' version)
"Not What These Hands Have Done"
"O the Deep, Deep Love of Jesus"
"Sing Alleluia to the Lord"
"The Church's One Foundation"
"The Mystery of Godliness" (O'Donnell)
"The Power of the Cross (Oh to See the Dawn)"
"There Is a Redeemer"
"Wonderful, Merciful Savior"
"Worthy Thou, O Christ" (O'Donnell)
"You Have Been Given"

Songs of Response

"Amazing Grace"
"And Can It Be That I Should Gain?"
"Be Still My Soul"
"Be Thou My Vision"
"Beneath the Cross"
"Breathe on Me, Breath of God"
"Come to the Waters"
"Come, Ye Sinners, Poor and Needy"
"Every Promise of Your Word"
"Forgive Our Sins as We Forgive"
"God, You Keep Us"
"Great Is Thy Faithfulness"
"How Deep the Father's Love for Us"
"How Firm a Foundation"
"I Love Thy Kingdom, Lord"
"I Need Thee Every Hour"
"I Want to Walk as a Child of the Light"
"I Will Sing of My Redeemer"

"If Thou but Suffer God to Guide Thee"
"It Is Well with My Soul"
"Just As I Am"
"Lead On, O King Eternal"
"Lift High the Cross"
"May the Mind of Christ My Savior"
"My Heart Is Filled with Thankfulness"
"My Soul Magnifies the Lord/Song of Mary" (O'Donnell)
"My Strength, My Song, My Salvation" (O'Donnell)
"Not What These Hands Have Done"
"O Church Arise"
"O for a Thousand Tongues to Sing"
"O Love That Will Not Let Me Go"
"Our King God Doth Exalt" (O'Donnell)
"Take My Life"
"The Church's One Foundation"
"The Gift of Love"
"The Servant Song"
"Though the Fig Tree Blooms Not" (O'Donnell)

Communion Hymns

"A Purple Robe, A Crown of Thorns"
"Ah, Holy Jesus"
"Beneath the Cross"
"Fairest Lord Jesus"
"Go to Dark Gethsemane"
"How Great Thou Art"
"I Need Thee Every Hour"
"I Will Sing of My Redeemer"
"Lamb of God"
"Let Thy Blood in Mercy Poured"
"Man of Sorrows, What a Name"
"My Jesus, I Love Thee" (followed by "I Love You, Lord")
"O Sacred Head Now Wounded"
"Stricken, Smitten, and Afflicted"
"The Power of the Cross"
"Were You There?"
"What Wondrous Love Is This?"
"When I Survey the Wondrous Cross"
"Worthy Is the Lamb"

Kent also asked Dan Kreider (minister of music at Grace Immanuel Bible Church in Jupiter, Florida) to compile a list of songs and hymns for various church seasons and occasions. Below are Dan's excellent selections. These are also listed in part in four of the other chapters.

Hymns and Songs by Season/Event

The hymnody of each generation has been a reflection of the depth of its theology. Accompanying the recent resurgence of modern hymns has been the rediscovery and revival of the best hymns of the Reformation and beyond. Some of these old hymns are appearing unaltered and paired with their original tunes, while some are textually altered or set to completely new music, or both.

All the songs listed below are rich in doctrine, appropriate for corporate expressions of praise, and easily sung by a congregation.

Since the Internet and its search engines have become so universally accessible, it is no longer necessary to provide extensive details for locating resources. For both older, established hymns and newer hymns and songs, we have listed enough information that the reader should be able to easily find lyrics and other information.

Advent
Old Hymns
  "Come, Thou Long-Expected Jesus" (Wesley)
  "Comfort, Comfort Ye My People" (Olearius)
  "Hark, the Glad Sound!" (Doddridge)
  "Joy to the World!" (Watts)
  "Let All Mortal Flesh Keep Silence" (Liturgy of St. James)
  "Lo, He Comes with Clouds Descending" (Wesley)
  "O Come, O Come Emmanuel" (Latin hymn)
  "On Jordan's Bank the Baptist's Cry" (Coffin)
  "Rejoice, Rejoice Believers" (Laurenti)
  "Savior of the Nations, Come!" (Ambrose)
  "Thou Didst Leave Thy Throne" (Elliott)
  "Wake, Awake, For Night Is Flying!" (Nicolai)

New Hymns
  "Awake! Awake, and Greet the New Morn" (Haugen)
  "Exult in the Savior's Birth" (Carson/Boswell)
  "O Come, Our World's Redeemer, Come" (Perry)
  "O Savior of Our Fallen Race" (6th c.)

"People, Look East" (Farjeon)
"Wonderful Counselor" (Mark Altrogge)

Christmas
Old Hymns
"All My Heart This Night Rejoices" (Gerhardt)
"Angels from the Realms of Glory" (Montgomery)
"Gabriel's Message" (Basque carol)
"Good Christian Men, Rejoice" (Suso)
"Hark! The Herald Angels Sing" (Wesley)
"How Great Our Joy" (trad. German carol)
"Lo, How a Rose E'er Blooming" (15th c.)
"O Come, All Ye Faithful" (Wade)
"O Holy Night" (Cappeau)
"Of the Father's Love Begotten" (Prudentius)
"On This Day Earth Shall Ring" (*Piae Cantiones*)
"Once in Royal David's City" (Alexander)
"Silent Night! Holy Night!" (Mohr)
"The First Noel" (trad. English carol)
"What Child Is This?" (Dix)

New Hymns
"Anthem for Christmas" (Gaither/Smith)
"Christ the Lord Is Born Today" (Altrogge)
"From the Squalor of a Borrowed Stable" (Townend)
"Glory Be to God" (Wesley; alt. Kauflin)
"Jesus, Joy of the Highest Heaven" (Getty/Getty)
"Joy Has Dawned" (Getty/Townend)
"Thou Who Wast Rich Beyond All Splendour" (Houghton)

Palm Sunday
Old Hymns
"All Glory, Laud, and Honor" (Theodulph of Orleans)
"Hail to the Lord's Anointed" (Montgomery)
"Ride On, Ride On in Majesty" (Milman)

New Hymns
"Come, People of the Risen King" (Townend)
"Lift High the Name of Jesus" (Getty/Cash/de Barra)
"Make Way" (Kendrick)
"The King of Glory Comes" (Jabusch)

Good Friday
Old Hymns

"Ah, Holy Jesus! How Hast Thou Offended?" (Heermann)
"Go to Dark Gethsemane" (Montgomery)
"Jesus, Priceless Treasure" (Franck)
"Jesus, Thy Blood and Righteousness" (von Zinzendorf)
"My Song Is Love Unknown" (Crossman)
"O Sacred Head Now Wounded" (Bernard of Clairvaux)
"Sing, My Tongue, the Glorious Battle" (Fortunatus)
"The Love of Christ Is Rich and Free" (Gadsby)
"Were You There?" (spiritual)
"What Wondrous Love Is This?" (American folk hymn)
"When I Survey the Wondrous Cross" (Watts)

New Hymns

"Amazing Love, O What Sacrifice" (Kendrick)
"Beneath the Cross of Jesus" (Getty/Getty)
"Gethsemane" (Getty/Townend)
"His Robes for Mine" (Anderson)
"How Deep the Father's Love for Us" (Townend)
"In the Cross Alone I Glory" (Petak)
"Lamb of God" (Paris)
"Let Us Draw Near!" (Clarkson)
"Man of Grief and Man of Sorrows" (Kendrick/Getty)
"My Jesus Fair" (Anderson)
"On the Cross" (Baker)
"The Look" (Newton; alt. Kauflin)
"The Power of the Cross" (Getty/Getty)
"Through the Precious Blood" (Altrogge)

Resurrection Sunday
Old Hymns

"All Praise to Thee" (Tucker)
"Christ Jesus Lay in Death's Strong Bands" (Luther)
"Christ the Lord Is Risen Today" (Wesley)
"Crown Him with Many Crowns" (Bridges)
"The Day of Resurrection" (John of Damascus)
"The Head That Once Was Crowned with Thorns" (Kelly)
"The Strife Is O'er, the Battle Won" (12th c.)
"Thine Be the Glory" (Budry)

New Hymns

"Alleluia! Jesus is Risen" (Brokering)
"Behold Our God" (Baird/Baird/Altrogge/Baird)
"Christ Is Risen" (Maher)
"Christ Is Risen, He Is Risen Indeed" (Getty/Getty/Cash)
"Hail the Day" (Wesley; alt. Cook/Cook)
"In Christ Alone" (Getty/Townend)
"Jesus Lives" (Romanacce/Kauflin)
"See What a Morning" (Getty/Townend)

Communion

Old Hymns

"At the Lamb's High Feast We Sing" (6th c.)
"O Living Bread from Heaven" (von Rist)

New Hymns

"All Who Are Thirsty" (Perry)
"Behold the Lamb (The Communion Hymn)" (Getty/Getty/Townend)
"Gathered 'Round Your Table" (Clarkson)
"Merciful God" (Getty/Getty/Townend)
"Now the Feast and Celebration" (Haugen)

Weddings

"Although I Speak with Angel's Tongue" (Donaldson)
"Beloved, God's Chosen" (Cherwien)
"O God, Beyond All Praising" (Perry)
"This is a Day, Lord, Gladly Awaited" (Rowthorn)
"Where Love Is Found" (Schutte)

Funerals

Old Hymns

"Abide with Me" (Lyte)
"All Things New" (Bonar; new music, Wells)
"Be Still, My Soul" (von Schlegel)
"For All the Saints" (How)
"God Moves in a Mysterious Way" (Cowper)
"It Is Well with My Soul" (Spafford)

New Hymns

"All Must Be Well" (Bowley-Peters; alt. Smith)
"It Is Not Death to Die" (Malan; alt. Kauflin)
"O Father, You Are Sovereign" (Clarkson)

"Out of the Depths (Psalm 130)" (Kauflin)
"Still, My Soul, Be Still" (Getty/Getty/Townend)
"The Perfect Wisdom of Our God" (Getty/Townend)
"There Is a Hope" (Townend/Edwards)

SHEPHERDING THROUGH SONG: PERSONAL DEVOTIONS

Another way a pastor can shepherd his people is by suggesting songs for personal devotions. The following songs were selected based on lyrical excellence (they adapt scriptural texts or are reflective of scriptural themes) and fine tunes (simple yet rich melodies that are especially fitting for the human voice without musical accompaniment). Also, we have selected a blend of classic devotional hymns (songs every Christian should know or learn) as well as contemporary praise songs ("contemporary" in the sense of composed recently). The focus on the cross of Christ is intentional, as is the selection of songs that contain first-person singular pronouns.[55]

We selected only seventy songs. If you give your people this list and encourage them to sing five songs per week, they will be able to sing them all through at least three times a year. Lord willing, in a few years, they will have all seventy memorized. We also recommend teaching them to sing the Doxology and the *Gloria Patri* daily (perhaps before or after they read their Bibles). If you do not know some songs listed below, you can listen to them on www.cyberhymnal.org or where listed in the footnotes.

There is a trend today of setting old hymn texts to new tunes. This trend is valuable in that it helps the younger generation return to some of the church's classic texts (texts certainly worth singing). However, in our view, work needs to be done to improve most of the new tunes. The ones we think highly of (some are even improvements on the old tunes) are listed in the footnotes. For non-English songs, we have listed only the lyricist (e.g., Martin Luther, 1529), not the English translator (e.g., Frederic Henry Hedge, 1853). For the sake of space, some titles and names have been shortened (e.g., Katharina Amalia Dorothea von Schlegel to Katharina von Schlegel). A good number of the songs below can be found in *The Christian Life Hymnal* (Peabody, MA: Hendrickson Worship, 2006).

Songs for Personal Devotion
"A Mighty Fortress" (Luther)
"Ah, Holy Jesus" (Heerman)

---

[55] On the use of personal pronouns in Scripture and Christian song, see O'Donnell, *God's Lyrics*, 128–131.

"Alas! And Did My Savior Bleed?"[56] (Watts)
"And Can It Be That I Should Gain?" (Wesley)
"Be Still My Soul" (von Schlegel)
"Be Thou My Vision" (attr. Forgaill)
"Before the Throne of God Above" (Bancroft)
"Beneath the Cross" (Getty/Getty[57])
"Breathe on Me, Breath of God" (Hatch)
"Come Thou Fount of Every Blessing" (Robinson)
"Come to the Waters" (Boice[58])
"Come, Ye Disconsolate"[59] (Moore)
"Come Ye Sinners, Poor and Needy" (Hart)
"Fairest Lord Jesus" (*Münster Gesangbuch*)
"Give Me Jesus" (spiritual)
"Great Is Thy Faithfulness" (Chisholm)
"Habakkuk 3" (Deliyannides[60])
"Holy God, We Praise Thy Name" (attr. Franz)
"Holy, Holy, Holy" (Heber)
"Holy Is the Lord" (traditional American folk tune)
"How Deep the Father's Love for Us" (Townend)
"How Great Thou Art" (Boberg/Hine)
"I Bind Unto Myself Today" (attr. St. Patrick)
"I Greet Thee" (John Calvin)
"I Heard the Voice of Jesus Say"[61] (Bonar)
"I Love Thy Kingdom, Lord" (Dwight)
"I Want to Walk as a Child of the Light" (Thomerson)
"I Will Sing of My Redeemer" (Bliss)
"If Thou But Suffer God to Guide Thee" (Neumark)
"Immortal, Invisible, God Only Wise" (Smith)
"In Christ Alone" (Getty/Townend)
"In the Bleak Midwinter" (Rossetti)
"It Is Well with My Soul" (Spafford)

---

[56] Listen also to Greg Thompson's new tune at http://hymnbook.igracemusic.com/hymns/alas-and-did-my-savior-bleed-thompson and a sample of Greg Wilbur's new tune at www.amazon.com/My-Cry-Ascends-Parish-Psalms/dp/B003NMSDB0/ref=sr_1_1?s=music&ie=UTF8&qid=1310657086&sr=1-1 or www.ligonier.org/store/my-cry-ascends-new-parish-psalms-cd/
[57] For samples of the Gettys' music, go to www.gettymusic.com.
[58] From James Montgomery Boice and Paul Steven Jones, *Hymns for a Modern Reformation* (Philadelphia: Tenth Music, 2000). To hear samples of these songs, go to www.amazon.com/Hymns-for-a-Modern-Reformation/dp/B00192N52S/ref=tmm_msc_title_0
[59] Listen also to a sample of Greg Wilbur's new tune at www.amazon.com/My-Cry-Ascends-Parish-Psalms/dp/B003NMSDB0/ref=sr_1_1?s=music&ie=UTF8&qid=1310657086&sr=1-1
[60] A. B. Deliyannides and Peter Wallace from Michiana Covenant Presbyterian Church have written new Scripture songs that are worth singing (http://michianacovenant.org/worship/psalms-hymns-and-spiritual-songs/).
[61] Listen also to Kevin Twit's new tune at http://hymnbook.igracemusic.com/hymns/i-heard-the-voice-of-jesus-say

"Jesus, Lover of My Soul"[62] (Wesley)
"Jesus Paid It All" (Hall)
"Jesus, What a Friend for Sinners" (Chapman)
"Just as I Am" (Elliot)
"Lamb of God" (Paris)
"Lord Jesus, Think on Me"[63] (Synesius of Cyrene)
"May the Mind of Christ My Savior" (Wilkinson)
"More Love to Thee" (Prentiss)
"My Heart Is Filled with Thankfulness" (Getty/Townend)
"My Jesus, I Love Thee" (Featherstone)
"My Song Is Love Unknown"[64] (Crossman)
"Not What These Hands Have Done" (Bonar)
"O Great God"[65] (Kauflin)
"O Sacred Head, Now Wounded"[66] (Bernard of Clairvaux)
"O the Deep, Deep Love of Jesus" (Francis)
"O Worship the King" (Grant)
"Of the Father's Love Begotten" (Prudentius.)
"Praise, My Soul, the King of Heaven"[67] (Lyte)
"Praise to the Lord, the Almighty" (Neander)
"Stricken, Smitten, and Afflicted" (Kelly)
"Take My Life, and Let It Be" (Havergal)
"Tell Out My Soul" (Dudley-Smith)
"The Gift of Love" (Hopson)
"The God of Abraham Praise" (ben Judah)
"The Gospel Song"[68] (Kauflin/Jones)
"The King of Love My Shepherd Is" (Baker)
"The King Shall Come" (anon.)
"The Power of the Cross" (Getty/Townend)
"There Is a Higher Throne" (Getty/Getty)
"There Is a Redeemer" (Green)
"'Tis the Church Triumphant Singing"[69] (Kent)
"Were You There?" (spiritual)

---

[62] Listen also to Greg Thompson's new tune at http://hymnbook.igracemusic.com/hymns/jesus-lover-of-my-soul

[63] Listen also to a sample of Greg Wilbur's version at www.amazon.com/My-Cry-Ascends-Parish-Psalms/dp/B003NMSDB0/ref=sr_1_1?s=music&ie=UTF8&qid=1310657086&sr=1-1

[64] Listen also to a sample of Edwin T. Childs's version at http://edwintchilds.com/recordings-songs-through-endless-ages.html

[65] Listen to a sample at http://www.sovereigngracemusic.org/Songs/O_Great_God/35

[66] Listen also to James Falzone's version at www.cdbaby.com/cd/gracechicago

[67] Listen also to Christopher Miner's new tune at http://hymnbook.igracemusic.com/hymns/praise-my-soul-the-king-of-heaven-miner

[68] Listen to a sample at http://www.sovereigngracemusic.org/Songs/The_Gospel_Song/35

[69] Listen also to the college group at College Church in Wheaton's new tune at www.cdbaby.com/cd/restorationproject

"What Wondrous Love Is This?" (Appalachian folk hymn)
"When I Survey the Wondrous Cross" (Watts)
"When You Prayed Beneath the Trees"[70] (Idle)
"Wonderful, Merciful Savior" (Rogers/Wise)
"You Have Been Given" (Kauflin)

ADDITIONAL RESOURCES

It has been said that Charles Wesley wrote the first and best systematic theology of the Methodist Church through his thousands of hymns, songs with attractive tunes matched to compelling poetry. This is similar to what has been observed about the Levitical musicians in the Old Testament, who "catechized the nation of Israel through the singing of psalms."[71] As pastors, we must recognize that music is important to congregational life as a partner to preaching—as a musical minister of the Word—and it is our prayer that this chapter will help you to better lead others in worship of our great God.

For further resources, we suggest below a list of books on the topic (or topics related to it), followed by helpful Internet sites.

Books on Christian Worship Music

Begbie, Jeremy S., and Steven R. Guthrie. *Resonant Witness: Conversations between Music and Theology*, Calvin Institute of Christian Worship Liturgical Studies Series. Grand Rapids: Eerdmans, 2011.

Best, Harold. *Music through the Eyes of Faith*. New York: HarperOne, 1993.

Jilian, John. *Dictionary of Hymnody*. New York: Dover, 1957.

Johansson, Calvin M. *Discipling Music Ministry: Twenty-first Century Directions*. Peabody, MA: Hendrickson, 1992.

Jones, Paul S. *Singing and Making Music*. Phillipsburg, NJ: P&R, 2006.

———. *What Is Worship Music?* Basics of the Faith. Phillipsburg, NJ: P&R, 2012.

McCall, Sally, and Rosalie Milne, eds. *Church Musicians' Handbook*. Kingsford, Australia: Matthias Media, 1999.

Mouw, Richard J., and Mark A. Noll. *Wonderful Words of Life: Hymns in American Protestant History and Theology*. Grand Rapids: Eerdmans, 2004.

Noll, Mark A., and Edith L. Blumhofer. *Sing Them Over Again to Me: Hymns and Hymnbooks in America*. Tuscaloosa, AL: University of Alabama, 2006.

O'Donnell, Douglas Sean. *God's Lyrics: Rediscovering Worship through Old Testament Songs*. Phillipsburg, NJ: P&R, 2010.

---

[70] Listen to this at www.sheetmusicplus.com/title/When-You-Prayed-Beneath-the-Trees/7537953.
[71] Payton, "How Shall We Sing to God?" 193.

Payton, Leonard. *Reforming Our Worship Music*. Wheaton, IL: Crossway, 1999.

Quasten, Johannes. *Music and Worship in Pagan and Christian Antiquity*, trans. Boniface Ramsey. Washington, DC: National Association of Pastoral Musicians, 1983.

Schalk, Carl F. *Luther on Music: Paradigms of Praise*. St. Louis: Concordia, 1988.

———. *First Person Singular: Reflections on Worship, Liturgy, and Children*. St. Louis: MorningStar, 1998.

Scheer, Greg. *The Art of Worship: A Musician's Guide to Leading Modern Worship*. Grand Rapids: Baker, 2006.

Westermeyer, Paul. *Te Deum: The Church and Music*. Minneapolis: Fortress, 1998.

Wilson-Dickson, Andrew. *The Story of Christian Music*. Minneapolis: Fortress, 1992.

INTERNET RESOURCES

In *Christ-Centered Worship: Letting the Gospel Shape our Practice*, Bryan Chapell lists "Worship Resources on the Internet" and brief descriptions.[72] Below we list our top seven from his list (in alphabetical order) and using his descriptions:

> http://www.calvin.edu/worship/. The Calvin Institute of Christian Worship provides many resources for the study and practice of Christian worship. Devoted to the renewal of worship by continuity with great traditions of the church while respecting modern contributions, the institute's Worship Sourcebook in print and CD form is the most recommended single resource now available for worship service creation in the Reformed tradition.

> http://www.cardiphonia.com/. The website of Redeemer Church in Indianapolis is devoted to enhancing worship by sharing its many insights and resources regarding the aesthetics of ancient and modern worship. (On the Psalms, see http://cardiphonia.org/2010/05/12/resources-on-using-the -psalms-in-worship/)

> http://www.cyberhymnal.org. Probably the most used and extensive website for searching out hymns by title or text. Users can copy and paste

---

[72] Bryan Chapell, *Christ-Centered Worship: Letting the Gospel Shape Our Practice* (Grand Rapids: Baker Academic, 2009), 305–306.

the text if they want to include it in their bulletin. They also have the ability to listen to the tune on the page on which the text appears. There are many other features available on this site that are helpful to worship planners and musicians.

http://www.hymnary.org. Seeks to combine the best features of numerous sites devoted to hymn study, sharing, and research.

http://www.hymnary.org/dnah. The Dictionary of North American Hymnology searchable website, with the contexts of 4,876 hymnals published in North America between 1640 and 1978, including over one million hymns contained in these publications.

https://itunes.apple.com/us/album/new-york-hymns/id318475749. Redeemer Music is a resource for new Christian music in the jazz, classical, and folk traditions with texts that uphold the centrality of the gospel message. Originally created for worship services at Redeemer Presbyterian Church in New York City, this music is now heard at churches throughout the United States and overseas.

http://www2.cpdl.org/wiki/index.php/Main_Page. The Choral Public Domain Library includes traditional church music that is in the public domain. It can be copied without charge.

To this excellent list we will add:

http://www.ccel.org/index/subject/hymn. The Christian Classics Ethereal Library hosts an amazing array of nearly seventy websites on everything from "Christian Hymns of the First Three Centuries" to John Jilian's two-volume "Dictionary of Hymnology." If you want to find "Hymns from the Russian Church," "Sacred Hymns from the German," "Scottish Psalter and Paraphrases," "Sweet Singers of Wales," or "Southern Harmony," it is all there!

http://thegospelcoalition.org/blogs/tgcworship/. Hosted on the Gospel Coalition website, this multicontributor blog "seeks to promote gospel-centered worship throughout the church by training and equipping leaders in the Word-shaped ministry of singing, songwriting, and service planning." Here you can find thought-provoking articles as well as the latest resources.

http://www2.wheaton.edu/isae/hymns.html. The Hymnody in American Protestantism Project is the findings of a three-year study on American

Protestant hymnody, including Stephen Marini's list of the three hundred most frequently published American hymns. It also features a link to a CD project that contains new choral arrangements to hymns from nine of America's leading arrangers of church music.

8

Baptism

This promises to be a fascinating chapter because the writers are Kent Hughes (a Baptist) and Douglas O'Donnell (a paedobaptist). Five hundred years ago, two men from such disparate positions could not have written such a chapter, but today we can because we understand that what binds us together transcends our views on baptism. As it stands, the two of us are nearly identical in the classic theological categories and share similar approaches to ministry, as the chapters of this book repeatedly attest. Morally and ethically, we stand shoulder to shoulder. John Calvin's commitment to *lectio continua* ("continuous reading" of Scripture) has shaped our homiletical agendas as Bible expositors; we both preach through the books of the Bible chapter and verse, and have conducted preaching workshops together for the Charles Simeon Trust. For us both, the text is sovereign.

Yet here is the curious thing: we disagree over baptism and are convinced of our positions. And it is not because we don't understand the other's arguments. I (Kent), for example, understand the paedobaptist reasoning that whereas circumcision was an outward sign of admission into the old covenant community, so baptism is the outward sign of admission into the new covenant community. And as regards infants, while circumcision was gender specific (eight-day-old male infants), water baptism is open to and incumbent for all infants in the new covenant community, male and female alike. I also follow the logic that just as the Passover was replaced by the Lord's Table, so circumcision has been replaced by baptism. Lastly, the argument that the "household baptisms" of the New Testament included young children is clear enough. So why do I not accede to these arguments? Because I think they treat the biblical texts tendentiously in order to support the covenantal construct. In some places, they ignore the plainest meaning of the text. This may sound dismissive, but it is not. The arguments of the paedobaptists are substantial and well reasoned, and have been articulated through the centuries by many of the great minds and heroes in church history, but to debate them here is beyond the intention and scope of this book.

Likewise, Doug understands the Baptist arguments. He says:

> The Baptist position argues—exegetically as well as via example—that water baptism is not a replacement for circumcision and that regeneration and faith always precede the new sign of the new covenant (i.e., water baptism). Saving faith is the prerequisite for baptism. Moreover, from the Apostle Paul to Cornelius's household, there is no clear example of an infant baptism in the New Testament.

There is more to say, obviously, on both sides; and we will say more in what follows. However, for the primary purpose of this chapter, we agree to disagree, because the one thing that we agree on, and which is more foundational, is that baptism is not optional. As Christians, we are to obey Christ's Great Commission command to be baptized (Matt. 28:19).

That foundational unity stated, we hope that dividing the chapter into two sections—under the subheadings "The Protestant Believer's Baptism View and Practice" and "The Protestant Infant Baptism View and Practice"—will continue to promote unity while recognizing diversity. We hope this approach will be of great practical help, as each section will begin with our observations about baptism and then offer practical advice about preparing for baptism and outlines of liturgies for administering baptism.

THE PROTESTANT BELIEVER'S BAPTISM VIEW AND PRACTICE

The following discussion is shaped under five major headings. The first is a brief discussion of the theology of baptism; the second two headings deal sequentially with the spiritual preparations of the candidates for baptism and the preparations for a service of baptism; and the final two provide multiple full-text examples of baptism liturgies, including a full liturgy for baby dedications.

THEOLOGY OF BAPTISM

Mode

The only mode of baptism described in the New Testament is immersion; a new believer is submersed under the water and lifted out. The Greek word *baptizo* literally means "to plunge, dip, immerse." The prepositions *in, out of*, and *into* used variously in the baptism passages are concomitant with immersion (cf. Mark 1:5, 10; John 3:23; Acts 8:36–39).[1]

Symbolism

The theological symbolism of immersion and elevation from the water throbs with the movement of the gospel. Submersion pictures our union with Christ in his death and burial, elevation our being raised with him to newness of life. This is certainly the gospel movement of Romans 6:3–4, where Paul says: "Do you not know that all of us who have been baptized into Christ Jesus were baptized into his death? We were buried therefore with him by baptism into death, in order that, just as Christ was raised from the dead by the glory of the Father, we too might walk in newness of life." And again in Colossians 2:12, "[You have] been buried with him in baptism, in which you were raised with him through faith in the powerful working of God, who raised him from the dead." This is the explicit movement of the apostolic gospel according to Paul:

> Now I would remind you, brothers, of *the gospel* I preached to you, which you received, in which you stand, and by which you are being saved, if you hold fast to the word I preached to you—unless you believed in vain. For I delivered to you as of first importance what I also received: that Christ *died* for our sins in accordance with the Scriptures, that he was *buried*, that he was *raised* on the third day in accordance with the Scriptures. (1 Cor. 15:1–4)

This is magnificent symbolism. And there is further gospel symbolism in immersion, because the waters of baptism are emblematic not only of our death, burial, and resurrection with Christ, but also of our washing and cleansing from sin that occurs concurrent with conversion. As Ananias commanded Saul when he was saved, "Rise and be baptized and wash away your sins, calling on his name" (Acts 22:16).[2]

Therefore, believers' baptisms are occasions for gospel theater in the non-Broadway (original) sense of the word—a time to view intently and observe the movements of the gospel. Calvin viewed the bread and the wine of Communion as visible words, and in a similar way baptism is such a word. As pastors and leaders of the flock, it is our responsibility to teach these truths of baptism clearly and to use the joyous occasion of a believer's baptism as a gospel opportunity.

---

[1] Wayne Grudem, *Systematic Theology: An Introduction to Biblical Doctrine* (Grand Rapids: Zondervan, 1994), 967.
[2] Ibid., 969.

Subjects

The New Testament consistently records that baptism was reserved for those who professed faith in Christ—believers only. Following Peter's sermon at Pentecost, we read, "Those who received his word were baptized" (Acts 2:41). Of Philip's preaching of the gospel in Samaria, we read, "When they believed Philip as he preached good news . . . they were baptized, both men and women" (Acts 8:12). Likewise, when Peter preached to the Gentile audience in Cornelius's household, he commended baptism for those who heard the word and received the Holy Spirit, declaring: "'Can anyone withhold water for baptizing these people, who have received the Holy Spirit just as we have?' And he commanded them to be baptized in the name of Jesus Christ" (Acts 10:47–48). The so-called "household baptisms" of the household of Lydia (Acts 16:14–15), the Philippian jailer's family (Acts 16:32–33), and the household of Stephanas (1 Cor. 1:16) are, as Grudem explains, "really not decisive for one position or another. When we look at the actual examples more closely, we see that in a number of them there are indications of saving faith on the part of all of those baptized."[3] The New Testament is clear that baptism symbolizes the beginning of the Christian life and is for the regenerate alone.

Imperative

Of course, baptism is not necessary for salvation. A symbol cannot save. The crucified repentant thief went straight from his cross to paradise (Luke 23:42–43). The imperative is simply to obey Christ, who commanded baptism for all who believe. Here the immediacy with which the command was carried out must be noted. Immediately upon the apostle Paul's conversion, Ananias said to him, "And now why do you wait? Rise and be baptized and wash away your sins, calling on his name" (Acts 22:16), and the parallel account earlier in Acts pictures the haste with which it was carried out: "And immediately something like scales fell from his eyes, and he regained his sight. Then he rose and was baptized; and taking food, he was strengthened" (9:18). He didn't even take time to stay his hunger before baptism. The same immediacy is evident in the Ethiopian eunuch's exclamation: "See, here is water! What prevents me from being baptized?" (Acts 8:36). Less dramatic but similar immediacy is seen in the accounts that were just referenced in regard to Pentecost and the preaching of the gospel in Samaria and to Cornelius's house. Too much can be made of the apostolic immediacy, but it

---

[3] Ibid., 978.

appears that ideally baptism should take place in reasonable proximity to salvation.

PREPARATION FOR BAPTISM

Today few churches in the revivalist tradition baptize immediately upon profession of faith. Instead, most churches take a less spontaneous approach because they want to know first if the profession is real. And this is not a new practice, because the early church came to require a lengthy catechism of converts before baptizing them, due to a spate of unregenerate converts. Today, with the winds of modernity and postmodernity blowing around and even through the church, loving care needs to be extended to converts before they are baptized. At the same time, the immediacy with which baptism was administered in the apostolic church tells us that the time of preparation must not be overly long. New birth and its symbol belong as close together as possible.

Assessment of the Candidates

As churches seek to discern the readiness of a professing believer for baptism, the following factors should be considered:

- *Regenerate?* Preparation begins with discerning whether the person is truly regenerate. People sometimes come seeking baptism because of the pressure of a worried friend or relative, or because they feel an inner stirring and want to do a "religious" thing. And what could be more religious than getting baptized? So pat answers—such as, "I asked Jesus into my heart when I was six" or "I went forward at camp"—need to be kindly probed. There are diagnostic questions, of course, such as, "If you were to die tonight and stand before God, and he were to say, 'Why should I let you into my heaven?' what would you say?" But better yet is to ask how the person understands the cross. Personal probings such as, "Tell me about your prayer life" will get beyond the surface answers. This said, a person can be a true believer and not be able to adequately describe the gospel. Any church contains a wide range of mental ability and articulateness. But a patient, loving pastor who takes the time can discern belief.
- *Repentant?* Along with this, the prospective candidate must have turned from known sins and must desire to live a righteous life. Here again, probing questions are a pastoral responsibility. To enter the waters of baptism without a repentant spirit gives a distorted picture of the beauty of the gospel.

- *Old enough?* There are other necessary considerations, such as the question of age. Here the Bible gives no parameters. Wisdom would dictate that when a child is able to express an understanding of the gospel and give a transparent, unprompted profession of faith in Christ, he or she may be baptized. Also, the parents, who naturally know the child best, must provide enthusiastic support. I once baptized a six-year-old boy because: (1) the father came to me at the boy's request, (2) the son bore remarkable testimony to the cross and his faith in Christ, and (3) his father and mother said that he was ready. It was a beautiful thing. But we must always remember that every child has a different interior clock, and God's grace works when he pleases and as he pleases in the lives of his children.

Preparation of the Candidates

Preparing Christian brothers or sisters for baptism is a huge opportunity to disciple them, especially if they are fresh converts. The rush of new life has energized their souls, their sins are completely gone, the Word of God has become alive to them, they are naturally bearing witness to Christ, and the Holy Spirit has poured God's love into their hearts with the result that they are receptive, teachable, and impressionable. Preparing these tender souls for baptism follows a very natural curriculum.

Instruct Them as to What Baptism Is

That is to say, teach them the gospel. The very movements that they will undergo in baptism are divine theater that will portray what happened to them when they met Christ. When they are submerged momentarily in baptism, it is emblematic of their death and burial with Christ (and when baptized, they ought to think about it). When they are raised from the waters, it is a picture of being raised with Christ (they ought to think about that, too). Christ died our death and raised us to life in himself.

This is an opportunity to acquaint them with something of the cross-centered theology of their redemption, not in a rigorous exploration, but with simple explanations and illustrations of Christ's substitutionary atonement (cf. John 1:29; 1 Pet. 1:18–19; 1 John 1:7) and of the imputed righteousness that comes by faith (Gen. 15:6; Rom. 3:21–22; 4:1–12; Phil. 3:9). And, of course, you should reiterate that it is all of grace: "For by grace you have been saved through faith. And this is not your own doing; it is the gift of God, not a result of works, so that no one may boast" (Eph. 2:8–9).

Because they are so teachable at this tender time in their lives, these truths will sink indelibly into their souls, so that as life unfolds, they will become gospel men and women who affirm with increasing conviction the words of Paul: "For I am not ashamed of the gospel, for it is the power of God for salvation to everyone who believes" (Rom. 1:16).

Help Them Prepare Testimonies for Baptism

Every redeemed soul has a unique narrative. It is his or hers alone, though God is the ultimate author. All can tell of a chain of divine providences that led to their salvation, a chain that began in the womb (Ps. 139:16). Some of the links are visible (some of those are sad, others joyful), but the chain led ineluctably to the moment their eyes were opened and they saw Jesus. Their experiences of salvation varied. Some were thunderstruck, and they can still whiff the spiritual ozone of that wondrous event. For others, it was like a long dawn, where the cosmic light increased so imperceptibly that the converts cannot say when they first saw it. Most narratives fall somewhere between these extremes. But ultimately, for every regenerate soul, there is the experience of forgiveness, not the therapeutic or communal forgiveness of television talk show hosts, but *real* theological forgiveness for *real* theological sin. And with the forgiveness comes the removal of the leaden gravity of guilt—"I have often walked down this street before, but the pavement always stayed beneath my feet before," to quote the *My Fair Lady* song in a different context. Along with this comes joy and an intense love for God through the Holy Spirit (Rom. 5:5, cf. Matt. 22:36–38; Gal. 5:22–23).

Every Christian has so much to tell, but some believers lack the confidence to compose and deliver a public testimony. Pastors and church leaders, this again is a sweet gospel opportunity. The way to do it is simple and salutary. Just engage the person in a one-on-one conversation (or perhaps a conversation with one or two other baptismal candidates) about his or her conversion, and tease it out with questions about life before coming to Christ, the experience of coming to Christ, and life after coming to Christ. By some gentle probing, honest fascination, and genial humor and generous affirmations, the story of God's grace will emerge with its own unique beauty. From this, a concise gospel testimony can be composed, using the *before* and *after* outline.

For use in a baptismal service, the testimony should be short, preferably under three minutes. For some, this is easy; most will find it doable; others will find it impossible. Many people today cannot write a comprehensible paragraph. So when you ask them to do it, you should, in the same breath, offer your help if needed. This will avoid humiliation and embarrassment, the last thing you want associated with their baptism. Personally, I have found this to be a simple thing to do and an opportunity for further personal ministry. And when and however it is done, a significant family document will have come into existence.

The wonderful thing about composing a personal testimony is that it articulates the power of the gospel in the most personal way, and for some it will become the bones for repeatedly sharing Christ over the subsequent years.

As to the use of written testimonies in a service of baptism, they can be read or recited by the candidate before each baptism or printed out for the congregation to read. Pastors must also bear in mind that some people simply cannot utter more than a monosyllable before a crowd, especially if they are about to be baptized.

Help Them Prepare Spiritually for Baptism

This obviously begins with individual preparation of the heart by confessing and repenting of one's sins, reading God's Word, and regular prayer. There is nothing extraordinary here, and there should not be. If such discipline is presented as a way to achieve an extraordinary state so as to experience a special exaltation of soul at the moment of baptism, then the discipline becomes a means of spiritual arrogation. This said, to undergo baptism while sinning or refusing to confess one's sins can do damage to the soul.

One other key to spiritual preparation for baptism is to pray regularly for those who will be attending because baptisms are often witnessed by unbelieving family members, as well as non-Christian friends and neighbors. This places the emphasis outside the one being baptized and on the gospel. An effective thing to do is ask each candidate to give you a copy of his or her list of visitors so that you too can pray for them. This is gospel power!

Preparation for the Baptism Service

Baptisms take place is such differing venues—in swimming pools, rivers, lakes, even in the ocean. I recall, during the rise of Costa Mesa's Calvary Chapel, seeing well over a thousand people standing in line to be baptized in the waters of Corona Del Mar. For many, baptism takes place in a church, though even there the location varies—the baptismal pool may be in the floor, behind the pastor, over the choir, or in the courtyard. Clergy and candidate attire also varies widely—from the preacher in black waders and gown baptizing those clad in white surplices to the preacher in surfing gear baptizing other surfers in—where else?—the surf. Most preachers do their baptisms regularly in the church building, though at times they conduct baptisms alfresco, well aware of the biblical precedent. The advice that follows is given with the regular services in mind, but most of it is transferable to any context.

Most of this is boilerplate common sense, but if it is ignored, the event will likely not go smoothly. The reader should note that the church contexts from which this advice comes are quite different. The first is the Midwest setting of nondenominational College Church in Wheaton, Illinois, and the second is the First Baptist Church in rural Lindale, Texas. FBC Lindale is a fine, thriving, midsized Southern Baptist church with a commitment to biblical exposition. The practical preparations of College Church (as they were when I was pastor) will be presented first, and then the more precise preparations of FBC Lindale.

Letters to the Candidates
Sample from College Church in Wheaton, Illinois
The week before a Sunday evening when baptisms were scheduled, I (Kent) sent a letter to the candidates that read as follows:

> Dear _____,
> This next Sunday night you will give testimony through baptism of your faith that Christ died on the cross for your sins and then triumphed over death by his resurrection from the dead and that when you came to believe this you were baptized by the Holy Spirit in the body of Christ (cf. 1 Cor. 12:13). So this Sunday when you are immersed in baptism, it will symbolize that you have been united with Christ in his death, and when you are lifted from the water, it will testify that you have been raised in him to new life—and ultimate resurrection. Your baptism will proclaim the gospel!
> As your pastor, I can tell you that we all are looking forward to this event. I have been praying that you will find great satisfaction in testifying about your coming to faith in Christ. You have written a fine testimony, and your listeners will be inwardly cheering you on. Also, may you sense God's smile as you undergo the waters of baptism. [Note: if the candidate will not be giving a testimony verbally, the words "your listeners" would be replaced with "as the people read it, they."]
> _____, I have included a few things that you must do to ensure that the evening goes well.
>
> - Bring suitable clothes for baptism. Men, a polo shirt and jeans or chinos work well. Women: similar dress. No shorts, and nothing that becomes "see through" when wet.

- Bring a beach towel or large bath towel.
- You may want to bring a hair dryer.
- Most importantly, be at the church at ____, which is forty-five minutes before the service begins. We will do a "dry run" ☺ through the motions of baptism, review the questions that you will be affirming, and then pray together.

Should you have any questions or concerns this week, please call me at _____.

Again, your baptism is a special time for you and for the church. God bless you.

Sample from First Baptist Church in Lindale, Texas

First Baptist Church's baptisms are normally scheduled for the third Sunday of the month and are done in the morning worship service. They are more formal than the evening baptisms at College Church. The following comprehensive letter is sent to all who request to be baptized and initiates the pastoral interaction and care in preparation for baptism. The latter half of this letter contains excellent advice and examples for preparing a testimony:

Dear _____,

We're so glad that you've decided to be baptized. Jesus gave us his example to follow, the apostles declared its importance, and we continue the practice today. It's a joyous celebration and an important event! Here's FBC's doctrinal statement regarding baptism:

We believe that Christian Baptism is the immersion in water of a believer, into the name of the Father, and Son, and Holy Spirit; to show forth in a solemn and beautiful emblem, our faith in the crucified, buried, and risen Savior, with its effect, in our death to sin and resurrection to a new life; that it is pre-requisite to the privileges of a church relation.

What a glorious testimony you'll be proclaiming! We want you to be able to relax and focus on this message rather than on the details of the baptism. That's why we've created this sheet. Read over it, and take care of all of the details long before the morning of your baptism. That way you'll be able to focus on the spiritual significance of the event rather than the technical details.

1. You will work closely with one of our pastors, who will walk you through the process. Be sure you schedule a meeting with him as soon as you can.

2. You will work with Pastor _____ to schedule your baptism in a Sunday morning service. He can be reached at the church office at _____ or by e-mail at _____@_____. We try to schedule baptisms on the third Sunday of each month, but will gladly make exceptions when necessary. You need to have a few dates in mind when you contact _____, including the worship service (8:15 a.m. or 11 a.m.) in which you'd like to be baptized.

3. Write out your testimony. You can find a guide attached to this sheet. Your pastor will walk you through this guide and help you shape your testimony if you'd like. Also find a recent digital photo of yourself (and only yourself). If you don't have one, or if the picture you have won't work for our system, we will take one for you. We use this information to put together your testimony sheet, which we'll insert in the bulletin so people can "meet" you and pray for you. Find a time to meet with your baptizing pastor to give him your testimony and picture.

4. Be sure to wear a modest swimsuit or other clothing beneath the baptismal robe (which will be provided for you on the morning of your baptism). The robes are white and will get wet—they are not intended to be a cover-all; plan accordingly so that you don't embarrass yourself and others. You'll also want to bring a change of clothes and any other items you'll need to clean up after yourself. Bring a towel and a bag to store your wet clothes until you can take them home.

5. The stairs to the baptistery are located behind the Worship Center platform (in the hallway by the choir room). You will be greeted by one of our deacons, who will guide you in the remainder of the process. Family members are welcome to stay in the baptistery to witness the baptism and assist with the details, but they are not required to do so. Plan to arrive *fifteen minutes before* the service begins so that you have plenty of time to take care of any last minute details.

Your baptizing pastor is available for any additional questions you may have.

We're looking forward to this wonderful occasion!

Writing a Testimony for Baptism

The fact that a holy God has provided a way for sinners like you and me to be reconciled to him is amazing. There is nothing we have done or could have done to deserve his forgiveness for our sins. So whether you were saved at a young age and went to church most of your life or whether you weren't saved until much later in life, you have an amazing gift. You should be telling others about God's gift of salvation and how he has worked in your life and sharing that gift as God has instructed us to do.

Because your testimony will be published instead of spoken, we ask that you limit what you write to 275 words (just short of half a page). A lot can be said in this amount of words, and the limit will help you focus on the most important aspects of your testimony.

Testimonies should state how you were saved. You should tell people how you came to realize you were a sinner, how you came to understand that Jesus died for your sins, and why you decided to put your faith in Jesus as Savior and Lord. A good testimony will show how God has been at work in your heart and in your life. A testimony is not simply your life story. It needs to clearly point others to God. Therefore, it must be Christ-centered and gospel-centered. Choose to include biographical details that highlight the basic gospel truths taught in the Bible.

Use *at least* one passage of Scripture in your testimony. It should relate to what you write.

Three sample written testimonies are included below.

Your baptism is an exciting event, and we delight to share in this joy. We are praying for you as you write out your testimony, and we know the church will rejoice to hear of God's work in your life.

Sample testimony #1: My name is _____. I'm getting baptized today out of obedience to Jesus's command and to show everybody that I want to follow Jesus. God blessed me in allowing me to be born into a Christian family. I have seen up close that my parents are different because of Jesus. When I was young, I understood that I was a sinner and that Jesus died for my sins. I believed in Jesus. That belief has grown as I've come to understand just how ugly my sinful nature can be and as I've come to understand that Jesus took the penalty of my sins upon himself at the cross. But Jesus didn't stay dead. He defeated sin and death, and now he gives me the strength to walk as a new creation. I'm still far from perfect, but it's encouraging as I see God's Spirit making small changes in me. Second Corinthians 5:17 says, "If anyone is in Christ, he is a new creation. The old has passed away; behold, the new has come." I know God has worked that miracle in me, and that is why I'm getting baptized today.

Sample testimony #2: My name is _____, and I was born and raised in Lindale. Those who've known me might have thought I was a good man. I didn't get into too much trouble as a youth, and I went away to college and got a degree. I have been a good husband and have faithfully attended church. The problem is that I never fully understood that I was a slave to my sin. I thought that I was doing the right things, so God would accept me. But I am a slave to my sin. And as I've heard God's Word preached, I've seen that very clearly. I am a man in desperate need of a Savior! That's why I praise God that he sent his Son to die on the cross for my sin. The Bible says, "For our sake he made him to be sin who knew no sin, so that in him we might become the righteousness of God" (2 Cor. 5:21). I used to believe that Jesus existed and that he died on a cross. Now I have put my faith in Jesus as my Lord and Savior. My life is fully his, and I want to follow him with all my heart. My baptism today is a symbol of my union with my beloved Savior.

Sample testimony #3: My name is _____. Those who knew me five years ago would find it hard to believe that I'd be getting baptized as a Christian today. Back then I was trying to fill my life with all sorts of things of this world. I'd divorced my wife, and I wasn't a good dad. Looking back on those days, my heart breaks. But I am so thankful that God did not give up on me. "While we were still sinners, Christ died for us" (Rom. 5:8). I feel so free. I am a different man. I have trusted Jesus for the forgiveness of sins. And Jesus has changed me. I want everyone to know that I belong to Jesus. That's why I'm getting baptized. Praise the Lord!

ADMINISTRATIVE PREPARATIONS FOR BAPTISM (LOGISTICS)

College Church

Readying College Church for baptisms was initiated by my assistant making two calls. The first was to the custodian, requesting that the baptistery be filled with *warm* water. On one occasion, this was not done, which made the midwinter baptism a memorable event, not unlike a polar dip in Lake Michigan! On another occasion, the drain was not closed, leaving about four inches of water in the baptismal tank, which necessitated a lot of splashing to effect an "immersion." Today I have things checked out ahead of time. The second call was to the deaconesses, who always came through with an extra towel for each of the baptized, a couple of extra hair dryers, and some maternal tendernesses for their charges.

First Baptist Church

First Baptist Church has a more thorough template for preparing for baptisms that covers everything down to skimming any bug from its East Texas baptismal tank. This is practical contextualization!

Week of Baptism

- The appropriate deacon and wife (if needed) are contacted in order to assist in the upcoming baptism (deacons assist male candidates, and wives assist female candidates).

- The baptizing pastor calls the candidate, no later than Tuesday before the baptism, to confirm the baptism date and time.
- The baptizing pastor is responsible to get each testimony text and candidate's picture to be produced for the bulletin insert.
- The pastor notifies the individual responsible for filling the baptistery and setting the water temperature.
- Signs that include the candidates' names are made and placed on the appropriate baptistery door.

Morning of Baptism

- A deacon assists the males, and his wife assists the females.
- The deacon arrives fifteen minutes early to meet the candidates and assist in their preparations.
- The deacon should make sure to have the baptismal skimmed of any bugs before the baptism.
- During the baptism, the deacon should be available to assist the candidate(s) and the pastor with clothes/robes/waders and with the process of moving in and out of the waters.
- The pastor should arrive at least ten minutes early to meet with the candidates, review the details of the mechanics of the baptism, and pray with them.

Subsequent to Baptism

- The attending deacon is responsible for washing, drying, folding, and returning the towels to the dressing room.
- The pastor relays the baptism information to the church secretary on Monday morning so the candidates' names and their baptism date can be entered into the church records.

THE FULL TEXTS OF FIVE BAPTISM LITURGIES

In briefest terms, the rite of baptism consists of two things. First, a *credo* ("I believe"), answering questions about the gospel. Sometimes the questions are contained in a single sentence and require a single "I do." Other times they are a series of questions answered by sequential affirmations. Second, a Trinitarian pronouncement accompanies the baptism: "I baptize you in the name of the Father and of the Son and of the Holy Spirit." The only variations here are the introductory words and the placement of the person's name.

Five examples of baptism liturgies follow. Three have been used variously at College Church (two of which contain brief explanations of the significance of baptism). The fourth example is from Tom Buck, pastor of First Baptist Church in Lindale, Texas. And the fifth example is from Christ Church in Pleasanton, California, pastored by Bob Evans (the author of this book's chapter on "Pastoral Counseling").

Sample Baptism Liturgy #1

Opening Remarks

This is a joyous occasion because it is a celebration of new life and the power of the gospel. We exult with the apostle that we are "not ashamed of the gospel, for it is the power of God for salvation to everyone who believes" (Rom. 1:16), and we have seen this gospel power in the lives of these who are about to undergo the waters of baptism. All of the candidates have met with the pastors and certain of the elders and have borne clear confession of their faith and changed lives, as you can read [or will hear] in the testimonies.

Prayer

Our Father, those of us who are Christians remember the spiritual genesis of our own lives when we first believed in Christ, our sins were taken away, our consciences were made clear, and we experienced a flood of deep love for your Son.

So on this day/night, we pray for these in the springtime of their spiritual lives; that your Spirit would continue to pour the love of Christ into their hearts; that your Word would become their food; that you would protect them from the world, the flesh, and the Devil; that you would use them to spread the gospel; that you would use them to build up your church; and that one day, when they stand before you, they will hear you say, "Well done, good and faithful servant" (Matt. 25:23).

Our loving Father, in these blessed moments, help each one grasp even more of the wonder of having been buried with Christ in his death and raised with him in his resurrection. We pray this in Jesus's name. Amen.

Brief Comments on Baptism

These who are being baptized today/tonight have received the essential inner baptism of the Spirit, as the apostle Paul explained: "For in one Spirit we were all baptized into one body—Jews or Greeks, slaves or free—and all were made to drink of one Spirit" (1 Cor. 12:13).

Today/tonight they are identifying themselves with Christ; their baptism is a public statement of their union with him. "Do you not know that all of us who have been baptized into Christ Jesus were baptized into his death? We were buried therefore with him by baptism into death, in order that, just as Christ was raised from the dead by the glory of the Father, we too might walk in newness of life" (Rom. 6:3–4).

And more, they are not only identifying themselves with Christ, but also with the church, his body. "For in one Spirit we were all baptized into one body" (1 Cor. 12:13).

Baptism symbolizes their new life, as the apostle says in conclusion: "So you also must consider yourselves dead to sin and alive to God in Christ Jesus" (Rom. 6:11).

The Baptism

(Note: this liturgy would be repeated sequentially for each person being baptized.)

1. The pastor (standing in the baptismal tank) announces the first candidate's name, and he or she descends the steps into the water.

2. The pastor asks three questions, each of which is answered with a single affirmation:

- Do you believe that Jesus Christ is the Son of God? *I do.*
- Do you believe that he died on the cross for your sins and was raised on the third day? *I do.*
- Do you trust in Christ alone for your salvation? *I do.*

3. The pastor then baptizes the candidate, saying: "_____ (full name), I baptize you in the name of the Father and of the Son and of the Holy Spirit. Amen."

Then, a very nice touch, the congregation sings a stanza of a hymn or song. This allows time for the one just baptized to exit the baptismal tank and the next to be ready for entrance. Some stanzas that work well are from the following hymns:

- "My Heart Is Filled with Thankfulness"
- "My Jesus, I Love Thee"
- "Praise the Name of Jesus"
- "How Deep the Father's Love for Us"
- "I Love Thee"

Doxology

Benediction

Sample Baptism Liturgy #2

Opening Remarks

Inasmuch as our Lord Jesus Christ has given authority and command-ment to his disciples to baptize all nations in the name of the Father, the

Son, and the Holy Spirit, let us now with one accord invoke the blessing of God.

Prayer

Our merciful Father, tonight we present these your children who have trusted Christ alone for their salvation. By grace they have received the free gift of eternal life, and you have seated them "with him in the heavenly places in Christ Jesus" (Eph. 2:6). So they are here to bear witness to their salvation through baptism. Father, as they enter the waters tonight, refresh them to the reality that they have died with Christ and have been resurrected in him to new life. May our souls also be refreshed to the reality that Christ's death and resurrection is the greatest work ever done in time or eternity. We pray this in Jesus's name. Amen.

Scripture

"Now if we have died with Christ, we believe that we will also live with him. We know that Christ, being raised from the dead, will never die again; death no longer has dominion over him. For the death he died he died to sin, once for all, but the life he lives he lives to God. So you must also consider yourselves dead to sin and alive to God in Christ Jesus" (Rom. 6:8–11).

"But God, being rich in mercy, because of the great love with which he loved us, even when we were dead in our trespasses, made us alive together with Christ—by grace you have been saved—and raised us up with him and seated us with him in the heavenly places in Christ Jesus" (Eph. 2:4–6).

Brief Comments on Baptism (optional)

The Baptism

(Note: this liturgy would be repeated sequentially for each person being baptized.)

1. The pastor (standing in the baptismal tank) announces the first candidate's name, and he or she descends the steps into the water.

2. The pastor asks three questions, each of which is answered with a single affirmation:

- Do you believe that Jesus Christ is the Son of God? *I do.*
- Do you believe that he died on the cross for your sins and was raised on the third day? *I do.*
- Do you trust in Christ alone for your salvation? *I do.*

3. The pastor then baptizes the candidate, saying: "_____ (full name), upon your profession of faith in the Lord Jesus Christ, I now

baptize you in the name of the Father and the Son, and the Holy Spirit. Amen."

Litany

In this service, four people were baptized, so a litany was improvised wherein after each candidate came out of the water, the assisting pastor read a line of Scripture from Romans 6, and the congregation responded, "Amen!"

After the first baptism: "We were buried therefore with him by baptism into death, in order that . . . as Christ was raised from the dead . . . we too might walk in newness of life" (v. 4). "Amen!"

After the second baptism: "For if we have been united with him in a death like his, we shall certainly be united with him in a resurrection like his" (v. 5). "Amen!"

After the third baptism: "For one who has died has been set free from sin" (v. 7). "Amen!"

After the fourth baptism: "So you also must consider yourselves dead to sin and alive to God in Christ Jesus" (v. 11). "Amen!"

Doxology

Benediction

Sample Baptism Liturgy #3

Opening Remarks

Tonight we have the privilege of witnessing the baptisms of _____ (full names).

Jesus commanded his followers to go and make disciples of all nations, baptizing them in the name of the Father, the Son, and the Holy Spirit (Matt. 28:19–20), and that is exactly what the disciples did after Jesus's ascension. The narratives of Acts tell of multiple instances of people coming to belief and being baptized. Faith, repentance, and baptism were bound tightly together.

Brief Comments on Baptism

Baptism is an external sign of an internal reality. The internal reality is that, by the grace of God, believers have become new creations in Christ; the old has passed away, and the new has come (see 2 Cor. 5:17). Their sins have been removed as far as the east is from the west (cf. Ps. 103:12). And with that, the love of Christ has been poured into their hearts by the Holy Spirit, so that the Spirit bears witness with their spirits that they are children of God (cf. Rom. 8:16).

These being baptized tonight have all borne testimony to their faith in Christ and have been under the care of the church leadership, who are now joyously supporting them as they come to be baptized. This is a time for the church family to celebrate the grace of our Lord Jesus Christ.

Let us together continue in a joyous and prayerful spirit as our brothers and sisters proceed to baptism.

Prayer
Merciful Father, we praise you for sending your Son to be our Savior. And we praise you, Christ Jesus, for leaving heaven to be born among us and become sin for us (2 Cor. 5:21).

Father, Son, and Holy Spirit, calm the hearts of these about to be baptized, and fill us all with gratitude as we reflect on your mercy to us. May we love you even more. We pray these things in Jesus's name. Amen.

Scripture
"What shall we say then? Are we to continue in sin that grace may abound? By no means! How can we who died to sin still live in it? Do you not know that all of us who have been baptized into Christ Jesus were baptized into his death? We were buried therefore with him by baptism into death, in order that, just as Christ was raised from the dead by the glory of the Father, we too might walk in newness of life" (Rom. 6:1–4).

The Baptism
(Note: This liturgy would be repeated sequentially for each person being baptized.)

1. The pastor (standing in the baptismal tank) announces the first candidate's name, and he or she descends the steps into the water.

2. The pastor asks four questions, each of which is answered with a single affirmation:

- Do you believe that Jesus Christ is the Son of God? *I do.*
- Do you believe that he died on the cross for your sins and was raised on the third day? *I do.*
- Do you trust in Christ alone for forgiveness and the hope of eternal life? *I do.*
- By God's grace, do you intend to be his disciple, obey his Word, and live out his love? *I do.*

3. The pastor then baptizes the candidate, saying: "_____ (full name), I baptize you in the name of the Father and of the Son and of the Holy Spirit. Amen."

Doxology

Benediction

Sample Baptism Liturgy #4

The following service is used by First Baptist Church in Lindale, Texas. Pastor Tom Buck writes: "Since we believe baptism should be done when the maximum number of members and visitors are present to observe, we conduct them in the Sunday morning services. Members of the church can celebrate the picture of gospel work in the life of fellow believers and welcome them into the visible body of Christ—the church. It also allows unbelievers to receive explanation and to see the powerful picture of the effectual work of the gospel. In addition, we incorporate the baptism into the flow of the morning service because we want it to be seen as a part of the church's worship."

Opening Remarks

This morning we have the privilege of celebrating together the baptisms of _____ (candidates' names). They have responded to the call of the gospel by repenting of their sin and by faith trusting in the death and resurrection of Jesus Christ for salvation. You will find their personal testimonies inside your bulletin, and we encourage you to read how God brought each of them to believe the wonderful truth of the gospel. We rejoice with them as they come to publicly profess their faith in the Lord Jesus Christ and obey his first command to believers: to be baptized (Matt. 28:18–20).

Brief Comments on Baptism

Fundamentally, baptism is an outward physical sign of an inward spiritual reality. Nothing magical or supernatural takes place because someone is immersed in these waters. The act of baptism does not save you, but only is a symbol pointing to the reality of your salvation. You could liken it to a wedding ring that, in and of itself, does not make you married, but serves as a sign to the world that you have committed yourself in marriage to your lifelong spouse. Therefore, baptism is a beautiful picture given by the Lord Jesus Christ that points to the spiritual transformation that takes place when one rightly responds to the gospel message. Romans 6:1–4 teaches that baptism serves as a visible picture of our death and burial with Christ, along with our spiritual resurrection with him, and that it identifies us with him as our representative head. In addition, baptism not only identifies the new believer with Christ, but also identifies us as members of God's people—the church.

Prayer

Our heavenly Father, we thank you for these who have come this morning to make public their belief in the gospel of the Lord Jesus Christ. We praise you for your great mercy, having caused them to be born again to a living hope through the resurrection of Jesus Christ from the dead. We rejoice in the wonderful picture of baptism that points to their spiritual burial with Christ and ultimate resurrection to walk in newness of life. May we once again exult in the wonderful reality that through the power of the gospel we do not come into judgment, but have passed from death to life. We pray these things in the name of Jesus. Amen.

The Baptism

(Note: This liturgy would be repeated sequentially for each person being baptized.)

1. The pastor (standing in the baptismal tank) announces the first candidate's name, and he or she descends the steps into the water.

2. The pastor asks three questions, pausing after each question to allow the individual to give an affirmative response:

- Have you come this morning to make a public profession that you have placed your faith and trust in Jesus Christ as your Lord and Savior? *I have.*
- Do you believe that Jesus died in accordance with the Scriptures, that he was buried, and that he was raised on the third day in accordance with the Scriptures (1 Cor. 15:3–4)? *I do.*
- Have you repented of your sins and trusted in the Lord Jesus Christ's death and resurrection for the forgiveness of your sins? *I have.*

3. The pastor then baptizes the candidate, saying: "_____, it is therefore my privilege to baptize you, my brother/sister, in the name of the Father and of the Son and of the Holy Spirit." He adds, as the candidate goes under and comes out of the water, "Buried with Christ in baptism, raised to walk in newness of life."

4. After the final baptism, the congregation joins together in response with a song of worship.

Sample Baptism Liturgy #5

Dr. Bob Evans describes the hands-on pastoral care given to those who have come to Christ in the intimate fellowship of Christ Church:

(1) Prospective candidates for baptism are invited to meet with me, during which time they share their testimony and reasons for desiring

394 *Parts of the Worship Service*

baptism; (2) we discuss how baptism is both a sign and a symbol; (3) we make clear that baptism does not save, or add to the salvation of the person, but is a public statement of faith in obedience to Christ; (4) we usually perform our baptisms in connection with a church-wide celebratory meal, to which the candidates may invite their family and friends; (5) at the time of baptism, I provide a brief statement that surveys the above, so that those witnessing are clear about what is (and is not) happening; and (6) we invite the candidates to share their conversion and growth in faith that has brought them to this point. This tends to be quite powerful, as extended family members and friends are usually present. Rarely is there a dry eye.

Opening Remarks

I warmly welcome you to this special occasion for joyous celebration as we gather to witness the baptisms of _____ (give names). It is the fervent prayer of each of those who will be baptized that you join with them in giving all glory to God for the wondrous gift of his Son, Jesus, through whom each has been graciously saved. Let's commit this time to our heavenly Father and ask for his richest blessings upon the same.

Prayer

Our Father and our God, we come before you this day/evening with hearts that are brimming with thankfulness both for who you are and for what you have done for us in providing the sole means by which we can be reconciled to you. How grateful we are that, seeing us in our lost and helpless state, you did not turn away, but made a way for us to be redeemed—by grace alone, through faith alone, as we place our full trust in the substitutionary and atoning work of Jesus Christ at Calvary alone as payment of the penalty for our sins. And we particularly praise you this day/evening for these lives that have been made new—trophies to the gospel of grace. Heavenly Father, cause their hearts to soar as they consider afresh your boundless love and tender mercies by which you have drawn them to yourself and with which you continue to lavish them as your precious children. Impress the significance of these moments deeply upon their hearts and minds, and bless our time together, for the cause of your glory and our good. Amen.

Scripture

People often say that which is most important to them just prior to departing. For that reason, we do well to consider Jesus's final words; they are recorded for us in Matthew 28:19–20:

"Go therefore and make disciples of all nations, baptizing them in the name of the Father and of the Son and of the Holy Spirit, teaching them to observe all that I have commanded you. And behold, I am with you always, to the end of the age."

In keeping with our Lord's final commission, we gather this afternoon/morning/evening to baptize _____ (insert names).

Brief Comments on Baptism

What is the meaning of baptism? The apostle Paul addresses that question in Romans 6:1–11. Writing about the folly of a Christian persisting in unrepentant sin so that grace will abound all the more, Paul draws specific attention to the link between baptism and the new life that is ours through being united with Jesus Christ in his death and resurrection:

Do you not know that all of us who have been baptized into Christ Jesus were baptized into his death? We were buried therefore with him by baptism into death, in order that, just as Christ was raised from the dead by the glory of the Father, we too might walk in newness of life. (vv. 3–4)

Baptism, then, is an act of obedience and faith—a public declaration of our spiritual identification with Jesus Christ in his death and resurrection. In baptism, we proclaim the fact that we have been united with Christ—our sins put to assured death through his sacrificial death, our souls renewed to imperishable life through the power and promise of his resurrection.

What a glorious gospel is symbolized in these baptisms today—that, by grace, through faith and repentance, we may be grafted into Christ and that God will accept his Son's accomplished work at the cross and in the resurrection, and will apply the benefits of the same to all who will believe—forgiveness of sins and newness of life.

The Baptism

(Note: This liturgy would be repeated sequentially for each person being baptized.)

1. The pastor (standing in the baptismal tank) announces the first candidate's name, and he or she descends the steps into the water.

2. The pastor asks two questions, each of which is answered with a single affirmation:

- _____, do you believe that Jesus is the Christ, the very Son of God, and have you turned to him and confessed your need for forgiveness of sin and acknowledged who he is and what he accomplished for you at Calvary, and do you now stand before us this day professing Jesus Christ as your Savior and the Lord of your life? *I do.*

• _____, having repented of your sins and having placed full faith in Jesus Christ alone as your Savior and Lord, do you now promise to joyfully and faithfully follow after him all the days of your life? *I do.*

3. Then the pastor baptizes the candidate, saying: "_____ (full name), upon your profession of faith and the stated desire to follow faithfully after him, I recognize you as my brother/sister in Christ and hereby baptize you in the name of the Father and of the Son and of the Holy Spirit. Amen."

Baby Dedications

Consider this: Though you were to travel a hundred times the speed of light, past countless yellow-orange stars, to the edge of the galaxy, then swoop down to the fiery glow located a few hundred light years below the plane of the Milky Way; though you were to slow down to examine the host of hot young stars luminous among the gas and dust; though you were to observe, close up, the protostars poised to burst forth from their dusty cocoons; and though you were to witness a star's birth, in all your stellar journeys, you would never see anything equal to the birth and wonder of a human being. A tiny baby girl or boy is the apex of God's creation. But the greatest wonder of all is that the child is created in the image of God (the *imago Dei*). That child was once not, but now, as a created soul, he or she is eternal. He or she will exist forever. When the stars of the universe fade away, that soul shall live on.

Notwithstanding the fall, which eradicated the original righteousness of the soul of every child born into the world, the image of God still persists in sinful humanity (cf. Gen. 9:6; James 3:9), so that every child bears the *imago Dei* and holds vast eternal potential. And this wondrous potential ought to inform the church's dedications of every baby—the possibility of eternal ignominy or eternal glory, living out the colossal fullness of the image of God in Christ for all eternity (Col. 1:15; 2:9–10).

For this reason, when a couple stands before God's people and dedicates their child to God, it is an occasion of immense spiritual significance. This is because if the parents live consistent Christian lives that testify to their child of the reality of Christ and are committed to the local body of Christ so that the family sits under the regular teaching of the Word and participates in the fellowship of Christ's body, and if the body of Christ truly loves that child and nurtures and prays for his or her soul, *that child is in a favored position to trust Christ* and become his devoted follower. Of course, there are no guarantees, but a child in such a blessed position has rather a high probability of receiving the endless grace of Christ.

This is why, as a pastor, I took great interest and pleasure in baby dedications. In fact, when dedications were scheduled for Sunday, I found myself smiling in anticipation of seeing the parents, so proud and earnest; of taking their little girl or boy in my arms (a hot star fallen from heaven!) and holding the child up for all the smiling congregation to admire; and of uttering a specially prepared blessing on the child's name before I handed the little one back to the parents for their covenant and prayer.

Liturgy for Baby Dedications

Invitation to Parents
Will the parents of (full name[s] of the child/children) bring him/her/them forward for dedication to the Lord? (The parents ascend the platform with babies in arms and children at their sides.)

Remarks on Dedication
Option #1: "Hannah conceived and bore a son, and she called his name Samuel. . . . And she brought him to the house of the LORD at Shiloh. . . . And she said, '. . . I am the woman who was standing here in your presence, praying to the LORD. For this child I prayed, and the LORD has granted me my petition. . . . Therefore I have lent [*given*] him to the LORD. As long as he lives, he is lent [*given*] to the LORD'" (1 Sam. 1:20–28).

This is a happy and significant occasion, because, like Hannah of old, you have brought your child to "the house of the LORD" (here the assembly of the body of Christ) to present your child in joyful and solemn dedication.

It is fitting that you do this while your hearts are filled with wonder and fresh gratitude for God's gift to you.

Option #2: The psalmist rejoices over children, saying:

> Behold, children are a heritage from the LORD,
>   the fruit of the womb a reward.
> Like arrows in the hand of a warrior
>   are the children of one's youth.
> Blessed is the man
>   who fills his quiver with them! (Ps. 127:3–5a)

Today you have come with a fresh arrow for your family quiver, and the sense of divine blessing lingers in your hearts. It is fitting that you bring your child before God's people in joyful and solemn dedication. May the trajectory of this new arrow (these new arrows) be graced as it courses (they course) through the years.

Blessing Based on the Child's Name (optional)

(Note: The inclusion of this element in the liturgy will enhance the brief moments of the baby dedication because: 1) it allows time to focus briefly on each child, 2) it removes any sense of the "perfunctory" from the ceremony, 3) it provides an opportunity for hands-on pastoral involvement, and 4) it provides immense pleasure for the whole body of Christ.)

The pastor takes each child in his arms, cradles the child so that the congregation can get a good look, and pronounces a blessing based on the child's given name, as the following examples demonstrate:

Caitlyn Lyn (surname): Caitlyn is the Gaelic form of Kathryn, which comes from the Greek word *katharos*, which means "clean" or "pure." Lyn is an old English word that signifies a place of respite and rest. Caitlyn Lyn, may the blood of Christ wash you clean of your sins, and may your life provide rest and refreshment of Christ to many souls in this needy world.

James Andrew (surname): James comes from the Hebrew name Jacob, who was a man who, despite his many faults, treasured the blessings of God. Andrew means "manly," and is the name of the apostle most known for bringing people to Jesus. James Andrew, may you keep seeking the things that are above, where Christ is seated at the right hand of God; and as you do, be the man who is always pointing others to Christ.

(Note: composing brief meditations on a child's name takes only a few minutes. Several books give the meanings of names, or they can be easily researched on the Internet.)

Parental Covenant

The pastor then says to the parents:

The purpose of this service is to help you as parents fully embrace the sacred call to raise up your children in the nurture and admonition of the Lord. And so, in keeping with that purpose, will you now respond together to the following covenant:

- Do you now present your child before God in solemn dedication? *We do.*
- Do you consecrate yourselves as parents to bring up your child in the nurture and admonition of the Lord? *We do.*

- Do you promise to instruct her/him/them in the gospel of Jesus Christ and in the practice of prayer and to guide her/him/them in the development of a Christlike character? *We do.*
- Do you promise to try, by God's grace, so to shape the home life of your child, both by example and family devotions and by your word and conduct, that at the proper time she/he/they will come to an open confession of Christ and membership in his church? *We do.*

Inasmuch as you have promised before God and his people to raise your child in the nurture and admonition of the Lord, we charge you to set yourselves to that task by the grace of God.

Congregational Covenant

The pastor asks the people to stand and affirm their commitment as printed in the bulletin.

Minister: "Do you, the body of Christ, promise to receive these children in love, pray for them, help instruct them in the faith, and encourage and sustain them in the fellowship of believers?"

Congregation: "We do, God helping us."

Prayer

In most instances it may be best to close the baby dedications with an extemporaneous prayer, inspired by the joy of the commitments just made. At other times, a thought-through, written prayer may be in order. Here is one that may supply some inspiration for such a prayer:

> Our Father and the Author of life, our hearts well with gratitude for these beautiful children who were knit in their mothers' wombs—their tiny valved hearts, the complex rainbow tapestries of their veins and nerves, their exquisite hands, hinged and so wondrously wrought.
>
> And all of this, Father, is just a hint of the subtlety of their persons—the immense intelligences just now learning to communicate, the poetry and art in their souls, the God-sized capacity for you, Father God, as they have been created in your image.
>
> Father, on this the day of their dedication, we pray that in the years to come, the prayers and love of their parents, their families, and this church would be used by your Spirit to open their hearts to you, so that they serve you all of the days of their lives. In Jesus's name. Amen.

THE PROTESTANT INFANT BAPTISM
VIEW AND PRACTICE

This is Doug writing now. Kent has allotted me one hundred words or less to give a biblical defense for infant baptism (I write jokingly). To help, he sent me his favorite tract, "What the Bible Says about Infant Baptism." I opened it. It was blank. Pure white. Nothing.[4]

This is not the first time I have been persecuted for righteousness' sake. When I served as the associate pastor at Christ the King Church, I was the only elder who held the paedobaptist position, and my family was the first family to have an infant baptized.[5] When my oldest daughter, Lily, was born, I felt compelled to offer a written defense to the elders and the church for my position. I called that treatise "Why a Lily Needs Water." It was an attempt to win favor and appease wrath. In it, I argued from a biblical, historical, and theological perspective that "the children of Christian parents are rightly to be baptized as infants."

Did my penetrating logic—e.g., "Are we truly to believe that with four household baptisms recorded in the New Testament there were no infants or young children as part of those households, especially when ancient 'households' included the extended family as well as servants and their children?"—change minds? No. Did my scattering of quotations from Christian heroes—e.g., "Nothing, I believe, would astonish a Jewish convert so much as to tell him his children could *not* be baptized?" (J. C. Ryle)—win the day? No. Did my clear exegesis—"How is it possible for children to be commanded to obey their parents 'in the Lord' (Eph. 6:1–2; Col. 3:20) if they are not already and in some sense *in Christ*?"—clarify the matter once and for all? No. Was I better understood? Perhaps. Did the church love my daughter on the day of her baptism? Yes. Did they love her more? No. But come on, what does that matter, for at least the essay was therapeutic for me.

Years later, I was asked to debate my good friend Pastor Jay Thomas. The event was held in a booth at Quigley's Irish Pub in downtown Naperville. At least five men (and one poor wife) were in attendance. Below are some points I walked through that night. As I reflect afresh on what I said then, I know now how I have further developed in my thought. Yet what I said then has a beautiful simplicity to it, one that I hope would promote charity as well as a desire for further exegetical observations and synthesis.

---

[4] Okay, that is an exaggeration. Kent didn't send the tract—he told me about it over the phone.
[5] Wisely, I had my colleague, Niel Nielson, then a pastor at College Church, perform the ceremony. I let him take the direct heat!

Baptism Texts in the New Testament

Here are some insights and observations on the New Testament texts:

- Regarding the four Gospels, other than the end of Matthew (Matt. 28:19; cf. the longer ending in Mark 16:16), there are no references to *Christian* baptism (i.e., the baptism of new believers into Christ). And from the Matthew text we learn that baptism is to be done in the name of the Trinity and with water.

- Regarding the Acts of the Apostles, three important facts need to be considered: (1) this sacred history only highlights the first generation of Christians and their faith response to the gospel, yet (2) Peter in his Pentecost sermon (Acts 2:38–39) includes "children" as being heirs of the promise, and (3) Luke records nearly as many household baptisms as individual baptisms.

- Outside of Acts, very little is said on the sacraments. Baptism is mentioned in only six epistles and only nine times total—Romans 6:3–4; 1 Corinthians 1:14–17; 10:2; 12:13; 15:29; Galatians 3:27; Ephesians 4:5; Colossians 2:12; and 1 Peter 3:21. Moreover, in all of those passages, very little is said about baptism theologically (this is what baptism is about) or practically (this is how to baptize).

- Of those nine references, one is the discussion on the matter of baptism for the dead (1 Cor. 15:29), and another certainly uses the word *baptism* metaphorically and not in reference to Christian water baptism (1 Cor. 10:2). In Romans 6:3–4, Galatians 3:27, Ephesians 4:5, and Colossians 2:12, it is difficult to tell whether Paul is referencing water baptism or baptism in the Spirit (see Matt. 3:11; John 1:33; Acts 1:5), for if Paul is referring to water baptism, it would be the only time he speaks of the sacraments or uses sacramental language in those epistles. The use of *into* also suggests metaphorical usage (see its use in 1 Cor. 10:2; cf. how Jesus speaks of his death using the metaphorical language of baptism, Mark 10:38; Luke 12:50).

- First Peter 3:21 is a tough text. In my mind, it either stresses (like Mark 16:16) the close connection between Spirit and water baptism, or it is using *baptism* metaphorically again—i.e., Spirit baptism as related to faith. Spiritual baptism makes good sense of the language of "baptism" being "an appeal to God for a good conscience."

- In 1 Corinthians 1:10–17, we certainly have reference to water baptism. However, there Paul downplays the significance of such baptisms in light of church unity and the gospel. Furthermore, he references baptizing individuals and a household.

Here are some further thoughts:

- There were two signs of the covenant in the Old Testament—circumcision and the Passover. It is fairly clear that the Lord's Supper replaces the Passover. That baptism replaces circumcision seems logical (a point from Colossians 2:11–12?), but the exegetical connection is not certain.
- Some of the important texts on infant baptism are not "baptism" texts, notably Abraham and his new covenant faith (Romans 4) and Paul's view of the children of believers (1 Cor. 7:12–14; Eph. 6:1). Are we still under the Abrahamic covenant, the covenant of grace? If so, how should we treat our children? Perhaps like Abraham treated Isaac—as an heir of the covenant.
- Titus 3:3–7 is important for at least two reasons: (1) it shows the link between regeneration and Spirit baptism using the water metaphor, and (2) the water metaphor is *pouring*.

Here is a final thought:

- I'm always right and Jay is always wrong.

Mode, Symbolism, and Subjects

The purpose of the second half of this chapter is not to provide a full apologetic for infant baptism; rather, it is to offer some practical advice and assistance for pastors who serve in fellowships that administer baptism to the children of believers. Since I agree with many of the points Kent made regarding baptism (and have used his liturgies when I have baptized believers via immersion), below I address three differences.

Mode

While Kent argues that "the only mode of baptism described in the New Testament is immersion" (citing Mark 1:5, 10; John 3:23; Acts 8:36–39), my view is that such a mode of baptism *could* have been immersion, but it likely was not. For example, when Jesus "came up out of the water" (Mark 1:10), it was *after* his baptism, not as part of it. The phrase "out of the water" simply means that he was walking *out of* the Jordan River. This is similar to what happened to the Ethiopian eunuch. Both he *and Philip* "went down into the water" and "came up out of the water" (Acts 8:38–39). This very likely does not mean that Philip was immersed as he baptized the new believer.

Instead of immersion, it is more likely that New Testament believers were baptized by sprinkling or pouring. Sprinkling would have followed the ceremonial washings of the Old Testament, and that linguistic connection is made by the author of Hebrews in Hebrews 9:10, where "ceremonial *washings*" (NIV) or "*cleansing* ceremonies" (NLT) is used to translate *baptismois* in the Greek.[6] Pouring fits how the earliest Christians spoke of the Holy Spirit.

> Whenever the mode in which the Holy Spirit was given is described, it is consistently described as a *pouring out*, or as a *descending*. The disciples are not lowered into the "water" of the Holy Spirit. Rather, the "water" of the Spirit is poured out upon them. They are not placed *in* Him; He is placed *on* them. The evidence for this is overwhelming (Acts 2:3, 16–17, 33; 10:44–45; 11:15–16; Mt. 3:16–17; Jn. 1:32; Lk. 3:22; Is. 44:3).[7]

Symbolism

When Kent spoke of the symbolism he pointed to the gospel, focusing on the death and resurrection of Christ and our union with him through faith. Amen to that! The only potential difference in practice is that of emphasis. For the paedobaptist, the emphasis always falls on the objective work of Christ. As Douglas Wilson illustrates and explains:

> Too often parents haul their infants down to the front of the church for a feel-good Kodak moment. The baby is cute, the baptism is performed, and the flesh applauds. But the true meaning of baptism is *objective*, and rests outside of all hypocrisies and doctrinal misunderstandings. It means the mark of Christ has been placed on that person, and that he now has an additional obligation to repent and believe. A baptized individual has the obligation to have his life point the same direction his baptism does—to Christ and to His righteousness.[8]

For the family that comes to bring their son or daughter to the water, there is no confusion of what the baptism symbolizes. It is not an arrow pointing in, symbolizing internal regeneration and/or an external public confession of faith; rather, it is an arrow pointing heavenward—to the Trinity's sovereign initiative in salvation and God's objective covenantal claim on a child's life. Like Esau, the child may sell his birthright. But every believing parent, pastor, and church member hopes and prays for Jacoblike faith in the promises of God.

---

[6] Cf. "I will sprinkle clean water on you, and you shall be clean from all your uncleannesses" (Ezek. 36:25).
[7] Douglas Wilson, *Mother Kirk: Essays and Forays in Practical Ecclesiology* (Moscow, ID: Canon, 2001), 99.
[8] Ibid., 96–97.

Subjects

I agree with the language and theology of the Westminster Standards:

> Baptism is not to be administered to any that are out of the visible church, till they profess their faith in Christ, and obedience to him; but the infants of such as are members of the visible church are to be baptized. (Westminster Shorter Catechism, A95)

> Baptism is not to be administered to any that are out of the visible church, and so strangers from the covenant of promise, till they profess their faith in Christ, and obedience to him, but infants descending from parents, either both, or but one of them, professing faith in Christ, and obedience to him, are in that respect within the covenant, and to be baptized. (Westminster Larger Catechism, A166)

> Not only those that do actually profess faith in and obedience unto Christ, but also the infants of one, or both, believing parents, are to be baptized. (Westminster Confession of Faith, 28.4)

That said, the necessary clarification follows:

> The efficacy of Baptism is not tied to that moment of time wherein it is administered; yet, notwithstanding, by the right use of this ordinance, the grace promised is not only offered, but really exhibited, and conferred, by the Holy Ghost, to such (whether of age or infants) as that grace belongs unto, according to the counsel of God's own will, in His appointed time. (Westminster Confession of Faith, 28.6)

PROTESTANT INFANT BAPTISM PRACTICE

Before we walk through the baptism ceremony, let's begin with three preliminaries: the parent interview, the letter to the parents, and administrative preparations.

Parent Interview

If the parents are members of the church, the interview is short. We trust that our membership process was thorough enough and that those who profess their faith through taking membership vows are part of Christ's visible church. Nevertheless, I have a brief discussion with them about their faith and their reasons for baptizing their child or children. If someone has not yet joined the church (e.g., they recently moved into the area, had a baby, and want the child to be baptized as soon as possible), we welcome them to partake of this sacrament. Obviously, in this case, the questioning is more comprehensive.

Letter

A few weeks before the baptism, a letter is sent to the parent/s of the child being baptized. A reminder e-mail is also sent, or a phone call made, a few days before the service. Below is the last baptism letter I wrote at New Covenant Church:

Dear _____,

I'm looking forward to _____'s baptism on 7/21/13. Here are a few details. I'll call you next week to walk through them.

First, I will invite you up to the platform at the beginning of the service. This will be right after the creed.

Second, I will ask you the following questions, to which you will respond to each, "We do."

- Do you acknowledge your son's need of the cleansing blood of Jesus Christ and the renewing grace of the Holy Spirit?
- Do you claim God's covenant promises on your son's behalf, and do you look in faith to the Lord Jesus Christ for his salvation, as you do for your own?
- Do you now unreservedly dedicate your son to God and promise, in humble reliance upon divine grace, that you will endeavor to set before him a godly example, that you will pray with and for him, that you will teach him the doctrines of our holy faith, and that you will strive, by all the means of God's appointment, to bring him up in the nurture and admonition of the Lord?

Third, I will take _____ from you and say something about why you chose his names and something of the historical, biblical, and/or morphological significance of the names. *Please e-mail me the reasons why you chose his name.*

Then I will return him to you. Soon after, I will ask you, "What is the Christian name of this child?" (Father's name) will give your son's first and middle names. Then I will baptize _____.

I will close with prayer, give you a certificate, and then you may be seated as the congregation sings "Gift from the Lord."

Looking forward to this wonderful event!

Pastor O'Donnell

Administrative Preparations

At least six details need to be covered prior to the baptism. First, the office staff (or pastor) should print a baptism certificate. Double-check the names with the parents. Also make sure you receive from them some personal information on the name selections.

Second, on Sunday morning, pour warm water into the baptismal font. Remember, babies scream easily—no cold water! If you want the sacramental water to be more visible and audible to the congregation, you could wait to pour the water in the font at the start of the service, during the creed, or right before the baptism itself.

Third, meet the parents before the service and walk through the ceremony with them. Make them feel comfortable. Remind them when they are to come up, where they are to stand, and what they are to say. Pray with them.

Fourth, bring a handkerchief. You can use this if you cry, but its primary purpose is to wipe your hands after the baptism. You will shake the parents' hands and then give them the certificate.

Fifth, at New Covenant Church, we typically print in the bulletin our policy on baptism. This is important because we offer both infant baptisms and baby dedications. Obviously whoever makes the bulletin should make sure this insert is included.

Sixth, make sure any special songs (such as the one we sing at New Covenant; I have also included what is sung at Covenant Chicago) are printed in the bulletin or made as overhead slides. The song below was written by Dr. Gary Rownd for Holy Trinity Church in Chicago,[9] and it is used for infant baptisms and dedications there, as well as at Christ the King Church in Batavia, Illinois, and at New Covenant Church.

CHARITABLE POLICY ON BAPTISM

One of the central mottos of New Covenant Church comes from a saying of the ancient church: "In essentials unity, in non-essentials liberty, in all things charity."

We believe baptism by water in the name of the Trinity is an essential of the Christian faith. We also believe that a personal faith in Jesus Christ as Lord and Savior is a necessary requirement for baptism.[10] We at New Covenant do not, however, believe that a certain mode of baptism—immersion

---

[9] Used with permission.

[10] This *faith* refers to either the faith of the individual being baptized or the faith of the parents (or parent) presenting the child for baptism.

or pouring—is essential for Christian unity. Nor do we believe it is right for us, as a Protestant interdenominational church, to accept only one view of baptism as opposed to another—e.g., a Baptist view (only believers should be baptized) but not a Presbyterian one (believers and the children of believers should be baptized).[11] Thus, in charity and for the sake of a greater unity, we allow the parents of young children to determine, in counsel with the pastors, both the time and mode of baptism for their children.

While we recognize this is not the normal practice of most churches, we embrace it as a God-honoring practice, seeking to acknowledge fully the importance of this sacrament, while also honoring, despite our differences, the greater commandment of love. In fact, Pastor Andrew Fulton and I embody well—in our own convictions and practices—our church's view. Pastor Fulton is a Baptist, while I am a Presbyterian. And believe it or not, we still love each other and respect each other's positions (while knowing perfectly well one of them is right and the other wrong).

We hope this attitude reflects yours. We are not asking you to throw away your convictions, if they are from Scripture and have come with much prayer, study, and thought. We are merely asking you to embrace what C. S. Lewis called "mere Christianity" and thus to be willing to fellowship and even celebrate this day—with its infant baptism or believer's baptism—under the banner not of "Christian relativism" but of Christian liberty and love.

Sample Infant Baptism Liturgy

The Apostles' Creed (optional)
Since the Apostles' Creed, or an early form of it, was used in the baptismal rite of the early church, it has symbolic ecclesial value. Thus, it is good to have the congregation recite it before the baptism. One idea is to include it by following the ancient practice of renunciation.

> Do you renounce Satan and all the spiritual forces of evil that rebel against God?
> *I renounce them!*
> Do you renounce all sinful desires that draw you from the love of God?
> *I renounce them!*
> Do you turn to Jesus Christ?
> *Yes! I trust him as my Lord and Savior.*

---

[11] We do not hold to baptismal regeneration, as taught in Roman Catholic theology. In other words, the waters of baptism are insufficient in themselves to save anyone.

Gift from the Lord

Gary Rownd

Do you intend to be Christ's faithful disciple, trusting his promises, obeying his Word, honoring his church, and showing his love as long as you live?
Yes! God helping me. . . .[12]
Do you believe in God, the Father?
I believe in God, the Father almighty. . . .
Do you believe in Jesus Christ, the Son of God?
I believe in Jesus Christ, God's only Son, our Lord. . . .
Do you believe in God the Holy Spirit?
I believe in the Holy Spirit. . . .[13]

A Word on Infant Baptism

Before I invite the parents whose child is being baptized to come forward with their child, let me first clarify our church's view regarding baptism, especially the baptism of infants.

First, regarding baptism in general: As a church we believe:

1. Baptism in the name of the Trinity in water is very important because it was commanded by our Lord Jesus to symbolize our spiritual union with him.

2. Thus, it is a sin to condemn or neglect this ordinance.

3. Yet someone can still be saved without ever being baptized (God's grace is in no way limited). *And* just because someone has been baptized (as an infant, a child, or even an adult), it does not guarantee salvation. As question forty-five of the New City Catechism has it:

Q. Is baptism with water the washing away of sin itself?
A. No, only the blood of Christ and the renewal of the Holy Spirit can cleanse us from sin.

That is our view of baptism in general. Now, regarding the issue of infant baptism, our church—in Christian charity and for the purpose of promoting Christian unity—has agreed to disagree. Since we are a non-denominational or interdenominational church, we leave one's view of baptism (within reason) up to one's own conscience and understanding of Scripture, and so we both baptize as well as dedicate the infants of believers.

With that said, I joyfully ask the parents of _____ to bring your son forward for Christian baptism.

Instruction

"For as there was no salvation outside Noah's ark when the world perished in the flood; so we believe that there is no certain salvation outside

---

[12] *The Worship Sourcebook*, 2nd ed. (Grand Rapids: Calvin Institute of Christian Worship/Faith Alive/Baker, 2013), 272 (6.2.4)
[13] Ibid., 274 (6.2.9)

of Christ."[14] Baptism is a sign and a seal of God's covenant promise to his own: that he will be their God and they will be his people.

Our Lord Jesus said, "'Let the children come to me; do not hinder them, for to such belongs the kingdom of God. Truly, I say to you, whoever does not receive the kingdom of God like a child shall not enter it.' And he took them in his arms and blessed them, laying his hands on them" (Mark 10:14b–16).

Optional Instruction

"The ordinance of baptism by the church is in obedience to the command of Christ that the nations should be converted, baptized, and taught all that Christ has commanded (Mt 28:19, 20). Baptism represents and seals our union with Christ (Rom 6:1ff), the outpouring of the Holy Spirit (Jn 1:33), and resulting regeneration, adoption, and cleansing from sin (Titus 3:5, 6). By baptism we are admitted into the covenant community (Acts 2:41; 1 Cor 12:13), and made members of the body of Christ."[15]

Optional Instruction

"Baptism is a celebration that conveys several layers of meaning. It is at once a sign of the washing away of sin, a sign of our union with Jesus' death and resurrection, a sign of the promise of new birth in Christ, a sign of incorporation in the church, a sign of the promise of the Holy Spirit, and a sign of the covenant and kingdom of God."[16] Then any or all of the following Scripture texts could be read: Genesis 17:3–4, 7; Isaiah 43:1–2; Jeremiah 31:31–34; Ezekiel 36:25–28; John 1:12–13; Acts 2:38–39; Romans 6:3–4; 8:14–17; 1 Corinthians 12:12–13; Galatians 3:26–28; Ephesians 4:4–6; Colossians 2:11–12; Titus 3:4–8; 1 Peter 2:9–10.

Optional Instruction

"Let us recall the teaching of Scripture concerning the sacrament of baptism. The water of baptism signifies the washing away of our sin by the blood of Christ and the renewal of our lives by the Holy Spirit. It also signifies that we are buried with Christ. From this we learn that our sin has been condemned by God, that we are to hate it and to consider ourselves as having died to it. Moreover, the water of baptism signifies that we are raised with Christ. From this we learn that we are to walk

---

[14] The Second Helvetic Confession, Chap. 27.
[15] Terry L. Johnson, ed., *Leading in Worship: A Sourcebook for Presbyterian Students and Ministers Drawing from the Biblical and Historical Forms of the Reformed Tradition* (Powder Springs, GA: Tolle Lege, 2013), 101. In a few places, I have inserted portions of Johnson's liturgy from Independent Presbyterian Church, Savannah, Georgia, as included in his book.
[16] *The Worship Sourcebook*, 6.1.2.

with Christ in newness of life. All this tells us that God has adopted us as his children: 'Now if we are children, then we are heirs—heirs of God and co-heirs with Christ' (Rom. 8:17). Thus in baptism God seals the promises he gave when he made his covenant with us, calling us and our children to put our trust for life and death in Christ our Savior, deny ourselves, take up our cross, and follow him in obedience and love. God graciously includes our children in his covenant, and all his promises are for them as well as for us. Jesus himself embraced little children and blessed them, and the apostle Paul said that children of believers are holy. So, just as children of the old covenant received the sign of circumcision, our children are given the sign of baptism. We are therefore always to teach our little ones that they have been set apart by baptism as God's own children."[17]

Minister: "_____ (parents), as you have brought your son for baptism, I now charge you with the following confession":

- Do you acknowledge your son's need of the cleansing blood of Jesus Christ and the renewing grace of the Holy Spirit?
- Do you claim God's covenant promises on _____'s behalf, and do you look in faith to the Lord Jesus Christ for his salvation, as you do for your own?
- Do you now unreservedly dedicate your son to God and promise, in humble reliance upon divine grace, that you will endeavor to set before him a godly example, that you will pray with and for him, that you will teach him the doctrines of our holy faith, and that you will strive, by all the means of God's appointment, to bring him up in the nurture and admonition of the Lord?[18]

Parents: We do.

Name/s

(The pastor takes the child in his arms. The baby should be facing the congregation. The pastor is mostly talking to the child, with the congregation overhearing what he says).

Maxton Paul, I see that you draw a crowd. We should have you baptized every Sunday! Perhaps the reason for the crowd—your extended family—is because of the historical significance of your baptism. Did you know that your mom's sister (your aunt) was baptized in this church using this baptismal font in 1984? Today we are celebrating God's grace extended throughout the years to your family.

---

[17] Ibid., 6.1.19.
[18] These questions, with slight revision, are taken from the Book of Church Order, 56.5, of the Presbyterian Church in America.

Maxton is an old Scottish clan name, and your great-grandfather is Scottish. The name is likely connected to the Latin word for "great" or "greatest."

Paul is your grandfather's name on your mom's side, and of course the name of the apostle Paul. The name Paul is Latin (*Paulus*), and it means "small." So you are both great and small (or the greatest and most humble)!

Maxton Paul (surname), may you embrace Jesus Christ as Savior and Lord, and may you live in light of his teaching on greatness—that the greatest in the kingdom must be the most humble and the servant of all.

Remarks

_____ (parents), since you have confessed Jesus Christ as Lord and acknowledge that he alone is your salvation, and since it is your desire to bring up _____ in the nurture and admonition of the Lord, you now bring him to be baptized as a covenantal sign and an earnest of your desire that at the proper age he will confess Christ as Savior, thereby receiving the washing of regeneration by the Holy Spirit.

Baptism

Minister: "What is the Christian name of this child?"
Father responds with child's first and middle name.
Minister: "_____, I baptize you in the name of the Father and of the Son and of the Holy Spirit."

Optional Blessing

"The blessing of God Almighty, Father, Son, and Holy Spirit, descend upon you, and dwell in your heart forever. Amen."[19]

Optional Blessing

"The Lord bless you and keep you. The Lord be kind and gracious to you. The Lord look upon you with favor and give you peace. Alleluia! Amen" (based on Num. 6:24–26).

Optional Blessing

"O Lord, uphold (name) by your Holy Spirit. Give him/her the spirit of wisdom and understanding, the spirit of counsel and might, and the spirit of knowledge and the fear of the Lord, the spirit of joy in your presence, both now and forevermore. Amen."[20]

---

[19] Johnson, *Leading in Worship*, 105.
[20] *The Worship Sourcebook*, 6.4.4.

I invite the congregation to stand and please respond to the question by saying, "We do."

Minister: "Do you, the people of the Lord, promise to receive this child in love, pray for him, help instruct him in the faith, and encourage and sustain him in the fellowship of believers?"

Congregation: "We do."

Congregational Charge and Welcome (optional)

Minister: "Brothers and sisters, we now receive _____ into Christ's church. I charge you to nurture and love him and to assist him to be Christ's faithful disciple(s)."

Congregation: "With joy and thanksgiving, we now welcome you into Christ's church, for we are all one in Christ. We promise to love, encourage, and support you and to help you know and follow Christ."[21]

Minister: "Before we pray, I invite you (after the prayer) to join us in singing, "Gift from the Lord."[22]

Prayer

Heavenly Father, we acknowledge, that insofar as _____ did not choose his parents, neither did we first choose you. And so we take this occasion to thank you for the physical breath with which you bless us and the spiritual breath by which we were graciously and mercifully born again. Lord, we ask that you would be pleased to impart to this precious baby, in whom you have already bestowed physical life, spiritual life; and we pray that, toward this end, your grace would rest mightily and mercifully upon his parents. We ask this in the name of Jesus Christ, our Savior and Lord. Amen.

Two Other Sample Prayers

"Give thanks to God for the gift of this child and for His covenant promises; pray that God will grant the inward reality that corresponds to the outward washing; that the child will be received into the protection and care of Christ and His church; that even as He has been the God of the child's parents, that the Lord would be the child's God as well; that the child would be granted the gift of the Holy Spirit; that (his/her) heart would be renewed and regenerated; that (he/she) would grow up never knowing a day apart from Christ; like John filled with the Holy Spirit from the womb (Lk 1:15); like David, trusting God while still a nursing infant (Ps 22:9, 10)."[23]

---

[21] Ibid., 6.5.1.
[22] See words and music on page 408.
[23] Johnson, *Leading in Worship*, 104. Johnson calls this prayer a "Prayer of Consecration" and uses it before the baptism.

"Praying Almighty God for His sovereign grace in Christ Jesus; praying that the Lord will guide and protect this child; that (he/she) will grow daily in the love and knowledge of Christ; that (he/she) will serve God all (his/her) days and live for His glory; that (his/her) parents will show wisdom, discernment, and diligence as they seek to rear (him/her) in the nurture and admonition of the Lord; that (he/she) will live so as to be credit to (his/her) family and church."[24]

Seat the congregation and present the parents with a handshake and the certificate. The parents and children may return to their seats.

CONFIRMATION

We conclude this chapter with a service of confirmation, contributed by Dr. Niel Nielson. Whether your church includes a formal liturgy or formal process (e.g., offering youth membership and/or admission to the Lord's Supper to those who have been baptized, have been approved by the elders, and made a public profession of faith), the church must stress that their hope is that every child who was baptized as an infant will *confirm* his/her baptismal vows through genuine Christian confession, obedience, and service to Christ as Lord. For example, note point j below (emphasis mine). I cite this entire section from the Book of Church Order, 56.4, of the Presbyterian Church in America because it helps fill in any theological gaps and can be used during a baptism or confirmation ceremony.

Before baptism, the minister is to use some words of instruction, touching the institution, nature, use, and ends of this sacrament, showing: a. That it is instituted by our Lord Jesus Christ; b. That it is a seal of the Covenant of Grace, of our ingrafting into Christ, and of our union with Him, of remission of sins, regeneration, adoption, and life eternal; c. That the water, in baptism, represents and signifies both the blood of Christ, which taketh away all guilt of sin, original and actual; and the sanctifying virtue of the Spirit of Christ against the dominion of sin, and the corruption of our sinful nature; d. That baptizing, or sprinkling and washing with water, signifies the cleansing from sin by the blood and for the merit of Christ, together with the mortification of sin, and rising from sin to newness of life, by virtue of the death and resurrection of Christ; e. That the promise is made to believers and their children; and that the children of believers have an interest in the covenant, and right to the seal of it, and to the outward privileges of the Church, under the Gospel, no less than

---

[24] Ibid., 105. For other example prayers of thanksgiving and intercession, see *The Worship Sourcebook*, 6.3 and 6:5.

the children of Abraham in the time of the Old Testament; the Covenant of Grace, for substance, being the same; and the grace of God, and the consolation of believers, more plentiful than before; f. That the Son of God admitted little children into His presence, embracing and blessing them, saying, "For of such is the kingdom of God"; g. That children by Baptism, are solemnly received into the bosom of the Visible Church, distinguished from the world, and them that are without, and united with believers; and that all who are baptized in the name of Christ, do renounce, and by their Baptism are bound to fight against the devil, the world, and the flesh; h. That they are federally holy before Baptism, and therefore are they baptized; i. That the inward grace and virtue of Baptism is not tied to that very moment of time wherein it is administered; and that the fruit and power thereof reaches to the whole course of our life; and that outward baptism is not so necessary, that through the want thereof, the infant is in danger of damnation; j. By virtue of being children of believing parents they are, because of God's covenant ordinance, made members of the Church, but this is not sufficient to make them continue members of the Church. When they have reached the age of discretion, they become subject to obligations of the covenant: faith, repentance and obedience. *They then make public confession of their faith in Christ*, or become covenant breakers, and subject to the discipline of the Church.

Confirmation Liturgy (Niel Nielson)

A preface is intended to keep the service warm and engaging. Either the pastor can say a few words about the confirmants (those making their confirmation), especially noting how they came to faith, or the confirmants can share brief testimonies (printed in the bulletin or recorded on a video that is shown to the congregation). Then the pastor introduces the service (why we are gathered) and begins with a prayer. He then says:

> *Minister*: "As a church, we make provision for those who have been baptized at an early age and come later to salvation through a personal faith in Jesus Christ to confirm their belief publicly when they are old enough to do so. At this time, I invite _____ to come to the platform."

> *Minister* (to the confirmants): "Hear the words of our Lord Jesus Christ":

> - "You did not choose me, but I chose you and appointed you that you should go and bear fruit" (John 15:16a).
> - "Everyone who acknowledges me before men, I also will acknowledge before my Father who is in heaven" (Matt. 10:32).

"Jesus Christ has chosen you and, in baptism, has set his great and glorious promises upon you. He has called you, together with us, into the church, which is his body. Now he has brought you to this time and place and has given you the faith and desire that you may confess his name before men and go out to serve him as faithful disciples."

Then the pastor calls each person by name. Following this, he addresses each candidate in turn, asking the following questions, each of which is answered with a single affirmation:

- Do you believe that Jesus Christ is the Son of God, and do you believe that he died on the cross for your sins and was raised on the third day? *I do.*
- Do you trust in Christ alone for forgiveness and hope of eternal life? By God's grace, do you intend to be his disciple—to obey his Word and to proclaim Christ's glory? *I do.*

Following this confession of faith, the confirmants kneel as a group for confirmation. The pastor says each name, followed by:

Upon your public profession of faith, we do now acknowledge your faith in Jesus Christ as your Lord and Savior and his saving grace in your life that was foreshadowed in your baptism and has now been received by grace through faith. He has chosen you; he has commissioned you. Live in his love, and serve him.

This continues until all candidates have been so addressed. The pastor concludes, saying:

"And let the peace of Christ rule in your hearts, to which indeed you were called in one body. And be thankful. Let the word of Christ dwell in you richly, teaching and admonishing one another in all wisdom, singing psalms and hymns and spiritual songs, with thankfulness in your hearts to God. And whatever you do, in word or deed, do everything in the name of the Lord Jesus, giving thanks to God the Father through him" (Col. 3:15–17). Amen.

This Scripture is followed by a final prayer.

9

Communion

Presiding over the Communion service, the Lord's Supper, is one of the pastor's most precious and profound privileges and ministries.

The word *transcendence* wasn't a part of my third-grade vocabulary, but that is what I (Kent) now think that I sensed as I sat next to my newly widowed mother in hushed silence before the Communion Table of Vermont Avenue Presbyterian Church in Los Angeles.

Dr. Ed Caldwell's opening words of institution ("For I received from the Lord what I also delivered to you, that the Lord Jesus on the night when he was betrayed . . ."); the kindly elders in their blue serge suits, white carnations in their lapels, reverently distributing the elements; my mother prayerfully partaking; the rhythm of the footfall back to the Table; the silence; and again echoing words ("For as often as you eat this bread and drink the cup, you proclaim the Lord's death until he comes") filled me with inarticulate wonder that marked the beginning of my coming to Christ in the summer before my freshman year of high school.

Fifty years later, I am the pastor standing behind the Table, about to preside over the Communion of the body and blood of Christ in College Church in Wheaton, Illinois, as I had done on hundreds of previous occasions. The sermon has been delivered, the pastors have taken their places behind the Table, the elders and deacons have assumed their seats, and I give the invitation to Communion (borrowed from The Book of Common Worship).

Brothers and sisters, as we draw near to the Lord's Table to celebrate the Communion of the body and blood of Christ, we are grateful to remember that our Lord instituted this ordinance:

- For the perpetual memory of his dying for our sakes and the pledge of his undying love.

- As a bond of our union with him and each other as members of his mystical body.
- As a seal of his promises to us and a renewal of our obedience to him.
- For the blessed assurance of his presence with us who are gathered here in his name.
- As an opportunity for us who love the Savior to feed spiritually on him who is the Bread of Life.
- As a pledge of his coming again.

The immense theology of the invitation (memory, bond, seal, assurance, opportunity) refreshes my heart, as well as those of the congregation, and compels all of us to ponder afresh what Christ has done for us.

The Communion prayer, followed by the words of institution and then the partaking of the bread and the cup, is anything but perfunctory. The prayers offered for the elements are thought-through and from the heart; the hymns sung and played in the background have been prayerfully chosen, the pace slowed for reflection on the body and blood of Christ and interspersed with silence for individual prayer.

The atmosphere is one of serious joy in the deep contemplation of what Christ has done for us—gospel joy. And God's people leave refreshed and hungry for more of Christ. As Bernard of Clairvaux put it in his hymn "Jesus, Thou Joy of Loving Hearts":

> We taste Thee, O Thou living Bread,
> And long to feast upon thee still;
> We drink of Thee, the Fountainhead,
> And thirst our souls from Thee to fill.

Indeed the gospel has been preached that morning in a way that was ordained and instituted by Christ himself. The church assembled is in communion (*koinonia*) in the gospel: "The cup of blessing that we bless, is it not a participation [*koinonia*] in the blood of Christ? The bread that we break, is it not a participation [*koinonia*] in the body of Christ?" (1 Cor. 10:16). Thus, the church has fellowship in the cross of Christ. And there are likely some sitting there, observing, who experience seismic movement in their souls as they begin to be drawn ineluctably to Christ—perhaps even a young boy who cannot articulate what he feels.

And this points to a great concern for the contemporary church, because the Lord's Table has suffered increasing neglect and even abuse in evangelical contexts. Large churches find the logistics daunting and thus limit the observance of Communion to once or perhaps twice a year. Others see it as taking time away from "worship" or as a hindrance to evangelism because of its exclusive nature. And in many churches, the observance has devolved into a perfunctory, robotic service with brief monotone prayers offered at a "Let's get it over with" pace, affording no time or pause for reflection.

To be sure, this is a caricature, and most of this book's readers do not abuse the Lord's Table, but rather desire to give it care and observance consonant with Jesus's command, "Do this in remembrance of me" (Luke 22:19). To help meet that desire, in this chapter we will review the history of the Lord's Table, restate its profound theology, and provide practical advice and substance for its observance.

THE HISTORY OF THE LORD'S TABLE

THE EARLY CHURCH

Historian Hughes Oliphant Old summarizes his investigation of the celebration of the Lord's Supper in the New Testament with these observations:

> The celebration by the earliest Christians was in liturgical form very much like the Passover seder. It was, like the Passover meal, a covenant meal, but it was shared with the risen Christ as a celebration of his passage from death to life and as a prophetic sign of the heavenly banquet in the last day. By the end of the New Testament period the Christian celebration of this meal had undergone a number of modifications. First, it had become a weekly celebration held every Lord's Day morning in celebration of Christ's resurrection. Second, it was no longer a rite observed by a small group of ten people, but a celebration of the whole Christian community. . . . Third, the celebration was closely connected with the proclamation of the gospel. It is not clear whether the service of the Word and the service of the Supper had been joined into a single liturgy in New Testament times, but surely this was beginning to happen. Fourth, the sacrament already has diaconal significance. The meal was to be shared with the poor, the widowed, and the hungry. It was a sign of concern for those who were in need. Fifth, the content of the prayers had been changed so that they were a thanksgiving for God's mighty acts of redemption in Christ. Finally, the whole service was a memorial of God's mighty acts that the church proclaimed to the world "until he comes."[1]

---

[1] Hughes Oliphant Old, *Worship: Reformed According to Scripture* (Louisville: Westminster John Knox, 2002), 120.

This view of the Supper informed worship well into the middle of the second century. The *Didache* indicates that the Communion service remained liturgically much like the Passover seder, though there is a hint of the idea of Eucharistic sacrifice because, before partaking, Christians were directed to confess their sins in order that "their offering be pure."[2] Justin Martyr (ca. 100–ca. 165) tells us that shortly after mid-century, the multiple prayers of the seder had been incorporated into a single lengthy extemporaneous prayer of thanksgiving to which the entire congregation said "Amen." This is the origination of the term *Eucharist* (Greek for "thanksgiving").[3]

At the beginning of the third century, the bread and wine came to be regarded as a sacrifice, though the original sense is not clear. In the *Apostolic Constitutions*, Hippolytus (ca. 170–ca. 236) records that the bread and wine were called an offering/oblation that was offered to God with the priestly assignation "because thou hast biden us to stand before thee and minister as priests to thee." From that time on, Communion was regarded increasingly as a sacrifice, and the prayer of thanksgiving became the means of transforming the bread and wine into a sacrifice to God.[4]

By the end of the fourth century, Ambrose of Milan (ca. 339–397) preached a series of sermons entitled *De sacramentis*, in which he taught that in the prayer of thanksgiving, the eucharistic prayer, when the words of Jesus were quoted, the bread and the wine were *transformed* into the body and blood of Christ, which were then sacrificed to God. In logical consequence, Christians began to come to church to see the Communion service performed. In addition, Cyril of Jerusalem (ca. 315–386) authored the *Mystagogical Catechism*, an explanation of the redemptive events of Christianity, a kind of divine theater for the ignorant masses.[5] About the same time, a devotional attitude of fear was encouraged in reference to the celebration of the Eucharist. In the East, the consecration of the host was moved behind a screen, an iconostasis, to shield the holy moment. In the West, the prayer of consecration was spoken by the priest in muted reverence that was inaudible to the congregation. The sacred moment of the consecration was indicated by the ringing of bells and the prostration of the celebrants. Though the people could not hear the prayers, they could see the elevation of the host from afar as they bowed to the floor.[6]

Augustine countered Cyril's mysticism by reemphasizing the biblical

---

[2] Ibid., 121.
[3] Ibid., 121–122.
[4] Ibid., 122.
[5] Ibid.
[6] Ibid., 123.

teachings about the Lord's Supper—namely, the meal's covenantal nature, God's initiative in the Supper, the meal as a sign of God's grace, and Augustine's famous explanation of the sacrament as the Word of God made visible. Nevertheless, the die had been cast, and much of what Augustine said would be misunderstood or interpreted in a mystical way. Significantly, the Reformers would pick up on certain of Augustine's insights nearly a millennium later.[7]

THE MIDDLE AGES

Much good can be said of the so-called Middle Ages, such as the Bible translation work of John Wycliffe and Miles Coverdale, the protests and sacrifices of the Lollards and Hussites, the fidelity of the Roman Church to ancient creeds, certain admirable monastic enterprises (copying the Scriptures, serving the poor), and some brilliant theological contributions, such as Thomas Aquinas's *Summa*. However, during the Middle Ages, the theological trajectory of the doctrine of transubstantiation reached its apotheosis as the Lord's Supper became the sacrifice of the Mass. Dr. Old summarizes:

> It was a sacred drama that reenacted the sacrifice of Christ on the cross, a most solemn mystery celebrated in a language unknown to the common people. It was, in the eyes of many, a magical ceremony that transformed the bread and wine into the body and blood of Christ and made God present on the altar, there to be worshipped and adored in sumptuous religious rites. The awesome idea of eating Christ's flesh and drinking his blood led to the practice of receiving communion but once a year; even then, only the bread was eaten, and the cup withheld from the people. Many churches were filled with dozens of altars, and every day flocks of priests would offer the sacrifice of the mass for the salvation of the living and the dead. The private mass had become an institution. The whole concept of covenant fellowship among the faithful was lost. The splendid celebration of the Roman Mass in a Rhineland cathedral in the year 1500 had developed into something quite different from the celebration of the Passover seder that Jesus observed with his disciples in the upper room.[8]

THE REFORMATION

The theological genesis of the Reformation occurred when Martin Luther came to understand that "the righteousness of God" in Romans 1:17 was

---

[7] Ibid., 125.
[8] Ibid.

not the condemning righteousness wherein God is righteous and punishes the unrighteous sinner, but rather the gift of righteousness from God. "Thus," Luther would write, "that place in Paul was for me the gate to paradise."[9] Ultimately, that which made Luther's heart sing and declare, "Here I felt that I was altogether born again and had entered paradise itself through open gates,"[10] was the understanding that the gift of righteousness comes by faith, literally "from faith to faith" ("from faith for faith," Rom. 1:17), meaning that righteousness comes entirely by faith. Thus, the good news of the gospel is that salvation is by faith alone, *sola fide.*

The effect was seismic. Among the immediate results was the rejection of the Mass and the painstaking reform of the celebration of Communion. The Reformers rightly understood the gospel issues at stake and the life-and-death importance of getting it right. Luther led the way with his *Formula missae,* detailing his proposals for reform. The resulting interaction by the leaders of the Reformation (Martin Bucer, Ulrich Zwingli, Johannes Oecolampadius, John Calvin, Peter Martyr Vermigli, and, across the channel, Thomas Cranmer and John Knox) produced theology and liturgies that are reflected in today's observances of the Lord's Table.

The Reformers rejected the doctrine of transubstantiation out of hand. Luther replaced it with consubstantiation, which understands Jesus's words "this is my body" in a quasi-literal sense, arguing that while the bread and wine do not *become* the body and blood of Christ, the physical body of Christ is present "in, with and, under" the bread. This view was rejected by the rest of the Reformers because it calls for (as Luther taught) the ubiquity of Christ's human nature after the resurrection, a most tenuous theological assertion. Furthermore, Luther's view actually does not take "this is my body" in the normal literal sense, in which Jesus used physical objects to express spiritual realities (cf. John 6:27–59).[11]

The other Reformers (save Zwingli) and most Protestants today (excepting some Baptists) understand the bread and wine to be not only symbolic of the body and blood of Christ, but visible signs that Christ is spiritually present. This will be discussed in the next section of this chapter.

The result of the Reformers' theologizing and hard thinking was massive liturgical renovation and innovation:

---

[9] Quoted in John Dillenberger, ed., *Martin Luther, Selections from His Writings* (Garden City, NY: Anchor, 1961), 11.
[10] Quoted in Timothy F. Lull and William R. Russell, eds., *Martin Luther's Basic Theological Writings,* 3rd ed. (Minneapolis: Fortress, 2012), 497.
[11] Wayne Grudem, *Systematic Theology: An Introduction to Biblical Doctrine* (Grand Rapids: Zondervan, 1994), 994–995.

- The finality and sufficiency of Christ's sacrifice was reasserted as Jesus's words from the cross, "It is finished" (John 19:30), were allowed their full sense. The Mass's repeated sacrifice of Christ was rejected as wholly unbiblical.
- The significance of the celebration of the Lord's Table on the Lord's Day (Resurrection Day) was emphasized. Communion was not a funeral, but a recognition of the triumph of the cross.
- The Eucharist ("thanksgiving") was restored in the literal sense of the word.
- Latin as the liturgical language of Communion was replaced with the vernacular languages of the people.
- The administration of Communion was no longer the domain of priests.
- The celebration of the Lord's Table was conducted as a meal for the whole body of Christ.
- Communion was celebrated as a ministry of the Word. Sermon and Supper went together.
- Ecclesiastical furnishings changed as the altar was replaced by the Table, and the pulpit was moved to the center of the church.
- Simplicity became the operative word in forming Communion liturgies.

THE BIBLICAL THEOLOGY OF THE LORD'S TABLE

OLD TESTAMENT THEOLOGY

The theological ground for the New Testament observance of the Lord's Table was the Passover, when God commanded each Israelite household to offer an unblemished yearling male lamb by slaying it at twilight and then applying the lamb's blood to the lintel over the door and the two doorposts (directives redolent with Christ, the ultimate Passover Lamb; see 1 Cor. 5:7). The Passover lamb was then roasted with bitter herbs and consumed hastily at a common meal within the house by the family, which was dressed and ready for the exodus. Those households that faithfully followed God's directives were spared the loss of their firstborn, for when the Lord passed by that night, he saw the blood (Ex. 12:1–13).

Significantly, God issues four directives that the Passover be observed as a *memorial*, an occasion to remember in detail how the Lord delivered them from bondage in Egypt. The first directive is to all Israelites: "This day shall be for you a memorial day, and you shall keep it as a feast to the LORD; throughout your generations, as a statute forever, you shall keep it as a feast" (Ex. 12:14). The other three directives instruct the fathers to recount the story of the Passover to their children on the day of the feast (12:26–27; 13:6–10, 14–16). Clearly, God tells Israel that remembering his saving work and memorializing it is crucial to the ongoing spiritual life and health of his people. Moreover, this theology of remembrance extends to the Communion Table and Christ's directive, "Do this in remembrance of me" (Luke 22:19). Thus, we see that a primary function of the Lord's Table is to help us *remember* in depth the substitutionary death of Christ our Passover— a function, incidentally, that the Catholic Mass obscured with its putative resacrifice of Christ.

Here it must also be noted that the Lord Jesus chose the 14th of Nisan, the annual culmination of the Passover Feast, while he sat at table with his disciples, to institute the Communion of his body and blood—the Lord's Supper.

New Testament Theology
New Covenant

By New Testament times, the Passover seder had morphed into a ceremony that included, in addition to the unleavened bread, the partaking of four cups of wine. Jesus imbued the ceremony with ultimate redemptive significance when he broke the bread, saying, "This is my body, which is given for you" (Luke 22:19), and then took the third cup of wine, "the cup of blessing" (see 1 Cor. 10:16), and gave the wine new meaning, saying, "This cup that is poured out for you is the new covenant in my blood" (Luke 22:20). Just as the blood of the Passover lamb had shielded God's people from death, now the blood of the ultimate Passover Lamb would shield his followers from judgment and death. Indeed, Jesus's shed blood initiated the new covenant blessings of Jeremiah 31:31–34, which provide in effect a spiritual profile of those who sit at the Lord's Table:

> For this is the covenant that I will make with the house of Israel after those days, declares the LORD: I will put my law within them, and I will write it on their hearts. And I will be their God, and they shall be my people. And no longer shall each one teach his neighbor and each his brother, saying, "Know the LORD," for they shall all know me, from the least of them to the greatest, declares the LORD. For I will forgive their iniquity, and I will remember their sins no more. (vv. 33–34)

The new covenant in Christ's blood effects a radically transformed and radically forgiven community that can then sit in communion at the Lord's Table. The repeated divine "I wills" of the new covenant tell us that it is all because of his initiative. Indeed, the very language in and around Communion speaks of this. It is the *Lord's* Supper, the *Lord's* Table, and the *Lord's* cup because he is the host who rose on the third day, which is now the *Lord's* Day! Whenever we gather to celebrate Communion, we must remember that the meal is all from him and that he is the host.

Memory

As we have seen, the Passover observance was instituted as a *memorial* of redemption, a day to remember the saving acts of God: "You shall tell your son on that day, 'It is because of what the LORD did for me when I came out of Egypt.' And it shall be to you as a sign on your hand and as a memorial between your eyes . . ." (Ex. 13:8–9). Likewise, at the Paschal feast, the Lord Jesus twice commanded remembrance, saying of the bread and then the cup, "Do this in remembrance of me" (cf. 1 Cor. 11:24–25). These divine imperatives tell us that volitional remembering of what Christ did on the cross whenever we eat the bread and drink the cup is crucial to the proper celebration of Communion and the health of our souls. Jesus was not calling for a perfunctory recollection, a nod to God over the bread and the wine, but rather deep reflection. This ought to sound the alarm over the bland "fast forward" observances of the Lord's Supper with their dispassionate recitations and prayers. Whenever we take the bread, we must remember the Lord's body, broken on the cross as he became sin for us. And when we take the cup, we must remember the source of the new covenant, which is the remission of sins through his shed blood. And more, we pastors who administer the bread and the cup must do so with our hearts in full passionate engagement, leaving our people space and time to actually remember.

Communion

As we noted at the beginning of this chapter, the Lord's Table is literally a *koinonia*, which our translations render as "fellowship," "communion," or "participation." All three renderings speak well enough to what happens when the body of Christ partakes of the cup and the bread: "The cup of blessing that we bless, is it not a participation in the blood of Christ? The bread that we break, is it not a participation in the body of Christ? Because there is one bread, we who are many are one body, for we all partake of the one bread" (1 Cor. 10:16–17). The theological reality is that all believers are members of Christ's body (1 Cor. 12:12–13) and that when we partake of the Lord's Table, we experience a deepened sense of communion with

Christ and one another. As a member of the Brethren Church remarked with a smile to a friend who greeted him after the service, "I already met you in the bread." Indeed.

Presence

But there is yet another deep reality rooted in our Communion in the blood and body of Christ, and that is the experience of Christ's *spiritual presence*. This is, of course, the classic Reformed understanding of the Lord's Table. The Westminster Larger Catechism explains: "The body and blood of Christ . . . are spiritually present to the faith of the receiver, no less truly and really than the elements themselves are to their outward senses." Therefore, the communicants "feed upon the body and blood of Christ, not after a corporal and carnal manner; yet truly and really, while by faith they receive and apply to themselves Christ crucified, and all the benefits of his death" (Answer 170).[12]

Theologian Wayne Grudem agrees, noting that most Protestants today would say that while the bread and the wine symbolize the body and blood of Christ, "Christ is also *spiritually present* in a special way as we partake of the bread and wine." Grudem argues that if Christ is specially present when Christians gather to worship, we should expect that he will be present in a special way when they sup at the Lord's Table.[13] The famed Victorian preacher Charles Spurgeon exulted in the Lord's spiritual presence at the Table through his Holy Spirit, saying: "He comes to us at the Lord's Supper in a way more real than our simply remembering him or simply our being granted his grace. . . . Christ is indeed present to us at the Lord's Supper, but not according to the flesh. His presence is a personal presence. This is not some sort of spiritualized presence, but rather a presence through the Holy Spirit."[14] The force of this truth ought to tell us that the spiritual health of today's occasional church attender is greatly diminished by living apart from the regular benefits of the Lord's Table, and also that the church that rarely observes Communion or does it in a perfunctory way is not providing proper care to the souls of the flock.

Gospel

The words of institution conclude with the sonorous pronouncement, "For as often as you eat this bread and drink the cup, you proclaim the Lord's death until he comes" (1 Cor. 11:26). This is by no means a gloomy, funereal

---

[12] *The Confession of Faith Together with The Larger Catechism and Shorter Catechism with the Scriptural Proofs*, 3rd Edition (Atlanta: The Committee for Christian Education and Publications, 1990), 129.
[13] Grudem, *Systematic Theology*, 994.
[14] Quoted in Old, *Worship*, 145.

pronouncement, as some have likely heard it. Rather, it means that the Lord's Table proclaims the gospel. In point of fact, the apostle Paul reminded his hearers of the gospel that he preached to them, saying, "For I delivered to you as of first importance what I also received: that Christ died for our sins in accordance with the Scriptures, that he was buried, that he was raised on the third day in accordance with the Scriptures" (1 Cor. 15:3–4). Proclaiming the Lord's death until he comes involves proclaiming the Lord's Day, Resurrection Day—the gospel!

Richard Phillips, onetime assistant to Dr. James Montgomery Boice, describes one memorable Lord's Day. After preaching from Matthew's Gospel about Christ's death for sinners, Dr. Boice approached the Table gravely and read the words of institution. Then he looked out on the congregation of Philadelphia's Tenth Presbyterian Church and stopped. Phillips recalls, "Gazing into the eyes seemingly of every man, woman, and child present, he solemnly exclaimed: 'Let no one here today, in life and in death, ever claim that you have not heard the Gospel of Jesus Christ.'" He concluded by pressing home the need to respond to the gospel. Phillips concludes, "The simplicity and directness of his presentation worked a memorable solemnity upon the proceedings, so that the word and sacrament combined to powerfully set forth the gospel's demand."[15]

RESOURCES FOR THE LORD'S TABLE

In the extensive section that follows, we have provided multiple options under each subheading for enhancing your observance of the Lord's Table. A relaxed read through these pages will provide many fresh ideas that can be used in full or in part to elevate your corporate worship. As you read, you will find a prayer here and there; a line or a suggestion that may inspire a prayer of your own; or a liturgical tweak that will enhance your congregation's Communion of the body and blood of Christ.

Sample Invitations to Communion

Sample Invitation #1

> What language shall I borrow to thank Thee, dearest friend,
> For this Thy dying sorrow, Thy pity without end?
> O make me Thine forever, and should I fainting be,
> Lord, let me never, never outlive my love to Thee.[16]

---

[15] Richard D. Phillips, "The Lord's Supper: An Overview," in *Give Praise to God: A Vision for Reforming Worship: Celebrating the Legacy of James Montgomery Boice* (Phillipsburg, NJ: P&R, 2011), 193.
[16] From the hymn "O Sacred Head, Now Wounded" by Bernard of Clairvaux, 1091–1153.

We gather now around this Table to express our love—our love for one another and our love for our Lord, Jesus Christ. We also gather around this Table to remember. To remember when Jesus took the bread and broke it and said, "This is my body, given for you; eat this in remembrance of me." And to remember when he took the cup and said, "This is the cup of the new covenant in my blood, shed for you; drink this in remembrance of me."

We gather to show our love for Jesus and for one another, and to remember the cross.

Sample Invitation #2

My song is love unknown,
My Savior's love to me;
Love to the loveless shown,
That they might lovely be.
O who am I, that for my sake
My Lord should take frail flesh and die?[17]

Who are we that we find ourselves, like Noah and his family, on that ark of salvation, escaping the judgment of God, as the floodwaters prevail upon the earth? And who are we that, like Israel of old, the angel of death should pass over us? And who are we that Jesus, the very Creator and Sustainer of this world, should take on frail flesh and suffer and die?

We come to this Table this day with a sense of awe and gratitude for our salvation and for our Savior. For we have been saved—saved from our sin, saved from eternal death, saved from the wrath of God. And for such a salvation we celebrate today this good and holy meal.

Sample Invitation #3

Our Lord Jesus gave thanks on the day he instituted this sacrament. He broke the bread, and he gave thanks.

And as he was thankful at that Last Supper for the Passover (for God's provision for his people of a perfect lamb and the lamb's blood, shed for their sins), so we now give thanks for this, our perpetual Passover meal, and for the ultimate Lamb of God, the Lord Jesus himself, who shed his blood so that we, through faith, might claim it as our protection and as our provision.

My brothers and sisters, this is a day to give thanks. This is a time to give thanks. This is the meal at which to give thanks, to give thanks for

---

[17] From the hymn "My Song Is Love Unknown" by Samuel Crossman, ca. 1624–1683.

Jesus, the Lamb of God who came to take away the sins of the world, to give thanks to the Son of God who feeds us even now through his supreme sacrifice.

This morning, I invite all those who profess a sincere faith in Christ and all those who are living according to his Word and with a clear conscience to join me in partaking of this thanksgiving meal.

Our Lord Jesus Christ is now exalted at the right hand of the Father, and he calls us, through partaking of this sacrament, to commune with him. And through this bread and cup he calls us to remember and proclaim his death until he comes to make his enemies his footstool. So I ask those here this morning who love the Lord Jesus, trust in his atoning death, and find refuge in his eternal priesthood to join me in solemnly celebrating this sacred meal, the Lord's Supper.

Augustine's words, "Where Christ is, there is the church," assure us of Christ's presence with us this morning. He sits by us and walks our aisles, so to speak. And when we come to the Table, while human hands distribute the bread and the cup, it comes ultimately from his unseen hands. Christ is our host this day! May joy and reverence fill our souls as we come to the Lord's Supper.

We are grateful for your presence with us. It is our hope that all will find food for their souls.

Sample Invitation #4

This morning, through our celebration of the Lord's Supper, we proclaim the death of Christ. These elements, which represent the body and blood of Christ, are a visible sermon to us; they are the gospel in tangible form.

They proclaim to us the great drama of redemption in Christ: salvation in the *present* ("for as often as you eat this bread and drink the cup"), salvation in the *past* ("you proclaim the Lord's death"), and salvation in the *future* ("until he comes," 1 Cor. 11:26).

In light of such a salvation, the apostle Paul warns us, "Whoever, therefore, eats the bread or drinks the cup of the Lord in an unworthy manner will be guilty concerning the body and blood of the Lord" (v. 27). Before we partake of the Supper, let us examine ourselves this morning, recognizing both the gravity of our sin and the weight of Christ's glorious sacrifice.

Sample Invitation #5

The Westminster Confession of Faith says this of the Lord's Table:

Our Lord Jesus, in the night wherein he was betrayed, instituted the sacrament of his body and blood, called the Lord's Supper, to be observed in his church, unto the end of the world, for the perpetual re-membrance of the sacrifice of himself in his death; the sealing of all benefits thereof unto true believers, their spiritual nourishment and growth in him, their further engagement in and to all duties which they owe to him; and, to be a bond and pledge of their communion with him, and with each other, as members of his mystical body.[18]

For how great it is to dwell upon the benefits given to us in this meal. The Lord's Supper is a *seal* that binds us to Christ. It is a *food* for our soul; it is a means of God's grace that provides for us spiritual nourish-ment and growth. And it is a covenantal *bond* of communion with God and with one another, with the church, with those who believe.

Sample Invitation #6

The following is taken from *Common Prayer: Resources for gospel-shaped gatherings*:

Brothers and sisters in Christ,
    We who come to receive the holy communion of the body and blood of our Saviour Christ can come only because of his great love for us. For, although we are completely undeserving of his love, yet in order to raise us from the darkness of death to everlasting life as God's sons and daughters, our Saviour Christ humbled himself to share our life and to die for us on the cross. In remembrance of his death, and as a pledge of his love, Jesus instituted his holy sacrament, which we are now to share. But those who would eat the bread and drink the cup of the Lord must examine themselves, and amend their lives. They must come with a re-pentant heart and steadfast faith. Above all, they must give thanks to God for his love towards us in Christ Jesus.[19]

Sample Invitation #7

The following is taken from *Common Prayer: Resources for gospel-shaped gatherings*:

At the heart of the Christian life is active trust in the Lord Jesus Christ and his sacrificial death for sin.
    In this symbolic meal, originating from Jesus's Last Supper with his disciples, we express and strengthen our trust in him, as we eat and drink with our brothers and sisters in Christ.

---

[18] *The Confession of Faith*, 91.
[19] *Common Prayer: Resources for gospel-shaped gatherings* (Sydney: Anglican Press, 2012), 37.

The Lord's Supper is an outward and visible sign of the grace shown to us in the death of our Saviour. As we share the bread and the wine together, we are invited to feed on him in our hearts by faith with thanksgiving. We are faced again with God's love for the unworthy and are strengthened by faith in the one whose body was given and whose blood was shed for us.

Come then with heartfelt repentance and genuine trust in the Lord Jesus, recognizing the significance of sharing this way.

If in good conscience it would not be right for you to participate, please use this time to reflect on God's love for us in Christ.[20]

Sample Prayers for Communion

Almighty God, we come to you this morning admitting our unworthiness to partake of this holy meal. And yet, with confidence, sincerity, truth, and joy, we come to this Supper through the sacred blood of Jesus, our Lord and Savior. We praise you for your mercy and grace, and ask you through this bread and cup to commune with us now as we commune with you and one another. Amen.

Heavenly Father, as we now celebrate this meal that you have prepared for us (a heavenly meal that reminds us of earthly realities), this bread and this cup are tangible and visible reminders of our sin and also of the supreme sacrifice of your Son (his body broken and his blood shed for us and for our salvation).

So, Lord, as we meditate on the realities of our sin and your salvation, we ask for your help in fully *confessing our sins in the silence* as we prepare to solemnly partake of the body and blood of your Son.

Father in heaven, we bow our heads now because Jesus bowed his head and gave up his spirit. We bow in reverence, in respect, in awe, and in adoration for the *person* of Christ, the *words* of Christ, and today for the *cross* of Christ.

Now fill us afresh with your Holy Spirit, so that our worship in this moment will bring true honor to you—Father, Son, and Holy Spirit—and genuine consolation to our souls. We pray this in Jesus's name. Amen.

Almighty God, the Table that you have set before us calls us to deepest ongoing remembrance of your death for us. So now, Lord, quiet our hearts, still our souls, remove all distractions, so that when we take the bread we remember your body hanging impaled, writhing in the darkness

---

[20] Ibid., 51.

as you, who knew no sin, became sin for us, that we might become the righteousness of God (cf. 2 Cor. 5:21). And when we take the cup, may we remember that you bled out on the cross for us as the perfect Passover Lamb, paying an infinite price for our sin.

May we partake of the bread and partake of the cup with perpetual, indelible, saving remembrance. Amen.

The following is taken from *Common Prayer: Resources for gospel-shaped gatherings*:

We do not presume to come to your table, merciful Lord, trusting in our own righteousness, but in your many and great mercies. We are not worthy so much as to gather up the crumbs under your table. But you are the same Lord whose nature is always to have mercy. Grant us, therefore, gracious Lord, so to eat the flesh of your dear Son Jesus Christ, and to drink his blood, that we may evermore dwell in him, and he in us. Amen.[21]

Following are two Communion prayers, one by John Knox and the other by Richard Baxter. Though the language is archaic, we have included them because they provide extraordinary substance for our Communion prayers due to their profound theology and magnificent expression.

John Knox's Thanksgiving (Eucharistic Prayer) for the Lord's Table (1560), the last two paragraphs, reads:

O Father of Mercy, and God of all consolation! . . . [At] the commandment of Jesus Christ our Lord, we present ourselves at this table, which he hath left to be used in remembrance of his death, until his coming again: to declare and witness before the world, that by him alone we have received liberty and life; that by him alone thou dost acknowledge us thy children and heirs; that by him alone we have entrance to the throne of grace; that by him alone we are possessed in our spiritual kingdom to eat and drink at his table, with whom we have our conversation presently in heaven, and by whom our bodies shall be raised up again from the dust, and shall be placed with him in that endless joy, which thou, O Father of Mercy, hast prepared for thine elect before the foundation of the world was laid.

And these most estimable benefits we acknowledge and confess to have received of thy free mercy and grace, by thine only beloved Son Jesus Christ: for the which, therefore, we thy congregation, moved by thine Holy Spirit, render all thanks, praise, and glory, for ever and ever. Amen.[22]

---

[21] Ibid., 40.
[22] Quoted in Old, *Worship*, 136–137.

Richard Baxter's invocation of the Holy Spirit (*epiclesis*) on the Lord's Table in his Reformed Liturgy of 1662 reads:

> Most Holy Spirit, proceeding from the Father and the Son: by whom Christ was conceived; by whom the prophets and apostles were inspired, and the ministers of Christ are qualified and called: that dwellest and workest in all the members of Christ, whom thou sanctifiest to the image and for the service of their Head, and comfortest them that they may shew forth thy praise: illuminate us, that by faith we may see him that is here represented to us. Soften our hearts, and humble us for our sins. Sanctify and quicken us, that we may relish the spiritual food, and feed on it to our nourishment and growth in grace. Shed abroad the love of God upon our hearts, and draw them out in love to him. Fill us with thankfulness and holy joy, and with love to one another. Comfort us by witnessing that we are the children of God. Confirm us for new obedience. Be the earnest of our inheritance, and seal us up to everlasting life. Amen.[23]

SAMPLE PRAYERS OF CONFESSION

Our loving Father, your Word tells us: "If we say we have no sin, we deceive ourselves, and the truth is not in us. If we confess our sins, he is faithful and just to forgive us our sins and to cleanse us from all unrighteousness" (1 John 1:8–9).

So now, in these moments, we silently confess our sins.

"My little children, I am writing these things to you so that you may not sin. But if anyone does sin, we have an advocate with the Father, Jesus Christ the righteous. He is the propitiation for our sins" (1 John 2:1–2a).

Heavenly Father, we come to this meal that you have prepared for us to remind us of our sin and of your sacrifice, and to help us even now to grow in grace. So, Lord, do help us, in this time of meditation before we eat of this bread, to confess our sins to you, to acknowledge our indebtedness to your free grace, and to be grateful for your steadfast love. We pray this in Jesus's name. Amen.

Our gracious God, it is because you have restored our sight, it is because you have opened our eyes to see the truth of your gospel, that we can freely confess this morning our love for and dependence on Christ and can joyfully partake of his body broken for us and his blood shed for us. Help us now, O Lord, as we think on both our sin and our Savior,

---

[23] Quoted in ibid., 138.

to confess the worthiness of Christ and him alone. We pray this in his name. Amen.

The following is taken from the 1956 Book of Common Worship:

ALMIGHTY GOD, Father of our Lord Jesus Christ, maker of all things, Judge of all men; We acknowledge and confess our manifold sins; Which we, from time to time, most grievously have committed; By thought, word, and deed; Against Thy Divine majesty. We do earnestly repent; And are heartily sorry for these our misdoings; The remembrance of them is grievous unto us. Have mercy upon us, most merciful Father; For Thy Son our Lord Jesus Christ's sake; Forgive us all that is past; And grant that we may ever hereafter serve and please Thee in newness of life; To the honor and glory of Thy name; Through Jesus Christ our Lord. Amen.[24]

The following two prayers are taken from *Common Prayer: Resources for gospel-shaped gatherings*:

To be prayed together.
Almighty God
Father of our Lord Jesus Christ,
you made all things,
and you call everyone to account.
With shame we confess
the sins we have committed against you,
in thought, word and deed.
We rightly deserve your condemnation.
We turn from our sins
and are truly sorry for them;
they are a burden we cannot bear.
Have mercy on us, most merciful father.
For the sake of your Son our Lord Jesus Christ,
Forgive us all that is past.
Enable us to serve and please you in newness of life,
to your honour and glory,
through Jesus Christ our Lord. Amen.[25]

Knowing that we are all sinners saved by grace, and that we regularly sin in thought and word and deed, let us confess our sins together.

---

[24] The Book of Common Worship (Philadelphia: The Board of Education of the Presbyterian Church in the United States of America, 1956), 166.
[25] *Common Prayer: Resources for gospel-shaped gatherings*, 37.

Heavenly Father,
you have loved us with an everlasting love,
but we have often gone our own way
and rejected your will for our lives.
We are sorry for our sins
and turn away from them.
For the sake of your Son who died for us
forgive us, cleanse us, and change us.
By your Holy Spirit enable us to live for you
and to please you in every way,
for the glory of our Lord Jesus Christ. Amen.[26]

SAMPLE PRAYERS FOR THE BREAD

Almighty God, you have written in your Word, "Christ, our Passover Lamb, has been sacrificed. Let us therefore celebrate the festival, not with the old leaven, the leaven of malice and evil, but with the unleavened bread of sincerity and truth" (1 Cor. 5:7b–8). We come to you this morning admitting our unworthiness to partake of this holy meal. And yet with confidence, sincerity, truth, and joy, we come to this Supper through the sacred blood of Jesus, our Lord and Savior.

We praise you for your mercy and grace, and we ask you through this bread to commune with us now as we commune with you. Amen.

Our dear Lord, the bread that we are about to partake of is symbolic of the human body in which you dwelt incarnate among us, sinless, for thirty-three years. And when you were crucified, you bore our sins in your body on the tree, that we might die to sin and live to righteousness. And by your wounds we were healed (see 1 Pet. 2:24). You took our place and paid a price that we could never pay.

Seal this to our hearts as we eat the bread, representative of your body broken for us. Amen.

Christ Jesus, when you came into the world you said to the Father, "Sacrifices and offerings you have not desired, but a body have you prepared for me; in burnt offerings and sin offerings you have taken no pleasure. Then I said, 'Behold, I have come to do your will, O God, as it is written of me in the scroll of the book'" (Heb. 10:5–7). Then you came in the incarnation, and by the single offering of your body on the cross, you did what all the offerings on Israelite altars could never accomplish—the complete forgiveness of our sins.

---

[26] Ibid., 61.

Bread of heaven, as we now partake of the symbol, ravish our hearts and refresh our souls. Amen.

Lord Jesus, you said: "I am the living bread that came down from heaven. If anyone eats of this bread, he will live forever. And the bread that I will give for the life of the world is my flesh" (John 6:51). Shocking words, prophetic of the cross.

Now as we eat this bread, help us to ride the symbol to the deepest reality. You bore our sins in your body, you became sin for us, you suffered death in your body, and you were resurrected in your body. Bread of heaven, we feast in remembrance of your body given for us. Amen.

Sample Directives for Partaking of the Bread

Scriptural directives

[Jesus] said, "This is my body which is for you. Do this is remembrance of me." (1 Cor. 11:24)

[Jesus] said, "Take, eat; this is my body." (Matt. 26:26)

Classic Directives

Here is a contemporary rendering of Thomas Cranmer's directive:

The body of our Lord Jesus Christ, which was given for you, preserve your body and soul to everlasting life. Take and eat this in remembrance that Christ died for you, and feed on him in your hearts by faith with thanksgiving.

A shortened version is:

Take and eat this in remembrance that Christ died for you, and feed on him in your heart by faith with thanksgiving.[27]

Sample Prayers for the Cup

Our gracious God, we thank you this day for the new covenant, the covenant sealed through the blood of Jesus Christ. And we drink this cup in remembrance of Christ's sacrifice for our sins, asking him even now, through the Spirit, to commune with us as we commune with each other. With grateful hearts, O Christ, we drink to you and of you. Amen.

---

[27] Ibid., 53–54.

Our gracious and merciful God, we know from your Word that we cannot claim to be righteous apart from your righteousness, the righteousness that has been given to us through faith in Christ. We praise and honor you for this new covenant, the covenant sealed through the death of your Son and our Lord and Savior Jesus Christ. And we drink this cup in remembrance of Christ's sacrifice for our sins, asking him even now, through the Spirit, to commune with us as we commune with each other. With grateful hearts and sober minds, we pray this in Christ's name. Amen.

Our Lord, your Word tells us that when Cain rose up and killed his brother, Abel's blood cried out to God from the ground, and Cain came under the curse of judgment. But your Word tells us that in the church, we come "to Jesus, the mediator of a new covenant, and to the sprinkled blood that speaks a better word than the blood of Abel" (Heb. 12:24). Abel's blood cried for vengeance, but Christ's blood shouts the better word of forgiveness. As we ponder the cup, we rejoice for the better word that rises before us—complete forgiveness because of the shed blood of Jesus. Thank you for this better word. Seal it to our hearts as we partake. Amen.

Jesus, lover of our souls, in Gethsemane you looked into the cup that you would have to drink in order to redeem us from our sins, and it was so awful that you prayed: "Abba, Father, all things are possible for you. Remove this cup from me. Yet not what I will, but what you will" (Mark 14:36). And then you did the hardest thing ever done in time and eternity as you shed your blood to secure our salvation, so that we might come to your Table and partake of the cup in deep remembrance of what you did for us on the cross. Thank you, Lord Jesus. Amen.

Our dear Lord, as we ponder partaking of the cup, our hearts affirm:

> This is all my hope and peace,
> Nothing but the blood of Jesus;
> This is all my righteousness,
> Nothing but the blood of Jesus.[28]

SAMPLE DIRECTIVES FOR PARTAKING OF THE CUP

Scriptural Directive

Jesus said, "Drink of it, all of you, for this is my blood of the covenant, which is poured out for many for the forgiveness of sins" (Matt.

---

[28] From the hymn "Nothing but the Blood" by Robert Lowry, 1876.

26:27–28), and, "This cup is the new covenant in my blood. Do this, as
often as you drink it, in remembrance of me" (1 Cor. 11:25).

Classic Directives

A contemporary rendering of Archbishop Cranmer's directive reads:

> The blood of our Lord Jesus Christ, which was shed for you, preserve
> your body and soul to everlasting life. Drink this in remembrance that
> Christ's blood was shed for you, and be thankful.

A shortened version is:

> Drink this in remembrance that Christ's blood was shed for you, and be
> thankful.[29]

CREEDS AND THE TABLE

Many traditional Protestant liturgies include a congregational recitation of
the Apostles' Creed. If your church rarely or never uses a creed, introducing one as part of the Communion service might be a way to start. You can
always argue that many great Protestant leaders did the same!

In Zwingli's Zurich Liturgy, after a Gospel reading from John 6:47–48,
63, "the server brings the first line" of the creed, followed by an antiphonal
response from the men, then women (back and forth fifteen times), concluding together with "Amen."[30]

In Calvin's "The Manner of Celebrating the Lord's Supper," he advocates
for the Strassburg Liturgy, saying: "Then, after the accustomed prayers have
been offered, the Congregation, in making confession of the faith, *sings
the Apostles' Creed* to testify that all wish to live and die in the Christian
doctrine and religion. Meanwhile, the Minister prepares the bread and wine
of the Table."[31] Elsewhere, Calvin introduces the creed for his Communion
service, saying: "We shall beseech our Father to give us steadfast, living, and
perfect faith, and to increase and enlarge the same in us, by which we may
be able to overcome all the malice of our enemy. We shall express our desire
to live in that faith by making our confession of it, saying: I believe in God
the Father Almighty, Maker of heaven, etc."[32]

In the English Rite—The First and Second Prayer Books of King Edward

---

[29] *Common Prayer: Resources for gospel-shaped gatherings*, 54.
[30] Bard Thompson, *Liturgies of the Western Church* (Philadelphia: Fortress, 1980), 152–153.
[31] Ibid., 204 (emphasis added).
[32] Ibid., 221–222.

VI—the 1549 liturgy followed the medieval elements: introit, *Kyrie eleison*, *Gloria in excelsis*, collect, epistle and Gospel readings, creed, and sermon.[33] The Book of Common Prayer describes it as follows: "The priest or deacon, then shall reade the Gospel: after the Gospell ended, the priest shall begin: 'I beleue [believe] in one God.' The clerkes shall syng the rest."[34]

In Richard Baxter's Savoy Liturgy, he advocates that "one of the Creeds [note the plural!] be read by the Minister." The pastor is to say, "In the profession of this holy Christian Faith we are here assembled." Then a line from the Apostles' Creed and Nicene Creed are given, followed by the comment, "And sometimes Athanasius' Creed."[35]

Many other selections from the historic Protestant confessions can be used as well. In fact, their focus on various theological topics, such as "sin" or "the Lord's Supper," fits perfectly. An excellent resource to see what the Belgic Confession of Faith (1561), Heidelberg Catechism (1563), Second Helvetic Confession (1566), Canons of Dort (1618–1619), and the Westminster Standards (1647–1648) teach is Joel R. Beeke and Sinclair B. Ferguson, *Reformed Confessions Harmonized* (Grand Rapids: Baker, 2002).

For example, your church could use questions/answers from the Westminster Shorter Catechism:

Q. 96. What is the Lord's Supper?
A. The Lord's Supper is a sacrament, wherein, by giving and receiving bread and wine, according to Christ's appointment, his death is showed forth; and the worthy receivers are, not after a corporal and carnal manner, but by faith, made partakers of his body and blood, with all his benefits, to their spiritual nourishment, and growth in grace.

Q. 97. What is required for the worthy receiving of the Lord's Supper?
A. It is required of them that would worthily partake of the Lord's Supper, that they examine themselves of their knowledge to discern the Lord's body, of their faith to feed upon him, of their repentance, love, and new obedience; lest, coming unworthily, they eat and drink judgment to themselves.

FENCING THE TABLE

Because the Lord's Supper is meant only for those who have been born again and are walking faithfully with their Lord, we must warn those in our congregations of these serious matters. Sample comments follow.

---

[33] Ibid., 234.
[34] Ibid., 248.
[35] Ibid., 386.

As a minister of the gospel, it is my solemn duty to guard the Lord's Table from those who do not yet trust in our Lord Jesus Christ for their salvation *and* from those who do trust in Christ for their salvation but who now are living in secret and unrepentant sin. If this describes you, for your own spiritual well-being, it is my duty to ask you not to participate in this holy meal lest you partake unworthily, eating and drinking condemnation upon yourselves.

Yet, as a gospel minister, it is also my solemn duty to open this Table for repentant and trusting sinners, for this Table is not for those who are free from sin, but for those who are humble of heart and contrite in spirit. God invites to this Supper all sinners who confess utter dependence for pardon and cleansing based on the perfect sacrifice of Christ, sinners who base their hope of eternal life upon his perfect obedience and righteousness, and sinners who seek by the power of the Spirit to crucify their old natures and to continue to follow Christ.

Let us therefore, heeding the instructions given by the apostle Paul in 1 Corinthians, examine our minds and hearts to determine whether or not we should partake of this meal. And if we decide to partake, may it be to the end that we eat and drink to the glory of God and to our growth in the grace of Christ.

How great it is to dwell upon the benefits given to us in this meal. The Lord's Supper is a *seal* that binds us to Christ. It is *food* for our soul. It is a *means* of God's grace that provides for us spiritual nourishment and growth. And it is a covenantal *bond* of communion with God and with one another, with the church, with those who believe.

So with this great thought in mind, I invite those who believe, those who are in fellowship/communion with God through Christ, to partake gladly of this body broken for you and blood shed for the salvation of your soul. And for those who have yet to come to faith, I ask that you let the elements pass you by. We pray that in time, through God's work on your heart, you too would be able to join us at this Table.

So, my fellow believers, we come together this morning to eat and to drink so as to remember who we are in Christ, strangers in this world. And so I invite all those who are Christians (and only those who are believers in Jesus Christ) to partake of this gracious meal that has been prepared and provided for you, for your growth in grace.

Those of you here this morning who have not come to profess and know Jesus Christ as Savior and Lord, we ask you to let the bread and cup pass you by (others will be doing the same). But those of you who have welcomed Christ into our lives to be the King of our hearts, please solemnly and joyfully partake of the meal.

This sacred time at the Lord's Table is for believers who have rested all their hope on the death and resurrection of Christ. If you are not yet a believer, you should refrain from partaking until you come to faith in Christ—and then joyfully partake along with the body of Christ.

We encourage those who are believers to examine your hearts, so that you can partake in a worthy manner. If your heart is not right, refrain until you can come freely to partake.

The apostle Paul warns us, "Whoever, therefore, eats the bread or drinks the cup of the Lord in an unworthy manner will be guilty concerning the body and blood of the Lord" (1 Cor. 11:27). Before we partake of the Supper, let us examine ourselves this morning, recognizing both the gravity of our sin and the weight of Christ's glorious sacrifice.

SAMPLE COMMUNION BENEDICTIONS

Sample Scriptural Benedictions

The LORD bless you and keep you; the LORD make his face to shine upon you and be gracious to you; the LORD lift up his countenance upon you and give you peace. (Num. 6:24–26)

The grace of the Lord Jesus Christ and the love of God and the fellowship of the Holy Spirit be with you all. (2 Cor. 13:14)

But you have come to . . . Jesus, the mediator of a new covenant, and to the sprinkled blood that speaks a better word than the blood of Abel. (Heb. 12:22, 24)

Now to him who is able to keep you from stumbling and present you blameless before the presence of his glory with great joy, to the only God, our Savior, through Jesus Christ our Lord, be glory, majesty, dominion, and authority, before all time and now and forever. Amen. (Jude 24–25)

Revelation 7:10, 12 (responsive benediction):

> *Minister*: "Salvation belongs to our God who sits on the throne, and to the Lamb!"
> *Congregation*: "Amen! Blessing and glory and wisdom and thanksgiving and honor and power and might be to our God forever and ever! Amen."

Sample Traditional Benedictions

The 1662 Book of Common Prayer:

> The peace of God, that passes all understanding, keep your hearts and minds in the knowledge of the love of God, and of His Son Jesus Christ our Lord; and the blessing of God Almighty, the Father, the Son, and the Holy Spirit, be upon you, and remain with you always. Amen.

John Calvin's prayer of dedication at the end of Communion:

> Now grant us this . . . benefit: that thou wilt never allow us to forget these things; but having them imprinted on our hearts, we may grow and increase daily in the faith which is at work in every good deed. Thus may we order and pursue all our life to the exaltation of thy glory and the edification of our neighbor. Amen.[36]

SAMPLE COMMUNION LITURGIES

This section begins with the outlines of four historic communion liturgies: Calvin's Genevan Psalter of 1542, the Puritans' 1651 Westminster Directory for Worship, the 1661 Savoy Liturgy, and the 1662 Book of Common Prayer. There are, of course, other rich liturgies from which we could learn much, but space does not allow their inclusion in this book. But these liturgies together will acquaint the reader with the historic structures that preceded and inform today's observances. These will be followed by some examples of contemporary liturgies.

Our purpose here is not to prescribe how pastors ought to structure their churches' observance of the Lord's Table, but to enhance the observance of Communion. It should be noted that the outlines are skeletal, and where the liturgies do not have titles for sections, we have inserted headings that help make the structure visible. These liturgies pick up variously after the preaching of the Word.

The Genevan Psalter of 1542

The Singing of the Creed
Invocation

Four conjoined prayers: a prayer of invocation, an *epiclesis* (a prayer of thanksgiving for Christ's redemptive work), a prayer renewing covenant vows, and the Lord's Prayer.

---

[36] Calvin, quoted in Old, *Worship*, 134.

Words of Institution
  1 Corinthians 11:23–25
Fencing of the Table
Distribution of the Bread and Wine
  Congregation sings Psalm 138, a song of thanksgiving
A Prayer of Thanksgiving
Final Hymn of Praise
  Commonly Psalm 103 or 113
Aaronic Benediction
  Numbers 6:23–26[37]

The Puritan Celebration of the Lord's Table, 1651

The Puritan celebration of the Lord's Table was preceded the prior Sunday or during the week by a Preparatory Service so "that all may come better prepared to that heavenly feast."[38] Then, following the prescriptions of the Westminster Directory for Worship of 1651, Communion was ordered as follows:

Exhortation
  The proper use of the sacrament
Table
  The people were seated around or at a table for the sacred meal.
Words of Institution
  1 Corinthians 11:23–25
Eucharistic Prayer
  Thanksgiving for the great benefits of redemption
Invocation (*epiclesis*)
  The pastor asks the Holy Spirit to sanctify the bread and wine and bless his own ordinance.
Distribution of the Bread and Wine
Post-Communion Prayer
Communion Psalms
  Selected from their favorites: Psalms 23, 24, 34, 103, 113, 116, 118, and 133
Collection of Alms
  Given to the deacons for distribution to the poor.[39]

---

[37] Ibid., 129–130.
[38] Ibid., 218.
[39] Ibid.

RICHARD BAXTER'S SAVOY LITURGY OF 1661

Baxter's work is noted for its Scripture-infused phraseology, especially evident in the liturgy's exquisite prayers. The profound theology and rich devotional mood of his Communion service is that of the consummate pastor and theologian, which he was. We encourage our readers to read the full text of The Savoy Liturgy (outlined below) in Bard Thompson's *Liturgies of the Western Church*.[40]

> *The Order of Celebrating the Sacrament of the Body and Blood of Christ*
> **Explication**
>> The nature, use, and benefits of the sacrament (optional)
> **Exhortation**
>> A call for the people to come to the Lord's Table
> **Prayer**
>> Of confession, forgiveness, and full partaking
> **Blessing of the Bread and Wine**
> **Words of Institution**
> **Consecration of the Bread and Wine**
> **Breaking of the Bread and Pouring of the Wine**
> **Prayer** (*epiclesis*)
>> For the illumination and ministry of the Holy Spirit
> **Partaking of the Bread and the Cup** (optional liturgies)
> **Post-Communion Prayer**
> **Exhortation** (if time allows)
> **Hymn**
>> An appropriate Psalm (Psalms 23, 116, 100, 103, etc.), sung in meter
> **Blessing/Benediction**
>> (Hebrews 13:20, 21)

THE BOOK OF COMMON PRAYER, 1662

> **Exhortation**
>> A warning not to partake unworthily and calls to repent, to give "humble and hearty thanks" for Christ's atoning death, to give thanks for his "exceeding great love."
> **Invitation**
>> An invitation for the people to draw near in faith and "make your humble confession to Almighty God."

---

[40] Thompson, *Liturgies*, 393–405.

Confession
    A set prayer offered up in unison by all
Absolution
    Pronounced by the presiding priest or the bishop
Comfortable Words
    Comforting words of Christ, beginning with Matthew 11:28, followed by John 3:16, 1 Timothy 1:15, and 1 John 2:1. Concluded by a brief congregational response
Proper Preface
    A brief, single-sentence prayer ascribing all glory to God, concluding with a brief song or spoken response
Communion Prayer
    A prayer containing the affirmation, "We are not worthy so much as to gather up the crumbs from under Thy Table."
Prayer of Consecration
    Offered after the priest breaks the bread and takes the cup in his hands. Note: this prayer consecrates the bread and the wine for the "perpetual memory" of Christ's death, three times employing the dominical descriptive "remembrance."
Communion
    Served with Archbishop Cranmer's matchless injunctions
The Lord's Prayer
    The priest prays, with the people repeating every petition.
Prayer for Commitment and Heavenly Benediction
Doxology
    Said or sung
Blessing and Departure
Collection
    Given to the deacons for distribution to the poor.[41]

THE COMPLETE TEXTS OF THREE COMMUNION SERVICES FOR TODAY

Today, the strands of those early Protestant liturgies variously inform our observances of Communion across the spectrum of worship styles. Virtually all feature an invitation to the Lord's Table, a Communion prayer, the words of institution, prayers over the bread and wine, Christ's injunctions for partaking, a prayer of thanksgiving, and a benediction.

    Beyond that, contemporary liturgies vary widely in the use of the Lord's Prayer, doxologies, creeds, confessions, congregational responses, methods

---

[41] *The Book of Common Prayer* (Cambridge: Cambridge University Press, n.d.), 249–259.

of partaking, hymns and songs, offerings for the poor, and the fencing of the Table.

This said, all celebrations of the Lord's Table must be done with prayerful premeditation and intentionality because of the life-and-death theology that attends the Table, which seals the blessings of the new covenant to believers. It fires our remembrance of his body and blood broken and shed for us; it enhances the reality of our communion with Christ and one another as it is a participation in the body and blood of Christ; and it lifts the gospel high, as by eating the bread and drinking the cup we "proclaim the Lord's death until he comes" (1 Cor. 11:26).

The following sample Communion liturgies have been assembled using the "Resources" and "Hymns and Songs" sections of this chapter and the chapter on the creeds. We have done this to illustrate how to use this book to create your own services for your own contexts. Admittedly, these samples are done from a more traditional slant, but your choice of music will generally contextualize your observance of the Lord's Table. Also, the sample prayers need not be given word for word, but will serve well as templates or inspiration for "extemporaneous" prayers.

SAMPLE COMMUNION LITURGY #1

(Note: the service that preceded this observance of the Lord's Table included the Apostles' Creed, a prayer of confession, and the Lord's Prayer. Thus, none of these are included in this Communion liturgy. Here the sermon has concluded with prayer, and the pastors have descended the platform and have taken their places before the Table as the standing congregation sang a hymn.)

Invitation

Brothers and sisters, as we draw near to the Lord's Table to celebrate the Communion of the body and blood of Christ, we are grateful to remember that our Lord instituted this ordinance:

- For the perpetual memory of his dying for our sakes and the pledge of his undying love;
- As a bond of our union with him and each other as members of his mystical body;
- As a seal of his promises to us and a renewal of our obedience to him;
- For the blessed assurance of his presence with us who are gathered here in his name;

- As an opportunity for us who love the Savior to feed spiritually on him who is the Bread of Life; and
- As a pledge of his coming again.

Communion Prayer

Father in heaven, we bow our heads now because Jesus bowed his head and gave up his spirit. We bow in reverence, in respect, in awe, and in adoration for the *person* of Christ, the *words* of Christ, and today for the *cross* of Christ.

Fill us now and afresh with your Holy Spirit, so that our worship in this moment will bring true honor to you—Father, Son, and Holy Spirit—and genuine consolation to our souls.

We pray this in Jesus's name. Amen.

Fencing

This sacred time at the Lord's Table is for believers who have rested all their hope on the death and resurrection of Christ. If you are not yet a believer, you should refrain from partaking until you come to faith in Christ—and then joyfully partake along with the body of Christ.

We encourage those of you who are believers to examine your hearts, so that you can partake in a worthy manner. If your heart is not right, refrain until you can come freely to partake.

As the bread and the cup are served, we ask that you hold them, so that we all partake together.

The Bread

"For I received from the Lord what I also delivered to you, that the Lord Jesus on the night when he was betrayed took bread, and when he had given thanks, he broke it, and said, 'This is my body which is for you. Do this in remembrance of me'" (1 Cor. 11:23–24).

Prayer for the Bread

Christ Jesus, when you came into the world, you said to the Father: "Sacrifices and offerings you have not desired, but a body you have prepared for me; in burnt offerings and sin offerings you have taken no pleasure." Then you said, "Behold, I have come to do your will, O God, as it is written of me in the scroll of the book" (Heb. 10:5–7).

And then you came in the incarnation, and by a single offering of your body on the cross you achieved what all the offerings on Jewish altars could never accomplish—the complete forgiveness of our sins. Bread of heaven, as we now partake of the symbol, ravish our hearts and refresh our souls. Amen.

Distribution

Elders rise, receive the bread, and serve the congregation. Music (instrumental or choral) begins midway through the distribution of the bread so as to coincide with the completion. There are many wonderful hymns and songs to select from (see the list on page 455). For example, the congregation might sing together a line from "Come, Ye Disconsolate":

> Come, ye disconsolate, where'er ye languish,
> Come to the mercy seat, fervently kneel.
> Here bring your wounded hearts, here tell your anguish;
> Earth has no sorrow that heaven cannot heal.[42]

Partaking of the Bread

Jesus said: "This is my body which is for you. Do this in remembrance of me" (1 Cor. 11:24).

Silence

The Cup

"In the same way also he took the cup, after supper, saying, 'This cup is the new covenant in my blood. Do this, as often as you drink it, in remembrance of me'" (1 Cor. 11:25).

Prayer for the Cup

Our gracious God, we thank you this day for the new covenant, the covenant sealed through the blood of Jesus Christ, your Son. And we drink this cup in remembrance of Christ's sacrifice for our sins, asking him even now, through the Spirit, to commune with us as we commune with each other. With grateful hearts, O Christ, we drink of you and to you. Amen.

Distribution

Elders rise, receive the cup, and serve the congregation. As with the bread, music begins midway through the serving of the cup so as to coincide with the completion. Perhaps sing a line from "O Sacred Head Now Wounded":

> What language shall I borrow to thank Thee, dearest friend,
> For this Thy dying sorrow, Thy pity without end?
> O make me Thine forever, and should I fainting be,
> Lord, let me never, never outlive my love to Thee.

Partaking of the Cup

Jesus said, "Do this, as often as you drink it, in remembrance of me" (1 Cor. 11:25b).

---

[42] From the hymn "Come, Ye Disconsolate, Where'er Ye Languish" by Thomas More, 1816, and Thomas Hastings, 1832. For a newer rendition of this wonderful hymn, see Greg Wilbur's version at http://greyfriars press.com/?page_id=26

Silence

Care Offering

As we conclude this service, we provide opportunity for people to give to the care offering, which is used to assist people going through times of financial need. If you are aware of such needs in the body of Christ, please let us know by contacting an elder or pastor.

Hymn/Song

Benediction

"The grace of the Lord Jesus Christ and the love of God and the fellowship of the Holy Spirit be with you all" (2 Cor. 13:14). Amen.

SAMPLE COMMUNION LITURGY #2

Apostles' Creed

Let us all affirm our faith before coming to the Lord's Table. Christian, what do you believe?

I believe in God the Father Almighty,
creator of heaven and earth.
I believe in Jesus Christ,
his only Son, our Lord,
who was conceived by the Holy Spirit,
born of the virgin Mary,
suffered under Pontius Pilate,
was crucified, died, and was buried;
he descended into hell.
On the third day he rose again from the dead;
he ascended into heaven,
and is seated at the right hand of the Father;
from there he will come to judge
the living and the dead.
I believe in the Holy Spirit,
the holy catholic church,
the communion of the saints,
the forgiveness of sins,
the resurrection of the body,
and the life everlasting. Amen.

Invitation

This morning, through our celebration of the Lord's Supper, we proclaim the death of Christ. These elements, which represent the body and blood of Christ, are a visible sermon to us; they are the gospel in tangible form.

They proclaim to us the great drama of redemption in Christ: salvation in the *present* ("for as often as you eat this bread and drink the cup"), salvation in the *past* ("you proclaim the Lord's death"), and salvation in the *future* ("until he comes [again]," 1 Cor. 11:26).

It is our privilege to partake of this visible sermon.

Fencing

In the light of such a salvation, the apostle Paul warns us, "Whoever, therefore, eats the bread or drinks the cup of the Lord in an unworthy manner will be guilty concerning the body and blood of the Lord" (1 Cor. 11:27).

Before we partake of the Supper, let us examine ourselves, recognizing both the gravity of our sin and the weight of Christ's glorious sacrifice.

Institution

"For I received from the Lord what I also delivered to you, that the Lord Jesus on the night when he was betrayed took bread, and when he had given thanks, he broke it, and said, 'This is my body which is for you. Do this is remembrance of me.' In the same way also he took the cup, after supper, saying, 'This is the new covenant in my blood. Do this, as often as you drink it, in remembrance of me.' For as often as you eat this bread and drink the cup, you proclaim the Lord's death until he comes" (1 Cor. 11:23–26).

Communion Prayer and Confession

Heavenly Father, as we now celebrate this meal that you have prepared for us (a heavenly meal that reminds us of earthly realities), this bread and this cup are tangible and visible reminders of our sin and also of the supreme sacrifice of your Son (his body broken and his blood shed for us and for our salvation). So, Lord, as we meditate on the realities of our sin and your salvation, we ask for your help in fully confessing our sins in the silence as we prepare to solemnly partake of the body and blood of your Son.

Silence

Amen.

Prayer for the Bread

Lord Jesus, you said, "I am the living bread that came down from heaven. If anyone eats of this bread, he will live forever. And the bread that I will give for the life of the world is my flesh" (John 6:51). Shocking words, prophetic of the cross. Now, as we eat this bread, help our souls to ride the symbol to the deepest reality. You bore our sins in your body, you became sin for us, you suffered death in your body, and you were resurrected in your body. Bread of heaven, we feast in remembrance of your body given for us. Amen.

Distribution

Elders rise, receive the bread, and serve the congregation. Music (instrumental or choral) begins midway through the distribution of the bread and concludes when the elders are seated.

> What wondrous love is this, O my soul, O my soul!
> What wondrous love is this, O my soul!
> What wondrous love is this
> That caused the Lord of bliss
> To bear the dreadful curse for my soul, for my soul,
> To bear the dreadful curse for my soul![43]

Partaking of the Bread

The body of our Lord Jesus Christ, which is given for you, preserve your body and soul to everlasting life. Take and eat this in remembrance that Christ died for you, and feed on him in your heart by faith with thanksgiving.

Silence

Prayer for the Cup

Our dear Lord, as we prepare to drink the cup, we affirm with all our hearts:

> This is all my hope and peace,
> Nothing but the blood of Jesus;
> This is all my righteousness,
> Nothing but the blood of Jesus.

Distribution

Elders rise, receive the cup, and serve the congregation. As with the bread, the music begins midway through the distribution.

> See from His head, His hands, His feet,
> Sorrow and love flow mingled down!
> Did e'er such love and sorrow meet,
> Or thorns compose so rich a crown?[44]

Partaking of the Cup

The blood of our Lord Jesus Christ, which was shed for you, preserve your body and soul to everlasting life. Drink this in remembrance that Christ's blood was shed for you and be thankful.

---

[43] From the hymn "What Wondrous Love Is This," American folk hymn.
[44] From the hymn "When I Survey the Wondrous Cross" by Isaac Watts, 1707.

Silence

Hymn/Song of Thanksgiving

Benediction

The Lord bless you and keep you;
the Lord make his face shine upon you and be gracious to you;
the Lord lift up his countenance upon you and give you peace.
(Num. 6:24–26)

Sample Communion Liturgy #3

(Note: The sermon has concluded with prayer, and the pastors have descended the platform and taken their places before the Table as the standing congregation sang a hymn.)

Invitation

Listen to the inviting words of the Lord to his children: "Come to me, all who labor and are heavy laden, and I will give you rest" (Matt. 11:28). Listen also to the apostle Paul: "The saying is trustworthy and deserving of full acceptance, that Christ Jesus came into the world to save sinners" (1 Tim. 1:15). Finally, hear the apostle John: "But if anyone does sin, we have an advocate with the Father, Jesus Christ the righteous. He is the propitiation for our sins" (1 John 2:1–2).

With these words we invite you to the Lord's Table, which he has set for all his children. So let us now reverently and joyfully take our places.

Institution

Hear the words of institution: "For I received from the Lord what I also delivered to you, that the Lord Jesus on the night when he was betrayed took bread, and when he had given thanks, he broke it, and said, 'This is my body which is for you. Do this is remembrance of me.' In the same way also he took the cup, after supper, saying, 'This is the new covenant in my blood. Do this, as often as you drink it, in remembrance of me.' For as often as you eat this bread and drink the cup, you proclaim the Lord's death until he comes" (1 Cor. 11:23–26).

Communion Prayer

Merciful Lord, we do not presume to come to your Table trusting in our own righteousness, but in your many and great mercies. We are not worthy so much as to gather up the crumbs under your table. But you are the same Lord whose nature is always to have mercy. Grant us, therefore, gracious Lord, so to eat the flesh of your dear Son Jesus Christ and to drink his blood that we may evermore dwell in him and he in us. Amen.

Confession

Knowing that we are all sinners saved by grace and that we regularly sin in thought, word, and deed, let us confess our sins together:

Heavenly Father,
you have loved us with an everlasting love,
but we have often gone our own way
and rejected your will for our lives.
We are sorry for our sins
and turn away from them.
For the sake of your Son who died for us,
forgive us, cleanse us, and change us.
By your Holy Spirit, enable us to live for you
and to please you in every way,
for the glory of our Lord Jesus Christ. Amen.

"If we confess our sins, he is faithful and just to forgive us our sins and to cleanse us from all unrighteousness" (1 John 1:9).

Fencing

This is a meal for believers. Christians believe that Jesus truly lived, died, and rose from the dead. Christians also personally appropriate those historical realities. We believe that Jesus died for *our* sins. We believe that he was raised for *our* justification. We believe that he will return again in glory as the Lord of lords and King of kings.

If you do not yet believe this, we encourage you to refrain until you can partake worthily in full belief.

Prayer for the Bread

Our dear Lord, the bread that we are about to partake of is symbolic of the human body in which you dwelt incarnate among us, sinless, for thirty-three years. And when you were crucified, you bore our sins in your body on the tree, that we might die to sin and live to righteousness. And by your wounds we were healed (see 1 Pet. 2:24). You took our place and paid a price that we could never pay.

Seal this to our hearts as we eat the bread, representative of your body broken for us. Amen.

Distribution

Elders rise, receive the bread, and serve the congregation. Music (instrumental or choral) begins midway through the distribution of the bread and concludes when the elders are seated.

Partaking of the Bread

Take and eat this in remembrance that Christ died for you, and feed on him in your heart by faith with thanksgiving.

Silence

Prayer for the Cup

Jesus, lover of our souls, in Gethsemane you looked into the cup that you would have to drink in order to redeem us from our sins, and it was so awful that you prayed, "Abba, Father, all things are possible for you. Remove this cup from me. Yet not what I will, but what you will" (Mark 14:36).

And then you did the hardest thing ever done in time and eternity—you shed your blood to secure our salvation, so that we might sit here today at your Table and partake of the cup in deep remembrance of what you did for us on the cross. Thank you, Lord Jesus. Amen.

Distribution

Elders rise, receive the cup, and serve the congregation. As with the bread, the music begins midway through the distribution.

Partaking of the Cup

Drink this in remembrance that Christ's blood was shed for you, and be thankful.

Silence

Doxology

Praise God, from whom all blessings flow;
Praise Him, all creatures here below;
Praise Him above, ye heavenly host;
Praise Father, Son, and Holy Ghost.
Amen.

Benediction

Now to him who is able to keep you from stumbling and to present you blameless before the presence of his glory with great joy, to the only God, our Savior, through Jesus Christ our Lord, be glory, majesty, dominion, and authority, before all time and now and forever. Amen. (Jude 24–25)

HYMNS AND SONGS FOR COMMUNION

There are many wonderful songs to sing during or after Communion. A short list follows.[45]

---

[45] For more songs, see "Hymns and Songs by Season/Event," in Chapter 4.

OLD HYMNS

"Ah, Holy Jesus! How Hast Thou Offended?" (Heermann)
"Alas! And Did My Savior Bleed?" (Watts)
"Alleluia! Sing to Jesus" (Dix)
"At the Lamb's High Feast We Sing" (6th c. Latin)
"Come, All Ye Hungry, Pining Poor" (Steele)
"Go to Dark Gethsemane" (Montgomery)
"Jesus, Thy Blood and Righteousness" (von Zinzendorf)
"Jesus! What a Friend for Sinners" (Chapman)
"Let Thy Blood in Mercy Poured" (Greek hymn)
"Man of Sorrows, What a Name" (Bliss)
"My Song Is Love Unknown" (Crossman)
"O Bread of Life from Heaven" (trans. Schaff)
"O Living Bread from Heaven" (von Rist)
"O Sacred Head Now Wounded" (Bernard of Clairvaux)
"O the Deep, Deep Love of Jesus" (Francis)
"Stricken, Smitten, and Afflicted" (Kelly)
"The King of Love My Shepherd Is" (Baker)
"Were You There?" (spiritual)
"What Wondrous Love Is This" (American folk hymn)
"When I Survey the Wondrous Cross" (Watts)

NEWER HYMNS

"A Purple Robe, a Crown of Thorn" (Dudley-Smith)
"All Who Are Thirsty" (Perry)
"Behold the Lamb (Communion Hymn)" (Getty/Getty/Townend)
"Beneath the Cross of Jesus" (Getty/Getty)
"Communion Hymn for Christmas" (Clarkson)
"How Deep the Father's Love for Us" (Townend)
"I Am the Bread of Life" (Toolan)
"Lamb of God" (Paris)
"Lift Up Your Hearts unto the Lord" (Stassen)
"Merciful God" (Getty/Getty/Townend)
"Now the Feast and Celebration" (Haugen)
"So This Is the Day When His God Does Not Answer" (Idle)
"The Love of Christ Who Died for Me" (Dudley-Smith)
"There Is a Redeemer" (Green)

SPECIAL COMMUNION SERVICES

Many churches hold two or three special Communion services a year—a
Christmas Communion on a Sunday evening during the Advent season,

another on Good Friday, and perhaps a New Year's Communion service on the Sunday night before the new year or on New Year's Eve.

A typical New Year's Communion features extended singing, planned and/or spontaneous testimonies from the congregation, and a brief sermon followed by the observance of the Lord's Table. Such occasions often evince a lingering sweetness among Christ's gathered family, with memorable testimonies and an unhurried communal meal. Unlike Christmas, Good Friday, and Easter services, which have specific biblical texts, hymns, and songs that focus on the birth, death, and resurrection of Christ, these special Communion services have a more general theme of fellowship, notwithstanding the gospel proclamation of the Table. Thus, a relaxed, "unplanned" approach works well.

Christmas and Good Friday Communions naturally require more planning. Chapter 2, "Annual Services," contains three extensive liturgies for Good Friday. Here we provide an order for Christmas Communion to be observed on a Sunday evening of Advent, traditionally the Sunday before Christmas.

SAMPLE CHRISTMAS COMMUNION SERVICE

(Note: The Lord's Table here has been preceded by a choir singing "Hurry to Bethlehem!" followed by an opening hymn, a welcome and prayer, an extended carol sing interspersed with an offering and prayers, the preaching of the Word, a hymn, and then the affirmation of the Nicene Creed.)

Words of Institution
Communion Prayer
Fencing
Preparation for the Bread

> Lord Jesus, you said, "I am the living bread that came down from heaven. If anyone eats of this bread, he will live forever. And the bread that I will give for the life of the world is my flesh" (John 6:51). Shocking words that are prophetic of the cross.
>
> Now as we eat this bread, help our souls to ride the symbol to the deepest reality. You bore our sins in your body, you became sin for us, you suffered death in your body, and you were resurrected in your body. Bread of heaven, we feast in remembrance of your body given for us. Amen.

Distribution
Choral Meditation

> "The Blessed Son of God," R. Vaughan Williams

Before partaking of the bread, the congregation sings:

> Let all mortal flesh keep silence,
> And with fear and trembling stand;
> Ponder nothing earthly minded,
> For with blessing in his hand
> Christ our God to earth descendeth,
> Our full homage to demand.[46]

Partaking

The blood of our Lord Jesus Christ, which was shed for you, preserve your body and soul in everlasting life. Drink this in remembrance that Christ's blood was shed for you, and be thankful.

Preparation for the Cup

Jesus, lover of our souls, in Gethsemane you looked into the cup that you would have to drink in order to redeem us from our sins, and it was so awful that you prayed: "Abba, Father, all things are possible for you. Remove this cup from me. Yet not what I will but what you will" (Mark 14:36). And then you did the hardest thing ever done in time and eternity—you shed your blood to secure our salvation, so that we might sit here today at your Table and partake of the cup in deep remembrance of what you did for us on the cross. Thank you, Lord Jesus. Amen.

Distribution

A choir sings "The Cross" by Craig Courtney and Pamela Martin.

Before partaking of the cup, the congregation sings:

> King of kings, yet born of Mary,
> As of old on earth he stood,
> Lord of lords, in human vesture,
> In the body and the blood;
> He will give to all the faithful
> His own self for heavenly food.[47]

Partaking

The blood of our Lord Jesus Christ, which was shed for you, preserve your body and soul to everlasting life. Drink this in remembrance that Christ's blood was shed for you, and be thankful.

Benediction

"The grace of the Lord Jesus Christ and the love of God and the fellowship of the Holy Spirit be with you all" (2 Cor. 13:14). Amen.

---

[46] From the hymn "Let All Mortal Flesh Keep Silence," from Liturgy of St. James, 5th c. Adapted by Gerard Moultrie, 1864.

[47] Ibid.

Hymn
"Hark! The Herald Angels Sing"

COMMUNION QUESTIONS
FREQUENCY?

The biblical evidence about the frequency of Communion lends support to both ends of the spectrum—annual Communion and weekly Communion. Those who hold to an annual observance of the Lord's Table argue that it was instituted by Christ at the annual celebration of the Passover meal, when he sat at table with his disciples in the upper room. Additionally, the "as often" in the final sentence of his solemn words of institution ("For as often as you eat this bread and drink the cup," 1 Cor. 11:26) would have been understood by his observant Jewish disciples to mean an annual observance.

Those who hold to a weekly observance of the Lord's Table point to the texts that record the frequent observance of table fellowship in the apostolic church. One such text is Acts 2:46: "And day by day, attending the temple together and breaking bread in their homes, they received their food with glad and generous hearts." Yet, it can be questioned as to whether the "breaking bread" was always done sacramentally. The Corinthian church, so it seems, frequently held a putative sacramental observance of the Lord's Supper that (notwithstanding their scandalous abuse of it) argues for at least weekly, if not more frequent, observance. Thus, it seems probable that the apostolic church weekly came to the Lord's Table.

However, it does not follow *ipso facto* that the practice of the apostolic house churches is incumbent on all the succeeding gatherings of the church. Indeed, both Roman Catholic[48] and Protestant church history shows otherwise. Subsequent to the Reformation, Calvin argued for a weekly observance, but the Geneva city council chose to celebrate the Table quarterly.[49] Many churches in the Puritan and Scottish Presbyterian traditions elected to celebrate it only once a year because of their concern to fence the table, ensuring that only the regenerate partake and that they not partake unworthily.[50]

So what are we to do? At the very least, infrequent observance (or nonobservance!) of the Lord's Table is not optional. It is incumbent on all faithful believers under the new covenant to come to the Table regularly, just as the

---

[48] Old, *Worship*, 126 explains: "By the end of the Middle Ages, the Lord's Supper had already a long time before become the sacrifice of the Mass. . . . The awesome idea of eating Christ's flesh had led to the practice of receiving communion but once a year; even then, only the bread was eaten, and the cup was withheld from the people."
[49] Phillips, "The Lord's Supper," 220.
[50] Ibid.

observance of Passover was incumbent on all faithful Jews under the old covenant. Those who ignore the Lord's Supper disobey the divine imperatives to "Do this in remembrance of me" (Luke 22:19; cf. 1 Cor. 11:24). And by doing so, they imperil their spiritual health, if not their very souls. This is the great tragedy of today's "church hitchhiking culture," which leads professing believers to live apart from the regular ministry of the Word, without recognizing the spiritual benefits of church discipline and the Lord's Table.

What about the weekly observance of Communion? Certainly it has precedence in the apostolic church. Also, its practice means that every service ends centered on the gospel—the visible words of the bread and the wine. However, notwithstanding the protestations of the Brethren, Lutherans, and others, weekly observance runs the risk of becoming ritually rote and even commonplace if not ministered with great thought and prayerful care. And dare we enter the secular thought of logistics, because large churches, with two or three Sunday morning services (that cannot exceed specific time restraints), would necessarily have to shorten the length of the Scripture readings, the prayers, and the preaching of the Word to allow for a proper observance of the Table. There are some answers for a church that has multiple morning services, such as making the first service a Communion service, with the necessary abbreviations. Another is to observe Communion in the evening.

As for the majority of churches that observe Communion quarterly or monthly (frequencies that the Bible does not mention), the responsibility lies with the pastoral leadership to schedule the Lord's Table in a way that best serves the spiritual life of the people and then to spiritually prepare them in advance to partake and, of course, to conduct the service with fresh, prayerful thought and diligence.

PARTICIPATION?

When we fence the Table, we answer the question of who should take part: only those who believe in Christ. The Table is our *participation*, along with fellow believers, in the body and blood of Christ. A nonbeliever cannot truly participate and must not effect a seeming participation. The apostle Paul warns that alien participation may wreak havoc on the participant's soul: "For anyone who eats and drinks without discerning the body eats and drinks judgment on himself" (1 Cor. 11:29).

A second question centers on baptism. Many argue that only a baptized believer may participate in Communion, the logic being that baptism is a symbol of the *beginning* of the Christian life, while Communion is a symbol of *continuing* the Christian life. The former must precede the latter. But others, such as Grudem, object to such a restriction. Grudem argues:

> A different problem arises if someone who is a genuine believer, but not yet baptized, is *not* allowed to participate in the Lord's Supper when Christians get together. In that case the person's nonparticipation symbolizes that he or she is *not* a member of the body of Christ which is coming together to observe the Lord's Supper in a unified fellowship (see 1 Cor. 10:17: "Because there is one bread, we who are many are one body, for we all partake of the one bread"). Therefore churches may think it best to allow non-baptized believers to participate in the Lord's Supper but urge them to be baptized as soon as possible. For if they are willing to participate in an outward symbol of being a Christian, there seems no reason why they should not be willing to participate in the other, a symbol that appropriately comes first.
>
> Of course, the problems that arise in both situations (when unbaptized believers take Communion and when they do not) can be avoided if new Christians are regularly baptized shortly after they come to faith. And, whichever position a church takes on the question of whether unbaptized believers should take communion, in the teaching ministry of the church, it would seem wise to teach that the ideal situation is for new believers to be baptized and then to provide the Lord's Supper.[51]

This is tempered, thought-through, theological, and practical advice for readers who are of a Baptist persuasion. But for readers who are of the Reformed denominations (indeed, all paedobaptists), the questions and answers are necessarily different. The big question among the Reformed is, when may a baptized child participate in the Lord's Table? None have an indifferent attitude about the question, but some are more relaxed about it than others, believing that participation should be left to the discretion of the parents, who best know the hearts and theological comprehension of their own children. They argue that children by definition are not mature. However, as Douglas Wilson explains:

> Nowhere does the Scripture require *mature* faith in order to be built up by the grace of God. We speak English to our children before they understand it. This is how they come to understand it. We should instruct them through the Supper in a similar way. If children are mature enough

---

[51] Grudem, *Systematic Theology*, 996–997.

to receive simple instruction from their parents as they take the Supper, then they should be included in it. If the children are consistently bearing bad fruit (rebellion, defiance, etc.), then the parents should bring the concern to the elders, who should consider suspension from the Supper, accompanied by instruction.[52]

Clearly this approach places a child's initial participation in Communion wholly at the discretion of the parents. This will likely work well if the parents are themselves well-grounded in the Scriptures, spiritually mature, and discerning. But this is not the case with many young parents today, though they may be members of fine churches.

Therefore, others counsel a more conservative, structured approach that recognizes the distinction between communing and non-communing members of the church, the non-communing members being baptized children who have not been admitted to the Lord's Table. In this approach, the children are taken through a process of confirmation to ensure that they have been adequately instructed in the faith and have given clear testimony of saving faith in Christ before being admitted to the Lord's Table as full communing members. See the discussion on a service of confirmation in chapter 8, "Baptism."

In the delicate deliberation about who may participate in the Lord's Table, both Baptists and paedobaptists must avoid rigid, intractable application of rules, especially in respect to children. Children's spiritual calendars vary greatly. The observable growth of their bodies makes this clear. Some shoot up tall and gangly as preadolescent giants, only to be dwarfed by some late-bloomers in high school. It is the same with spiritual development. Some sprout early, while others destined for equal or greater spiritual growth grow later, according to their own mysterious spiritual clocks. The church is not Microsoft Corp.—it is a family.

PARTAKING WORTHILY?

The apostle Paul addresses the subject, declaring: "Whoever, therefore, eats the bread or drinks the cup of the Lord in an unworthy manner will be guilty concerning the body and blood of the Lord. Let a person examine himself, then, and so eat of the bread and drink of the cup. For anyone who eats and drinks without discerning the body eats and drinks judgment on himself. That is why many of you are weak and ill, and some have died" (1 Cor. 11:27–30).

---

[52] Douglas Wilson, *Mother Kirk: Essays and Forays in Practical Ecclesiology* (Moscow, ID: Canon, 2001), 107.

Those who unworthily partook did so because they did not "discern the body." This can be understood in two ways. First, it may be that *body* is a synecdoche (literary shorthand, where the part refers to the whole), so that it refers to the body and the blood of Christ symbolized in the bread and the cup—Christ's atoning death. Second, *body* may refer to the church, the body of Christ. This seems to be what is meant here, because earlier in the discussion Paul says, "The bread that we break, is it not a participation [*koinonia*] in the body of Christ?" (1 Cor. 10:16b).

Thus, we understand that to partake "in an unworthy manner" was to partake of the Lord's Table with disregard for others in the body of Christ. And this is apparently what the "haves" were doing in Corinth, as Paul describes it: "When you come together, it is not the Lord's supper that you eat. For in eating, each one goes ahead with his own meal. One goes hungry, another gets drunk. What! Do you not have houses to eat and drink in? Or do you despise the church of God and humiliate those who have nothing? What shall I say to you? Shall I commend you in this? No, I will not" (1 Cor. 11:20–22). Partaking worthily of the Table begins with remembering the union and fellowship that believers share in Christ and treating everyone with deference and loving respect. If one partakes of the Lord's Supper with disrespect or disregard for others at the Table, it is no longer the Lord's Supper.

We partake worthily:

- By discerning the body of Christ sharing the meal with us and loving one another and giving preference to all. This is the primary emphasis of the text.
- By confessing all known sins, especially as they relate to others. We cannot partake in a worthy manner while refusing to repent.
- By reverently partaking, not like the gluttonous me-first denizens of the Corinthian church.
- By conscious, volitional remembrance, seriously internalizing Christ's "Do this in remembrance of me" commands.
- By never allowing the Table to become routine, as if the Table somehow functioned *ex opere operato* and all we have to do is eat and drink what is passed to us.

Every Lord's Table is an occasion for self examination—"Let a person examine himself . . . and so eat of the bread and drink of the cup" (1 Cor. 11:28). The sense of the word is serious self-examination. This done, we can eat the bread and drink the cup, and thereby joyfully proclaim the Lord's death until he comes!

PART 3

MINISTERIAL DUTIES

10

Pastoral Counseling

By Robert W. Evans[1]

As always, he was clear and concise. My good friend Kent Hughes had called me to ask if I would contribute a chapter on pastoral counseling to this book. "Bob," he said, "be comprehensive and detailed, yet completely accessible; informal and casual, yet buttoned-up theologically, psychologically, and pastorally. Be sure to make it highly practical, including useful tidbits for the pastor, even some humor. You have eight thousand to ten thousand words . . . fifteen thousand if you like . . . or more if you want."

Instructions in hand, I hung up the phone, gently leaned back in my chair, breathed out a slow and heavy sigh, and stared out my office window for a few quiet moments. It wasn't long before my mind had drifted and recovered a faint memory of an old final exam joke that had made the rounds a number of years ago: "Define the universe. Give three examples." It seemed that the project before me was of a similar magnitude. "Shouldn't be a problem," I had cheerfully replied to Kent before we ended our conversation. For the life of me, I don't know what I was thinking at the time. But such is my task.

Of course, it is unrealistic to think that I could summarize thirty-plus years of counseling education, training, and experience, and provide you with everything that you need to know to be a competent pastoral counselor, in a single book chapter. Nor could I hope to produce an academic piece of writing that exhaustively canvasses the literature, evenhandedly sifts through

[1] Robert W. Evans is pastor-teacher at Christ Church in Pleasanton, California, and president of Veritas Ministries International. He has a PhD in clinical psychology and a PhD in systematic theology, having received his education at UCLA, UC Berkeley, Fuller Theological Seminary, Trinity Evangelical Divinity School, and Harvard University, among others. Prior to his call to full-time ministry, he was a psychologist in both hospital and private practice.

various theories and data, and advances the field of clinical pastoral counseling. Space limitations will also necessarily put many important questions and tensions associated with pastoral counseling broadly, and the relationship between psychology and theology specifically, to the side. Elsewhere, I have given my voice to a small sliver of some of those issues.[2] Here my aim is far more modest. I strive to offer a rather sweeping and largely unapologetic introduction to the basics of effective pastoral counseling—essentials of theory and practice, if you will—that I have found useful over my years of working with others in the counseling context. Should these insights and suggestions result in God's greater glory, advance the cause of Christ and his gospel, and further equip you to minister more faithfully and effectively to those in need, I will be especially grateful.

A BIBLICAL-THEOLOGICAL RATIONALE FOR PASTORAL COUNSELING

We have been called to pastor, a word that means "shepherd." Perhaps more than any other passage, the sustained imagery of Jesus as the Good Shepherd of the sheep in John 10 paints for us the portrait of our calling as shepherds in the care of God's people.[3] Jesus is our exemplar—the pattern for how we are to serve those who have been entrusted to our temporal pastorage.

The main focus of John's Gospel is christological—he is keen to reveal Jesus as the divine Christ—and John 10 ushers that primary purpose to center stage. Throughout John 10, Jesus makes frequent use of the shepherd/sheep motif to illustrate his unique relationship with the Father and his sacrificial and sustaining relationship with those entrusted to him by the Father. Jesus is most immediately addressing those who have been calling into question his identity and purposes, and contrasting himself with them. Jesus is the Good Shepherd who calls and cares for his Father's sheep. By contrast, the religious leaders were derelict shepherds—"thieves and robbers," Jesus said, who gain unauthorized access to the sheep and abuse them (John 10:1).

---

[2] For example, see Robert W. Evans, "The Jurisprudence of Moral Responsibility: Toward a Descriptive Theory of the Relative Contributions of Moral Philosophy, Christian Theology, and Behavioral Medicine to the Origins and Historical Development of the Insanity Defense and Mental Elements of Crime" (PhD dissertation, Trinity Evangelical Divinity School, 2000); Robert W. Evans, "Neuropsychological Aspects of Aging and Their Implications for Decision-Making Among the Elderly," in *Aging, Death, and the Quest for Immortality*, C. Ben Mitchell, Robert D. Orr, and Susan A. Salladay, eds. (Grand Rapids: Eerdmans, 2004), 75–86; and R. W. Evans, "Recent Developments in Behavioral Neurology and Their Implications for the Existence and Care of Human Souls," paper presented at the Evangelical Theological Society Annual Meeting (Washington, DC, November 2006).

[3] For an excellent treatment of the shepherd/sheep theme in John 10, see D. A. Carson, *The Gospel According to John*, Pillar New Testament Commentary (Grand Rapids: Eerdmans, 1991), 379–395.

It is interesting that Jesus assumes two different metaphorical roles within the overarching sheep/shepherd theme in John 10. First, Jesus says that he is the Good Shepherd, who presents himself at the gate and calls out his own; his sheep hear his voice and push through the other woolies to follow him (John 10:2–4). Second, he says that he is the door through which the sheep enter and are saved, and thus gain access to pasture (John 10:7–9). Each metaphor within a metaphor, if you will, is instructive for pastoring.

In the first instance, we are to imagine a large enclosed pen, perhaps near the town, in which several shepherds placed their sheep at night. The shepherds would entrust the care of their sheep to a watchman—an under-shepherd—who guarded the gate to the fold.[4] In the morning, the shepherds would return to the mixed fold of sheep, present themselves to the watch-man, and call for their sheep. In Jesus's case, he calls out his own sheep by name and leads them out (John 10:3). The shepherd knows his sheep, his sheep know him, and his flock responds to his voice and follows only him.

In the second instance, we are to imagine that the sheep are being kept not in a mixed fold in a pen adjacent to the town, but as a flock with their own shepherd out in the countryside at night. With no available natural enclosures, the shepherd would construct a pen from rocks or thicket, lead his sheep in, and lay down across the opening, thereby serving as the protec-tive gate. In the morning, the sheep were led out to safe pasture, where they would feed.

Reading the opening verses of John 10, one hears echoes from the Old Testament, perhaps most notably Ezekiel 34, where many of the same roles and responsibilities of shepherding appear.[5] As in John 10, Ezekiel 34 in-volves a contrast between faithful and unfaithful shepherding.

In Ezekiel 34, God denounces "the shepherds of Israel" (v. 1) for fleecing and brutalizing his sheep. The leaders had slaughtered the best of the ani-mals, fed themselves the choicest portions, clothed themselves in the finest wool, and completely shirked their responsibilities in caring for the people, so God sharply rebukes them: "Thus says the Lord GOD: Ah, shepherds of Israel who have been feeding yourselves! Should not shepherds feed the

---

[4] While commentators and preachers are surely right to focus on the role of Jesus as the Good Shepherd in John 10 in keeping with John's central christological concern, we should not overlook mention of "the gatekeeper," who functions as an undershepherd (John 10:3). It is to the undershepherd that the shepherd entrusts primary care for his sheep while he departs home for a time. But the shepherd's absence is only temporary. He will soon return and present himself to the undershepherd to collect his sheep. Of course, with the entrustment of his sheep to the undershepherd comes the expectation that his sheep—those whom he loves and knows by name—will be well tended, fed, and protected during his leave. The implications for pastoring (i.e., undershepherding) are numerous and clear.
[5] Similar themes are found in Ps. 23; 80:1; Isa. 40:11; 56:9–12; Jer. 23:1–14; 25:32–38; Zech. 11.

sheep? You eat the fat, you clothe yourself with the wool, you slaughter the fat ones, but you do not feed the sheep. The weak you have not strengthened, the sick you have not healed, the injured you have not bound up, the strayed you have not brought back, the lost you have not sought, and with force and harshness you have ruled them" (vv. 2b–4). What an indictment! As a consequence of their selfishness and brutality, God said that his sheep were starving and scattered—left helpless, vulnerable, and alone (vv. 6, 8). Those are heavy words.

It is difficult to imagine a more desperate situation for sheep than to be abused by the very ones who are charged with their care. Sheep don't fare well on their own—they require faithful shepherds whom they know and trust. Sheep need a good shepherd. They need the kind of shepherd that God describes in the verses that follow after his denouncement of the treacherous shepherds in Ezekiel 34: "Therefore, you shepherds, hear the word of the LORD. . . . I will rescue my sheep. . . . I myself will search for my sheep. . . . I will bring them out from the peoples and gather them from the countries. . . . I will feed them with good pasture. . . . I myself will make them lie down. . . . I will bind up the injured, and I will strengthen the weak, and the fat and the strong I will destroy. I will feed them in justice. . . . I will rescue my flock; they shall no longer be a prey" (vv. 9–22a). What a beautiful picture of faithful shepherding.

If Jesus is pulling forward various Old Testament shepherd/sheep metaphors in his encounter with the religious leaders of his day in John 10 and bringing them to bear on what he means when he refers to himself as "the good shepherd" (v. 11), then we glean important and practical lessons that instruct us on the proper heart and task of faithful shepherding. Five themes emerge from the recurring sheep/shepherd theme found in John 10 and Ezekiel 34:

1. *Faithful shepherds feed their sheep.* "Should not shepherds feed the sheep? . . . And I will feed them on the mountains of Israel, by the ravines, and in all the inhabited places of the country. I will feed them with good pasture, and on the mountain heights of Israel shall be their grazing land. There they shall lie down in good grazing land, and on rich pasture they shall feed on the mountains of Israel. . . . And I will set up over them one shepherd, my servant David, and he shall feed them: he shall feed them and be their shepherd" (Ezek. 34:2b, 13b–14, 23).

2. *Faithful shepherds know their sheep.* "To him the gatekeeper opens. The sheep hear his voice, and he calls his own sheep by name and leads them out. . . . I am the good shepherd. I know my own and my own know

me. . . . My sheep hear my voice, and I know them, and they follow me" (John 10:3, 14, 27).

3. *Faithful shepherds love their sheep.* "I am the good shepherd. The good shepherd lays down his life for the sheep. He who is a hired hand and not a shepherd, who does not own the sheep, sees the wolf coming and leaves the sheep and flees, and the wolf snatches them and scatters them. He flees because he is a hired hand and cares nothing for the sheep. I am the good shepherd. . . . I lay down my life for the sheep. . . . For this reason the Father loves me, because I lay down my life that I may take it up again. No one takes it from me, but I lay it down of my own accord. I have authority to lay it down, and I have authority to take it up again. This charge I have received from my Father" (John 10:11–14a, 15b, 17–18).[6]

4. *Faithful shepherds lead their sheep.* "For thus says the Lord GOD: Behold, I, I myself will search for my sheep and will seek them out. As a shepherd seeks out his flock when he is among his sheep that have been scattered, so will I seek out my sheep, and I will rescue them from all places where they have been scattered on a day of clouds and thick darkness. And I will bring them out from the peoples and gather them from the countries, and will bring them into their own land. . . . I will seek the lost, and I will bring back the strayed, and I will bind up the injured" (Ezek. 34:11–16a). "The sheep hear his voice, and he calls his own sheep by name and leads them out. When he has brought out all his own, he goes before them, and the sheep follow him, for they know his voice" (John 10:3a–4).

5. *Faithful shepherds protect their sheep.* "I will rescue my flock; they shall no longer be a prey. . . . I will make with them a covenant of peace and banish wild beasts from the land, so that they may dwell securely in the wilderness and sleep in the woods. . . . And the trees of the field shall yield their fruit, and the earth shall yield its increase, and they shall be secure in their land. And they shall know that I am the LORD. . . . They shall no more be a prey to the nations, nor shall the beasts of the land devour them. They shall dwell securely, and none shall make them afraid" (Ezek. 34:22a, 25, 27–28). "So Jesus again said to them, 'Truly, truly, I say to you, I am the door of the sheep. . . . I am the door. If anyone enters by me, he will be saved and will go in and out and find pasture. The thief comes only to steal and kill and destroy. I came that they may have life and have it abundantly. . . . I give them

---

[6] The depth of Jesus's love for his sheep is brought home with tremendous force when we compare his statements in John 10 with what he said as recorded in John 15:12–13: "This is my commandment, that you love one another as I have loved you. Greater love has no one than this, that someone lay down his life for his friends."

eternal life, and they will never perish, and no one will snatch them out of my hand. My Father, who has given them to me, is greater than all, and no one is able to snatch them out of the Father's hand'" (John 10:7, 9–10, 28–29).

The faithful shepherd is the one who feeds, knows, loves, leads, and protects God's sheep. Supremely, the Good Shepherd is Jesus. But proximately, the role of shepherding has been given to pastors; we are the undershepherds, if you will, who have been called and charged with both the responsibility and privilege of faithfully feeding and caring for God's flock.

Frequently, shepherding involves getting in front of the gathered flock and leading them to pasture and safety. However, even a quick glance through the various biblical sheep/shepherd images reveals the personal care that the Good Shepherd extends to individual sheep. Like Jesus, the faithful undershepherd leaves the ninety-nine to go after the one (Matt. 18:12), seeks out every scattered sheep (Ezek. 34:11–12a), rescues every sheep (Ezek. 34:12b), brings back every stray sheep (Ezek. 34:16a), binds up the wounds of every injured sheep (Ezek. 34:16b), strengthens every weak sheep (Ezek. 34:16c), protects every sheep (John 10:28–29), and dies a death that is individually applied to every one of his sheep (John 6:35–40).

So there is both a corporate and an individual aspect to the care that faithful undershepherds provide for God's sheep. On this view, we might say that pastoral counseling is individual sheep-tending, fulfilling our calling as undershepherds in the care of one (or a couple) of sheep in need of specific attention, and doing so after the example of the Good Shepherd.

WHAT IS PASTORAL COUNSELING?
The Philosophy of Pastoral Counseling

To our great comfort and joy, the apostle Paul confidently asserts, "And I am sure of this, that he who began a good work in you will bring it to completion at the day of Jesus Christ" (Phil. 1:6). Shortly thereafter Paul writes, "it is God who works in you, both to will and to work for his good pleasure" (Phil. 2:13). Mindful that it is God who is at work, and that it is "he who began a good work" in us who brings it to completion, the pastoral counselor seeks to create an interpersonal environment that is conducive to God's Spirit doing his work in the life of another.

It is the Spirit's interior presence that persistently refines the believer's life.[7] Progressive renovation follows thorough regeneration, and the Christian is inexorably moved further along in the spectrum of spiritual maturity

---

[7] I address working with unbelievers later in this chapter.

and conformity to Christ—such is the process of sanctification. The day will come when all things will be put right and the final vestiges of sin will be fully and finally removed, but until we enter into that blessed state on the other side of glory, God's Spirit will continue renewing our spiritual lives.

Of course, the spiritual branches of our new life in Christ rarely flower and bear fruit without pruning. The writer of Hebrews reminds us that God trims with the tool of discipline the one he loves (Heb. 12:5–6).[8] Times of pruning can be as confusing as they are painful; it is little wonder that we so easily lose sight of the fact that God is lovingly working *all things* together for his greater glory and our ultimate good.[9]

Properly understood, God's discipline is an expression of his grace toward us. And, far from being something we should seek to avoid, it is a part of the refining process in which we are to participate actively. As the writer of Hebrews put it, we are to "lay aside every weight, and sin which clings so closely" as we run the race of faith (12:1). We are to cooperate with God's Spirit in our sanctification. But we often need help identifying weights, putting off sin, and remaining encouraged and supported through the renovation process. It is often the feelings of confusion and seeming defeat associated with times of pruning and spiritual refinement that precipitate a request for pastoral counseling among those within whom God "began a good work."

The spiritual life also occasionally stumbles because we live as fallen people in a fallen world, and the enemy of our souls seeks toeholds in our hearts and minds from which to launch assaults on our growth in the gospel. When Satan is successful in tempting one to sin, expect him subsequently to wield the double-edged sword of doubt and discouragement in the life of that believer—features that are often present in those who come for pastoral counseling.

Whatever the reason for referral, the faithful pastoral counselor works in cooperation with the Holy Spirit to help God's people live and grow into maturity in Christ. Practically, that involves, among other things, reminding people of the greatness of God and the presence, power, and provisions of his Spirit in their lives. It involves bringing the Christian back to God's Word as the final source for determining what is holy, true, and good, and the grounding for all comfort, encouragement, and hope. It involves helping bewildered, wounded, weak, neglected, discouraged, and wandering sheep

---

[8] The writer of Heb. 12:5–6 bundles together Prov. 3:11–12; Job 5:17; Ps. 94:12; 119:67, 75.
[9] By "good," Rom. 8:28 means that which serves God's purpose in conforming us to the image of Christ, in contrast to what feels, seems, or looks "good" from the human vantage point, as that term has come to be more commonly understood today.

locate their individual life stories within the trajectory of God's overarching story of redemptive history. It involves feeding, knowing, loving, leading, and protecting through instruction, encouragement, support, and example—always with a view toward restoration and reconciliation—those who are part of God's flock, that they may grow in the grace of the gospel and be properly related to the Father and others. In short, the attitudinal posture of the pastoral counselor is to shepherd God's sheep as the Good Shepherd shepherds God's sheep. Keep that attitude in mind as you approach and counsel others.

THE NATURE OF PASTORAL COUNSELING

Most broadly described, pastoral counseling is a structured relationship between an individual and a pastor that is directed at providing help in discovering, choosing, and attaining specific appropriate goals consistent with Scripture and spiritual growth. In describing the pastoral counseling relationship as structured, I am distinguishing pastoral *counseling* from pastoral *care*, which may be described as the relatively unstructured conversations and involvements that pastors have with others.

Most pastors are involved in daily pastoral care, whether they provide counseling or not. Pastoral-care encounters are often spontaneous and may occur either inside or outside the church. Wherever we go as pastors, we serve as public symbols of the sacred and often find that people turn to us for spiritual and emotional encouragement and support, whether in a home, a restaurant, a grocery aisle, a neighborhood park, a hospital room, a funeral home, or following services and church meetings, to name just a few examples.

By contrast, pastoral counseling usually occurs when someone either desires or needs more intensive and focused pastoral involvement, and when such is offered within the context of a specified time arrangement and in a specified place. Furthermore, pastoral counseling focuses on realizing specific, observably manifest changes in thinking, feeling, and/or behaving, in contrast to pastoral care, which is not usually goal-directed, but is rather an interaction that offers more general affirmation, encouragement, and support. Of course, pastoral-care contacts sometimes transition into pastoral-counseling opportunities.

Doubtless, some with clinical counseling training see similarities between pastoral counseling and psychotherapy, but I also draw distinctions here. Like pastoral counseling, psychotherapy entails specified time and setting arrangements, but psychotherapy is usually more open-ended than counseling and often focuses on helping others understand the underlying dynamics that have conspired to shape their thoughts, feelings, and/or behavior rather than on realizing specified goals. That is not to say that psychotherapy is unconcerned with behavioral changes, but to emphasize that psychotherapy tends to place greater emphasis on the past than does counseling. At the risk of oversimplifying, we might say that psychotherapy is primarily concerned with understanding the past in ways that affect the present, whereas pastoral counseling is primarily concerned with understanding the present in ways that will affect the future. Accordingly, psychotherapy tends to be somewhat less goal-directed and more reflective than pastoral counseling, though, as we shall see, pastoral counseling is not merely telling people what to do or not do.

CHARACTERISTICS OF EFFECTIVE PASTORAL COUNSELORS

Your effectiveness as a counselor (or a pastor, for that matter) is far more dependent upon who you are than upon what you know or what you do. Now, please don't misunderstand me. I am not diminishing the importance of education, training, or experience. We must have our doctrine right, labor hard at preaching well and thinking clearly, and take advantage of every sound opportunity to put a fine edge on our pastoral skills. But ministry is, essentially, a character calling, and no amount of education, training, or experience will offset a flawed character.

Of course, you need not be perfect—none save Christ is—but to engage in faithful and effective pastoral counseling, you need to give irreproachable evidence of having been truly redeemed by the grace of the gospel and authentically bent toward God's heart. Typically, the effective pastoral counselor:

1. Is genuinely redeemed by the glorious gospel of grace, through faith and repentance, and strives daily to live in obedience to Christ's commands;
2. Has crafted a mature, responsible, and integrated biblical-theological worldview and sees others, and contemporary events and issues, through the lens of that worldview;
3. Is a man marked by authenticity and honesty, matched by personal maturity and humility;
4. Displays a warm and gracious spirit that communicates care, gentleness, and respect for others;
5. Is approachable;

6. Has an understanding heart;
7. Is unusually gifted at listening actively, deeply, and patiently;
8. Is able to reach out and help others without becoming personally affected;
9. Has a keen ability to bring one's issues and problems into clear focus and direct them toward a future goal;
10. Carries himself with a demeanor that inspires trust, credibility, hope, and confidence in others;
11. Is deeply reflective, understands himself, and thinks about his actions, feelings, commitments, and motivations;
12. Has well-defined limits and exceptional self-control;
13. Respects himself and does not use others to satisfy his own desires or needs;
14. Possesses a specific fund of biblical-theological knowledge and is exceedingly wise in applying the same in ways that are helpful to another;
15. Seeks to understand, not harshly judge, others—is not judgmental in attitude (Matt. 7:1), but "judge[s] with right judgment" (John 7:24);
16. Possesses the ability to reason systematically and to conceptualize issues;
17. Is able to discern unconscious themes and self-defeating patterns;
18. Is skillful at helping others to see themselves for who they *truly* are and envisioning who God would have them be; and
19. Possesses nonspecific factors of an effective counselor—in other words, there are some who, for reasons difficult to describe or measure, are just the kind of people to whom others are drawn when in need; perhaps it is a sense of the personal presence of God's Spirit in the life of the counselor.

I wish I could say that I have always modeled these characteristics. The truth is that I have fallen far short. It is with considerable embarrassment that I openly confess that I have not always been the kind of man that I have described above. I have had to do hard work with God, and he with me—a work that is, gratefully, ongoing. But I have traveled the path of discipleship long enough to know that I am likely not alone in having to make that admission.

Men, I encourage you to take honest and prayerful inventory of the characteristics listed above. Take before the Lord those character issues that need attention and seek, by God's gracious aid and in an accountability relationship with another, to bring those areas under the Father's control. Do that before offering yourself as a counselor, for we cannot credibly bring others to a spiritual place where we have not ourselves gone.

SPIRITUAL AND PSYCHOLOGICAL
CHARACTERISTICS OF HEALTHY PEOPLE

Many people are fascinated by the mechanisms of a deviant mind. Hollywood understands that curious allure and has turned it into a series of highly successful television programs, such as *Profiler, Criminal Minds, Law & Order: Criminal Intent,* and *Hannibal,* and a raft of movies, including the blockbuster 1991 movie *The Silence of the Lambs* and its sequels. Universities and colleges also understand the attraction and often reserve one of their larger lecture halls for undergraduate courses in abnormal psychology, where astonished freshmen sit in rapt silence as the various disorders and deviances of the human psyche are descriptively put on display.

In graduate school, one must complete a certain number of hours in "abnormal psychology" to satisfy degree and eligibility requirements to become licensed as a psychologist. These graduate courses in abnormal psychology often take psychologists-in-training deep into the recesses of all things psychiatrically askew. It's riveting stuff, even if it does spoil one for enjoying psychological thrillers and late-night reruns of *The Bob Newhart Show.*

The chief publication with which psychologists become thoroughly familiar is the *Diagnostic and Statistical Manual of Mental Disorders* (DSM), a publication of the American Psychiatric Association that categorizes all the mental-health disorders of both children and adults.[10] Mental-health professionals use this manual in order to better understand what is "abnormal" about the patterns of thinking, feeling, and behaving that they encounter in counseling situations and to help generate possible treatment protocols and file paperwork for insurance reimbursement.[11]

But for all the courses that I took in "abnormal psychology," I never had a course in "normal psychology." Curiosity mingled with mild humor one day, and I leaned over to a classmate during a lecture on some mental disorder and whispered, "OK, so I know what they *shouldn't* be thinking and doing, but what *should* they be thinking and doing?" Quite frankly, we received little instruction on what constitutes a "healthy" person. However, one thing was made abundantly clear: the absence of disease is not the same thing as the presence of health. So what are the characteristics of fully functioning, healthy people?

[10] The designation DSM is followed by a number that identifies its edition (e.g., DSM-V). When an edition is revised, an "R" is placed after the edition number (e.g., DSM-III-R). When text sections are updated and the revisions are more modest, the designation TR "text revision" is appended (e.g., DSM-IV-TR).
[11] It is common for those in the mental-health field to causally refer to the DSM as their "bible," an unfortunate label that has, understandably, served to heighten distrust of the mental-health professions among some Christians.

Of course, Scripture provides the definitive statement on what is normal, healthy, and desirable character and behavior. The Bible teaches that the life truly transformed by the grace of the gospel and submitted in joyful obedience to God gives unmistakable evidence of conversion. Salvation involves transformation. Surely when all things become new, it is unimaginable to think that changes will not occur and be made manifest in thought, feeling, and action (e.g., 2 Cor. 5:17; Eph. 2:4–10; Col. 3:5–17; Heb. 10:19–25). And the apostle Paul writes that the indwelling presence, power, and provisions of God's Spirit in the redeemed life produces spiritual fruit (Gal. 5:22–26). In short, all behavior, thoughts, and feelings are to be ultimately measured, nurtured, and tested by the Word of God.

With that said, I want to offer some characteristics commonly believed to mark psychological health. I offer these qualities not to supplant Scripture, but because they correlate well with spiritual maturity.

1. *Authenticity*. Healthy people are consistent with themselves and consistent across situations; they know who they really are, don't bluff or put on airs, and are genuinely themselves at all times and in all circumstances.
2. *Commitment*. Healthy people are able to make commitments and follow through on the same; they are trustworthy, reliable, and dependable.
3. *Self-control*. Healthy people are aware of their impulses, tendencies, and desires, and they keep their emotions and behavior in check.
4. *Competence*. Healthy people are proficient at things; they realize their relative strengths (and weaknesses) and derive enjoyment in doing what they are good at and satisfaction in exercising their giftedness and talents for the benefit of others.
5. *Creativity*. Healthy people express their thoughts and feelings in ways that inspire, encourage, help, and build up others.
6. *Self-awareness*. Healthy people are aware of their personality and individuality, including their traits, tendencies, feelings, and behavior.
7. *Tolerance of ambiguity*. Healthy people are able to hold certain thoughts, beliefs, and feelings in tension as necessary; they avoid clichés and hackneyed catchphrases, and eschew oversimplifying those mysteries that God has seen fit, according to his great wisdom, to keep veiled.

Now, this list is certainly not exhaustive, but it captures important features associated with personal maturity and psychological health. I find that these characteristics are useful in helping to develop a quick "snapshot" of the emotional and psychological development of the counselee, establishing a baseline against which to measure counseling progress and identifying portals through which to enter and explore the underlying spiritual condition of the person.

THE PRACTICE OF EFFECTIVE COUNSELING

I have sketched some very basic introductory thoughts concerning the biblical-theological rationale for pastoral counseling, the philosophy and nature of pastoral counseling, the qualities that make for an effective pastoral counselor, and the characteristics of a Spirit-filled and psychological healthy person. Let me now turn from theory to practice.

Receiving Referrals for Pastoral Counseling

Ideally, the prospective counselee initiates contact and makes a direct request of you for counseling. The benefits of a counselee-initiated request are tremendous: first, it suggests that the counselee has some awareness that there is a problem; and second, it suggests that there is some level of motivation to do something about it.

When I was in private practice as a psychologist, I was sometimes assigned court-ordered therapy referrals. Rarely was counseling effective under those circumstances, as the counselee sensed little, if any, need for service or desire to invest into the process. Acknowledgment of a problem and the desire to see things change are critical elements for counseling success, and self-referrals usually provide you with the best early gauge of the same.

Occasionally a third party approaches me about seeing someone not present. "Pastor, Susie seems to be pretty down, and I was wondering if she should see you for counseling? Maybe you could call her." In most cases, I reply: "I appreciate your concern for her and your confidence in me. Would you please ask her to contact me? Here's my card. And please tell her that I am happy to receive her call and that I am very much looking forward to speaking with her." I have found that approach highly effective.[12]

Of course, there are some conditions under which a self-referral is unrealistic. For example, I initiate contact when the prospective counselee is hospitalized, legally detained, suicidal, intoxicated, gravely disabled, or otherwise so situated that she could not reasonably make her own request for help. I also take the initiative if the prospective counselee is either actively engaged in or seriously contemplating an unbiblical, immoral, or illegal course of

---

[12] I am alternating between the use of masculine and feminine pronouns throughout much of this chapter, though the principles and examples discussed should be understood to apply equally to men and women, unless otherwise indicated by direct reference or context. The reader's understanding of the difficulty posed by this limitation in the English language is appreciated.

action. Though many of those situations may begin as pastoral contacts, I understand that they will likely transition into pastoral-counseling opportunities. In short, encourage self-referrals whenever possible, but be like the Good Shepherd, who goes after his sheep whenever necessary.

Preparing for the First Session

Effective pastoral counseling begins with the selection of a proper time and place to meet. As you want to give the counselee your full and undivided attention, meet at a time and in a setting that is free from distractions and interruptions. I conduct nearly all of my pastoral counseling in my church office. If you plan to use your office for counseling, instruct your assistant to hold your calls during the session. Turn off your computer and place your cell phone on "Silent," if possible.

Prior to the meeting, give the counselee specific instructions on where, when, and how to arrive. If the counselee will check in with someone before seeing you, provide the counselee with that person's name. Ideally, have him arrive, enter, and wait in a place that minimizes contact with others so he does not feel the need to explain his presence. You should arrive before your counselee and be prepared to meet him. Unless unavoidable, don't make your counselee wait for you.

Your office should be prepared for counseling—no music, birthday balloons left over from a celebratory staff lunch, janitorial personnel, or interns perusing your personal library or the like. You can reduce unexpected surprises by directly leaving your office to meet your counselee.

Keep your office decor simple, clean, and modest, and avoid displaying accolades. Don't make the dejected young man who is seeking your pastoral support because he just got cut from his high school baseball team sit underneath your college "All America" certificate, facing a trophy case jammed with gleaming medals and MVP awards. And be careful about setting up a shrine in tribute to the blessedness of married life. The couple that is struggling in their relationship and contemplating divorce may find the constant visual reminder of what they don't have a very difficult thing to have to stare at throughout their sessions. I have a picture of my wife and kids near my desk, but it is out of view of the counselee sitting in the "counseling area" of my office.

Pay attention to lighting and temperature. The counseling setting should feel more like a family room than an examination room. I prefer indirect lighting when available. I tend to run "warm" and keep my office rather chilly, but I tap up the thermostat a bit so that counselees don't have to sit through counseling sessions wearing down parkas, scarves, and mittens.

Greeting the Counselee and Constructing the Counseling Environment

When it comes to counseling, *everything* is on the table, so to speak. Accordingly, good counselors start working in the waiting room. I begin by taking note of when the counselee arrives for his session. A scheduled appointment is a responsibility, and how one manages responsibilities reveals something about one's personality—assuming either too little or too much responsibility are both problematic.

When I arrived for the first day of a graduate class in psychological assessment, I was greeted by an empty room and the following line written on the board: "If you are early, you're anxious; if you are late, you're hostile; and if you are right on time, you are obsessive-compulsive." I grinned, checked my watch, self-diagnosed, and went out into the hallway—I was apparently anxious for the class. Chuckles aside, I have been surprised to find that, when applied to patterns of behavior, there is an element of truth in that little maxim.[13]

Greet your counselee where you have instructed him to wait for you. Do not merely tell your assistant to "send him up." Upon meeting your counselee, be gentle and pleasant in demeanor, but use as few words as necessary. Chances are good that your counselee is anxious to meet you. You may find it helpful to see how he handles his anxiety—an opportunity lost, at least temporarily, should you reduce his anxiety with small talk. Much better is a warm and simple "Hello" or "Good morning/evening."

I usually extend my hand upon greeting the counselee, though not always. Members of certain cultural groups may find handshaking a bit much upon a first meeting. Further, if the counselee presents as distraught or tearful, I usually forgo a handshake, which feels somewhat forced under such conditions. Use your best judgment here, and when in doubt err on the reserved side. Most importantly, other than possibly initiating an appropriately cordial handshake, do not engage in any other contact with the counselee.

After the greeting, I often offer a counselee something to drink. Dry mouth is a common side effect of many psychotropic medications, and fluid intake usually goes up as a result. And, interestingly, the act of drinking (and eating) is generally incompatible with experiencing feelings of anxiety, which

---

[13] Other details that can be readily observed that may provide useful information include clothing, excessive makeup, reading literature brought to the session, and jewelry, to name but a few. But be careful—it is easy to get carried away and read too much into things that may signify nothing more than what they are.

is one of the reasons that you are offered snacks and beverages on flights. Because of those considerations, I usually offer only decaffeinated beverages.

From the waiting area, escort the counselee to your office. I usually gesture in the direction of my office and say something like, "Please, come on back," then try to follow along behind the counselee, if possible and appropriate. This gives me an opportunity to observe body posture, gait, personal tempo, and any overt problems with judgment, orientation, and gross motor control. I say "if appropriate" because I usually do not follow behind those who might feel uncomfortable having a man following behind them (e.g., those who seem quite timid, the paranoid, women whom I know are seeing me pursuant to having been abused, children, etc.).

If you are following, the counselee will often stop at your office door. If you are in the lead, you should stop at your office door. Either way, invite him to enter your office ahead of you. I usually say something like, "Please come on in and make yourself comfortable" or "Come on in—anywhere that you like to sit is fine" as I remain at the office door and gesture in the direction in which I would like him to be seated. When anxious, counselees sometimes enter the office and, without sitting down, ask, "Where do *you* sit?" I usually reply, "I'm happy to sit anywhere, so please, make yourself comfortable." I give these instructions because these procedures (1) provide the counselee with some immediate sense of being in control and (2) provide me with some immediate feedback on his general disposition—the anxious person wanting direction, the depressed person favoring the corner, the dominant spouse instructing the passive spouse where to sit, angry couples choosing to sit apart, etc.

As you can see, it is helpful to have different types of seating options. A couch is useful, especially if you have room to offer at least two or three additional chairs. It's all systems go when a couple enters your office and chooses individual seats over sitting together on a couch or chooses to sit at opposite ends of the couch. Rarely, but occasionally, I direct highly aggressive or oppositional individuals to move to a different specific chair after they have made their seat selection. I am not particularly interested in where they sit; rather, I want to establish control and boundaries at the beginning of the session. A simple thing like having someone change chairs—"You know, come to think of it, I'd like you to sit over here, please, and I'll move over there"—can help manage the aggressive or insubordinate counselee.

If possible, try to sit at eye level or, especially if you are tall, slightly lower than those whom you counsel. You don't want to be looking down on a cowering counselee, either figuratively or literally. By assuming a slightly lower seated position than the counselee, you can help diffuse any feelings of anxiety and intimidation. Standing at about 6'5", I am often challenged on this point—particularly when the counselee chooses the couch and leaves me with a selection of higher chairs. In those cases, I try to sit low, without slouching, and make myself small, so to speak.

Avoid sitting between the counselee and an exit. The last place that you want to be positioned is between a terrified or violent counselee and the door when he suddenly senses an immediate need to "escape." I don't mean to alarm you, but I have known of unwary counselors who were injured when a counselee, like a startled moose, unexpectedly took to flight. And do not counsel from behind your desk—that places too much "distance" between you and the counselee, and is quite certain to interfere with your effectiveness.

If possible, arrange one part of your office in a casual "family room" style that is conducive to relaxed conversation. Choose your artwork carefully. For example, a painting of the crucified Savior writhing in agony may be spectacular from an artistic standpoint, but it will likely pull some strong feelings from counselees inclined toward depression or persecutory ideation. I like to place on the walls a neutral painting or two that offer some "vistas" to encourage reflection and projection.

During my years in private practice, I hung over the couch a painting of sailors diligently working on the deck of a clipper ship. On the horizon, the skies were thick, dark, and menacing. However, it was unclear whether the ship was sailing into or away from the tempest. I was struck by the number of counselees who, early in their counseling, paused in front of the painting and remarked, "Wow, that's exactly how I feel" before going on to explain that the ship appeared to be heading into a violent storm. And it was a good sign when, later in counseling, they walked in my office, paused at the painting, and said, "You know, now that I look at it more closely, they are not sailing *into* the storm—they've passed through it and are coming into safe harbor," quite unaware of how their projections onto the painting served as a metaphor for their progress. In short, consider the themes of your artwork and decor, and the feelings they may elicit from the counselee.

Placing a coffee table between you and the counselee can add to the casual "family room" style of the counseling area and further help reduce feelings of anxiety or intimidation. Casual and convenient table surfaces can also serve useful purposes. For example, I place a box of tissues on my coffee table—occasionally and discretely repositioning it closer to counselees during moments when they become more visibly sad or tearful. That simple act is often sufficient to invite counselees to feel and express their emotions openly.

Door Closed or Door Open/Ajar?

Few issues have sparked as much discussion and controversy as the question of whether the office door should be closed or remain open/ajar during pastoral-counseling sessions. That may seem like a trivial concern, but many ministries and marriages have been ruined by what has begun behind closed doors between pastor and counselee.

Counseling often involves engaging in a close and deeply personal interaction with an emotionally vulnerable and bewildered person, bringing to the surface intense feelings, unrealized hopes, and conflicted desires. Merely sensing that one is being truly heard in counseling is a powerful dynamic that can engender strong feelings for the counselor. When the counselor is unaware of the counselee's transferred feelings or is unaware of his own unconscious motives and desires that are satisfied in receiving such transferred feelings, the results can be disastrous. The wise pastoral counselor is aware of these dangers and takes precautions.

The issues involved in this debate are many and thorny, and I will not pretend that I can exhaustively summarize every view and resolve every question or concern. Rather, in keeping with our aim and limitations here, I will advance a few points on both sides of the divide.

There are those who believe that keeping the office door open/ajar (with, perhaps, an assistant sitting outside) is an effective way of reducing, if not eliminating, inappropriate behavior between the counselor and counselee.[14] Arguably, the risk of being overheard talking about material that is clearly unrelated to any legitimate counseling focus helps keep things on target—an informal means of accountable "supervision." And, of course, engaging in inappropriate physical/sexual contact becomes much more difficult if there is the chance that someone could pass by the office door and catch a glimpse of what is going on inside. In addition to guarding against inappropriate conversations and contact, the door open/ajar policy may also help guard the pastoral counselor against a false accusation lodged by a disgruntled or disturbed counselee. These are no small protections.

Those who advocate for a door-closed policy point out that confidenti-

---

[14] Some pastors take this line of thinking a step further and tell counselees that they do not keep any secrets from their wives, and, therefore, "Don't tell me anything that I cannot tell my wife." Still other pastors take a long stride further, refusing to counsel woman parishioners unless their wives are also present during the counseling sessions. Such measures, of course, amplify both the advantages and disadvantages noted in the discussion.

ality is of utmost importance to ethical counseling. Keeping the office door open/ajar presents a real opportunity for sensitive and potentially damaging information to reach the ears of uninvolved third parties. Having the door open/ajar may also affect the openness of the counselee, who senses the desire or need to edit what is shared for fear of being overheard.

It is further argued that counseling with the door open/ajar significantly changes the dynamics of the counseling session. For example, a door-open/ ajar policy (especially with an assistant stationed nearby) may unwittingly cause the counselee to call into question the very issue of integrity that the counselor is seeking to guard: "If he doesn't trust himself enough to meet with me without having a door open and someone sitting just on the other side, why should I trust him? Is an open door all that separates him from acting inappropriately with me?" Conversely, the counselee may get the impression that you don't trust her: "I wonder what he thinks of me if he feels the need to protect himself by keeping the door open and someone positioned nearby?"[15]

Some critics of the door-open/ajar approach also point out that the pastoral counselor may not always be in a situation where he can so easily counsel with an open door, place reliance on passing foot traffic, or find someone who is available to sit quietly outside his office while he counsels.[16] Moreover, the pastoral counselor can be lulled—whether immediately or gradually—into a sense of false security associated with counseling under a door-open/ajar policy. Interestingly, most of the morally fallen pastors with whom I have worked over the years got themselves into trouble while providing counseling with their office door open/ajar.

I know many solid pastors and counselors who line up on both sides of the debate, and a consensus of opinion on this issue is not likely forthcoming. But whatever your view and practice, there are at least two aspects of this matter that are beyond dispute.

First, if you think that you are invulnerable to sexual temptation and have no need to put safeguards in place when counseling, you are playing the fool. I have yet to work with a pastor who got embroiled in sexual sin who didn't say, "I never thought that could happen to me." The wise and safe counselor takes precautions.

Second, ministry is a character calling, and relying on external room

---

[15] Such concerns are not merely hypothetical. I have had counselees come to me and state that they felt uncomfortable working with their previous counselors because the door was left open during their sessions. The sample quotes provided in the body of the text summarize and reflect the essence of actual concerns that counselees have shared with me.

[16] There have been numerous times when I have been called to a home or the church office after midnight to meet with a distressed counselee. Frequently no one else has been around.

configurations to guard against acting inappropriately with others is a poor substitute for personal integrity and godly self-control. Sexual sins don't begin with the body, they begin with the eyes—we look with our eyes, we linger in our thoughts, we long in our hearts, and then we lust. Many morally fallen pastors have told me at the beginning of counseling, "It was just a single moment of weakness—one little spontaneous slipup. I don't know what the big deal is; it won't happen again." But that's naive.

Moral failure involves a long and subtle process of compromise. Seemingly innocent digressions at critical choice points shave nearly imperceptible microns off of one's resolve. Each ensuing divergence of thought, feeling, or behavior escapes notice because that instance of compromise stands so very near where one was just yesterday. It's much like watching hair grow—the changes are simply too minuscule to detect.

An open door may keep some counselors from acting on their feelings, but such is a precautionary step taken far too late. Men, we need to be guarding our eyes and hearts long before we should be relying on open and ajar doors. Job had it right: "I have made a covenant with my eyes . . ." (Job 31:1). We need to guard against affairs of the heart, which usually begin because we look, linger, long, and lust.

I counsel with the door closed, but never locked. My office is on the ground floor and features floor-to-ceiling tinted windows, permitting someone to see that there are people in the office without easily discerning who they are—they see little more than silhouettes. I also have an interior window adjacent to my office door that provides a passerby full view of the study end of my office, and the backs of those seated in the chairs and the legs of those seated on the couch at the counseling end of the office. The arrangement protects everyone's identity. With the assistance of our property owner, I strategically modified the counseling end of my office so that I can maintain both confidentiality and accountability.

There is much more that I could say about this topic, but for now I encourage you to consider carefully how you will arrange for a counseling environment that is conducive to open and honest disclosure while protecting confidentiality and reputations. I write about putting additional safeguards in place later in this chapter.

Starting the Counseling Session

How do you begin the pastoral counseling session? I usually open with a brief prayer that sets the tone and trajectory for the session. For example, once seated, I briefly pause and say to the counselee, "Let's pray." The following represents what I might pray in opening a counseling session:

> Our Father and our God, we praise you for who you are and for your many gracious provisions to us; most significantly, what you did for us in giving your Son and our Savior, Jesus. And we thank you for this opportunity to meet together to discuss matters that weigh upon our hearts and minds. We lay our lives before you and ask that you search us and direct us in our time together. We know that you are very present with us and attentive to our every thought and need, and in that we take comfort, joy, and hope. Father, we ask for wisdom, mercy, strength, and peace, and for the courage to cooperate with your Spirit to make changes where necessary, so that we are living fully and faithfully in accordance with your Word and will. Lord, we invite you to be our Counselor in these moments, and we give you the praise and glory for what you will accomplish in us, with us, and through us, for your greater glory and our good. Amen.

If particularly anxious, a counselee may begin talking about what is on his mind while being escorted to the office or while in the process of selecting his seat. When that occurs, I usually do not interrupt the flow of the session by pausing for opening prayer, but instead close the session with prayer.

After opening the initial session in prayer, I often say, "What would you like to talk about today?" "What brings you to see me today?" or "How can I be of help to you today?" I often use the word *today* in my opening question both to keep the counselee focused on his present problem(s) and to convey that I am committing myself only to the session that we have before us. Occasionally the counselee says, "I don't know where to begin." When that happens, I usually respond, "What happened that initially prompted you to call me?" If the counselee remains unsure of where to begin, I often say, "Well, tell me about some of the thoughts and feelings you had as you were preparing to come and see me." During subsequent sessions, I often open in prayer, pause, warmly smile, and look for a brief moment or two at the counselee. He often takes that as his cue to begin talking. If he doesn't launch in, I may say, "Please tell me about your week" or "How would you like to use our time today?"

Humor is an effective defense against anxiety. Accordingly, some counselees will engage in levity, if not outright foolishness, at the beginning of a session (or throughout). Understand that the counselee is employing humor in an attempt to control feelings of uneasiness, but don't go there with him;

rather, simply redirect. For example, you might say: "I realize that it is not easy to know where to begin or what to say when starting counseling, and I can appreciate that you might be feeling a bit anxious right now. That's okay. Maybe you could just start by telling me what's on your mind today." That usually works to bring things back to center and will likely reduce future detours into silliness. And now you're off.

Listen intently while the counselee is talking, and observe everything carefully. Pay attention to changes in the volume or speed with which the counselee talks; conflicted material is often embedded in offhand remarks and in speech that is slightly rushed or produced at a lower volume. Emotional reactions that are disproportionate to the topic or situation are also suggestive of unresolved issues. Make a mental note of those instances, as you will want to go back later and probe them further.

I usually don't take notes during the session so that I can be fully "present" with the counselee. An occasional nod of the head signals that you are tracking with him—I say occasional because continually nodding your head may be distracting. I try to be as silent as possible and remain mostly motionless while listening. Work to understand and not judge the counselee, and receive whatever the counselee tells you with minimal reaction—ideally none. The counselee is likely concerned about what you will think of him once he tells you what he is thinking, feeling, or has done.

Occasionally a counselee begins the initial session(s) by presenting a non-issue—a "trial balloon" concern, if you will. Sometimes the non-issue is put forward in an attempt to assess your competency as a counselor. Other times the counselee wants to see how you will react to what he shares before deciding whether or not to venture into the real problem(s). Registering disapproval, shock, or disgust—either verbally or facially—to the non-issue is likely to sabotage the counseling process and may prevent you from getting to the core issue(s). I have had people come and confess to me that they have maintained a "second family" in another city, have engaged in serial affairs, have actively served as ministers while actually disbelieving in the existence of God and the truthfulness of what they preach from Scripture, and have committed multiple murders (among many, many other things far too disturbing and sordid to mention or print), and I try to receive it all with the same disposition as if I were listening to a midday PBS discourse on the declension of the adjectival aspects of Greek participles.

It is very easy to substitute conversation for counseling. Especially in the first session, work hard to keep your comments to a minimum. The more the counselee says without prompting, the better. As counselees talk, they invest more into the process—like dropping coins into a piggy bank—and the more invested they become, the better the potential outcome. Accordingly, you should say only what is necessary to keep the ball rolling by providing the very slightest verbal "kick," as necessary.

Many people are uncomfortable with silence and feel the need to fill it by saying something—anything. If you are to become an effective counselor, you need to grow comfortable with silence. Most novice counselors speak far too much and far too soon. Silence is the incubator of thoughts and feelings—space that you should learn to appreciate and work hard to stay out of for as long as you can.

When the counselee stops talking, I usually wait silently to see if he will spontaneously reengage. I especially remain silent when the counselee has stopped talking and has averted his eyes away from looking at me; that's usually a sign that something is getting processed in silence, and that should not be interrupted. The counselee may remain silent for moments—or longer.[17] Resist the temptation to break the silence by saying something. The counselee will signal you when he is done silently processing his thoughts or feelings by turning his gaze back to you, at which time I continue to wait until he either says something or nonverbally indicates that he doesn't know what to say.[18] A simple and soft "You look like you are thinking about something" or "Can you say a little more about [whatever he was talking about just before stopping]?" will be sufficient to keep the discussion moving forward.

When provided an opportunity to respond, it is helpful to summarize very briefly what you understand based on what has been disclosed to that point. Summarizing from time to time keeps the session focused, conveys that you are listening, and does not allow you to stray too far from accurately tracking with what the counselee is trying to communicate. I often summarize by saying, "If I understand you right, it sounds like you are saying that . . ." I try to keep my summary statement to a single sentence, if possible. Again, I want to keep the session progressing and have the counselee keep talking.

---

[17] During a practicum experience as a graduate student in the early 1980s, I opened the session, only to have the counselee spend the following forty minutes in absolute silence. He alternated between staring out the window and looking at the floor, all laced with occasional periods of tearfulness. I didn't say a word. When, toward the end of the session, he finally raised his eyes to look at me, I quietly said, "I was wondering what our time together today was like for you." He broke down and sobbed, saying, "You are the only person that I know with whom I can sit and not feel compelled to say something." The experience proved invaluable for both of us. I learned to appreciate the incredible power of silence, and the counselee used the experience in subsequent sessions to launch into an exploration of his bitterness toward his father over seemingly "always being told what to do and what to think without any consideration of how I feel."

[18] Some of the common nonverbal clues signaling that the counselee has finished talking or is "stuck" may include smirking, pursing the lips, shrugging shoulders, and sighing.

Controlling Excessive Emotion in Pastoral Counseling

Give careful attention to how your counselee starts her session. As previously mentioned, I allow those with whom I work to begin by talking about whatever they want. Frequently it is not what people say but what they omit that is critical. For example, it is significant when a wife, whose husband filed for divorce three days earlier, opens her session with a casual twenty-minute story about how she just had her carpets shampooed. That's a huge elephant to ignore—sitting on a damp shag rug.

I allow people to tell their stories and wander as they wish—for a while. Frequently, the counselee is not oblivious to the elephant in the room, but is trying to ease into the material without getting overwhelmed. Talking about facts helps control emotions, and wise counselors know when counselees may be trying to keep themselves from going over the edge by focusing on seemingly trivial stuff. But if the counselee does not show signs of redirecting herself, I gently point her toward the edge, so to speak. I may say: "I notice that you talked about getting your carpets cleaned this week. I am wondering if that is really the most significant thing that has recently happened in your life." That is usually sufficient to move the counselee into the emotionally laden material.

If you have to redirect the counselee, it is probably for very good reason, and the lengths to which the counselee has gone to avoid talking about the most pressing issues is roughly proportionate to the depth of her defended feelings. As such, redirection usually triggers a lot of emotion, and you should be prepared for it. Control your own emotions, especially when those around you are losing control of theirs; in short, the more out of control the counselee is, the more calm and controlled you need to be. Don't panic, and don't "rescue" your counselee from feeling her feelings, but stay on your counseling toes and become more active. Focus on what I call "dosing" the counselee's feelings.

By "dosing" feelings, I mean that you should permit the counselee to experience her feelings as long as she is able to tolerate it without becoming overwhelmed. The distraught counselee is usually unable to paddle herself out of the torrent of her emotions and will need your help. If you see uncontrollable sobbing, clenched fists, confused and incoherent speech, or others signs suggesting that your counselee is being swept away, you must step in and "dose" her off of her feelings. You can do that by asking very specific, non-emotional questions that have short, objective, and concise answers, such as, "Mary, remind me, where were you born?" (answer);

"And, again, where did you go to school?" (answer); "How long have you
lived in [name of your city]?" (answer). Stay with that line of questioning
until the counselee has calmed down and has emotionally reconstituted. You
can then gently "dose" her back into the emotional material: "Thank you,
Mary. That's helpful. Now, you were talking about how sad you have been
feeling lately." Again, allow your counselee to experience her feelings as
deeply (and for as long) as she can tolerate without becoming overwhelmed
before "dosing" her back to factual material through redirected questioning.
Repeat as necessary.

Setting Goals in Pastoral Counseling

Your objective in the first session is to observe carefully, listen intently, and
begin thinking about establishing the goal for pastoral counseling. But that
is often easier said than done. Those who come for pastoral counseling are
usually confused and hurting, and they frequently have little idea of what
they want, other than to have whatever is bothering them "go away." Rarely
is the counselee able to present clear and concise objectives for counseling.
Rather, new counselees are often so fixated on their present problems that
they have difficulty envisioning their desired future.

You may find that new counselees start and stop, change directions,
pause and repeat themselves, engage in self-loathing, and cry over their in-
ability to put words to their feelings and thoughts. It is not uncommon to
hear new counselees say things like "I don't know why I'm here," "I don't
know what's wrong with me," "Actually, I'm not sure what's the problem,"
"You must think I'm crazy," or other remarks that reveal their bewilderment
and anguish.

When counselees start to get rattled and look to me for help in sorting
things out, I seek to reassure them and keep them talking: "You are doing
fine. You were saying something about [insert the last issue they talked
about]." That usually puts them back on track. They may spend the entire
first session pouring out their feelings and problems without settling on
anything for a focus. That is usually fine with me, as long as they can leave
without any "open wounds." Sometimes people simply need to be heard by
a sympathetic set of ears—and being *really* heard is, in and of itself, wonderfully helpful. Such people will often compliment you on how good the session
was for them and how much they appreciate your help, even though you may
feel that you made little progress. That's fine—they'll very likely be back.

Whether in the first session or the following, you want to start helping your counselee sort through the various issues presented for counseling and settle on your counseling goal. A counseling goal is a biblical, moral, healthy, and desirable change in thinking, behavior, or feelings that a person wants to make happen. As such, effective counseling works from the present to the future.

If counseling is to be successful, future goals(s) must be:

1. *Specific.* Each counseling goal should be reduced to a clear statement specifying the future changes that will occur in thinking, behavior, and/or feelings.
2. *Observable.* Each counseling goal should result in specific future changes in thinking, behavior, and/or feelings that are visibly manifest.
3. *Contextualized.* Each counseling goal should connect the specific future changes in thinking, behavior, and/or feeling to the specific conditions where such changes are visibly made manifest.

When the counselee presents numerous issues for potential focus, help him select just one and turn that focus into a goal, as per above. When a laundry list of genuine problems is recited, often the first one mentioned is most important. Subsequent sessions should center on working toward the identified goal. Counseling ends when the desired goal has been realized or after a specified number of counseling sessions, whichever comes first.

When selecting an appropriate counseling goal, consider the length of time that you can reasonably offer to the counselee. Unless you are well-trained, I advise pastors to consider seeing a counselee for no more than six to eight sessions. The length of counseling is discussed at the time that the goal is established and in large measure depends upon the nature of the goal. Counseling that is directed at making a specific choice (e.g., helping a high school senior choose between different college options) will likely require less time than an issue that is relational or long-standing (e.g., dealing with a trust issue in marriage counseling).

During the last of your agreed-upon number of sessions, take time with the counselee to evaluate the effectiveness of the counseling. If you are making limited progress in keeping with your established goal, realistically evaluate how far the counselee has come and if there is a reasonable expectation that a few more sessions might realize the goal. If so, consider extending counseling an additional two to four sessions, but no more. If not, you may either need to reevaluate your goal or refer the counselee to someone with more training and experience. Don't interpret that as a failure—even the very best of highly trained and competent psychologists make frequent referrals. Wise counselors make wise referrals.

When taking inventory of the various problems that the counselee has presented, consider whether any of the issues may actually cluster together and be symptomatic of a larger, overarching issue. For example, marital sexual dissatisfaction and communication difficulties often walk hand in hand and are usually symptoms of a more fundamental problem. If you were to select either the sexual or communication issue as your goal, you could spend a couple of months addressing a "symptom" and not the real problem. Conversely, if you worked on respect/trust issues or on establishing/ reestablishing a proper biblical understanding of marriage, you might find that the "symptom" of marital sexual dissatisfaction and/or communication difficulties also eases or evaporates. In short, see if you can group the main problems under a heading, and then consider selecting the heading as the goal—you may resolve several issues with one goal.

You need not work on everything initially presented as a problem. Work on one goal at a time to completion and then reevaluate; perhaps you will later agree that there is another thorny issue that needs to be turned into a goal. However, I frequently find that by selecting and working through a single goal to resolution, the counselee develops the insight and transferable skills to tackle additional problems independently with greater confidence and hope.

Establishing and Working toward the Goal in Pastoral Counseling

Counseling is more than simply telling people what to do—that's coaching, not counseling. Under most conditions, the wise counselor avoids giving advice—even when the counselee directly asks. Of course, there are times when it is appropriate (necessary even) to step in and give specific instructions to a counselee. For example, you should not allow a counselee to seriously contemplate behaving in a way that is unbiblical, immoral, illegal, or absurd. Further, if I am asked a question that the counselee cannot reasonably answer without assistance, I gladly respond.[19] But those are exceptions, not the rule.

Those of us who have been married for a while have likely heard our wives tell us, "When I share my feelings with you, I just want you to listen to me and not try to fix everything." That's good counsel for the counselor.

---

[19] I am frequently asked by non-Christian counselees, "Pastor, would you tell me about this Jesus you preach about?" Such a question deserves a full and direct answer. Similarly, I am happy to provide direct answers to questions about the Bible, theology, etc., which, in many cases, are not discoverable through human reason or counseling insight (e.g., "What does it mean to be baptized?" "Why do we take Communion?" or "Why do I need to trust Jesus?").

Don't be too eager to rush in and try to offer the "solution." Remember, you may not have heard the *real* problem yet. If you quickly step in and "fix the problem," counselees may sense that you are not really listening to what's truly on their hearts. Rather, the wise counselor *guides* counselees through careful questioning in such a way that they "solve" their own problems, in conformity with God's Word and will, of course.

Helping counselees generate their own solutions to their problems has tremendous benefits. First, people are more likely to believe that the answer/change/plan is the "right" one if they have come up with the solution on their own. Second, people better respond and are more likely to follow through on the answer/change/plan if they arrive at their own insight and generate their own solution. And, third, people are more likely to generalize the approach and be successful at independently addressing other problems in their lives if they come up with their own solutions. None of this should be interpreted as suggesting that we allow the counselee to arrive at just any solution—that's not true. Pastoral counseling involves assisting people in identifying, choosing, and realizing biblically sound and morally proper goals. But counselees are better helped if they are shepherded into biblical truth and spiritual maturity.

If you are having a difficult time guiding a counselee to see possible solutions, you can suggest different options for him to consider. When counselees get stuck at generating possible solutions to their problems, I sometimes say, "What do you think would happen if you [propose an option]?" If they answer the question and then ask, "Do you think that's what I should do?" I often reply: "Well, I like the way that you have thought and talked your way through that, and it is one option. What might be some alternatives to that potential solution?" My response differentiates between guiding feedback and directive advice, and usually results in the counselee coming up with additional possible solutions. In those rare instances when the counselee can't think of any additional alternative solutions, I repeat the process. I have found that the approach works quite well.

Once the counselee has identified several possible solutions to his problem, you may find it useful to summarize each alternative and write them all down. Of course, even as you hear the counselee talk about various solutions, you may immediately recognize that some of them will not work or are unbiblical, immoral, or otherwise undesirable, but that's okay *for the moment*. Avoid editing possible solutions as they are being generated by the counselee. Once the various alternative solutions are summarized and written down, begin guiding the counselee through the process of assessing each possible option. This is a bit like helping someone try on different pairs of shoes—the counselee discovers that some solutions "fit," others don't.

Take one possible solution at a time, and help the counselee consider the values that inform the same. All behavior is to be purposeful and directed by biblical and/or moral commitments—that's the point from which you want to begin guiding your counselee in evaluating each option. As Christians, our moral commitments are biblically informed, shaped, and determined; collectively, they form our worldview. The biblical-moral worldview may be likened to a template that is laid over every choice point and decision-making process in life, guiding us to biblical, moral, and healthy ends.

Many people, including counselees, begin at the wrong end of the process and predestine where they want to end up, *then* construct their values and commitments to justify their predetermined decisions and goals. But that's backward. Scripture ought to direct thinking, behaving, and feeling, not the reverse. The godly, wise, and faithful counselor helps others place those elements in their proper order.

Once the counselee's biblical-moral template is constructed, help him evaluate each of his proposed solutions in light of the same. You will likely need to be patient and engage in much redirection, as most people are not used to working from biblical-moral commitments to changes in thinking, behavior, and feeling.

For example, I counseled a man who came to me to confess an affair. He discussed the problems in his marriage and his feelings of "love" for the other woman. He had set the possibility of divorcing his wife and marrying the woman with whom he was having the affair among his alternatives. Instead of confronting him and saying, "You can't do that," "God does not permit such a decision," or "The Bible says . . . ," I walked him through a series of questions designed to elicit his biblical-moral worldview. I patiently asked the following questions, among others: "What is your understanding of marriage?"; "What do you understand the Bible to say about marriage?"; "Talk to me about what it means to make a vow"; "What is your understanding of love?"; and "What does God's Word say about the meaning of marriage/love/commitment?" Repeatedly throughout the process, the man returned to his predetermined goal: "But I don't love my wife, and I love this other woman and want to be with her." Each time he relapsed into a recitation of his desired endgame, I would bring him back to the biblical-moral beginning by patiently and gently asking, "Help me square that with your stated commitment to honor God and his Word." We cycled through this process several times before he eventually came to understand that his biblical-moral commitments needed to determine his goal.

After you have helped guide the counselee in eliminating all of the unbiblical, immoral, and unhealthy options through an evaluation of his underlying values, turn to helping the counselee understand the consequences of the remaining biblical, moral, and healthy alternatives. Thought experiments may prove helpful at this point.

For example, you might take a proposed biblically appropriate solution and ask, "If you were to [fill in the option], talk about how you envision that playing out over time." Be sure to help your counselee evaluate each appropriate option objectively, and honestly discuss the strengths and weaknesses of each proposed course of action. Of course, there are some decisions for which there is no simple "right or wrong" answer, but there is always a right and wrong way of going about making decisions. Your role as counselor is to ensure that the biblical wisdom for which we are instructed to pray is guiding the entire process of establishing and working toward the goals of counseling, including goal selection (e.g., James 1:5–8).

Once the ultimate goal is selected, establish both intermediate and immediate "mile markers" along the way that will confirm that you are making progress toward the goal. You might think of these "mile markers" as minigoals—points that lie between where the counselee is at the time that counseling begins and where you aim to arrive at its conclusion. Like the ultimate goal of counseling, the "mile markers" need to be reduced to clear statements about the specific, observable, and contextualized changes in thinking, behavior, and feeling that are going to be realized as the counselee progresses toward the goal. You work toward the established biblical, moral, and healthy goal of counseling by helping the counselee first achieve immediate and then intermediate changes as defined by the "mile markers" statement.

I have likened the counseling process to that of backpacking. There are few activities that I enjoy quite as much as strapping a fly rod on a backpack and disappearing into the wilderness for a couple of weeks. But I don't just traipse off into the woods—I create a plan. In advance of my trip, I purchase the best topographical map I can get my hands on; study the various streams, rivers, and lakes; assess trail options; select my destination and route; and choose those places where I will establish my campsites along the way.[20] I then identify a number of prominent landmarks that appear on the map that

---

[20] I am an old-school Eagle Scout (think flint and steel) and have yet to own a handheld GPS for use in the wilds—I understand that they are whiz-bang. I mean no disrespect when I say that, to a considerable extent,

I should expect to either reach or be able to see clearly between the trailhead and my ultimate destination. I make note of the mileage of each landmark from both the trailhead and the destination, and write it down in the margin of the map.

Before setting off down the trail, I consult my map and make sure that I am at the right trailhead. Confident of the same, I strike out. My favorite itinerary is a loop trip, alternating between a day of backpacking and a day of fishing. While hiking, I make frequent checks of my location with my map and compass, triangulating my previously selected landmarks to place myself on the map. In this way, I know that I am on the right trail and heading in the right direction; can calculate my distance traveled and remaining; and can estimate when I should expect to arrive at my evening campsite and ultimate destination.

With a little practice, you can become quite proficient with a map and compass. In fact, if you make a careful study of your map and know what to look for along the route, you can almost envision yourself walking along the little dotted trail markings on the topographical map and anticipate what you might see around the next bend. Few experiences are as satisfying as seeing the sapphire-blue alpine lake that you had expected when arriving at the crest of a hill. Of course, if you go with a professional guide, you will hike and camp with much greater confidence.

The analogy is transparent enough and has served me well in orienting counselees to the counseling process. While there may be numerous possible destinations (goals) on the map, we select but one and determine our route for getting there. Once established, we have a better idea of how long the journey will take and what we expect to encounter along the way. We will want to check our progress toward the goal frequently by "triangulating" our position in counseling against the established landmarks ("mile markers"). I will serve as the trail guide, but counselees must do their own walking and carry their own packs. As we walk together, my job is to help the counselee keep focused on the goal, remain motivated to move forward, identify and deal with obstacles that hinder progress, assist in offloading weight and sin, act as a porter when necessary, and celebrate the arrival at the established "mile markers" en route to the destination.

As you work toward the immediate and intermediate "mile markers," attend to both the content and process. In other words, provide feedback on both what is being said and on the counselee's self-defeating patterns of

---

I trek off into the backcountry to get away from the technological world, not to see how much of it I can schlep with me.

thinking, behaving, and feeling that interfere with making progress toward his goal.

For example, you might observe that a female counselee returns for her second and third sessions without having completed an immediate "mile marker" assignment of speaking to her husband about a recent purchase that he made that has placed stress on the family finances. She explains: "I haven't been home much lately. Several friends from church have been reaching out to me, and I haven't wanted to turn anyone down for fear that they might get upset with me." You might respond by saying, "And I suppose that remaining busy might also help you avoid having a rather uncomfortable discussion with your husband." If there is good rapport and trust between you and the counselee, she will likely receive the feedback with little resistance and acknowledge how she has employed busyness as a defense against feeling her anxiety. By gently lifting unconscious patterns to consciousness, counselees are helped to make behavioral changes consistent with their insight in counseling.

When giving feedback to the counselee, it is important to *describe* behavior, not *label* behavior. Describing behavior involves commenting on what you see and hear. By describing behavior, you better align yourself as an ally with the counselee, minimize opportunities for defensiveness, provide valuable feedback to the counselee on how he is coming across to others, and convey both the opportunity and hope for change. Labeling behavior involves making statements about who a person is. Labeling behavior goes to the person's "fixed" traits or character, and tends to communicate a sense of inevitability and unchangeableness.

Labeling may be reduced by avoiding "You are . . ." statements. For example, it is better to tell a counselee, "I notice that you are crying . . . you look sad" rather than, "You are depressed." The first statement better conveys warmth of feeling, is unlikely to prompt defensiveness, and keeps counseling moving along. Crucially, we *always* want to instill hope in our counselees and help them understand that, regardless of how bleak or desperate things may appear, no one is beyond the reach of God's grace. Counselees sense more room for hope when there are fewer labels.

Celebrate the arrival at the established "mile markers" along the way to the goal, pointing out even small positive changes in the counselee's pattern of thinking, behaving, and feeling. Take some time during each session to summarize progress to date, review the goal, and sharpen focus on the next "mile marker." Then encourage your counselee to keep moving forward, assured of your continued support and prayers. This process continues until the goal is realized.

Pacing in Pastoral Counseling

When I was in private practice, I usually scheduled my sessions on the hour and ran them for fifty minutes, using the remaining ten minutes for note-taking and review. In more recent years, I have allotted ninety minutes for most counseling sessions, and I enjoy the more leisurely pace.

The counseling session divides fairly neatly into three sections—an opening, a middle, and an end—with each section lasting roughly one-third the allotted time. I don't force transitions from one section into the next, but rather unobtrusively maneuver the counselee through the progressive sections of the session.

The counselee usually spends much of the initial session presenting various thoughts and feelings associated with her perceived problems, as previously described. I become a bit more active during the final third of the first session as I work with the counselee to establish the goal and "mile markers" that will be monitored along the way. Occasionally, the presenting problems are too numerous or thorny, or the counselee is too confused or upset, to permit us to sort completely through everything in a session or two and establish the goal and "mile markers." Should that occur, the pastoral counselor is wise to consider referring.

Provided that the goal and progress markers have been established, subsequent sessions proceed through each section in turn. During the opening section, counselees usually report on changes that they made during the previous week. In the middle section, feedback on what has been reported is provided, and the focus for that session is developed and explored. In the end section of the session, the conversation moves to a discussion of those changes that the counselee intends to implement as a result of the insight he has gained during the session. The counselor helps seamlessly pace the counselee through those three main sections of the session.

The primary focus for each section of the counseling session is usually "introduced" by the counselor. That is especially the case early in counseling with a new counselee who may not know how to effectively use the session time. While I usually allow counselees to begin their sessions by talking about what they wish, I redirect them into reporting on their changes and observations from the previous week if they wander too far or too long. I find that most counselees learn how to start and use the opening section of the counseling sessions after only a week or two of redirection.

Here are some statements and questions that can help move a counselee through each of the three major sections of a typical counseling session:

Opening Section

- "So, tell me about your week."
- "As I recall, you were going to talk with your husband this past week. How did that go?"
- "How have you been doing since I last saw you?"

Middle Section

- "You have put several important issues out on the table for discussion. Which seems most important to you right now?"
- "What are some of your thoughts and feelings about the changes that you tried out this past week?"
- "I noticed that when you talked about your husband, your voice was hushed and you looked uncomfortable."
- "I'm struck by the fact that you have yet to bring up [fill in the avoided issues here]."

End Section

- "So, I am wondering what you perceive as your options."
- "What do you think is the way forward?"
- "Well, it seems to me that you tried _____, and that didn't work out well, you said. So, what are you thinking of doing differently this week?"

The session should proceed smoothly and seamlessly. I don't specifically identify the three sections for the counselee or announce transitions. In fact, quite often my counselees learn to pace themselves through their sessions.

I have counseled throughout my career with a clock in my office that sounds the Westminster chimes at the quarter-hour. I initially placed it in my office to help me keep my attention on the counselee and pace through the session without having to look at my watch or glance at a clock.[21] But shortly thereafter, I noticed that the chimes were having an effect on the counselees. I remain amazed by the number of my counselees who unconsciously learn to pace themselves by the subtle chiming of the clock. It is almost amusing to hear someone say, upon hearing the chimes, "Well, perhaps we should talk some about what I can do differently this week," quite unaware that they have cued their transition into the final section of the session by my clock. Not a single counselee over the decades has ever mentioned the pacing influence of the Westminster chimes.

Given that the end of the session is more specifically goal-directed and

---

[21] Avoid the bad habit of looking at your watch or glancing at the clock. Many counselees notice what you are doing and have a difficult time interpreting your apparent concern with time as anything other than unconcern for them.

future-focused, you want to try to move the counselee away from emotional-toned material during the closing section. Do not allow a counselee to leave your office immediately after having processed deep, conflicted, or distressing feelings. Take adequate time to ensure that he is "contained" and not at risk for emotionally disintegrating when he leaves your office—he may not have anyone around to help "dose" him off his overwhelming feelings and may not think clearly enough to reach out for help when near the edge.

Closing the Session

Before ending the initial (or, if necessary, second) session, make sure that you and the counselee are clear on the goal and "mile markers" that will be checked along the way. I often take a few minutes to explain the counseling process and what the counselee should expect in subsequent sessions. I also invite the counselee to ask any questions. I usually close sessions in prayer.

I spend the closing minutes of each subsequent counseling session pulling together the main points discussed, revisiting the goal, assessing and reinforcing changes the counselee has made, reviewing the next steps/objectives, giving any necessary pastoral instructions, and concluding with some words of encouragement, support, and hope. Here is a sample of how I might end a session.

> *Counselor*: "I appreciate our time together today; you are doing some very good work. We have talked about several things that I think are important—you seem to better understand how unrealistic expectations can so easily lead to feelings of disappointment, and I am delighted to hear that you have acknowledged that to your husband and apologized for your angry outbursts. That takes a lot of courage, and I'm very pleased that you are learning to submit that area of your life more fully to the Father's control. And I am grateful that God has graciously blessed your obedience to him by moving in your husband's heart to forgive you—you mentioned that you hadn't expected that, had you?"
> *Counselee*: "No . . . not at all."
> *Counselor*: "Forgiveness is a wonderful thing, isn't it?"
> *Counselee*: "Oh, yes!"
> *Counselor*: "Now, during this next week, I understand that you will be calling your daughter to confess some of the same things to her and to ask for her forgiveness as well, in an effort to repair that relationship and live as God would have us live, right?"
> *Counselee*: "Right."

Counselor: "That's great. I trust that you understand that if you are unable to connect with your daughter before Sunday, I must ask that you refrain from taking Communion, right?"

Counselee: "Yes, I understand."

Counselor: "We need to come to the Table with clean hands and a pure heart, and I want you to be able to celebrate the reconciling power of the gospel that is ours as a result of Christ's death—both with God and with others. I know that you want that, too, right?"

Counselee: "I do, pastor."

Counselor: "Great. Before we close in prayer, I want to tell you what a joy it is for me to see God's Spirit so actively involved in your life these past few weeks, and how thrilled I am that you are cooperating with him as he does his work. Keep it up! We'll plan to meet next Tuesday at 3 p.m.—does that still work for you?"

Counselee: "Yes, that works fine, and I have it on my calendar."

Counselor: "Good. I look forward to seeing you then. Remember, if something changes or you need to get in touch with me—especially if you notice any changes in your sleep patterns or appetite—you are to call me, okay?"

Counselee: "Yes, I know to do that, and I will."

Counselor: "Wonderful . . . let's pray."

After we pray, I then escort the counselee back to where I had initially met him prior to the session. I usually keep the conversation to a minimum when walking him back to the waiting area to avoid having issues raised that cannot be adequately or appropriately addressed in a more public setting. I then extend a handshake and bid him a good day/evening.

COMMON PITFALLS TO EFFECTIVE PASTORAL COUNSELING

When the pastoral counselor doesn't know what to do, he should know what *not* to do, including the following.

1. *Don't play the role of the Holy Spirit.* Our role as pastoral counselors is to provide an environment that is conducive to the Holy Spirit doing his work in the lives of our counselees. While we want to cooperate with God's Spirit in bringing about his desired changes in the lives of those with whom we counsel, we must realize that the Spirit often works in ways and at a pace that are quite different from what we might either desire or expect. Particularly when the focus for counseling involves sin, and repentance is biblically demanded, we need to be careful not to rush ahead of the Spirit's convicting

work. I have worked with numerous people over the years who have desperately wanted to deal with their sin and be restored to God and others, but who felt that the approach taken by their church and/or its leaders was so stern that it became oppressive and drove them away. Pastoral counseling—including matters involving church discipline—must always have biblical restoration (to God and to others) as its primary aim. Don't ignore or wink at sin, and don't compromise the biblical demands and processes for restoration, but don't confuse your role with that of the Holy Spirit. Trust God's Spirit to use you to accomplish his work in the life of your counselees, and allow him to bring conviction and change in his time.

2. *Don't say that you "understand."* Saying that you understand may seem like a tender expression that conveys your sympathy to the counselee, but the reality is that you don't actually understand what it is like to be another person and to experience his feelings and problems within the constellation of his personality, constitution, and life experiences. Many counselors have expressed their "understanding," only to have the counselee snap back: "No, you don't! How could you? You're not me!" It is more accurate and effective to say something like "I can only imagine what this must be like for you." Such a statement conveys your heart without risking defensiveness.

3. *Don't endorse or "buy in" to a counselee's pathology or problem.* Avoid responding to the counselee who says, "My wife is really a jerk" with "Yeah, mine, too" or "She has always seemed that way to me." It is better to ask a question (e.g., "Can you tell me more about that?") than to agree and effectively endorse the validity of the statement or perspective. Similarly, if a counselee violates the parameters of reality and states that, for example, he is from a moon revolving around Jupiter, don't say, "Oh, yeah, which one?" If he is serious, you should grab your phone and dial 911.

4. *Don't engage in physical contact.* Other than an appropriate handshake, as previously mentioned, don't touch the counselee. Period.

5. *Don't ask "Why?"* Asking "Why?" calls for a defense and places the other person in a position where he senses the immediate need to justify himself. That, in turn, sets you in a psychologically adversarial relationship with your counselee. If at all possible, you want to stand alongside the counselee, not stand against him. You can elicit the same information that the question "Why?" is designed to get at by turning the last thing that the person said into a reflected question (e.g., "You're thinking of quitting your job?") or by asking, "Can you say a little more about that?" or "Can you help me better understand that?"

6. *Don't feel compelled to fill silence.* We are strangers to silence. Grow

comfortable with it, learn to read the counselee's nonverbal clues so that you can properly manage it (as previously discussed), and realize that some of the best counseling work occurs when seemingly nothing is going on.

7. *Don't oversell yourself.* Realize your relative strengths and weaknesses as a person, a pastor, and a counselor—we all have them. Stay well within the boundaries of your competency level, and err on the side of caution and underestimation when it comes to the problems that you can effectively handle. Compassion and humility mark the faithful Christian, and they are indispensable qualities in the pastoral counselor. Practice underselling and overdelivering.

8. *Don't raise unrealistic expectations.* Promising a counselee that you can make his problem go away or otherwise setting the counselee up for disappointment is a sure way to harm another person and tarnish your reputation.

9. *Don't make promises you can't or won't keep.* If you make a representation, follow through and do it. Your faithfulness as a pastor and your effectiveness as a counselor hinge on your character, of which trustworthiness is an essential component.

10. *Don't introduce humor into a serious situation or moment.* Ministerial comic relief is in vogue these days. Rare today is the preacher who has not turned comedian in the pulpit. For many pastors, stories—especially funny stories—*are* the sermon, and the closer they skate to unbridled hilarity, the better. Sadly, this buffoonery is too often brought into the counseling context, where serious counselee disclosures are sprinkled with sarcastic and "witty" verbal footnotes. Such is the mark of immaturity, and the wise pastoral counselor learns to restrain himself and save his humor for appropriate times and circumstances.

11. *Don't be both punisher and counselor.* When working with a counselee who has fallen into sin, consider having the remaining church leadership administrate any disciplinary processes. It is generally easier for people to be open and honest with and confess everything to someone whom they view as a "priest" rather than a "judge."

12. *Don't fail to collaborate and refer.* No counselor is good enough to do it all. Learn to refer to trusted professionals with whom you have nurtured a good working relationship, and do so often and early. One of my saddest experiences as a psychologist was speaking with an elderly Christian man and church leader who had killed his dear wife of many decades by repeatedly stabbing her with a knife. He had been seeing a pastoral counselor for some time who had failed to refer him when there were clear signs

and symptoms indicating that he should have done so. It is hard to make a mistake by referring.

13. *Don't violate confidentiality.* Generally only under emergency conditions may you breach confidentiality without the counselee's express permission. I always get the counselee's permission in writing. Should you be served a subpoena to testify in a matter involving your counselee, you are wise to consult an attorney. In some cases, the courts cannot compel a minister to divulge information shared in confidence.

14. *Don't fail to get supervision.* Even the best psychologists and psychiatrists are involved in continuing education and receive ongoing supervision. Having another set of eyes looking over your shoulder is a tremendous advantage in pointing out blind spots, understanding issues, unraveling complex scenarios, generating options and intervention strategies, assessing progress, removing obstacles, and more. I continue to consult with former psychology professors and training supervisors, and I am greatly helped in ministry by discussing theological and ministerial challenges with fellow pastoral colleagues, past seminary professors and classmates, and Christian leaders. In turn, I appreciate having opportunities to walk my present and former students through tricky counseling and theological quandaries. I have never lost respect for someone who asked for help or said "I don't know." The wise and competent pastor is continually learning and seeking supervision from more mature Christians and experienced counselors.[22]

15. *Don't use yourself as an example.* There is little to gain and much to lose when you hold yourself out as either a positive or negative example. If you project a positive image of yourself, the counselee may feel further diminished by your apparent "success." If you project a negative image of yourself, the counselee may be inclined to diminish the severity of his problem. "After all," he may surmise, "if the pastor has done the same thing or something nearly as bad, then why am I feeling guilty and sensing that I need to make changes?"

EMERGENCY SITUATIONS AND MAKING REFERRALS IN PASTORAL COUNSELING

I have taught college and seminary courses in pastoral counseling for many years, and I sometimes, with tongue in cheek, introduce the course as "How

---

[22] One effective way of gaining greater competency as a counselor is to produce a "tape-script" of an actual counseling session. With the counselee's prior informed and written consent, a recording is made of the counseling session and subsequently transcribed. The pastoral counselor then reviews both the tape and script with a senior colleague or supervising professional. Be sure to "sterilize" the script of all identifying information unnecessary to supervision, and properly destroy all recordings and transcripts after supervision has concluded.

to Make a Referral." There is some humor in that, but only a little. Many counselors are ineffective (or downright dangerous) at counseling because they don't know what they don't know. Counselees are not always reliable historians when it comes to their thoughts, behavior, or feelings, and they are unaware of unconscious material and motives that can escape detection by even the most seasoned psychologist. The wise counselor quickly recognizes when he is in over his head and knows how to make efficient and appropriate referrals.

EMERGENCIES

You should stop counseling and, when appropriate, advise the counselee that you need to make an immediate call for help if he begins talking about harming himself or someone else, committing a crime, abusing/neglecting a child or elderly person, or showing signs of being gravely disabled. By "gravely disabled" I mean any disturbance in the quality of his thinking (e.g., the counselee's speech is odd or confused), reality testing (e.g., the counselee is saying or doing things that suggests he is not connected to the real world), or his ability to care for his own or a dependent's health and/or safety needs (e.g., appearing disheveled, malnourished, at risk for placing himself or another in a potentially harmful situation, lacking basic hygiene, or intending to drive while intoxicated).

Counselees often deny feeling suicidal, and I avoid using the loaded word *suicide* in the counseling context. Rather, I ask, "Have you recently felt so badly that it just seemed worth it to you to end it all?" I have had many counselees admit to such feelings, even though they would have otherwise rejected the thought that they were "suicidal."[23] If your counselee seems to be hinting at self-harm, ask the previous question. If he answers in the affirmative, get immediate help.

Psychiatrists and psychologists are professionally trained to assess lethality, abuse, health and safety concerns, and major mental illness. Such matters should be immediately referred to them by placing a 911 call and briefly explaining to the operator the nature of your concern. The operator will most likely dispatch the police, who will evaluate the situation and arrange for the counselee's transport to a proper mental health facility.

If I can satisfactorily explain to the counselee my need to call for help

---

[23] Similarly, I avoid asking my counselees if they are "depressed." Many counselees find the word too clinical and bristle at the thought that they are "depressed." Rather, I ask, "Have you recently noticed feeling sadder or more down than usual?" Such captures the feeling of depression and gets at the information that I need without creating an unnecessary obstacle in the mind of the counselee.

and he appears to concur that such is necessary, I often have him remain with me while I place the call from my office. If it is clear that I am unable to meaningfully communicate with the counselee, or I am concerned about how he may react to my calling for emergency help in his presence, I often ask him to remain in my office while, without explanation, I excuse myself and place the call from another room. When I find it prudent to leave my office in order to call for emergency help, I ask an assistant to bring his cell phone and remain outside my office door. Should the counselee attempt to leave, the assistant is to gently encourage the counselee to remain. If the assistant's efforts are unsuccessful and the counselee tries to leave, the assistant is to call me and follow the counselee until help arrives. No one should attempt to restrain a fleeing counselee.

I cannot overstate the importance of this topic. Failure to make an appropriate and immediate emergency referral under the above-cited conditions has repeatedly, and unnecessarily, led to tragic consequences. Know when you are in an emergency situation, know what to do, and don't delay in getting your counselee immediate help.

"Must Referrals"

Competent counselors are aware of signs (i.e., what you observe) and symptoms (i.e., what you are told) that indicate that a professional referral is needed. The majority of these signs and symptoms are associated with two conditions: anxiety and depression. Take some time to become familiar with the basic features of these two conditions, as they present frequently in pastoral counseling contexts.

Characteristics of Anxiety
- Worry (apprehensive expectation)
- Difficulty controlling concerns
- Restlessness or a feeling of being "keyed up"
- Becoming easily fatigued
- Difficulty concentrating
- Irritability
- Muscle tension
- Disturbance in sleep

Characteristics of Depression
- Disturbance in sleep/fatigue
- Disturbance in appetite

- Loss of pleasure
- Sadness/tearfulness
- Slow personal tempo
- Irritability
- Feelings of worthlessness/inappropriate guilt
- Difficulty with attention/concentration/decisiveness
- Recurrent thoughts of death

You will notice that several characteristics are common to both anxiety and depression, including disturbances in sleep, fatigue, difficulty with concentration, and irritability. Those with typical major depression often have trouble staying asleep, awaken early in the morning and are troubled by intrusive thoughts, have difficulty falling back asleep, and experience chronic daytime fatigue and a general suppression in appetite—but not always. Sometimes depressed people have an increase in sleep and appetite—signs and symptoms suggestive of "atypical depression." And, of course, it is sometimes difficult to differentiate between depression and anxiety, as the overlap in signs and symptoms reveals.

To simplify matters, I often encourage pastoral counselors to pay specific attention to and make regular inquiries concerning two features: disturbances in sleep and appetite.

I inquire about any changes in sleep or appetite before concluding nearly every session. If your counselee reports either a disturbance in sleep (either sleeping too little or too much) or appetite (either eating too little or too much), you should bring that to the attention of the counselee's primary-care physician. I usually place the call to the physician from my office, briefly explain my concern, and then allow the counselee to speak directly with the physician or nurse to make an appointment. Trust me when I say that any competent physician will be grateful for your assistance in this matter.

There are two other conditions that must trigger a referral. First, if the presenting problem(s) for counseling is/are beyond your proficiency, you should refer. Sometimes the counselor quickly knows when he is not equipped to help someone responsibly with a particular problem. Psychologists and psychiatrists understand that there are conditions they are simply not competent to treat, and referrals between highly skilled professionals are very common occurrences. I have made more referrals than I have accepted over my career. I know the conditions with which I work well (and with what and with whom I don't), and I understand my limitations.

Admittedly, proficiency is sometimes difficult to gauge. If after a few sessions you find that you are not arriving at your established "mile markers" en route to the counseling goal, either the goal should be reevaluated or a referral is in order. And should there be no progress at all after three or four sessions, you should refer.

Second, there is a vast difference, on one hand, between counseling people through a marital crisis or a difficult decision, improving communication skills, and helping to encourage spiritual growth, and, on the other hand, doing psychotherapy with those suffering from major mental illness or long-standing and pervasive disorders in mood or identity. Pastoral counselors are rarely equipped to handle the latter types of disorders and conditions, and ought to refer to a professional. Under those circumstances, you might explore with the treating professional how you can best be of pastoral support and encouragement to the counselee, without interfering with the treatment. Under no circumstances should a pastoral counselor meddle in medication regimens or professionally prescribed treatment protocols. If you have a concern regarding medication and/or professional treatment regimens, make an inquiry of the treating professional, but don't contravene or contradict professional involvement.

Effective pastoral counselors have cultivated a referral relationship with at least one mental-health professional. You should be aware that there are different kinds of professionals, with different kinds of education, training, and experience, offering different kinds of help with different kinds of people and conditions. Some pastors form a close relationship with a single trusted psychiatrist or psychologist to whom they refer all necessary and appropriate cases, allowing the professional in turn to assign the case to a suitable treating provider or facility. This single-provider approach has many advantages, including ease of referral-making and professional competency. Other pastors assemble a network of providers and triage their own cases for referral. However, the latter approach works only if the pastor possesses unusual skills at psychiatric differential diagnosis. In the majority of cases, it is best to refer to the counselee's primary-care physician or to a psychologist or psychiatrist, who will make the subsequent referrals for you as necessary and appropriate.

I offer one more word about making referrals. I am often asked about referral-making to non-Christian mental-health providers. Like the door-closed, door-open/ajar debate previously discussed, opinions here tend to run strong and loud. All things being equal, I refer to a *competent* Christian psychologist or psychiatrist when that option is available. However, I refer

508 Ministerial Duties

to a competent non-Christian psychologist or psychiatrist before I refer to an *incompetent* Christian psychologist or psychiatrist, if I must choose.

Psychologists and psychiatrists practice in accordance with ethical and professional standards that require that they work within the counselee's presenting worldview and/or religious framework; otherwise, they must refer to someone who will. For example, when I was in practice as a psychologist, I referred to another provider a same-sex couple seeking counseling for issues related to sexual dysfunction. I was ethically bound to do so, as I was biblically-theologically unable to work within the moral framework presented to me by the couple. The standards cut both ways, and an ethical psychologist or psychiatrist who accepts a Christian for counseling will either work within the biblical-theological worldview of the counselee or make an appropriate referral.

If you will be making referrals to a non-Christian professional, I advise that you get to know him first. Take the psychologist or psychiatrist for coffee or a meal and explain who you are, the kinds of people that you would like to refer, and the biblical-theological values that inform Christian goal-setting. Ask if he would be comfortable working with such people and within such a framework. I don't know of a single ethical, competent, professional psychologist or psychiatrist who wouldn't appreciate having such a discussion. As for myself, if those conditions were satisfied and I had no realistic alternatives for referring to a competent Christian professional, I would feel comfortable making a referral to an unbelieving psychologist or psychiatrist.

"Should Referrals"

Be careful about the number of counselees that you take on and the number of counseling hours that you provide. Actively listening and effectively working with people in counseling is all-consuming, and you will be emotionally and mentally drained after a session or two. Since entering full-time pastoral ministry, I average fewer than four counselees at any given time, rarely five—never more. You may want to consider starting by offering fifty-minute sessions, as appropriate. That would translate into between two to four hours of counseling a week. That's plenty. Additional requests for counseling might best be referred to others, depending on the nature of the issue or problem. You can probably safely put off for several weeks the high school senior who needs to make a college decision in twelve months, but other issues may not be so easily, or wisely, postponed. Refer rather than overextend yourself.

Some counseling needs may be suitable for referral to a ministerial colleague, church leader, or other gifted person within your church. Fellow pastors in the community who you know and trust and who are equipped and reliable may also be good candidates for receiving your referrals. At any given time, I am usually counseling with at least one person referred to me by a local pastor.

Make your referrals from your office with the counselee present and, when possible, introduce him on the phone to the one to whom you are making the referral, allowing the counselee to make his own appointment. Again, taking the initiative in seeking help correlates with a better outcome in counseling. You want to pass the counselee along personally, smoothly, and efficiently. Such is the practice of professionals, and the benefits are many.

ACCEPTING REIMBURSEMENT

I do not charge any fees associated with my counseling services. I view counseling as part of my ministerial duties.[24] Research suggests that those who pay for services tend to do better in counseling, presumably because they are more invested in the process. However, given that I provide counseling services primarily to those who are associated with the church I serve, it is likely that most of my counselees are contributing financially to the ministry.[25] Occasionally, someone receiving counseling asks if he can pay me. Such requests come more commonly from those who do not attend the church I pastor. I suggest that if he wishes to make a contribution, he can make an undesignated gift to the church.

If you choose to accept fees, I advise that you first consult with an attorney who specializes in nonprofit (ideally, church) tax laws. There may be legal and/or state agency regulations that have bearing on accepting fees for service, and you want to be very sure that you are not opening yourself personally, or the church more broadly, to either legal liability or possible charges of professional malpractice.

SAFEGUARDS FOR PASTORAL COUNSELING

Pastoral failure usually involves touching the gold, the girls, or the glory, and many pastors have shipwrecked their ministries on the shoals of temptations

---

[24] I hold a valid and active license as a psychologist, but I neither advertise nor hold myself out to the public as offering professional psychological services, and I make it clear to counselees that I am counseling them in my role as a minister.

[25] At my request, I do not receive any information related to individual giving. I want to be available to minister fully to everyone in my sphere of service, and I do not want knowledge of giving habits or amounts to exert any influence—unconsciously or otherwise—on my pastoring.

encountered in the counseling context. Men, I can't exhort you strongly enough to keep your hands off those three. The wise pastoral counselor takes precautions to guard against unprofessional, unethical, illegal, and immoral behavior.

Psychologists receive education and training that helps them identity situations and exchanges that can potentially lead to ethical/professional violations and turn them into opportunities for effective counseling or care. Furthermore, many psychologists-in-training are required to undergo their own therapy, in part, to identify unconscious drives, motivations, desires, and tendencies that can place them at risk for inappropriately acting out with counselees. Few pastors have received such education, training, or therapy, and what you don't know—the unconscious needs and desires that drive you—can render you exceedingly vulnerable in a counseling context.

As I have argued, there is no substitute for godly character and spiritual maturity when it comes to ministering to others. However, there are a number of safeguards that the pastoral counselor can put in place to help eliminate unbiblical and inappropriate behavior with counselees.

1. *Conduct yourself at all times in an irreproachable manner.* Speak and behave in ways that project the unambiguous and consistent message "I'm not available in any inappropriate way." Establish a barrier against unwanted and improper advances by publicly affirming your committed love, complete devotion, and uncompromising faithfulness to your wife. Those with whom you have contact should have the clear sense that you prefer your wife to the exclusion of everyone else and that you would rather die than violate your wedding vows or your wife's trust. Now, I'm not suggesting that you act surly, stiff, or suspicious in an effort to keep others at an arm's distance. Much less am I proposing that you and your wife behave in such ways that you become an uncomfortable spectacle at church. But people ought to both see and sense that you have eyes for no one else on the face of the earth—nor will you ever.

2. *The godly and trustworthy pastor puts off all coarse and crass language, suggestive speech, sexual innuendo and double entendré, tasteless remarks, and humor that is questionable, much less risqué.* I realize that it is currently fashionable for pastors to come across as "manly men of the world," replete with the vocabulary, attire, and cool factor of a recently paroled rapper. However, an indelicate temperament or conversational style is not only unbecoming of a man of God, but courts serious trouble in the counseling context. I don't think more highly of an invasive cardiac surgeon

because he has street cred or acts and talks like a thug. Men, how much higher is our calling as "doctors of the soul."[26]

3. *Always sit across from counselees, not next to them.* Sit at a comfortable and appropriate conversational distance.

4. *Other than a proper handshake, don't touch the counselee.* Resist any temptation to place your arm around an upset counselee in a counseling context. Physical contact is easily misinterpreted, may unconsciously encourage emotional upset in order to elicit future instances of physical closeness, and is a significant step in the direction of serious trouble.

5. *Be aware that it is not uncommon for some female parishioners to idealize their pastors—even fantasize about them.* In many ways, you represent the "ideal man" in the minds of some women. Publicly, you are viewed as a godly, educated, charismatic, accomplished, and gifted spiritual leader upon whom the Lord's hand rests. You do what few can do—stand in front of others and effectively speak for God—and do so for the cause of his glory and the good of those who come to hear you preach. And if you don't look like Godzilla or have a third eye growing out of your forehead, that's a plus. As such, some women may be smitten by you from the pew, perhaps becoming infatuated with you. Once in the counseling context, appreciation and admiration can easily turn to attraction and desire as the counselee comes to experience you as gentle, understanding, tender, helpful, nonjudgmental, and an effective listener, among other things. If she is unhappy in her marriage, she may be especially vulnerable to unconsciously viewing you as the paragon of everything that her husband is not. Now imagine a scenario in which such conditions exist and the female counselee is seeking to validate her self-worth, desirability, and attractiveness—those things that she feels are lacking in her marriage. If you are not exceedingly careful, you could easily get the impression, unconsciously, that she is attracted to *you* rather than to what you represent in her life and act out on her unconscious overtures. Such is but one example of the kind of disastrous consequences that can occur when pastoral counselors are not aware of the unconscious desires and motives of their counselees—or their own. When you hear a female counselee say things like "I wish that my husband understood me like you do"; "You are such a great listener; I have never felt so comfortable with anyone before"; or "Your wife sure is a lucky woman," be on guard. Don't act out, but rather redirect if you can. And if you can't, refer.

6. *Men, if you are having difficulties in your own personal life or marriage, don't counsel others until you get those issues resolved.* If you find

---

[26] See Eph. 4:1–16.

yourself attracted to the one you are counseling, refer the case to another counselor.

7. *Do not be seen in public with another woman without your wife's prior knowledge.* My wife knows where I am at all times. If I am called away from the church office to meet a woman in public, I contact my wife and let her know where I will be. Should anyone in the church see you in public with another woman and report the incident to your wife, you want her to be in a position to calm any concerns and defend your integrity. Most specifically, I tell my wife when I have a counseling appointment and when I expect to be done and home, though I never disclose whom I am counseling or the details of my counseling appointments.[27]

8. *Be accountable to your wife and frequently reassure her of your complete faithfulness.* On a personal note, I offer the following. From the beginning of my marriage, I have made it my practice to hold my wife, look directly in her eyes, and tell her that I have been faithful to her upon returning from an overnight trip—regardless of the setting, purpose, or duration. After approximately six months of marriage, I returned from a psychology conference, held my wife, and said, "Honey, I want you to know that I love you and that I have been faithful to you." She replied: "I know that you are a faithful man. You don't have to say that to me anymore." I told her: "I must, because I say it as much for my benefit as yours. I know when I leave that I will return to you and will tell you that I have been faithful. Knowing that, and knowing that you would know if I tried to say that and it was not true, is a part of my accountability." Men, if you want to adopt my practice, feel free.

9. *Give a circle of men permission to speak into your life and to look you in the eye and ask the hard questions that we each need to have repeatedly asked of us.* Brothers, don't be a "lone ranger" in ministry. (Remember, even the Lone Ranger had Tonto.) Surround yourself with godly, gracious, and disciplined men who genuinely love you and who are fully committed to God's very best for you. A man who resists appropriate accountability is a spiritual danger to himself and others.

SPECIAL SITUATIONS IN PASTORAL COUNSELING

I have provided a basic structure, along with some specific techniques, for the practice of effective pastoral counseling that I trust may be usefully applied

---

[27] Again, I hold a valid and active license as a psychologist, so I am bound to the ethical and professional standards of the psychology profession, including the manner and context in which I provide counseling.

to a wide array of situations and problems. However, there are at least three issues that present themselves in pastoral counseling with sufficient frequency to warrant separate attention.

Effective Premarital Counseling

I realize that we need to define terms carefully and that statistics can become rather slippery depending upon who is handling them and for what purposes, but the majority of indicators suggests that the divorce rate among self-professed Christians—including self-identified "evangelicals"—is not appreciably different from the prevalence rate within American society at large. Such is bad enough. However, when one considers that the statistics do not capture the number of Christian couples who feel compelled to remain in unhappy marriages for reasons of fear (e.g., fear of violating Scripture's teaching on divorce) or shame (e.g., facing church discipline or being ostracized by families, churches, or Christian friends) that do not constrain unbelievers in the same ways, the picture looks more grim. We need to do far more than we are at present if we are to turn the tide of unhappy marriages and significantly correct the trend in the divorce rate.

I receive a fairly steady stream of younger married couples in counseling who are dissatisfied and disillusioned, if not completely disgusted, and common to nearly all is inadequate premarital counseling. The overwhelming majority of couples with whom I have worked has described their premarital counseling as "nonexistent," "completely useless," or "a joke." Sadly, much of what passes for premarital counseling today sounds more like wedding planning. Rarely do I hear of pastors offering an intentional and systematic approach to premarital counseling. And while even the most thorough and effective premarital counseling will not make a marriage bulletproof, most of the issues that eventually surface in marriage counseling are those that are foundational to a healthy marriage and that should have been first addressed in premarital counseling.

I require every couple whom I marry to complete a minimum of eight ninety-minute premarital sessions with me—no exceptions.[28] Each session explores a different brick in the foundation of marriage upon which the couple will build their relationship. We discuss: (1) the meaning and "mystery" of marriage, (2) expectations for marriage, (3) roles and responsibilities, (4) family backgrounds, personality styles, in-laws, and "crossing family

---

[28] I once conducted premarital counseling with a couple that was separated by a considerable distance. The woman came to my office at 10:00 p.m. for their sessions, and her fiancé, who was in the military and stationed halfway around the globe, participated via weekly conference calls.

lines," (5) communication patterns, decision-making, conflict resolution, and "fighting fair," (6) financial matters, including debt and budget-setting, (7) sexual purity before and sexual intimacy after marriage, and (8) family planning and contraception.

In cases of remarriage, I explore the previous marriage, reasons for the dissolution, the length of time since the dissolution, and spiritual/emotional growth since the dissolution before agreeing to initiate premarital counseling. This process can take a while. If I agree to provide premarital counseling, I add a session to discuss the impact of the marriage on any children and parenting issues, as necessary.

I have the couple use a premarital guide/workbook that requires between one and three hours of homework each week, which I supplement with my own materials.[29] If the couple balks at the length of premarital counseling or the assignment of a workbook and homework, that is a caution flag. I told one hesitant couple, "You can either choose to see me for eight weeks now when you are happy or raise your risk of having to see me in seven years for twelve weeks when you are not." They chuckled and signed up on the spot.

I have found it helpful to have the couple write out their respective expectations for marriage. I assign this writing project a couple of weeks prior to the session when we will discuss the same. Their lists should include their expectations for both themselves and their partner in marriage, and I ask that they not discuss the items on their lists or collaborate on the project. The session during which these lists are reviewed is often incredibly useful, as each becomes aware of his or her previously unspoken expectations of the other. In at least one case, this project prompted a discussion that subsequently led one couple to decide against marrying one another. They both eventually married different partners, and each has repeatedly remarked to me how grateful they are for having been asked to go through such a thorough assignment.

Countless wide-eyed young people are gleefully bounding down the aisle every year and standing before us to vow before God their lifelong devotion to a person whom they don't really know, covenant to live in a "mystery" that they don't really understand, and assume roles and responsibilities based

---

[29] There is a need for more and better resources for use in premarital counseling. I have used David Boehl, Brent Nelson, Jeff Schulte, and Lloyd Sharach, *Preparing for Marriage: The Complete Guide to Help Discover God's Plan for a Lifetime of Love*, ed. Dennis Rainey (Little Rock, AR: FamilyLife, 1997) with good success. I have also scanned but have yet to use John Henderson, *Catching Foxes: A Gospel-Guided Journey to Marriage* (Bedford, TX: Association of Biblical Counselors, 2011). Additional areas for premarital counseling that I believe need to be covered (as listed in the text) are addressed through sermon and lecture materials that I have prepared. There is a lot of fluff out there on both marriage and premarital counseling. Carefully review any proposed materials.

upon expectations that they don't really share. It seems that most couples spend more time preparing for a two-week cruise than for a fifty-year marriage. Those of us who are pastors bear a large part of the blame. We are right to preach about biblical marriage in our pulpits, teach about it in our churches, and work to preserve it in our counseling, but let us do more than merely rail against the divorce epidemic. Let us roll up our sleeves to help prepare people for biblical, healthy, and satisfying marriages.

EFFECTIVE MARRIAGE COUNSELING

Especially in Christian circles, where stigmas about "counseling" remain deeply entrenched, many couples do not seek help for their problems until it is in the very late innings. It is not uncommon for couples to make an appointment to see me and begin their first session by saying something like, "Well, we have decided to get a divorce, and we want you to help us do this amicably for the sake of the children."

Top of the ninth, down by twenty-six runs, bases loaded, no outs—"Hey, preacher, step up here and pitch us out of this thing."

In such cases, I usually assume a more active role in counseling and ask to see the couple at least twice per week. I ask the couple to make a commitment to attend a fixed number of sessions (usually eight) and to put off all decisions until the sessions have been completed. In many cases, the couple is relieved, as they had been hoping for a reason to hope but simply could not see a way forward.

Some couples wait until the marriage is broken before one or the other can't take it anymore and makes a plea for help. Frequently, it is the discovery of an affair, marital separation, talk of divorce, or some other major crisis that precipitates counseling. Under those conditions, it is not uncommon for "marriage counseling" to begin with only one spouse. While I am pleased initially to accept one spouse for "marriage counseling," I realize that I will eventually need to have both partners in the room in order to be of significant help to the marriage.

If "marriage counseling" begins with only one spouse in the room, I understand that I am receiving only a part of the story—most often, tilted. Usually it is the "aggrieved" party that first comes to the pastoral counselor's attention, and he can use much of the early session(s) to convince the counselor that he is the "victim." Be prepared to hear a lot of nasty stuff about the spouse not present and for attempts—both overt and subtle—aimed at gaining your sympathies and assent that the absent spouse is largely, if not

516   Ministerial Duties

totally, at fault. Resisting such attempts can be difficult, and your seeming reluctance to buy the story wholesale and declare the "victim" the victim can be met with anger, disappointment, increased attempts at manipulation, or rejection.

Despite what you may hear during marriage counseling sessions, understand that *both* partners are contributing in significant, though perhaps different, ways to the downfall of the marriage. That is not to say that each is contributing equally, but rather that there is very rarely a completely "innocent" party when a marriage turns sour. As such, efforts to assign "blame" are largely fruitless. Listen carefully and warmly accept what is shared, but avoid passing judgment or making pronouncements. If asked by an unaccompanied spouse in "marriage counseling" about what I think regarding what has been shared, I find it best to comment upon what I have observed and express my appreciation for the feelings shared while endorsing very little and not rendering any judgments. For example, I might say something like, "I can see that you are very upset and that this is weighing very heavily upon you. The look of sadness I see in your eyes shows me how deeply you are hurting. I very much want to help you through this." That usually gets the conversation going.

When you are providing marriage counseling, the marriage itself becomes the "counselee," so to speak. As such, you eventually need to work at getting both partners in the room. I find that the absent spouse is usually quite resistant to counseling, and the longer the first spouse has seen me, the more difficult it is to get the absent spouse to come. Frequently, the absent spouse senses you are biased against her, given that her partner got to tell his story first—a suspicious and distrustful perception that tends to become more deeply entrenched the longer I see just one of the partners in counseling.

One of the most effective ways that I have found to get a resistant partner into counseling is to call and request her help with my efforts to help her spouse. For example, with the presenting spouse's knowledge and permission, I call and say: "Hi, Carol, this is Pastor Evans calling from Christ Church. As you may be aware, I have been meeting with your husband, Bill, over the past few weeks to help him walk through some stuff, and I am calling to see if you might be kind enough to help me do that. Your perspective on things would be of tremendous help to me. Might you be willing to help me out please?" I don't give details to the absent spouse related to my request for help. I have found that an absent spouse generally has a difficult time refusing a humble request for assistance, even when it involves a spouse for whom she harbors very hard or hurtful feelings.

I have also found that by identifying the first spouse as, in essence, "the one in need of help" (known as the "identified patient" in professional circles), the resistant spouse may relax her concerns that I am biased against her or that I view her as "the problem spouse" and be more willing to enter the process as my "therapeutic ally" in the "treatment" of her husband.

I prepare the first spouse for the joint session, and once the resistant partner enters in, I begin summarizing a few of the issues that the first spouse has identified as problematic and request the resistant spouse's feedback. The resistant spouse is frequently all too happy to share with me what's "wrong" with her spouse. With increased investment comes increased involvement in counseling, and I have seen many initially resistant spouses become actively engaged through this approach.

When counseling with a resistant spouse (or individual for that matter), there are a few things that are useful to keep in mind. Resistant people are far more likely to respond favorably to positive reinforcement than to criticism, punishment, or threat. Avoid using "should" statements that may trigger anger and defensiveness, and keep the resistant spouse in the "helper" role. Closing the session by expressing my appreciation for the resistant spouse's help and asking if she would be willing to continue to help me a bit more usually brings her back. Gradually, after I have established trust and a good rapport through nonjudgmental caring with the resistant spouse, I gently begin to explore her contributions to the marriage that makes it difficult. Now I am treating the marriage.

A few words of caution are in order here. Once you have both partners in marriage counseling, avoid seeing either of them individually, unless it is for good reason. Frequently the absent spouse wants a report from the spouse with whom you met. Seldom are you fully and faithfully represented under such conditions, and the absent spouse may feel slighted, manipulated, gossiped about, or abused, or conclude that you violated confidentiality. When that occurs, the absent spouse sometimes discontinues marriage counseling, sensing that you have taken sides against her based upon what she was told by her spouse. Alternatively, the absent spouse may make her own request to see you privately, at which time she may want to "fact-check" what she was told. This scenario rarely ends well, and marriage counseling can get completely derailed. For the same reasons, I suspend a counseling session for the duration of a spouse's absence when one steps out of the office to use the restroom or accept a phone call. In short, avoid *ex parte* conversations once marriage counseling has begun, unless there is a very good reason.

Marriage counseling is framed by the same values and proceeds through the same stages as individual counseling; only the identification of the "counselee" has changed—counsel one marriage, not two individuals. Problems are mutually shared, goals are mutually developed, and progress is mutually pursued and monitored. I often assign some reading to a couple in counseling, which helps to keeps conversation and "counseling" moving between sessions.[30] Much of the real "work" of counseling takes place between sessions.

Sadly, some couples have already determined their fate and have made the firm decision to divorce long before they seek your involvement. For many couples—especially Christian couples—going to see someone for "marriage counseling" before divorcing is merely perfunctory. Most couples realize that they will carry the stigma of a failed marriage throughout their lives and will need to give a repeated account of what happened and why, as well as answer questions concerning the lengths to which they went to try and save their marriage. Most specifically, each will be asked if they "sought counseling." No one wants to answer that question in the negative; to divorce without having sought counseling seems insincere at best. It is believed much better to answer, "Oh yes, we even tried counseling, but it didn't work." With that box ticked, family members and friends usually feel at least some small measure of solace and can more easily say, "Well, that's too bad, but at least you did everything you could," as if marriage counseling is the very last resort.

If a couple has irrevocably decided to divorce and one of the partners seeks counseling, usually the other partner will want to attend at least one session—neither wants to go through life labeled as "the one unwilling to try to make things work." Accordingly, even when things are most desperate, you can often get in at least one session with both partners. During that session, I often tell couples who seem to be coming for no other reason than to satisfy a socially expected "requirement" before divorcing, "I suppose one thing that you gain by seeing me today will be the ability to tell people that you sought out counseling, but it didn't work." That feedback often leads into a fruitful discussion of their true motives for seeking counseling and whether they really want help or are merely looking to stamp their social

---

[30] There is no shortage of books on marriage—some of them are good, but many of them are appalling nonsense. You may find it useful to begin the process of assembling your eventual marriage counseling reading recommendations by consulting the various book reviews on marriage provided by The Gospel Coalition (www.thegospelcoalition.org). But be warned: a book review does not imply endorsement. Again, I strongly recommend that a pastor/counselor personally read any prospective materials before recommending them to others.

At the end of the chapter, I provide some resources as a convenience for those who wish to make a further study of pastoral counseling, explore my biblical-theological framework for pastoral counseling, and construct a possible reading list for use in marriage and premarital counseling. Inclusion in this list should not be construed as unqualified endorsement of either the author or resource.

passports for their lives after divorce. I have seen God do amazing things in seemingly doomed marriages.

Effective Counseling with Unbelievers

Counseling unbelievers can provide wonderful opportunities to encourage reflection on matters of eternal weight and consequence, demonstrate the tender mercies and compassion of Christ, and commend the gospel. Among my greatest joys in pastoral counseling is witnessing occasions when God graciously draws to himself an unbeliever in repentance and faith. Sometimes redemption is transacted in a counseling session; at other times, the counselee starts attending worship services and is exposed to the preaching of the gospel, through which God calls that one to himself. Accordingly, I am pleased to accept unbelievers for counseling, provided that the presenting issues of concern fall within my areas of competency. I follow the same guidelines that I have provided in this chapter for making that determination.

Of course, the pastoral counselor needs to be aware that the unbeliever lacks the presence, power, and provisions of God's Spirit, and so lacks both the conviction and ability to bring his life into unassisted conformity with God's Word and will. The unbelieving counselee is unlikely to recognize the spiritual dimension of his problem and may be unable to generate appropriate biblical goals for counseling. The pastoral counselor actively assists with both of those tasks.

Provided that the unbelieving counselee understands that you are offering *pastoral* counseling, it is highly probable that he will be open to exploring the spiritual aspects of his problems with you. I directly invite the unbelieving counselee to do that with me during the initial session. I might say: "As you are aware, I am a pastor, and I want you to know that I provide counseling consistent with my Christian convictions and biblical worldview. Knowing that, I am wondering if you are open to exploring the spiritual facet of your problem with me, in addition to everything else that we will talk about." I have yet to have anyone decline the offer.

It is not uncommon for the first "spiritual" discussion to occur during goal-setting. Lacking a biblical worldview, unbelieving counselees sometimes articulate incomplete, if not wholly inappropriate, goals for counseling. Having secured the counselee's permission to venture into spiritual territory, I often use the goal-setting stage to introduce biblical values. For example, I might say: "You mention that you see divorce as your only option. I wonder if there are not more options available to you that may be difficult for you to see right now because of how you are presently feeling." Some counselees are open to extending their list of options; others are not. If the counselee refuses to consider that there might be other available options, I might say, "You mentioned that you were open to exploring the spiritual aspects of your problem, and I am wondering if you would be willing to consider what the Bible has to say about your current situation and the options available to you?" That question has proven very fruitful. In all events, the faithful biblical counselor does not assist a counselee in pursuing unbiblical goals.

CONCLUSION

It is at once an extraordinarily lofty and profoundly humbling thought to consider that almighty God would choose to use failed and flawed human beings to accomplish his purposes. I wish, somehow, that I felt worthy to be called God's child and, as if that were not already enough, to have him see fit to use me as a herald of his gospel and an undershepherd in the rescue and restoration of his sheep. The truth is, I do not, and I am not. It is all as a result of undeserved grace—*all* of it.

I am continually reminded of my unworthiness and prompted to praise each time I see the same extreme grace extended to me at work in the life of another. What joy there is in watching the power of God unleashed through the preaching of the cross. And what wonder there is in seeing God's Spirit move in the life of a haggard sheep.

My aim here has been to help us become better equipped for useful service as pastoral counselors in the faithful shepherding of God's flock. I have sought to be "comprehensive and detailed, yet completely accessible; informal and casual, yet buttoned-up theologically, psychologically, and pastorally . . . highly practical, including useful tidbits for the pastor, even some humor," as Kent requested. If those purposes have been achieved and there be any profit in all of this, I'll let you judge, and I ask that the Chief Shepherd receive any praise and all glory.

May God bless and use you for the cause of his glory and the extension of his kingdom until that day when we shall all stand before him face to face and marvel at Christ.

SELECTED BIBLIOGRAPHY

Barnes, M. Craig. *The Pastor as Minor Poet*. Grand Rapids: Eerdmans, 2009.

Benner, David G. *Care of Souls: Revisioning Christian Nurture and Counsel*. Grand Rapids: Baker Books, 1998.

————. *Strategic Pastoral Counseling: A Short-Term Structured Model.* 2nd. ed. Grand Rapids: Baker Academic, 2003.

———— and Peter Hill, eds. *Baker Encyclopedia of Psychology & Counseling.* 2nd. ed. Grand Rapids: Baker Books, 1999.

Boehl, David, Brent Nelson, Jeff Schulte and Lloyd Shadrach. *Preparing for Marriage: The Complete Guide to Help you Discover God's Plan for a Lifetime of Love.* Ed. Dennis Rainey. Ventura, CA: Gospel Light, 1997.

Clinton, Timothy, and George Ohlschlager, eds. *Competent Christian Counseling: Foundations & Practice of Compassionate Soul Care, Vol. I.* Colorado Springs: Waterbrook Press, 2002.

Dittes, James E. *Pastoral Counseling: The Basics.* Louisville: Westminster John Knox Press, 1999.

Evans, Robert W. *Psychological Aspects of Injury and Illness.* Colorado Springs: self-published, 1992.

————. *Effective Counseling in the Margins of Life.* Sacramento, CA: Veritas, 1999.

————. "Neuropsychological Aspects of Aging and Their Implications for Bioethical Decision-Making Among the Elderly." In *Aging, Death, and the Quest for Immortality.* Ed. C. Ben Mitchell, Robert D. Orr, and Susan A. Salladay. Grand Rapids: Eerdmans, 2004, 75–86.

Henderson, John. *Catching Foxes: A Gospel-Guided Journey to Marriage.* Bedford, TX: Association of Biblical Counselors, 2011.

Hunter, Rodney, ed. *Dictionary of Pastoral Care and Counseling.* Nashville: Abingdon Press, 1990.

Johnson, W. Brad. *The Pastor's Guide to Psychological Disorders and Treatments.* New York: Haworth Pastoral Press, 2000.

Kornfeld, Margaret. *Cultivating Wholeness: A Guide to Care and Counseling in Faith Communities.* New York: Continuum, 2001.

Mason, Mike. *The Mystery of Marriage.* Colorado Springs: Multnomah, 1985/2005.

McMinn, Mark R., and Timothy R. Phillips, eds. *Care for the Soul: Exploring the Intersection of Psychology and Theology.* Downers Grove, IL: IVP Academic, 2001.

McMinn, Mark. *Sin and Grace in Christian Counseling: An Integrative Paradigm.* Downers Grove, IL: IVP Academic, 2008.

Moon, Gary, and David Benner, eds. *Spiritual Direction and the Care of Souls.* Downers Grove, IL: InterVarsity Press, 2004.

Piper, John. *This Momentary Marriage: A Parable of Permanence*. Wheaton, IL: Crossway, 2012.

Shields, Harry, and Gary Bredfeldt. *Caring for Souls: Counseling Under the Authority of Scripture*. Chicago: Moody Press, 2001.

Stone, Howard W., ed. *Strategies for Brief Pastoral Counseling*. Minneapolis: Fortress Press, 2001.

Wicks, Robert J., and Richard D. Parsons, eds. *Clinical Handbook of Pastoral Counseling, Vol. 1*. Mahwah, NJ: Integration Books, 1985/1993.

———. *Clinical Handbook of Pastoral Counseling. Vol. 2*. Mahwah, NJ: Integration Books, 1993.

11

Hospital Visitation

Over the years, a pastor will encounter the full range of emotions in hospital rooms—from the joyous birth of a newborn (a hot and living star fallen from heaven, so to speak) to the cold, lifeless stillborn who will never see the constellations. On another day, he will hear the unexpected wonderful news of an incredible life-giving surgery for one, and for another the bleak news of a terminal diagnosis. Through all of these experiences, he will witness the inner workings of families in times of deepest crisis. In the midst of both the bleak and the bright events, the pastor will have the opportunity to be a humble servant of Christ, to be his feet, hands, and lips to his people—and to the world. In all instances, he will be ministering to far more people than the sick and dying. And the deep needs and weaknesses to which he ministers will afford sweet opportunities for the gospel. This means that the visitation of the hospitalized is not something that derails the pastor from his ministry, but is something central to it.

HOSPITAL PROTOCOLS

How can we minister effectively in hospitals? In this chapter, we will consider a number of key factors.

All hospitals have unique conventions and protocols, and these can be easily learned by pastors who set aside ecclesial presumption and put on a genial smile. Generally all that is required is a visit to the front desk, followed by a stop at the nurses' station before entering the patient's room.

If the pastor knows what he will be encountering, he can be prepared by having already prayed and by having an appropriate Scripture reading in mind (see the detailed list of Scriptures below). Beyond that, everything must be done with prayerful sensitivity and with an eye to the care of the soul of the patient and the people who are present.

VISITING THE SICK

Here are some well-traveled don'ts and do's for the visit. First, the *don'ts*:

1. *Don't overstay.* Usually the patient and the family are glad to see you come and glad to see you go. It is a mistake to imagine that a long stay will be interpreted as a demonstration of love. This, of course, is not to be confused with a vigil with a family during a child's surgery or at the passing of a loved one. The omnipresent pastor may be meeting his own needs rather than that of the ill and the family.

2. *Don't read too much Scripture.* In most cases, the ill are in no state to listen attentively to long sections of God's Word, no matter how wonderful the truths. Sometimes it can be downright irritating to the one who is in pain. Be sensitive. Doing a religious thing may be just that and no more.

3. *Don't offer a lengthy prayer.* Remember the coda often attributed to Mark Twain: "I didn't have time to write you a short letter, so I wrote you a long one instead." Few patients want a long letter—or a long prayer!—when you come to visit. So keep your prayer biblical, thought-through, brief, and reverently to the point. That way the ill and the family can pray along with you.

4. *Don't offer a prognosis.* Leave that to the doctor. If you do offer one, the family will remember it, and you will turn out to either be a prophet or false prophet, neither of which is an enviable role to occupy in another's life.

5. *Don't promise too much.* It is tempting, when you are empathizing with someone in great need, to promise that you will be there every day or even twice a day, which is all good and fine if you do it, but sometimes you can't. Better just to do it rather than to break your pastoral word.

As to the *do's*, all visits vary, but generally you should:

1. *Quietly enter the room* and greet the ill and others who may be there. Take mental note of their names and relationships. Chat quietly with all, but do not get distracted.

2. *Focus on the patient.* Take your time in asking appropriate questions, and listen, wholly engaged. Do not press for responses, especially if the patient is in pain. And do not yield to filling any awkward silences with nervous banter.

3. *Be sensitive to all.* Sometimes it turns out that your ministry is to the spouse or parents.

4. *Read the Scriptures.* When you sense that you have stayed an appropriate length of time, ask if he/she would like you to read from God's Word. Read it well with understanding, and not too fast. Take your time.

5. *Pray.* Ask if you may pray. If possible, take his/her hand in yours, or place your hand on the ill, and offer a compassionate, faith-filled prayer in the name of the Lord Jesus Christ.

6. *Make a ministry-minded exit.* As you excuse yourself, give a word of encouragement to each person in the room by name, offering your prayers and services. Also remember that if there is another patient in the room, he or she may have been listening. So quietly ask if he or she would like you to pray. It may be a divine appointment. Then make yourself available to others who may want to interact in the hallway or lounge. Sometimes this is where the greatest work is done.

MINISTERING TO THE DYING
To Unbelievers

If the dying person is an unbeliever, your job is simple—present the gospel in the clearest way that you know. This, of course, must be preceded by both your fervent prayers and the prayers of others. The unbelieving heart is veiled, and only God can remove the veil (2 Cor. 3:16–18). Along with the classic gospel texts (such as John 3:16, Acts 16:29–33, Rom. 10:9–13, Eph. 2:8–9, 1 Tim. 1:15–16, and 1 Pet. 2:23–24), the go-to passage is Luke 23:39–43 and Jesus's words to the dying thief, "Truly, I say to you, today you will be with me in Paradise." The thief's redemption assures us that it is never too late to turn to Christ. Samuel Johnson was fond of quoting a hopeful epitaph for those who despair. The image is that of a man being pitched to his death from horseback.

> Between the stirrup and the ground,
> I mercy ask'd, I mercy found.[1]

It is never too late! The thief's reward was heaven to its fullest—Paradise face to face with Jesus. In Jesus's parable of the workers in the vineyard (Matt. 20:1–16), the workers who were hired for the last hour were paid the same as those who had labored all day. The landowner's response to the workers' response was: "'Take what belongs to you and go. I choose to give to this last worker as I give to you. Am I not allowed to do what I choose with what belongs to me? Or do you begrudge my generosity?' So the last will be first, and the first last" (vv. 14–16).

Luke's account of the cross is not about a good thief but about a bad thief and a good Savior! Jesus loves to save sinners:

---

[1] James Boswell, *The Life of Samuel Johnson* (1791; repr., London: Penguin, 1979), 299.

Waft it on the rolling tide:
Jesus saves! Jesus saves!
Tell to sinners far and wide:
Jesus saves! Jesus saves![2]

To Believers

In the late 1970s, Margie, a thirty-eight-year-old mother of four, was hooked up to a ventilator. Unlike most other patients, she was not heavily sedated. She and her husband had just been told that she had only a few days to live because of the total respiratory failure she had experienced that very morning. Young Margie took a writing pad and asked her pastor, Dr. Darryl Bodie, the bare question "How do you die?" In the providence of God, Pastor Bodie had been studying the last words of Jesus from the cross and was led to use them to frame a template for what to do when dying. In the next few hours, Margie did all the seven last words. Her final breath was, "Father, into your hands I . . ."

The following template has been used over the years to help believers finish their journey. Note: these are not strict applications of Jesus's words, but principled applications of his dying expressions and actions, which may help believers die well.

First word: "Father, forgive them, for they know not what they do" (Luke 23:34).
Who do you need to forgive? Will you let them know? Is reconciliation possible?

Second word: "Truly, I say to you, today you will be with me in Paradise" (Luke 23:43).
Who in your life do you need to talk to about salvation?

Third word: "Woman, behold, your son! . . . [John,] behold, your mother!" (John 19:26–27).
For whom do you need to make provisions as you depart?

Fourth word: "My God, my God, why have you forsaken me?" (Matt. 27:46).
Because Jesus suffered this separation for you, you will never suffer separation from God. You need not be afraid.

Fifth word: "I thirst" (John 19:28).
As your dying physical needs cry out, take the help offered.

---

[2] From the hymn "We Have Heard a Joyful Sound" by Priscilla Jane Owens, 1892.

Sixth word: "It is finished" (John 19:30).
You can rest in Christ's finished work on the cross and anticipate the beginning of eternal life with him in heaven.

Seventh word: "Father, into your hands I commit my spirit!" (Luke 23:46).
You will enter the hands of a loving heavenly Father who will care for you from now on. What a comforting thought!

ESSENTIAL SCRIPTURES FOR HOSPITAL VISITATION (BY SUBJECT)

The following Scripture passages have been organized for quick reference under subject headings that are especially useful to the pastor in ministering to the sick.

BREVITY OF LIFE

Job 8:9: "For we are but of yesterday and know nothing, for our days on earth are a shadow."

Psalm 39:4–5: "O LORD, make me know my end and what is the measure of my days; let me know how fleeting I am! Behold, you have made my days a few handbreadths, and my lifetime is as nothing before you. Surely all mankind stands as a mere breath!"

Psalm 90:10: "The years of our life are seventy, or even by reason of strength eighty; yet their span is but toil and trouble; they are soon gone, and we fly away."

Psalm 103:15–16: "As for man, his days are like grass; he flourishes like a flower of the field; for the wind passes over it, and it is gone, and its place knows it no more."

James 4:13–15: "Come now, you who say, 'Today or tomorrow we will go into such and such a town and spend a year there and trade and make a profit'—yet you do not know what tomorrow will bring. What is your life? For you are a mist that appears for a little time and then vanishes. Instead you ought to say, 'If the Lord wills, we will live and do this or that.'"

COMFORT

Numbers 6:24–26: "The LORD bless you and keep you; the LORD make his face to shine upon you and be gracious to you; the LORD lift up his countenance upon you and give you peace."

Psalm 103:13–14: "As a father shows compassion to his children, so the LORD shows compassion to those who fear him. For he knows our frame; he remembers that we are dust."

Matthew 10:29–31: "Are not two sparrows sold for a penny? And not one of them will fall to the ground apart from your Father. But even the hairs of your head are all numbered. Fear not, therefore; you are of more value than many sparrows."

John 14:1: "Let not your hearts be troubled. Believe in God; believe also in me."

2 Corinthians 1:3–5: "Blessed be the God and Father of our Lord Jesus Christ, the Father of mercies and God of all comfort, who comforts us in all our affliction, so that we may be able to comfort those who are in any affliction, with the comfort with which we ourselves are comforted by God. For as we share abundantly in Christ's sufferings, so through Christ we share abundantly in comfort too."

2 Corinthians 13:14: "The grace of the Lord Jesus Christ and the love of God and the fellowship of the Holy Spirit be with you all."

CONFIDENCE

John 16:33b: "In the world you will have tribulation. But take heart; I have overcome the world."

1 Corinthians 15:57–58: "But thanks be to God, who gives us the victory through our Lord Jesus Christ. Therefore, my beloved brothers, be steadfast, immovable, always abounding in the work of the Lord, knowing that in the Lord your labor is not in vain."

Galatians 2:20: "I have been crucified with Christ. It is no longer I who live, but Christ who lives in me. And the life I now live in the flesh I live by faith in the Son of God, who loved me and gave himself for me."

DEATH

Psalm 116:15: "Precious in the sight of the LORD is the death of his saints."

Ecclesiastes 3:1–2a: "For everything there is a season, and a time for every matter under heaven: a time to be born, and a time to die."

Ecclesiastes 5:15: "As he came from his mother's womb he shall go again, naked as he came, and shall take nothing for his toil that he may carry away in his hand."

Ecclesiastes 12:1–8: "Remember also your Creator in the days of your youth, before the evil days come and the years draw near of which you will say, 'I have no pleasure in them'; before the sun and the light and the moon and the stars are darkened and the clouds return after the rain, in the day when the keepers of the house tremble, and the strong men are bent, and the grinders cease because they are few, and those who look through the windows are dimmed, and the doors on the street are shut—when the sound of the grinding is low . . . they are afraid also of what is high, and terrors are in the way; the almond tree blossoms, the grasshopper drags itself along, and desire fails, because man is going to his eternal home, and the mourners go about the streets—before the silver cord is snapped, or the golden bowl is broken, or the pitcher is shattered at the fountain, or the wheel broken at the cistern, and the dust returns to the earth as it was, and the spirit returns to God who gave it. Vanity of vanities, says the Preacher; all is vanity."

Hebrews 9:27: "It is appointed for man to die once, and after that comes judgment."

Revelation 1:17–18: "When I saw him, I fell at his feet as though dead. But he laid his right hand on me, saying, 'Fear not, I am the first and the last, and the living one. I died, and behold I am alive forevermore, and I have the keys of Death and Hades.'"

GOD

His Faithfulness

Psalm 36:5: "Your steadfast love, O LORD, extends to the heavens, your faithfulness to the clouds."

Psalm 89:1–2: "I will sing of the steadfast love of the LORD, forever; with my mouth I will make known your faithfulness to all generations. For I said, 'Steadfast love will be built up forever; in the heavens you will establish your faithfulness.'"

Lamentations 3:22–23: "The steadfast love of the LORD never ceases; his mercies never come to an end; they are new ever morning; great is your faithfulness."

His Goodness

Psalm 34:8: "Oh, taste and see that the LORD is good! Blessed is the man who takes refuge in him!"

Psalm 86:5: "For you, O Lord, are good and forgiving, abounding in steadfast love to all who call upon you."

Psalm 100:5: "For the LORD is good; his steadfast love endures forever, and his faithfulness to all generations."

Psalm 145:8–9: "The LORD is gracious and merciful, slow to anger and abounding in steadfast love. The LORD is good to all, and his mercy is over all that he has made."

Nahum 1:7: "The LORD is good, a stronghold in the day of trouble; he knows those who take refuge in him."

Matthew 7:11: "If you then, who are evil, know how to give good gifts to your children, how much more will your Father who is in heaven give good things to those who ask him!"

His Grace

Romans 11:6: "But if it is by grace, it is no longer on the basis of works; otherwise grace would no longer be grace."

2 Corinthians 8:9: "For you know the grace of our Lord Jesus Christ, that though he was rich, yet for your sake he became poor, so that you by his poverty might become rich."

Ephesians 2:8–9: "For by grace you have been saved through faith. And this is not your own doing; it is the gift of God, not as a result of works, so that no one may boast."

Hebrews 4:16: "Let us then with confidence draw near to the throne of grace, that we may receive mercy and find grace to help in time of need."

His Knowledge

Psalm 33:13–15: "The LORD looks down from heaven; he sees all the children of man; from where he sits enthroned he looks out on all the inhabitants of the earth, he who fashions the hearts of them all and observes all their deeds."

Psalm 139:1–6, 11–16: "O Lᴏʀᴅ, you have searched me and known me! You know when I sit down and when I rise up; you discern my thoughts from afar. You search out my path and my lying down and are acquainted with all my ways. Even before a word is on my tongue, behold, O Lᴏʀᴅ, you know it altogether. You hem me in, behind and before, and lay your hand upon me. Such knowledge is too wonderful for me; it is high; I cannot attain it. . . . If I say, 'Surely the darkness shall cover me, and the light about me be night,' even the darkness is not dark to you; the night is bright as the day, for darkness is as light with you. For you formed my inward parts; you knitted me together in my mother's womb. I praise you, for I am fearfully and wonderfully made. Wonderful are your works; my soul knows it very well. My frame was not hidden from you, when I was being made in secret, intricately woven in the depths of the earth. Your eyes saw my unformed substance; in your book were written, every one of them, the days that were formed for me, when as yet there were none of them."

Psalm 147:4–5: "He determines the number of stars; he gives to all of them their names. Great is our Lord, and abundant in power; his understanding is beyond measure."

Romans 11:33–36: "Oh, the depth of the riches and wisdom and knowledge of God! How unsearchable are his judgments and how inscrutable his ways! 'For who has known the mind of the Lord, or who has been his counselor?' 'Or who has given a gift to him that he might be repaid?' For from him and through him and to him are all things. To him be glory forever. Amen."

His Love

Psalm 136:1–26: (twenty-six duplicate refrains of, "for his steadfast love endures forever").

John 16:27: "The Father himself loves you, because you have loved me and have believed that I came from God."

Romans 8:38–39: "For I am sure that neither death nor life, nor angels nor rulers, nor things present nor things to come, nor powers, nor height nor depth, nor anything else in all creation, will be able to separate us from the love of God in Christ Jesus our Lord."

1 John 4:8–10: "Anyone who does not love does not know God, because God is love. In this the love of God was made manifest among us, that

God sent his only Son into the world, so that we might live through him. In this is love, not that we have loved God but that he loved us and sent his Son to be the propitiation for our sins."

His Mercy and Compassion

Exodus 34:5–6: "The Lord descended in the cloud and stood with him there, and proclaimed the name of the Lord. The Lord passed before him and proclaimed, 'The Lord, the Lord, a God merciful and gracious, slow to anger, and abounding in steadfast love and faithfulness.'"

Psalm 103:1–5, 8–14: "Bless the Lord, O my soul, and all that is within me, bless his holy name! Bless the Lord, O my soul, and forget not all his benefits, who forgives all your iniquity, who heals all your diseases, who redeems your life from the pit, who crowns you with steadfast love and mercy, who satisfies you with good so that your youth is renewed like the eagle's. . . . The Lord is merciful and gracious, slow to anger and abounding in steadfast love. He will not always chide, nor will he keep his anger forever. He does not deal with us according to our sins, nor repay us according to our iniquities. For as far as the heavens are above the earth, so great is his steadfast love toward those who fear him; as far as the east is from the west, so far does he remove our transgressions from us. As a father shows compassion to his children, so the Lord shows compassion to those who fear him. For he knows our frame; he remembers that we are dust."

Psalm 130:1–8: "Out of the depths I cry to you, O Lord! O Lord, hear my voice! Let your ears be attentive to the voice of my pleas for mercy! If you, O Lord, should mark iniquities, O Lord, who could stand? But with you there is forgiveness, that you may be feared. I wait for the Lord, my soul waits, and in his word I hope; my soul waits for the Lord more than watchmen for the morning, more than watchmen for the morning. O Israel, hope in the Lord! For with the Lord there is steadfast love, and with him is plentiful redemption. And he will redeem Israel from all his iniquities."

Proverbs 28:13: "Whoever conceals his transgressions will not prosper, but he who confesses and forsakes them will obtain mercy."

Isaiah 54:10: "'For the mountains may depart and the hills be removed, but my steadfast love shall not depart from you, and my covenant of peace shall not be removed,' says the Lord, who has compassion on you."

Isaiah 55:6–7: "Seek the Lord while he may be found; call upon him while he is near; let the wicked forsake his way, and the unrighteous man his thoughts; let him return to the Lord, that he may have compassion on him, and to our God, for he will abundantly pardon."

Lamentations 3:22–23: "The steadfast love of the Lord never ceases; his mercies never come to an end; they are new every morning; great is your faithfulness."

Titus 3:5–7: "He saved us, not because of works done by us in righteousness, but according to his own mercy, by the washing of regeneration and renewal of the Holy Spirit, whom he poured out on us richly through Jesus Christ our Savior, so that being justified by his grace we might become heirs according to the hope of eternal life."

Hebrews 4:16: "Let us then with confidence draw near to the throne of grace, that we may receive mercy and find grace to help in time of need."

His Power

Isaiah 44:24: "Thus says the Lord, your Redeemer, who formed you from the womb: 'I am the Lord, who made all things, who alone stretched out the heavens, who spread out the earth by myself.'"

John 1:1–3: "In the beginning was the Word, and the Word was with God, and the Word was God. He was in the beginning with God. All things were made through him, and without him was not anything made that was made."

1 Corinthians 8:6: "Yet for us there is one God, the Father, from whom are all things and for whom we exist, and one Lord, Jesus Christ, through whom are all things and through whom we exist."

Colossians 1:16–17: "For by him all things were created, in heaven and on earth, visible and invisible, whether thrones or dominions or rulers or authorities—all things were created through him and for him. And he is before all things, and in him all things hold together."

Hebrews 1:1–3: "Long ago, at many times and in many ways, God spoke to our fathers by the prophets, but in these last days he has spoken to us by his Son, whom he appointed the heir of all things, through whom also he created the world. He is the radiance of the glory of God and the exact imprint of his nature, and he upholds the universe by the word of his power."

Revelation 4:10b–11: "They cast their crowns before the throne, saying, 'Worthy are you, our Lord and God, to receive glory and honor and power, for you created all things, and by your will they existed and were created.'"

His Presence

Psalm 139:7–10a: "Where shall I go from your Spirit? Or where shall I flee from your presence? If I ascend to heaven, you are there! If I make my bed in Sheol, you are there! If I take the wings of the morning and dwell in the uttermost parts of the sea, even there your hand shall lead me."

Jeremiah 23:23–24: "Am I a God at hand, declares the LORD, and not a God far away? Can a man hide himself in secret places so that I cannot see him? declares the LORD. Do I not fill heaven and earth? declares the LORD."

Acts 17:24–28: "The God who made the world and everything in it, being Lord of heaven and earth, does not live in temples made by man, nor is he served by human hands, as though he needed anything, since he himself gives to all mankind life and breath and everything. And he made from one man every nation of mankind to live on all the face of the earth, having determined allotted periods and the boundaries of their dwelling place, that they should seek God, and perhaps feel their way toward him and find him. Yet he is actually not far from each one of us, for 'In him we live and move and have our being'; as even some of your own poets have said, 'For we are indeed his offspring.'"

His Protection

Psalm 23:1–6: "The LORD is my shepherd; I shall not want. He makes me lie down in green pastures. He leads me beside still waters. He restores my soul. He leads me in paths of righteousness for his name's sake. Even though I walk through the valley of the shadow of death, I will fear no evil, for you are with me; your rod and your staff, they comfort me. You prepare a table before me in the presence of my enemies; you anoint my head with oil; my cup overflows. Surely goodness and mercy shall follow me all the days of my life, and I shall dwell in the house of the LORD forever."

Psalm 27:1–4: "The LORD is my light and my salvation; whom shall I fear? The LORD is the stronghold of my life; of whom shall I be afraid?

When evildoers assail me to eat up my flesh, my adversaries and foes, it is they who stumble and fall. Though an army encamp against me, my heart shall not fear; though war rise against me, yet I will be confident."

Psalm 46:1–11: "God is our refuge and strength, a very present help in trouble. Therefore we will not fear though the earth gives way, though the mountains be moved into the heart of the sea, though its waters roar and foam, though the mountains tremble at its swelling. Selah. There is a river whose streams make glad the city of God, the holy habitation of the Most High. God is in the midst of her; she shall not be moved; God will help her when morning dawns. The nations rage, the kingdoms totter; he utters his voice, the earth melts. The LORD of hosts is with us; the God of Jacob is our fortress. Selah. Come, behold the works of the LORD, how he has brought desolations on the earth. He makes wars cease to the end of the earth; he breaks the bow and shatters the spear; he burns the chariots with fire. 'Be still, and know that I am God. I will be exalted among the nations, I will be exalted in the earth!' The LORD of hosts is with us; the God of Jacob is our fortress. Selah."

Psalm 91:1–6: "He who dwells in the shelter of the Most High will abide in the shadow of the Almighty. I will say to the LORD, 'My refuge and my fortress, my God, in whom I trust.' For he will deliver you from the snare of the fowler and from the deadly pestilence. He will cover you with his pinions, and under his wings you will find refuge; his faithfulness is a shield and buckler. You will not fear the terror of the night, nor the arrow that flies by day, nor the pestilence that stalks in darkness, nor the destruction that wastes at noonday."

Psalm 121:1–8: "I lift up my eyes to the hills. From where does my help come? My help comes from the LORD, who made heaven and earth. He will not let your foot be moved; he who keeps you will not slumber. Behold, he who keeps Israel will neither slumber nor sleep. The LORD is your keeper; the LORD is your shade on your right hand. The sun shall not strike you by day, nor the moon by night. The LORD will keep you from all evil; he will keep your life. The LORD will keep your going out and your coming in from this time forth and forevermore."

Romans 8:37–39: "In all these things we are more than conquerors through him who loved us. For I am sure that neither death nor life, nor angels nor rulers, nor things present nor things to come, nor powers, nor height nor depth, nor anything else in all creation, will be able to separate us from the love of God in Christ Jesus our Lord."

Romans 14:8–9: "For if we live, we live to the Lord, and if we die, we die to the Lord. So then, whether we live or whether we die, we are the Lord's. For to this end Christ died and lived again, that he might be Lord both of the dead and of the living."

His Providence

Genesis 50:20: "As for you, you meant evil against me, but God meant it for good, to bring it about that many people should be kept alive, as they are today."

Jeremiah 29:11: "For I know the plans I have for you, declares the LORD, plans for welfare and not for evil, to give you a future and a hope."

Romans 8:28: "And we know that for those who love God all things work together for good, for those who are called according to his purpose."

HEAVEN

John 14:1–3: "Let not your hearts be troubled. Believe in God; believe also in me. In my Father's house are many rooms. If it were not so, would I have told you that I go to prepare a place for you? And if I go and prepare a place for you, I will come again and will take you to myself, that where I am you may be also."

2 Corinthians 4:13–18: "Since we have the same spirit of faith according to what has been written, 'I believed, and so I spoke,' we also believe, and so we also speak, knowing that he who raised the Lord Jesus will raise us also with Jesus and bring us with you into his presence. For it is all for your sake, so that as grace extends to more and more people it may increase thanksgiving, to the glory of God. So we do not lose heart. Though our outer self is wasting away, our inner self is being renewed day by day. For this light momentary affliction is preparing for us an eternal weight of glory beyond all comparison, as we look not to the things that are seen but to the things that are unseen. For the things that are seen are transient, but the things that are unseen are eternal."

2 Corinthians 5:1–5: "For we know that if the tent that is our earthly home is destroyed, we have a building from God, a house not made with hands, eternal in the heavens. For in this tent we groan, longing to put on our heavenly dwelling, if indeed by putting it on we may not be found naked. For while we are still in this tent, we groan, being burdened—not that we would be unclothed, but that we would be further clothed, so

that what is mortal may be swallowed up by life. He who has prepared us for this very thing is God, who has given us the Spirit as a guarantee."

Revelation 14:13: "And I heard a voice from heaven saying, 'Write this: Blessed are the dead who die in the Lord from now on.' 'Blessed indeed,' says the Spirit, 'that they may rest from their labors, for their deeds follow them!'"

Revelation 21:1–4: "Then I saw a new heaven and a new earth, for the first heaven and the first earth had passed away, and the sea was no more. And I saw the holy city, new Jerusalem, coming down out of heaven from God, prepared as a bride adorned for her husband. And I heard a loud voice from the throne saying, 'Behold, the dwelling place of God is with man. He will dwell with them, and they will be his people, and God himself will be with them as their God. He will wipe away every tear from their eyes, and death shall be no more, neither shall there be mourning, nor crying, nor pain anymore, for the former things have passed away.'"

Revelation 22:1–5: "Then the angel showed me the river of the water of life, bright as crystal, flowing from the throne of God and of the Lamb through the middle of the street of the city; also, on either side of the river, the tree of life with its twelve kinds of fruit, yielding its fruit each month. The leaves of the tree were for the healing of the nations. No longer will there be anything accursed, but the throne of God and of the Lamb will be in it, and his servants will worship him. They will see his face, and his name will be on their foreheads. And night will be no more. They will need no light of lamp or sun, for the Lord God will be their light, and they will reign forever and ever."

RESURRECTION

Job 19:23–27: "Oh that my words were written! Oh that they were inscribed in a book! Oh that with an iron pen and lead they were engraved in the rock forever! For I know that my Redeemer lives, and at the last he will stand upon the earth. And after my skin has been thus destroyed, yet in my flesh I shall see God, whom I shall see for myself, and my eyes shall behold, and not another. My heart faints within me!"

John 5:25–29: "Truly, truly, I say to you, an hour is coming, and is now here, when the dead will hear the voice of the Son of God, and those who hear will live. For as the Father has life in himself, so he has granted the Son also to have life in himself. And he has given him authority to execute judgment, because he is the Son of Man. Do not marvel at this, for an hour is coming when all who are in the tombs will hear his voice and come out, those who have done good to the resurrection of life, and those who have done evil to the resurrection of judgment."

John 11:21–27: "Martha said to Jesus, 'Lord, if you had been here, my brother would not have died. But even now I know that whatever you ask from God, God will give you.' Jesus said to her, 'Your brother will rise again.' Martha said to him, 'I know that he will rise again in the resurrection on the last day.' Jesus said to her, 'I am the resurrection and the life. Whoever believes in me, though he die, yet shall he live, and everyone who lives and believes in me shall never die. Do you believe this?' She said to him, 'Yes, Lord; I believe that you are the Christ, the Son of God, who is coming into the world.'"

1 Corinthians 15:50–58: "I tell you this, brothers: flesh and blood cannot inherit the kingdom of God, nor does the perishable inherit the imperishable. Behold! I tell you a mystery. We shall not all sleep, but we shall all be changed, in a moment, in the twinkling of an eye, at the last trumpet. For the trumpet will sound, and the dead will be raised imperishable, and we shall be changed. For this perishable body must put on the imperishable, and this mortal body must put on immortality. When the perishable puts on the imperishable, and the mortal puts on immortality, then shall come to pass the saying that is written: 'Death is swallowed up in victory.' 'O death, where is your victory? O death, where is your sting?' The sting of death is sin, and the power of sin is the law. But thanks be to God, who gives us the victory through our Lord Jesus Christ. Therefore, my beloved brothers, be steadfast, immovable, always abounding in the work of the Lord, knowing that in the Lord your labor is not in vain."

Philippians 3:20–21: "But our citizenship is in heaven, and from it we await a Savior, the Lord Jesus Christ, who will transform our lowly body to be like his glorious body, by the power that enables him even to subject all things to himself."

1 Thessalonians 4:13–18: "But we do not want you to be uninformed, brothers, about those who are asleep, that you may not grieve as others do who have no hope. For since we believe that Jesus died and rose again, even so, through Jesus, God will bring with him those who have fallen asleep. For this we declare to you by a word from the Lord, that we who are alive, who are left until the coming of the Lord, will not precede those who have fallen asleep. For the Lord himself will descend from heaven with a cry of command, with the voice of an archangel, and with the

sound of the trumpet of God. And the dead in Christ will rise first. Then we who are alive, who are left, will be caught up together with them in the clouds to meet the Lord in the air, and so we will always be with the Lord. Therefore encourage one another with these words."

SUFFERING

Romans 8:18: "For I consider that the sufferings of this present time are not worth comparing with the glory that is to be revealed to us."

2 Corinthians 4:16–18: "So we do not lose heart. Though our outer self is wasting away, our inner self is being renewed day by day. For this light momentary affliction is preparing for us an eternal weight of glory beyond all comparison, as we look not to the things that are seen but to the things that are unseen. For the things that are seen are transient, but the things that are unseen are eternal."

Philippians 1:29: "For it has been granted to you that for the sake of Christ you should not only believe in him but also suffer for his sake."

Philippians 3:10: ". . . that I may know him and the power of his resurrection, and may share his sufferings, becoming like him in his death."

Appendix

Sample Wedding Services
from Various Churches

In the texts of the various denominational services in this appendix, we have inserted uniform designations to identify the various sections of the services in order to make it easy for the pastor/reader to select the finest elements to construct his wedding services. These designations (in bold type in the text) include: Presentation, Call to Worship, Preface, Consent, Prayer/Invocation, Homily, Vows, Rings, Pronouncement, Prayer(s) and Benediction, and Introduction (of newly married couple).

ANGLICAN, 1662
The Form Of Solemnization Of Matrimony[1]

First the Banns of all that are to be married together must be published in the Church three several Sundays, during the time of Morning Service, or of Evening Service, (if there be no Morning Service) immediately after the second Lesson; the Curate saying after the accustomed manner, I publish the Banns of Marriage between M. of _____ and N. of _____.
If any of you know cause, or just impediment, why these two persons should not be joined together in holy Matrimony, ye are to declare it. This is the first [second, or third] time of asking.

And if the persons that are to be married dwell in divers Parishes, the Banns must be asked in Both Parishes; and the Curate of the one Parish shall not solemnize Matrimony betwixt them, without a Certificate of the Banns being thrice asked, from the Curate of the other Parish.

At the day and time appointed for solemnization of Matrimony, the persons to be married shall come into the body of the Church with their

[1] The Book of Common Prayer, 1662 (Cambridge: Cambridge University Press, n.d.), 301–309.

friends and neighbours: and there standing together, the Man on the right hand, and the Woman on the left, the Priest shall say,

Preface

DEARLY beloved, we are gathered together here in the sight of God, and in the face of this Congregation, to join together this man and this woman in holy Matrimony; which is an honourable estate, instituted of God in the time of man's innocency, signifying unto us the mystical union that is betwixt Christ and his Church; which holy estate Christ adorned and beautified with his presence, and first miracle that he wrought, in Cana of Galilee; and is commended of Saint Paul to be honourable among all men: and therefore is not by any to be enterprized, nor taken in hand, unadvisedly, lightly, or wantonly, to satisfy men's carnal lusts and appetites, like brute beasts that have no understanding; but reverently, discreetly, advisedly, soberly, and in the fear of God; duly considering the causes for which Matrimony was ordained.

First, It was ordained for the procreation of children, to be brought up in the fear and nurture of the Lord, and to the praise of his holy Name.

Secondly, It was ordained for a remedy against sin, and to avoid fornication; that such persons as have not the gift of continency might marry, and keep themselves undefiled members of Christ's body.

Thirdly, It was ordained for the mutual society, help, and comfort, that the one ought to have of the other, both in prosperity and adversity. Into which holy estate these two persons present come now to be joined. Therefore if any man can shew any just cause, why they may not lawfully be joined together, let him now speak, or else hereafter for ever hold his peace.

Charge

And also, speaking unto the persons that shall be married, he shall say,

I REQUIRE and charge you both, as ye will answer at the dreadful day of judgment, when the secrets of all hearts shall be disclosed, that if either of you know any impediment, why ye may not be lawfully joined together in Matrimony, ye do now confess it. For be ye well assured, that so many as are coupled together otherwise than God's Word doth allow are not joined together by God; neither is their Matrimony lawful.

At which day of Marriage, if any man do allege and declare any impediment, why they may not be coupled together in Matrimony, by God's law, or the laws of this Realm; and will be bound, and sufficient sureties with him to the parties; or else put in a caution (to the full value of such charges as the persons to be married do thereby sustain) to prove his allegation: then the solemnization must be deferred, until such time as the truth be tried.

Consent

If no impediment be alleged, then shall the Curate say unto the Man,

M. WILT thou have this woman to thy wedded wife, to live together after God's ordinance in the holy estate of Matrimony? Wilt thou love her, comfort her, honour, and keep her, in sickness and in health; and, forsaking all other, keep thee only unto her, so long as ye both shall live?

The Man shall answer, I will.

Then shall the Priest say unto the Woman,

N. WILT thou have this man to thy wedded husband, to live together after God's ordinance in the holy estate of Matrimony? Wilt thou obey him, and serve him, love, honour, and keep him, in sickness and in health; and, forsaking all other, keep thee only unto him, so long as ye both shall live?

The Woman shall answer, I will.

Presentation

Then shall the Minister say,

Who giveth this woman to be married to this man?

Vows

Then shall they give their troth to each other in this manner.

The Minister, receiving the Woman at her father's or friend's hands, shall cause the Man with his right hand to take the Woman by her right hand, and to say after him as followeth.

I M. take thee N. to my wedded wife, to have and to hold from this day forward, for better for worse, for richer for poorer, in sickness and in health, to love and to cherish, till death us do part, according to God's holy ordinance; and thereto I plight thee my troth.

Then shall they loose their hands; and the Woman, with her right hand taking the Man by his right hand, shall likewise say after the Minister,

I N. take thee M. to my wedded husband, to have and to hold from this day forward, for better for worse, for richer for poorer, in sickness and in health, to love, cherish, and to obey, till death us do part, according to God's holy ordinance; and thereto I give thee my troth.

Rings

Then shall they again loose their hands; and the Man shall give unto the Woman a Ring, laying the same upon the book with the accustomed duty to the Priest and Clerk. And the Priest, taking the Ring, shall deliver it unto the Man, to put it upon the fourth finger of the Woman's left hand. And the Man holding the Ring there, and taught by the Priest, shall say,

With this ring I thee wed, with my body I thee worship, and with all my worldly goods I thee endow: In the Name of the Father, and of the Son, and of the Holy Ghost. Amen.

Then the Man leaving the Ring upon the fourth finger of the Woman's left hand, they shall both kneel down, and the Minister shall say,

Let us pray.

O ETERNAL God, Creator and Preserver of all mankind, Giver of all spiritual grace, the Author of everlasting life: Send thy blessing upon these thy servants, this man and this woman, whom we bless in thy Name; that, as Isaac and Rebecca lived faithfully together, so these persons may surely perform and keep the vow and covenant betwixt them made, (whereof this ring given and received is a token and pledge) and may ever remain in perfect love and peace together, and live according to thy laws; through Jesus Christ our Lord. Amen.

Pronouncement

Then the Priest shall join their right hands together, and say,

Those whom God hath joined together let no man put asunder.

Then shall the Minister speak unto the people.

FOR AS MUCH as M. and N. have consented together in holy wedlock, and have witnessed the same before God and this company, and thereto have given and pledged their troth either to other, and have declared the same by giving and receiving of a ring, and by joining of hands; I pronounce that they be man and wife together, In the Name of the Father, and of the Son, and of the Holy Ghost. Amen.

Benedictions

And the Minister shall add this Blessing.

GOD the Father, God the Son, God the Holy Ghost, bless, preserve, and keep you; the Lord mercifully with his favour look upon you, and so fill you with all spiritual benediction and grace, that ye may so live together in this life, that in the world to come ye may have life everlasting. Amen.

Then the Minister or Clerks, going to the Lord's Table, shall say or sing this Psalm following.

Beati omnes. Psalm 128

BLESSED are all they that fear the Lord: and walk in his ways.

For thou shalt eat the labour of thine hands: O well is thee, and
　　happy shalt thou be.

Thy wife shall be as the fruitful vine: Upon the walls of thy house;

Thy children like the olive branches: round about thy table.

Lo, thus shall the man be blessed that feareth the Lord.

The Lord from out of Sion shall so bless thee that thou shalt see
Jerusalem in prosperity all thy life long;

Yea, that thou shalt see thy children's children: and peace upon
Israel.

Glory be to the Father, and to the Son, and to the Holy Ghost;

As it was in the beginning, is now, and ever shall be: world without
end. Amen.

Or this Psalm

Deus misereatur. Psalm 67

GOD be merciful unto us, and bless us: and shew us the light of his
countenance, and be merciful unto us:

That thy way may be known upon earth: thy saving health among
all nations.

Let the people praise thee, O God: yea, let all the people praise
thee.

O let the nations rejoice and be glad: for thou shalt judge the folk
righteously, and govern the nations upon earth.

Let the people praise thee, O God: yea, let all the people praise
thee.

Then shall the earth bring forth her increase: and God, even our
own God, shall give us his blessing.

God shall bless us: and all the ends of the world shall fear him.

Glory be to the Father, and to the Son and to the Holy Ghost;

As it was in the beginning, is now, and ever shall be: world without
end. Amen.

*The Psalm ended, and the Man and the Woman kneeling before the
Lord's Table, the Priest standing at the Table, and turning his face towards them, shall say,*

Lord, have mercy upon us.

Answer. Christ, have mercy upon us.

Minister. Lord, have mercy upon us.

Our Father which art in heaven, Hallowed be thy Name. Thy kingdom come. Thy will be done in earth. As it is in heaven. Give us this day
our daily bread. And forgive us our trespasses, As we forgive them that
trespass against us. And lead us not into temptation; But deliver us from
evil. Amen.

Minister. O Lord, save thy servant, and thy handmaid;

Answer. Who put their trust in thee.

Minister. O Lord, send them help from thy holy place;

Answer. And evermore defend them.

Minister. Be unto them a tower of strength,

Answer. From the face of their enemy.

Minister. O Lord, hear our prayer;

Answer. And let our cry come unto thee.

Minister. O GOD of Abraham, God of Isaac, God of Jacob, bless these thy servants, and sow the seed of eternal life in their hearts; that whatsoever in thy holy Word they shall profitably learn, they may in deed fulfil the same. Look, O Lord, mercifully upon them from heaven, and bless them. And as thou didst send thy blessing upon Abraham and Sarah, to their great comfort, so vouchsafe to send thy blessing upon these thy servants; that they obeying thy will, and always being in safety under thy protection, may abide in thy love unto their lives' end; through Jesus Christ our Lord. Amen.

This Prayer next following shall be omitted, where the Woman is past child-bearing.

O MERCIFUL Lord, and heavenly Father, by whose gracious gift mankind is increased: We beseech thee, assist with thy blessing these two persons, that they may both be fruitful in procreation of children, and also live together so long in godly love and honesty, that they may see their children christianly and virtuously brought up, to thy praise and honour; through Jesus Christ our Lord. Amen.

O GOD, who by thy mighty power hast made all things of nothing; who also (after other things set in order) didst appoint, that out of man (created after thine own image and similitude) woman should take her beginning; and, knitting them together, didst teach that it should never be lawful to put asunder those whom thou by Matrimony hadst made one: O God, who hast consecrated the state of Matrimony to such an excellent mystery, that in it is signified and represented the spiritual marriage and unity betwixt Christ and his Church: Look mercifully upon these thy servants, that both this man may love his wife, according to thy Word, (as Christ did love his spouse the Church, who gave himself for it, loving and cherishing it even as his own flesh) and also that this woman may be loving and amiable, faithful and obedient to her husband; and in all quietness, sobriety, and peace, be a follower of holy and godly matrons. O Lord, bless them both, and grant them to inherit thy everlasting *kingdom;* through Jesus Christ our Lord. Amen.

Then shall the Priest say,

ALMIGHTY God, who at the beginning did create our first parents, Adam and Eve, and did sanctify and join them together in marriage;

Pour upon you the riches of his grace, sanctify and bless you, that ye may please him both in body and soul, and live together in holy love unto your lives' end. Amen.

After which, if there be no Sermon declaring the duties of Man and Wife, the Minister shall read as followeth.

ALL ye that are married, or that intend to take the holy estate of Matrimony upon you, hear what the holy Scripture doth say as touching the duty of husbands towards their wives, and wives towards their husbands.

Saint Paul, in his Epistle to the Ephesians, the fifth Chapter, doth give this commandment to all married men; Husbands, love your wives, even as Christ also loved the Church, and gave himself for it, that he might sanctify and cleanse it with the washing of water, by the Word; that he might present it to himself a glorious Church, not having spot, or wrinkle, or any such thing; but that it should be holy, and without blemish. So ought men to love their wives as their own bodies. He that loveth his wife loveth himself: for no man ever yet hated his own flesh, but nourisheth and cherisheth it, even as the Lord the Church: for we are members of his body, of his flesh, and of his bones. For this cause shall a man leave his father and mother, and shall be joined unto his wife; and they two shall be one flesh. This is a great mystery; but I speak concerning Christ and the Church. Nevertheless, let every one of you in particular so love his wife, even as himself.

Likewise the same Saint Paul, writing to the Colossians, speaketh thus to all men that are married; Husbands, love your wives, and be not bitter against them.

Hear also what Saint Peter, the Apostle of Christ, who was himself a married man, saith unto them that are married; Ye husbands, dwell with your wives according to knowledge; giving honour unto the wife, as unto the weaker vessel, and as being heirs together of the grace of life, that your prayers be not hindered.

Hitherto ye have heard the duty of the husband toward the wife. Now likewise, ye wives, hear and learn your duties toward your husbands, even as it is plainly set forth in holy Scripture.

Saint Paul, in the aforenamed Epistle to the Ephesians, teacheth you thus; Wives, submit yourselves unto your own husbands, as unto the Lord. For the husband is the head of the wife, even as Christ is the head of the Church: and he is the Saviour of the body. Therefore as the Church is subject unto Christ, so let the wives be to their own husbands in every thing. And again he saith, Let the wife see that she reverence her husband.

And in his Epistle to the Colossians, Saint Paul giveth you this short lesson; Wives, submit yourselves unto your own husbands, as it is fit in the Lord.

Saint Peter also doth instruct you very well, thus saying; Ye wives, be in subjection to your own husbands; that, if any obey not the Word, they also may without the Word be won by the conversation of the wives; while they behold your chaste conversation coupled with fear. Whose adorning, let it not be that outward adorning of plaiting the hair, and of wearing of gold, or of putting on of apparel; but let it be the hidden man of the heart, in that which is not corruptible; even the ornament of a meek and quiet spirit, which is in the sight of God of great price. For after this manner in the old time the holy women also, who trusted in God, adorned themselves, being in subjection unto their own husbands; even as Sarah obeyed Abraham, calling him lord; whose daughters ye are as long as ye do well, and are not afraid with any amazement.

It is convenient that the new-married persons should receive the holy Communion at the time of their Marriage, or at the first opportunity after their Marriage.

ANGLICAN, 1978

A Service for Marriage

FIRST FORM[2]

Preface

1 *At the day and time appointed for solemnization of matrimony, the persons to be married come into the church with their friends and neighbours; and there standing together, the man on the right hand, and the woman on the left, the priest says*

We have come together here in the sight of God, and in the presence of this congregation, to join together this man and this woman in holy matrimony; which is an honourable state of life, instituted from the beginning by God himself, signifying to us the spiritual union that is between Christ and his Church.

Christ adorned and beautified matrimony with his presence, and with the first sign by which he revealed his glory, at the marriage in Cana of Galilee; and holy scripture commands that all should hold it in honour.

It is therefore not to be entered upon unadvisedly, lightly, or merely to satisfy physical desires; but prayerfully, with careful thought, and with reverence for God, duly considering the purposes for which it was ordained.

---

[2] An Australian Prayer Book: for use together with The Book of Common Prayer, 1662 (Sydney: The Standing Committee of the General Synod of the Church of England in Australia, 1978), 548–558. Used with permission.

It was ordained for the procreation of children and that they might be brought up in the nurture and instruction of the Lord, to the praise of his holy name.

It was ordained so that those to whom God has granted the gift of marriage might live a chaste and holy life, as befits members of Christ's body.

And it was ordained for the mutual companionship, help, and comfort, that the one ought to have of the other, both in prosperity and adversity.

Into this holy manner of life N and N come now to be joined. Therefore if anyone can show any just cause why they may not lawfully be joined together, let him speak now, or hereafter remain silent.

2 *Speaking to the persons to be married, the priest says*

I charge you both, as you will answer before God, who is the judge of all and from whom no secrets are hidden, that if either of you know any reason why you may not lawfully be joined together in matrimony, you now confess it. For be assured that those who marry otherwise than God's word allows are not joined together by God, neither is their matrimony lawful in his sight.

Consent

THE CONSENT

3 *If no impediment be alleged, the priest says to the man*

N, will you have N as your wife,
to live together, as God has ordained,
in the holy state of matrimony?
Will you love her, cherish her,
honour and protect her,
in sickness and in health;
and, forsaking all others,
be faithful to her, as long as you both shall live?

The man answers

I will.

4 *Then the priest says to the woman*

N, will you have N as your husband,
to live together, as God has ordained,
in the holy state of matrimony?
Will you love him, obey him,
honour and protect him,
in sickness and in health;

and, forsaking all others,
be faithful to him, as long as you both shall live?

The woman answers

I will.

5 If the bride is to be given away, the priest says

Who gives this woman to be married to this man?

And he receives her at her father's or friend's hands, taking her by the right hand.

Vows

The Betrothal and Wedding

6 They give their troth to each other in this manner.

They face each other, and the minister causes the man with his right hand to take the woman by her right hand and to say

I N take you N to be my wife,
according to God's holy ordinance:
to have and to hold
from this day forward,
for better for worse,
for richer for poorer,
in sickness and in health,
to love and to cherish,
until we are parted by death.
And to this I pledge you my word.

7 Then they loose their hands; and the woman, with her right hand taking the man by his right hand, says

I N take you N to be my husband,
according to God's holy ordinance:
to have and to hold
from this day forward,
for better for worse,
for richer for poorer,
in sickness and in health,
to love and to obey,
until we are parted by death.
And to this I pledge you my word.

Rings

8 They again loose their hands, and the man gives the woman a ring, placing it on the book. [While the ring is on the book the priest may say

Lord, we pray that this ring may be to your servants a token of their solemn vows, and a pledge of pure and abiding love; through Jesus Christ our Lord. Amen.*] The priest takes it and gives it to the man to put it on the fourth finger of the woman's left hand. The man holds the ring there, and says*

With this ring I wed you,
with my body I worship you;
with all that I am and all that I have
I honour you:
in the name of the Father,
and of the Son,
and of the Holy Spirit.
Amen.

9 *They both kneel. The minister says*

Let us pray.
Eternal God,
creator and preserver of all mankind,
giver of all spiritual grace
and author of everlasting life:
send your blessing upon this man and this woman
whom we bless in your name;
that as Isaac and Rebecca lived faithfully together,
so N and N may surely perform and keep
the vow and covenant made between them,
of which this ring given and received is a token and pledge,
and may ever remain in perfect love and peace together,
and live according to your laws;
through Jesus Christ our Lord. Amen.

If the bride is to give the bridegroom a ring, she does so after §8.

10 *Then the priest joins their right hands together and says*

Those whom God has joined together
let not man put asunder.

Pronouncement

THE DECLARATION OF MARRIAGE

11 *The priest addresses the people*

N and N have now witnessed to their mutual consent
before God and this company;
they have pledged their solemn word to each other;
and they have confirmed it

by the giving and receiving of a ring
and by the joining of hands.
I therefore declare them to be husband and wife:
in the name of the Father,
and of the Son,
and of the Holy Spirit.
Amen.

Benediction
And he adds this blessing:

God the Father,
God the Son,
God the Holy Spirit,
bless, preserve, and keep you;
the Lord mercifully with his favour look upon you
and fill you with all spiritual blessing and grace,
that you may so live together in this life,
that in· the world to come you may have life everlasting.
Amen.

12 *One of the following Psalms is said or sung. The minister, followed by the man and the woman, may go to the Lord's table during the reading or singing of the psalm.*

Psalm 128

¹ Blessed is everyone who fears the Lord:
and walks in the confine of his ways.
² You will eat the fruit of your labours:
happy shall you be and all shall go well with you.
³ Your wife within your house:
shall be as a fruitful vine;
⁴ Your children around your table:
like the fresh shoots of the olive.
⁵ Behold thus shall the man be blessed:
who lives in the fear of the Lord.
⁶ May the Lord so bless you from Zion:
that you see Jerusalem in prosperity
all the days of your life.
⁷ May you see your children's children:
and in Israel let there be peace.

Glory to God: Father Son and Holy Spirit;
As in the beginning so now: and for ever. Amen.

Psalm 37:3–7

³ Trust in the Lord and do good:
and you shall dwell in the land,
and feed in safe pastures.
⁴ Let the Lord be your delight:
and he will I grant you your heart's desire.
⁵ Commit your way to the I Lord:
trust him and he will act.
⁶ He will make your righteousness
shine as clear as the light:
and your innocence as the noonday.
⁷ Be still before the Lord:
and wait patiently for him.

Glory to God: Father Son and Holy Spirit;
As in the beginning so now and for ever. Amen.

Psalm 67

¹ Let God be gracious to us and bless us:
and make his face shine upon us,
² That your ways may be known on earth:
your liberating power among all nations.
³ Let the peoples praise you O God:
let all the peoples praise you.
⁴ Let the nations be glad and sing:
for you judge the peoples with integrity
and govern the nations upon earth.
⁵ Let the peoples praise you O God:
let all the peoples praise you.
⁶ Then the earth will yield its fruitfulness:
and God our God will bless us.
⁷ God shall bless us:
and all the lands of the earth will fear him.

Glory to God: Father Son and Holy Spirit;
As in the beginning so now: and for ever. Amen.

13 *One or more passages of scripture may be read (see Note 4) and a sermon declaring the duties of husband and wife may be preached here or later in the service. If no sermon is preached, Ephesians 5:20–33 at least must be read.*

Hear now the teaching of Saint Paul on the duties of husband and wife.

Always give thanks for everything to God the Father, in the name of our Lord Jesus Christ. Submit yourselves to one another, because of your reverence for Christ.

Wives, submit yourselves to your husbands, as to the Lord. For a husband has authority over his wife in the same way that Christ has authority over the church; and Christ is himself the Saviour of the church, his body. And so wives must submit themselves completely to their husbands, in the same way that the church submits itself to Christ.

Husbands, love your wives in the same way that Christ loved the church and gave his life for it. He did this to dedicate the church to God, by his word, after making it clean by the washing in water, in order to present the church to himself, in all its beauty, pure and faultless, without spot or wrinkle, or any other imperfection.

Men ought to love their wives just as they love their own bodies. A man who loves his wife loves himself. (No one ever hates his own flesh. Instead, he feeds it and takes care of it, just as Christ does the church; for we are members of his body.) As the scripture says, 'For this reason, a man will leave his father and mother, and unite with his wife, and the two will become one.' There is a great truth revealed in this scripture, and I understand it applies to Christ and the church. But it also applies to you: every husband must love his wife as himself, and every wife must respect her husband. Ephesians 5.20–33 (TEV)

14 *Then, the people kneeling, and the man and the woman kneeling before the Lord's Table, the priest stands at the Table and, turning towards them says*

The Lord be with you.
And also with you.
Let us pray.

Our Father in heaven,
hallowed be your Name,
your kingdom come,
your will be done
on earth as in heaven.
Give us today our daily bread.
Forgive us our sins
as we forgive those who sin against us.
Lead us not into temptation,

but deliver us from evil.
For the kingdom, the power, and the glory are yours
now and for ever. Amen.

Lord, save your servants,
who put their trust in you.

Lord, send them help from your holy place,
and evermore defend them.

Be to them a tower of strength,
against every enemy.

Father, hear our prayer,
through Jesus Christ our Lord.

A prayer for the blessing of eternal life

God of Abraham,
God of Isaac,
God of Jacob,
bless these your servants
and sow the seed of eternal life in their hearts,
that whatever they learn in your holy word
they may indeed fulfill.
Look in love upon them, Father,
and bless them with the blessing you sent on Abraham and Sarah
that, obeying your will and secure in your protection,
they may abide in your love to their lives' end;
through Jesus Christ our Lord.
Amen.

A prayer for the blessing of children

We praise you, Father,
for creating us in your own image
and for your gracious gift whereby mankind is increased;
give to N and N the blessing of children,
and grant them the wisdom and grace to bring them up
in the discipline and instruction of the Lord,
to your praise and honour;
through Jesus Christ our Lord.
Amen.

A prayer for the blessing of mutual love and faithfulness

Almighty God,
who by joining man and woman together
taught us from the beginning

that we should not separate what you have joined as one;
we praise you that you have consecrated the state of matrimony to
        such an excellent purpose
that in it is signified the spiritual marriage and unity between Christ
        and his Church.
Look mercifully on these your servants,
that this man may love his wife, according to your word,
as Christ loved his bride the Church,
and gave himself for it,
cherishing it as himself;
and also that this woman may be loving and generous,
responsive and faithful to her husband.
O Lord, bless them both,
and grant them to inherit your everlasting kingdom;
through Jesus Christ our Lord.
Amen.

or

Lord God,
you have consecrated marriage
to be a sign of the spiritual unity between Christ and his Church;
bless these your servants
that they may love, honour, and cherish each other
in faithfulness, patience, wisdom, and true godliness;
may their home be a place of love and peace;
through Jesus Christ our Lord.
Amen.

15 *Then the priest says*

Almighty God,
who created our first parents
and sanctified and joined them together in marriage,
pour upon you the riches of his love,
sanctify and bless you,
that you may please him both in body and soul,
and live together in holy love to your lives' end.
Amen.

or

God the Father enrich you with his grace,
God the Son make you holy in his love,
God the Holy Spirit strengthen you with his joy.

The Lord bless you and keep you in eternal life.
Amen.

16 *If there is no Communion, the minister concludes*
And the grace of our Lord Jesus Christ, and the love of God, and
the fellowship of the Holy Spirit, be with us all evermore. Amen.

PRESBYTERIAN CHURCH IN THE
UNITED STATES OF AMERICA, 1946
Order for the Solemnization of Marriage[3]

Preface
The Persons to be married shall present themselves before the Minister,
the Man standing at the right hand of the Woman. Then, all present
reverently standing, the Minister shall say:
DEARLY beloved, we are assembled here in the presence of God,
to join this Man and this Woman in holy marriage; which is instituted
of God, regulated by His commandments, blessed by our Lord Jesus
Christ, and to be held in honor among all men. Let us therefore reverently remember that God has established and sanctified marriage, for
the welfare and happiness of mankind. Our Saviour has declared that
a man shall leave his father and mother and cleave unto his wife. By
His apostles, He has instructed those who enter into this relation to
cherish a mutual esteem and love; to bear with each other's infirmities
and weaknesses; to comfort each other in sickness, trouble, and sorrow; in honesty and industry to provide for each other, and for their
household, in temporal things; to pray for and encourage each other
in the things which pertain to God; and to live together as the heirs of
the grace of life.

Forasmuch as these two Persons have come hither to be made one in
this holy estate, if there be any here present who knows any just cause
why they may not lawfully be joined in marriage, I require him now to
make it known, or ever after to hold his peace.

Charge
Then, speaking unto the Persons who are to be married, the Minister
shall say:
I CHARGE you both, before the great God, the Searcher of all hearts,
that if either of you know any reason why ye may not lawfully be joined

[3] The Book of Common Worship (Philadelphia: The Board of Christian Education of the Presbyterian Church in the United States of America, 1946), 183–188. Used with permission.

together in marriage, ye do now confess it. For be ye well assured that if any persons are joined together otherwise than as God's Word allows, their union is not blessed by Him.

Then, if no impediment appear, the Minister shall say:
Let us pray.

ALMIGHTY and ever-blessed God, whose presence is the happiness of every condition, and whose favor hallows every relation: We beseech Thee to be present and favorable unto these Thy servants, that they may be truly joined in the honorable estate of marriage, in the covenant of their God. As Thou hast brought them together by Thy providence, sanctify them by Thy Spirit, giving them a new frame of heart fit for their new estate; and enrich them with all grace, whereby they may enjoy the comforts, undergo the cares, endure the trials, and perform the duties of life together as becometh Christians under Thy heavenly guidance and protection; through our Lord Jesus Christ. Amen.

Consent
Then the Minister, calling the Man by his Christian name, shall say:
N., wilt thou have this Woman to be thy wife, and wilt thou pledge thy troth to her, in all love and honor, in all duty and service, in all faith and tenderness, to live with her, and cherish her, according to the ordinance of God, in the holy bond of marriage?

The Man shall answer:
I will.

Then the Minister, calling the Woman by her Christian name, shall say:
N., wilt thou have this Man to be thy husband, and wilt thou pledge thy troth to him, in all love and honor, in all duty and service in all faith and tenderness, to live with him, and cherish him, according to the ordinance of God, in the holy bond of marriage?

The Woman shall answer:
I will.

Presentation
Then the Minister shall say:
Who giveth this Woman to be married to this Man?

Vows
Then the Father, or Guardian, or Friend, of the Woman shall put her right hand in the hand of the Minister, who shall cause the Man with his right hand to take the Woman by her right hand and to say after the Minister as follows:

I, N., take thee, N.,
To be my wedded wife;
And I do promise and covenant;
Before God and these witnesses;
To be thy loving and faithful husband;
In plenty and in want;
In joy and in sorrow;
In sickness and in health;
As long as we both shall live.

Then shall they loose their hands; and the Woman, with her right hand taking the Man by his right hand, shall likewise say after the Minister:

I, N., take thee, N.;
To be my wedded husband;
And I do promise and covenant;
Before God and these witnesses;
To be thy loving and faithful wife;
In plenty and in want;
In joy and in sorrow;
In sickness and in health;
As long as we both shall live.

Rings

Then if a ring be provided, it shall be given to the Minister, who shall return it to the Man, who shall then put it upon the fourth finger of the Woman's left hand, saying after the Minister:

This ring I give thee;
In token and pledge;
Of our constant faith;
And abiding love.

Or,

With this ring I thee wed;
In the name of the Father;
And of the Son;
And of the Holy Spirit.
Amen.

Before giving the ring, the Minister may say:

Bless, O Lord, this ring, that he who gives it and she who wears it may abide in Thy peace and continue in Thy favor unto their life's end; through Jesus Christ our Lord. Amen.

If a second ring be provided, a similar order shall be followed, the Woman saying the same words after the Minister.

Then the Minister shall say:

Let us pray.

MOST merciful and gracious God, of whom the whole family in heaven and earth is named: Bestow upon these Thy servants the seal of Thine approval, and Thy Fatherly benediction; granting unto them grace to fulfill, with pure and steadfast affection, the vow and covenant between them made. Guide them together, we beseech Thee, in the way of righteousness and peace, that, loving and serving Thee, with one heart and mind, all the days of their life, they may be abundantly enriched with the tokens of Thine everlasting favor, in Jesus Christ our Lord. Amen.

Then the Minister and People shall say:

OUR Father, who art in heaven;
Hallowed be Thy name.
Thy kingdom come.
Thy will be done;
On earth as it is in heaven.
Give us this day our daily bread.
And forgive us our debts;
As we forgive our debtors.
And lead us not into temptation;
But deliver us from evil;
For Thine is the kingdom, and the power, and the glory, forever.
Amen.

Pronouncement

Then shall the Minister say unto all who are present:

BY THE authority committed unto me as a Minister of the Church of Christ, I declare that N. and N. are now Husband and Wife, according to the ordinance of God, and the law of the State: in the name of the Father, and of the Son, and of the Holy Spirit. Amen.

Then, causing the Husband and Wife to join their right hands, the Minister shall say:

Whom therefore God hath joined together, let no man put asunder.

Benediction

It is fitting that the Bride and Groom kneel to receive the Benediction:

THE Lord bless you and keep you: the Lord make His face to shine upon you, and be gracious unto you: the Lord lift up His countenance upon you, and give you peace: both now and in the life everlasting. Amen.

Or,

GOD the Father, God the Son, God the Holy Spirit, bless, preserve, and keep you; the Lord mercifully with His favor look upon you, and fill you with all spiritual benediction and grace; that ye may so live together in this life that in the world to come ye may have life everlasting. Amen.

LUTHERAN[4]

Call to Worship
Minister: O Lord, open my lips,
Congregation: and my mouth will declare your praise.
Minister: Make haste, O God, to deliver me.
Congregation: Make haste to help me, O Lord. Glory be to the Father and to the Son and to the Holy Spirit; as it was in the beginning, is now, and will be forever. Amen. Praise to you, O Christ. Alleluia.

(The following Psalm may be sung or said.)

The Lord is good and His love endures forever. His faithfulness continues through all generations. Shout for joy to the Lord, all the earth. Serve the Lord with gladness; come before Him with joyful songs. Know that the Lord is God. It is He who made us, and we are His; we are His people, the sheep of His pasture. Enter His gates with thanksgiving and His courts with praise; give thanks to Him and praise His name. For the Lord is good and His love endures forever; His faithfulness continues through all generations. Glory be to the Father and to the Son and to the Holy Spirit; as it was in the beginning, is now, and will be forever. Amen. The Lord is good and His love endures forever. His faithfulness continues through all generations. (Antiphon, Ps. 100:5; Ps. 100)

(Scripture)

Two or more of the following portions of Holy Scripture are read:

Genesis 2:18–25
Ephesians 5:21–33
John 2:1–11
John 15:12–15
Matthew 19:4–6

Ephesians 5:21–33 and Matthew 19:4–6 are always read.

Submit to one another out of reverence for Christ. Wives, submit to your husbands as to the Lord. For the husband is the head of

[4] Adapted from the Lutheran Worship Agenda © 1984 Concordia Publishing House. Used with permission. All rights reserved. www.cph.org.

the wife as Christ is the head of the church, his body, of which he is the Savior. Now as the church submits to Christ, so also wives should submit to their husbands in everything. Husbands, love your wives, just as Christ loved the church and gave himself up for her to make her holy, cleansing her by the washing with water through the word, and to present her to himself as a radiant church, without stain or wrinkle or any other blemish, but holy and blameless. In this same way, husbands ought to love their wives as their own bodies.

He who loves his wife loves himself. After all, no one ever hated his body, but he feeds and cares for it, just as Christ does the church—for we are members of his body. "For this reason a man will leave his father and mother and be united to his wife, and the two will become one flesh." This is a profound mystery—but I am talking about Christ and the church. However, each one of you also must love his wife as he loves himself, and the wife must respect her husband. (Eph. 5:21–33, NIV)

"Have you not read," he replied, "that at the beginning the Creator 'made them male and female,' and said, 'For this reason a man will leave his father and mother and be united to his wife, and the two will become one flesh'? So they are no longer two, but one. Therefore what God has joined together, let man not separate." (Matt. 19:4–6, NIV)

Minister: O Lord, have mercy on us.
Congregation: Thanks be to God.

(Homily)
(Hymn)

Charge
We are gathered here in the sight of God and of His Church that this man and this woman may be joined together in holy matrimony, which is an honorable estate, which God Himself has instituted and blessed, and by which He gives us a picture of the very communion of Christ and His Bride, the Church. God has both established and sanctified this estate and has promised to bless therein all who love and trust in Him and who seek to give Him their faithful worship and service, for the sake of our Lord Jesus Christ.

God has ordained marriage for the good of man and woman in lifelong companionship according to His good pleasure and that children may be nurtured to the praise of His holy name.

He has further ordained marriage so that the love you have for each other may be hallowed and fulfilled according to His bountiful purposes, both in prosperity and adversity all your days.

Christian marriage consists in your mutual consent, sincerely and freely given, which you now solemnly declare before God, these witnesses, and each other.

Consent
(Declaration of Intent)

(G)_____, will you have this woman to be your wife; to live with her in holy marriage according to the Word of God? Will you love her, comfort her, honor her and keep her, in sickness and in health and, forsaking all others, be husband to her as long as you both shall live?

(G) *I will.*

(B)_____, will you have this man to be your husband; to live with him in holy marriage according to the Word of God? Will you love him, comfort him, honor him, obey him, and keep him, in sickness and in health and, forsaking all others, be wife to him as long as you both shall live?

(B) *I will.*

Presentation
(Giving of the Bride)

Minister: Who gives this woman to be married to this man?

Vows
(Exchange of Vows)

I (G) in the presence of God and these witnesses, take you (B) to be my wife; to have and to hold from this day forward, for better for worse, for richer for poorer, in sickness and in health, to love and to cherish, till death us do part. I pledge you my faithfulness.

I (B) in the presence of God and these witnesses, take you (G) to be my husband; to have and to hold from this day forward, for better for worse, for richer for poorer, in sickness and in health, to have and to cherish, till death us do part. I pledge you my faithfulness.

Grant your blessing, O Lord, to these your servants, that they may be ever mindful of their solemn pledge and, trusting in Your mercy, abound evermore in love through all their days; through Jesus Christ our Lord.

Congregation: Amen.

Rings
(Said by both.) Receive this ring as a pledge and token of wedded love and faithfulness.

Pronouncement
(Pronouncement of Marriage)

Minister: Join your right hands and kneel.

Forasmuch as _____ and _____ have consented together in holy marriage and have declared the same before God and these witnesses, I therefore pronounce them husband and wife, in the name of the Father and of the Son and of the Holy Spirit. Amen.

What God has joined together, let no one put asunder.

Congregation: Amen.

(Hymn)

Prayers and Benedictions
(Blessing)

Minister: The almighty and gracious God abundantly grant you His favor, and sanctify and bless you with the blessing given our first parents in paradise that you may please Him both in body and soul, and live together in holy love until life's end.

The eternal God, the Father of our Lord Jesus Christ, bestow upon you His Holy Spirit, be with you, and richly bless you forever.

Congregation: Amen.

(The Lord's Prayer)

Minister: In peace, let us pray to the Lord:

Our Father who art in heaven, hallowed be Thy name.
Thy kingdom come: Thy will be done,
on earth as it is in heaven.
Give us this day our daily bread.
And forgive us our trespasses
as we forgive those who trespass against us;
and lead us not into temptation.

Or,

Our Father in heaven, hallowed be Your name.
Your kingdom come; Your will be done,
on earth as in heaven.
Give us today our daily bread.
And forgive us our sin,
as we forgive those who sin against us,
Lead us not into temptation,
but deliver us from evil.
For Thine is the kingdom

and the power and the glory
forever and ever. Amen.

Minister: The Lord be with you.

Congregation: And with your spirit.

(Prayer)

Minister: Let us pray to the Lord.

Almighty, everlasting God, our heavenly Father, having joined this man and woman in holy marriage, grant that by Your blessing they may live together according to Your Word and promise. Strengthen them in faithfulness and love toward each other. Sustain and defend them in all trial and temptation, and help them to live in faith toward You in the communion of Your holy Church and in loving service to each other that they may ever enjoy your (heavenly family's) blessing; through Jesus Christ, Your Son, our Lord, who lives and reigns with You and the Holy Spirit, one God, now and forever.

Congregation: Amen.

(Hymn)

(Benediction)

Minister: The Lord bless you and keep you. The Lord make His face shine on you and be gracious to you. The Lord lift up His countenance on you and give you peace.

Congregation: Amen.

BAPTIST[5]

Preface
CHARGE

Dear friends (or dearly beloved, or beloved friends), we are here assembled in the presence of God to unite _____ and _____ in marriage.

The Bible teaches that marriage is to be a permanent relationship of one man and one woman freely and totally committed to each other as companions for life. Our Lord declared that man shall leave his father and mother and unite with his wife in the building of a home, and the two shall become one flesh.

Presentation
(Bride given away)

Who gives the bride to be married?

[5] Adapted from Franklin M. Segler, *The Broadman Minister's Manual* (Nashville: Broadman, 1969). Used with permission.

(Homily)

The home is built upon love, which virtue is best portrayed in the thirteenth chapter of Paul's first letter to the Corinthians. "Love is patient and kind; love is not jealous or boastful; it is not arrogant or rude. Love does not insist on its own way; it is not irritable or resentful; it does not rejoice at wrong, but rejoices in the right. Love bears all things, believes all things, hopes all things, endures all things. Love never ends; . . . So faith, hope, love abide, these three; but the greatest of these is love" (1 Cor. 13:4–13, RSV).

Marriage is a companionship which involves mutual commitment and responsibility. You will share alike in the responsibilities and the joys of life. When companions share a sorrow the sorrow is halved, and when they share a joy the joy is doubled.

You are exhorted to dedicate your home to your Creator. Take His Word, the Bible, for your guide. Give loyal devotion to His church, thus uniting the mutual strength of these two most important institutions, living your lives as His willing servants, and true happiness will be your temporal and eternal reward.

(Prayer)

Let us pray. O Lord of life and love, bestow Thy grace upon this marriage, and seal this commitment of Thy children with Thy love.

As Thou hast brought them together by Thy divine providence, sanctify them by Thy Spirit, that they may give themselves fully one to the other and to Thee. Give them strength and patience to live their lives in a manner that will mutually bless themselves and honor Thy holy name; through Jesus Christ our Lord. Amen.

Vows

(Exchange of Vows)

(G), will you take (B) to be your wife; will you commit yourself to her happiness and her self-fulfillment as a person, and to her usefulness in God's kingdom; and will you promise to love, honor, trust, and serve her in sickness and in health, in adversity and prosperity, and to be true and loyal to her, so long as you both shall live?
(G) I will.

(B), will you take (G) to be your husband; will you commit yourself to his happiness and his self-fulfillment as a person, and to his usefulness in God's kingdom; and will you promise to love, honor, trust, and serve him in sickness and in health, in adversity and prosperity, and to be true and loyal to him, so long as you both shall live?
(B) I will.

Rings

(Exchange of Rings)

The wedding ring is a symbol of marriage in at least two ways: the purity of gold symbolizes the purity of your love for each other, and the unending circle symbolizes the unending vows which you are taking, which may be broken honorably in the sight of God only by death. As a token of your vows, you will give and receive the rings (or ring).

(G), you will give the ring and repeat after me: (B), with this ring I pledge my life and love to you, in the name of the Father, and of the Son, and of the Holy Spirit.

(B), you will give the ring and repeat after me: (G), with this ring I pledge my love and life to you, in the name of the Father, and of the Son, and of the Holy Spirit.

(In the case of a single ring ceremony, the bride will say, (G), I accept this ring and pledge to you my love and life, in the name of the Father, and of the Son, and of the Holy Spirit.)

(Scripture)

Will both of you please repeat after me:

Entreat me not to leave you
or to return from following you;
for where you go I will go,
and where you lodge I will lodge;
your people shall be my people,
and your God my God. (Ruth 1:16, RSV)

Pronouncement

Since they have made these commitments before God and this assembly (or, these witnesses), by the authority of God and the laws of this state, I declare that _____ and _____ are husband and wife.

And, _____ and _____, you are no longer two independent persons but one. "What therefore God has joined together, let no man separate" (Matt. 19:6, NASB).

(Prayer)

(The Lord's Prayer)

Our Father which art in heaven, hallowed be Thy name. Thy kingdom come. Thy will be done in earth, as it is in heaven. Give us this day our daily bread. And forgive us our debts, as we forgive our debtors. And lead us not into temptation, but deliver us from evil: For thine is the kingdom, and the power, and the glory, for ever. Amen.

Benedictions

(Benediction)

The Lord bless you and keep you: The Lord make His face to shine upon you, and be gracious to you: The Lord lift up His countenance upon you, and give you peace (Num. 6:24- 26, RSV).

Or

The grace of the Lord Jesus Christ and the love of God and the fellowship of the Holy Spirit be with you all (2 Cor. 13:14, RSV).

Amen.

A SAMPLE WEDDING CEREMONY[6]

Any etiquette book may be consulted about the seating of family members of the bride and groom, the lighting of candles, and appropriate music before the ceremony begins. There is usually a solo during the seating of the parents. Sometimes the mothers of the groom and bride will light the candles that are on either side of a unity candle. The pastor, the groom, and his groomsmen may come to the front of the church from the side and stand in front of the platform. (The pastor mounts the platform and takes his place behind the kneeling bench, if one is used.)

The bride, preceded by her bridesmaids and flower girl and/or ring-bearer, will come down the aisle on the arm of her father to meet the groom at the front of the platform. The groomsmen and bridesmaids will go directly to their places as the bridesmaids arrive at the front. They will stand at an angle facing the congregation, so that they will see the bride as she comes down the aisle. The bride's mother, standing up as the bride comes down the aisle, will signal the congregation to stand as well.

Presentation

As the bride comes to the base of the platform on her father's left arm, the groom will stand next to the bride's father. Then the pastor will ask, "Who gives this woman to be married to this man?" The father will answer either "I do" or "Her mother and I." Then the father will step back, placing the bride's right hand on the left arm of the groom. They will then ascend the steps leading up to the platform and stand in front of the pastor or kneeling bench, if there is one. As the couple climbs the steps, the wedding party will turn at an angle toward the couple. The bride's father will take his seat beside his wife. The pastor will say, "The congregation may be seated."

---

6 James W. Bryant and Mac Brunson, *The New Guidebook for Pastors* (Nashville: Broadman & Holman, 2007). Used with permission.

At this point the bride should pass her bouquet to the maid of honor. The pastor will say,

"A wise man once said, 'There are three things which are too wonderful for me, yes, four which I do not understand: The way of an eagle in the air, the way of a serpent on a rock, the way of a ship in the midst of the sea, and the way of a man with a virgin'" [Prov. 30:18–19, NKJV].

Preface

"We are gathered here together today (or tonight) to witness the exchanging of wedding vows between [groom's full name] and [bride's full name]. It is appropriate that this wedding takes place in the church because marriage is an institution ordained by God. No one except God could have thought of anything as wonderful as marriage. It was God Himself who placed that first man and woman together in the garden to love one another, to complete one another, and to provide that unique companionship found in the marriage union. In His wonderful book, the Bible, God tells us the duties and responsibilities of each marriage partner whereby they might have the blessing of God on their home."

Charge

"[Groom's name], to you God gives a wonderful assignment: 'Husband, love your wife, even as Christ loved the Church and gave Himself for her. . . . So the husband ought to love his wife as his own body; he who loves his wife loves himself. For no one ever hated his own flesh, but nourishes and cherishes it, just as the Lord does the Church' [see Eph. 5:25–29 NKJV].

"[Bride's name], God says to you, 'Wife, submit yourself unto your own husband, as to the Lord. For the husband is head of the wife, as also Christ is head of the church, and He is the Savior of the body. Therefore, just as the church is subject to Christ, so let the wife be subject to her own husband, in everything' [see Eph. 5:22–24 NKJV].

"As your lives are put together today in the legal and Christian manner, I pray that it is just the beginning of God taking two hearts and making them into one heart, which ought never to be broken, except by death."

Vows

"Now you have declared to me in private that there is nothing according to the laws of God or the laws of this state that would keep you from becoming husband and wife. You have made known to your family and friends gathered here together your intentions of giving yourselves each to the other as long as you both shall live. Now will you face each other and join right hands as you exchange these wedding vows.

"[Groom's name], will you take this woman, [bride's name], whom you hold by the hand, as your lawful wedded wife? Will you love her tenderly, comfort her in times of sorrow, keep her in times of prosperity or poverty, sickness or health? Will you cherish her and keep her close to your side and to your heart as long as both of you live?" (The groom answers, "I will.")

"[Bride's name], will you take this man, [groom's name], whom you hold by the hand, as your lawful wedded husband? Will you love him tenderly, comfort him in times of sorrow, keep him in times of prosperity or poverty, sickness or health? Will you obey him and keep him close to your side and to your heart as long as both of you live?" (The bride answers, "I will.")

Rings
"Now each of you brings a ring as a sign and token of your love for each other." (The maid of honor and the best man should then place both rings in the pastor's hand. He will hold his hand with the rings out to the groom.)

"[Groom's name], please take your ring and place it on the third finger of [bride's name] left hand. Hold it there for a moment, look deep into her eyes and into her heart, and repeat these words after me: (The pastor will pause at the end of each line.)

"May this ring be a reminder / To you and to me / Of the love and devotion I now pledge / This day to you."

"Now [bride's name], please take your ring and place it on the ring finger of [groom's name] left hand. Hold it there for a moment, look deep into his eyes and into his heart, and repeat these words after me: (The pastor will pause at the end of each line.)

"May this ring be a reminder / To you and to me / Of the love and devotion I now pledge / This day to you."

The couple then holds hands and faces the pastor.

"Let these rings, circles of gold, mark the purity, the value, and the constancy of true wedded love. Let them be now and for the rest of your lives a twofold seal of the vows you have taken here before your family and friends and in heaven before God."

If there is a unity candle to be lit, a solo may be sung or an organ interlude played while the couple lights the unity candle and then returns to their place before the pastor. After the solo is over, the pastor says,

"Now let us pray." The couple will kneel if there is a kneeling bench. Otherwise they will bow their heads as the pastor prays. Sometimes the Lord's Prayer is sung at this time. If it is, the pastor, at the close of the song, will say, "Amen."

If the Lord's Prayer is not sung, the pastor will pray something like this:

"Our Father in heaven, we ask you to bless [groom's name] and [bride's name] as they join hands together to climb the hill of life. May their blessings be doubled as two share them together rather than each alone. May the inevitable hardships of life be made bearable as two bear them together instead of each alone. If you bless this union with children, may they be raised in the nurture and admonition of the Lord. May Christ dwell at the center of the home that is hereby established today (or tonight). As [groom's name] and [bride's name] grow closer to Him, may they grow closer to one another than they ever felt previously. We pray this prayer in Jesus's name."

Pronouncement

If the couple has been kneeling, they will stand. Then the pastor will say:

"[Groom's name] and [bride's name], upon your solemn vows that you have made here today (or tonight), and upon your sacred pledge to love one another for the rest of your lives, in accordance with the laws of God and of this state, it gives me great delight to pronounce you husband and wife, in the name of the Father, and of the Son, and of the Holy Spirit. And what God has joined together, let no man put asunder. You may kiss your bride."

After the kiss, as the couple turns toward the congregation and the bride retrieves her bouquet, the pastor will say,

"Ladies and gentlemen, may I present to you Mr. and Mrs. [groom's full name]."

The recessional takes place as rehearsed. The pastor will stand in place until the family members have been escorted from the church. Then he will either invite everyone to the reception and tell them how to get there, or he will simply say, "You are dismissed."

CHOICE OUTTAKES

We now offer some helpful outtakes from sequential sections of various standard wedding ceremonies (not all of which are included in this appendix).

Call to Worship
Methodist
Dear friends, we are gathered together in the sight of God to witness and bless the joining together of _____ and _____ (full names) in Christian marriage. The covenant of marriage was established by God, who created us male and female for each other. With his presence and power Jesus graced a wedding in Cana of Galilee, and in his sacrificial love gave us the example for the love of husband and wife.

_____ and _____ (first names) come to give themselves to one another in holy covenant.

(*The United Methodist Hymnal* [Nashville: United Methodist Publishing House, 1989], 864.)

Nondenominational
Our Lord Jesus said: "From the beginning of Creation, God made them male and female. For this reason, a man shall leave his father and mother and be joined to his wife, so they are no longer two but one."

Let us worship God as we now witness the marriage of _____ and _____ (full names).

May God be glorified this day in the lives of this couple, and in the years to come.

Preface
Anglican
We have come together here in the sight of God, and in the presence of this congregation, to join together this man and this woman in holy matrimony; which is an honorable state of life, instituted in the beginning by God himself, signifying to us the spiritual union that is between Christ and the Church.

Christ adorned and beautified matrimony with his presence, and with the first sign by which he revealed his glory, at the marriage in Cana of Galilee; and holy scripture demands that all should hold it in honour.

It is therefore not to be entered upon unadvisedly, lightly, or merely to satisfy physical desires; but prayerfully, with careful thought, and with reverence for God, duly considering the purposes for which it was ordained.

It was ordained for the procreation of children and that they might be brought up in the nurture and instruction of the Lord, to the praise of his holy name.

It was ordained so that those to whom God has granted the gift of marriage might live a chaste and holy life, as befits members of Christ's body.

And it was ordained for the mutual companionship, help and comfort, that the one ought to have to the other, both in prosperity and adversity.

(Adapted from An Australian Prayer Book: for use together with The Book of Common Prayer, 1662 [Sydney: The Standing Committee of the General Synod of the Church of England in Australia, 1978].)

Presbyterian

Dearly beloved, we are assembled here in the presence of God, to join this man and this woman in holy marriage: which is instituted by God, regulated by his commandments, blessed by our Lord Jesus Christ, and to be held in honor among all men. Let us therefore reverently remember that God has established and sanctified marriage, for the welfare and happiness of mankind. Our Savior has declared that a man shall leave his father and mother and cleave unto his wife. By His apostles he has instructed those who enter into this relation to cherish a mutual esteem and love; to bear with each other's infirmities and weaknesses; to comfort each other in sickness, trouble, and sorrow; in honesty and industry to provide for each other, and for their household, in temporal things; to pray for and encourage each other in the things which pertain to God; and to live together as heirs to the grace of life.

(Adapted from The Book of Common Worship [Philadelphia: The Board of Christian Education of the United Presbyterian Church, 1978].)

CHARGE

Methodist

I require and charge both of you, as you stand in the presence of God, before whom the secrets of all hearts are disclosed, that, having duly considered the holy covenant that you are about to make, you do now declare before this company your pledge of faith, each to the other. Be well assured that if these solemn vows are kept inviolate, as God's Word demands, and if steadfastly you endeavor to do the will of your heavenly Father, God will bless your marriage, will grant you fulfillment in it, and will establish your home in peace.

(Adapted from *The Book of Worship for Church and Home* [Board of Publications of the Methodist Church, Inc., 1964, 1965]).

Nondenominational

Today you are presenting yourselves before this congregation to declare your intention of uniting your lives voluntarily and honorably for the service of God and man. You are making a double dedication: to each other, in a lasting and indivisible union that shall endure for the remaining years of your lives; and to God, that he may make you his dual instrument for the accomplishment of his purpose both in and by your personalities. The achievement of this purpose will require appreciation of each other's abilities and virtues, forgiveness of each other's faults, and unfailing devotion to each other's welfare and development. There must be on your part a united consent to the purpose of God as he progressively reveals it to you by his Word and by his Spirit, and an unhesitant acceptance by faith of the challenges that he sets before you.

I charge you, therefore, first of all, to consider that your promises to each other are made in the presence of a God who remembers your pledges and who holds you responsible for performing them. They must be kept inviolable before him.

I admonish you to keep in mind that each of you is the object of Christ's redemption, and should be valued accordingly. Neither should be neglected or belittled by the other. Esteem each other as God's gift for mutual aid, comfort, and joy, and as a repository of complete confidence and trust.

I encourage you to share willingly and sympathetically your joys and worries, your successes and your struggles, and to be neither conceited by the former nor depressed by the latter. Whichever may prevail, cling closely to each other, that defeats may be met by united strength, and victories by united joy.

I charge you to make your home a place where you can have a refuge for the storms of life, not only for yourselves, but also for others who may be your guests. Let it be a haven for the weary, a source of uplift for the discouraged, and a convincing testimony to a cynical world.

In short, recognize the Lord Jesus Christ as head of the house, the ruler of your destinies, and the object of your deepest affection. If you do, He will confirm your marriage by his guidance and will overshadow it by his peace.

I charge you to love each other, to support each other, and to serve Him with sincere hearts and determined wills until your mutual service for Him shall be completed.

(Dr. Merrill Tenney)

Presbyterian

(G) _____, wilt thou have this woman to be thy wife, and wilt thou pledge thy troth to her, in all love and honor, in all duty and service, in all faith and tenderness, to live with her and cherish her, according to the ordinance of God, in the holy bond of marriage?
I will.

(B) _____, wilt thou have this man to be thy husband, and wilt thou pledge thy troth to him, in all love and honor, in all duty and service, in all faith and tenderness, to live with him and cherish him, according to the ordinance of God, in the holy bond of marriage?
I will.

(Adapted from The Book of Common Worship.)

Lutheran
Christian marriage consists of your mutual consent, sincerely and freely, which you now solemnly declare before God, these witnesses and each other.

(G) _____, will you have this woman to be your wife; to live with her in holy marriage according to the Word of God? Will you love her, comfort her, honor and keep her, in sickness and in health and, forsaking all others, be husband to her as long as you both shall live?
I will.

(B) _____, will you have this man to be your husband; to live with him in holy marriage according to the Word of God? Will you love him, comfort him, honor him, obey him, and keep him, in sickness and in health and, forsaking all others, be wife to him as long as you both shall live?
I will.

(Adapted from Lutheran Worship Agenda [St. Louis: Concordia Publishing House, 1984].)

PRAYER/INVOCATION AND VOWS
Presbyterian
Most gracious God, fountain of life and love and joy, look with merciful favor upon your servants now to be joined in holy wedlock, and enable them ever to remember and truly keep the vows which they make as they enter into covenant with one another and with you, in accordance with the Holy Word through Jesus Christ our Lord. Amen.

Here the parties join their right hands, and the minister says to the man:
Do you (G) _____ take (B) _____ whom you now hold by the right hand to be your lawful and wedded wife, and do you promise in the presence of these witnesses to be to her a faithful, loving and devoted husband, so long as you both shall live?

The man answers: *I do.*

The minister then says to the woman: Do you (B) _____ take (G) _____ whom you now hold by the right hand to be your lawful and wedded husband, and do you promise in the presence of God and these witnesses to be to him a faithful, loving and obedient wife, so long as you both shall live?

The woman answers: *I will.*

(From The Book of Church Order of the Presbyterian Church in America, 6th ed. [Atlanta: Committee for Christian Education and Publications, 2006].)

Episcopalian

I (G) _____ take (B) _____ to be my wife, to have and to hold from this day forward, for better for worse, for richer for poorer, in sickness and in health, to love and to cherish, until we are parted by death. This is my solemn vow.

(Adapted from the The Book of Common Prayer [Kingsport, TN: Kingsport Press, 1997].)

Rings

Anglican

In a traditional Anglican ceremony, only the man gives a ring, placing it on the book, and the presiding minister prays: "Lord, we pray that this ring may be to your servants a token of their solemn vows, and a pledge of pure and abiding love: through Jesus Christ our Lord. Amen." Then he takes it and gives it to the man to put on the fourth finger of the woman's left hand. The man holds the ring there, and says:

> With this ring, I wed you,
> With my body I worship you;
> With all that I am and all that I have
> I honour you:
> In the name of the Father,
> And of the Son,
> And of the Holy Spirit.
> Amen.

Presbyterian

Before the ring, the minister may say:

"Bless, O Lord, this ring, that he who gives it and she who wears it may abide in Thy peace, and continue in Thy favor, unto their life's end; through Jesus Christ our Lord. Amen."

(said by both)

This ring I give thee, in token and pledge, our constant faith and abiding love.

Or

With this ring I thee wed; in the name of the Father, and of the Son, and of the Holy Spirit. Amen.

(Adapted from The Book of Common Worship.)

Methodist

The wedding ring is the outward and visible sign of an inward spiritual grace, signifying to all the uniting of this man and this woman in holy matrimony, through the Church of Jesus Christ our Lord.

Let us pray: "Bless, O Lord, the giving of these rings, that they who wear them may abide in your peace, and continue in your favor, through Jesus Christ our Lord."

(said by both groom and bride in sequence)

In token and pledge, of our constant faith, and abiding love; with this ring I thee wed. With all that I am, and all that I have, I wish to honor you. So this ring is a sign of my unending devotion, and commitment to you. I give this to you, in the name of the Father, and of the Son, and of the Holy Spirit. Amen.

PRONOUNCEMENT

Anglican

N and N have now witnessed to their mutual consent
before God and this company;
they have pledged their solemn word to each other;
and they have confirmed it
by the giving and receiving of a ring
and by the joining of hands.
I therefore declare them to be husband and wife:
in the name of the Father,
and of the Son,
and of the Holy Spirit.
Amen.

(From An Australian Prayer Book, 552.)

Methodist

Forasmuch as _____ and _____ have consented together in holy wedlock, and have witnessed the same before God and this company, and thereto have pledged their faith to each other and have declared the same by the joining of hands and by giving and receiving rings; I pronounce that they are husband and wife together, in the name of the Father, and of the Son, and of the Holy Spirit. Those whom God has joined together let no one put asunder. Amen.

(Adapted from *The Book of Worship for Church and Home* [Nashville: The Board of Publication of the Methodist Church, Inc., 1964, 1965].)

PRAYER

Anglican
Prayer of blessing after the pronouncement of marriage:

God the Father,
God the Son,
God the Holy Spirit,
bless, preserve and keep you,
the Lord mercifully with his favour look upon you
and fill you with all spiritual blessing and grace,
that you may live together in this life,
that in the world to come you may have life everlasting.
Amen.

BENEDICTIONS

Lutheran
The almighty and gracious God abundantly grant you His favor, and sanctify and bless you with the blessing given our first parents in paradise that you may please Him both in body and soul, and live together in holy love until life's end.

The eternal God, the Father of our Lord Jesus Christ, bestow upon you His Holy Spirit, be with you, and richly bless you forever.

Congregation: "Amen."

(Adapted from Lutheran Worship Agenda)

Methodist
God the Father, the Son, and the Holy Spirit bless, preserve, and keep you; the Lord graciously with his favor look upon you, and so fill you with all spiritual benediction and love that you may so live together in this life that in the world to come you may have everlasting life. Amen.

(Adapted from *The Book of Worship for Church and Home*.)

Aaronic Blessing (Num. 6:24–26)
"The LORD bless you and keep you;

the Lord make his face to shine upon you and be gracious to you;
the Lord lift up his countenance upon you and give you peace."

2 Corinthians 13:14
This is the most often used of all benedictions:

"The grace of the Lord Jesus Christ and the love of God and the
fellowship of the Holy Spirit be with you all."

Books for Further Reading

As we mentioned in the preface, we chose to limit the topics we addressed in *The Pastor's Book* for various reasons. One of those reasons is that many excellent books and articles already have been written on some topics. The following is a list of some of the best of these resources, as suggested by several of our trusted colleagues. We hope these resources will help you find information or guidance on subjects we have not addressed.

CALLING TO MINISTRY

- Os Guinness, *The Call: Finding and Fulfilling the Central Purpose of Your Life* (Nashville: Word, 1998).
- Dave Harvey, *Am I Called: The Summons to Pastoral Ministry* (Wheaton, IL: Crossway, 2012).
- Charles Jefferson, *The Minister as Shepherd* (New York: Thomas Y. Crowell, 1912).
- D. B. Knox, *Sent by Jesus: Some Aspects of Christian Ministry Today* (Edinburgh: Banner of Truth, 1992).
- John MacArthur, *Rediscovering Pastoral Ministry: Shaping Contemporary Ministry with Biblical Mandates* (Dallas: Word, 1995).
- R. Albert Mohler, Donald S. Whitney, Dan Dumas, *The Call to Ministry* (Louisville, KY: The Southern Baptist Theological Seminary Press, 2013).
- Stephen J. Nichols, *What Is Vocation?* (Phillipsburg, NJ: P&R, 2010).
- Charles Spurgeon, *Lectures to My Students* (1897; repr., Grand Rapids: Zondervan, 1954).

PERSONAL CHARACTER

- Charles Bridges, *The Christian Ministry: With an Inquiry into the Causes of Its Inefficiency* (1830; repr., London: Banner of Truth, 1967).
- D. A. Carson, *A Call to Spiritual Reformation: Priorities from Paul and His Prayers* (Grand Rapids: Baker, 1992).

- R. Kent Hughes, *Disciplines of a Godly Man* (Wheaton, IL: Crossway, 1991).
- John Piper and D. A. Carson, *The Pastor as Scholar and the Scholar as Pastor: Reflections on Life and Ministry*, ed. Owen Strachan and David Mathis (Wheaton, IL: Crossway, 2011).
- J. C. Ryle, *Holiness* (1875; repr., Grand Rapids: Baker, 1976).
- Alexander Strauch, *Biblical Eldership: An Urgent Call to Restore Biblical Church Leadership* (Littleton, CO: Lewis & Roth, 1995).
- Paul David Tripp, *Dangerous Calling: Confronting the Unique Challenges of Pastoral Ministry* (Wheaton, IL: Crossway 2012).

FAMILY LIFE

- Brian and Cara Croft, *The Pastor's Family: Shepherding Your Family through the Challenges of Pastoral Ministry* (Grand Rapids: Zondervan, 2013).
- Kent and Barbara Hughes, *Disciplines of a Godly Family* (Wheaton, IL: Crossway, 2004).
- Andreas Köstenberger, with David W. Jones, *God, Marriage, and Family: Rebuilding the Biblical Foundation* (Wheaton, IL: Crossway, 2004).
- Wayne A. Mack, *Your Family, God's Way: Developing and Sustaining Relationships in the Home* (Phillipsburg, NJ: P&R 1991).

PREACHING

- Peter Adam, *Speaking God's Words: A Practical Theology of Preaching* (Leicester: Inter-Varsity, 1996).
- Jay E. Adams, *Preaching with Purpose: A Comprehensive Textbook on Biblical Preaching* (Grand Rapids: Baker, 1982).
- Christopher Ash, *The Priority of Preaching* (Fearn, Ross-shire: Christian Focus, 2009).
- Bryan Chapell, *Christ-Centered Preaching: Redeeming the Expository Sermon* (Grand Rapids: Baker, 1994).
- David R. Helm, *Expositional Preaching: How We Speak God's Word Today* (Wheaton, IL: Crossway, 2014).
- John MacArthur, *Rediscovering Expository Preaching* (Dallas: Word, 1992).
- Jason C. Meyer, *Preaching: A Biblical Theology* (Wheaton, IL: Crossway, 2013).
- John Piper, *The Supremacy of God in Preaching* (Grand Rapids: Baker, 1990).

LEADING A PASTORAL STAFF

- Mark Dever, *Nine Marks of a Healthy Church* (Wheaton, IL: Crossway, 2004).
- John Piper, *Brothers, We Are Not Professionals: A Plea to Pastors for Radical Ministry* (Nashville: Broadman & Holman, 2002).
- Alexander Strauch, *Leading with Love* (Littleton, CO: Lewis & Roth, 2006).

WORKING WITH ELDERS

- Gene A. Getz, *Elders and Leaders: God's Plan for Leading the Church* (Chicago: Moody, 2003).
- John MacArthur, *Pastoral Ministry: How to Shepherd Biblically* (Nashville: Thomas Nelson, 2005).
- Jeramie Rinne, *Church Elders: How to Shepherd God's People Like Jesus* (Wheaton, IL: Crossway, 2014).
- Alexander Strauch, *Biblical Eldership: An Urgent Call to Restore Biblical Church Leadership* (Littleton, CO: Lewis & Roth, 1995).
- Alexander Strauch, *Meetings That Work: A Guide to Effective Elders Meetings* (Littleton, CO: Lewis & Roth, 2001).
- Timothy Z. Witmer, *The Shepherd Leader: Achieving Effective Shepherding in Your Church* (Phillipsburg, NJ: P&R, 2010).

CHURCH DISCIPLINE

- Mark Dever, *Nine Marks of a Healthy Church* (Wheaton, IL: Crossway, 2004).
- Jonathan Leeman, *Church Discipline: How the Church Protects the Name of Jesus* (Wheaton, IL: Crossway, 2012).
- Jonathan Leeman, *The Church and the Surprising Offense of God's Love: Reintroducing the Doctrines of Church Membership and Discipline* (Wheaton, IL: Crossway, 2010).
- John MacArthur, *The Master's Plan for the Church* (Chicago: Moody, 1991).

CHURCH PLANTING

- Aubrey Malphurs, *Planting Growing Churches for the 21st Century: A Comprehensive Guide for New Churches and Those Desiring Renewal* (Grand Rapids: Baker, 1998).
- Mike McKinley, *Church Planting Is for Wimps: How God Uses Messed-up People to Plant Ordinary Churches That Do Extraordinary Things* (Wheaton, IL: Crossway, 2010).

- David T. Olson, *The American Church in Crisis: Groundbreaking Research Based on a National Database of over 200,000 Churches* (Grand Rapids: Zondervan, 2008).
- Darrin Patrick, *Church Planter: The Man, the Message, the Mission* (Wheaton, IL: Crossway, 2010).
- Tony Payne and Colin Marshall, *The Trellis and the Vine* (Kingsford, NSW: Matthias Media, 2009).

Downloadable Resources

The following resources included in *The Pastor's Book* are available in downloadable form at the following Internet links:

Sample Wedding Questionnaire (p. 131)
Crossway.org/WeddingWorksheet1

Sample Wedding Ceremony Planning Worksheet (pp. 144–45)
Crossway.org/WeddingWorksheet2

Sample Funeral Information Worksheet (pp. 188–89)
Crossway.org/FuneralWorksheet1

Sample Funeral Service Planning Worksheet (p. 189–90)
Crossway.org/FuneralWorksheet2

Index